Contemporary American
Foreign Policy

CQ Press, an imprint of SAGE, is the leading publisher of books, periodicals, and electronic products on American government and international affairs. CQ Press consistently ranks among the top commercial publishers in terms of quality, as evidenced by the numerous awards its products have won over the years. CQ Press owes its existence to Nelson Poynter, former publisher of the *St. Petersburg Times,* and his wife Henrietta, with whom he founded *Congressional Quarterly* in 1945. Poynter established CQ with the mission of promoting democracy through education and in 1975 founded the Modern Media Institute, renamed The Poynter Institute for Media Studies after his death. The Poynter Institute (*www.poynter.org*) is a nonprofit organization dedicated to training journalists and media leaders.

In 2008, CQ Press was acquired by SAGE, a leading international publisher of journals, books, and electronic media for academic, educational, and professional markets. Since 1965, SAGE has helped inform and educate a global community of scholars, practitioners, researchers, and students spanning a wide range of subject areas, including business, humanities, social sciences, and science, technology, and medicine. A privately owned corporation, SAGE has offices in Los Angeles, London, New Delhi, and Singapore, in addition to the Washington DC office of CQ Press.

Contemporary American Foreign Policy

Influences, Challenges, and Opportunities

Richard Mansbach
Iowa State University

Kirsten L. Taylor
Berry College

Los Angeles | London | New Delhi
Singapore | Washington DC

Los Angeles | London | New Delhi
Singapore | Washington DC

FOR INFORMATION:

CQ Press

An Imprint of SAGE Publications, Inc.

2455 Teller Road

Thousand Oaks, California 91320

E-mail: order@sagepub.com

SAGE Publications Ltd.

1 Oliver's Yard

55 City Road

London EC1Y 1SP

United Kingdom

SAGE Publications India Pvt. Ltd.

B 1/I 1 Mohan Cooperative Industrial Area

Mathura Road, New Delhi 110 044

India

SAGE Publications Asia-Pacific Pte. Ltd.

3 Church Street

#10-04 Samsung Hub

Singapore 049483

Senior Acquisitions Editor: Michael Kerns

eLearning Editor: Allison Hughes

Editorial Assistant: Zachary Hoskins

Development Editor: Elise Frasier

Production Editor: Tracy Buyan

Copy Editor: Michelle Ponce

Typesetter: C&M Digitals (P) Ltd.

Proofreader: Sarah Duffy

Indexer: Terri Morrissey

Cover Designer: Gail Buschman

Marketing Manager: Amy Whitaker

Printed in the United States of America

Library of Congress Cataloging-in-Publication Data

Names: Mansbach, Richard W., 1943- | Taylor, Kirsten L.

Title: Contemporary American foreign policy : influences, challenges, and opportunities / Richard Mansbach, Kirsten L. Taylor.

Description: First edition. | CQ Press, an imprint of SAGE Publications, 2017. | Includes bibliographical references and index.

Identifiers: LCCN 2015039391 | ISBN 9781452287232 (pbk. : alk. paper)

Subjects: LCSH: United States—Foreign relations—1989-

Classification: LCC E840 .M348 2017 | DDC 327.73009/04—dc23 LC record available at http://lccn.loc.gov/2015039391

This book is printed on acid-free paper.

16 17 18 19 20 10 9 8 7 6 5 4 3 2 1

Brief Contents

PART IV. CONCLUSION

Detailed Contents

PART I. POLICY ORIENTATIONS

1 | Sources of American Foreign Policy   6

2 | Competing Currents in U.S. Foreign Policy   36

PART II. CHALLENGES IN KEY ISSUE AREAS

3 | American Military Strategy in an Era of Power Diffusion 65

8 | Energy and the Environment: The Limits of U.S. Leadership

PART III. CHALLENGES IN KEY REGIONS AND COUNTRIES

9 | America and the Palestinian-Israeli Imbroglio

10 | Arab Spring or Arab Winter? 299

11 | America and Radical Islam 326

12 | The United States and China: Engagement or Containment?

Part IV. Conclusion

15 | Conclusion: America, a Wary Hegemon

Features and Illustrations

FEATURES

FIGURES

TABLES

MAPS

Preface

In our new book, *Contemporary American Foreign Policy: Influences, Challenges, and Opportunities*, we've set out to examine the outstanding issues confronting American foreign policy today, as well as the foreign policies of other key global actors in the foreseeable future. We systematically explore the forces that influence decisions among alternative policies and carefully outline the potential advantages and disadvantages of those alternatives. Since we know that few students have significant historical exposure, we begin each chapter with a section on historical background of the issue at hand and a description of the nature of the problem. However, the major emphasis of the text is the analysis of alternative policy options available to the United States with the potential positive and/or negative outcomes associated with each alternative, a critical aspect of the foreign policymaking process that is seldom covered in other texts on the subject. Our text assumes that most policies are not the result of perfect rationality of political leaders. Instead, it assumes that policy is usually made in a complex environment and takes form owing to myriad pressures from domestic interest groups in society, bureaucratic and political factors, and the idiosyncrasies of individual leaders. Each chapter concludes by addressing the alternative policies available to the United States and, in each case, the influences pushing Washington to select one or another option and possible consequences of each alternative.

To help students of foreign policy and international studies master new terminology and ideas, we have employed a variety of learning aids including timelines, maps, figures, tables, illustrations, cartoons, discussion questions, and a glossary of bolded key terms to help them study and review. The text also includes boxed features that contain excerpts of original documents, present policy controversies, and highlight significant details and facts. Additional student and instructor resources are available online, including chapter summaries and learning objectives, PowerPoint slides, discussion questions and ideas, class activities, question banks, practice quizzes, and flashcards.

ORGANIZATION OF THE BOOK

In this book, we explain decisions that Washington has made in meeting critical contemporary challenges and describe those policies as well as alternative policies that might be adopted. To accomplish this, all of the chapters are divided into three parts—"past" (what policies were historically pursued), "present" (what policies are currently pursued), and "future" (alternative policies and their potential costs and benefits).

Part I. Policy Orientations

Part I consists of two chapters. The first examines the various influences on foreign-policy decisions, influences that preclude purely rational decision making and that push policymakers toward one or another alternative. The influences are both domestic and external and, in most cases, force leaders to compromise and to sacrifice clear and decisive decisions in favor of incremental change. The second chapter reviews some of the enduring and competing emphases in American foreign policy: isolationism versus internationalism, unilateralism versus multilateralism, and interventionism versus non-interventionism. The material in these two chapters will reappear in assessing U.S. foreign policy in subsequent chapters.

Part II. Challenges in Key Issue Areas

Part II consists of several chapters concerning challenges confronting American policymakers in key issue areas: American military strategy, the proliferation of weapons of mass destruction, trade and investment policies, democracy and human rights promotion, relations with the less developed regions of the world like Africa and Latin America, and the global environment.

Part III. Challenges in Key Regions and Countries

Part III consists of chapters that focus on American relations with and policies toward regions and countries of particular importance to U.S. security and well-being: Israel-Palestine, the Arab world, Islamic extremism and terrorism, "rising" China, Europe and the North Atlantic Treaty Organization (NATO), and resurgent Russia. The final chapter consists of several conclusions about American leadership in a changing world.

PEDAGOGICAL TOOLS

To enhance students' learning experience, the book identifies key terms with boldface, and these are defined in a glossary at the end of the book. The book also includes such features as excerpts from key documents, end-of-chapter discussion questions, and "DID YOU KNOW?" and "Controversy" boxes.

ONLINE RESOURCES

for CQ Press

SAGE edge offers a robust online environment featuring an impressive array of tools and resources for review, study, and further exploration, keeping both instructors and students on the cutting edge of teaching and learning. SAGE edge content is open access and available on demand. Learning and teaching have never been easier!

edge.sagepub.com/Mansbach

SAGE edge for Students provides a personalized approach to help students accomplish their course-work goals in an easy-to-use learning environment.

- Mobile-friendly **eFlashcards** and **quizzes** strengthen understanding of key terms and concepts.

- A customized online **action plan** allows students to individualize their learning experience.

- **Chapter summaries** with **learning objectives** reinforce the most important material.

- EXCLUSIVE! Access to full-text **SAGE journal articles** to support and expand on concepts presented in each chapter.

SAGE edge for Instructors supports teaching by making it easy to integrate quality content and create a rich learning environment for students.

- **Test banks** provide a diverse range of prewritten options as well as the opportunity to edit any question and/or insert personalized questions to effectively assess students' progress and understanding.

- **Sample course syllabi** for semester and quarter courses provide suggested models for structuring one's course.

- Editable, chapter-specific **PowerPoint® slides** offer complete flexibility for creating a multimedia presentation for the course.

- EXCLUSIVE! Access to full-text **SAGE journal articles** to support and expand on concepts presented in each chapter to encourage students to think critically.

ACKNOWLEDGMENTS

We would like to acknowledge Sarah Calabi, Elise Frasier, and Raquel Christie at CQ Press for their generous assistance at all stages of writing and publishing this book and the following reviewers, who provided many thoughtful and helpful suggestions:

Benn L. Bongang, Savannah State University

Matthew Caverly, University of North Florida

Mark Cichock, University of Texas–Arlington

Martha Cottam, Washington State University

Alan Eastham, Hendrix College

Ivan Ivanov, University of Cincinnati

Thomas Kolasa, Troy University

Sanford A. Lakoff, University of California, San Diego

Alynna Lyon, University of New Hampshire

Klejda Mulaj, Exeter University

Jim Seroka, Auburn University

James R. Stocker, Trinity Washington University

Brian Urlacher, University of North Dakota

Rhoda and Rachael Mansbach, no husband or father could ask for more

RWM

Ron Taylor, husband and friend

KLT

Introduction

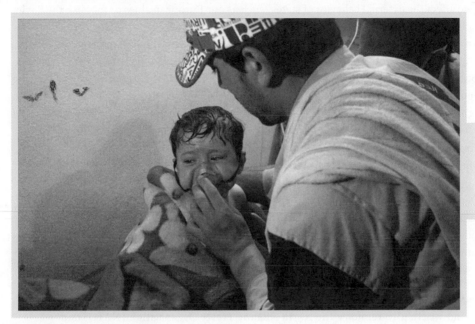

A Syrian child receives treatment following a suspected gas attack by the Assad regime.

Firas Taki/Anadolu Agency/Getty Images

In August 2013, as the brutal civil war in Syria between the regime of President Bashar al-Assad and his Sunni foes continued, a neighborhood in the country's capital was the target of a gas attack. As a horrified world became aware of the effects of toxic chemical weapons, a debate unfolded about whether or not Washington should use military force to punish the Syrian government for using this weapon against its own citizens.

Few moments in recent history have been as exciting and unpredictable as the current era. The distribution of global military and economic power is changing, and American dominance of global affairs, so pronounced at the end of the Cold War, is eroding as new centers of power in Asia, Europe, and elsewhere are emerging on the world stage. American decision makers are confronting a world that is rapidly changing. Dramatic challenges to American security and well-being confronted President Barack Obama as he took office for a second term in January 2013. With America having withdrawn from Iraq and planning an end its war in Afghanistan, the administration seemed to grow warier about using military force and more willing to employ diplomacy. Responding to doubts about entering into negotiations with Iran and participating in a peace conference seeking to end Syria's civil war, the president declared, "We're testing diplomacy; we're not resorting immediately to military conflict. . . . Tough talk and bluster may be the easy thing to do politically, but it's not the right thing for our security."[1] As Obama's first secretary of defense, Robert Gates, asked rhetorically, "Haven't Iraq, Afghanistan, and Libya taught us something about the unintended consequences of military action?"[2]

America faces foreign-policy challenges far different than those it confronted during the Cold War. Political scientist Michael Mandelbaum suggests that during the Cold War, U.S. foreign policy "was all about how we affect the external behavior of states" such as our European allies or foes like the Soviet Union. Domestic conditions in those countries were largely ignored; Turkey and Pakistan, for instance, were American allies against the USSR even though both were governed my military dictatorships. However, as Mandelbaum points out, contemporary U.S. foreign policy is largely about "affecting the internal composition and governance of states" such as Iraq, Egypt, Syria, and Afghanistan and altering their political culture and society. But "guns, money, and rhetoric—simply don't work for these new tasks. It is like trying to open a can with a sponge." This leads to his conclusion, "With the traditional tools of foreign policy, we can stop some bad things from happening, but we cannot make good things happen," such as transforming Iraq and Afghanistan into democratic societies.[3]

The following are some of the crucial issues facing American leaders:

- China's growing economic, political, and military muscle led American policymakers to announce a "strategic pivot" from the Middle East to Asia, and now officials have to decide whether to emphasize containing or engaging a new generation of Chinese communist leaders.

- Renewed Russian military power poses difficult choices for Washington, such as whether or not to go forward with an antiballistic system that Russian leaders bitterly oppose and whether to reinforce the North Atlantic Treaty Organization (NATO) and send arms to Ukraine, which is a victim of Russian aggression.

- Global economic and financial crises challenge recovery from the global recession. Crises threaten the future of Europe's Eurozone and even the survival of the European Union; political gridlock in Washington limits defense spending even as the U.S. economy improves; and even China's dramatic economic growth, a key element in global economic growth, has slowed.

- Potential foes like Iran and North Korea have acquired or were acquiring weapons of mass destruction (WMD). In the case of Iran, negotiations with Tehran sought to reduce that threat. Officials now must oversee implementation of the deal completed in 2015.

- Political revolution and counterrevolution have swept across North Africa and the Middle East, promising a new era of democracy in some countries and the prospect of growing civil strife in others, while destabilizing long-time political relationships like that between the United States and Israel, and challenging the security of pro-American regimes in the Persian Gulf. The spread of violence in the Middle East also threatens to increase the influence of violent Islamic extremists.

- Disputes in East Asia, notably those involving rival territorial claims of China, Taiwan, and Japan and China, Vietnam, and the Philippines to offshore islands, threaten to ignite violence that might entangle Washington in a conflict with China.

- At a time of growing strains in the long-time U.S.-Israeli alliance, durable conflicts in the Middle East, especially that between Israel and the Palestinians, continue to threaten regional stability. Iran's aid to groups like Hezbollah and its involvement in Syria, Iraq, Yemen, and Lebanon further destabilize the Middle East.

- Smoldering conflicts in several African countries such as Somalia, Mali, Nigeria, and the Democratic Republic of Congo threaten humanitarian disasters and regional instability.

- Several Latin American countries, notably Venezuela, Bolivia, and Ecuador, have pursued increasingly hostile policies toward the United States, but Washington ended its long-time embargo on Cuba.

- Political and religious extremists organized in terrorist groups in Afghanistan, Iraq, Pakistan, Indonesia, Nigeria, Somalia, and Yemen, and especially Iraq and Syria remain significant threats to America's national security as well as to American friends and allies in Europe, Africa, and Asia.

COMPETING MODELS OF U.S. FOREIGN POLICY

Some students of foreign policy believe that there is an objective and discernible **national interest** that should guide the foreign-policy choices that policymakers make—whether in responding to dramatic events or more ordinary, ongoing activities like managing trade agreements, working in international and regional organizations, or enhancing homeland security. That premise shapes the belief that foreign-policy decisions can be made in a rational fashion that serves the national interest. This assumption is the basis of Graham Allison's and Philip Zelikow's **rational actor model** that views states as purposive unitary actors analogous to individuals who are seeking to minimize costs and maximize gains in order to achieve coherent objectives and goals. This model assumes that an observer will have successfully "explained an event when he can show an action was reasonable given the strategic reasons or preferences of the state."[4] The model may seem useful to observers because it requires little detailed information about the actual process of decision making, which is difficult to access even at home or in other countries.

This simplified model of foreign-policy decision making assumes **rationality**. This implies awareness of alternatives and sufficient knowledge to allow leaders to weigh accurately the costs and benefits of each and the capacity to implement policies in a consistent fashion such that one policy does not contradict other policies. Although we can imagine individual decision makers reaching conclusions in what they perceive as a rational manner, in the complex external and domestic political arenas every **bureaucracy** and **interest group** defines its own interests and opinions as constituting the "national interest" and thereafter calculates its preferences. Such groups and institutions pursue their own agendas, and the arena of choice is characterized by interactions among them.

The making and implementation of foreign policy in *any* country is a complex process. This is especially the case in a great power like the United States with its innumerable bureaucracies, pressure groups, political perspectives, and partisan preferences. Although precisely which societal groups or government bureaucracies and which individuals will seek to have a place at the table in formulating and/or implementing policy varies by issue, the results are likely to be uneasy compromises that incorporate diverse opinions and perspectives. Allison and Zelikow present two alternatives to their rational actor model that take account of this complexity and look within the state and other actors.

The **organizational process model** considers how the processes of large bureaucracies such as standard operating and organizational procedures explain their behavior.[5] Bureaucracies that confront challenges rarely look at them holistically but instead tap subgroups or individuals within the organization to deal with pieces of the issue. Moreover, owing to time constraints such organizations fall back either on existing contingency plans or on policies and repertoires that have been useful in the past.

In the second alternative model, the **government politics model**, Allison and Zelikow conceive of policy as the outcome of bargaining among the various participants and contestants.[6] Compromises and incrementalism are crucial because of the necessity to reach consensus among numerous players, representing a variety of interests and with differential influence to pursue those interests. The two models are not necessarily incompatible, describing as they do processes *within* and *among* bureaucratic or societal groups. They are significant for highlighting the complexity of the foreign-policymaking process that is absent in the rational actor model.

ORGANIZATION OF THE BOOK

Like Allison and Zelikow, we seek to explain decisions that Washington has made in meeting critical contemporary challenges and describe those policies as well as alternative policies that might be adopted. To accomplish this, all of the chapters are divided in three parts—"past" (what policies were historically pursued), "present" (what policies are currently pursued), and "future" (alternative policies and their potential costs and benefits).

Part I, "Policy Orientations," examines the various influences on foreign-policy decisions that preclude purely rational decision making and that often compel leaders to compromise and to sacrifice clear and decisive policies. Part I also introduces the enduring and competing emphases in American foreign policy that will reappear in subsequent chapters: isolationism and internationalism, unilateralism and multilateralism, and interventionism and noninterventionism.

Part II, "Challenges in Key Issue Areas," consists of several chapters concerning challenges confronting American policymakers in important functional areas. The first of these issues involves designing American military strategy in a dangerous world in which threats range from nuclear and large-scale conventional conflict down to civil wars, ethnic violence, and terrorism by small groups of extremists. The second examines the problem posed by the proliferation of weapons of mass destruction to potential foes such as North Korea and Iran. The third describes the difficulties entailed in crafting consistent trade and investment policies in a world beset by economic and financial crises and characterized by economic globalization and economic interdependence. The fourth chapter in this section examines the conundrum resulting from the tension between idealistic policies aimed at spreading democracy and enhancing human rights and the pragmatic needs of engagement with authoritarian governments in order to minimize conflict and promote other policy objectives. The fifth examines U.S. policies toward the less developed regions of the world like Africa and Latin America that are growing in importance and salience owing to economic, strategic, and humanitarian considerations. The sixth describes the evolution of American policies that deal with the deteriorating global environment, especially climate change and the need for new sources of energy.

Part III, "Challenges in Key Regions and Countries," consists of chapters that focus on American relations with and policies toward regions and countries of particular importance to U.S. security and well-being. These include Israel-Palestine, the Arab world and the consequences of the "Arab Spring," Islamic extremism and terrorism, "rising" China, America's friends and allies in Europe and the North Atlantic Treaty Organization (NATO), and resurgent Russia. The final chapter consists of several conclusions about American leadership in a changing world.

KEY TERMS

bureaucracy (p. 3)

dictatorships (p. 2)

foreign policy (p. 2)

government politics
    model (p. 4)

interest group (p. 3)

national interest (p. 3)

organizational
    process model
    (p. 4)

rational actor
    model (p. 3)

rationality (p. 3)

weapons of mass destruction
    (WMD) (p. 2)

1

Sources of American Foreign Policy

Fed Chairman Ben Bernanke testifies before Congress about America's great recession.

AP Photo/Evan Vucci

Our first chapter examines key influences on U.S. foreign-policy formulation and implementation. It begins by discussing how the foreign and domestic arenas have become intermingled in a globalized world and then identifies the several sources of foreign policy.

THE LINKAGE OF DOMESTIC AND FOREIGN POLICIES

With America's economy sputtering, interest rates near zero, and the threat of a second recession looming, America's Federal Reserve announced a third round of "quantitative easing" (QE3) in September 2012. The Fed would purchase up to $40 billion a month of U.S. mortgage-backed bonds to increase America's money supply and provide financial institutions with additional capital that could be loaned to businesses and individuals who would spend the funds, thereby stimulating the domestic economy and reducing unemployment. The action, advocated by Fed Chairman Ben Bernanke, had domestic objectives but, owing to **globalization**, would have a powerful impact abroad. Foreign critics, notably in Brazil, China, and Russia, contended that the Fed's action would weaken the U.S. dollar, raise the value of their currencies, and harm their ability to export, while triggering volatile investment flows from America to the developing world. Brazil's finance minister described QE3 as "selfish" and expressed fear about a currency war of competitive devaluations. Bernanke responded that the Fed's policy would hasten America's economic recovery, thereby aiding the global economy because Americans would be able to buy more foreign goods. As the Fed's decision illustrates, the domestic and foreign arenas are no longer isolated from each other.

Recent decades have witnessed growing links between the domestic and foreign arenas. President Barack Obama came to office in 2008 promising a foreign policy based on domestic **values**. America's domestic policies were profoundly affected by wars in Korea and Vietnam and, more recently, by wars in Afghanistan and Iraq. International organizations and agreements such as the World Trade Organization and the North American Free Trade Agreement have a direct impact on America's domestic economy. Conversely, domestic policies on trade, taxation, economic investment, and even civil rights have a significant impact overseas. Frequently issues that arise in a domestic context have major consequences overseas. Thus, the appearance of a 14-minute U.S. film trailer posted in July 2012 on YouTube, featuring a blasphemous treatment of the Prophet Muhammad, produced rage throughout the Islamic world after it appeared on Egyptian television.

All countries are subject to external influences, and their external environment is in turn affected by domestic events. Foreign policy is the point at which influences arising in the global system cross into the domestic arena and domestic politics is transformed into external behavior. The traditional **state-centric** view was that America, like other states, is sovereign and, as such, controls its boundaries and territory, is subject to no higher external authority, and is the legal equal of other states. This perspective assumes that sovereign states have a clear and unitary national interest, and that their governments interact directly with one another and with international organizations. It also assumes that publics and domestic interest groups in different societies do not interact directly with those in other societies. Instead, they present their views to their own governments, which then represent them in relations with other governments. Figure 1.1 illustrates this perspective in which interstate politics remains distinct from domestic politics.

The traditional model is inadequate to describe the full range of factors shaping foreign policy. In the words of former Secretary of State Hillary Clinton, "increasing global interconnectedness now necessitates reaching beyond governments to citizens directly and broadening the U.S. foreign policy portfolio to include issues once confined to the domestic sphere, such as economic and environmental regulation, drugs and disease, organized crime, and world hunger. As those issues spill across borders, the domestic agencies addressing them must now do more of their work overseas, operating out of embassies and consulates."[1]

Figure 1.2 presents a picture of a **transnational** world in which external and domestic factors interact directly. The domestic pyramid of policy formation is penetrated at several levels, and links among governments and domestic groups are multiplied to reflect the complex exchanges that occur. Thus, there is interaction among interest groups at home and abroad and governments,

FIGURE 1.1   Model of State-Centric World

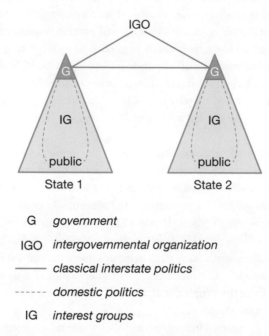

G	*government*
IGO	*intergovernmental organization*
——	*classical interstate politics*
- - - -	*domestic politics*
IG	*interest groups*

Source: Adapted from Robert O. Keohane and Joseph S. Nye, Jr., "Transnational Relations and World Politics: An Introduction," *International Organization,* Summer 1971: 332–334.

among interest groups in different states, and among interest groups and both international and **nongovernmental organizations.**

The complexity of relations between societies and states at home and abroad was reflected by American recognition of Israel. Israel declared its statehood in 1948, a presidential election year in America. Both candidates had to take a position about whether to recognize Israel, but it was especially important that Harry Truman, the incumbent Democrat, adopt a favorable attitude toward the new state because he sought Jewish political and financial support in key states like New York. For Truman, Israelis constituted a significant constituency because of their links with America's Jewish community. Truman adopted a pro-Israeli policy, despite objections from the Departments of Defense and State, which feared that recognizing Israel would alienate oil-rich Arab states. Figure 1.3 represents schematically the links among groups in 1948 that interacted in relation to the question of recognizing Israel. Arrows represent the flow of communications among key actors. To understand Truman's decision, we would have to describe communications between him and other government officials, between the government and groups like the Jewish community and the Democratic Party, and between the U.S. government and those of other countries.

A similar link between the domestic and external arenas involving the Middle East was evident during the 2012 U.S. presidential election. President Obama and Republican candidate Mitt Romney in a televised debate on October 16, 2012, vigorously disputed the assault on the U.S. consulate in Benghazi,

FIGURE 1.2   Model of Transnational World

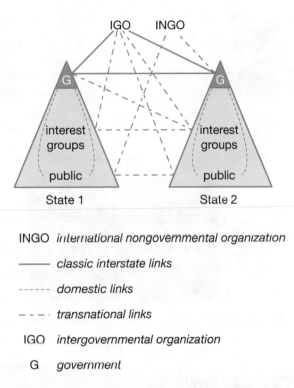

INGO   *international nongovernmental organization*

——————   *classic interstate links*

------   *domestic links*

– – – ·   *transnational links*

IGO   *intergovernmental organization*

G   *government*

Source: Adapted from Robert O. Keohane and Joseph S. Nye, Jr., "Transnational Relations and World Politics: An Introduction," *International Organization,* Summer 1971: 332–334.

Libya, that climaxed with the death of America's ambassador. Earlier in the campaign, Governor Romney had visited Israel, where he depicted Obama as hostile to Israel and weak toward Iran. Injecting himself in the campaign, Israeli Prime Minister Benjamin Netanyahu gave a speech at the United Nations in which he declared that Iran was approaching the point where it could produce a nuclear weapon and urged Washington to act before it was too late. As this case suggests, affiliations and identities that cut across national boundaries are important factors in foreign policy. Thus, analyzing only diplomatic relations among governments is insufficient to explain foreign policy, and studying foreign policy entails awareness that traditional boundaries between "foreign" and "domestic" policies have eroded.

Moreover, globalization has facilitated the movement of persons, things, and ideas across national boundaries, making them increasingly porous. Even a superpower like America is "penetrated" by flows of illegal migrants, illegal drugs, and subversive ideas. For its part, Washington employs a variety of tools to penetrate foreign societies—propaganda favoring democracy and human rights in countries like China and Russia, covert assistance to opposition groups in hostile states like Iran, foreign aid to friendly governments, and financial and political support for American corporations like Boeing.

FIGURE 1.3   Communication Model Israeli Recognition Process, 1948

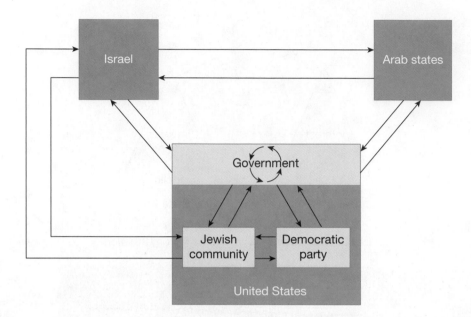

Source: Raymond F. Hopkins and Richard W. Mansbach, *Structure and Process in International Politics* (New York, NY: Harper & Row, 1973), 135.

SOURCES OF FOREIGN-POLICY INFLUENCE

Let us now examine the major sources of influence on U.S. foreign policy. We shall discuss five categories of factors that influence American policymaking: **external factors**, **government factors**, **role factors**, **societal factors**, and **individual factors**.[2] The degree to which these affect foreign policy varies by country. For example, the United States is a large **democracy** with a high level of **economic development**. As such, it has a large government with numerous foreign-policy agencies and bureaucracies as well as innumerable societal pressure groups. And, increasingly, interest groups at home and abroad are linked transnationally. External factors, while important in shaping U.S. policies, are likely to have a greater impact on small countries like Denmark or Singapore because they are more dependent on trade and allies for economic and military security, while societal factors are likely to have less of an impact in countries like Russia and China that have **authoritarian governments** that limit the freedom of social groups, unlike the United States, which is an open society, governed by democratic **norms** and the rule of law. In addition, in large countries like America, the impact of particular individuals like the president, while substantial, is likely to be constrained by the many bureaucratic and social actors competing to have their views taken account of.

Israeli Prime Minister
Benjamin Netanyahu
warns the United
Nations about
Iranian weapons of
mass destruction
(WMD).

AP Photo/Seth Wenig

External Factors

Globalization itself is perhaps the leading external constraint on foreign policy because **interdependence** dilutes American **sovereignty**, makes the United States increasingly vulnerable to the actions of other countries and, as the opening paragraphs of this chapter reflect, makes those countries more vulnerable to U.S. policies. Globalization also is a key source for the disappearing distinction between domestic and foreign policy. President Obama explicitly recognized growing global interdependence when, on entering office, he spoke of the need for multilateral cooperation and "common problems." Thus, globalization and the interdependence of the U.S. economy with economies worldwide were largely responsible for the rapid spread worldwide of America's subprime mortgage crisis in 2007 to 2008, and Obama declared that restoring U.S. influence abroad required reinvigorating the economy at home. In a word, America's recession became a global contagion.

The porosity of U.S. borders makes it vulnerable to flows of people, things, and ideas from abroad, for instance, cyberattacks, extremist political views, drugs, diseases, terrorists, and any interruption in patterns of trade. One such interruption was triggered by the 2011 earthquake and tsunami in Japan and the subsequent nuclear crisis that interrupted global supply chains in a variety of transnational industries including the production of and trade in automobiles and consumer electronics.

Other external factors of great significance are the distributions of resources and attitudes in the global system. America's own resources—economic, military, political, and social—are part of the country's domestic environment, but the *distribution* of such factors elsewhere is external and must be considered by decision makers in Washington. American decision makers must ask what U.S. capabilities are *relative* to those of potential friends and foes rather than what is the *absolute* level of American capabilities. Thus, American military and economic capabilities have declined since the end of the Cold War in relative though not in absolute terms.

Although some observers conclude that America is losing the military and economic dominance it enjoyed after the Cold War,[3] this does not mean that America is in the midst of absolute decline. China, for example, is "rising" but remains behind the United States on most dimensions. As political scientist Joseph Nye observes: "The word 'decline' mixes up two different dimensions: absolute decline, in the sense of decay, and relative decline in which the power resources of other states grow or are used more effectively." This leads Nye to conclude, "A smart-power narrative for the twenty-first century is not about maximizing power or preserving hegemony. It is about finding ways to combine resources in successful strategies in the new context of power diffusion and 'the rise of the rest.'"[4] Nye also reminds us of the interdependence of domestic and foreign policy in arguing that challenges to U.S. strength include remedying the American economy, ending the political stalemate between Republicans and Democrats, and reforming immigration policy to encourage the inflow of talented individuals from overseas.

Americans have also become increasingly preoccupied with domestic issues which they believe should take precedence over involvement abroad. Nevertheless, it is not that the United States has less military or economic **capability**—"**hard power**"—than it did in the 1990s but rather that other countries such as China and India have significantly increased their own military and economic capabilities. America remains the world's only superpower, but new centers of military and economic power have emerged in the global system.

The distribution of political views and **ideologies** is equally important. If emerging centers of military and economic power are American allies and friends, the relative decline in U.S. resources matters less than if those new centers are American enemies or potential enemies. The fact that Great Britain, France, and Israel have nuclear weapons does not concern Washington because they have been allies for many years. Indeed, as U.S. allies they enhance America's military reach and capability. By contrast, the growth in China's nuclear capability and the acquisition of weapons of mass destruction by Iran and North Korea would pose serious problems for American national security because those countries are rivals and possibly enemies of the United States.

The importance of **attitudes** becomes apparent in other ways as well. The wars in Afghanistan and Iraq and the Great Recession at home sapped American global influence, especially its reputation or "**soft power**"—a positive reputation that helps a country attract and persuade others—a fact reflected in the hostile attitudes of growing numbers of Muslims toward the United States. Indeed, one reason why President Obama in June 2009 spoke in Cairo of "a new beginning" was that American popularity among Muslims globally had fallen precipitously owing to wars in Iraq and Afghanistan, tensions with Iran, and U.S. support for Israel. According to the White House Press Secretary, Egypt had been selected because it "is a country that in many ways represents the heart of the Arab world, and I think will be a trip, an opportunity for the President to address and discuss our relationship with the Muslim world."[5]

Geographic location is also an external factor of importance though perhaps less so than in past decades. Historically, the United States enjoyed the protection of two great oceans, the Atlantic and the Pacific, that also served as highways for trade with Europe and Asia respectively. In addition, America's northern and southern neighbors, Canada and Mexico, are relatively weak militarily and are close political and economic partners of the United States. Contrast the security historically afforded America by geography with the insecurity of a country like Israel whose dangerous neighborhood includes adversaries such as Iran and Syria and nonstate terrorist groups such as Hezbollah in Lebanon to the north and Hamas in the Gaza Strip to the southwest. It is hardly surprising that Israel, surrounded by foes and with a relatively small population and territory (both societal factors) remains preoccupied with military security and has both literally and figuratively sought "to wall itself off."

Globalization has, however, reduced the overall impact of geography. Notwithstanding the protection of the oceans, America is vulnerable to Russian or Chinese intercontinental ballistic missiles (ICBMs) as well as terrorists and cyberattacks. It depended until recently on energy sources, especially oil, and raw materials located thousands of miles from its shores. Economic and financial interdependence, the growth of global markets, and the growing role of technology in the movement of funds globally make Americans vulnerable to economic decisions or difficulties in all corners of the world.

Other external factors also affect policy decisions. As noted above, alignments and **alliances,** such as the North Atlantic Treaty Organization (NATO) and the U.S.-Japanese Treaty of Mutual Cooperation

MAP 1.1   Israel and Neighboring States

and Security, combined with the strong political, economic, and social ties among the members of such alliances, enhance overall U.S. capabilities and facilitate the projection of U.S. power around the world. On the other hand, alliances also limit the autonomy of the United States by obliging Washington legally and morally to act in certain ways to aid or protect its allies and friends.

A final set of external factors are the policies and actions of other countries toward the United States. Many of these are themselves reactions to U.S. policies and actions toward those countries. Indeed, reciprocity explains a good deal of foreign policy. As a rule, friendly acts trigger friendly responses, and hostile acts produce hostile responses. One problem, of course, is that another country's intentions are not always clear, and that its actions may be misunderstood by those in government. For example, as we saw at the beginning of this chapter, Brazil's finance minister interpreted the action of the Fed's renewed purchase of U.S. securities as unfriendly when the Fed's intention probably took little account of the consequences of its actions for Brazil.

→ ← CONTROVERSY

Realists and Liberals

Foreign-policy analysts and practitioners are frequently divided into "realists" and "liberals." These are ideal types, and most policymakers do not fit neatly into either category. Those who describe themselves as "realists" focus on external factors. They infer the national interest by examining the distribution of power globally, especially military power, and caution against intervention except where substantial American interests are at stake or where powerful rivals such as China or Russia are likely to profit. Alexander Hamilton was a "realist" who cautioned his young but vulnerable nation to remain out of the quarrels between England and revolutionary France. Realists largely ignore domestic factors, instead regarding states as "unitary" actors that reason like rational individuals. They also largely ignore normative questions, denounce ideologies, and regard as foolish idealistic efforts to extend democracy or human rights.

By contrast, those who describe themselves as "liberals" focus on norms rather than power and were termed "idealists" and "utopians" by realists. Liberals pay attention to domestic factors as sources of foreign policy and are more concerned than realists by threats to human security—climate change, global pandemics, and famine. Some, like Hamilton's political foe Thomas Jefferson, see normative objectives such as democratization and human rights as laudable foreign-policy objectives and are prepared to intervene overseas for humanitarian reasons. They also consider soft power as important as hard power.

Let us turn to the impact of governmental factors on foreign policymaking.

Government Factors

Such factors as the nature of government institutions; the distribution of influence among them; the means by which personnel are selected, recruited, and promoted; the bureaucratic and societal interests that are their constituents; and the degree to which government institutions are accessible to societal concerns are all relevant to American foreign policy. The size of government bureaucracies also matters. Thus, the larger and more complex are such bureaucracies, the more information they can absorb and the greater the attention they can pay to problems. On the other hand, as bureaucracies grow larger, more individuals must approve decisions, "red tape" increases, and, in general, it takes longer to make policy decisions.

Separation of Powers Among the constitutional factors that influence U.S. foreign policymaking is "**separation of powers**" among the branches of government—executive, legislative, and judicial. The authors of the Constitution intended that by distributing authority among the branches of government and constructing a system of **checks and balances**, it would prevent any branch from accumulating too much power. The separation ensures that there will be a fragmentation of decision-making authority in American policymaking.

Constitutionally, the president is "Commander in Chief of the Army and Navy of the United States, and of the Militia of the several States" and has responsibility for overseeing the major foreign-policy bureaucracies—the Departments of State and Defense, the Central Intelligence Agency (CIA), the National Security Council (consisting of the vice president, the secretary of state, the secretary of Treasury, the secretary of defense, and the national security adviser)—that serve to coordinate foreign-policy planning for the president. Other agencies with both domestic and foreign-policy responsibilities include the Treasury; the Office of Management and Budget; the Office of National Drug Control Policy; the Federal Bureau of Investigation (FBI); the Bureau of Alcohol, Tobacco, Firearms and Explosives; and the Departments of Homeland Security, Agriculture, Justice, and Commerce. Some of these agencies have grown more important in recent decades. For example, the Treasury and Commerce Departments and the U.S. Trade Representative have growing responsibilities in an era of economic globalization, and the intelligence agencies, along with Homeland Security, have a special role in combating terrorist threats.

These agencies frequently have overlapping responsibilities—for example, the State Department and the National Security Council—and may compete with one another for primacy in particular issue areas. Indeed, the position of national director of intelligence was established in 2004 with an eye toward coordinating intelligence activities following intelligence failures regarding 9/11 and Saddam Hussein's alleged program for developing WMD. Nevertheless, coordinating the activities of powerful intelligence agencies such as the CIA, the Defense Intelligence Agency, the National Security Agency, the Department of Homeland Security, the FBI, and the State Department's Bureau of Intelligence and Research remains a daunting task.

Presidents share their role in making foreign policy with Congress. Article II, Section 2 of the Constitution states: "He shall have Power, by and with the Advice and Consent of the Senate, to make Treaties, provided two thirds of the Senators present concur; and he shall nominate, and by and with the Advice and Consent of the Senate, shall appoint Ambassadors, other public Ministers and Consuls." Moreover, the Congress is vested with responsibility to "provide for the common Defense," "raise and support armies," and declare war.

On some occasions, presidents have asked for and received resolutions from Congress short of declarations of war, while on others, they have used NATO and United Nations (UN) resolutions as the basis for committing troops to combat. The presidency affords considerable latitude in foreign affairs and, despite the constitutional requirement that only Congress can declare war, the presidential prerogative to commit U.S. combat forces overseas has grown dramatically since President Franklin D. Roosevelt had to cope with an isolationist Congress before World War II. There were no official declarations of war for conflicts in Korea (1950–1953), Vietnam (1965–1973), the Persian Gulf (1990–1991), Afghanistan (2001–2014), or Iraq (2003–2011). To rein in presidential power to go to war, Congress passed the War Powers Resolution in 1973 by which Congress must approve troop commitments in conflicts lasting over 60 days. President Richard Nixon vetoed the act but was overridden by Congress, and every later president regarded the law as an intrusion on presidential authority. Nevertheless, in 2014 when President Obama decided to launch airstrikes in Iraq against the Islamic State in Iraq and Syria (ISIS), he welcomed congressional approval but declared he could do so regardless owing to his power as Commander in Chief. When he decided to expand the strikes to Syria, he also invoked Congress's 2001 Authorization for the Use of Military Force against terrorists and its 2002 Authorization of Military Force against Iraq as providing authority to go forward. Thereafter, however, he decided to seek congressional authorization for his military campaign against ISIS while limiting it to three years, ruling out ground combat, and rescinding the 2002 authorization.

Congress retains the power of the purse—the authority to levy taxes and determine public expenditures without which foreign and security policies could not be implemented. A host of committees and subcommittees in the House of Representatives and the Senate deal with foreign-policy legislation, among which the most important are the Senate Foreign Relations, Homeland Security, and Armed Services committees, and the House of Representatives Select Committee on Intelligence, Foreign Affairs, Armed Services, Homeland Security, and Intelligence committees. These committees and their subcommittees are managed by powerful chairpersons, can hold hearings on foreign policy, and play a role in determining budget appropriations. But the power of the purse is a blunt instrument, and Congress rarely uses it if a president argues that national security is at risk.

If either house of Congress is dominated by a different political party than the president's, there will almost certainly be partisan disagreements. Thus, congressional Republicans blamed Presidents Roosevelt and Truman for the communization of Eastern Europe after World War II and for the defeat of China's anticommunists by Mao Zedong in 1949. And although congressional Democrats initially supported President George W. Bush's decision to invade Iraq, they later sought to limit the president's freedom of action once it appeared that the war would continue after the fall of Iraqi President Saddam Hussein. More recently, the Republican-controlled Congress tried to force President Obama to declare additional sanctions against Iran even while negotiations were continuing with Tehran regarding its nuclear aspirations, and John Boehner, the Republican Speaker of the House of Representatives, invited Israeli Prime Minister Netanyahu to address Congress about the dangers posed by Iran and Islamic terrorists, issues that Republicans believed Obama did not take sufficiently seriously. The president, who did not get on well with Netanyahu, with whom he disagreed strongly on several issues, was not consulted and declared he would not see Netanyahu when he came to Washington. Thereafter, Netanyahu authorized expansion of West Bank settlements, which Obama opposed. Obama regarded Boehner as exceeding his role as House Speaker and intruding on the president's leading role in foreign affairs. He also regarded Netanyahu's acceptance of the invitation to speak and the actions of Israeli Ambassador Ron Dermer as gratuitous interference in America's domestic affairs. Susan Rice, President Obama's national security adviser, termed Netanyahu's acceptance of Speaker Boehner's invitation as "disastrous" for U.S.-Israeli relations. Following the March 2015 framework agreement with Iran, the Senate, led by Bob Corker (R-TN), chairperson of the Foreign Relations Committee, sought to force the president to obtain its approval for a final agreement. Obama agreed to let Congress reject the agreement, but its vote could be vetoed by the president.

Although congressional influence on foreign policy fluctuates, Congress rarely sways the executive branch on major issues. Congressional weakness in formulating foreign policy partly reflects lack of information and the exigencies of time, especially if situations require prompt action. Although some members of Congress, notably committee chairs who have served on key committees for lengthy periods, come to be foreign-policy experts, most members of Congress know little about foreign policy. America's intervention in Iraq provoked little congressional opposition until public frustration with the war led to Democratic control of the House and Senate in 2006. Congress has also asserted itself periodically during the Obama years, especially after Republicans took control of the House of Representatives in 2010. After taking control of the Senate in 2015, 47 Republican senators wrote a letter to Iranian leaders without consulting the White House, warning them that any agreement concluded with Tehran by Obama could be reversed by a future president, and the permanent end of sanctions against Iran would need congressional approval. The White House accused the senators of undermining U.S. foreign policy. Nevertheless, congressional criticisms of presidential decisions failed to alter significantly Obama's cautious approach to foreign policy.

Although the judicial branch is less frequently involved in foreign policy than the executive or legislative branches, it, too, has from time to time an important input. The Supreme Court confirmed the supremacy of the government in foreign policy in *United States v. Curtiss-Wright Export Corp.* (1936) when it decided that Curtiss-Wright could not defy a U.S. arms embargo during the Chaco War between Bolivia and Paraguay. In *Missouri v. Holland* (1920), the Court ruled that international treaties took precedence over states' rights after Missouri declared that the federal government had no right to enforce a treaty regulating migratory birds.

The Supreme Court has also adjudicated disagreements between the president and Congress. Under the "political question doctrine," federal courts "will not adjudicate certain controversies because their resolution is more proper within the political branches," and "it has regularly been invoked in lower federal courts in cases concerning foreign policy."[6] In general, the Supreme Court has supported the president's prerogatives as Commander in Chief. One analysis reviewed 347 cases dealing with foreign policy that the Court decided between 1789 and 1996 and concluded that it had ruled in favor of the executive branch in over two-thirds of these. "The executive branch was more likely to emerge victorious when the case involved the President's constitutional powers, the supremacy of federal over state law, and when the case involved foreign actors."[7] Thus, the court ruled in 2015 that Congress could not require the State Department to indicate in passports that Jerusalem belonged to Israel because it undermined presidential foreign-policy authority.

Nevertheless, in *Youngstown Sheet & Tube Co. v. Sawyer* (1952), the Court ruled that President Harry Truman, who had nationalized Youngstown Sheet & Tube to prevent a strike from closing it during the Korean War, did not have the authority to seize private property. Nor has the Court been reluctant to overrule the executive branch in cases involving foreign policy if they touch on civil rights. For example, in *Hamdi v. Rumsfeld* (2004), the Court ruled that, while the government could detain those judged to be "enemy combatants" indefinitely, it could not deprive an American citizen of the right of **habeas corpus** and, therefore, had to allow Yaser Esam Hamdi (a U.S. citizen captured in Afghanistan in 2001) the right to challenge his detention and status as an enemy combatant in an American court.

In contrast to the United States, parliamentary democracies like that in Britain do not have separation of powers among the branches of government. In consequence, although prime ministers may be constrained by the need to consult other parties in coalition governments, as leaders of a majority party or a coalition, they are usually assured of a legislative majority for their foreign policies and defense budgets.

Policy Incrementalism Conflict among different branches of government constitutes only one of the impediments to foreign-policy consensus in America. The executive branch consists of a host of agencies and departments that define the national interest from their own perspective. The need to gain agreement among the branches of government or among the bureaucracies that constitute the foreign-policy community impedes making bold policies that diverge significantly from past policies or that change in a major way America's orientation to the world. Instead, foreign policymaking tends to be pragmatic and incremental, a style of decision making that Roger Hilsman, director of the State Department's Bureau of Intelligence and Research during the Kennedy administration, described as "an uneasy . . . compromise among competing goals. . . . A government does not decide to inaugurate the nuclear age, but only to try to build an atomic bomb before its enemy does. . . . Rather than through grand decision on grand alternatives, policy changes seem to come through a series of slight modifications of existing policy, with new policy emerging slowly and haltingly by small and usually tentative steps, a process of trial and error in which policy zigs and zags, reverses itself, and then moves forward."[8]

Most American foreign policy consists of routine procedures in maintaining relations with other countries and of bureaucratic competition in pursuit of institutional goals. With imperfect information and inability to foresee accurately the consequences of their decisions, leaders tend to proceed cautiously. Radical shifts in policy are also inhibited by the numerous cross pressures to which policymakers are subject, failure to reach consensus in the face of competing interests, and different perceptions. All this fosters minimal decisions even on important issues. Thus, the process by which American troop strength in Vietnam grew from 760 in 1959 to over 536,000 in 1968 was a gradual one, consisting of numerous discrete decisions in response to specific events that led to modest troop increases without any single decision to intervene massively. As we shall see, policymakers are bound by their own roles, the push and pull of parochial interest groups, and competition among bureaucracies, the topic to which we now turn.

Bureaucratic Competition **Incrementalism** presupposes the existence of a government that consists of "a conglomerate of semi-feudal, loosely allied organizations, each with a substantial life of its own."[9] Although presidents are in charge of the executive branch, they cannot always bend foreign-policy bureaucracies to do their bidding. They need the bureaucracies to collect, process, and interpret information, as well as allocate resources and responsibilities for performing important tasks. It is often difficult to determine whether the information bureaucracies provide is slanted to support a particular policy, and it is sometimes impossible to determine whether they implement policy in the manner leaders wish. Large foreign-policy organizations like the Departments of State and Defense have their own "culture" based on collective memories, routines, and sources of information that is perpetuated by selective recruitment of similarly minded employees.

Bureaucracies devise **standard operating procedures** for dealing with routine issues. Such procedures are especially helpful in dealing with recurring issues because high-ranking policymakers in the executive and legislative branches have neither the time nor expertise to do so. On such issues, low-echelon bureaucrats can act within policy guidelines set by political leaders. But routine decisions can have serious consequences. President Dwight Eisenhower authorized a series of "spy flights" over the Soviet Union to gather intelligence, and decisions about individual missions were made routinely by the CIA. On the eve of a summit conference to be held in May 1960 with Soviet leader Nikita Khrushchev, such a flight was authorized. However, a U-2 spy plane, piloted by Francis Gary Powers, a civilian working for the Lockheed Aircraft Corporation under government contract, was shot down over the USSR. The news was released by Khrushchev, who demanded an American apology. The incident was deeply embarrassing to Eisenhower, who had been unaware that a flight was taking place. The administration denied that the violation of Soviet airspace was intentional, but its claims were shown to be false, and the summit was abruptly cancelled by the Soviet leader. Presidents can alter standard operating procedures, priorities, and institutional perspectives, but such alteration is usually a complex undertaking.

Nor do American leaders usually have the time, information, or expertise to supervise the implementation of policy. At best they may concentrate on those aspects of immediate importance to them, ignoring other issues. President Obama was intimately involved in the three-month review of the Afghanistan war leading to a decision to add 30,000 U.S. troops in the 2009 "surge." He spent so much time on the issue, including eleven hours on the day after Thanksgiving that he joked, "I've got more deeply in the weeds than a president should, and now you guys need to solve this."[10] Presidents who expect to give orders and have them carried out as they desire will be disappointed. President Truman said of Eisenhower, his successor: "He'll sit here and he'll say, 'Do this! Do that!' *And nothing will happen.* Poor Ike—it won't be a bit like the Army. He'll find it very frustrating."[11] Even President Franklin Roosevelt, noted for his ability to control his executive departments, was so frustrated by the effort he exclaimed:

> The Treasury is so large and far-flung and ingrained in its practices that I find it almost impossible to get the action and results. . . . But the Treasury is not to be compared with the State Department. You should go through the experience of trying to get any changes in the thinking, policy, and action of the career diplomats and then you'd know what a real problem was. But the Treasury and the State Department put together are nothing as compared with the Na-a-vy. . . . To change anything in the Na-a-a-vy is like punching a feather bed. You punch it with your right and you punch it with your left until you are finally exhausted, and then you find the damn bed just as it was before you started punching.[12]

The existence of large bureaucracies encourages competition. Much of foreign policy is the product of interaction among members of government and nongovernmental organizations and groups. The belief that "rational" decisions are based on "national interest" is remote from reality. Instead, much of foreign policy is the outcome of politicized bureaucratic processes involving competition and bargaining in which the outcome depends as much on the relative power of the participants as on the wisdom of their arguments. The budgetary process is often an important battleground for competing interests. Some argue that bureaucratic rivalry can be reduced through reorganization, but as one observer put it: "The 'best' organization is that which distributes power and responsibility in such a fashion as to facilitate the policies you favor."[13]

Bureaucratic competition is especially common in situations when time is available for debate, and decisions may lead to the distribution or redistribution of resources among bureaucracies. The Defense Department may argue for a larger share of the overall budget, declaring that military threats from overseas are increasing and are more important than concerns about the economy, the environment, or other issues. Rivalry is also common among the Army, Navy, Air Force, and Marines for a larger share of the defense budget, each arguing that its role is more important for national defense than that of the others. Sometimes a decision may be aimed at protecting bureaucratic interests by following "accepted practice." Thus, the military services may agree to maintain an existing distribution of funds in order not "to rock the boat." Bureaucratic competition encourages the formation of coalitions across organizational boundaries. Thus, the Defense Department may ally with members of Congress who favor high defense spending, especially from districts or states with high employment in defense industries, as well as with those industries. Defense-related industries in return may provide campaign contributions to those who favor defense spending. This coalition was termed by Eisenhower the "**military-industrial complex.**"

The Military Industrial Complex

DID YOU KNOW?

Shortly before leaving office, President Dwight Eisenhower gave a television address in which he warned the American public about what he regarded a threat to democracy. "In the councils of government, we must guard against the acquisition of unwarranted influence, whether sought or unsought, by the military-industrial complex. The potential for the disastrous rise of misplaced power exists, and will persist."[14]

Small Groups Unlike day-to-day issues that engage large foreign-policy bureaucracies, **international crises**—high-threat issues that arise unexpectedly and necessitate rapid decisions—require that decisions be made by small groups of top-level leaders. In the 1962 Cuban missile crisis, President John Kennedy bypassed the ordinary mechanisms of policy formation and set up a small group of about fifteen trusted advisers, which came to be known as the "Ex Comm" (the Executive Committee of the National Security Council). The need for secrecy, speed, imagination, and consensus limits the size of decision-making groups during crises.

Small-group decision making differs from that of large organizations in several ways. First, the parochial interests of the group members' bureaucratic organizations (in which the individuals occupy high positions) tend to be subordinated to the purposes of the ad hoc group, which is under pressure to behave cooperatively and expeditiously. The shortage of time in which to make decisions and the threatening nature of the situation generate stress. Although individuals tend to perform less effectively under intense stress, moderate stress may increase productivity and efficiency, heighten morale, and enhance problem-solving abilities in small groups. Moderate stress also reduces selfish behavior and increases group cohesion. Under time pressure, groups are more able to reach agreement quickly. Such cooperation may facilitate decisions but may also produce bad ones, especially if no one offers divergent views. Attorney General Robert Kennedy argued that if his brother President Kennedy and his advisers had been forced to make a decision during the missile crisis twenty-four hours before they did, they would have chosen to initiate an airstrike against Soviet bases in Cuba with potentially disastrous consequences.

In conditions of stress and limited time, the members of small groups tend to rely on their own memories of past events, drawing simplified comparisons and analogies between the present and the past. President Truman's determination that the invasion of South Korea in 1950 should not be "another Munich" and Robert Kennedy's concern lest his brother be viewed as "another Tojo" (Japan's Prime Minister who ordered the surprise attack on Pearl Harbor on December 7, 1941) suggest that simple analogies may prove potent in the decisions of small groups. Except in crises, foreign-policy decision making is more open to public view in democracies like America than in countries with authoritarian regimes that can determine foreign policy without consulting citizens.

Regime Type The type of government or regime is seen by many observers as a crucial factor in foreign policy. Thus, according to **democratic peace theory**, democracies do not go to war with one another because they are constrained by voters who are reluctant to do so. America is a democracy and, although democracy has many virtues, some critics argue that foreign-policy decision making is not among them. In an oft-recited passaged, French political thinker Alexis de Tocqueville, writing early in the 19th century, declared: "Foreign policy does not require the use of the good qualities peculiar to democracy but does demand the cultivation of almost all those which it lacks," and "a democracy finds it difficult to coordinate the details of a great undertaking and to fix on some plan and carry it through with determination in spite of obstacles. It has little capacity for combining its measures in secret and waiting patiently for the result."[15] This pessimistic analysis suggests that the role of public opinion, which we discuss below, is shaping decisions in democratic societies and is the source of democracies' foreign-policy errors.

Societal Factors

Several societal factors have an impact on foreign-policy decision makers.

Political Culture Societal factors reflect America's **political culture**, that is, the pattern of beliefs, identities, and values held by members of society. American history, myths, education, language, experience, and ideology all affect national identity and common goals. American politicians routinely try to appeal to values such as democracy, individual liberty, equality of opportunity, the virtues of capitalism, and entrepreneurial initiative. Public opinion broadly reflects America's political culture, but the nature of its impact on foreign policy is highly contested.

Public Opinion   Observers differ about what the "public" is and whose views matter. **Public opinion** exists even though it only episodically affects policy directly and is difficult to identify or even measure. The public's "mood" fluctuates as does its attention to foreign affairs. Thus, Alexander Hamilton declared that "the people" are "turbulent and changing" and "seldom judge or determine right."[16] Relatively few people are well informed about foreign policy or have more than superficial views about it, and much of the time the public is divided in its views and unable to articulate those views clearly.

Although public opinion is diffuse, there are social elites, or **opinion leaders,** who can guide the public in certain directions. Religious leaders assume positions that can influence their flocks, the mass media popularize some policies and criticize others, and educators have an impact in shaping the beliefs of their students. Business and labor leaders, like other socioeconomic elites, frequently help shape the views of those whom they represent. Politicians persistently seek to persuade partisan followers of the virtues of particular courses of action. Congressional hearings on foreign policy routinely feature opinion leaders with different views testifying about policies that they support or oppose.

How significant is public opinion? The fickle nature of public opinion in bringing an end to America's war in Korea in the 1950s, its intervention in Vietnam in the 1970s or, more recently, in Iraq and Afghanistan, lends credence the claims of de Tocqueville and Hamilton. The American public was aroused in 1992 by televised images of the effects of famine in Somalia and in 2001 by television coverage of al-Qaeda's attack on New York's Twin Towers. In 2014, grisly images of two Americans being decapitated by the Islamic State in Iraq and Syria (ISIS) in Syria rapidly transformed public opinion from aversion to intervention following wars in Iraq and Afghanistan to support for attacking ISIS in Iraq and Syria.

In crises, the public typically rallies around its leaders, especially if Washington makes an effort to mobilize public support for U.S. commitments overseas. As foreign threats loom, congressional efforts to oversee executive actions tend to lessen. Thus, the events of 9/11 united Americans. Congress quickly authorized President Bush to use force "against those nations, organizations, or persons, he determines planned, authorized, committed, or aided the terrorist attacks," and public opinion willingly accepted the resulting American intervention in Afghanistan and the effort to capture Osama bin Laden. In September 2014, Congress quickly gave approval to President Obama's request for authorization to train and arm Syrian rebels in the face of ISIS with majorities of "hawks" in both parties supporting the request. Such events reinforced, at least temporarily, the role of the president as the principal architect of foreign policy. However, presidents often have to "oversell" what they are trying to accomplish with slogans such as "leader of the free world" or "making the world safe for democracy."

Overselling, however, makes it difficult for leaders to change course. Once an adversary has been demonized and depersonalized and once blood and treasure have been expended, it is difficult to back away from those commitments without facing an angry electorate. Thus, political scientist Gabriel Almond described the public's mood as prone to "dangerous overreactions,"[17] and diplomat George Kennan compared the public to a dinosaur in the sense that "you practically have to whack his tail off to make him aware that his interests are being disturbed; but once he grasps this, he lays about him such blind determination that he not only destroys his adversary but largely wrecks his native habitat."[18]

Nevertheless, we should not overestimate the impact of public opinion. First, relatively few Americans pay much attention to foreign affairs except when sensational events occur like the 9/11 terrorist attacks. In 2012, only 12 percent of the U.S. electorate regarded foreign policy among their top three concerns, only 15 percent regarded defense as one of their three main concerns,[19] and in a national exit poll only 5 percent regarded foreign policy as the major issue in the 2012 elections.[20] Indeed, some analysts argue that, far from influencing leaders, in most cases leaders have the capability to shape public opinion. Hence, the Florentine political philosopher Niccolò Machiavelli cynically declared that "men are so simple and so ready to obey present necessities that one who deceives will always find those who allow themselves to be deceived."[21] This reflects an elitist model in which leaders can shape and manipulate public opinion and use the media to do so.

Others, however, like Thomas Jefferson, accept a **pluralist** model and view public opinion as shaping the view of foreign-policy elites who are aided by the media in doing so. Thus, political scientist William Caspary concluded that "American public opinion is characterized by a *strong* and *stable* 'permissive mood' toward international involvements."[22] Almond perhaps best captured the role of the American public in foreign policy when he wrote that "the function of the public in a democratic-making process is to set certain policy criteria in the form of widely-held values and expectations, leaving to those who have a positive and informed interest the actual formation of policy."[23]

In sum, what is perceived as public opinion may actually reflect the views of relatively small but highly vocal minorities, and, though few Americans have consistent views of foreign policy, those that do pay attention may feel intensely about particular issues. Public opinion can flow into the foreign-policy process through various channels—elections, mass media, political parties, Congress, and interest groups. Although most of the public is not organized and only a small proportion is attentive to foreign policy, vocal minorities are frequently associated with interest groups that use political and economic influence to shape policy and frequently contribute financially to the campaigns of politicians whose views they support. American political parties are especially important in this respect because they combine interests of many stripes into broad coalitions.

Interest Groups   Major socioeconomic groups in America enjoy access to the government arena and can exercise indirect or even direct influence on decisions. Such groups represent ethnic and religious communities (e.g., Cuban, African-American, Jewish, Catholic, Islamic, Mexican-American, Indian, and Greek), labor and business, veterans, farmers, and women among others. Some groups have broad agendas, but many are single-issue groups that focus solely on what they regard as most important—for example, global warming, birth control and abortion for women overseas, human rights in Tibet or Cuba, and so forth. The influence of such groups varies depending on their ability to gain access to and lobby policymakers, their capacity to provide campaign contributions and deliver votes, and their overall public support. As a result, decisions with foreign-policy consequences are frequently made to satisfy domestic constituencies rather than deliberately to shape the external environment.

The Israel Lobby

Political scientists John Mearsheimer and Stephen Walt published an article in 2006, which later became a book, in which they contended that U.S. policy toward the Middle East was responsive to the "Israel lobby" in America, and that regional and strategic interests took a back seat to the domestic influence of this lobby. Critics contended that Mearsheimer and Walt exaggerated the lobby's influence and that moral, ideological, political, and military considerations dominated policymaking toward the region. What follows is an extract from their book.

"The real reason why American policymakers are so deferential is the political power of the Israel lobby. The lobby is a loose coalition of individuals and organizations that actively works to move U.S. foreign policy in a pro-Israel direction. . . . It is not a single unified movement with a central leadership, and it is not a cabal or conspiracy that 'controls' U.S. foreign policy. It is simply a powerful interest group, made up of both Jews and gentiles, whose acknowledged purpose is to press Israel's case within the United States and influence American foreign policy in ways that its members believe will benefit the Jewish state. . . . These groups want U.S. leaders to treat Israel as if it were the fifty-first state. Democrats and Republicans alike fear the lobby's clout. They all know that any politician who challenges its policies stands little chance of becoming president."[24]

Political scientist Aaron Friedberg characterized the argument as "a stunning display of intellectual arrogance,"[25] and Dennis Ross, chief U.S. diplomat for the Middle East under Presidents George H. W. Bush and Bill Clinton concluded: "Republican and Democratic presidents have consistently believed in a special relationship with Israel because values matter in foreign policy."[26] Shlomo Ben-Ami, former Israeli foreign minister, contended that Mearsheimer and Walt "portray U.S. politicians as either being too incompetent to understand America's national interest, or so undutiful that they would sell it to any pressure group for the sake of political survival" and that "petitioning the government in favor of a given foreign policy is not the same as manufacturing it."[27] By contrast, others like the German writer Christoph Bertram praise the authors for "their desire and the courage to break taboos."[28]

Even supposedly apolitical research groups—"think tanks"—like the Brookings Institution and the Center for Strategic and International Studies receive funding from foreign governments that effectively make them lobbyists for those governments. The Center, for example, has many foreign donors, all of whom hope the Center will publicize their views.

George Kennan recalled that his first lesson on becoming a diplomat was that "one of the most consistent and incurable traits of American statesmanship—namely, its neurotic self-consciousness and introversion, the tendency to make statements and take actions with regard not to their effect on the international scene to which they are ostensibly addressed but rather to their effects on those echelons of American opinion, congressional opinion first and foremost, to which the respective statesmen are anxious to appeal."[29] Political scientist Robert Putnam makes a similar point when he writes of "two-level games." "At the national level, domestic groups pursue their interests by pressuring the government to adopt favorable policies and politicians seek power by constructing coalitions among those groups. At the international level, national governments seek to maximize their own ability to satisfy domestic pressures, while minimizing the adverse consequences of foreign developments."[30]

Indeed, sometimes Washington tries to modify or oppose the efforts of domestic interest groups to act in ways that policymakers believe will alienate other countries. Armenian-Americans in California have repeatedly sought to persuade Congress to declare the murderous actions of Ottoman Turkey in 1915 as "genocide," and every year on April 24 that community reiterates its demands publicly. For its part, the Turkish government vociferously denies that what took place constituted genocide and warns Washington that a congressional resolution that labeled the event genocidal would harm relations between two countries that have enjoyed a long history of friendship. Repeatedly, presidents have sought to prevent congressional action, but in 2007 and 2010, the House Foreign Affairs Committee passed nonbinding resolutions over the objections of Presidents George W. Bush and Obama. And in 2007 and again in 2010, Turkey recalled its ambassador to Washington "for consultations" in protest. During the 2008 presidential campaign, Obama promised to declare the events of 1915 a genocide, thereby illustrating the link between the foreign and domestic arenas, but altered his position after the election. Although the resolution failed to gain congressional approval on those occasions, a similar bill was referred to committee in March 2012.

☞ *KEY DOCUMENT*

S.RES.399: Affirmation of the United States Record on the Armenian Genocide Resolution

112th CONGRESS

2d Session

S. RES. 399

IN THE SENATE OF THE UNITED STATES

March 19, 2012

Resolution

Calling upon the President to ensure that the foreign policy of the United States reflects appropriate understanding and sensitivity concerning issues related to human rights, crimes against humanity, ethnic cleansing, and genocide documented in the United States record relating to the Armenian Genocide, and for other purposes

Findings

Sec. 2. The Senate finds the following:

(1) The Armenian Genocide was conceived and carried out by the Ottoman Empire from 1915 to 1923, resulting in the deportation of nearly 2,000,000 Armenians, of whom 1,500,000 men, women, and children were killed, 500,000 survivors were expelled from their homes, and the elimination of the over 2,500-year

(Continued)

(Continued)

presence of Armenians in their historic homeland.

(2) On May 24, 1915, the Allied Powers of England, France, and Russia jointly issued a statement explicitly charging for the first time ever another government of committing 'a crime against humanity'

(7) The Armenian Genocide and these domestic judicial failures are documented with overwhelming evidence in the national archives of Austria, France, Germany, Great Britain, Russia, the United States, the Vatican and many other countries,

and this vast body of evidence attests to the same facts, the same events, and the same consequences

(15) As displayed in the United States Holocaust Memorial Museum, Adolf Hitler, on ordering his military commanders to attack Poland without provocation in 1939, dismissed objections by saying 'who, after all, speaks today of the annihilation of the Armenians?' and thus set the stage for the Holocaust

Source: Library of Congress, Bill Text, 112th Congress (2011–2012), S.RES.399. IS, http://thomas.loc.gov/cgi-bin/query/z?c112:S.RES.399.

Individuals rarely have an impact on legislators or bureaucrats through letters or visits because, without the aid of interest groups or political parties, most lack sufficient organization or resources. There are, of course, exceptions to this. For example, the billionaire casino owner Sheldon Adelson contributed roughly $100 million to Mitt Romney's 2012 presidential campaign because he believes that Republicans are more likely than Democrats to support Israel's security. Others include Charles and David Koch, owners of the conglomerate Koch Industries, who "have funded opposition campaigns against so many Obama Administration policies—from health-care reform to the economic-stimulus program—that, in political circles, their ideological network is known as the Kochtopus."[31]

Members of Congress, however, are seldom swayed by the opinions of those who have no direct interest in the foreign-policy issue being discussed. Thus, the influence of interest groups frequently involves economic issues and is exercised by professional lobbyists (often former politicians or bureaucrats who have friends in Washington). Interest groups are likely to exercise greater influence on issues that affect them directly. Labor unions, for instance, are likely to enjoy access to political allies on issues that involve the outsourcing of American jobs to other countries. Sometimes informal coalitions develop between interest groups and congressional committees or executive agencies responsible for selected areas of policy.

If government and society constitute complex systems, individuals are the parts of those systems. The following sections examine the impact of individuals in formulating and implementing foreign policy. The first describes the impact of the roles of officeholders and policymakers, and the second deals with the characteristics of individuals that are unique to them. The roles of policymakers comprise the demands that their positions place on their actions. A role constitutes a piece of a larger organization and intervenes between that organization and an individual's personal preferences and perceptions.

Role

A role is a set of socially prescribed behaviors associated with individuals occupying similar official positions in a political system that encourages them to view foreign-policy issues in similar ways. An individual's role entails a set of responsibilities and tasks associated with the organization in which he or she is involved. As a rule, those with similar roles confront their tasks in similar ways, using the organization's standard operating procedures. Thus, American diplomats and military officers, however different in personal attributes, occupy similar roles in the government and will handle routine and repetitive tasks in similar ways that have in the past proved efficient and effective.

Roles can be modified by the interaction of individual officeholders' interpretation of what is expected of them, their actual behavior, and the expectations of those who are responsible for their recruitment or career advancement. When individuals assume new positions, their knowledge of role norms is based on the behavior of previous occupants of those positions as well as legal statutes, job descriptions, organizational charts, and peer groups. Thus, those who are promoted to the ranks of U.S. Army generals will likely behave like their predecessors and act in ways expected by the higher officers who promoted them.

A role, therefore, is partly shaped by what superiors expect. Individuals who wish to retain their positions or advance their careers try to behave in ways that they think are expected of them and to meet the obligations to the organization of which they are members rather than following personal convictions. In this sense, an individual's role involves a commitment to serve the interests of that individual's institutional home. From a role perspective, where individuals "stand depends on where they sit." Military officers are expected to support increased budgets for defense and improvements in the status of the military profession in society. Those who behave otherwise will find it difficult to advance in their profession. The highly competitive promotion systems in organizations like the Departments of State and Defense and the CIA tend to limit creativity and encourage conformity. Since key factors in promotions are the efficiency reports written by superiors, they can deter the forthright expression of views on foreign policy that differ from the views of supervisors. Only a courageous foreign-service officer would have publicly taken issue with the Bush administration's intervention in Iraq in 2003 or have expressed doubt about whether Saddam Hussein was seeking WMD at that time.

The obligations of role occupants to superiors shape their perceptions of foreign-policy issues. A member of Congress is likely to take positions that conform to the interests of constituents—those who elected him or her to office—rather than to the interests of the country as a whole. Thus, members of Congress see no conflict between seeking to close down military bases to reduce the budget while opposing closing bases in *their* districts. Institutional loyalty also narrows the frame of reference for interpreting information and, not surprisingly, stimulates rivalries among executive organizations.

Role prescriptions can be passed on to individuals in various ways but primarily through socialization and recruitment. Government bureaucracies recruit individuals with beliefs and backgrounds similar to those in the existing elite. Role prescriptions are thus perpetuated by self-selection. Those who are recruited and able to gain promotion have usually been able to internalize role prescriptions, that is, to adopt them as their own views. As such, prescriptions are generally resistant to change.

If a position occupied by an individual is new, that individual may enjoy greater latitude in defining his or her role. George Washington set significant precedents as America's first president. His interpretation of the constitutional requirement (Article II, Section 3) that the president "shall from time to time give to Congress Information of the State of the Union" led him to deliver the first State of the Nation address to Congress on January 8, 1790. After he delivered a second State of the Nation address the following year, he established a precedent that later presidents followed in reporting to Congress either in a speech or, beginning with Thomas Jefferson, in a formal written letter. In 1913, President Woodrow Wilson reverted to speaking annually before a joint session of Congress. Until recently, presidents sometimes spoke directly to Congress and sometimes followed Jefferson's custom. Washington's original precedent has dominated recent decades, however, owing to the unique opportunity offered presidents in advocating policies in an annual televised speech with officials from all three branches of government in attendance.

As time passes, role norms become set, precedents grow, and expectations become more widely shared and deeply anchored. It is thus difficult for an occupant, even a president, to impose his or her personality on or remold well-established roles. For that reason, high officials find themselves with few alternatives even if a particular policy violates their personal principles. Whether individuals can modify role norms depends upon the strength of role prescriptions, the force of their personality, and the uniqueness of the problems they confront. Robert McNamara's career as secretary of defense for Presidents Kennedy and Lyndon Johnson illustrates how such factors can enlarge a role. Between 1961 and 1968, McNamara gradually expanded his role vis-à-vis Congress and the military services, reviewing programs of the Defense Department and introducing novel cost-effectiveness techniques that assisted him to evaluate them comparatively. "McNamara innovated both in the types of decisions that he did make and in the manner in which he made and carried them out. Both types of innovation stemmed from a conception McNamara had of his office—a conception unlike that of any of his predecessors."[32] McNamara's career illustrated how role and personal characteristics combine in fostering the views and actions of policymakers.

An individual like McNamara can rationalize a decision by referring to the demands of his role. Presidents do so as well, and overall Americans tend to accept a president's policy in foreign affairs more readily than in domestic affairs. In a 2002 speech delivered at West Point, President George W. Bush explained that after 9/11 his role demanded that he take extraordinary steps to meet his obligation to provide security for Americans. "Homeland defense and missile defense are part of a stronger security, and they're essential priorities for America. Yet the war on terror will not be won on the defensive. We must take the battle to the enemy, disrupt his plans, and confront the worst threats before they emerge. In the world we have entered, the only path to safety is the path of action. And this nation will act."[33]

Unlike presidents, however, other role occupants have more limited scope for individual initiatives, and the role expectations of their organizations reflect more parochial interests. In sum: "Role, in and of itself, cannot explain the positions adopted by individuals; after all, the very notion of role implies a certain latitude over how to play the role," but "role occupiers do become predisposed to think in certain bureaucratic ways, and for a variety of psychological reasons they tend to adopt mind-sets compatible with those of their closest colleagues."[34] Thus, role explains only part of how individuals affect foreign policy. We have seen that in new or top-level political posts, individuals like McNamara may be able to take initiatives or follow their personal beliefs rather than the positions dictated by their roles. Let us now examine some of the individual traits that can have an impact on foreign policy.

Individual Factors

The 19th-century Scottish essayist and historian Thomas Carlyle attributed nearly all change and drama in history to the wills of great men. That Netanyahu and Obama disliked each other complicated efforts to achieve peace in the Middle East, while the close rapport between Obama and Indian Prime Minister Narendra Modi facilitated overcoming policy differences between their countries. But history is the product of both people *and* their times. We can distinguish those characteristics of individual leaders and their behavior—personality, experience, intellect, values, and political style—that make them unique.

🔑 *KEY DOCUMENT*

Thomas Carlyle, "On Heroes, Hero-Worship, and the Heroic in History"

"We have undertaken to discourse here for a little on Great Men, their manner of appearance in our world's business, how they have shaped themselves in the world's history, what ideas men formed of them, what work they did;—on Heroes, namely, and on their reception and performance; what I call Hero-worship and the Heroic in human affairs. . . . Universal History, the history of what man has accomplished in this world, is at bottom the History of the Great Men who have worked here. They were the leaders of men, these great ones; the modelers, patterns, and in a wide sense creators, of whatsoever the general mass of men contrived to do or to attain; all things that we see standing accomplished in the world are properly the outer material result, the practical realization and embodiment, of Thoughts that dwelt in the Great Men sent into the world: the soul of the whole world's history, it may justly be considered, were the history of these."

Source. Thomas Carlyle, Lecture I, The Hero as Divinity (May 5, 1840), "On Heroes, Hero-Worship, and the Heroic in History," The Project Gutenberg EBook, July 26, 2008, http://www.gutenberg.org/files/1091/1091-h/1091-h.htm.

Since decision making is partly the product of environmental and psychological predispositions, the relevance of individual traits is significant. During the 1962 Cuban missile crisis, American leaders had to make informed assumptions about the belief system of Soviet leader Nikita Khrushchev. How would he interpret and respond to American moves? Would he view them as a personal challenge, or would he seek to avoid a nuclear cataclysm? Data on psychological predispositions, however, are difficult to obtain and are subject to different interpretations. During the crisis, Llewellyn Thompson, Ambassador-at-Large and former Ambassador to the Soviet Union, was brought into the decision process to "act" the part of Khrushchev. During the discussion among American leaders who were members of the Ex Comm, some of the participants argued that Washington should remain firm but avoid forcing Khrushchev into a corner and making him respond defensively. Others argued that the United States should adopt an unambiguously hard line because Khrushchev would back down in the face of superior American military power. In part, the disagreement arose from different interpretations of Khrushchev's personality.

Personality Among the most interesting individuals are those with personality characteristics that lead to aberrant behavior. Sometimes such behavior reflects an individual's unconscious attempt to cope with inner conflict or need—in political scientist Harold Lasswell's classic formulation, the displacement of private motives onto public objects.[35] Lasswell was concerned with what he called "social psychiatry," which he believed clarified the process of policymaking.[36]

Certain emotional issues tend to evoke aberrant behavior. For example, ego-defensive behavior occurs in agitation for or against communism, pacifism, birth control, and obscenity. Studies of prejudice suggest that certain individuals have greater needs than do others to defend their identities. Their behavior, often hostile, may compensate for unconscious needs and personality defects. Garry Wills analyzed how Richard Nixon acted during a press conference in 1962 after he had been defeated in California's election for governor. "Nixon entered, laboring unsuccessfully at the game smile of politicians who have submitted to the judgment of voters and now must accept it. But as he advanced to the podium, his eyes picked out this or that face in the press corps; and behind the faces—behind pens slanting in a hostile scrawl, mikes held up for every slip—he could see again the words they used against him, headlines, leads, last paragraphs all stored in his retentive memory bank, that library of grievances."[37]

When individual factors have an impact, studying leaders' life histories can help us to understand their adult behavior. Their relations with their parents, their education, and their **socialization** as children and adolescents may have created enduring frustrations or anxieties. An analysis of President Woodrow Wilson's behavior concluded that his unwillingness to compromise with political opponents and, therefore, his failure to get the Senate to agree to America's entry in the League of Nations were consequences of childhood competition with his strict Presbyterian father. The authors suggest that Wilson repressed his rebellion against his father but unconsciously refused to submit to him. As a result, Wilson "could brook no interference. *His* will must prevail if he wished it to. He bristled at the slightest challenge to his authority. Such a characteristic might well have represented a rebellion against the domination of his father, whose authority he had never dared openly to challenge. Throughout his life his relationship with others seemed shaped by an inner command never again to bend his will to another man's."[38]

Wilson, who set out to "make the world safe for democracy," was described by political scientist John Stoessinger as "the classical crusader," that is, an individual who "tends to sacrifice unwelcome facts on the altar of a fixed idea." Stoessinger contrasted crusaders, who are frequently moralists, with "pragmatists" like Harry Truman. "The pragmatist always tests his ideas against the facts of his experience. If the design does not hold up against the facts, the design will have to change."[39] Bruce Bartlett, an adviser to President Ronald Reagan, argues that President George W. Bush became a crusader during his presidency. Bush was "clear-eyed about Al Qaeda and the Islamic fundamentalist enemy" whom he understood "because he's just like them." Bush "truly believes he's on a mission from God. Absolute faith like that overwhelms a need for analysis."[40]

Individuals motivated by repressed hostility may also assume a posture of moral superiority toward those with whom they are in conflict, and this may lead to poor decisions. Those in the foreign-policy establishment with such attitudes may encourage ethnocentric behavior, that is, behavior reflecting suspicions of other societies and nations and showing little respect for them. **Ethnocentrism** produces hostility. For example, many Pakistanis believe that American leaders are haughty and disrespectful because Washington persists in sending unmanned drones over their country to kill Islamic militants, thereby violating Pakistani sovereignty. Such personality factors contribute to an individual's beliefs.

Beliefs The beliefs of leaders and the strength with which those beliefs are held may have an impact on the way in which they deal with new information, including information that seems to contradict those beliefs. People usually have coherent attitudes toward and beliefs about the world that reflect their values and preferences. The stronger their attitudes and beliefs, the greater the contradictory evidence and information needed to alter them. When confronted with evidence that contradicts strong beliefs, policymakers must alter their beliefs, deny the evidence, or rationalize it so that it no longer seems contradictory.

An analysis of Secretary of State John Foster Dulles by political scientist Ole Holsti concluded that he consistently explained changes in Soviet behavior during the Cold War, including conciliatory actions, in terms of hostility, weakness, or treachery, which eliminated the need for him to alter his beliefs in the face of new evidence. "Dulles selected two aspects of Marxist theory—materialism and atheism—for special emphasis," and "after pointing out that the free world had such high moral standards as to preclude the use of immoral methods, Dulles concluded that 'atheists can hardly be expected to conform to an ideal so high.'" Thus, "he attributed the characteristics of the Soviet leaders—insincerity, immorality, brutality, and deceitfulness—primarily to their atheism."[41] Dulles's experience in negotiating with Soviet leaders had contributed to his suspicions of their motives. As in the case of Dulles, people's experiences can shape their beliefs and foreign-policy preferences.

Experience The experiences of policymakers help them interpret the challenges they face. Different experiences are likely to endow officeholders with unique qualifications that may or may not be suitable for solving the problems at hand. George C. Marshall, who served as secretary of defense from 1950 to 1951, had been a five-star general of the army and chief of staff. More than any other secretary of defense, Marshall understood the difficulties confronting the military services. In addition, having also served as secretary of state, he was in a position to judge between the military services and the political objectives they were supposed to serve.

In contrast to Marshall, Charles E. Wilson had been president of General Motors before becoming secretary of defense in 1953. His previous experience equipped him to cut military expenditures and design military plans that would enable the Eisenhower administration to maintain a balanced budget. Wilson had little military training, and toward the end of the Eisenhower years, professional officers complained that American military forces had been permitted to grow obsolete. More recently Ashton Carter replaced Chuck Hagel as secretary of defense, largely because Carter's wide experience in the formulation of defense policy made him more willing to consider using force, a trait sought by hardliners in Congress.

Age is also an important aspect of experience. The events of the era in which individuals were socialized are likely to be reflected in the ways in which they consider problems. Such individuals have different points of reference and concerns from others of a different generation. Thus, policymakers who were socialized before and during World War II are more likely to be concerned about "appeasing" a foe than those raised earlier during World War I or later during Vietnam. The generations that came of age during the slaughter of World War I, the American defeat in Vietnam, or the frustrating wars in Afghanistan and Iraq are likely to be less concerned about appeasing others if such a policy would avoid war. The experiences of policymakers may also affect their leadership style, that is, how they approach making decisions.

Leadership Style   Leadership style refers to the ways in which policymakers reach decisions. President Eisenhower, who had served much of his adult life as a high-ranking army staff officer, expected as president to coordinate the work of others and consult widely with advisers and subordinates. Not only did Eisenhower solicit the advice of others and delegate authority to them, he tried not to impose his views on them in order to achieve consensus. Although this approach minimized conflict among decision makers, it also tended to blur the lines of responsibility and produce decisions at the "lowest common denominator."

President Bill Clinton was a "policy wonk" who took great pleasure in engaging subordinates and advisers in discussion and debate. That style was also characteristic to some extent of President Obama. Obama was less able than Eisenhower or George W. Bush to operate hierarchically and less willing than Eisenhower or Bush to let others narrow the alternatives presented to him. Obama "had very little foreign policy experience" and "lacked any executive-management experience." He was "deliberative to a fault and an inveterate seeker of the middle ground" and was not "inclined to develop strong bonds with most of his cabinet members or to empower them or agency heads, which is essential in a sprawling U.S. government that is the world's largest and most complex organization."[42] His reliance on a small circle of advisers made it more difficult to cope with the multiple and simultaneous challenges to America during his second term—confrontation with Russia over Ukraine, the Ebola epidemic, the Islamic State of Iraq and Syria, civil war in Syria, and Chinese truculence. "Personal relationships," declared a former U.S. diplomat, "are not his style" unlike Presidents Clinton and George W. Bush who "yukked it up with everybody."[43] Indeed, former CIA director and defense secretary Leon Panetta criticized President Obama for his leadership style. "Too often, in my view, the president relies on the logic of a law professor rather than the passion of a leader."[44]

In contrast to Obama, President Franklin Roosevelt, previously assistant secretary of the Navy and governor of New York, encouraged subordinates to compete with one another, making it necessary for him to serve as ultimate arbiter in the disputes that inevitably erupted. He let situations develop and crystalize, and "the competing forces had to vindicate themselves in the actual pull and tug of conflict; public opinion had to face the question, consider it, pronounce upon it—only then, at the long frazzled end, would the President's intuitions consolidate and precipitate a result." Roosevelt "organized—or disorganized—his system of command to insure that important decisions were passed on to the top."[45]

Leon Panetta and David Petraeus, very different CIA directors

United States Department of Defense   Darren Livingston (Central Intelligence Agency)

Different leadership styles are apparent when comparing General David Petraeus and his ebullient predecessor Leon Panetta as director of the Central Intelligence Agency. Petraeus, a former four-star army general who was prominently involved in America's wars in Iraq and Afghanistan, had a quieter and less public demeanor than Panetta, a former congressman with considerable political experience. According to a friend of Petraeus, "He thinks he has to be very discreet and let others in the government do the talking."[46] Fearful of leaks, Petraeus, unlike Panetta, gave few interviews and kept a low profile.

Finally, foreign-policy decision making can also be affected by the physical and mental health of policymakers.

Health Leaders are frequently old and less able to act with the vigor and dynamism they had when they were younger. The strain of high public office in Washington is great. Both Eisenhower and Woodrow Wilson, for example, suffered serious illnesses while in office, which lessened their control over decisions. President Roosevelt was already ill when he met Soviet leader Joseph Stalin at Yalta in February 1945. He died two months later, and some observers claim Roosevelt was unfit to negotiate effectively with the Soviet dictator.

As the stress of making life-and-death decisions increases, mental illness may become a problem. James Forrestal, the first American secretary of defense, took his own life in 1949 by throwing himself from the sixteenth floor of the Bethesda Naval Hospital, where he was undergoing psychiatric treatment. "The most lasting tribute to James Forrestal," wrote his biographer, "would be a massive effort to reduce the incidence of physical and mental breakdown in political life."[47] Indeed, although America requires military officers in charge of nuclear weapons to undergo extensive psychological tests, it provides no such safeguards for the president who would order their use in the event of war.

CONCLUSION

This chapter has examined several of the key sources of influence on the formulation and implementation of American foreign policy. We have seen how foreign and domestic policies have become increasingly entangled in recent decades. In a large democratic country like the United States, it is difficult to identify a unitary national interest that is the outcome of individual rationality. Instead, many government and societal groups as well as individuals define the national interest from their own perspective.

External factors like globalization and accompanying international and transnational interdependence have limited sovereign independence, and the relative distribution of power constrains what is possible while the distribution of attitudes shapes what is probable in foreign policy. A host of government characteristics such as separation of powers and the competitive views of government bureaucracies shape the way foreign policy is made and the outcomes of policymaking. Societal factors such as the lobbying of interest groups and public opinion also influence policy outcomes. The roles that individuals have in government and society influence their perceptions and actions, as do individual characteristics such as their personality, beliefs, and health. In sum, American foreign policy is the outcome of a complex, continuous, and messy process in which alternatives are put forward by many individuals and interests and frequently are the outcome of domestic conflict and compromise rather than rational consensus.

The relative potency of these sources of influence varies over time and by issue. The next chapter examines how these influences have affected the contours of American foreign policy historically and the changing patterns in policy over time.

DISCUSSION QUESTIONS

1. How do the "transnational" and "state-centric" models of foreign policy differ? Which is closer to the reality of a globalized world?

2. In a globalized world, the foreign and domestic political arenas are increasingly linked. Discuss and give illustrations.

3. What are major sources of influence on American foreign policy? How do they differ?

4. How do you think the relative impact of the different influences on foreign policy might differ in the United States and China?

5. Do you think U.S. influence in foreign affairs is declining? Why or why not? How would an American decline change global politics?

6. How do you think the relative impact of the several sources of foreign policy might differ in dangerous crises like the 1962 Cuban missile crisis and in noncrisis situations?

KEY TERMS

affiliations (p. 9)

alliance (p. 13)

attitudes (p. 12)

authoritarian government (p. 10)

capability (p. 12)

checks and balances (p. 15)

democracy (p. 10)

democratic peace theory (p. 21)

economic development (p. 10)

ethnocentrism (p. 31)

external factors (p. 10)

globalization (p. 7)

government factors (p. 10)

habeas corpus (p. 18)

hard power (p. 12)

identities (p. 9)

ideologies (p. 12)

incrementalism (p. 18)

individual factors (p. 10)

interdependence (p. 11)

international crises (p. 20)

liberals (p. 14)

military-industrial complex (p. 20)

nongovernmental organizations (p. 8)

norms (p. 10)

opinion leaders (p. 22)

pluralist (p. 23)

political culture (p. 21)

propaganda (p. 9)

public opinion (p. 22)

realists (p. 14)

role factors (p. 10)

separation of powers (p. 15)

socialization (p. 30)

societal factors (p. 10)

soft power (p. 12)

sovereignty (p. 11)

standard operating procedures (p. 19)

state-centric (p. 7)

transnational (p. 7)

two-level games (p. 24)

values (p. 7)

SAGE edge™
for CQ Press

Sharpen your skill with SAGE edge at **edge.sagepub.com/mansbach**

SAGE edge for Students provides a personalized approach to help you accomplish your coursework goals in an easy-to-use learning environment.

2

Competing Currents in U.S. Foreign Policy

Policy continuity under Obama

Paresh Nath, The Khaleej Times, UAE

This chapter continues our discussion of influences on American foreign policy, focusing on how these influences have produced competing orientations in foreign policy. The conventional narrative describes America as isolationist until World War II, after which it accepted the mantle of global leadership and became permanently engaged in global life. The narrative becomes more complicated in the 21st century after 9/11, depicting U.S. foreign policy as unilateralist and interventionist under President George W. Bush and increasingly multilateralist under President Barack Obama. The reality is more complicated. Multilateralism was never completely abandoned under Bush, and unilateralism did not disappear during the Obama years. Thus, Obama shocked many who expected him to be a norm-driven multilateralist when in receiving the 2009 Nobel Peace Prize he reminded the world of the role U.S. military power had played, emphasizing that "the world must remember that it was not simply international institutions—not just treaties and declarations—that brought stability to a post–World War II world," and "the plain fact is this: The United States of America has helped underwrite global security for more than six decades with the blood of our citizens and the strength of our arms."[1]

Employing power to pursue U.S. interests *and* values is described as "multilateralism with teeth"[2] and has been a frequent theme under Obama, just as in many earlier administrations. Foreign policy is an area where presidents have considerable latitude, but they are not free of constraints. Their policies are the product of competing interests that seek a variety of goals and also competing values. Many public and private actors are involved in this process, as we saw in chapter 1. Even if these actors may share fundamental ideals like democracy and individualism, they may disagree about how to pursue such values. Moreover, interests are frequently incompatible, and policies are often compromises that achieve minimal common interests. In sum, America is not a rational, unified actor coherently acting in the "national interest." Nonetheless, there are some patterns that have emerged in foreign policy over the course of American history. In various eras, U.S. leaders have placed more or less relative emphasis on values or interests in its conduct of foreign policy. At the same time America's relationship with the rest of the world has involved **isolationism** and **internationalism, unilateralism** and **multilateralism**, and **interventionism** and **noninterventionism**. Students of U.S. history cite the interwar period as isolationist or the Cold War period as interventionist, and America's post-9/11 policy as interventionist *and* unilateral or **bilateral** in the case of countries like Poland that provided detention centers for suspected terrorists. As we shall see, however, no era has been immune to debates about America's place in the world. This chapter is the most historical in the book, and the account will emphasize symbolic events and actors that highlight enduring tendencies and tensions in U.S. foreign policy.

COMPETING CURRENTS

American foreign policy is often described in dichotomies: pursuit of values *versus* interests, isolationism *versus* internationalism, unilateralism *versus* multilateralism, and interventionism *versus* noninterventionism. These contrasts are often false. In every era, several perspectives coexist and compete for influence, even though one may dominate. Foreign policy has *always* been a concern of U.S. leaders and a topic of debate, and whether leaders explicitly acknowledge it or not, through much of America's history, they have been guided by a reasonably consistent and coherent view of America's interests in foreign affairs. Such a structured worldview is called **grand strategy**.[3]

Contemporary grand strategy refers to a broad framework that structures a country's approach to foreign affairs. According to historian Paul Kennedy, it is "the capacity of the nation's leaders to bring together all the elements, both military and nonmilitary, for the preservation and enhancement of the nation's long-term"[4] interests, however defined. In this sense, it encompasses a coherent articulation of core interests, a clear understanding of key threats, and an awareness of resources and capabilities that can be mobilized to advance those interests. It represents the logic by which a government employs the tools of foreign policy to achieve the greatest advantage in its pursuit of core interests.[5] Grand strategy reveals the nexus of foreign and domestic politics because it "is precisely about the broader, often ignored, context of building and reinforcing the domestic political and economic foundations of American national power."[6] It guides leaders when they confront new challenges in foreign affairs and helps them use resources wisely, avoid overstretch, and maintain policy coherence across the range of foreign-policy issues. However, as we shall see, not all presidents have a grand strategy, and even when they do, it may be insufficient to meet foreign-policy challenges.

Although for much of U.S. history there existed no such label to identify core interests or the strategies for accomplishing them, key foreign-policy initiatives reflected implicit grand strategies. We begin by examining the tension that exists between considerations of interests and values in American foreign policy and then turn to the competing currents of isolationism and internationalism, unilateralism and multilateralism, and interventionism and noninterventionism in the pursuit of interests and values.

Interests and Values

In explaining the shifts between the several dimensions of American foreign policy, it is important to recognize that decisions are *simultaneously* the outcome of considerations of interests *and* values. The former reflects the role played by concerns about American security and preservation of its geopolitical interests, emphasizing power and expediency. The latter involves the maintenance and spread of American norms—democracy, human rights, **rule of law, free-market capitalism,** and **individualism.** Those who describe themselves as "realists" believe that interests should dominate foreign policy, while "liberals" argue that pursuing values should take precedence. In fact, power and values are not antithetical. No policy is shaped that does not involve seeking security against foes and preserving America's ideals. The attraction of American values constitutes "soft power" because it influences others to accept American policies, while "hard power" such as military and economic capabilities is necessary to preserve those values and project them abroad.

Timeline

1700	1800	1900
1775–1783 American Revolution	**1803** Louisiana Purchase	**1904** Roosevelt Corollary extends the Monroe Doctrine
	1812 War of 1812	**1917–1918** United States and World War I
	1823 Monroe Doctrine	**1921–1922** Washington naval conference
	1844–1848 Mexican-American War	**1928** The Kellogg-Briand Pact renouncing war
	1845 Annexation of Texas	**1930** London naval conference
	1848 Addition of California, Arizona, and New Mexico	
	1898 Spanish-American War, annexation of Hawaii and acquisition of the Philippines and Puerto Rico	

Conflicts can arise, however, about which to emphasize, and successful foreign policies require a balance between the two that changes depending on circumstances. Efforts to export American values to countries with inimical beliefs are likely to meet with failure. Thus, despite America's overwhelming military superiority, efforts to spread its values to Vietnam in the 1960s and 1970s failed because they did not win Vietnamese "hearts and minds" as well as the absence of an effective South Vietnamese government. By contrast, the defeat of Germany, Japan, and Italy in World War II led to a transformation that made those societies "more like us."

Power and values are related in other ways. Insufficient power makes it dangerous to try to spread values abroad. During its formative years in the late 18th and early 19th centuries, America was weak militarily and dependent on European trade, and efforts to spread values would have endangered U.S. security and, therefore, also placed at risk the values it sought to preserve. By contrast, the effort to use power to impose American values on others as in Iraq after 2003 can appear as bullying and produce a backlash. Even more dangerous is when such efforts appear to threaten others' security. Thus, U.S. efforts to encourage democracy in post–Cold War Russia were viewed as endangering the stability of its regime.

The changing balance between power and values will arise repeatedly as we examine American policies in later chapters. Chapter 3 on military strategy focuses on changing security considerations, while the discussion of human rights and democracy in chapter 6 examines the role of American ideals. Subsequent chapters concerning U.S. policy toward particular regions or countries also assess the role of security and **ideals**. Ultimately, their role is impossible to weigh accurately. Did America enter World War I to make the world safe for democracy as President Woodrow Wilson declared, or did it do so to preserve a balance of power? Did the United States go to war with Spain in 1898 to liberate Spain's colonies and infuse them with the ideals of **independence** and freedom, or did it do so to extend American power? The answer is "both."

Isolationism versus Internationalism

One outcome of the interplay of interests and values is the choice between isolationism and internationalism—concepts used to describe U.S. **disengagement** or **engagement** in world affairs. Isolationism had deep roots in American foreign policy even before President George Washington advised Americans

1900 (Continued)

1941–1945 United States and World War II
1947 Truman Doctrine
1950–1953 Korean War
1964–1975 Vietnam War
1991 First Persian Gulf War
1992 The Cold War ends

2000

September **2001** Al-Qaeda terrorist attacks in New York and Washington, D.C.
2001–2014 Afghanistan War
March **2003** U.S.-led invasion of Iraq
2011 Withdrawal of U.S. forces from Iraq

to avoid "entangling alliances." Isolationism gained widespread currency in the 1930s and came to be associated with avoiding "political and military commitments to or alliances with foreign powers, particularly those of Europe."[7] In fact, isolationism does not require that a state remain uninvolved in world affairs. Instead, an isolationist government is one that exercises restraint in its ambitions and maximizes its freedom of action. Such a policy is "based on the belief that most of what happens outside of America's borders poses no military threat to the country; the belief that America's military power, short of war, can accomplish little to shape that environment; and the belief that it is not worth the costs and risks of waging war to do so."[8] In U.S. foreign policy, isolationism refers to reliance on American power—mixed with xenophobia, costs of intervention, and even disinterest—to ensure freedom of action, including an aversion to multilateral treaties or international organizations that may limit **autonomy**.[9]

Although its foreign policy has often been described as isolationist, America has never been completely disengaged from world affairs. "External assistance was essential to the birth of an independent United States; concerns about international commerce and foreign threats decisively influenced the form of government created in the Constitutional Convention of 1787. Foreign Policy molded the political culture of the new nation."[10] Complete isolation has never been an option, and America has always relied on international trade and a "complex web of international cultural connections."[11] The country's founders did not seek to be cut off from the rest of the world, but instead sought to "safeguard the independence of a new and not yet powerful nation by avoiding, whenever possible, involvement in the military and political affairs of the major powers while, at the same time, expanding trade and commerce as a means of fostering national development."[12] Today's "neo-isolationists" regard themselves as conservatives who look to the example of the country's founders.

Like isolationism, internationalism is often oversimplified and is frequently used to describe "any U.S. involvement overseas, even if it is action undertaken unilaterally or in the narrow case of American national interest, simply because it is international in a geographic sense."[13] Other interest-based interpretations stress international involvement "as a means of realizing and protecting goals."[14] By contrast, others insist that internationalism must also include efforts to promote cooperation, including establishing law and institutions to achieve a more just and peaceful world—that is, values in addition to interests. American internationalists share "the vision of a peaceful world ordered by law"[15] and believe that U.S. involvement is necessary to create this world. America, they believe, should act as a leader in a partnership of democratic nations and that the national interest is best sought by cooperation within a larger community, a perspective incorporating both interests and values.

Internationalism and isolationism are not incompatible. The emphasis may change, but even if one is dominant, elites debate the merits of both. "Isolationism and Internationalism have a somewhat symbiotic relationship and need to be understood as longstanding features of American politics beyond the typically accepted highpoint of the 'twenties and thirties.'"[16]

Unilateralism versus Multilateralism

The debate about acting alone or cooperating with others in foreign policy has long been debated in America. *Uni*-lateralism involves "acting alone," while *multi*-lateralism involves working with others. Unilateralism is "a tendency to opt out of a multilateral framework (whether existing or proposed) or to act alone in addressing a particular global challenge rather than choosing to participation in collective action."[17] Multilateralism has several meanings. It may simply describe policy coordination among three or more states.[18] Sometimes there is an implication regarding the nature of such coordination, for example, the normative idea that coordination must be consistent with principles that "specify appropriate conduct for a class of action, without regard to the particularistic interests of the parties or the strategic exigencies that may exist in any specific occurrence." Multilateralism, then, is "a highly demanding institutional form"[19] that is achieved less frequently than bilateralism or unilateralism. Identifying policies as unilateral or multilateral is further complicated by the reality that, in actual practice, "there are many possible gradations between the two orientations and there may be complex situations where elements of unilateralism and multilateralism coexist."[20]

→ ← ## *CONTROVERSY*

Partisanship and U.S. Foreign Policy

According to conventional wisdom, the two U.S. political parties are deeply divided on foreign policy, with Democrats "feckless multilateralists" and Republicans "reckless unilateralists."[21] Are these characterizations accurate? A 2012 survey of U.S. foreign policy professionals found that there are "genuine partisan differences" between Republicans and Democrats, but there is also more overlap than one might expect. The survey finds that both parties believe multilateralism increases policy effectiveness but emphasize different factors in evaluating "effectiveness." Republicans emphasize sovereignty and freedom of action and oppose policies that infringe on sovereignty. Democrats, by contrast, evaluate multilateralism according to its impact on "vulnerabilities created by interdependence and [what] is perceived as legitimate by other countries."[22] The findings suggest that Republicans are really "sovereignty-minded multilateralists," and Democrats are "interdependence-oriented multilateralists."[23]

A survey of congressional staffers also found important areas of agreement among staffers from both parties. Over 60 percent from both believe America cannot solve problems alone, and that cooperation is more efficient than acting alone. Majorities have positive views of alliances like the North Atlantic Treaty Organization (NATO), but partisan divisions existed over issues like climate change. "The intense partisanship of today's political environment often leads policymakers to oppose each other for political reasons, even when their views do not differ greatly in substance," but "it should still be possible for U.S. foreign-policymakers to work together—both across the aisle and down the length of Pennsylvania Avenue—on some important issues."[24]

The first century of American foreign policy was characterized by unilateralism as leaders sought to remain aloof from European **power politics**. American leaders wished to craft policies to increase U.S. strength by encouraging trade and economic development, enlarging U.S. territory, and reducing foreign influence on the continent. Multilateralism is a more recent current in foreign policy. While there was support for involvement in multilateral institutions in the early 20th century, U.S. leaders did not pursue a sustained policy of multilateralism until after World War II. As that war ended and the Cold War began, Washington helped establish several multilateral organizations like the United Nations (UN) and the Bretton Woods economic institutions to manage global politics and economics and to establish global rules that were compatible with U.S. interests and values. Although these institutions remain, U.S. influence in them has declined with the emergence of new states in Africa and Asia after **decolonization**. Today, Washington often turns to institutions where it has more influence as well as bilateral arrangements when these alternatives offer more favorable outcomes. And American leaders have always retained the right to act unilaterally when vital interests are at stake. The tendency to adopt multilateralism when it offers a favorable solution to challenges is an **"instrumental"** multilateralism that fits the narrower definition of multilateralism above.

Interventionism versus Noninterventionism

Another enduring debate involves intervention—"unsolicited interference by one state in the affairs of another,"[25] often *military* intervention for **humanitarian** ends. In practice, intervention can take the form of military, economic, or diplomatic interference for a variety of purposes, expedient and altruistic. Intervention rarely occurs for purely selfless motives and on various occasions in U.S. history has involved adding territory or enhancing security. Nonintervention is the avoidance of "unsolicited" interference. Analysis of intervention-nonintervention is complicated by norms favoring intervention. In the 18th and 19th centuries, for example, intervention was permitted under international law and was even considered a sovereign *right* of states. For Europe's rulers, intervention sanctioned by the **balance of power** and **Concert of Europe** was considered a moral duty "to uphold their common culture and to protect the political status quo."[26] Today, the normative climate generally prohibits intervention except to rectify violations of international law or protect vital interests. America's position on the legality of intervention has generally been broad, accepting that states have a right to determine which interests are sufficiently vital to justify it. Even in eras when U.S. leaders have practiced nonintervention, they have retained the *right* to intervene when vital interests are at stake.

PAST: COMPETING CURRENTS IN HISTORICAL PERSPECTIVE

During much of its first century, America was a weak, former colony, and its leaders were preoccupied in securing independence from the "Old World." When intervention occurred, its purpose was to consolidate control over territory or prevent European meddling. America avoided intervening to acquire Canada because of the possibility of war with Britain. American leaders could not afford to emphasize values in their foreign policy but had to secure U.S. interests. Unilateralism and later interventionism served as bases for a grand strategy to ensure independence and evict Europe's powers from the Americas. As America amassed economic and military power in the 20th century, core interests expanded to include interests and values, and grand strategy became difficult to design. The early Cold War was a golden age of U.S. grand strategy defined by containing Soviet power. Although America practiced nonintervention in the Soviet sphere of influence, it repeatedly intervened in support of noncommunist governments outside that sphere. Multilateralism and interventionism were combined to achieve containment. The strategic landscape changed dramatically with the collapse of the USSR, the emergence of nonstate terrorists, and transnational threats such as nuclear proliferation, financial crises, and climate change.

Isolationism or Unilateralism? The Foreign Policy of a Young Nation

There was an isolationist element in American politics in the colonial era and the early years of the new republic. The first colonists had left Europe to escape wars and religious intolerance, and, "in venturing to the New World, they had accepted the prospect of a life of virtual isolation from the Old World."[27] But wanting and achieving isolation were very different objectives. Complete isolation was never possible, nor was it desirable. The dilemma for early Americans was how to maintain trade relationships without becoming dangerously entangled in European politics.

This dilemma persisted beyond the American Revolution although tension remained between the desire to remain free of foreign entanglements and the need for foreign support to ensure the country's independence. Several events during George Washington's presidency (1789–1797) forced American leaders to consider carefully their place in the world. The Neutrality Proclamation (1793), declaring American neutrality in the war between France and Britain, and Washington's Farewell Address (1796) are often cited as the sources of American isolationism. But Washington was not an isolationist. Rather, he recognized that America was too weak to become embroiled in foreign conflicts, notably the wars that France waged against other European powers following its revolution. The question hinged less on *whether* to ally and more on *with whom* to ally. Should America aid its fellow democracy France or assist its trading partner and the world's leading naval power, Britain, to combat the war waged by France's revolutionary government? Public opinion sided with France. Washington, however, refused to do so, fueling domestic debate. Federalists led by Alexander Hamilton sought to refrain from involvement in Europe. Democratic-Republicans led by Thomas Jefferson supported France in gratitude for French assistance to the colonies during the Revolutionary War. And Washington's predilection to remain neutral in Europe's conflicts did not prevent him from negotiating several treaties to ensure America's military security and economic prosperity, including the 1794 Jay Treaty with Britain that granted commercial rights to both countries and the 1795 Treaty of San Lorenzo with Spain that resolved their territorial disputes and gave American ships access to the Mississippi River.

Debate about America's engagement with the world continued beyond Washington's presidency. Although at times isolationism seemed to dominate, internationalism never vanished. The first century or so of American foreign policy was less an era of isolationism and more a "regional era" in which leaders "sought to expand the country's borders, provide security to its peoples, and promote capitalism"[28] to enhance American security and power. Two events that illustrated the tension between isolationism and internationalism were the 1803 Louisiana Purchase and the 1823 Monroe Doctrine.

KEY DOCUMENT

Excerpt from George Washington's Farewell Address (1796)

Upon retiring from public office, George Washington offered to "Friends and Fellow-Citizens" reflections on threats to the Union. Some, like those posed by political factions, were domestic, but several were foreign. In articulating the risks of "foreign influence" and "permanent alliances," Washington encouraged his successors to craft foreign policies that were honorable and prudent—that were consistent with American values but that also would protect American interests: "The great rule of conduct for us in regard to foreign nations is in extending our commercial relations, to have with them as little political connection as possible. So far as we have already formed engagements, let them be fulfilled with perfect good faith. Here let us stop. Europe has a set of primary interests which to us have none; or a very remote relation. Hence she must be engaged in frequent controversies, the causes of which are essentially foreign to our concerns. . . . Our detached and distant situation invites and enables us to pursue a different course. . . . Why forego the advantages of so peculiar a situation? . . . Why, by interweaving our destiny with that of any part of Europe, entangle our peace and prosperity in the toils of European ambition, rivalship, interest, humor or caprice? It is our true policy to steer clear of permanent alliances with any portion of the foreign world; so far, I mean, as we are now at liberty to do it."

Source: "Washington's Farewell Address 1796," The Avalon Project, Yale Law School, http://avalon.law.yale.edu/18th_century/washing.asp.

The Louisiana Purchase involved the purchase of 530 million acres of territory from Napoleon Bonaparte in 1803 for $15 million, doubling the size of the United States. The transaction had profound implications for American foreign policy. Sought by President Thomas Jefferson to safeguard U.S. control of the mouth of the Mississippi River, the purchase enjoyed wide public support, while also igniting political controversy. There was a question of whether Jefferson was constitutionally authorized to make such a purchase. Equally important was the question of whether prior treaty obligations allowed Napoleon to sell the territory. There were also concerns about its impact on domestic politics, especially the citizenship of "foreigners" and the shifting political balance of power among American states after the addition of so many new citizens. Nevertheless, in providing control of the Mississippi River, the acquisition enhanced U.S. security, enabled westward expansion, provided commercial advantages, and marked the initial retreat of European powers from the Western hemisphere while establishing a precedent for expansion into neighboring territories.

MAP **2.1**   The Louisiana Purchase

The tension between isolationism and internationalism again appeared in the Monroe Doctrine. In his annual message to Congress in December 1823, President James Monroe outlined two principles of U.S. policy relating to the emerging political order in the Americas—noncolonization and nonintervention. Regarding the former, the Monroe Doctrine is recalled for the warning that "the American continents, by the free and independent condition which they have assumed and maintain, are henceforth not to be considered as subjects for future colonization by any European power." But Monroe's address also affirmed that America would not intervene in the "internal affairs" of European powers and declared that it "should consider any attempt on their part to extend their system to any portion of [the Western] hemisphere as dangerous to [American] peace and safety."[29] Some Europeans were outraged that Monroe would presume to issue such a statement given America's military weakness. Austrian statesman Klemens von Metternich called it "a new act of revolt," and the Russian government regarded it with "only the profoundest contempt." Decades later, Prussian Chancellor Otto von Bismarck would call it "a species of arrogance peculiarly American and inexcusable."[30] Latin American leaders, many of whom perceived no threat from Europe, were more anxious about U.S. ambitions in the region. In fact, the doctrine had been suggested by British Foreign Minister George Canning and was premised on British naval power preventing Spain or France from regaining colonies in Latin America. In 1826 Canning famously declared, "I called the New World into existence to redress the balance of the Old."

The doctrine's promise that America would not tolerate European interference in its hemisphere became a cornerstone of American foreign policy and has long been equated with isolationism. Better viewed as an example of unilateralism (or bilateralism), the Monroe Doctrine ushered in a new era in American foreign policy in which America was more engaged in hemispheric *and* world affairs. Indeed, one can see "Monroe thinking" in the many interventions that the United States undertook in the 19th and 20th centuries.[31] Let us now examine the following era in American foreign policy, often described as isolationist but involving unilateralism and emerging interventionism.

Interventionism: America Expands, 1823–1914

For the rest of the 19th century and into the early 20th century, isolationist sentiment remained strong in America, and its leaders continued to avoid war with European powers. The era also featured a steady expansion of U.S. trade and interventionism. Attention was focused on westward expansion to curtail European influence on the continent. America expanded into new territories that would eventually become states, beginning with Texas (annexed in 1845), then California, Arizona, and New Mexico (1848), Alaska (1867), and Hawaii (1898). Washington also intervened aggressively in hemispheric affairs and added links with Asia, reflected in commercial treaties with China (1844) and Japan (1853). Following Spain's defeat in the Spanish-American War (1898), America also acquired the Philippines and Puerto Rico. The era reflected competing isolationist, internationalist, and interventionist tendencies in the idea of **Manifest Destiny** that fueled westward expansion and growing interest in the stability of smaller countries in the Americas.

Manifest Destiny (1842–1848)   The idea of territorial expansion dominated American foreign policy during this period. To some extent, interests fueled the desire to spread westward. America's population was growing rapidly, and revolutions in communication and transportation technologies made it possible to absorb this growth. Americans also feared Europeans would expand into this "empty, unused"[32] land if they did not. But the idea that America was divinely destined to expand and had a superior claim to the territory stretching to the Pacific and beyond was influential in driving territorial expansion. By this logic, the American people and institutions were uniquely virtuous and so Americans were obliged to "remake the world in their image."[33] Manifest Destiny was **nationalistic**, idealistic, and entwined with concerns about national security. It was controversial, and political parties differed on the value of expanding, with Democrats viewing it as the "solution to the problems of modernization" and Whigs fearful that uncontrolled growth would create economic disparities and fuel internal conflict.[34]

Manifest Destiny was instrumental in President James K. Polk's reinterpretation of the Monroe Doctrine in 1845 and the Mexican-American War (1846–1848) that followed—America's first major occupation of foreign soil. Polk's desire to annex Texas, Mexican California, and the Oregon Territory played a central role in his presidential campaign. European efforts to thwart Polk prompted the new president to extend the Monroe Doctrine to prohibit European interference with American expansion.

When Polk's effort to purchase land in northern Mexico failed, he sent troops to the disputed U.S.-Texas border, triggering a controversial war. Although Polk had expected a brief war, it took a year for U.S. troops to occupy the territories he sought because Mexico, Secretary of State Daniel Webster argued, was an "ugly enemy"; "She will not fight—and will not treat."[35] Mexico refused to negotiate and used guerrilla warfare to resist occupation. Finally, in 1848, by the Treaty of Guadalupe Hidalgo, Polk achieved his aims, including acquiring Texas. As a result, America increased its territory by one-third, including most of Arizona, New Mexico, California, Colorado, Texas, Nevada, Utah, Kansas, Oklahoma, and Wyoming.

The war had consequences at home and abroad. The acquisition of new territories elevated the slavery issue on the national agenda and propelled the country toward civil war—a war that posed foreign-policy challenges for both the North and the South. Elsewhere in the Americas, governments grew fearful that the "colossus of the North" had greater ambitions. These fears seemed to be confirmed in the Spanish-American War (1898) and the construction of the Panama Canal. The administration of Theodore Roosevelt began two interventionist decades during which America acquired Puerto Rico, Guam, the Philippines, Hawaii, Samoa, and the Panama Canal Zone. This last was viewed as so important that America enabled Panama to become independent of Colombia and repeatedly intervened in countries near the canal to ensure political stability, including treaties with governments in the Americas securing the right to intervene.

Guantánamo Bay, Cuba

DID YOU KNOW?

America maintains a perpetual lease to the site of the Guantánamo Bay naval base in Cuba, owing to a 1901 amendment to a joint congressional resolution known as the Platt Amendment. This amendment was incorporated into a treaty with Cuba permitting Washington to buy or lease land for naval bases and granted America the right to intervene in Cuban affairs "for the preservation of Cuban independence, the maintenance of a government adequate for the protection of life, property, and individual liberty, and for discharging the obligations with respect to Cuba imposed by the Treaty of Paris on the United States, now to be assumed and undertaken by the Government of Cuba." Although the Platt Amendment was repealed in 1934, the lease on Guantánamo remained.

Interventionism and the Roosevelt Corollary   Until the turn of the 20th century, U.S. foreign policy could, with the exception of the Mexican-American War, be characterized by the effort to avoid foreign conflicts. Reluctance to become engaged in Europe's affairs began to recede with Theodore Roosevelt's presidency owing to new overseas interests after the Spanish-American War as well as Roosevelt's desire to make the country more influential internationally and his belief that the United States should "accept responsibility for order and stability in its own region."[36]

The Roosevelt Corollary was formalized in 1904 after attempts by European governments to use naval power to collect debts owed them by Latin American countries. To end these efforts, Roosevelt extended the Monroe Doctrine, proclaiming a right to use military force in the Americas to keep Europeans out *and* (his corollary) the prerogative to intervene to restore stability in unstable countries in the Americas. He insisted that, when disputes arose between European powers and governments in the Western Hemisphere, the United States would intervene, adding, "Chronic wrongdoing, or an impotence which results in a general loosening of the ties of civilized society, may in America, as elsewhere, ultimately require intervention by some civilized nation, and in the Western Hemisphere the adherence of

The Big Stick in
the Caribbean

THE BIG STICK IN THE CARIBBEAN SEA

the United States to the Monroe Doctrine may force the United States, however reluctantly, in flagrant cases of such wrongdoing or impotence, to the exercise of an international police power."[37] His corollary served as justification for later interventions, often by "gunboat diplomacy," in Venezuela, Cuba, Nicaragua, Haiti, and the Dominican Republic. In 1931, Marine General Smedley Butler recalled, "I helped make Mexico safe for American oil interests in 1914. I helped make Haiti and Cuba a decent place for the National City Bank boys to collect revenue in. I helped purify Nicaragua for the international banking house of Brown Brothers. . . . I brought light to the Dominican Republic for American sugar interests in 1916. I helped make Honduras 'right' for American fruit companies in 1903. Looking back on it, I might have given Al Capone a few hints."[38]

While Roosevelt is remembered for his "big stick" diplomacy in the Americas and his imperialist views, he was also a strong internationalist who recognized "that the United States was affected by events around the globe and believed that it was in the country's best interest to work with other developed nations to maintain peace and stability."[39] He largely succeeded, although U.S. public opinion generally remained opposed (as in previous eras) to involvement in European disputes. Although Roosevelt recognized the limits posed by public opinion, he brought America into international institutions to help settle international disputes. In 1902, he called upon the Permanent Court of Arbitration at The Hague to hear a longstanding dispute between America and Mexico, the first taken to the body after its establishment in 1899. In 1904, at the request of the Inter-Parliamentary Union, he called for a second Hague Conference to develop the laws of war. And the following year he offered his good offices to help end the 1905 Russo-Japanese War, for which he was awarded a Nobel Peace Prize.

A Global Leader Emerges, 1914–1945

The early 20th century again witnessed tensions among isolationism, unilateralism, and interventionism in U.S. policy. As in earlier eras, American policy was to avoid involvement in Europe's wars—that is, until those wars posed a clear threat to American interests. America only reluctantly entered World War I after Germany's adoption of unrestricted submarine warfare threatened U.S. commercial interests and risked American lives. Washington pursued a noninterventionist policy before World War II and only joined that conflict after Japan's attack on Pearl Harbor. American power and prestige grew after these conflicts, setting the stage for Washington to accept the mantle of global leadership.

World War I and Wilsonian Diplomacy (1914–1920) America reluctantly entered World War I, having demanded that the belligerents respect American rights as a neutral party. Noninvolvement in the Great War was a cornerstone of President Woodrow Wilson's foreign policy during his first term in office and aided his reelection in 1916, with Democrats campaigning on the slogan "He kept us out of war!" The potential for conflict among America's diverse immigrant populations was only one reason for remaining neutral. Equally important was a desire to trade with both sides—a policy only a neutral could follow. However, U.S. neutrality was undermined by the large loans it made to Britain and France.

As war raged, Americans debated their role in the world and how to promote U.S. interests and values. Conservative internationalists saw Germany's defeat as necessary for establishing a new international order based on law and collective security whereas progressive internationalists argued for peace as necessary to advance domestic social and economic reform, including labor reform and women's rights. Isolationists advocated sticking to America's "long-standing tradition of noninvolvement as a way of safeguarding the nation's way of life."[40] Several factors persuaded Wilson to rethink his views by 1916. In 1915, Germany launched a submarine campaign that resulted in American deaths, notably the sinking of the British-registered *Lusitania*. In 1917, when Germany declared an official policy of unrestricted submarine warfare, the threat to U.S. vessels grew, and pressure to enter the war intensified. As German U-boats sank U.S. ships, Americans learned that Germany had offered Mexico an alliance and support for Mexican efforts to regain Texas, New Mexico, and Arizona. On April 2, 1917, Wilson asked Congress to declare war on Germany.

Woodrow Wilson sought a generous peace at the conclusion of World War I. An idealistic, liberal interventionist, Wilson represented America at the 1919 Versailles Peace Conference. His Fourteen Points encapsulated his goals for a postwar world, including renunciation of secret treaties, free trade, independence and self-determination for subject peoples, and the creation of a League of Nations to preserve peace. Wilson's idealistic internationalist objectives were, however, largely thwarted by the opposition of British and French leaders. Nevertheless, his proposal for a League of Nations based on collective security under which members would unite to repel aggression was incorporated into the Treaty of Versailles. A political battle ensued when the treaty was brought to the U.S. Senate for ratification.

Many observers interpret what happened as a battle between isolationists and internationalists, the latter represented by Wilson and the former by Henry Cabot Lodge, a Republican and Senate majority leader. In fact, there was a small bipartisan group of "irreconcilables" in the Senate, who were opposed to the treaty under any circumstances, though for different reasons. Some thought it protected liberal ideals insufficiently, while others viewed it as a threat to U.S. sovereignty and feared League membership might involve America in war without congressional approval. This group, only 14 senators, received support from influential industrialists, including Andrew Mellon and Henry Clay Frick. Lodge was not himself an irreconcilable but represented a larger group that was willing to consider ratification *if* reservations could be included that preserved the right of Congress to determine whether the country would go to war. Wilson refused to compromise, and the Senate failed to ratify the treaty by a vote of 38 in favor and 52 opposed.

Renewed isolationism is too simple an explanation for the Senate's refusal to ratify, but there was a turn inward in America after World War I. A number of policies reflected an "America-first" mentality, including new tariffs imposed on foreign goods to protect American manufacturers and quotas on immigration. Following the Great Depression, the U.S. public became increasingly isolationist, opposing American involvement in conflicts in Europe and Asia (although seeking increased trade with Latin America).

American Isolationism in the 1930s Fueled by the Great Depression and the experience of World War I, including a belief that bankers and arms manufacturers had pushed America into war, U.S. public opinion and government policies became increasingly isolationist in the 1930s. Isolationists, much as in earlier eras, sought to avoid involvement in foreign conflicts and foreign entanglement more generally to preserve the country's freedom of action in foreign affairs. Isolationists were united in the belief that American "participation in war would weaken the United States and indeed place her survival as a free republic in jeopardy."[41] Otherwise, isolationists were a diverse lot. Some were conservatives who believed that war would lead to inflation and price and wage controls that would threaten the foundations of capitalism. Others were liberals who feared that war would bring Franklin Roosevelt's New Deal to an end and fuel "armament economics" that would threaten labor rights and civil liberties. Indeed, isolationists were powerful because they were diverse and faced no organized, consistent opposition from internationalists.

→ ← | CONTROVERSY

The Social Costs of War

As chairman of the Special Committee on Investigation of the Munitions Industry (1934–1936), Senator Gerald P. Nye (R-SD) investigated the role that the munitions and banking industries, so-called merchants of death, played in fueling World War I and concluded that profiteering was a key factor in America's involvement in the war. A staunch isolationist, Nye feared the social costs of war:

> Think of the social benefits the world has sacrificed to pursue a war which brought us all only a depression and more war! . . . When the appropriations for the Office of Education

comes before Congress, the legislators begin at once to quibble. . . . But when the appropriations for the maintenance of the army and navy come before Congress, our economists in the House and the Senate are as silent as the grave. There isn't any fear then about increasing budgets. . . . Now, what possible explanation can be found for this inconsistency and madness?[42]

Nye's comment mirrors the concerns of those who were critical of what President Eisenhower called the "military-industrial complex" during the Cold War. A similar concern led to sequestration in 2013. Across-the-board spending cuts threatened the military in particular, raising anxiety that American security might be endangered. Polling data indicated that the American public, while generally supportive of across-the-board cuts to reduce the federal deficit, does not back large across-the-board military cuts.[43]

Isolationism led Congress in the 1930s to pass the Neutrality Acts, a series of laws intended to ensure America would remain neutral as conflicts developed in Europe and Asia. These acts prevented Americans from exporting arms and ammunition to countries at war and made it difficult for Washington to aid Britain and France to resist Nazi aggression. This era highlighted the challenges presidents may face in implementing foreign policy. President Franklin D. Roosevelt was an internationalist, but his actions were constrained by isolationist sentiment. FDR sought to help quarantine "the epidemic of world lawlessness." In 1940, he argued America could best defend its interests by supporting Britain because "the best immediate defense of the United States is the success of Great Britain in defending itself," which he justified both by America's "historic and current interest in the survival of democracy in the world as a whole" and "from a selfish point of view of American defense."[44]

Isolationists opposed policies that would, they argued, trigger war with Germany. All the while, there were influential internationalists fighting the isolationist current. Henry Luce, for example, the founder of *Time, Life,* and *Fortune* magazines and an influential voice for internationalism, argued that Americans "accept wholeheartedly our duty and our opportunity as the most powerful and vital nation in the world"[45] by supporting Britain and create a new world order based upon American principles. Those principles were encompassed in what Roosevelt called the "four freedoms"—freedom of speech, freedom of worship, freedom from want, and freedom from fear. Congress finally abandoned neutrality in March 1941 with the passage of the Lend-Lease Act allowing America to provide supplies to Germany's foes. Then, in August, Roosevelt and British Prime Minister Winston Churchill agreed to the Atlantic Charter, publicly demonstrating U.S. support for Britain and laying out an internationalist agenda for the postwar world— freer trade, self-determination, disarmament, and collective security. Nonetheless, isolationist sentiment remained strong, and only Japan's attack on December 7, 1941, convinced the public to enter World War II.

Instrumental Multilateralism: Containing Strategic Challenges

U.S isolationism had ended by 1945. World War II had left power vacuums in Europe and Asia, and America emerged as a great power—with global interests and responsibilities.

The Cold War America was the first nuclear power, and U.S. leaders viewed the Soviet Union as the greatest threat in the postwar era. In the Cold War, Washington pursued a grand strategy that included multilateralist, unilateralist, interventionist, and noninterventionist policies. On the one hand, this was an internationalist and multilateralist era of foreign policy in which U.S. leaders encouraged the development of global institutions founded on liberal democratic and economic principles, including the UN, an outgrowth of the Atlantic Charter; the Bretton Woods financial institutions; the Marshall Plan; and NATO.

In other respects, however, America remained unilateral, even when dealing with multilateral institutions like the UN or NATO. America's European allies, for example, were repeatedly frustrated by the failure of American leaders to consult them on policies that had a direct bearing on NATO defense as in the decision to remove U.S. missiles from Turkey as part of an agreement with Moscow to end the 1962 Cuban missile crisis. Simultaneously, U.S. policy balanced interventionism and noninterventionism, with a tacit policy of noninterference in the Soviet bloc alongside interventionism to prevent the spread of Soviet influence into new areas, especially those in Washington's sphere of influence. In the Western Hemisphere, unilateral policies were pursued under the Hemispheric Defense Doctrine, an extension of the Monroe Doctrine, that claimed Latin America as part of the "free world" and thus under U.S. protection. This doctrine justified military interventions and covert operations to support anticommunist forces in Guatemala and Brazil (1954), Cuba (1961), the Dominican Republic (1965), Chile (1973), and Nicaragua (1980s).

After the Cold War With the fall of the Berlin Wall in 1989, the reunification of Germany in 1990, and the collapse of the USSR in 1991, the world radically changed. Suddenly, U.S. leaders no longer had a clear adversary, and its Cold War strategy was no longer relevant. For a time, observers were optimistic that a new, peaceful world order would ensue—one in which liberal institutions could flourish and in which America would no longer have to invest heavily in military preparedness. With the **peace dividend** produced by the end of the Cold War, Washington would have additional resources to invest in economic and social development. Reality did not match expectations. New, unanticipated threats emerged, and there has been significant continuity across post–Cold War administrations in managing this new environment.

Postwar administrations sought to maintain U.S. leadership and assumed that other countries sought that leadership.[46] All the presidents in this era—George H. W. Bush (1989–1993), Bill Clinton (1993–2001), George W. Bush (2001–2009), and Barack Obama (2009–2017)—were internationalists in the limited sense of seeking a major role for America in the world. They differed, however, about why that role was necessary and the means to sustain it. None was isolationist or exclusively unilateralist. As George W. Bush's first secretary of state, Colin Powell, observed in 2001, "You can't be unilateralist. The world is too complicated."[47]

Since the end of the Cold War there remains an enduring commitment to preserving sovereignty and maximizing flexibility in foreign affairs as well as elements of unilateralism and multilateralism. As in the past, "America behaves unilaterally when it can, and it is always at moments of nationalist crisis that the impulse is strongest."[48] Even when it does work through multilateral institutions, we see an instrumental multilateralism that seeks to preserve flexibility, even as America engages the world. We do not see a coherent grand strategy like containment, and there is no coherent sense of when to emphasize values over interests or which values and interests are worth fighting for. While observers have tried to find such strategies in the form of presidential "doctrines," in fact, none encompassed a comprehensive view of America's role in the world and the appropriate instruments for preserving that role.

As president when the Cold War ended, President George H.W. Bush devoted considerable attention to foreign affairs. He had extensive foreign policy experience having served as vice president under Ronald Reagan, ambassador to China and the UN, and CIA director. Perhaps owing to this experience, he had a multilateral orientation that shaped his approach to the 1991 Persian Gulf War, the Middle East peace process, famine in Somalia, and the emerging conflict in Yugoslavia. In the Persian Gulf War, he organized a UN-backed international coalition of thirty-four countries to force Iraq's withdrawal from Kuwait. The coalition's victory ushered in, Bush declared, a New World Order, "where the rule of law, not the law of the jungle, governs the conduct of nations . . . an order in which a credible United Nations can use its peacekeeping role to fulfill the promise and vision of the UN's founders."[49] In other words, America ought to use its power to support universal values.

At the same time, however, U.S. intervention in Panama in 1989 to oust Manuel Noriega signaled that Bush was willing to act unilaterally on matters of vital interest. Noriega, the military dictator of Panama since 1983, had supported U.S. anticommunist policies in Central America, but he also had a record of involvement in drug trafficking. In 1988, he was indicted by federal grand juries in Tampa and Miami on charges of drug smuggling and money laundering. The following year, he annulled a presidential election that would have brought the opposition to power. In December 1989, just a day after an off-duty U.S. Marine was killed by Panamanian soldiers, Bush authorized "Operation Just Cause" to overthrow Noriega. The president justified the invasion as necessary to combat drug trafficking, defend democracy in Panama, and protect the Panama Canal (permitted under the 1977 Torrijos-Carter Treaties). The operation was successful, and Noriega was tried and convicted by a U.S. court in 1992. The U.S. invasion, however, had violated international law and was denounced by the Organization of American States (OAS) and the UN.

Bush's New World Order was never realized, and as the first fully post–Cold War president, Bill Clinton faced a changed strategic environment. America had become the world's sole superpower with the collapse of the USSR. In the absence of a major challenger, Washington seemed free to pursue its own global agenda, but there would be less public support for engagement in international institutions and overseas involvement than before. Thus, the Clinton administration faced greater domestic constraints than previous administrations in pursuing foreign policy, especially after the Republicans gained a majority in the House of Representatives in 1994. Political foes like Senator Jesse Helms (R-NC), chair of the Senate Foreign Relations Committee, opposed much of Clinton's international agenda, including payment on UN dues and U.S. participation in global treaties, like the Kyoto Protocol for reducing greenhouse gas emissions and the Rome Statute that created the International Criminal Court (ICC).

Clinton's strategic vision involved advancing both values and interests, although the emphasis changed during his two terms in office. During his first term, Clinton emphasized the spread of democracy. This emphasis encompassed four goals that Clinton believed would produce security and prosperity: (1) "strengthen the community of market democracies," (2) "foster and consolidate new democracies and market economies where possible," (3) "counter the aggression and support the liberalization of states hostile to democracy," and (4) "help democracy and market economies take root in regions of greatest humanitarian concern."[50] Clinton's first term emphasized economic issues and in some ways foreshadowed the policies of his successor, George W. Bush.

A competing "**Clinton Doctrine**" emerged during his second term, and it is for this that he will be remembered. In a reaction to admitted foreign-policy failures in his first term—notably, the 1994 Rwandan genocide—the Clinton doctrine emphasized humanitarian intervention. This emphasis was shaped by recognition that U.S. citizens and interests faced a broad spectrum of threats including terrorism, ethnic unrest, and criminal violence, and that America had an interest in guaranteeing global stability and must maintain sufficient military force to operate against multiple adversaries simultaneously.[51] The crux of the doctrine was that Washington would intervene militarily, even without UN approval, to end human-rights abuses when it could do so at limited cost. According to one official, Clinton viewed "genocide as itself a national interest where we should act"[52]—a policy distinctive for the principle that intervention should serve moral ends.

Although Clinton was a multilateralist who valued international institutions and norms, his policies were frequently unilateralist and interventionist as well. Clinton unilaterally removed U.S. troops deployed in Somalia to implement a UN humanitarian mission after the death of U.S. soldiers in the 1993 Battle of Mogadishu, and he refused to form a coalition to prevent genocide in Rwanda. The Clinton administration also engaged in interventions in Haiti (1994), Bosnia (1995), and Kosovo (1999) and airstrikes in Afghanistan and Sudan in 1998 in retaliation for the bombing of U.S. embassies in East Africa, in Iraq in 1993 after an alleged assassination plot against former President George H. W. Bush and 1996 in response to interference with aircraft patrolling no-fly zones in Iraq. These actions were evidence of U.S. military power that no state or coalition of states could challenge. U.S. dominance was so great that French Foreign Minister Hubert Védrine argued the label "superpower" no longer did it justice. America had achieved the status of "hyperpower," a unique degree of power in all categories, including "this domination of attitudes, concepts, language and modes of life."[53] This designation called attention to what France and others viewed as growing U.S. unilateralism.

PRESENT: THE IMPACT OF 9/11

The 9/11 terrorist attacks transformed U.S. policy (chapter 11). The most notable shift was a resurgence of unilateralism.

The Unilateralist Turn

Examples of unilateralism after 9/11 included articulation of a **preemptive war** doctrine, military intervention in Iraq without UN authorization, the creation of new and less formal mechanisms for countering weapons of mass destruction (WMD) proliferation, the use of bilateral treaties to protect U.S. citizens from prosecution in the ICC, and the use of unmanned drones for targeted killing of suspected terrorists overseas. In an era in which enemies were often disparate and invisible, multilateralism was viewed as a luxury that America could not afford in dealing with threats requiring decisive action.

Effective multilateralism requires governments with different values and interests to agree on common objectives *and* appropriate means to achieve these. The process takes time and often leads to lowest-common-denominator policies. This is not to say that Washington abandoned multilateralism, but after 9/11 it used it selectively—especially in the security realm where interests frequently trump ideals.

CHAPTER 2   Competing Currents in U.S. Foreign Policy   55

The willingness of U.S. officials to practice interventionism was another trend, marked by wars in Afghanistan in 2001 and Iraq in 2003. More recently, there has been a reluctance to intervene in messy conflicts, notably Syria, as the American public grew weary of long and costly wars. Republican George W. Bush and Democrat Barack Obama had contrasting worldviews, but there was considerable continuity in their foreign policies.

Early in the Bush administration, foreign-policy leaders focused on state-based threats. Of key concern to Bush and his senior policy advisors were great powers, China and Russia, and rogue states Iraq, Iran, North Korea, and Libya. It was to deal with rogue states that Bush pursued an active missile-defense program (approved during the Clinton Administration) (chapter 14), a policy that heightened tension with Russia. Bush also rejected U.S. participation in several international treaties he viewed as potentially harmful to U.S. political and economic interests, including the Rome Statute and the Kyoto Protocol. It appeared that under the younger Bush, America would emphasize disengagement. This trend continued with the December 2001 abrogation of the 1972 Anti-Ballistic Missile Treaty and rejection in 2002 of a protocol to the Biological Weapons Convention.

But after 9/11 global terrorism became the highest priority, and the War on Terror (chapter 11) was framed as a struggle between good and evil. Interests and norms were integrated in the formulation of U.S. foreign policies that sought simultaneously to enhance security and spread liberal values. This new war was not just between America and al-Qaeda but targeted worldwide terrorism. America, Bush argued, could not afford to be defensive, reacting to terrorist attacks, but had to prepare to attack preemptively.

Anticipatory defense meant military engagement. By October 2001, America had invaded Afghanistan in search of al-Qaeda leaders responsible for the attacks and to oust the Taliban regime that had given sanctuary to al-Qaeda. Iraq also became part of this strategy (chapter 13). Saddam Hussein, who remained in power in Iraq after his defeat in 1991, "embodied the convergence of Bush's three fears—terrorism, tyrants and technologies of mass destruction."[54] America could not wait, in the words of Bush's national security advisor (later secretary of state), Condoleezza Rice, "for the smoking gun to be a mushroom cloud."[55] Bush turned to the UN Security Council, seeking international support for intervention, but when that failed, he crafted a "coalition of the willing" and invaded without UN approval. The fact that the Iraq war did not receive Security Council authorization reinforced perceptions of U.S. unilateralism and interventionism.

Democracy promotion was a second goal in Bush's strategy in the War on Terror, based on a belief that democracies do not go to war with one another. This gained greater prominence when formally articulated as the **Bush Doctrine** in his second inaugural address when he declared, "It is the policy of the United States to seek and support the growth of democratic movements and institutions in every nation and culture with the ultimate goal of ending tyranny in our world."[56] The Afghan and Iraq wars were not just about "regime change." They were also fought to establish stable democracies, a daunting goal, and both conflicts turned into costly protracted wars that were still continuing when Bush left office in 2009. Nonproliferation was a third, related, goal that ranked high on the post 9/11 security agenda (chapter 4). It reflected a disengagement from multilateral efforts like the Nuclear Nonproliferation Treaty and the Comprehensive Test Ban Treaty in favor of bilateral and informal arrangements like the Proliferation Security Initiative.

Bush also pursued an active foreign policy outside the security realm. In economic policy, his administration pursued free trade and investment, signing several free trade agreements. Critics countered that the emphasis on bilateral agreements and trade ties undermined multilateral efforts organized by the World Trade Organization. Washington also substantially increased its foreign aid commitments, with significant support going to fight global disease. Taken in its entirety, this agenda was mixed. Except for security, there was no clear strategy. Even as the administration championed democratization as a goal, it cut funding for democracy promotion. And democratization conflicted with other goals, like fighting terrorism.

Thus, U.S. foreign policy during Bush's first term shifted toward disengagement except for use of military force. Foreign policy reflected a dislike for international treaties and organizations that limited freedom of action, growing reliance on military preemption to cope with security threats, and military intervention to spread democracy. This reorientation was described by some as the "Bush revolution," but was it really? We see considerable continuity in the use of foreign policy to pursue historically American values[57] like liberty, democracy, free-market capitalism, and the belief in a unique responsibility to spread those values.

Bush was a Wilsonian (a staunch **liberal interventionist**) in his commitment to spread democracy, even by force. But Bush also represented an unapologetic return to the tradition of unilateralism. Unilateralism has never been repudiated by American leaders, who have consistently been willing to act on their own when they believed it was the best way to serve U.S. interests. Where the Bush administration's shift was distinct was the militant expansion of American power in reaction to security threats. Thus, the "Bush revolution" represented a shift in style, not substance, although the shift in style was dramatic.

Several factors contributed to this shift, beginning with the unprecedented gap in military power between America and other countries. The United States turned to unilateralism because, in the absence of other actors capable of challenging it militarily, it could do so. But while the global distribution of power partly explains American unilateralism and interventionism, it is not the only factor. One must also consider the president's personality. Bush came to office with little foreign-policy experience but with a **Manichean worldview** of good versus evil shaped by his religious faith. Perhaps because he had little foreign-policy experience, he relied on key advisers. In his first term, Bush had appointed a diverse foreign-policy team of staunch **neoconservatives** including Vice President Dick Cheney, Secretary of Defense Donald Rumsfeld, and Deputy Secretary of Defense Paul Wolfowitz *and* internationalists such as Secretary of State Colin Powell and Richard Armitage and Richard N. Haass, senior officials in the State Department.

After 9/11, Bush embraced the views of the hardline nationalists in his administration. The **rally-round-the-flag effect** of 9/11 on public opinion, which saw a 35-percentage-point increase in the president's approval ratings,[58] provided him with leeway to pursue unilateralist and interventionist policies. But the internationalist camp, represented by Condoleezza Rice and Secretary of Defense Robert Gates, gained influence in Bush's second term when it became necessary to underplay unilateralism and engage allies to make progress in nuclear proliferation and Middle East peace.[59]

Critics argued that the costs of this unilateralist and interventionist orientation were greater than the short-term advantages it produced. They claimed that it undermined U.S. **legitimacy** abroad, alienated allies, actually increased the threat of terrorism, and drove America into debt. Such critics were eager for a change of course with the election of Barack Obama in 2008, but they were frustrated when a decisive shift did not occur.

A Return to Multilateralism

On the campaign trail, then junior senator from Illinois Barack Obama called for a new "American moment" in which the United States would "provide global leadership grounded in the understanding that the world shares a common security and a common humanity."

> This century's threats are at least as dangerous as and in some ways more complex than those we have confronted in the past. They come from weapons that can kill on a mass scale and from global terrorists who respond to alienation or perceived injustice with murderous nihilism. They come from rogue states allied to terrorists and from rising powers that could challenge both America and the international foundation of liberal democracy. They come from weak states that cannot control their territory or provide for their people. And they come from a warming planet that will spur new diseases, spawn more devastating natural disasters, and catalyze deadly conflicts.[60]

Environmental issues aside, Obama's view of the threats facing America was not unlike that of his predecessor, but he had a different interpretation of how the world worked, emphasizing that threats had a transnational dimension, and that the American military might have a role to play in managing some of them but was unsuited for managing others. On the campaign trail, Obama opposed the war in Iraq and promised to withdraw U.S. troops within sixteen months, but he also espoused sending additional troops to Afghanistan, a conflict he regarded as more important than Iraq. He supported more open, multilateral diplomacy, arguing that diplomacy was necessary to rally global support for U.S. policies. He fostered nuclear nonproliferation efforts; leadership in climate negotiations; direct engagement with foes like Iran, Venezuela, North Korea, and Myanmar; and obeying international law—a commitment that extended to human-rights treaties and closing the Guantánamo Bay detention camp. These positions set him apart from his Republican opponent, Senator John McCain, but he also argued that military intervention still had a role in U.S. policy.[61] In the words of a national security advisor, Obama's foreign policy goals on entering office were to "wind down these two wars [Iraq and Afghanistan], reestablish American standing and leadership in the world, and focus on a broader set of priorities, from Asia and the global economy to a nuclear-nonproliferation regime."[62]

Presidents, however, are rarely able to pursue the foreign-policy agenda they wish. Once in office, they face unexpected challenges, have access to new information, and encounter constraints, both foreseen and unforeseen. Obama's supporters were eager to see his vision reflected in foreign policy to reverse what they saw as "cowboy" diplomacy. Obama's opponents, by contrast, believed his policies would erode U.S. influence and compromise American security. Both groups expected Obama to be a multilateralist who would reaffirm support for international law and institutions while disengaging from costly military ventures, reversing the unilateralism and interventionism that had characterized the Bush years. As it turned out, at least in his first term, Obama lacked a grand strategy. Americans got something different than what they had expected. As president, Obama turned out to be more pragmatic than ideological in both the formulation and implementation of foreign policy.

Retrospectively, it was premature for the Norwegian Nobel Committee to announce in 2009 that it would award the Nobel Peace Prize to President Barack Obama "for his extraordinary efforts to strengthen international diplomacy and cooperation between peoples." The committee noted that Obama had "as President created a new climate in international politics. Multilateral diplomacy has regained a central position, with emphasis on the role that the United Nations and other international institutions can play."[63] The award generated criticism at home and abroad. Former Polish president and 1983 Nobel Peace Prize recipient Lech Walesa summed up the controversy: "So soon? Too early. He has no contribution so far."[64] Obama was not the first American president to receive the prize, but he had been in office less than nine months, whereas past recipients Theodore Roosevelt, Woodrow Wilson, and Jimmy Carter were awarded the prize for actions while in office or after their presidency. Suggests one presidential historian, "The committee seems to have been saying, 'We had eight years without strong U.S. leadership for peace and now we have someone who will put the country's energies behind Middle East talks and nuclear arms control.'"[65]

Obama's wartime Nobel Peace Prize

Adam Zyglis, *The Buffalo News*

President Obama accepts the Nobel Peace Prize in 2009

Heidi Wideroe/Bloomberg via Getty Images

Obama was not a value-driven multilateralist but a practical leader who was realistic and cautious, evaluating policy options according to their likelihood of success. "In office Obama has been a progressive where possible but a **pragmatist** when necessary. And given the domestic and global situations he has faced, pragmatism has dominated."[66] His caution was related to a second factor—the number and complexity of global challenges that faced America as he took office. As later chapters demonstrate, much of the complexity of Obama's foreign-policy dilemmas stemmed from linkages among issues. These dilemmas appeared across a range of issues and made it virtually impossible to shape a one-size-fits-all vision of foreign policy. A third factor that constrained Obama's efforts to pursue the visionary, multilateral foreign policy he had promised as a candidate was public and congressional suspicion of internationalism. The country was divided over core values, and, while public opinion was broadly internationalist, there was vocal opposition from neoconservatives, **new sovereignists,** and others influential in the previous administration that continued to oppose deeper cooperation with international institutions or new treaty commitments in arms control, climate change, and human rights.

Budget constraints were another factor that yielded pragmatism in foreign affairs. Implementing grand strategy is expensive because it tends to lead to extensive commitments, as it did for Monroe, Harry S. Truman, and George W. Bush. Thus, arguments about U.S. involvement abroad became almost inseparable from arguments about restoring fiscal discipline.

Obama's rhetoric reflected an ideological commitment to multilateralism. Addressing the UN General Assembly in 2009, he urged, "Those who used to chastise America for acting alone in the world cannot now stand by and wait for America to solve the world's problems alone. We have sought in word and deed a new era of engagement with the world, and now is the time for all of us to take our share of responsibility for a global response to global challenges."[67] And in his second inaugural address in 2013, he declared, "We will show the courage to try and resolve our differences with other nations peacefully— not because we are naïve about the dangers we face, but because engagement can more durably lift suspicion and fear. America will remain the anchor of strong alliances in every corner of the globe; and we will renew those institutions that extend our capacity to manage crisis abroad."[68]

Hybrid Multilateralism

Obama's multilateralism has been variously described as "hybrid multilateralism," "multilateralism with teeth," and "soft unilateralism." Depending on the issue, he has even been described as an outright unilateralist. Liberals who looked forward to an Obama revolution after his election found the president insufficiently multilateral, as did many citizens in other countries (Figure 2.1). During Obama's first term, America failed to adopt several high-profile multilateral treaties including the Law of the Sea Treaty, the Comprehensive Test Ban Treaty, the Ottawa Convention on Landmines banning antipersonnel mines, and the Rome Statute. After lengthy negotiations, Washington delayed action on an Arms Trade Treaty in 2012 that regulated the international trade in conventional weapons, delighting treaty opponents such as Russia, China, and Indonesia but vexing its supporters who charged Obama with abdicating U.S. leadership so as not to threaten his reelection prospects. Key military decisions were also taken without consultation with allies, including Obama's 2009 decision to send additional troops to Afghanistan, the 2011 raid that killed Osama bin Laden, and the continued use of drones in Pakistan.

Even policies that seemed multilateral, like the proposed Transatlantic Trade and Investment Partnership and the Trans Pacific Partnership, were criticized for their possible negative impact on *global* trade negotiations. On the other hand, relations with the UN improved during the Obama years, with a reversal of the Bush-era refusal to participate in the UN Human Rights Council and a willingness to seek Security Council approval for multilateral sanctions against North Korea and Iran for their proliferation efforts and for a NATO-led humanitarian mission in Libya. Obama also sought to improve U.S. standing in several regions, seeking a "reset" with Russia and a "pivot" to Asia in his first term, and during his second term, a "pivot back" to Europe (owing to Russo-American confrontation in Ukraine), nuclear talks with Iran, and a resumption of the Israeli-Palestinian peace process.

Although Obama argued that military intervention still had a place in American foreign policy, after lengthy wars in Afghanistan and Iraq, the president became wary of new foreign entanglements and armed intervention and only did so with multilateral support. By some accounts, the guiding principle of Obama's foreign policy was restrained multilateralism, or "retrenchment," reducing U.S. commitments abroad while shifting some of the burden for global leadership onto American partners,[69] a tendency that reflects less overall public support for U.S. involvement overseas (Figure 2.2). As explained by Secretary Gates in a speech at West Point, "any future defense secretary who advises the president to again send a big American land army into Asia or into the Middle East or Africa should 'have his head examined.'"[70] Thus, as we shall see, Obama showed pragmatic caution in crises in Libya, Mali, Egypt, Syria, and Ukraine. Skeptics worry about the long-term implications of such a low-key policy: "Step back too far from big sticks, and when America speaks, it may not be heard."[71] Supporters, by contrast, argued that this kind of leadership is required in a complex, interconnected world.

FIGURE 2.1   How Much Does the Unites States Consider Your Country's Interests?

➤ *Survey question: "In making international policy decisions, to what extent do you think the United States takes into account the interests of countries like (survey country)—a great deal, a fair amount, not too much, or not at all?"*

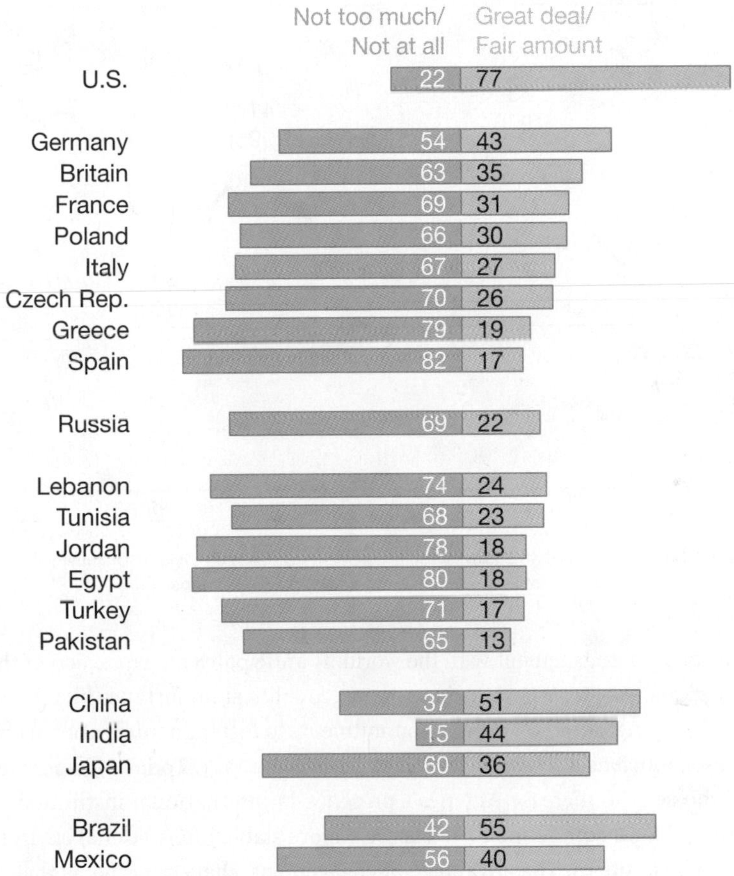

	Not too much/ Not at all	Great deal/ Fair amount
U.S.	22	77
Germany	54	43
Britain	63	35
France	69	31
Poland	66	30
Italy	67	27
Czech Rep.	70	26
Greece	79	19
Spain	82	17
Russia	69	22
Lebanon	74	24
Tunisia	68	23
Jordan	78	18
Egypt	80	18
Turkey	71	17
Pakistan	65	13
China	37	51
India	15	44
Japan	60	36
Brazil	42	55
Mexico	56	40

Source: "Views of the U.S. and American Foreign Policy," Pew Global Attitudes Project, June 13, 2012, http://www.pewglobal.org/2012/06/13/chapter-1-views-of-the-u-s-and-american-foreign-policy-4.

CONCLUSION: ENGAGEMENT OR DISENGAGEMENT?

Isolationism is no longer a real option in foreign policy. Even neo-isolationists recognize America cannot go it alone. Washington is unlikely, for example, to withdraw from the global economy or from international political organizations. Even the UN with which Washington has had a troubled relationship in recent decades is viewed by most Americans as playing a necessary role in global affairs.[72] The question becomes, *how engaged* will America be? American leaders have two possible options, both with historical roots.

FIGURE 2.2   Majority Says United States Should "Mind Its Own Business" Internationally

➤ *Graph shows percentage of respondents agreeing with the following statement: "The U.S. should mind its own business internationally and let other countries get along the best they can on their own."*

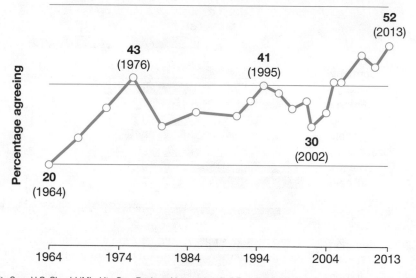

Source: "Majority Says U.S. Should 'Mind Its Own Business' Internationally," Pew Research Center, December 3, 2012, http://www.people-press.org/2013/12/03/public-sees-u-s-power-declining-as-support-for-global-engagement-slips.

The first entails greater engagement with the world. It anticipates an expansion of the U.S. commitments to influence global events, especially in areas of geopolitical importance like the Middle East and Asia. As a **shaper**, Washington would expand commitments to foster an international order favorable to pursuing its interests, much as it did at the outbreak of the Cold War. Today's shapers tend to be liberal internationalists who seek to increase America's presence in international institutions and are willing to extend international legal commitments to ensure a more stable international environment that they see as beneficial to all countries. The advantage of engagement, shapers argue, is that America retains its global leadership.

Continuing security commitments, shapers contend, reduce conflict in key regions and constrain potential rivals, and alliances reduce the risk of involvement in unwanted conflicts by giving America greater influence over weaker partners. Continued U.S. engagement also maintains an open world economy and affords influence in economic negotiations that shape the global economy in ways that benefit U.S. interests and cooperate with others in managing global economic crises. Although one estimate in 2013 predicted that U.S. military expenditures in Afghanistan, Iraq, and Pakistan would ultimately cost over $4 trillion,[73] some argue that engagement is possible at a reasonable cost.[74]

The second option, disengagement or retrenchment, involves a retreat from global commitments. **Retrenchers**, or restrainers, seek a limited foreign policy in which an overextended, indebted America withdraws from all but vital foreign commitments. Restrainers are *not* isolationists who want to cut off ties to the outside world. Rather, they wish to align U.S. commitments with U.S. interests, resources, and public opinion.[75] They believe that by allowing other countries to take greater responsibility for their own security, America can focus on economic recovery and military reform. Restrainers come from a variety of traditions. Some are liberal multilateralists who emphasize nation building at home as the way to restore American stature. Others represent a more conservative position associated with a sort of neo-isolationism that assumes the United States is sufficiently powerful that by disengaging from marginal commitments abroad it can insulate itself from dangerous overextension. Restrainers argue that current levels of engagement are too expensive in budget and manpower costs. American defense budgets are much higher than those of allies or adversaries, and the United States subsidizes its allies' security. Restrainers want allies like Japan to shoulder greater responsibility for their own security. They also argue that military involvement produces foreign enemies, while alliances risk trapping America in wars it does not seek.

Some retrenchers go further, arguing that engagement dilutes American sovereignty,[76] a belief apparent in America's rejection of the Comprehensive Test Ban Treaty, the Ottawa Convention on Landmines, the Rome Statute, the Kyoto Protocol, and the Convention on the Rights of the Child. America's hegemonic strategy—the desire to control events globally—in particular reflected in seemingly endless wars in Afghanistan and Iraq, retrenchers claim, should give way to restraint. "This undisciplined, expensive, and bloody strategy has done untold harm to U.S. national security."[77]

The debate over how engaged the United States should be persists. In the chapters that follow, we examine how this debate affects a variety of issues, regional problems, and relations with other major powers.

DISCUSSION QUESTIONS

1. To what extent should the United States try to spread its values globally? Do you think that exclusive concern with interests would be beneficial or harmful to America? Illustrate with a case.

2. Should the United States remain deeply engaged in regional and global issues, or should it disengage itself from some of these? What issues do you believe are vital to the United States?

3. Should the United States increasingly act multilaterally or unilaterally? What are the advantages and disadvantages of each?

4. Is isolationism a feasible alternative for the United States? What possible arguments could be made for isolationism before World Wars I and II or today?

5. How and why did the orientation of U.S. policy change after the Cold War?

6. In what ways did the orientation of President Obama's foreign policy differ from that of President Bill Clinton and President George W. Bush?

7. Would you be a foreign-policy shaper or retrencher? Explain.

KEY TERMS

autonomy (p. 40)

balance of power (p. 42)

bilateralism (p. 41)

Bush Doctrine (p. 55)

Clinton Doctrine (p. 54)

Concert of Europe (p. 42)

decolonization (p. 42)

disengagement (p. 39)

engagement (p. 39)

free-market capitalism
    (p. 38)

grand strategy (p. 37)

humanitarian (p. 42)

ideals (p. 39)

independence (p. 39)

individualism (p. 38)

instrumental (p. 42)

internationalism (p. 37)

interventionism (p. 37)

isolationism (p. 37)

legitimacy (p. 56)

liberal interventionist (p. 56)

Manichean worldview
    (p. 56)

Manifest Destiny (p. 46)

multilateralism (p. 37)

nationalistic (p. 46)

neoconservative (p. 56)

neo-isolationists (p. 40)

neutrality (p. 49)

New Deal (p. 50)

new sovereignists (p. 59)

noninterventionism (p. 37)

peace dividend (p. 52)

power politics (p. 42)

pragmatist (p. 59)

preemptive war (p. 54)

rally-round-the-flag effect
    (p. 56)

retrenchers (p. 62)

rule of law (p. 38)

shaper (p. 62)

unilateralism (p. 37)

for CQ Press

Sharpen your skill with SAGE edge at **edge.sagepub.com/mansbach**

SAGE edge for Students provides a personalized approach to help you accomplish your coursework goals in an easy-to-use learning environment.

3

American Military Strategy in an Era of Power Diffusion

Air Force Space
Command Network
Operations &
Security Center in
Colorado Springs

Reuters / Rick Wilking

U.S. policymakers have struggled since the Cold War to craft a coherent grand strategy to meet contemporary challenges, that is, a comprehensive approach to foreign policy that coordinates goals and the tools to pursue them. Administrations face pressure to design grand strategies that will guide America's involvement in the world and communicate U.S. interests to others. Shaping a grand strategy was challenging even when there existed a single unifying threat as there did during the Cold War. Today, it is more difficult, owing to a diffusion of power that enables other actors to challenge U.S. interests. The result has been instability in Europe, the Middle East, and Asia that critics at home and abroad blame on the absence of a grand strategy. Without it, they argue, there is no clear sense of America's interests, and neither allies nor foes know what Washington seeks—for what issues it will or will not go to war. Thus, foes are more willing to test U.S. resolve. Whether considered an era of "nonpolarity" or "disorder"[1] in which many actors exercise different types of power or "compounding complexity" in which challenges grow exponentially and interact with one another, the contemporary strategic environment is challenging.

This chapter examines U.S. military strategy in this complex era, focusing on how America has used military force and threats to achieve its interests and values and how its armed forces have had to adapt strategies and adopt new technologies to manage threats posed by a diffuse cast of actors.

SOURCES OF U.S. MILITARY STRATEGY

Several factors help explain the formulation of U.S. military strategy. External factors are critical—the distribution of power, the rise of new challengers, the proliferation of nonstate terrorists and militias, and the emergence of new technologies. Immediately after the Cold War, threats to the hegemon—America—were minimal. As additional power centers emerged, the more complex policymaking became. During the Cold War, U.S. officials were preoccupied with the USSR, and military strategy was directed toward containing Soviet expansion. In issues and areas beyond the bipolar confrontation, Washington enjoyed considerable latitude in foreign policy. In an increasingly multipolar world, however, U.S. officials must interact with other actors that pose threats or offer opportunities. Although America still enjoys military preponderance globally (in 2012 it accounted for 41 percent of global defense spending),[2] examining all the elements of power (military, economic, diplomatic, social, and cultural) lessens that preponderance. Although there is no clear *global* challenger, major states like Russia, China, and Iran pose regional challenges, and groups like al-Qaeda threaten instability in areas where Washington has geostrategic interests like the Middle East.

New technologies pose another external challenge. Some are "low-tech," like the improvised explosive devices used against U.S. troops in Iraq. Such asymmetric weapons enable weak adversaries to increase American casualties. At the other end of the spectrum, "high-tech" tools like

Timeline

1900	2000
1947 Truman Doctrine	**2001–2014** War in Afghanistan
1950–1953 Korean War	**2003–2011** Iraq War
1959–1975 Vietnam War	**2009** Stuxnet cyber-attack against Iran
1962 Cuban missile crisis	**2010** President Obama announces an end to the War on Terror.
1972 SALT I arms control agreement	**2011** NATO intervention in Libya
1989 Fall of the Berlin Wall	**2014** U.S. intervention against ISIS
1991 Persian Gulf War	
1992–1994 U.S. involvement in Somalia	
1999 Kosovo War	

cyber-espionage—network-hacking to access sensitive consumer, industrial, and military data—and **cyberattacks** on infrastructure like transportation networks can cause substantial harm. In 2012, Secretary of Defense Leon Panetta warned of a "cyber Pearl Harbor," and cautioned that a cyber-terrorist attack "could paralyze the nation and create a profound new sense of vulnerability."[3] In 2015, the Obama administration began to outline circumstances under which America would employ cyberattacks either to retaliate or as an offensive weapon for conflict.

Governmental factors are also important in formulating and implementing U.S. grand strategy. One of these is the constitutional separation of powers. The president is commander-in-chief of the armed forces, and the Defense Department is in the executive branch. Congress, as noted earlier, enjoys the power of the purse and war-making authority. The authority to determine when, where, and for how long U.S. troops can be engaged in conflicts overseas has frequently been debated, with the president repeatedly authorizing combat missions without a formal congressional declaration of war. In 1973, Congress enacted the War Powers Resolution, requiring the president to notify Congress within forty-eight hours after sending U.S. troops into action and to seek authorization to allow troops to remain in combat beyond sixty days. Despite the War Powers Resolution, members of Congress continued to accuse presidents of circumventing their authority. Thus, in 2014, Senators John McCain (R-AZ) and Tim Kaine (D-VA) sought to replace the War Powers Resolution with a War Powers Consultation Act to "establish a constructive and practical means by which the judgment of both the President and Congress can be brought to bear when deciding whether the United States should engage in a significant armed conflict."[4]

Congress's power of the purse—including the defense budget—also constrains presidential policymaking. In fiscal 2013, across-the-board spending reductions ("sequestration") required by the 2011 Budget Control Act would have cut $54.6 billion from the Pentagon's operating budget (later reduced to $37.2 billion by the Taxpayer Relief Act) and $500 billion over ten years. Secretary Panetta warned that such cuts would trigger "the most serious readiness cuts that this country is going to confront in a decade" and "degrade our ability to respond to crisis precisely at the time of rising instability across the globe."[5] Others disagreed. As a proportion of America's defense budget, the cuts were no deeper than those mandated after the world wars and later conflicts. Indeed, austerity might force an administration to be more "strategic" in its policy choices.

Interservice rivalries can be as damaging to the formulation and implementation of military strategy as budget cuts. Rivalries have always existed among the military services, but budget cuts and force reductions have intensified conflict over competing missions and technologies. The Army, the Navy, and the Air Force, for instance, all have unmanned drone capabilities, with the Navy and Air Force each arguing for a single capability that it would control. Similarly, the Army and Marines have battled as each crafted new missions that rely on small quick-response forces that require helicopters based on naval vessels. Redundant capabilities and missions complicate efforts to develop a coherent military strategy.

In his role as commander-in-chief, the president decides when to order U.S. military action, as Barack Obama did in 2014 when he announced a military campaign against the Islamic State of Iraq and Syria (ISIS). "I think that it is absolutely true that we're going to need Sunni states to step up, not just Saudi Arabia, our partners like Jordan, the United Arab Emirates, Turkey," said Obama.[6] As secretary of state, John Kerry sought to mobilize broad support for the military campaign and promised to build "the broadest possible coalition of partners around the globe to confront, degrade and ultimately defeat ISIS."[7] In his role as defense secretary, Chuck Hagel challenged White House officials regarding the new strategy, arguing for a clearer plan for dealing with Syria in order not to undermine previous gains against ISIS (chapters 10 and 11). In congressional testimony Hagel claimed that restoring stability in Syria and Iraq required strengthening a moderate Islamic opposition as an alternative to Syrian President Assad as well as using military means to expel ISIS from territory it occupied.

Society plays a role in military strategy, but it is complex. Public opinion influences the decision to deploy troops, the role they will play in conflicts (a bombing campaign and/or "boots on the ground"), and the length of their deployment. After U.S. marines who were part of the UN humanitarian mission "Operation Restore Hope" in Somalia were killed in Mogadishu in 1993 and their bodies dragged through the streets, America's public was so traumatized that Washington was less willing to act in later humanitarian crises in Rwanda and Darfur (chapter 6). For several years after 9/11, the public supported military intervention in Afghanistan. But by 2014, after two long wars in Afghanistan and Iraq, public war fatigue made leaders reluctant to commit military forces in later crises like the Syrian civil war and Russia's aggression in Ukraine. Americans also questioned Washington's role as global leader. Sensing that U.S. influence was declining, they questioned America's international engagement, especially overseas military commitments.[8]

Public attitudes toward committing troops overseas also influence America's military choices. If the public opposes placing U.S. soldiers at risk, leaders may favor using strategic bombing and drone warfare that allow Washington to use force with the loss of fewer U.S. lives.

The experiences and attitudes of individuals also shape policy. As we noted earlier, President George H. W. Bush had substantial foreign-policy experience—United Nations ambassador, ambassador to China, CIA director, and vice president. Indeed, critics argued that he was *too* interested in foreign policy in contrast to domestic economic and social issues. Bush also faced criticism for emphasizing political stability over human rights as protests spread across China and Eastern Europe. President Bill Clinton, by contrast, had no foreign policy experience on entering office and prioritized domestic issues throughout his term even as ethnic conflicts swept Rwanda, Bosnia, and Kosovo. Presidents Jimmy Carter and George W. Bush both claimed their styles and policies were shaped by their religious faith, and President Obama, who campaigned in 2008 with a lofty foreign-policy vision of multilateralism and internationalism, became a pragmatic policymaker.

The Cold War was, perhaps, the heyday of U.S. military strategy. America emerged from World War II as a global superpower and soon became embroiled in conflict with the other superpower, the Soviet Union. In this context, a grand strategy was necessary and relatively easy to formulate though it had to be refined to prevent a nuclear war.

PAST: MANAGING SUPERPOWER RIVALRY

Two strategies dominated U.S. policy from the early Cold War until the fall of the Berlin Wall in 1989—containment and deterrence.

Containment and U.S. Grand Strategy

Following World War II, mutual suspicion characterized U.S.-Soviet relations. America's liberal ideology emphasized individual rights and capitalism, whereas Soviet communism prioritized equality and collective responsibility. Leaders in each country thought their counterparts sought to expand their values, by force if necessary. A regional power imbalance reinforced mutual fear. Europe's major states had been devastated by war. Britain and France had suffered immense losses. Germany was in shambles and remained divided among the victors. Washington and Moscow both feared the other would take advantage of Europe's **power vacuum** to assert preeminence in the region. U.S. fears intensified after Moscow reneged on the promises it had made at the Yalta and Potsdam conferences (1945) to demobilize its forces in Eastern Europe and allow free elections in those countries or withdraw troops from Iran as promised in the Tehran Declaration (1943). Fear of Soviet westward expansion led to a reorientation of U.S. foreign policy, reflected in the 1947 Truman Doctrine, which promised to support all peoples resisting control by "armed minorities or outside pressures."

This policy was **"containment**," a defining component of U.S. grand strategy throughout the Cold War. Containment was initially based on political and economic power with a military component added later. Harry Truman's presidency is often viewed as strategy's golden age—"a time when a determined President and a group of talented subordinates laid down enduring policies for containing Soviet power and stabilizing a shaken global order."[9] Truman and Secretary of State Dean Acheson believed that the Great Depression and World War II were consequences of America's failure to intervene until late in World War I and interwar isolationism. Europe's power vacuum, they believed, had to be filled by Washington.

Containment's architect was George Kennan. Kennan, who was stationed at America's Moscow embassy, provided the intellectual rationale for the policy in the "Long Telegram" he sent in 1946 in response to questions about Soviet conduct. Kennan viewed Washington and Moscow as inevitable foes, concluding that the USSR sought to undermine America's political and social systems but would not use military force to do so. Instead, Moscow would promote social and industrial unrest, seek to overthrow noncommunist governments, and destroy all forms of personal independence, "economic, political, or moral."[10] Kennan publicly laid out his strategy to deal with the Kremlin in an article anonymously published in 1947 under the pseudonym "Mr. X" in the journal *Foreign Affairs*. He argued that Washington should "contain" the spread of Soviet power by strengthening the political, social, and economic institutions in countries threatened by Soviet power. Paul Nitze, head of the State Department's Policy Planning Staff, articulated a more muscular version of containment in National Security Council Document 68 (NSC-68) that recommended a massive buildup of U.S. military power to counter Soviet expansionism. Eventually Nitze's more aggressive vision triumphed, serving as the rationale for extending nuclear deterrence to U.S. allies, a worldwide alliance system, and conventional military buildups to shift the global military balance in America's favor.

The foundation of U.S. containment strategy was an alliance network that allowed Washington to project power across the globe and signaled to foes that U.S. interests were worldwide. The first of the multilateral alliances were the 1947 Inter-American Treaty of Mutual Assistance (Rio Treaty), among 19 countries in the Americas (later expanded to 21), and the 1949 North Atlantic Treaty Organization (NATO) among the United States, Canada, and European states. Other multilateral alliances included the Australia, New Zealand, U.S. (ANZUS) Treaty (1951), the Southeast Asia Treaty Organization (SEATO) (1954), and the 1955 Baghdad Pact linking Turkey, Pakistan, Iraq (until 1959), Iran, and Britain. Washington also negotiated bilateral defensive pacts with the Philippines, Japan, South Korea, and Taiwan.

In 1949, the Chinese Communist Party's triumph in China's civil war fueled fears of communist expansionism. A year later, the Korean War evoked fears that communists were prepared to use force. Korea was left divided after 1945, with the North in the Soviet sphere of influence and the

South in the U.S. sphere. On June 25, 1950, North Korea invaded South Korea. Secretary Acheson had previously indicated that South Korea was outside the U.S. defense perimeter, and U.S. officials believed the invasion was a probe to see what Washington would tolerate. Truman feared the worst: "If we let Korea down, the Soviet [sic] will keep right on going and swallow up one piece of Asia after another. . . . If we were to let Asia go, the Near East would collapse and no telling what would happen in Europe."[11] The belief that if one country were allowed to fall to communism others would follow became known as the "**domino theory**" and intensified support for the militant form of containment. Thereafter, containment justified the buildup of conventional and nuclear forces, the institutionalization of military alliances, and military intervention in Southeast Asia and Latin America to aid anticommunist regimes.

Washington's most extensive Cold War intervention was in Vietnam, a former French colony divided between a communist-governed North and a noncommunist South after the French withdrawal from Indochina in 1954. Seeking to prevent Vietnam's unification under North Vietnam's Ho Chi Minh, Washington backed Ngo Dinh Diem in South Vietnam, providing advisors, supplies, and training to fight communist guerrillas in the South. President Lyndon Johnson escalated U.S. involvement in Vietnam after Diem was overthrown in 1963, but U.S. troops were ill prepared to fight the guerrilla-style war of the communist Vietcong. The Pentagon estimated about $111 billion was spent fighting the Vietnam War in which 57,000 American soldiers died.[12] The war also proved divisive at home. On entering office in 1969, with no victory in sight, President Richard Nixon implemented a "Vietnamization" policy, reducing U.S. troops and giving the South Vietnamese responsibility to fight North Vietnam and the Vietcong. Direct U.S. military involvement ended in 1973, and two years later North Vietnamese forces captured Saigon, South Vietnam's capital. The conflict in Vietnam had spilled over into neighboring Laos and Cambodia, where civil wars also ended in 1975 with communist victories. Despite U.S. fears, however, communism did not expand in Asia beyond Indochina.

During the 1950s and 1960s, communism proved attractive in Latin America. Successive U.S. administrations supported anticommunist dictatorships in the region to prevent communists from coming to power in democratic elections (chapter 8), even if it meant undermining democratically elected governments. The Eisenhower administration backed a 1954 coup that overthrew Guatemala's democratically elected President Jacobo Arbenz, who administration officials believed was procommunist. Eisenhower viewed Guatemala through the lens of the domino theory. "My God," Eisenhower proclaimed, "just think what it would mean to us if Mexico went Communist!"[13] In later decades, domino theory and the containment of communism would be used to justify U.S. military intervention in Cuba and elsewhere in the developing world.

Deterrence and U.S. Cold War Grand Strategy

In 1945, the United States was the only nuclear-armed state, but in 1949, the USSR tested an atom bomb, igniting an arms race that became a defining feature of the Cold War. Each superpower sought to acquire a nuclear arsenal sufficient to deter the other from attacking. Washington pursued several distinct deterrence strategies, often simultaneously. Deterrence was intended to prevent Moscow from attacking America's homeland, but, during the early Cold War years, a conventional Soviet attack against America's

European allies was more likely. Thus, U.S. officials extended a "nuclear umbrella" to deter attacks against allies. In addition, a policy of general deterrence that relied on regional alliances and the development of new military technologies communicated the high costs that would be incurred by attacking American interests. Occasionally, as in the 1962 Cuban missile crisis, U.S. leaders employed a more immediate form of deterrence by issuing unambiguous threats verbally and deploying military assets in response to immediate challenges.

For most of the Cold War, deterrence relied on a threat of mutual retaliation that fueled the arms race. In 1953, Eisenhower adopted the doctrine of massive retaliation as part of a defense policy that sought to reduce the role of costly conventional forces in Europe (where Moscow had a conventional advantage) and take advantage of America's nuclear superiority by threatening nuclear retaliation if there were a Soviet conventional incursion. As the Soviet arsenal grew and its delivery capabilities improved, increasing the feasibility of a direct attack on U.S. territory, Washington refined its strategy to allow for an initial conventional response that would *not* entail immediate escalation to the nuclear level in the event of a conventional Soviet attack. After the 1960s, Washington continued to rely on this flexible deterrence doctrine.

Deterrence underwent additional refinement as America and the USSR acquired **second-strike capabilities** by burying missiles in underground silos, making them mobile, or deploying them on submarines that allowed them to survive and respond to a nuclear **first strike**. A mutual second-strike capability stabilized the relationship by reducing incentives to be the first to use nuclear weapons in a crisis. The new doctrine, **mutual assured destruction (MAD)**, assumed that only mutual vulnerability to nuclear attack could prevent nuclear war. If both superpowers viewed the costs of nuclear war as unacceptable, neither would start a war. The logic of MAD introduced a paradox into strategic policymaking. Nuclear weapons were widely viewed as *unusable*. Their value lay in successfully *threatening* their use in the event of an attack. Thus, MAD rested on *simultaneous* beliefs that nuclear weapons were unusable yet might be used under certain conditions.

MAD gradually lost support as the dangers associated with this paradox became apparent. Washington did not formally abandon the strategy until the 1980s, but by the 1960s several factors led both American hawks and doves to turn to **arms control** and **disarmament** to stabilize the superpower relationship. If nuclear weapons were unusable, then allies could not count on Washington for extended deterrence. Hawks realized that unrestrained growth in nuclear arsenals threatened that one side might develop an advantage that would undermine the strategic stability of MAD. If Moscow, for instance, were able to develop a workable missile defense shield to protect cities, a sense of invulnerability might encourage the Kremlin to initiate a nuclear war it believed it could win. Doves were persuaded that as arsenals grew so did the risk that nuclear weapons would be used, perhaps by accident or miscalculation, possibilities that arms control and disarmament could reduce.

ARMS CONTROL AND DISARMAMENT

The technological arms race accelerated in the 1960s. Both superpowers deployed tactical (short-range) nuclear weapons and in the 1970s added longer-range missiles with **multiple, independently targetable reentry vehicles** (warheads), or MIRVs, and more sophisticated missile defenses. U.S. and Soviet arsenals peaked at approximately 69,000 nuclear warheads and bombs in 1986.[14]

FIGURE 3.1   U.S. and Soviet/Russian Stockpiled Nuclear Warheads, 1945–2010

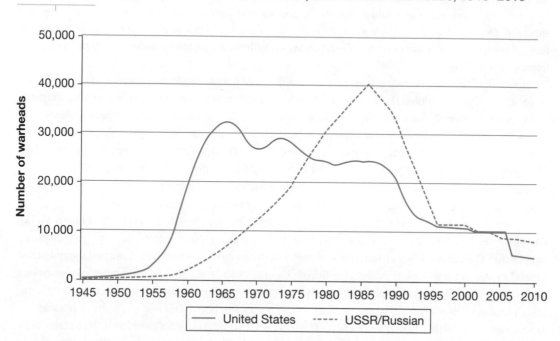

Source: Data from Robert S. Norris and Hans M. Kristensen, "Global Nuclear Weapons Inventories, 1945–2010," *Bulletin of the Atomic Scientists,* 66:4 (July/August 2010), 81–82.

The concern that nuclear war might erupt by design or miscalculation led to arms-control efforts in the 1970s, focused on limiting weapons that would offer strategic advantages that might alter the MAD calculus. Later efforts, which continue today, focused on disarmament to reduce the overall number of weapons in both countries' arsenals. For doves, managing and limiting the nuclear arms race contributed to preventing accidental war. For hawks, it was a way to stabilize the superpower relationship and make deterrence more credible. In 1961, strategic theorists Thomas Schelling and Morton Halperin observed: "We believe that arms control is a promising, but still only dimly perceived, enlargement on the scope of military strategy. It rests essentially on the recognition that our military relation with potential enemies is not one of pure conflict and opposition, but involves strong elements of mutual interest in the avoidance of a war that neither side wants, in minimizing the costs and risks of arms competition, and in curtailing the scope and violence of war in the event it occurs."[15]

Several nuclear arms-control agreements were negotiated in the 1970s. The Strategic Arms Limitation Talks consisted of bilateral negotiations between Washington and Moscow that aimed to limit the growth of long-range missiles and missile-defense systems. These negotiations produced SALT I (1972) and SALT II (1979). The most important of the 1972 agreements was the Anti-Ballistic Missile (ABM) Treaty and an interim agreement to limit offensive weapons. The ABM treaty limited the number of missile defenses—both systems and interceptors—each country could deploy to defend its population. Its purpose was to prevent either superpower from defending population centers because it might embolden that country to behave aggressively without fear of retaliation. The interim agreement froze the number of **intercontinental ballistic missiles** (ICBMs) and submarine-launched ballistic missiles (SLBMs) available to each side for five years, until SALT II could be negotiated.

SALT II negotiations were completed in 1979. Washington sought to equalize numbers of strategic delivery vehicles (ICBMs, SLBMs, and heavy bombers), cap the number of such vehicles, and limit development of new delivery systems that might undermine future stability.[16] Washington got much of what it sought. The treaty included a limit of 2,400 strategic nuclear delivery vehicles and 1,320 MIRV systems, prohibited construction of new land-based ICBM launchers, and limited the deployment of new types of strategic offensive arms.[17] Nonetheless, the treaty faced opposition in the Senate. Supporters argued it preserved a stable military balance and increased predictability by improving U.S. understanding of Soviet capabilities. Critics countered that the treaty did not go far enough and allowed Moscow to maintain existing military advantages.[18] Following the 1979 Soviet invasion of Afghanistan, President Carter asked the Senate to delay consideration of the treaty. It was never ratified.

Treaty Making in the U.S. System

The executive branch is responsible for negotiating treaties. Under U.S. law, all treaties acquire the status of federal legislation after ratification—a process that requires the approval of a two-thirds majority in the Senate.

With few exceptions, the treaty-making process is as follows: The secretary of state authorizes participation in negotiations. If the parties agree on the terms of a treaty and it is signed, the president must submit it to the Senate for approval. After a first reading, the treaty is referred to the Senate Foreign Relations Committee, which makes a recommendation to the full Senate, including amendments in the form of reservations, statements, understandings, or declarations.

Once a treaty is transmitted to the Senate, there are several possible outcomes. If the treaty does not have the necessary support, the Senate may choose not to hold a vote. This was the fate of SALT II. If the Senate refuses to consider a treaty or if a vote does not produce a two-thirds majority, the president may bring it back for another vote later, as President Obama pledged to do in his first term with the Comprehensive Test Ban Treaty that the Senate had rejected in 1999. If a treaty receives Senate approval, the president must sign an instrument of ratification and deposit the treaty with the designated depositary, either a government or an intergovernmental organization like the UN. Only then does the treaty enter into force.

DID YOU KNOW?

The first genuine U.S.-Soviet disarmament agreement was the 1987 Intermediate-Range Nuclear Forces Treaty that eliminated land-based nuclear missiles with ranges of 500 to 5,500 kilometers. The 1991 Strategic Arms Reduction Treaty (START I), signed just months before the collapse of the USSR, limited each side to 1,600 deployed delivery vehicles and 6,000 "accountable" nuclear warheads.[19] Washington and Russia continued to negotiate further reductions in their nuclear arsenals after the Cold War.

THE "UNIPOLAR MOMENT" AND NEW CHALLENGES TO NATIONAL SECURITY

The 1986 Goldwater-Nichols Defense Department Reorganization Act radically restructured the planning process in the Defense Department to improve military strategy and required the president to submit an annual national security strategy to Congress. Its purpose was to ensure the consistent formulation of a national military strategy and address institutional failures that might impede its implementation.[20] In the second of these reports, published in 1988 before the end of the Cold War, the administration identified Soviet military power and diplomacy as the principal threats to the survival of the United States as "a free and independent nation," healthy economic growth, a "stable and secure world, free of major threats to U.S. interests," the spread of human rights and liberal democratic and economic institutions, and "healthy and vigorous alliance relationships."[21]

Shortly thereafter, however, the world changed. The Cold War ended; the Soviet Union collapsed; the states of Eastern Europe rejected communism; and Germany was reunited. The post–Cold War world offered hope for a more peaceful world order but the reality—and the impact on U.S. strategy—was more complex.

The first challenge to this new **unipolar** world order was Iraq's 1990 invasion of Kuwait. Washington responded quickly, though some dissented from the decision to employ U.S. military power to compel Iraq to leave Kuwait. In what became known as the Powell Doctrine, General Colin Powell, then chairman of the Joint Chiefs of Staff, argued that America should only commit forces to battle when a clear vital interest was threatened, other means of protecting that interest had been exhausted, there was a clear exit strategy, and the use of force enjoyed broad domestic and international support. Powell did not view Kuwait as a vital interest and believed other strategies, including containment, would serve U.S. interests better. His view did not prevail, and President George H. W. Bush began building a multilateral coalition, eventually comprising thirty-four states, to drive Iraq from Kuwait should it not withdraw. While diplomatic efforts were underway, Bush began increasing U.S. troop levels in the Persian Gulf and diverting resources to the region, while lobbying the Security Council for economic and military sanctions against Iraq.

Despite pressure from Washington, the UN, and others, Saddam Hussein refused to comply with successive Security Council resolutions. In November 1990, the Council authorized member states to "use all necessary means" to implement previous resolutions and restore international peace and **security**[22] should Iraq not withdraw from Kuwait by January 15, 1991. As the deadline approached, Congress authorized the use of American troops. On January 17th, hostilities commenced with a massive bombing campaign that lasted six weeks and targeted Iraq's war-related infrastructure—communication facilities, utilities, and military bases. On February 24th, U.S. marines invaded Iraq and Kuwait, beginning a multinational ground offensive—"Operation Desert Storm"—that swiftly liberated Kuwait.

The outcome of the Persian Gulf War affected U.S. military strategy for decades, partly because it left Saddam Hussein in power. U.S. officials chose not to overthrow Saddam, believing his ouster would produce a power vacuum that would embolden revolutionary Iran. Saddam celebrated his survival as a victory, but U.S. officials hoped his domestic opponents would overthrow him. "Obviously," Bush reflected, "when the troops straggle home with no armor, beaten up, 50,000 . . . and maybe more dead, the people of Iraq will know."[23] Uprisings occurred in Iraq's Kurdish north and Shia south, but the regime crushed these with such brutality that the allied coalition established **no-fly zones** over those regions. Saddam Hussein remained in power until 2003.

The war was notable as an exercise in post–Cold War cooperation, only the second instance of collective security since the founding of the UN in 1945. It also demonstrated U.S. military superiority. America introduced F-117 stealth bombers, precision-guided munitions ("smart" bombs), infrared targeting, and global positioning technology that made it possible to win the war quickly with few U.S. casualties. (The Defense Department reported that 148 U.S. troops were killed in action or died of wounds.[24])

The end of the Cold War reduced superpower interest in conflicts in the developing world. During the Cold War, such conflicts were viewed through the prism of superpower competition, and each sought to prevent local conflicts in its sphere of influence from expanding into superpower confrontations. Local conflicts unrestrained by a superpower like Iraq's invasion of Kuwait proliferated after the Cold War. As the Persian Gulf War ended, ethnic tensions tore apart Yugoslavia. Between 1991 and 1999, several brutal wars were fought in the Balkans as ethnic groups in Yugoslavia sought their sovereign independence. As in Iraq, the remaining superpower felt compelled to act, though reluctantly, after its experience in Somalia.

In 1994, the Clinton administration took the lead in establishing a NATO peacekeeping mission to end violence in Bosnia. In the same year, genocidal war erupted in the small country of Rwanda in central Africa, during which nearly one million Rwandans, mostly ethnic Tutsis, were systematically murdered. The international community, including America, refused to acknowledge the conflict as genocidal until it was too late. It was not until later that President Clinton issued the Clinton Doctrine, committing America to use military intervention for humanitarian purposes, when it was likely to succeed.

Such conflicts reflected a new strategic environment. With the Cold War over, Leslie Gelb of the Council on Foreign Relations argued, "The danger today is that we may . . . think or at least act as if the world has changed less than it really has. And by so doing, we will exaggerate old threats and minimize new ones, and thus finally find ourselves overwhelmed by the all-corrosive danger that stares us down

The F-117 Stealth Bomber introduced in the Persian Gulf War

USAF Photo/Staff Sgt. Aaron Allmon II

daily—the teacup wars filled with countless bodies and horrors, the scourge of civil and ethnic violence."[25] Throughout the 1990s, U.S. leaders struggled to cope with this new strategic environment and formulate policies to manage "teacup wars." Traditional thinking continued to dominate the foreign-policy establishment. Nuclear deterrence remained a central element to U.S. military strategy. Containment—or more accurately "dual containment"—was employed to isolate Iraq and Iran and prevent either from dominating the Middle East. The Clinton administration also sought to expand NATO to include former Warsaw Pact members, a process seen as extending democracy and stability to those countries as much as enhancing European security. In only a few years, though, it became apparent that the world had so changed that Washington could no longer rely as heavily on old strategies.

9/11 AND GLOBAL TERRORISM

The world changed again on September 11, 2001, when al-Qaeda terrorists hijacked three U.S. airplanes and flew them into New York's World Trade Center and the Pentagon in Washington, D.C. Another plane was also hijacked, but passengers fought the hijackers, and the plane crashed in Pennsylvania before reaching its target. Nearly 3,000 people died in the attacks. Within weeks, Washington initiated war in Afghanistan to compel its strict Islamic Taliban rulers to hand over Osama bin Laden. On September 14, 2001, Congress passed the Authorization for the Use of Force Against Terrorists, authorizing the president "to use all necessary and appropriate force against those nations, organizations, or persons he determines planned, authorized, committed, or aided the terrorist attacks that occurred on September 11, 2001, or harbored such organizations or persons, in order to prevent any future acts of international terrorism against the United States by such nations, organizations or persons."[26]

The terrorist attacks exposed America's vulnerability and, President George W. Bush believed, called for a new approach to national defense. The old strategies of deterrence and containment that

🔑 KEY DOCUMENT
Bush's Speech at West Point, 2002

For much of the last century America's defense relied on the cold war doctrines of deterrence and containment. . . . But new threats also require new thinking.

Deterrence, the promise of massive retaliation against nations, means nothing against shadowy terrorist networks with no nation or citizens to defend. Containment is not possible when unbalanced dictators with weapons of mass destruction can deliver those weapons on missiles or secretly provide them to terrorist allies. . . .

Yet the war on terror will not be won on the defensive. We must take the battle to the enemy, disrupt his plans and confront the worst threats before they emerge.

Source: "Text of Bush's Speech at West Point," June 1, 2002, *New York Times,* http://www.nytimes.com/2002/06/01/international/02PTEX-WEB.html.

had managed state-based threats were insufficient to deal with transnational terrorists with an ability to strike without warning. Rather than wait for a threat to appear, Bush argued it was necessary to take the fight to the terrorists. The Bush Doctrine involved "preemptive and preventive action," or anticipatory self-defense that would serve as the rationale for lengthy conflicts in Afghanistan and Iraq.

Bush's strategy was articulated in America's 2002 National Security Strategy, which emphasized "anticipatory self-defense." U.S. goals, as defined in this document, emphasized both values and interests—"political and economic freedom, peaceful relations with other states, and respect for human dignity." To achieve them, America would "champion aspirations for human dignity"; "strengthen alliances to defeat global terrorism and work to prevent attacks against us and our friends"; "prevent our enemies from threatening us, our allies, and our friends, with weapons of mass destruction"; "ignite a new era of global economic growth through free markets and free trade"; "expand the circle of development by opening societies and building the infrastructure of democracy"; and "transform America's national security institutions."[27]

FIGHTING IRREGULAR WARS:
AFGHANISTAN (2001–2015) AND IRAQ (2003–2011)

The war in Afghanistan began as a traditional military operation, "Operation Enduring Freedom," to oust the Taliban government and end al-Qaeda's ability to use Afghanistan as a safe haven. Although the Taliban were quickly defeated, "Operation Enduring Freedom" became a counterinsurgency campaign and America's longest war. With a new Afghan government headed by Hamid Karzai, America and a UN-mandated force—International Security Assistance Force—maintained a troop presence in Afghanistan to provide security during the transition to a new government and to train Afghan police and army units to take over security functions.

Shortly after the initial defeat of the Taliban, Defense Secretary Donald Rumsfeld described the transformation underway in U.S. strategy to meet contemporary threats. America would no longer maintain as it had in the past military forces capable of fighting and occupying territory in a "two major-theater war," but would instead plan for "one massive counteroffensive" to achieve regime change in one enemy country while simultaneously defeating a second aggressor. Washington would shape a "capabilities-based" strategy, focusing less on *who* posed a threat and more on *how* they might threaten America. "Our job," he argued, is to "prepare for new forms of terrorism" as well as "attacks on U.S. space assets, cyberattacks on our information networks, cruise missiles, ballistic missiles, and nuclear, chemical, and biological weapons."[28] Deterrence remained important but would be sustained with smaller nuclear forces and enhanced high-tech conventional capabilities and missile defenses. Rumsfeld's new strategy, however, was not sufficient to meet the threats in Afghanistan and Iraq. It recognized terrorism as a threat but retained state-centric conceptions of "threat" and "security."

The initial defeat of the Taliban did not stabilize Afghanistan. In ensuing months, Taliban forces in Afghanistan and Pakistan regrouped, and warlords and militias also began competing for control of territories not under Kabul's control. Violence soon intensified, especially in border regions in the south and east along the Pakistani border. By early 2003, the violence in Afghanistan had become a full-scale insurgency—a form of irregular warfare that U.S. commanders were ill equipped to meet.

Insurgencies are "the organized use of subversion and violence to seize, nullify or challenge political control of a region."[29] They are political as well as military contests for the support (or at least acquiescence) of inhabitants. Insurgents are difficult to fight because they blend into the local population and coerce that population to support their cause. Their victory does not require the defeat of an enemy's conventional forces but involves prolonging the conflict and wearing down the enemy. Thus, insurgencies are protracted, asymmetrical conflicts. Afghanistan was not America's first counterinsurgency conflict. A RAND study after the Vietnam War noted that a conventional military force is "one hell of a poor instrument with which to engage insurgents."[30] Conventional combat operations involving airstrikes and massed infantry or armor are relatively ineffective against insurgents.

As the Afghan insurgency spread in 2003, Washington launched "Operation Iraqi Freedom" to force Iraq to abide by a decade of Security Council Resolutions calling on it to reveal all weapons of mass destruction (WMD) and verifiably dismantle its WMD programs, with an emphasis on nuclear disarmament. When U.S. troops failed to locate these weapons, Washington's principal goal became "regime change"—overthrowing Saddam Hussein. The initial military campaign that began in March ended with Iraq's defeat by May. But, as in Afghanistan, a violent insurgency erupted in the power vacuum left by dismantling Iraq's army and governing institutions. In 2004 and 2005, violence across Iraq escalated and took on a sectarian character as Sunni insurgents and Shia militias fought for control of towns and neighborhoods. In November 2005, U.S. officials announced a new counterinsurgency strategy that emphasized reconstructing local institutions. Violence intensified until 2007 when a "surge" strategy promoted by General David Petraeus, then commander of the Multi-National Force in Iraq, added 30,000 U.S. troops. In addition, a "Sunni Awakening" involving Sunni tribes to fight insurgents helped reduce violence. America's "surge" occurred with a shift to a strategy of "clear, hold, build" introduced by Petraeus that emphasized state-building—reconstructing infrastructure, reducing **sectarian violence**, protecting local populations, and encouraging reconciliation among Sunnis, Shias, and Kurds. Violence lessened, and Iraq was sufficiently stable to allow parliamentary elections in 2010. After the 2011 withdrawal of U.S. forces, however, sectarian violence resumed, and Iraq's weak political institutions were unable to cope with the heightened terrorism begun in 2014 by ISIS.

PRESENT: GRAND STRATEGY IN A CHANGING WORLD

After his election, President Barack Obama inherited the wars in Iraq and Afghanistan, and U.S. military strategy, especially during his first term, focused on conducting and winding down those wars. Obama came to office promising to emphasize multilateral and internationalist policies to advance U.S. interests. In practice, Obama's military strategy was *less* multilateral and internationalist than supporters hoped and *more* multilateral and internationalist than critics wished. Nevertheless, after Obama became president, U.S. troops left Iraq and were scheduled to leave Afghanistan. Both countries remained violent and unstable, but confronted by war fatigue, budget constraints, and other challenges, America is unlikely to resume major military intervention in those countries. Washington responded to Islamic terrorism, not with boots on the ground, but with air and drone strikes, the latter a technology allowing America to target suspected terrorists without risk to U.S. soldiers. Cyberwarfare is also a growing threat, with profound implications for U.S. military strategy. In what follows, we examine nuclear policy, counterinsurgency and counterterrorism warfare, and the adoption of drone and cyber technologies.

Nuclear Policy

Nuclear disarmament was a major theme in Obama's campaign and during his first year in office. Speaking in Prague, Czech Republic, he advocated a "world without nuclear weapons." Thereafter, Washington negotiated a new disarmament agreement with Russia to cut each country's strategic arsenals to between 2,200 and 1,500 deployed nuclear weapons (that was suspended after Russian aggression in Ukraine). Nuclear disarmament, Obama believed, was needed to facilitate nonproliferation efforts. Critics found the view naive. Without a nuclear arsenal, critics argued, America would be vulnerable to potential challengers, and there was no evidence that unilateral disarmament would be reciprocated. Even as Washington and Moscow negotiated, China, Pakistan, India, and North Korea were enhancing their

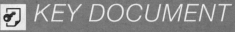

KEY DOCUMENT
Remarks by President Barack Obama, Prague, April 5, 2009

Some argue that the spread of [nuclear] weapons cannot be stopped, cannot be checked—that we are destined to live in a world where more nations and more people possess the ultimate tools of destruction. Such fatalism is a deadly adversary, for if we believe that the spread of nuclear weapons is inevitable, then in some way we are admitting to ourselves that the use of nuclear weapons is inevitable. . . .

First, the United States will take concrete steps towards a world without nuclear weapons. To put an end to Cold War thinking, we will reduce the role of nuclear weapons in our national security strategy, and urge others to do the same.

To achieve a global ban on nuclear testing, my administration will immediately and

aggressively pursue U.S. ratification of the Comprehensive Test Ban Treaty. After more than five decades of talks, it is time for the testing of nuclear weapons to finally be banned.

And to cut off the building blocks needed for a bomb, the United States will seek a new treaty that verifiably ends the production of fissile materials intended for use in state nuclear weapons. If we are serious about stopping the spread of these weapons, then we should put an end to the dedicated production of weapons-grade materials that create them.

Source: Excerpt, "Remarks by President Barack Obama," Hradcany Square, Prague, Czech Republic, April 5, 2009, http://www.whitehouse.gov/the_press_office/Remarks-By-President-Barack-Obama-In-Prague-As-Delivered.

arsenals. Thus, in 2009 Senate Republicans refused to ratify a treaty reducing America's nuclear arsenal without simultaneously modernizing remaining nuclear forces and manufacturing sites. To obtain Republican support, Obama promised $14 billion for nuclear renovations over the next decade. Thus, nuclear weapons continued to play a key role in U.S. military strategy, and with additional funding to modernize its forces, the arsenal is being rebuilt to enhance deterrence.

Since 2009, there has been little evidence that the world was moving toward the "Global Zero" that Obama envisioned. Critics assailed the president for failing to make promised cuts to the nation's nuclear arsenal and spending more to modernize that arsenal than his three predecessors. Nuclear weapons remained an important element of military strategy though the administration argued that deterrence could be achieved with a smaller arsenal. In 2010, the administration released a Nuclear Posture Review (NPR) that assigned a reduced role to nuclear weapons. "The massive nuclear arsenal we inherited from the Cold War era of bipolar military confrontation," the NPR stated, "is poorly suited to address the challenges posed by suicidal terrorists and unfriendly regimes seeking nuclear weapons." Yet the NPR also noted that key goals of America's nuclear-weapons program included strengthening regional deterrence and reassuring U.S. allies and partners.[31] In 2012, General James Cartwright, former commander of U.S. nuclear forces, argued that Washington could achieve its goals with an arsenal of 900 warheads. "The world has changed, but the current arsenal carries the baggage of the Cold War."[32] The 2014 Quadrennial Defense Review (QDR) continued to emphasize investment in modernizing nuclear weapons. "Our nuclear deterrent is the ultimate protection against a nuclear attack on the United States, and through extended deterrence, it also serves to reassure our distant allies of their security against regional aggression. It also supports our ability to project power by communicating to potential nuclear-armed adversaries that they cannot escalate their way out of failed conventional aggression."[33]

Even as the 2014 QDR was published, efforts to modernize the nation's aging nuclear arsenal had begun. Spending on modernization increased 11.6 percent in 2014 while other defense expenditures were cut, and the Congressional Budget Office estimated the overhaul would cost $348 billion (accounting for inflation) between 2015 and 2024.[34] Modernization involved rebuilding strategic delivery systems including ICBMs, SLBMs, ballistic missile submarines, and strategic bombers; refurbishing nuclear warheads and bombs; and building new uranium processing and nuclear weapons production facilities.[35]

Although Obama initially pursued these reforms to achieve a "smaller, more flexible" nuclear force, by 2014 concern was growing that America had to modernize to stay abreast of potential adversaries. Others, notably Russia, which was spending about $140 billion updating its nuclear weapons and testing new ICBMs, were also upgrading their nuclear forces.[36] President Vladimir Putin also indicated that Moscow would use **tactical nuclear weapons** to defend its **sphere of influence**, and Russia's invasion of Ukraine "made any measure to reduce the stockpile unilaterally politically impossible," concluded a former nuclear advisor to the Obama administration.[37]

From Counterterrorism to Counterinsurgency

Al-Qaeda remained a threat to U.S. interests. Its elimination was one object of U.S. global strategy and the wars in Afghanistan and Iraq. As Obama's first term drew to a close, he insisted that America would continue using military force to "finish the work of defeating" al-Qaeda and its affiliates. But by 2013, it was the affiliates—in Yemen, Nigeria, Syria, and Iraq—that posed the greater threat. Al-Qaeda "central" had been effectively defeated by U.S. military action in Afghanistan and drone strikes in Pakistan. Obama reflected on the change in a speech at the National Defense University in 2013: "What we can do—what we must do—is dismantle networks that pose a direct danger, and make it less likely for new groups to gain a foothold, all while maintaining the freedoms and ideals that we defend."[38] Force, argued Obama, would be only part of a comprehensive counterterrorism strategy that supplemented intelligence sharing, the deployment of irregular forces, and targeted drone strikes with new initiatives to offer advice and training to other countries. In 2013, Obama announced a counterterrorism fund for such activities.

Washington increasingly relied on Special Operations Forces like the Navy's SEAL Team Six that killed bin Laden in 2011 to conduct counterterrorist operations. Small teams, designed to conduct manhunts in combat zones, Special Operations Forces are agile and move "at the speed of war."[39] They work closely with intelligence agencies and other partners on the ground to train and advise local security forces. The indirect approach of Special Operations Forces promised significant benefits. Admiral William McRaven, head of Special Operations Command, noted, "the direct approach alone is not the solution to the challenges our nation faces today as it ultimately only buys time and space for the indirect approach. . . . [I]n the end, it will be such continuous indirect operations that will prove decisive in the global security arena."[40]

The Bush and Obama administrations invested heavily in Special Operations Forces, and the budget to support these missions grew from $2.3 billion in 2001 to $10.5 billion in 2012.[41] Although "special ops" have been successful in targeting terrorists, they involve risks. They can incur political costs when used to conduct raids, angering local populations whose homes are raided and whose relatives are killed when raids go wrong. When they operate without the local government's consent, they violate sovereignty and may embarrass and anger governments whose cooperation is needed for later counterterrorist operations. And when they are deployed to work closely with local security forces, the risk of "insider attacks" increases. In such "green on blue" attacks in Afghanistan, the enemy infiltrated local forces cooperating with the Special Operations teams and targeted U.S. soldiers and their allies. "Still," says one analyst, "the partnership option frequently represents the only realistic course for U.S. security policy between doing nothing and a unilateral military intervention."[42]

Cyber-Security and Drones

Changing technologies also reshaped U.S. military strategy. A revolution in military and computing technology revolutionized command and control capabilities, making it possible to project power further and more precisely without placing U.S. troops at risk. Drones and cyber-tools were at the forefront of this revolution. These technologies emerged so quickly that some analysts feared they were beginning to *drive* strategy, rather than remaining strategic *tools*. Moreover, there are dangers associated with these technologies. Washington has used drones and cyber-technologies effectively to achieve its goals, but too heavy a reliance on drones may produce a backlash in targeted regions that undermines U.S. interests. And other actors are already racing to exploit these technologies for themselves.

Cyber-Security **Cyber-security** poses new challenges to U.S. military strategy. Since the 1990s, securing cyberspace has been a growing concern. In 2014, it gained widespread attention when a group calling itself the Guardians of Peace hacked Sony Pictures, leaking thousands of documents and e-mails. The group threatened the Hollywood studio and theaters that showed the film *The Interview*, which included a plot to assassinate North Korean dictator Kim Jong-un. Washington quickly identified North Korea as involved with the hack—a discovery made possible by the hackers' "sloppy" efforts to conceal their identity, according to the FBI. Sony pulled the film from theaters, generating public anger. Senator McCain denounced Sony Pictures and the White House for setting "a troubling precedent" that would "only empower and embolden bad actors to use cyber as an offensive weapon even more aggressively in the future."[43]

America began pursuing cyber-defense in 1998, and after several hacking incidents targeting networks in the Defense Department and other agencies, President Obama declared that cyberspace would be considered a "strategic national interest" and efforts would be made to "deter, prevent, detect, and defend against attacks."[44] A Cyber Command was established in the Defense Department, and in 2011 the White House released its first International Strategy for Cyberspace. The new strategy defined the cyber-threat in traditional strategic terms: "When warranted, the United States will respond to hostile acts in cyberspace as we would to any other threat to our country . . . [and] reserves the right to use all necessary means—diplomatic, informational, military, and economic—as appropriate and consistent with international law, in order to defend our Nation, our allies, our partners and our interests."[45] Cyber-capabilities were integrated into all aspects of military planning. The first Commander of Cyber Command, General Keith Alexander, testified in 2013 that it was necessary to "normalize" cyber-operations into Pentagon thinking and operations—to adapt tactics, procedures, policies, and organizations and build "cyber-capabilities into doctrine, plans and training . . . in such a way that our Combatant Commanders can think, plan and integrate cyber-capabilities as they would capabilities in the air, land and sea domains."[46]

The details of America's offensive cyber capabilities are not publicized, but in 2010 it was revealed that a sophisticated cyber-weapon known as Stuxnet produced by America and Israel was responsible for damaging about 1,000 centrifuges in Iran's Natanz nuclear facility. The attack was believed to have delayed Iran's nuclear enrichment program by several years.

Cyber-threats are asymmetric. Any actor, state, or group, with access to computers and the Internet (which is not always necessary) can pose a cyber-threat. In cyberspace, the offense has an advantage. It is neither expensive nor difficult to hack U.S. or global networks, and attacks do not have to be sophisticated to be effective. Acknowledging the difficulty in deterring and defending against cyberattacks, Deputy Secretary of Defense William Lynn asserted, "speed and agility matter most. To stay ahead of its pursuers, the United States must constantly adjust and improve its defenses."[47] This is an issue where Washington faces both domestic and foreign criticism. In 2013, the Pentagon's Defense Science Board declared that America's military "dependence on vulnerable technology is a magnet to U.S. opponents . . . [that] yields a never-ending challenge"[48] without comprehensive technological solutions. The report recommended a balanced approach employing cyber, conventional, and nuclear capabilities to protect America's nuclear deterrent and war-fighting capability, improved defenses against low- and mid-level threats, improved intelligence collection and analysis, and "world-class cyber offensive capabilities."[49]

China has formidable cyberwar capabilities. Legal and illegal hacking is widespread in China, and hacking and cyber-security competitions attract military, academic, and corporate observers. China's military seeks clever hackers at universities and has a training center called the PLA Information Engineering University in Zhengzhou. The best hackers can earn high salaries from China's government and corporations.

Although sources of cyberattacks are difficult to trace because they are routed through computer servers elsewhere, the Pentagon's 2013 annual report concluded, "In 2012 numerous computer systems around the world, including those owned by the U.S. government, continued to be targeted for intrusions, some of which appear to be attributable directly to the Chinese government and military."[50] All the digital addresses of a hacking group that had stolen secrets from U.S. military contractors, chemical plants, mining companies, universities, and telecommunications corporations were traced by the cyber-security company Mandiant to a building in Shanghai on Datong Road that housed the People's Liberation Army's Shanghai Unit 61398, also called the "Comment Crew" or the "Shanghai Group." According to Mandiant, Unit 61398 had "drained terabytes of data from companies like Coca-Cola" and over 100 of Mandiant's clients. Stolen data included aerospace designs, clinical trial results, pricing documents, negotiating strategies, and wind-energy product schematics. According to Mandiant's chief security officer, "the same tools required to conduct digital espionage could allow intruders to go a step further and commit digital destruction."[51] Unit 61398 was only one of twenty Chinese hacker groups under U.S. intelligence surveillance. American officials in 2012 responded to complaints by U.S. companies about Chinese cyber-espionage, presenting Chinese officials with detailed evidence of such hacking.

Washington was especially sensitive to Chinese cyber-theft of industrial secrets from companies like U.S. Steel and Alcoa. If American companies complained, Beijing was liable to hack their computer systems in retaliation. In 2014, Washington indicted five members of Unit 61398 in absentia not for national security spying but for commercial espionage—for-profit theft—a step that triggered Chinese retaliatory threats. A private Commission on the Theft of American Intellectual Property run by former director of national intelligence Dennis Blair and former ambassador to China Jon Huntsman argued that Washington needed to adopt strong measures that would prove costly to China in response to Beijing's persistent cyber-espionage.[52] China has "an elaborate, comprehensive system for spotting foreign technologies, acquiring them by every means imaginable, and converting them into weapons and competitive goods."[53]

China cited information revealed by Edward Snowden that America had hacked numerous Chinese computer sites as evidence that Washington was the guilty party in cyberwar, a "hacker empire,"[54] in the words of a Chinese military analyst. "For many Chinese," declared *China Daily*, "it is bizarre how Washington can continue to pose as the biggest cyber-espionage victim and demand others behave well."[55] President Obama responded defensively, "Every country in the world, large and small, engages in intelligence gathering," adding that gathering intelligence was different than "a hacker directly connected with the Chinese government or the Chinese military breaking into Apple's software systems to see if they can obtain the designs for the latest Apple product," which was "theft, and we can't tolerate that." The timing was unfortunate for Obama because observers cannot easily distinguish between theft of intellectual property and spying. As China scholar Kenneth Lieberthal observed, "At a minimum, this has reduced our ability to cast ourselves as the injured party."[56]

Drone Warfare Another challenge involves the increasing use of drones (unmanned aerial vehicles; UAVs). Using drones for surveillance in warfare has a lengthy history. Electronic drones were used

A Predator drone

U.S. Marine Corps

for reconnaissance during the Vietnam War and for spotting targets in the 1991 Persian Gulf War and NATO's 1999 air campaign in Kosovo. Today's UAVs are used for both reconnaissance and attack. They are robotic weapons with profound implications for strategy because they "circumvent the domestic, operational, and diplomatic constraints that are imposed on their manned counterparts and, therefore, make otherwise unviable policies viable."[57] They are essential for U.S. power projection and counterterrorism but raise issues of strategy, legality, and human rights.

There are multiple U.S. drone programs: one run by the CIA in noncombat zones (Pakistan, Yemen, and Somalia) and another in the Defense Department operating in combat zones (Afghanistan, Iraq, and Libya). America's use of drones expanded dramatically after 9/11. By September 16, the CIA was operating Predator surveillance drones in Afghanistan, and once the ground war began in October, assault drones were introduced. The first lethal drone strike occurred in Afghanistan in November 2001, and the first "targeted killing" of a suspected terrorist outside a declared war zone occurred in Yemen the following year.

Piloting Drones

The military use of surveillance drones has expanded rapidly, and the Air Force has a shortage of pilots trained to fly them. It is a grueling job, in which pilots often work six fourteen-hour days and log an average of 900 to 1,100 hours flight time a year. (A jet fighter pilot might fly only 200 to 300 hours per year.)[58]

FIGURE 3.2   U.S. Drone Strikes

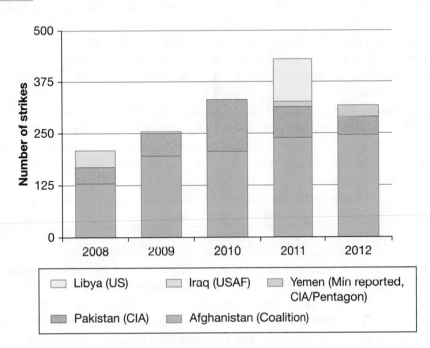

Source: Chris Woods and Alice K. Ross, "Revealed: U.S. and Britain Launched 1,200 Drone Strikes in Recent Wars," *The Bureau of Investigative Journalism*, December 4, 2014, http://www.thebureauinvestigates.com/2012/12/04/revealed-us-and-britain-launched-1200-drone-strikes-in-recent-wars.

The Bush administration used drones between 2002 and 2007 for "targeted strikes," but in 2008 drones acquired a central place in U.S. policy for "signature strikes" that targeted suspected terrorists who may not be identified but who "bear the characteristics of al-Qaeda or Taliban leaders on the run"[59]—a murkier criterion than that required for targeted killing. One such strike in 2015 accidentally killed an American and an Italian who were actually being held hostage by terrorists. President Obama escalated the signature strike policy in Pakistan, where strikes peaked in 2010 and then began to decline, possibly because there were fewer targets to attack. As strikes declined in Pakistan, they increased in Yemen, where forty-seven drone attacks targeting terrorists occurred in 2012.[60] Attack drones were also used to target al-Shabab terrorists in Somalia.

Drones were also used in combat. Afghanistan witnessed many drone strikes between 2004 and 2012, when they peaked at 245. As opposition to drone strikes increased, the Air Force stopped reporting Afghanistan strike data in 2013, stating it "disproportionately focused" on military assaults that only accounted for 3 percent of drone missions.[61] Armed drones were also used in Libya in 2011 to enforce a no-fly zone and protect civilians during NATO's intervention there.

Drones became central to U.S. military operations and strategy because, their advocates contend, they offer benefits in effectiveness and cost. They can be launched quickly and operate in areas where it is dangerous to send manned aircraft. They are also more discriminating than manned aircraft and target more precisely, and their warheads are smaller than those used by fighter jets, thus reducing civilian casualties. Drone advocates also note they are effective in killing terrorist leaders—so much so that there are ever fewer experienced terrorists in Pakistan and Afghanistan. All this comes at less cost in U.S. money and lives than a strategy relying on manned aircraft. Analyst Peter Singer argues that drones are "a game changer. . . . Using remotely piloted vehicles in the framework of intelligence, surveillance and reconnaissance is just the first step,"[62] perhaps to drones without any human involvement. This is reason for concern, argue critics.

Groups like Human Rights Watch claim that drones "take the humanity out of conflict"[63] with dangerous consequences. The technology removes much of the risk in warfare by enabling operators to pilot drones from a ground control station just off the battlefield or thousands of miles away, and that is problematic, insist critics. With soldiers no longer directly involved, the public cannot observe the consequences of war and may not insist on the same level of accountability as in past wars. This makes it is easier to remain in "a state of perpetual, low-level conflict underneath the public's radar."[64] The separation of soldier from battlefield threatens to produce a "moral hazard" in which leaders are more willing to take risks because they and their soldiers are removed from the consequences.

The signature strikes that target and kill unidentified individuals who appear to be terrorists are especially controversial, but all drone attacks raise questions about international law. Among the basic norms in humanitarian law about the conduct of war are that weapons must discriminate between combatants and noncombatants, and that the violence they involve must be proportional to the goals being sought. Analysts raise questions on both counts—drones, especially those used for signature strikes, fail to distinguish between terrorists and civilians and produce substantial collateral harm to civilians. Although it might seem to follow that smaller payloads and precision technology would reduce civilian casualties, a 2013 analysis found that U.S. drones caused *more* collateral damage than manned aircraft.[65] The Obama administration countered that it tries to minimize collateral deaths and that drone strikes are legal. Referring to drones, Obama reasoned, "We were attacked on 9/11. Within a week, Congress overwhelmingly authorized the use of force. Under domestic law, and international law, the United States is at war with al-Qaeda, the Taliban, and their associated forces. We are at war with an organization that right now would kill as many Americans as they could if we did not stop them first. So this is a just war—a war waged proportionally, in last resort, and in self-defense."[66]

Drones also pose political challenges. They alienate other governments, undermine the legitimacy of those who allow U.S. strikes in their territory, and have targeted Americans citizens without due process. The targeted killing in 2011 of U.S.-born Anwar al-Awlaki, a militant Muslim cleric who was masterminding terrorist plots for al-Qaeda's Yemen affiliate, started a debate about if and when American citizens could be killed without a trial. Critics were concerned that U.S. reliance on drones set a precedent for countries like China and Russia. Once more actors deploy assault drones, they may risk unintended escalation in conflicts for which there are as yet no clear rules of engagement.[67]

Some analysts are skeptical about drones' effectiveness. They contend that drones "are only useful where the United States has unfettered access to airspace, a well-defined target, and a clear objective."[68] Drones are also vulnerable: they are easily targeted by planes or anti-aircraft weapons, and the technology can be hacked. In 2011, Iran claimed it had successfully severed communications to a U.S. Sentinel drone and altered its GPS coordinates to direct it to land in Iran when it thought it was returning to its home base in Afghanistan. (U.S. officials claimed a malfunction, not a cyberattack, had downed the drone.)[69] Some analysts also fear that reliance on drones in Afghanistan, Pakistan, and Yemen may produce local resentment that attracts additional recruits to terrorist groups.

While drones are valuable for reconnaissance and are efficient weapons, some critics ask whether they foster America's long-term strategic interests. Are they an effective tool of counterterrorism? Can they degrade and destroy ISIS or other serious terrorist threats? "A campaign which is based on drones is quite good at dealing with the symptoms but it does little with the causes of an insurgency," says one observer. "In fact, it might exacerbate them. [Drones] are an attractive tactic but they are not necessarily a good strategy."[70] There has yet to be a sustained debate about their strategic role. Understanding the strategic context in which drones are deployed—and how it is different than past strategic contexts—"can help elevate debate on drones to the strategic level."[71]

FUTURE: ADAPTING TO A CHANGING ENVIRONMENT

Let us now examine policy options with regard to nuclear policy, counterterrorism and counterinsurgency, cyber-security, and drone warfare.

Nuclear Policy

On entering office, President Obama planned to reduce U.S. dependence on its nuclear arsenal and work toward a world in which nuclear weapons were obsolete—a **Global Zero**. America, he insisted, had a moral responsibility to lead an effort to eliminate nuclear weapons. America's example would enhance nonproliferation policies. And if Washington retained a nuclear component, what should it look like?

Policy Options

a. *Pursue complete disarmament and abandon nuclear deterrence as a component of military strategy,* an unlikely option. Those who advocate Global Zero argue that Washington must set an example. There is little evidence, however, that other nuclear-haves are interested in following that example. Nor is there reason to believe that U.S. disarmament would persuade nuclear aspirants to abandon their activities. Terrorist groups add another complication. It is unlikely that such groups could be deterred from using a nuclear weapon if they acquired it, owing to their extremist goals. Moreover, they might not operate from a territorial base that could be targeted in retaliation.

b. *Continued reliance on nuclear deterrence as a central element of U.S. strategy.* It is difficult to argue against some version of the status quo. While experts disagree about the extent nuclear deterrence has actually been responsible for preventing war and about how many nuclear weapons are needed to maintain effective deterrence, it is difficult to imagine abandoning the strategy as long as there are nuclear-armed foes. From this perspective, nuclear deterrence is insurance against future nuclear attack. The question then becomes, can nuclear deterrence be accomplished with fewer weapons?

c. *Pursue modest disarmament to achieve a more cost-effective and credible deterrent.* Advocates of this option argue that reductions would save money and enhance U.S. security. In addition to inducing other governments to reduce their arsenals or slow their growth, they claim, reductions would save Washington trillions of dollars earmarked for maintaining and modernizing nuclear arsenals and delivery systems. In an era when policymakers are concerned about budgets, Washington should reduce its nuclear arsenal. Senator Dianne Feinstein (D-CA) summed up this view: "It is time to think creatively about how to maintain a much smaller nuclear deterrent at an affordable cost."[72]

d. *Aggressively pursue nuclear modernization.* Proponents of this option contend that the aging U.S. nuclear arsenal needs modernization if it is to continue to have deterrent value. Russia is engaged in significant modernizing of its forces, replacing old Soviet-era weapons and delivery systems with cheaper modern systems. China has a smaller arsenal of 250 warheads, but it, too, is upgrading its delivery systems to create a more mobile nuclear force. Pakistan is developing new medium- and short-range rockets, and India is developing long-range delivery systems (to reach China).[73]

The danger, however, is that aggressive modernization might spark a new arms race. Critics also fear that modernizing nuclear arsenals is inconsistent with the Nuclear Nonproliferation Treaty, which requires the five recognized nuclear weapons states (America, Russia, China, Britain, and France) to "pursue negotiations in good faith on effective measures relating to cessation of the nuclear arms race."

Counterterrorism/Counterinsurgency

In 2014, with the U.S. public weary of conducting long, costly wars, it appeared that conventional ground wars to change regimes were obsolete. In 2011, only 27 percent of Americans believed Washington had an obligation to act in Libya. Low public support for military intervention likely influenced President Obama's decision to limit participation in the NATO bombing campaign in that country. As for regime change, "we went down that road in Iraq," the president argued. "Regime change there took eight years, thousands of American and Iraqi lives, and nearly a trillion dollars. That is not something we can afford to repeat in Libya."[74] Americans were equally averse to intervention in Syria in 2012—even as evidence accumulated that the Assad regime was using chemical weapons against civilians. Americans continued to oppose military intervention into 2014 as ISIS seized large swaths of Iraq and Syria. Public opinion only shifted after the release of video footage of the savage murders of U.S. journalists James Foley and Steven Sotloff. By February 2015, 65 percent of Americans viewed ISIS as a major threat, and 57 percent favored sending U.S. troops into Iraq and Syria to combat it.[75] A ground conflict with insurgents in Iraq or Syria would be asymmetrical. How should the U.S. conduct future **asymmetrical warfare**?

Policy Options

a. *Improve counterinsurgency (COIN) warfare.* Some analysts argue that COIN was successful in Iraq and Afghanistan to the extent it was actually employed. COIN cannot be effective, they argue, if strategy is limited by political constraints. Political leaders must be willing to commit enough troops to get the job done. At the height of the "surge," fewer than 170,000 troops were stationed in Iraq, whereas some observers argued that 400,000 troops were necessary to accomplish U.S. goals. In Afghanistan, troop levels never exceeded 100,000. And U.S. troop rotations that brought troops home after a year undermined COIN by removing experienced soldiers from conflict zones. It is also necessary, insist these analysts, to persuade local leaders to support U.S. counterinsurgency efforts. In Iraq, for example, removal of all employees of the former regime and dismantling the Iraqi army left political and military institutions without competent officials. Finally, COIN warfare requires more than military force to clear and hold territory. It also requires winning over the local population and rebuilding political and economic institutions. Military forces, which were used with mixed effect to achieve these goals in Iraq and Afghanistan, were not well suited to those tasks. Nonetheless Washington remained reluctant to commit civilian resources or integrate them with military efforts to accomplish successful nation building.

b. *Reduce reliance on COIN.* Not everyone agrees that COIN could have been done better in Iraq and Afghanistan. Counterinsurgency warfare is costly, hard to control, slow to produce results, and victory is always elusive, never decisive until functioning and legitimate political and economic institutions are established. Nation building involves more than restoring political and economic institutions that enable the state to fulfill basic functions like providing security and collecting taxes. As one analysis of nation-building efforts contends, "political engineering by outsiders seldom succeeds in radically altering the underlying conditions responsible for the state's ineffectiveness."[76] Militarily, such warfare is also difficult to conduct. Strategy and tactics must constantly evolve to counter innovations employed by the adversary and win over local populations. Armies are often fighting the last war and rarely demonstrate the flexibility to respond deftly to new methods of warfare. Done poorly, counterterrorist and counterinsurgent strategies perpetuate power vacuums that fuel sectarianism and extremism. Given the high costs over the time required to achieve success, it is difficult to sustain domestic political support for such conflicts.

c. *Focus counterterrorist strategies on efforts to protect Americans and U.S. interests at home and abroad.* A third option that is compatible with options a and b is to focus on enhancing counterterrorism to protect Americans at home and abroad by working to address underlying conditions that give rise to extremism and terrorism—poverty, economic inequality, and repressive government. To a large extent, this requires nonmilitary tools and "soft power." However, it can also involve military force to identify and target known and potential terrorists.

Cyber-Threats

Debate swirls about the extent of cyber-threats and whether they ought to be treated like conventional threats that demand a military solution or as acts of espionage and sabotage that can be dealt with short of war.

Policy Options

a. *Pursue multilateral responses.* Cyber-security is an area where multilateralism is complex. There is a UN process underway to examine possible multilateral efforts to combat cyber-threats, but the nature of such threats makes it difficult to manage them by treaties. Treaties are designed to deal with interstate issues, but threats to cyber-security are as likely to arise from nonstate groups as from states. States can play a role in bringing terrorists and individual hackers to justice, but these obligations are difficult to enforce. Cyber-security also confronts an "attribution problem," that is, it is difficult to determine who is responsible for an attack and whether the group is acting on its own or for a government. Finally, monitoring is difficult in the cyber realm, where almost any computer can be used for cyberattacks. For such reasons, treaties "are at best going to be of limited value."[77]

b. *Cyber-deterrence*. Deterrence does not transfer easily to the cyber realm. One view is that cyber deterrence may be impossible owing to the "attribution problem" noted above. Even if it were possible to track a hack to a particular computer or network, it remains difficult to identify who is behind the attack. This means that Washington cannot credibly threaten to retaliate against a cyberattack, no matter how robust its cyber offensive capabilities. Credibility, deterrence skeptics say, is compromised because it is difficult to demonstrate to potential hackers how U.S. cyber offensive capabilities can impose sufficient costs to persuade them to desist.

Even if the source of an attack were identified, how much damage must be done to justify responding with offensive cyber capabilities? Would Washington be willing to publicize cyber retaliation when doing so would likely reveal sensitive information about capabilities that might increase U.S. vulnerability to attack or sabotage? One way to overcome such limitations is to respond *outside* the cyber realm using economic or diplomatic pressure, including sanctions, or, if the attack is sufficiently severe, military force. Some observers insist that a military solution is neither appropriate nor credible because cyberattacks, at least in cases involving sabotage or espionage, do not "rise to the level of war."[78]

Others argue that deterrence is appropriate to prevent cyberattacks. Supporters of this view claim that this is why there have never been "strategically significant" cyberattacks "between equals." In other words, foes exercise strategic restraint in the cyber realm, just as in the nuclear realm.[79] But as cyber-threats become more complex, it may become necessary to "lean more heavily on deterrence by denial than during the nuclear age."[80] This means enhancing defenses to deny attackers success. "The challenge," said Deputy Secretary of Defense William Lynn, "is to make the defenses effective enough to deny an adversary the benefit of an attack despite the strength of offensive tools in cyberspace."[81] This assumes cyberattackers are rational and will only attack if they anticipate some benefit—an arguable claim. Attackers may probe for cyber vulnerabilities for several reasons, for example, embarrassing Washington or generating public fear not of attack but of personal vulnerability. Moreover, the nature of cyber-security is that there are always new vulnerabilities to be exploited. Even the best defenses must be constantly improved to anticipate the next threat.

c. *Increase cooperation between the public and private sectors*. Public-private sector information sharing is, says the chief information officer for American Express, "the single highest-impact, lowest-cost, fastest-[to]-implement capability we have at hand as a sector and a nation."[82] There have been several efforts to pass legislation in Congress to facilitate information exchanges to prevent and respond to data breaches.

In 2012, the proposed Cyber Intelligence Sharing and Protection Act encouraged greater information sharing for this purpose. The proposed bill would have allowed the government to notify companies if it detected a potential attack on their networks and required private companies to inform the government if they noticed activity suggesting a cyberattack. The proposal passed in the House of Representatives but not the Senate. House lawmakers unsuccessfully tried to resurrect the bill in 2013. Opposition stemmed from concerns about the impact of intelligence sharing on individual privacy. Senator Tom Carper (D-DE) reintroduced the bill in January 2015 after several high-profile data breaches, including the hacking of the Sony computing system. This time the bill included greater protection for individual privacy by minimizing identifying information and limiting how the government could use data. Private corporations, especially large Silicon Valley companies like Google and Facebook, opposed mandated security sharing that was not accompanied by changes in U.S. surveillance activities exposed by Edward Snowden in 2013 that allowed the systematic collection of private data in America and abroad and required them to allow the government access to private encrypted information.

President Obama, who had threatened to veto previous bills that failed to assure privacy, offered his own proposals in his 2015 State of the Union Address. These included greater public-private sector information sharing, greater punishments for cybercrimes, and new notification and cyber-defense standards. "We are making sure," said Obama, "our government integrates intelligence to combat cyber threats, just as we have done to combat terrorism."[83] Some weeks later, Obama issued an executive order to foster voluntary public-private sector information sharing, and in April 2015, the House of Representatives passed a cyber-security bill that would require increased public-private cooperation.

d. *Enhanced intelligence sharing.* In February 2015, President Obama announced the establishment of a Cyber Threat Intelligence Integration Center in the Office of the Director of National Intelligence to "fill the gaps" in efforts to share cyber-intelligence collected by the CIA, FBI, Cyber Command, the Department of Homeland Security, and other intelligence agencies. Much as the Department of Homeland Security and the Director of National Intelligence enhanced intelligence sharing among government agencies after the 9/11 attacks, the new center would coordinate the activities of agencies involved in gathering and analyzing cyber-intelligence to reduce vulnerabilities that follow when different agencies have independent intelligence capabilities. Critics, however, ask if another government agency is the answer or if it is merely another layer of redundancy.

Drones

There are several strategic and legal concerns surrounding the use of attack drones, but U.S. officials insist they constitute an effective counterterrorism tool. At present, there is limited government accountability for drone strikes.

Policy Options

a. *End the drone program,* an unlikely option. Ending the program would end the legal controversy, but Washington credits drone strikes with taking "dozens of highly skilled al Qaeda commanders, trainers, bomb makers, and operatives . . . off the battlefield,"[84] and disrupting plans to target America and its interests abroad. Ending the program would leave America without a valuable counterterrorism tool.

b. *Deploy drones for intelligence gathering only and let other governments kill identified targets in their territory.* This policy would avoid the appearance of violations of other countries' sovereignty, but again, it might undermine counterterrorism efforts. By the time friendly forces arrived, terrorists might have fled or taken cover. Any policy that required coordination of surveillance and targeting forces would entail a dangerous time lag. At worst, the drone presence would alert terrorists to their detection, making it possible for them to ambush security forces. For such a policy to work, Washington would have to be confident that the foreign government would be willing and able to carry out a successful military strike. U.S. experience with Pakistan has taught officials that while government officials privately might be willing to consent to the drone program, they are rarely willing to acknowledge their support publicly, and it is less likely they could be counted on to act against terrorists on U.S. intelligence.

c. *Place U.S. drones under another government's control,* thereby distancing Washington from concerns about violating sovereignty or international law. This would entail some of the difficulties previously discussed. Moreover, drones are a sensitive military technology that Washington is unlikely to share with other, especially unstable, governments. A related option would have Washington employ a "dual key" system that would enable other governments to veto a U.S. strike. Such arrangements, however, would require considerable trust among participants.[85]

d. *Reduce reliance on drones in America's counterterrorist strategy.* In 2013, the Obama administration announced that Washington would reduce its reliance on drones, but attack drones continued to be used in Yemen and Pakistan. Washington would need equally effective alternative tools before reducing the role of drones in protecting U.S. national security.

e. *Clarify the rules for targeting and killing suspected terrorists.* A combination of reducing reliance on drones and clarifying the rules by which they were used would eliminate some of the controversy surrounding these weapons. Moreover, if Washington were to clarify and set standards, it would be more difficult for other governments to employ drones for extrajudicial and extraterritorial killings.[86]

Obama sought to move in this direction by shifting all drone operations to the Defense Department, but it was unclear how quickly this would occur. Placing the entire drone program in the Pentagon would make it more transparent, but the Joint Special Operations Command that would oversee the program is also viewed as secretive, and it is not clear that the program would have greater congressional oversight than the CIA program.

CONCLUSION: A CHANGING STRATEGIC ENVIRONMENT

The strategic environment has dramatically changed since the Cold War ended, and change has accelerated in recent years, increasing uncertainty for policymakers and military strategists. Today's threats are complex and require solutions that did not seem thinkable a few years ago. Historically, when conflicts end, there is a peace dividend as defense spending falls and funding is reallocated to lower wartime deficits, taxes that were raised to pay for war are reduced, and nondefense spending is increased.[87] Anticipating the end of wars in Afghanistan and Iraq, U.S. officials began speaking of downsizing forces and reallocating defense budgets to new endeavors. But with persistent instability in Afghanistan and Iraq and new threats—including the ascendance of ISIS and Russian aggression in Ukraine—decisions made as recently as 2012 are controversial. As explained by General Raymond Odierno, Army Chief of Staff: "We made assumptions that we wouldn't be using Army forces in Europe the way we used to, we made assumptions that we wouldn't go back into Iraq—and here we are back in Iraq, here we are worried about Russia again."[88]

As we have noted, military strategy can no longer be considered in isolation from other policy areas. Decisions made to deploy or withdraw troops from abroad, employ Special Operations Forces to counter terrorists, and develop technologies to conduct warfare without placing U.S. troops in harm's way affect other interests besides national security. They incur economic costs in an era when Congress seeks to reduce deficits. They raise human-rights concerns. They raise sovereignty concerns for U.S. partners that may not fully agree with the strategies and tactics of American leaders. Finally, they may reduce long-time allies' confidence in the ability and willingness of Washington to meet longstanding commitments.

DISCUSSION QUESTIONS

1. How has America's grand strategy evolved since World War II?

2. Should the United States use force to spread its values globally?

3. Should the United States seek to achieve Global Zero? Why, or why not?

4. Explain the threat posed by cyber-weapons to the United States and possible ways to respond to it.

5. Describe the evolution of America's nuclear deterrence policy since World War II.

6. Under what circumstances should the United States be prepared to use nuclear weapons?

KEY TERMS

arms control (p. 71)

asymmetrical warfare (p. 88)

bipolar (p. 66)

containment (p. 69)

cyberattack (p. 67)

cyber-espionage (p. 67)

cyber-security (p. 82)

deterrence (p. 68)

disarmament (p. 71)

domino theory (p. 70)

first-strike capability (p. 71)

geostrategy (p. 66)

Global Zero (p. 87)

hegemon (p. 66)

insider attacks (p. 81)

intercontinental ballistic missiles (p. 73)

multiple, independently targetable reentry vehicles (p. 71)

mutual assured destruction (MAD) (p. 71)

no-fly zones (p. 74)

nonpolarity (p. 66)

power vacuum (p. 69)

second-strike capability (p. 71)

sectarian violence (p. 78)

security (p. 74)

signature strikes (p. 85)

sphere of influence (p. 80)

tactical nuclear weapons (p. 80)

targeted strikes (p. 85)

terrorists (p. 66)

unipolar moment (p. 74)

unipolarity (p. 74)

for CQ Press

Sharpen your skill with SAGE edge at **edge.sagepub.com/mansbach**

SAGE edge for Students provides a personalized approach to help you accomplish your coursework goals in an easy-to-use learning environment.

4

America and the Proliferation of Weapons of Mass Destruction

Kim Jong-un and his generals

Xinhua/KCNA via Corbis

Tensions ran high between America and North Korea in the spring of 2013, as evidence accumulated that North Korea was preparing a third nuclear weapons test. The year had begun with North Korea threatening a "higher level" nuclear test to follow those conducted in 2006 and 2009, along with long-range missile launches and threats that its weapons would target U.S. soil. These warnings came after United Nations (UN) **sanctions** imposed following a North Korean missile test. That missile, believed to have placed a satellite in orbit, threatened international security for what it represented—North Korea's progress toward developing long-range missiles that might someday send a nuclear weapon to North America.

North Korea then carried out its third nuclear test. Even China condemned North Korea's actions, and the UN imposed additional sanctions, but nothing reined in North Korea's leadership. Its threats continued—propaganda videos showing missiles falling on a U.S. city that appeared to be New York and on the White House and Capitol in Washington, an announcement that Pyongyang had deployed nuclear-tipped intercontinental ballistic missiles, and a photo showing North Korean leader Kim Jong-un and his generals meeting in front of a map depicting nuclear strike plans for America.

Observers scrambled to understand the reason for North Korea's threats. Some speculated that the country's young leader, Kim Jong-un, was consolidating his domestic position or was testing South Korea's new President Park Geun-hye. Because North Korea is a closed society, it was difficult to know how seriously to regard the threats, many of which were not credible. Nonetheless, events in the spring of 2013 focused attention on the dangers of **proliferation**, especially the spread of nuclear weapons to unpredictable governments like North Korea's.

Nuclear proliferation became a serious U.S. concern early in the nuclear age. American leaders in the Cold War wrestled with how widely nuclear weapons technology should be allowed to spread, if at all. America tested its first atomic device in 1945 but only retained its nuclear monopoly until 1949, when the USSR did the same. By 1964, Britain, France, and China also had acquired nuclear weapons, and America and the Soviet Union were engaged in a nuclear arms race. It was only later that biological and chemical weapons proliferation (also weapons of mass destruction, or WMD) reached America's foreign-policy agenda. America's nonproliferation agenda has empha- sized nuclear weapons over chemical and biological weapons (CBW), partly because nuclear weap- ons pose a special foreign-policy problem. Unlike biological and chemical weapons that are banned under international law, nuclear weapons are "legal in five countries, not illegal in three others, and forbidden essentially everywhere else."[1]

Timeline

1900	1900 (Continued)	2000
1945 America drops atom bombs on Hiroshima and Nagasaki.	**1975** America ratifies the 1925 Geneva Protocol and the 1972 Biological Weapons Convention.	**2002** President Bush labels Iran, Iraq, and North Korea an "axis of evil."
1949 The USSR detonates an atomic device.		**2003** North Korea withdraws from the NPT.
1968 The Nuclear Nonproliferation Treaty (NPT) is signed.		**2003** America invites ten states to join the Proliferation Security Initiative (PSI).
1969 President Nixon unilaterally ends America's bioweapons program.		**2003** Construction of Iran's first nuclear reactor begins.

This chapter examines U.S. nonproliferation policy beginning in the Cold War, as well as nonproliferation policy after the collapse of the USSR in the "second nuclear age," an era characterized by a range of state and nonstate actors seeking to acquire a WMD capability and expansion of U.S. policy to include unilateral and bilateral tools to plug the gaps in the multilateral nonproliferation regime.

PAST: PROLIFERATION IN THE FIRST NUCLEAR AGE

The first nuclear age began in 1945 with America's bombing of Hiroshima and Nagasaki. The era was defined by superpower confrontation, nuclear overkill, and the threat of mutual assured destruction. In this period, few countries had nuclear weapons, and the primary goal of U.S. nuclear policy was to manage the superpower conflict so as to avoid a nuclear Armageddon. Managing "horizontal proliferation," or the spread of nuclear weapons to additional actors, was a secondary consideration. Efforts to curb biological-weapons proliferation only began in the late 1960s and chemical weapons not until the late 1980s and early 1990s. Early U.S. nonproliferation policy relied heavily on the negotiation of bilateral and multilateral treaties to stop the spread of WMD.

Sources of Nonproliferation Policies in the First Nuclear Age

External factors provided the principle stimulus in defining the need for a nonproliferation policy. America was the world's first nuclear weapons state, but it maintained its monopoly for only a short time. By 1949, the USSR had a nuclear capability, and Britain and France followed in 1952 and 1960, respectively. When China, then a Cold War adversary, became a nuclear power in 1964, nonproliferation rose higher on the U.S. agenda. It was not inevitable that Washington would systematically pursue nuclear nonproliferation efforts. U.S. leaders were presented with a choice: halt proliferation entirely or encourage proliferation to allies to balance Soviet and Chinese capabilities.

2000 (Continued)

2003 Libya announces it will dismantle its WMD programs.

2006 North Korea tests its first nuclear device.

2009 North Korea conducts a second nuclear test.

2009 Iran admits building a uranium enrichment facility, rejecting an offer for enriching its uranium abroad.

2013 North Korea conducts a third nuclear test.

2013 Syria agrees to surrender its chemical weapons.

2000 (Continued)

2013 Iran signs a Joint Plan of Action to negotiate a comprehensive nuclear agreement.

March **2015** The P5+1 group and Iran reach a framework agreement for a final deal in June.

Key government bureaucracies took positions consistent with their obligation to advocate either complete nonproliferation or "selective proliferation." Secretary of State Dean Rusk had the latter role, arguing for a proposed NATO Multilateral Force. This arrangement would place nuclear weapons under the control of a force "jointly organized" by America and its NATO allies. It would give America's allies some control over NATO's strategic nuclear decisions but would not "contribute to national nuclear proliferation."[2] Others, notably the director of the newly formed Arms Control and Disarmament Agency, William Foster, argued that selective proliferation would encourage more countries to seek nuclear weapons and the status they conferred.[3] In 1965, President Lyndon Johnson commissioned a study to inform the choice. Known as the Gilpatric Report, it was the source of much debate, but eventually those advocating complete nonproliferation triumphed, and Johnson backed efforts to negotiate a nonproliferation treaty. Other presidents were also influential in seeking a non-proliferation policy—in their roles both as president and as individuals with different beliefs about the dangers proliferation posed.

President Dwight Eisenhower proposed the Atoms for Peace plan in a 1953 speech to the UN General Assembly. It was intended to transform nuclear power from a means of destruction to a tool for improving the human condition. It involved exchanging technical information, using nuclear materials and equipment for peaceful purposes, and creating an International Atomic Energy Agency (IAEA) to promote cooperation. Eisenhower's successor, John Kennedy, was personally committed to limiting the spread of nuclear weapons. In an address to the General Assembly, he argued, "The weapons of war must be abolished before they abolish us."[4] He also predicted in 1960 that "ten, fifteen or twenty nations will have a nuclear capacity"[5] by 1964. The 1962 Cuban missile crisis persuaded Kennedy to act. After the crisis, he resumed negotiations for a Comprehensive Test Ban Treaty; signed a Limited Test Ban Treaty with the USSR that prohibited atmospheric, space-based, and underwater nuclear tests; and floated the idea of a nuclear nonproliferation treaty.

After commissioning the Gilpatric Report, Johnson took up Kennedy's idea and advocated the **Nuclear Nonproliferation Treaty (NPT)**, which he signed in 1968. The NPT assumed that nuclear weapons ought never to be used, and that proliferation—particularly if it upset the superpower nuclear balance—would increase the possibility of catastrophic war. When negotiations for a nonproliferation treaty began, it was recognized that the existing nuclear powers would not soon relinquish their weapons. Consequently, the final treaty created two categories of states, nuclear-weapons states (NWS) and non-nuclear-weapons states (NNWS), with rules for each. The NWS included states that had exploded a nuclear device before January 1, 1967—America, the USSR, Britain, France, and China. Others fell into the category of NNWS.

The NPT prohibited nuclear-weapons states from transferring nuclear weapons, materials, or know-how to NNWS and required them to disarm eventually. NNWS insisted that the treaty required complete nuclear disarmament. Nuclear states argued that significant cuts, including those that occurred owing to bilateral disarmament treaties, were sufficient. All other states were prohibited from trying to make or acquire nuclear weapons, either on their own or with the aid of an NWS. To compensate NNWS for their promise not to acquire nuclear weapons, the treaty emphasized the right of *all* states to develop and use nuclear energy for peaceful purposes as long as they accepted international safeguards over their nuclear materials. The IAEA oversees these safeguards.

The treaty was signed in 1968, and by 1970 almost 100 states were participants. Treaty proponents cite the limited proliferation that has occurred since 1968 as evidence of the NPT's success in establishing a global nonproliferation norm. Critics counter that the treaty's effects have been exaggerated, and that a combination of superpower military might and the security guarantees provided to allies had prevented "nuclear-capable" states like Japan, Australia, and South Korea from acquiring nuclear weapons. From the start, there have been limitations to the NPT system. States that intended to acquire nuclear weapons like Israel, India, and Pakistan did not join. Additionally, the peaceful transfer of civilian nuclear technologies and materials encouraged by the NPT became a source of proliferation, as rogue states used those materials to produce nuclear fuel or engineer weapons. However, during the first nuclear age, few states took advantage of loopholes to pursue a nuclear-weapons program, and even fewer succeeded in building a bomb.

Limiting proliferation of chemical and biological weapons was not a U.S. priority in this era, and U.S. chemical and biological weapons programs expanded. America had maintained a biological warfare program during World War II, with research and development, testing, and production of agents including anthrax, botulism, cholera, and plague. That program expanded during the Korean War to develop more virulent and stable biological agents that were easier and less expensive to produce, and, in 1958, the first missile capable of carrying a biological warhead was deployed. A biodefense program was begun in 1953.[6]

America's chemical-weapons program preceded its biological-weapons counterpart. In 1918, the Army's Chemical Warfare Service was established to oversee the production of toxic chemicals like chlorine, mustard gas, and phosgene. In the interwar years, America stockpiled a chemical arsenal and began producing new chemical agents. Washington had signed the Geneva Protocol outlawing the use of chemical weapons in 1925 but did not ratify it until 1974. U.S. production of chemical weapons agents expanded during and after World War II, although Washington had a no-first-use policy and never employed these weapons.

If external and individual factors were central to America's nuclear nonproliferation policy, societal factors provided additional impetus for CBW nonproliferation, notably public opposition to the use of unconventional weapons in Cold War conflicts. During the Vietnam War, America's widespread use of chemical agents stirred opposition, especially the herbicide Agent Orange that defoliated enemy-controlled areas to enable locating enemy forces. Agent Orange caused serious health problems, including cancer and birth defects, for American soldiers and Vietnamese civilians who had been exposed to it. America's use of chemical agents became unpopular among publics at home and abroad, especially after high-profile chemical accidents highlighted the dangers associated with such weapons. Thus, President Nixon renounced biological weapons in 1969 and ordered destruction of existing U.S. stockpiles. Production facilities were to be converted to peaceful purposes including biodefense. Washington entered negotiations to outlaw biological weapons and in 1972 became an early signatory of the Biological Weapons Convention.

Efforts were also underway to limit U.S. chemical weapons. In 1969, Public Law 19-121 restricted the testing, transport, storage, and disposal of chemical agents, and Nixon signed an executive order halting production of unitary chemical weapons. (In unitary weapons, the chemical agent is toxic; in binary chemical weapons, separate non-lethal chemicals are combined before release to produce a highly toxic

MAP 4.1 Global Nuclear and Chemical Weapons

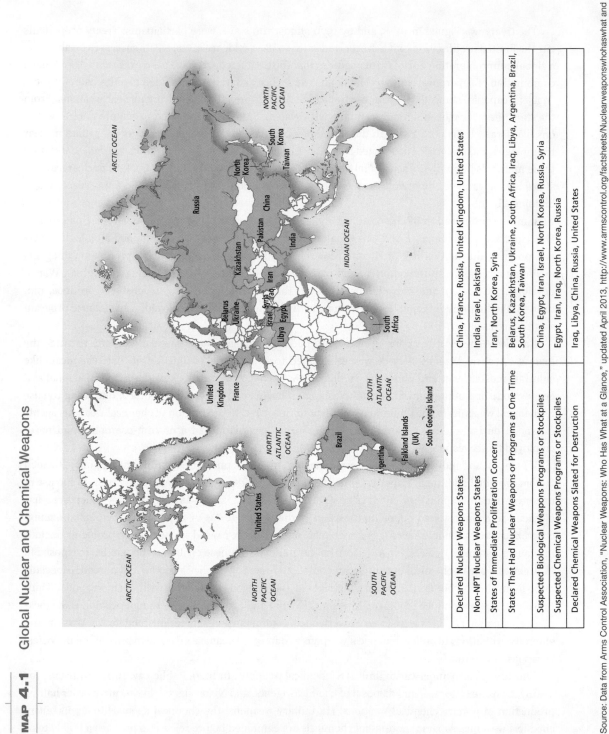

Declared Nuclear Weapons States	China, France, Russia, United Kingdom, United States
Non-NPT Nuclear Weapons States	India, Israel, Pakistan
States of Immediate Proliferation Concern	Iran, North Korea, Syria
States That Had Nuclear Weapons or Programs at One Time	Belarus, Kazakhstan, Ukraine, South Africa, Iraq, Libya, Argentina, Brazil, South Korea, Taiwan
Suspected Biological Weapons Programs or Stockpiles	China, Egypt, Iran, Israel, North Korea, Russia, Syria
Suspected Chemical Weapons Programs or Stockpiles	Egypt, Iran, Iraq, North Korea, Russia
Declared Chemical Weapons Slated for Destruction	Iraq, Libya, China, Russia, United States

Source: Data from Arms Control Association, "Nuclear Weapons: Who Has What at a Glance," updated April 2013, http://www.armscontrol.org/factsheets/Nuclearweaponswhohaswhat and Arms Control Association, "Chemical and Biological Weapons Status at a Glance," updated September 2013, http://www.armscontrol.org/factsheets/cbwprolif.

agent.) Washington continued developing and stockpiling binary agents into the 1980s. Again, public opinion spurred efforts to eliminate this class of WMD. This time, it was the use of chemical agents in the Iran-Iraq war (1980–1988) that led to public pressure on President George H. W. Bush to end America's chemical-weapons program and eliminate chemical stockpiles. In 1990, Bush and Soviet President Mikhail Gorbachev signed the Bilateral Destruction Agreement to end production of chemical weapons and require destruction of existing stockpiles. This spurred talks to draft a global treaty, the 1993 Chemical Weapons Convention (CWC). Washington ratified it in 1997.

PRESENT: PROLIFERATION IN THE SECOND NUCLEAR AGE

The end of the Cold War ushered in the second nuclear age, characterized by a growing awareness of threats from terrorists and rogue states and the emergence of new institutions to manage these threats. The threats that dominated American nonproliferation policy in this era were not new, but Washington's awareness of them had grown. The second nuclear age began when "actors realized they could no longer ignore something truly fundamental was taking place."[7] No longer preoccupied with the superpower rivalry, U.S. leaders began to concern themselves with new threats—horizontal proliferation of WMD, the possible theft of WMD materials or weapons from poorly guarded facilities in former Soviet states, and emergence of terrorists seeking WMD.

The second nuclear age differed from the first regarding horizontal proliferation. The earliest proliferators had sought a nuclear capability to gain an advantage in the Cold War. Proliferators in the second nuclear age sought nuclear arms not to alter the global nuclear balance but to enhance their own "power, legitimacy, and status"[8] or assure their own security. The addition of new nuclear-armed actors complicated strategic calculations. Late nuclear aspirants developed their programs covertly to avoid the nonproliferation regime and tended to be embroiled in regional conflicts. Significant investment in nuclear-weapons programs meant that less-developed countries had fewer resources for conventional forces or for social and economic development. With a reduced conventional capability, such countries were more likely to escalate to the nuclear level should a conflict erupt, and less investment in social and economic development risked political instability that endangered the security of nuclear weapons.

For America, the second nuclear age was characterized by concern with halting horizontal proliferation of *all* WMD, but unlike the earlier era, U.S. policy became less concerned with halting all proliferation and more concerned with limiting proliferation to "rogue" states. In his 2003 State of the Union Address, President George W. Bush argued that the greatest danger to America and the world was *not* nuclear proliferation per se, but "outlaw regimes that seek and possess nuclear, chemical, and biological weapons."[9] America continued to participate in the multilateral institutions like the NPT and the IAEA, and the Obama administration sought to join the Comprehensive Test Ban Treaty with the goal of developing a global consensus on nonproliferation. Washington, nevertheless, viewed these multilateral institutions as insufficient to cope with horizontal proliferation, and it adopted a strategy that relied increasingly on unilateral and bilateral initiatives and differentiated between "good" and "bad" proliferators. These initiatives emphasized eliminating the threat of unsecured WMD materials; restricting the transfer or sale of dual-use technologies; and employing missile defenses, preemptive war, and the threat of nuclear attack to prevent states and terrorists from acquiring WMD.

The United States and the Nonproliferation Regime

The NPT remained the cornerstone of the nonproliferation regime. Its early success was a product of the Cold War. America's policy of extended deterrence provided security guarantees to states that might otherwise have sought to acquire a nuclear capability, and where security guarantees were insufficient, both superpowers had the military muscle to dissuade countries in their sphere of influence from proliferating. In the early 21st century, America's nuclear umbrella continued to prevent proliferation in countries like South Korea that might go nuclear in the absence of U.S. protection. But neither Cold War superpower had the military might or moral authority to prevent proliferation.

The nonproliferation regime was also undermined by key omissions. India, Israel, and Pakistan never joined the NPT, and North Korea, which joined reluctantly in 1985, withdrew in 2003, having never complied with its treaty obligations. U.S. policymakers regarded noncompliance—or the concern that parties to the treaty would ignore their treaty obligations—as the biggest threat to the NPT. Thus, in the post–Cold War era, America has been at the forefront of efforts to shore up the nuclear nonproliferation regime by means of multilateral initiatives (through the UN Security Council or the IAEA), bilateral agreements, and ad hoc coalitions to make it difficult for potential proliferators to succeed. A key multilateral instrument for limiting proliferation is the IAEA inspections system. Nonnuclear weapons states are required by the NPT to negotiate comprehensive safeguards agreements with the IAEA in which they declare any nuclear facilities and materials and grant the IAEA access for routine inspections. This process for ensuring compliance was found wanting in the 1990s when a UN inspection team in Iraq found evidence that Baghdad had been working on a clandestine nuclear weapons program in undeclared facilities.

Thus, in 1997, the IAEA Board of Governors established a more comprehensive inspections agreement, known as the Additional Protocol. This was a voluntary agreement negotiated with NPT-member states that granted the agency authority to visit any location where nuclear materials might be present, whether a declared nuclear facility or not, to verify that the state was using its nuclear materials and facilities for peaceful purposes. The Additional Protocol did not give IAEA inspectors the right to inspect *any* facility at *any* time, but it gave them greater authority to verify that states had fully declared their nuclear facilities and materials. By September 2013, 145 countries had concluded an Additional Protocol with the IAEA, and most had entered into force. Many countries, including America, are requiring that trade partners sign an Additional Protocol before permitting nuclear-related exports.

Many non-nuclear NPT states viewed the reluctance of the nuclear-weapons states to disarm completely as a threat to nonproliferation efforts. They charged nuclear-weapons states with failing to make sufficient progress in eliminating their nuclear arsenals—a commitment reaffirmed at the 1995 NPT Review Conference. Proponents of the disarmament-proliferation link argued that America's massive arsenal reinforced a perception that nuclear arms were a source of power and therefore encouraged proliferation by rogue states. They also contended that Washington's conventional capabilities were so advanced that they rendered a large nuclear arsenal unnecessary.

Washington pointed to the reductions in the post–Cold War U.S. nuclear arsenal as evidence of progress in meeting this treaty obligation. NNWS, however, did not see these measures as progress toward eventual elimination of all nuclear weapons. Early in his first term, President Obama expressed a willingness to discuss "concrete steps towards a world without nuclear weapons"[10] and declared he intended

⚡ KEY DOCUMENT

2010 Nuclear Posture Review: Preventing Nuclear Proliferation and Nuclear Terrorism

"As part of our effort to move toward a world free of nuclear weapons, the United States will lead expanded international efforts to rebuild and strengthen the global nuclear non-proliferation regime and to accelerate efforts to prevent nuclear terrorism. Concerns have grown in recent years that unless today's dangerous trends are arrested and reversed, before long we will be living in a world with a steadily growing number of nuclear-armed states and an increasing likelihood of terrorists getting their hands on nuclear weapons. Therefore, for the first time, the 2010 NPR places this priority atop the U.S. nuclear agenda.

The United States is committed to renewing and strengthening the Nuclear Non-Proliferation Treaty (NPT) and the global nuclear non-proliferation regime it anchors to cope with the challenges of non-compliance and of the growth of nuclear power. . . . To strengthen the regime, the United States seeks to champion and reaffirm through its own actions the grand bargain that underpins the treaty: states without nuclear weapons will not acquire them, states with nuclear weapons will move toward disarmament, and all Parties can have access to peaceful nuclear energy under effective verification."

Source: U.S. Department of Defense, Nuclear Posture Review Report, April 2010, http://www.defense.gov/npr/docs/2010%20nuclear%20posture%20review%20report.pdf., 9.

to decrease the role of nuclear weapons in U.S. policy, reaffirming in the 2010 Nuclear Posture Review that America would not use nuclear weapons against nonnuclear states that were meeting their NPT obligations. However, domestic critics argued that these assurances damaged American credibility by raising questions about U.S. willingness to extend deterrence to allies like South Korea and Japan, limited America's ability to meet threats from Iran and North Korea, weakened America's position relative to Russia and China, and might actually *spur* nuclear proliferation.

Halting the Leakage, Trade, and Transfer of Weapons and Materials

The threats of the second nuclear era required new multilateral tools to manage proliferation. Today, 135 nuclear facilities around the world use **highly enriched uranium (HEU)** in quantities sufficient to make 400 nuclear weapons.[11] In the hands of terrorists, HEU could be used to build a crude nuclear device or a dirty bomb. UN Security Council Resolution 1540 (2004) tackled this challenge by requiring governments to "refrain from providing any form of support to non-State actors" that try to acquire nuclear, biological, or chemical weapons and their means of delivery; to adopt legislation prohibiting such actors from acquiring WMD or their means of delivery; and to establish domestic controls to prevent the proliferation of WMD (and related materials) and their means of delivery. The resolution called on UN members "in a position to do so" to assist others that did not have the "legal and regulatory infrastructure, implementation experience, and/or resources"[12] to meet these obligations.

U.S. efforts to prevent the spread of nuclear materials and technologies preceded Resolution 1540 by over a decade. Economic and political instability in Russia after the breakup of the USSR raised concerns about "nuclear leakage"–that is, that Russia would be unable to maintain control of its nuclear weapons and materials. Washington's answer was the highly successful Cooperative Threat Reduction Program (chapter 14). Other efforts included export controls, interdiction activities, and negotiations toward a fissile material cutoff treaty.

Export Controls The Nuclear Suppliers Group (NSG) is the principal export-control body for nuclear-related trade. It consists of 48 NPT members that have established and implemented export control guidelines to limit the sale of nuclear-related materials and technologies to potential proliferators. The NSG was born in 1975 in response to India's first nuclear test. India's nuclear detonation indicated that the NPT alone was insufficient to prevent horizontal proliferation. India's proliferation, "the most egregious abuse of peaceful nuclear assistance,"[13] was facilitated by the NPT requirement that developed countries share civilian nuclear technologies with less-developed states. The proliferation risk posed by the transfer of civilian nuclear materials was well known, for, in supplying India with heavy water for use in its nuclear power reactor, U.S. officials warned New Delhi not to divert this assistance to a nuclear weapons program.

Anti-proliferation efforts, and the NSG itself, may again be threatened by India's nuclear ambitions. India seeks to become a member of the NSG, and U.S. policy may enable it to do so. Because India had signed the NPT, it was barred from NSG membership, but that may change. NSG guidelines dictated that nuclear suppliers could not sell nuclear materials to India, partly as punishment for India's status as a nuclear "outlier"—a de facto but not a legal nuclear power. The prohibition also had a pragmatic aim because there was no way to verify that such materials would be used for peaceful purposes as long as India did not participate in the nonproliferation regime. The George W. Bush administration sought an NSG waiver to allow U.S.-Indian civilian nuclear cooperation and trade in nuclear materials worth some $150 billion.[14] Washington was eager to improve relations with India to increase support for U.S. military engagement in Iraq and Afghanistan and balance rising China.

India made improved relations contingent on America's accepting its status as a nuclear-weapons state. Critics of the agreement argued that this weakened global nonproliferation and reversed three decades of U.S. policy by granting India legitimacy as a nuclear-weapons state outside the NPT, thereby encouraging Pakistan, North Korea, and Iran to believe they also might be accepted as legitimate nuclear-weapons states. After Congress approved the agreement in 2008, India signed similar agreements with other countries, several of which also indicated they would support India's membership in the NSG.[15]

The Proliferation Security Initiative (PSI) In December 2002, the Bush administration, acting on intelligence that a North Korean freighter, the *So San,* was carrying ballistic missiles to Yemen, requested that Spanish warships on patrol in the Indian Ocean stop the vessel. By international law, ships on the high seas can only be stopped by officials of the country in which they are registered unless those ships are unregistered. U.S. officials claimed the right to board the *So San* because it appeared to be a "lawless, stateless vessel," flying no flag and having no official markings—they were painted over.[16] The Spaniards discovered missiles and drums of chemicals, hidden under bags of cement. The cargo was not technically illegal, and Spanish officials allowed the *So San* to continue on its way. The *So San* incident was notable for highlighting a gap in international law that enabled proliferation.

Thus, President Bush unveiled the **Proliferation Security Initiative** in 2003. The PSI is "an activity, not an organization," described in its mission statement as "a commitment by over 90 states to take action to interdict shipments, disrupt proliferation networks, and shut down the front companies that support them."[17] Today, over 100 countries cooperate "in developing best practices, joint training exercises, and information-sharing activities to improve multilateral interdiction efforts."[18]

The Bush and Obama administrations cited the PSI as successful in combatting trade in illicit WMD materials, but evidence is difficult to obtain because most interdictions are not made public. There are also limitations to the program. PSI participants have no legal authority to interdict vessels at sea beyond Security Council Resolution 1540, the UN Convention on the Law of the Sea, the Convention on the Suppression of Unlawful Acts (acts that may threaten the safety of maritime navigation), and bilateral agreements between themselves. Most interdictions, however, occur while vessels are in port, not at sea.

The informal nature of the PSI also can pose problems. It has no independent budget, coordinating mechanism, or legal framework to obligate members' participation. The Obama administration sought to rectify this problem. Obama declared, "We must . . . build on our efforts to break up black markets, detect and intercept materials in transit, and use financial tools to disrupt this dangerous trade. Because this threat will be lasting, we should come together to turn efforts such as the Proliferation Security Initiative . . . into durable international institutions."[19] Those who support institutionalizing the PSI believe doing so will enhance cooperation in intelligence gathering and enforcement. Critics counter that the absence of an institutional structure is an asset, giving the PSI flexibility to respond to threats.

Fissile Material Cut-Off Treaty (FMCT) The **Fissile Material Cut-Off Treaty**, proposed by President Bill Clinton in 1993, would ban production of fissile materials—those elements capable of sustaining "an explosive fission chain reaction." Highly enriched uranium and plutonium are fissile materials, but, except for trace amounts of plutonium, they are not found in nature. The proposed treaty would not address existing stockpiles, most of which are owned by nuclear-weapons states, but would limit the ability of the legal nuclear-weapons states (America, Russia, China, Britain, France) and non-NPT nuclear states (Israel, India, Pakistan, North Korea) to produce new fissile materials for weapons use. (The NPT had banned the production of fissile materials for weapons in NNWS NPT parties.) Of the five NPT nuclear-weapons states, all but China indicated they had ceased producing fissile material for nuclear weapons. De facto nuclear powers India and Pakistan continue to produce HEU and plutonium.

Efforts to negotiate the FMCT have continued since the 1990s, but progress has been slow owing to the opposition of key states. Pakistan, for instance, opposed the treaty because it would not address India's existing stockpile. The Bush administration was willing to participate in negotiations but expressed concern that "effective verification . . . would require an inspection regime so extensive that it could compromise key signatories' core national security interests and so costly that many countries will be hesitant to accept it."[20] President Obama reversed this position, announcing his intention to pursue the FMCT.

Although there is bipartisan congressional support for a treaty, there is also opposition to Obama's broader nuclear weapons agenda, and as long as Pakistan maintains its objections, the matter is moot.

Preventing Proliferation by Force: The Persian Gulf War

When other efforts prove inadequate, force becomes an option to prevent proliferation. America's 2002 National Security Strategy was controversial for advocating active defenses, including preemptive and preventive war, against WMD threats.

When Iraq invaded Kuwait in 1990, U.S. leaders were already concerned about Iraq's WMD. After the war, a UN Special Commission (UNSCOM) was established to enforce Security Council Resolution 687 (1991), requiring Iraq to "unconditionally accept, under international supervision, the destruction, removal or rendering harmless of its weapons of mass destruction, ballistic missiles with a range over 150 kilometers, and related production facilities and equipment."[21] It also established a system to monitor Iraqi compliance with the ban on these weapons. Inspectors discovered and dismantled facilities that Iraq had tried to hide.

Between 1992 and 2003, there was continual friction between Iraq and UNSCOM regarding access to Iraqi military facilities and production sites. In 1993, President Clinton ordered strikes on an Iraqi intelligence center because of a reported assassination plot against former president George H. W. Bush and on Iraq's air defenses after Iraqi troops moved into Iraq's Kurdish region. Security Council Resolution 1051 (1996) established a system to monitor Iraq's exports and imports related to WMD, and Resolution 1284 (1999) established the **UN Monitoring, Verification, and Inspection Commission** (UNMOVIC) to verify Baghdad's compliance with its obligation to eliminate chemical and biological weapons and illegal missiles, while the IAEA did the same regarding nuclear weapons. In the face of Iraqi obstruction, America and Britain launched three days of air and cruise missile strikes ("Operation Desert Fox") in 1998 against Iraqi targets believed to contribute to Iraq's ability to produce, store, and deliver WMD. Thereafter, Iraqi officials ceased cooperating with UN inspectors, and they were withdrawn until Iraq allowed their return in 2002.

Washington's concern that Baghdad was hiding WMD or the means to produce them served as a principal justification for the invasion of Iraq in 2003. At U.S. insistence, the Security Council unanimously adopted Resolution 1441 in November 2002, declaring that Iraq "has been and remains in material breach" of its previous commitments and was being given "a final opportunity to comply with its disarmament obligations" and set up "an enhanced inspection regime." The Security Council also demanded that Baghdad provide "a currently accurate, full, and complete declaration of all aspects of its programs to develop chemical, biological, and nuclear weapons, ballistic missiles, and other delivery systems" and provide "immediate, unimpeded, unconditional, and unrestricted access to any and all, including underground, areas, facilities, buildings, equipment, records, and means of transport which they wish to inspect, as well as immediate, unimpeded, unrestricted, and private access to all officials and other persons whom UNMOVIC or the IAEA wish to interview." The resolution warned Iraq that, in the event of noncompliance, it would "face serious consequences as a result of its continued violations of its obligations."[22] The following year, America, Britain, and Spain proposed an additional resolution, explicitly endorsing the use of force against Iraq, but it was withdrawn after it became clear it lacked majority support and would be vetoed by Russia, China, and/or France.

Washington claimed Resolution 1441 with its threat of "serious consequences" was sufficient to authorize the invasion, a claim that even some of America's closest allies rejected. In September 2004, UN Secretary-General Kofi Annan declared that the invasion "was not in conformity with the UN charter from our point of view, from the charter point of view, it was illegal."[23] Thus, America's 2006 National Security Strategy was revised to stipulate, "Our strong preference and common practice is to address proliferation concerns through international diplomacy, in concert with key allies and regional partners. If necessary, however, under long-standing principles of self-defense, we do not rule out the use of force before attacks occur, even if uncertainty remains as to the time and place of the enemy's attack."[24] In 2010, President Obama reaffirmed that force would be used after other options were exhausted, noting that if Iran and North Korea "ignore their international obligations, we will pursue multiple means to increase their isolation and bring them into compliance with international nonproliferation norms."[25]

Later it was discovered that Iraq did *not* have WMD, nor, according to the U.S.-led Iraq Survey Group, had it worked to develop them after the early 1990s. UNSCOM, UNMOVIC, and the IAEA had been successful, and the reason they could not find Iraq's WMD was that they no longer existed.

America's North Korea Predicament

North Korea has posed a challenge for U.S. nuclear proliferation policy for decades. Its nuclear-weapons program, which involves developing nuclear warheads and the missiles to deliver them, is cloaked in secrecy. American intelligence first detected that North Korea was developing nuclear weapons in the 1980s, and since then, the Clinton, Bush, and Obama administrations have been preoccupied with finding a mix of sanctions and rewards to curb that country's nuclear ambitions.

North Korean President Kim Il-sung began to seek nuclear weapons after the Korean War ended in 1953, leaving Korea divided at the 38th parallel, South Korea allied with America and the North allied with China and the USSR. Washington introduced nuclear weapons under American control into South Korea shortly after the armistice, and, by the 1960s, U.S. strategy to defend its ally relied heavily on nuclear weapons. Kim viewed an independent nuclear capability as a way to deter America and assure North Korea's security. Soviet assistance was crucial to its early proliferation efforts, beginning with a 1959 bilateral agreement on the peaceful use of nuclear energy. In 1974, Pyongyang joined the IAEA, and, in 1985, it acceded to the NPT because Moscow had made NPT membership a condition for its offer to provide nuclear reactors to produce electricity. North Korea's nuclear program continued into the 1980s but with little additional foreign assistance. During this time, its efforts focused on producing plutonium necessary to fuel a nuclear device.

North Korea emerged on America's proliferation agenda in 1992 when the IAEA found evidence that it had more plutonium than it had declared. The agency requested special inspections to determine how much plutonium North Korea had produced since 1989, but Pyongyang refused. As the crisis unfolded, North Korea refused to allow IAEA inspections of its nuclear facilities and the fuel rods it had removed from its Yongbyon reactor. Accusing the Clinton administration of appeasement, U.S. hardliners pressed for action to end North Korea's nuclear program, but Kim Il-sung only agreed to halt his country's nuclear activities after China notified him it would not veto economic sanctions that America had proposed in the Security Council. Pyongyang's decision opened the possibility of direct negotiations with Washington.

Fissile Materials

A nuclear weapon requires a fissile material to produce a nuclear blast (material capable of starting and sustaining a fission chain reaction in which atoms are split by neutrons). Uranium and plutonium are radioactive heavy elements that suit this purpose. Little plutonium is found in nature. Uranium is more readily available, but not all uranium is fissile. The most common form of uranium, U-238 (the number indicates its atomic weight), is stable, and its atoms do not easily split to produce nuclear energy, but a rare form of uranium, U-235, will split under the right conditions. For weapons purposes, naturally occurring uranium must be converted to plutonium or enriched to have a high proportion of the U-235 isotope. Fissile plutonium that is produced as Uranium-238 absorbs neutrons—a process that occurs when uranium is used as fuel in a nuclear reactor. Alternatively, centrifuges can be used to separate the fissile uranium from the (unspent) U-238, thereby enriching the uranium. Reactor-grade uranium, necessary to fuel a nuclear power plant, is only 3 to 5 percent U-235, but weapons-grade uranium, also known as highly enriched uranium, is 90 percent U-235. Thus, HEU requires thousands of fragile centrifuges, making it expensive and difficult to produce.

In 1994, Kim's son and successor, Kim Jong-il, accepted the U.S.-North Korean Agreed Framework. Pyongyang agreed to shut down and dismantle its gas graphite reactors that could produce weapons-grade plutonium, freeze and dismantle its plutonium reprocessing facilities, and allow the IAEA to monitor these activities and implement a safeguards agreement for inspection of related facilities. In return, North Korea would receive two proliferation-resistant light water reactors from an international consortium, fuel oil to replace energy production lost by closing its other reactors, and a formal assurance that Washington would not threaten or use nuclear weapons against North Korea.

Nevertheless, in 1995 Pyongyang denied IAEA inspectors permission to measure the amount of plutonium in spent fuel rods or the liquid waste at its reprocessing facility. American intelligence agencies continued to monitor installations that they suspected were nuclear weapons–related facilities, and North Korea continued to develop its long-range missile capability, testing an intermediate-range missile—the Taepo-dong 1—that demonstrated it had the technology to develop ICBMs able to reach U.S. territory. Negotiations stalled thereafter owing to U.S. concern that North Korea was building a secret nuclear facility.

After a three-month review, Washington offered to implement the Agreed Framework, but after George W. Bush's 2002 State of the Union address in which he labeled North Korea, Iraq, and Iran an "axis of evil, arming to threaten the peace of the world,"[26] Pyongyang again refused to allow inspections of its facilities, and each party accused the other of breaking the agreement. North Korea expelled nuclear inspectors and resumed reprocessing plutonium and, in January 2003, announced its intention to withdraw from the NPT, effectively terminating the Agreed Framework.

Negotiations shifted to a multilateral forum, the Six-Party Talks, involving North Korea, South Korea, Japan, China, Russia, and America. The Six-Party Talks were a series of negotiations held intermittently since 2003 hosted by China. This strategy has had both costs and benefits in that its success hinges not only on North Korea's interests but also on those of China, Japan, and South Korea. China has sought an outcome that maximize stability on its border. Japan has tried to link the talks to the issue of Japanese citizens abducted by North Korea and Pyongyang's provocative missile tests over the Sea of Japan, and South Korea has oscillated between hawkish and dovish policies toward Pyongyang.

In 2005, the talks produced an agreement by which North Korea would abandon its nuclear program, return to the NPT, and allow IAEA inspectors into the country in return for food and energy aid. Talks quickly broke down, however, over U.S. efforts to put financial pressure on the regime, and, in 2006, North Korea tested a long-range missile and its first nuclear device. In 2007, China persuaded Pyongyang to return to the table. This time, talks produced a denuclearization plan, and North Korea began dismantling its Yongbyong nuclear reactor with U.S. assistance. As North Korea made additional concessions, the Bush administration eased sanctions, removing the country from its list of state sponsors of terrorism, but Pyongyang still refused to agree to a new verification protocol. Tensions escalated again, and by late 2008, North Korea had restarted its nuclear program and refused access to inspectors.

While campaigning for president, Barack Obama promised he would be willing to engage North Korea on a bilateral basis, which Pyongyang had long sought. North Korea's persistent hostility toward America and South Korea made progress difficult. It continued to conduct missile tests and tested another nuclear weapon in 2009. In March 2010, a North Korean submarine torpedoed a South Korean navy corvette, and in November, Pyongyang revealed to U.S. experts that it was trying to enrich

MAP 4.2   North Korean Nuclear Enrichment and Test Sites

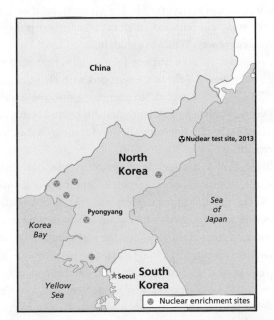

Sources: Data from http://www.atomicarchive.com/Reports/Northkorea/NKFacilities_static.shtml (enrichment sites) and http://www.stripes.com/news/pacific/n-korea-says-it-tested-miniaturized-more-powerful-nuclear-bomb-1.207552 (test sites).

uranium, offering the possibility of another fuel source for nuclear weapons, again ending the possibility of fruitful talks.

For years, observers speculated that North Korea's provocative rhetoric and threats to "go nuclear" were intended to attract international attention and economic assistance. Analysts, however, now believe that North Korea sought to become a full-fledged nuclear power. Following the collapse of a 2012 agreement that placed a moratorium on nuclear tests and uranium enrichment and resumed IAEA inspections in exchange for U.S. "nutritional assistance," North Korea specialist Victor Cha argued there was no longer any reason to believe North Korea was trying to trade nuclear weapons for aid. Instead, it wanted both.[27]

Relations with Pyongyang further deteriorated with North Korea's third nuclear test in 2013. It was unclear whether it had detonated a plutonium or uranium bomb. Previous tests were of plutonium bombs, but if the device was uranium-based, North Korea's arsenal had become more dangerous because it had two fuel sources. Uranium enrichment technology, moreover, would make it possible for Pyongyang to build a bomb compact enough to fit on an ICBM. And even as Washington was negotiating with Iran to prevent additional proliferation, North Korea was expanding its nuclear arsenal to the point where it might no longer be possible to halt its nuclear program.

Managing Iran's Nuclear Ambitions

Iran also poses a serious proliferation challenge. Mohammad Reza Shah Pahlavi, a U.S. ally, launched Iran's nuclear program in the 1950s. After Iran signed the NPT, it became a full participant in the nonproliferation regime. By the mid-1970s, however, the issue of control over uranium reprocessing had become a source of contention in U.S.-Iranian relations. The shah sought to turn Iran into a powerful modern state and pursued an ambitious nuclear policy to enable the country to produce electricity from nuclear power. While the shah insisted he did not seek nuclear weapons, he also asserted Iran's right to enrich its own nuclear fuel, a claim that contemporary Iranian leaders continue to make. U.S. officials viewed Tehran's intentions with skepticism, especially since no one in Tehran had "explained" how Iran expected "to absorb 23,000 megawatts-electric of additional power within the next 20 years."[28] Although Washington supported Iran's efforts to develop nuclear energy, it also tried to prevent Iran from pursuing fuel-cycle research that would give Tehran its own plutonium reprocessing capability.[29]

After the shah's overthrow, the Islamic regime of Ayatollah Ruhollah Khomeini resurrected Iran's nuclear program. In 1984, the Isfahan Nuclear Research Center opened with China's assistance and received aid from North Korea and Pakistani nuclear scientist Abdul Qadeer Khan's nuclear black market network. Iran's nuclear program accelerated when Russia agreed in 1994 to provide Iran with two 950-megawatt light-water reactors at Bushehr and the fuel to run them. In a separate secret agreement, Russia offered Iran a research reactor, a fuel fabrication plant, and a gas centrifuge facility to be used for peaceful, commercial purposes. Despite delays, the Bushehr plant was opened in 2011.

Iranian officials insisted that nuclear power was needed to meet growing domestic demand for energy. They had long insisted Iran was in compliance with the NPT, having declared all of its nuclear material and allowed inspectors to monitor its nuclear facilities, but the IAEA was unable to determine that all of Iran's nuclear material was intended for peaceful purposes. Was Iran seeking to develop nuclear

Pro-nuclear Iranian
demonstrators

Atta Kenare/AFP/Getty Images

weapons, as U.S. officials believed, or was it trying to develop commercial nuclear energy, as Iranian officials claimed? Resolving such questions was complicated by mistrust between the two governments that had severed diplomatic relations after Iran's 1979 revolution.

In 2002, it was revealed that Iran was pursuing a clandestine nuclear program involving several undeclared nuclear facilities, including a uranium enrichment facility and research laboratory under construction at Natanz and a heavy water reactor at Arak. The safeguard agreements negotiated with the IAEA in 1974 had only authorized its inspectors to monitor declared nuclear facilities. Moreover, countries were not required to report facilities until six months before nuclear material was introduced—at the time of the revelation there was no nuclear material at Natanz. Iran's efforts to conceal these facilities seemed to confirm U.S. suspicions that Iran sought to acquire nuclear weapons. The IAEA began to investigate Iran's nuclear program and called for a suspension of its uranium enrichment activities while the investigation was underway.

For a time, it seemed Iran might be willing to prove its peaceful intentions by reaching a voluntary agreement with France, Germany, and Britain to halt enrichment activities and sign an additional protocol with the IAEA granting the agency authority to inspect a wider range of undeclared nuclear-related facilities. It is unclear whether Iran's cooperation at the time reflected the policies of reformist President Mohammad Khatami or was a reaction to America's 2003 invasion of Iraq. But Iran's accommodating stance only lasted until 2005, when the George W. Bush administration pressed Iran to abandon all enrichment activities, and Khatami was succeeded by Mahmoud Ahmadinejad, a hardliner under whom enrichment activity was resumed. In the face of Iran's noncompliance, the IAEA referred the matter to the Security Council in 2006, after which Iran refused to implement the additional protocol. Later that year,

MAP 4.3   Iranian Nuclear Facilities

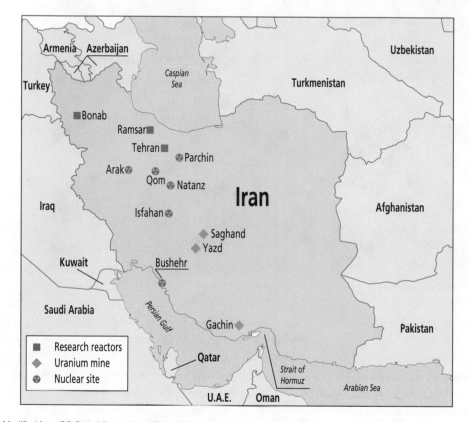

Source: Modified from *CQ Global Researcher*, "Rising Tension in Iran," February 7, 2012, p. 60.

China, France, Germany, Russia, Britain, and America—the **P5+1 group** referring to the five permanent members of the Security Council plus Germany—offered incentives to Tehran to address IAEA concerns.

President Bush tried to halt Iran's progress toward a nuclear-weapons capability by combining sanctions and refusing face-to-face talks with Iranian officials until Iran suspended uranium enrichment. As this proved unsuccessful, in July 2008, Washington altered its policy and signaled it was committed to a diplomatic path. From Iran's perspective, it was too little too late.

Although Barack Obama had run for office promising unconditional dialogue with Iran, events in 2009 made talks politically impossible during his first administration. These events included Tehran's manipulation of Iran's 2009 presidential election and its repression of the protests that followed, its admission that a new uranium enrichment facility was being built at Fordo, and tests of medium- and long-range missiles that threatened Israel and U.S. bases in the Persian Gulf. Instead, Washington pursued a two-track policy, participating in the P5+1 multilateral effort and imposing sanctions to pressure Tehran to cease enriching uranium. Iran refused, and, in 2010, America and the UN imposed unprecedented sanctions. A year later, the IAEA issued a report containing "credible evidence" that Iran was conducting nuclear weapons research, including work on fast-acting detonators and an indigenous nuclear weapon design.[30] Washington ramped up sanctions and, as America's 2012 presidential campaign began, pressure to consider a military response from both congressional conservatives and Israeli leaders mounted. Obama insisted "diplomacy backed by pressure" would work, but potential military action remained "on the table."

Washington combined several instruments to cripple Iran's nuclear program and induce Iranian leaders to participate in multilateral talks. It imposed robust sanctions to punish those who assisted Iran's development of WMD or advanced conventional weapons or invested in industries with dual use applications, including Iran's energy sector. Multilateral pressure steadily increased after 2006 when the first UN sanctions were imposed. By 2013, six Security Council resolutions had demanded that Iran cease enriching uranium, open its facilities to international inspection, and participate in multilateral talks. Several presidential executive orders and congressional acts provided legal authority for sanctions that were implemented by the Department of State's Office of Economic Sanctions Policy and Implementation and the Treasury Department's Office of Foreign Assets Control. U.S. legislation aimed to prevent the development of WMD and advanced conventional weapons, deny Iran access to materials to advance its nuclear program, ban trade and investment with Iran, and freeze the foreign assets of those believed to be supporting Iran's nuclear activities. After 2010, sanctions also targeted Iran's oil sector by penalizing financial institutions that conducted oil transactions with Iran.

The European Union imposed similar sanctions. In July 2012, it embargoed Iranian oil and prohibited European companies from insuring Iranian oil shipments. By mid-2013, the EU embargo had pushed Iran's oil exports to their lowest level in decades. Washington credited the sanctions regime, which has cost Iran billions in oil revenue and investment in its oil sector and caused soaring inflation, unemployment, and public debt and a steep decline in the value of its currency, with bringing Iran to the negotiating table.

In addition, America's CIA tried unsuccessfully to sabotage Iran's nuclear program by feeding faulty parts into its supply chain. In 2006, a program named "Olympic Games" pursued a new strategy. Along with a secret Israeli military unit known as 8200, NSA cyber-experts designed a sophisticated computer worm that instructed infected computers to accelerate abruptly or slow down, thereby making highly sensitive centrifuges used to enrich uranium in Iran's Natanz facility spin out of control while showing the control room that all was normal. In mid-2010, an error in the computer code allowed the worm to spread beyond Iran. Computer security experts identified the worm as a cyber-weapon called Stuxnet. Stuxnet was originally believed to have destroyed a fifth of Iran's nuclear centrifuges and delayed its progress toward building nuclear weapons by several years, but some analysts think its results were limited. Iran, for its part, also developed sophisticated cyber-weapons that are more usable and deniable than WMD.

The surprising election of moderate cleric Hassan Rouhani as Iran's president in June 2013 raised hopes that Iran might become more conciliatory. While condemning America's "warmongering pressure groups" in a UN speech, Rouhani insisted that Iran would never seek nuclear weapons and expressed hope that "we can arrive at a framework to manage our differences."[31] As Rouhani prepared to leave New York, he asked to speak with President Obama. Obama phoned Rouhani, and their brief conversation led them to agree that their governments should negotiate a deal over Iran's uranium enrichment program.

Obama observed, "The very fact that this was the first communication between an American and Iranian president since 1979 underscores the deep mistrust between our countries. . . . But it also indicates the prospect of moving beyond that difficult history."[32]

Following the historic conversation, Iran resumed negotiations with the IAEA and the P5+1. Initial talks achieved an agreement called the Joint Plan of Action (2013), containing an interim agreement to curtail Iran's nuclear activities in return for $7 billion in sanctions relief and a framework for reaching a comprehensive agreement by July 20, 2014. Iran agreed to eliminate its stockpile of 20 percent enriched uranium and take measures to ensure that existing equipment would not be used to enrich more uranium at that level. IAEA inspectors were authorized to visit enrichment facilities in Natanz and Fordo daily and gain access to centrifuge-production facilities. As the arrangement went into effect in January 2014, the IAEA's deputy director general indicated that "we have a very robust system in place with Iran"[33] to ensure its compliance.

Critics of the Joint Plan of Action believed Iran was already close to achieving a "critical capability," the point at which it could produce enough weapons-grade uranium from low-enriched uranium for one or more atom bombs without being detected. Congressional critics objected that the agreement allowed Iran to continue enriching uranium to 5 percent to produce fuel for civilian reactors. Although not weapons grade, such fuel, when enriched to 20 percent, can quickly be enriched to the 90 percent purity needed for nuclear weapons. Congressional hardliners believed Iran could not be trusted and had a record of deception. Others expressed concern that the deal benefitted Iran disproportionately by easing sanctions without requiring a comprehensive agreement to end uranium enrichment, limiting America's options in future negotiations. Critics were also concerned that sanctions would be difficult to reimpose if a comprehensive agreement were not reached. Administration officials insisted that sanctions would continue to pressure Iran, with Secretary of State Kerry contending that the sanctions relief was "just a drop in the bucket compared to the roughly $100 billion in foreign exchange holdings that are inaccessible to Iran."[34] Democrats, for the most part, applauded the agreement as a step in the right direction, and President Obama declared, "For the first time in nearly a decade, we have halted the progress of the Iranian nuclear program, and key parts of the program will be rolled back."[35]

U.S. allies Israel and Saudi Arabia condemned the deal. Israeli Prime Minister Benjamin Netanyahu insisted the deal "was a historic mistake," and that "for the first time, the leading nations in the world agreed to the enrichment of uranium in Iran by ignoring the decisions of the (UN) Security Council that they themselves led."[36] The Saudis, Sunni foes of Shia Iran, feared the deal would bolster Iran's status in the region. The deal so angered the Saudis that King Salman along with several other Arab leaders refused to attend a meeting at Camp David in May 2015 to smooth over differences with President Obama over policies toward Iran, sending instead lesser officials. At that meeting, the Saudis and several of their smaller Arab allies declared that if Iran were allowed to continue enriching uranium, they would also develop a similar capability.

Iran's opaque decision-making process complicated efforts to understand its intentions. The president is Iran's highest elected office but is constitutionally subordinate to Iran's Supreme Leader, Ayatollah Ali Khamenei. Shifts in nuclear policy have been attributed to the Supreme Leader, who insisted Iran had no interest in acquiring nuclear weapons, which he claimed to regard as a crime against humanity. In the days leading up to January 2014 negotiations over implementation, Ayatollah

Khamenei broadcast a list of grievances against America and denied that sanctions had made Iran negotiate. President Rouhani also sent mixed signals, promising at the 2014 World Economic Forum in Davos, Switzerland, that Iran had no desire to acquire nuclear weapons but would pursue "constructive engagement" as long as world leaders respected Iran. He also insisted that nuclear enrichment for commercial energy was Iran's sovereign right.

Nonetheless, by the July 2014 deadline, progress had been made, including stronger IAEA oversight and inspections and modifications to Iran's Arak heavy-water reactor to reduce its plutonium production. Major issues, however, remained unresolved, and the talks were extended to allow negotiators to decide how much existing uranium-enrichment infrastructure Iran would have to destroy and for how long, and what kind of research its scientists could pursue. While negotiations continued, America agreed to give Iran access to $2.8 billion in frozen assets, and Tehran agreed to dilute more of its uranium stocks or turn it into reactor fuel.

Then, in April 2015, the talks produced unexpectedly detailed "Parameters for a Joint Comprehensive Plan of Action" for a final agreement to be completed by June 30, 2015, to remain in force for 10 to 15 years. Negotiators admitted that details had to be worked out and differences remained. Both sides recognized they would have to sell the deal to domestic hardliners. Among the parameters, Iran agreed to retain 6,104 installed less-advanced centrifuges (more than Washington had sought) of the 19,000-plus it had, with all its centrifuges accessible to IAEA inspection. Tehran also agreed to reduce its stockpile of low-enriched uranium from 8 tons to 600 pounds and, while retaining centrifuges at its underground Fordo site, these would not be used for uranium enrichment for 15 years. IAEA inspectors would have access to Tehran's major nuclear facilities as well as its uranium mines and enjoy the right to investigate suspicious sites throughout Iran. Iran's Arak facility would be redesigned to prevent production of plutonium that could be used in nuclear weapons. In return, the P5+1 negotiators agreed to suspend sanctions in stages. Iran would retain all of its nuclear facilities, thereby confirming its right to develop peaceful nuclear energy.

Secretary of State Kerry and Energy Secretary Ernest J. Moniz, a nuclear physicist, contended that any clandestine cheating by Iran would be detected, and the agreement would prevent a "breakout" time of less than a year for Iran to acquire enriched uranium for a nuclear weapon. President Obama described it as "a historic understanding with Iran" that "cuts off every pathway" for Iran to develop nuclear weapons, while the former chief inspector of the IAEA declared, "It appears to be a fairly comprehensive deal with most important parameters," but that "Iran maintains enrichment capacity which will be beyond its near-term needs."[37] For President Obama, the deal was a triumph. "Right now, he has no foreign policy legacy," declared Cliff Kupchan, an Iran analyst. "A deal with Iran and the ensuing transformation of politics in the Middle East would provide one of the more robust foreign policy legacies of any recent presidencies."[38] Rhetorically, the president asked, "Do you really think that this verifiable deal, if fully implemented, backed by the world's major powers, is a worse option than the risk of another war in the Middle East," adding that if Congress blocked the deal "then it's the United States that will be blamed for the failure of diplomacy."[39]

Finally, after two years of negotiations, U.S. and Iranian officials announced in July 2015 that they had reached a deal. The Joint Comprehensive Plan of Action (JCPOA) did not stray far from the agreement of the previous April. Over the next 10 to 15 years, Iran agreed to operate only 6,104 less-advanced centrifuges, cut its stockpile of low-enriched uranium to 600 pounds, limit its research and development of advanced centrifuges, and to redesign its heavy-water reactor at Arak and refrain from building new heavy water reactors. Iran also agreed to continuous monitoring of enrichment and centrifuge production sites for 20 to 25 years and wider permanent inspections (consistent with its NPT obligations). The United States, in turn, agreed to implement sanctions relief once Iran took verifiable steps to meet its obligations. Within days of the agreement, the Security Council passed resolution 2231 endorsing the nuclear deal and arranging to lift UN sanctions once the deal was implemented.

Supporters viewed the deal as a "net plus," arguing that no better deal was to be found and that it had the potential to "reduce the risk of a destabilizing nuclear competition in a troubled region and head off a potentially catastrophic military conflict over Iran's nuclear program."[40] Moreover, they argued, sustained cooperation over 10 to 15 years could yield long-term stability by ending Iran's isolation. Opponents accused Obama of retreating from his goal of completely dismantling Iran's nuclear infrastructure and attacked the deal as too generous, fearing it would undermine nonproliferation, spark a nuclear arms race, and by easing sanctions enable Iran to ramp up support for regional actors like Hezbollah and Syria. Nonetheless, by September, Obama had secured enough votes to ensure the Senate would not block the agreement.

Syria and Chemical Weapons

Until recently, chemical weapons were not as central as nuclear weapons on Washington's nonproliferation agenda. America's intelligence community believed for years that Syria had an active chemical-weapons program. In 2012, allegations emerged that Syria was using chemical weapons against civilians in its civil war, and, in August, President Obama indicated that chemical weapons were a "red line" (chapter 10). When chemical attacks were reported in neighborhoods in Aleppo and Damascus, Syria's two principal cities, in March 2013, Syrian President Bashar al-Assad denied the allegations, claiming that rebels were responsible and asking for UN investigation.

Thus, UN Secretary General Ban Ki-moon announced that the UN, along with the World Health Organization and the Organization for the Prohibition of Chemical Weapons (OPCW), would conduct an investigation. This went nowhere after Assad denied the UN-led team permission to enter Syria. U.S. lawmakers pressed Obama to pursue limited military actions "that would require neither putting U.S. troops on the ground nor acting unilaterally."[41] In testimony before Congress, however, Ambassador Robert S. Ford declared that America still lacked strong evidence that chemical weapons had been used. Without such evidence, the president was unwilling to act. It was not until June 2013 that Washington concluded that Syrian forces had indeed used chemical weapons.

In late July, Assad finally allowed UN inspectors to enter Syria, and, while the UN team was in the country, a crisis erupted with accusations of a new, much more massive gas attack on civilians in rebel-controlled areas around Damascus. This was recognized as the most deadly chemical weapons attack since Saddam Hussein had used chemical weapons against his Kurdish population in 1988.

Debate again raged over who was to blame, the government or its foes. The Security Council debated the crisis but was unable to reach agreement, with China and Russia blocking approval for military strikes. U.S. officials cited evidence that the Syrian regime had been responsible for the attack and then tried to cover it up, and that it had "used chemical weapons over the last year primarily to gain the upper hand or break a stalemate in areas where it has struggled to seize and hold strategically valuable territory."[42]

Syria and the Chemical Weapons Taboo

The belief that chemical weapons are so inhumane led to their prohibition. The origins of this taboo date back to the 1925 Geneva Protocol that prohibited the use of chemical weapons in war and was reinforced in the 1993 Chemical Weapons Convention that outlawed the development, production, stockpiling, transfer, and use of these weapons.

Supporters of the taboo insisted that if violations were left unpunished, chemical weapons would become widely used, causing indiscriminate harm to civilians. Others countered that chemical weapons were not weapons of *mass* destruction, as "a single nuclear weapon can indeed inflict massive destruction; a single chemical weapon cannot."[43] America, they argued, should not undertake a destabilizing military intervention to uphold a taboo against weapons that really are not any more dangerous than conventional weapons—even if they are more "repugnant."[44]

Others viewed both perspectives as mistaken. The legal prohibition against chemical weapons existed because those weapons violate the norm of civilian protection: "Civilians died because Syria violated the taboo against deliberate attacks on civilians"[45]—by chemical *and* conventional means. From this perspective, America should have intervened to protect civilians in Syria long before.

On August 30, 2013, President Obama argued for action "to hold the Assad regime accountable for their use of chemical weapons, deter this kind of behavior, and degrade their capacity to carry it out."[46] As Congress debated whether to intervene in Syria, the president tried to build an international coalition at the G-20 summit in Russia. Only France, Turkey, Canada, and Saudi Arabia supported military strikes against Syria.

A breakthrough occurred when Secretary Kerry suggested off-the-cuff that military force might be avoided if President Assad surrendered his stockpile of chemical weapons. Russian Foreign Minister Sergei Lavrov quickly proposed to have Syria place its chemical weapons under international control and then destroyed. Syria welcomed the proposal, indicating its acceptance of the Chemical Weapons Convention, and international support rapidly grew, with Britain, France, the UN, and even U.S. lawmakers supporting the plan. Still unsure whether the proposal was a delaying tactic on the part of Russia and Syria, Obama asked Congress to delay voting on military action until Secretary Kerry could meet with his Russian counterpart to reach a deal. The president's willingness to abandon the military option in response to Russia's offer led to domestic criticism of Obama's strategy as vacillating and inconsistent and as letting others, notably Russia's President Vladimir Putin, shape U.S. policy.

Putin sought to influence U.S. opinion in a letter in the *New York Times* arguing against airstrikes on the grounds that Assad's foes had used the weapons, and that military intervention would fuel terrorism, undermine diplomatic efforts to halt Iran's nuclear program, and "could throw the entire system of international law and order out of balance."[47] In fact, U.S. public opinion was already opposed to airstrikes. Support for intervention broke along partisan lines, with most Republicans and Independents opposed to intervention and Democrats divided.[48] Most congressional Republicans were opposed to military intervention, because they either were opposed in principle or did not believe that the president had made a compelling case. Liberal Democrats were also skeptical, recalling intelligence errors that had led to the 2003 Iraq war.

The military option was taken off the table when U.S. and Russian officials in September revealed their Framework Agreement for Elimination of Syrian Chemical Weapons, a plan for a full accounting of Syria's chemical-weapons stockpile and dismantling those weapons. Responsibility for eliminating Syria's chemical weapons was given to the OPCW, "the implementing body of the Chemical Weapons Convention (CWC)"[49] that required destruction of such weapons. Syria had a week to submit a comprehensive inventory of its chemical-weapons stockpile and give OPCW inspectors access to all chemical-weapons sites. Initial inspections would be completed by November, and Syria's ability to make chemical weapons would be ended and all chemical weapons removed or destroyed by mid-2014.[50]

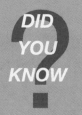

DID YOU KNOW?

The OPCW

On the same day the Security Council approved a plan to deploy a joint UN-OPCW mission to oversee the destruction of Syria's arsenal of chemical weapons, the OPCW was awarded the Nobel Peace Prize for previous efforts to pursue chemical-weapons disarmament.

Syria had to remove its stockpile by February 5, 2014, and have its weapons destroyed by June 30. The Syrian government missed the February deadline, blaming weather, civil war, and the dangerous journey along the highway connecting its facilities and its port in Latakia. The last of its chemical weapons were out of the country by June and shipped to facilities in America, Britain, and Finland (via Italy) for disposal after a U.S. vessel, the *MV Cape Ray,* had disarmed them. By August 18, Syria's deadliest chemical weapons had been destroyed, an accomplishment lauded by President Obama that "advances our collective goal to ensure that the Assad regime cannot use its chemical arsenal against the Syrian people and sends a clear message that the use of these abhorrent weapons has consequences and will not be tolerated by the international community."[51]

Questions, however, persist about whether Syria declared all its stockpiles of chemical weapons. Until policymakers are certain of Syria's compliance with the 2013 agreement, that country will remain on Washington's nonproliferation agenda.

NONPROLIFERATION AND THE FUTURE

Washington has several options regarding WMD proliferation. The most permissive would allow additional states to acquire nuclear, chemical, or biological weapons whereas the most restrictive would seek to prevent any additional states from acquiring WMD and reverse proliferation wherever

MAP 4.4   Route of Syrian Chemical Weapons to *MV Cape Ray*

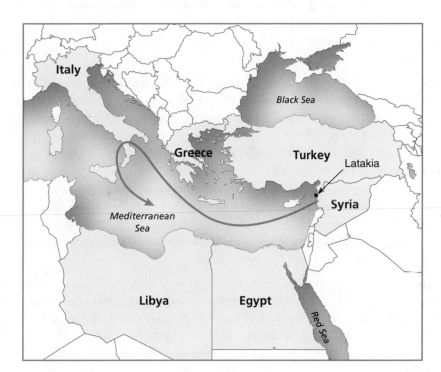

Source: Data from BBC, "US 'Concern' at Syria Chemical Weapons Delay," January 30, 2014, http://www.bbc.co.uk/news/world-middle-east-25968616.

it occurs. Some political scientists argue for a permissive policy on the grounds that proliferation is neither as threatening nor as destabilizing as believed. Allowing proliferation is the most unlikely choice, especially because America's Middle Eastern and Asian allies fear its consequences in their neighborhood. The other end of the spectrum, opposition to any proliferation, also poses problems. Does "halt proliferation," mean preventing new states from acquiring WMD or preventing additional states from achieving a breakout capability, even if they do not actually test weapons? And how far are we prepared to go to reverse proliferation if it occurs? The absolutist position is both difficult and risky, and history suggests that the United States and the global community are unwilling to accept the costs or risks to reverse proliferation.

North Korea

Pyongyang has tested three nuclear weapons since 2006 and is believed to have enough plutonium for four to eight nuclear weapons. It may also be developing a nuclear warhead that could be made small enough to fit on a ballistic missile. Pyongyang has also provided nuclear technologies to anyone who will pay, and given its political and economic isolation, it is likely to continue doing so. Washington and China would like to see a denuclearized North Korea, but American options are limited because North Korea already has a demonstrated nuclear capability. Most options either increase U.S., regional, and global insecurity or run counter to longstanding U.S. nonproliferation policies.

Policy Options

a. *Accept the status quo,* which would face strong domestic political opposition in America and be strategically risky. Even if North Korea cannot yet attack North America, it can strike South Korea and Japan. If Pyongyang acquires a significant nuclear capability, it would be difficult to deter a conventional attack on South Korea. Finally, North Korea remains a long-term threat to America, especially once it succeeds in building long-range ballistic missiles and a small nuclear warhead.

America can probably contain North Korea until the regime collapses or reforms. The regime's collapse has been frequently predicted, and with the death of Kim Jong-il the world hoped that his son, Kim Jong-un, would introduce reforms. Kim Jong-un, however, proved to be just as confrontational as his father. In early 2014, following a series of high-profile purges, including the execution of his uncle, it was clear that the younger Kim was as brutal as his predecessor. In sum, reform is not on the horizon, and the regime is going to do everything it can to prevent collapse.

b. *Preventive military strikes.* The political costs of preventive war and the low probability of success make it unwise to consider preventive strikes. Pyongyang's nuclear facilities are widely scattered, and the likelihood of destroying them all is low. Such attacks would also probably trigger a war on the Korean peninsula that could involve China, North Korea's neighbor and ally. They might also unintentionally legitimize North Korea's nuclear ambitions, justifying the defensive and deterrent goals of its program.

c. *Encourage South Korea and Japan to acquire WMD.* This option contradicts decades of U.S. nonproliferation policy and would undermine the credibility of American efforts to prevent proliferation elsewhere, including Iran. It is hard to predict the outcome of such a policy. It might persuade North Korea to abandon its nuclear program or simply ensure two new nuclear powers in the neighborhood. In either case, were American forces withdrawn from the region, it would be difficult to prevent South Korea and Japan from seeking their own nuclear capability.

d. *Expand sanctions.* North Korea is already among the world's most impoverished countries. A sanctions regime that bans the sale of luxury goods to its leadership and embargoes arms and nuclear and missile technologies has existed for years. It has had little impact, and Pyongyang remains defiant, partly because the leadership cares little about its people's welfare and because the sanctions regime has gaps. China, North Korea's major trading partner, has been reluctant to enforce sanctions that might lead to the collapse of the regime. Beijing fears that if the regime collapsed, it would face an influx of refugees and perhaps a U.S.-allied Korea next door. Expanding sanctions will not suffice to persuade Pyongyang to change course without Chinese participation. The Chinese-North Korean relationship deteriorated after Kim Jong-un came to power, but Beijing continues to aid North Korea although it dislikes Pyongyang's antics.

e. *Economic inducements* have been tried repeatedly, notably in the 1994 Agreed Framework and again in 2012. Every time America, Japan, or South Korea has offered inducements, North Korea has promised to slow its nuclear program only to renege on its commitment.

f. *Multilateral diplomacy* has been tried and failed. The Six-Party Talks collapsed after Pyongyang walked out in 2009. China has tried to get the parties back to the negotiating table, but Washington has been unwilling to return until North Korea honors past commitments. The effort to restart talks is likely to continue, but to succeed, they must include security guarantees for Pyongyang. A credible guarantee that America will not attack North Korea and is prepared to recognize the regime's legitimacy, along with economic aid, might persuade it to abandon its WMD. Such a guarantee would probably require improvements in North Korea's human-rights record and would trigger domestic opposition in both countries.

No single option will be successful. If Washington is to make headway in slowing or reversing North Korea's nuclear progress some combination of these policy options will be required.

Iran

Iran poses a different challenge. As it has not declared a nuclear capability, it remains possible for proliferation to be prevented. But the obstacles are great. As with North Korea, there is a history of deep mistrust on both sides. Iran's domestic politics are complicated and opaque. Even as Iran negotiated with the P5+1, it was unknown how committed the regime was to a nuclear deal. Both Ayatollah Khamenei and President Rouhani have sent mixed signals, but in July 2015, the P5+1 negotiators and Iran announced a final and detailed agreement. Much rides on whether that final agreement is honored and whether Israel and congressional hardliners can be persuaded to accept it. Their earlier uncompromising positions on key issues might have been a negotiating tactic, and, in the end, Iran may not be willing to concede more than it already has. To complicate matters, congressional hardliners believe Iran has not gone as far as it must to prove that its nuclear program is intended for peaceful purposes. U.S. options include allowing Iran to pursue nuclear weapons, prevent it from building nuclear weapons, or prevent it from achieving a breakout capability at which point it would not have nuclear weapons but would have the technology and materials to build them quickly.

Policy Options

a. *Allow Iran to proliferate,* the option least favored by U.S. officials, does have academic proponents. Political scientist Kenneth Waltz argued that those who are afraid of a nuclear Iran have misread the history of the nuclear era and misunderstand Iran's leaders, who neither are irrational nor wish to pursue policies that undermine their regime's security. Although Iranian leaders like former President Mahmoud Ahmadinejad have been confrontational, a nuclear and therefore secure Iran, in Waltz's view, would moderate its belligerence. Iran's entry into the nuclear club need not start a nuclear arms race. "Should Iran become the second Middle Eastern nuclear power since 1945," claimed Waltz, "it would hardly signal the start of a landslide. When Israel acquired the bomb in the 1960s, it was at war with many of its neighbors. Its nuclear arms were a much bigger threat to the Arab world than Iran's program is today. If an atomic Israel did not trigger an arms race then, there is no reason a nuclear Iran should now."[52]

It would, however, be difficult to persuade Israel or domestic critics in Congress to agree to this out-come and would trigger a domestic firestorm on the part of those who would see it as betrayal of a close ally in the region. It would also reduce the credibility of American commitments in the Middle East and Asia, where a belief would take root that Washington could not be trusted to assure security.

b. *Prevent Iran from achieving a breakout capability.* The Iranian situation is complicated by the fact that even if Iran can convince the world it does not presently seek a nuclear weapons program, its uranium enrichment activities may provide it with the expertise and material to allow it to build a bomb quickly should it choose to do so. Some U.S. critics will not be satisfied unless Iran can be prevented from ever acquiring a nuclear capability. They demand an agreement that prohibits Iran from engaging in *any* activities or research that could lead to a breakout capability and an eventual bomb. Their position, advocated by Israeli Prime Minister Netanyahu and hardliners in Congress, is that a comprehensive agreement should include "Four Nos": no uranium enrichment, no stockpile of enriched uranium, no centrifuges, and no Arak heavy water reactor. Those holding this position also insist an agreement must be permanent. This outcome may, however, not be realistic, as Iranian leaders indicated Iran will not surrender a right that they believe is theirs under the NPT. Although U.S. policymakers favor absolutely preventing Iran from acquiring *either* a nuclear weapons capability or a breakout capability, the 2013 interim deal and the 2015 agreement were negotiated to slow Iran's enrichment activities in exchange for easing sanctions. And so, the July 2015 deal effectively lengthens the breakout time to ten years if Iran participates in good faith.

c. *Threaten force to prevent Iran from acquiring nuclear weapons.* The completion of a deal in 2015 effectively removed force from the table. If, however, Iran were to violate the agreement, a mili-tary response might reemerge as a viable option. Throughout the diplomatic negotiations, proponents of a preventive attack believed that "diplomacy remains unlikely to neutralize the threat from Iran's nuclear program,"[53] and sanctions are unlikely to work. At best, argue hardliners, diplomacy will result in an agreement of limited duration. They contend that military action may be the only way to ensure that Iran never acquires a nuclear weapon or a breakout capability and insist that if a strike were launched early enough it would eliminate Iran's nuclear facilities and set Iran's nuclear program back by many years.

Opponents of the military option counter that, at present, there is no hard evidence that Iran is devel-oping nuclear weapons. And if it has a clandestine WMD program, it may also have facilities that U.S. intelligence is unaware of. Precision strikes would be useless when the number and location of targets remain unknown. Thus, an attack would have to be massive, and, even then, it would be impossible to know if all of Iran's nuclear facilities had been destroyed. Iranian leaders would view even a small pre-cision strike as an attack on the regime. The military option would also have spillover effects. Countries like Israel and Saudi Arabia would support U.S. intervention, but Iran could block the Strait of Hormuz, through which oil flows from the Persian Gulf, and could mobilize the region's Shia populations against U.S. interests. Military action would make Iran even more determined to acquire nuclear weapons to deter America from again attacking it, *and* Iran's public would rally around Iranian hardliners in support of this policy. Thus, argues one analyst, "Washington should not choose war when there are still other options, and it should not base its decision to attack on best-case analyses of how it hopes the conflict will turn out."[54]

d. *Expand or renew sanctions.* U.S. sanctions have damaged Iran's economy since Tehran's 1979 revolution. In the 1990s, Washington began applying additional pressure through expanded sanctions to get Tehran to curb its nuclear activities. During the Bush and Obama administrations, sanctions weakened Iran's economy, including its oil sector and its financial institutions, but sanctions alone rarely achieve success. Sanctions appear to work best when coupled with a diplomatic process that clearly defines what behavior by the targeted state will end them. A balance of "sticks" and "carrots" like those in the 2015 framework agreement are more likely than coercion alone to produce change.

Even while administration officials negotiated with Iran, members of Congress debated whether to impose new sanctions on Iran. Argued Senator Robert Menendez (D-NJ), former chair of the Senate Foreign Relations Committee, "Current sanctions brought Iran to the negotiating table and a credible threat of future sanctions will require Iran to cooperate and act in good faith at the negotiating table."[55] A bipartisan bill, the Nuclear Weapon Free Iran Act, would impose new sanctions if negotiations failed and would require that any final agreement preclude Iran's ability to enrich uranium *at any level*—a condition to which Iran will not agree. The bill also offered America's support for Israel should that country take unilateral military action to halt Iran's nuclear program. Initially introduced by 26 senators from both parties, by January 2014, nearly 60 senators had signed on (nearing the level needed for Congress to override a presidential veto). Hardline Iranian parliamentarians responded by drafting their own legislation that would *require* Iran to enrich uranium to near weapons grade if America implemented additional sanctions.

Critics of the bill argued it would sabotage negotiations by moving "the goalposts by making the new sanctions contingent not just on Iran's nuclear activities."[56] Iran could negotiate in good faith to limit or dismantle its nuclear program and *still* be targeted by new sanctions unless it agreed to end uranium enrichment, limit long-range missile development, and sever relations with Hezbollah. In late 2013, ten Senate committee chairs wrote then Senate Majority Leader Harry Reid (D-NV) imploring, "At this time, as negotiations are ongoing, we believe that new sanctions would play into the hands of those in Iran who are most eager to the see the negotiations fail."[57] Iran, critics insist, needs reassurance that America's negotiating position is credible and will not be undermined by Congress, which demanded the right to review any final deal, and that a successful diplomatic outcome will benefit Iran. Otherwise, what incentive would Iran have to negotiate?

Critics also argue there is no clear evidence that sanctions *alone* brought Iran to the negotiating table. During Ahmadinejad's presidency, sanctions imposed substantial costs on Iran but did not alter its unwillingness to negotiate. Enrichment activities actually *increased* under Ahmadinejad, causing the Bush and Obama administrations to extend sanctions. Iran's policy reversal, they say, was a result of sanctions *and* a domestic political climate in which frustration with the effects of Ahmadinejad's economic and political mismanagement reinforced the pain of sanctions. Without that domestic factor, additional sanctions would not sway Tehran but would undermine President Rouhani's authority and increase Iran's sense of vulnerability, pushing it to acquire WMD.

What if the parties cannot implement a comprehensive final agreement? If Washington adheres to a maximalist position, its negotiating partners may blame it for negotiating in bad faith. If Iran refuses

U.S.-Iranian
negotiations and
domestic politics

Peter Schrank

to cooperate, President Obama promised in his 2014 State of the Union address: "I will be the first to call for more sanctions and stand ready to exercise all options to make sure Iran does not build a nuclear weapon."[58] Such a "snap-back" mechanism was incorporated into the 2015 deal to put sanctions back in place if Iran violates any of its terms.

Syria

Embroiled in civil war, Syria posed a special proliferation challenge. Ongoing conflict complicated efforts to transport weapons to Latakia in 2014. But even after weapons had been destroyed, questions arose about whether Syria's *entire* chemical arsenal had been revealed to the OPCW. Indeed, after the last weapons had been removed, Syria continued to use chlorine gas (which it did not have to declare in the 2013 agreement).

Policy Options

a. *Work with multilateral institutions*, in particular the OPCW, to ensure Syria's complete disarmament. In 2014, it was President Obama's position that America would work with the OPCW "and the international community to seek resolution of these open issues, even as we broadly press the Assad regime to end the horrific atrocities it continues to commit against its people."[59] As long as Syria's civil war continues, however, this may prove impractical.

b. *Intervene in Syria.* In theory, the military option was never taken off the table, but military intervention to ensure Syria's compliance with the CWC is complicated by its civil war and the military campaign against ISIS. As those conflicts continue and violence spreads into neighboring countries, it is impossible to consider the chemical weapons issue apart from regional politics. Counter-proliferation measures that might weaken President Assad might also empower an even more hostile regime.

CONCLUSION: A DANGEROUS WORLD

Proliferation policy is not a relic of the Cold War and remains a high priority in America's foreign policy. Washington remains concerned about possible WMD proliferation to additional actors, but the environment in which nonproliferation is pursued is more complex today than during the Cold War. Relatively few states seek nuclear weapons, but they pose substantial challenges. North Korea and Iran, the countries dominating U.S. nuclear nonproliferation efforts, have opaque decision-making structures. It is difficult to know without understanding their goals or the logic of their policies what instruments are best suited to achieve nonproliferation (in the case of Iran) or counter-proliferation (in the case of North Korea). Nonproliferation efforts are complicated by a long history of mistrust between America and those countries, and their governments have a lengthy record of not cooperating with multilateral institutions.

Active or aspiring proliferators seek WMD for security and status and, as their regimes are not transparent, it is difficult to know how far they are willing to go to acquire such weapons. Nonproliferation policies also risk destabilizing entire countries and regions. In the cases of North Korea, Iran, and Syria, aggressive nonproliferation policies might unseat regimes, stoke anti-Americanism, or fuel conflicts that carry almost as many risks as proliferation itself.

DISCUSSION QUESTIONS

1. What lessons do American efforts to prevent North Korean acquisition of WMD suggest about U.S. policies to prevent Iran from acquiring nuclear weapons?

2. What should U.S. policy be toward North Korea now that that country possesses nuclear weapons?

3. Should Washington fear nuclear proliferation inasmuch as nuclear deterrence proved sufficient to deter the Soviet Union in the Cold War?

4. In what ways do the first and second nuclear ages differ? Do they pose different challenges?

5. If Iran developed nuclear weapons, should the United States use force to disarm Tehran, or would deterrence suffice?

6. To what extent has the NPT been a success? What are its strengths and weaknesses?

KEY TERMS

Fissile Material Cut-Off
   Treaty (p. 105)

highly enriched uranium
   (HEU) (p. 103)

Nuclear Nonproliferation Treaty
   (NPT) (p. 98)

P5+1 group (p. 112)

proliferation (p. 96)

Proliferation Security Initiative
   (PSI) (p. 105)

sanctions (p. 95)

UN Monitoring, Verification, and
   Inspection Commission
   (p. 106)

for CQ Press

Sharpen your skill with SAGE edge at **edge.sagepub.com/mansbach**

SAGE edge for Students provides a personalized approach to help you accomplish your coursework
goals in an easy-to-use learning environment.

5

An American Economic Conundrum

NEOLIBERALISM OR NEO-MERCANTILISM?

U.S.-EU free-trade
negotiations

USA - EU Free Trade Negotiations

Foreign economic policy is an area in which U.S. leaders have long had to balance values and interests. Indeed, on several occasions Washington has had to compare the utility of imposing sanctions on countries like Russia and China in the name of human rights that impose costs on U.S. firms.

During America's first century, Washington was more concerned about economic issues as a matter of domestic policy—to generate tax revenue, for example. As the U.S. economy grew in the 19th and 20th centuries, U.S. interests expanded, and economic policy became a more important element in foreign policy. After the United States became an acknowledged global power following World War II, economic policy became a crucial tool—along with multilateral diplomacy and military power—to advance American interests and values. U.S. interests rested on sustained economic growth enabled by a stable global economy, and U.S. ideals favored liberal policies that support free-market capitalism as the surest way to achieve growth and spread liberal political values and institutions. Washington promoted these values by promoting the establishment of global economic institutions—the International Monetary Fund (IMF), the World Bank (IBRD), and the General Agreement on Tariffs and Trade (GATT), in the immediate postwar period. Since then, Washington has used these institutions to advocate economic policies associated with economic growth and to strengthen liberal economic and political institutions globally. These institutions continue to operate, but their value as a means to foster U.S. interests and ideals is less certain in an era when U.S. economic influence is declining.

Despite its recovery from the 2008 financial crisis, U.S. economic primacy has been challenged in recent decades by the rise of competing actors—notably China—but also Brazil, Russia, and India (which, with China and South Africa, are known as the **BRICS**) even while the European Union has stagnated. **Neoliberals** emphasize **free trade** and investment and competitive markets globally. **Neomercantilists** (or economic nationalists) seek to protect domestic firms from foreign competition and limit access of foreign firms to the U.S. market. With the relative decline in U.S. economic power, the tension between neoliberalism and neomercantilism has intensified, and today there is a "fraying consensus" on the value of trade liberalization (values) versus economic protectionism (interests). And as U.S. power has waned so has its influence in global institutions. U.S. leaders seek to use their remaining influence to persuade others to accept Washington's preferred policies. Countries described as "**emerging economies**" are demanding changes to decision-making procedures in international institutions that increase their influence even as Washington is turning from global economic institutions to regional institutions that offer a more favorable climate or unilateral pursuit of U.S. interests.

Timeline

1900

1929 Great Depression begins in the United States.

1941 Atlantic Charter commits America and Britain to a liberal economic order after World War II.

1944 Bretton Woods Conference is held.

1948 GATT is signed.

1950 Senate rejects the International Trade Organization.

1900 (Continued)

1971 Washington abandons the gold standard.

1986–1993 Uruguay round of trade talks establishes the World Trade Organization (WTO).

1994 North American Free Trade Agreement (NAFTA) comes into effect.

1994 Bill Clinton proposes a Free Trade Area of the Americas.

Washington relies on multilateral, internationalist policies when doing so helps achieve its interests and values but turns to unilateral **protectionism** when multilateral approaches seem unpromising. Debates about multilateralism and unilateralism pervade deliberations over the pursuit of neoliberal or neomercantilist policies. Unilateralism underlies protectionist policies and multilateralism is associated with major trade agreements. Protectionism involves restricting trade to protect domestic jobs and uncompetitive industries but harms export-dependent industries, reducing consumer choice and raising prices. Shortly before the global financial crisis, Federal Reserve Chairman Ben Bernanke characterized efforts to restrict trade as economic isolationism, warning that "retreat from international competition would inexorably lead to lower productivity for U.S. firms and lower living standards for U.S. consumers."[1] By contrast, multilateral trade agreements benefit exporters and consumers.

SOURCES OF U.S. FOREIGN ECONOMIC POLICY

External factors play a pivotal role in driving U.S. foreign economic policy. The structure of the global economy offers constraints and opportunities, depending on the rates of economic growth of key actors and the distribution of economic wealth and power. At the end of World War II, as the current global economic system was emerging, America experienced high growth rates and had the world's largest economy, making it economically preponderant—an economic hegemon. In recent decades, the global economic structure has shifted, with emerging economies like China and India growing more quickly than the developed West. In this new economic world, Washington cannot call the shots.

Because different domestic constituents expect to benefit or suffer from foreign economic policies, it attracts intense interest domestically—more than in other areas like human rights where the effects of U.S. policies seem remote. Thus, examining foreign economic policy also requires discussing domestic economic issues. In government, the president and Congress are key actors, but many other agencies have a role in formulating and implementing economic policy. In trade, key agencies involved in developing policy, conducting negotiations, and coordinating trade policy include the Department of Commerce, the U.S. Trade Representative (USTR), and the International Trade Commission, but the Departments of

1900 (Continued)

1997 Congress refuses to grant the president "fast track" authority to negotiate trade agreements.

2000

2001 China joins the WTO.

2007 Financial crisis strikes the United States.

2009 European sovereign debt crisis begins.

2013 Negotiations begin for a Trans-Pacific Trade Pact and a Transatlantic Trade and Investment Partnership.

2015 Congress grants the president "fast track" trade authority and TPP agreement is reached in October.

Labor and Treasury also play important roles, and the interests of all of these agencies frequently collide. Free-trade policies pursued by the Department of Commerce and the USTR may threaten jobs that the Department of Labor seeks to protect.

Societal factors are especially important to foreign economic policy because whole sectors, firms, and households directly experience its effects. Groups like the Chamber of Commerce or the American Federation of Labor-Congress of Industrial Organizations (AFL-CIO) advocate policies that protect business and labor, respectively. Given the size and diversity of America's economy, different regions have distinct policy preferences, with those in the Midwest and the South generally favoring policies that protect agriculture and those in the Northeast supporting export-oriented policies that favor man-ufacturing. Unions, households, and individuals support policies that protect jobs and ensure price stability. Significantly, perceptions of trade policy are fluid over time and are not tightly correlated to political party affiliation, and education level is more highly correlated with views toward free trade, with the more educated viewing trade as beneficial.[2]

The president and Congress also have key roles in formulating economic policy. Before 1934, Congress played a central role in trade policy, but the Reciprocal Trade Agreements Act that year delegated much of its authority to the president. Congress continued to exercise a role in approving agreements but delegated more authority to the president in the Trade Act of 1974 by offering "**fast track authority**" (trade promotion authority)—the power to negotiate trade agreements that Congress can approve or reject but not amend. Between 1974 and 2007, with fast track authority presidents could negotiate trade agreements with little congressional interference, though they had to lobby later to get agreements rati-fied. Bill Clinton fought for ratification of the North American Free Trade Agreement (NAFTA) that had been negotiated by his predecessor. Fast track authority was granted on a temporary basis but extended

FIGURE 5.1   What Americans Think Foreign Trade Means for the Country

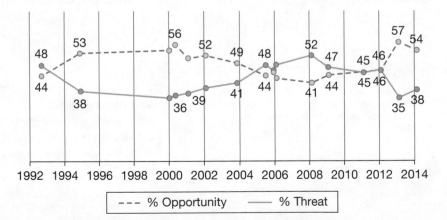

on several occasions to allow for negotiations in the framework of the GATT and, later, NAFTA. Presidents valued fast track authority still more after passage of the 1988 Omnibus Trade and Competitiveness Act that defined trade agreements as congressional-executive agreements requiring approval of both the House and the Senate. After 2007, Congress could amend trade agreements before ratification—a process that made other governments reluctant to commit to trade pacts and slowed negotiations. In monetary and financial policy, notably U.S. interest rates and the growth of the money supply, the chair of the Federal Reserve has great influence—and political independence from the president and Congress. It is the Federal Reserve that decides how much money should be in circulation, which directly affects inflation and employment.

Individuals also matter. Cordell Hull, FDR's secretary of state, strongly supported free trade and was instrumental in the passage of the 1934 Reciprocal Trade Agreements Act. More recently, Federal Reserve Chair Alan Greenspan (1987–2006) was described as a "wizard" and "rock star." His policy prescriptions were widely viewed as infallible during his tenure as Fed chair. After the financial crisis, however, he was personally blamed for irresponsible lending practices and poor oversight of financial institutions.

PAST: THE EVOLUTION OF U.S. FOREIGN ECONOMIC POLICY

Pre–World War I Economic Policy

Before World War I, U.S. interests, especially domestic conditions, largely drove economic policy. There was no foreign economic policy per se, although America was active in the global economy. By the turn of the 19th century, the United States was a major exporter, accounting for 3 percent of world exports with only 0.5 percent of the world's population. Many of its exports were agricultural products like tobacco and sugar. Washington was constitutionally prohibited from imposing taxes on exported goods and relied on duties ("**tariffs**") from imported goods for revenue. When trade with Europe (the destination of about 60 percent of U.S. exports) was interrupted during the Napoleonic Wars and the War of 1812, new industries emerged in America to provide previously imported goods like cotton, textiles, and iron. Once these wars ended and trade with Europe resumed, Washington turned to tariffs less for revenue than to protect its young industries from European competition.[3]

U.S. trade grew rapidly during the 19th century, but American trade policy remained domestic in its focus. With westward expansion, U.S. farmers began producing grain, and better transportation made it possible to move that grain to ports and ship it to Europe. By the 20th century, U.S. exports accounted for some 15 percent of world trade. During this era, tariffs generated revenue. They would be raised when coffers were low and reduced when coffers were full. The international economic system of the era had been designed by Britain and reflected British needs but also served U.S. interests, so there was little need for Washington to employ protectionism to influence the global economic order or other nations' economic policies.[4]

Early U.S. **monetary policy** also had domestic objectives and reflected interests rather than values. At the end of the Revolutionary War, America's national government was deeply in debt, owing over $5 million to foreign creditors. State governments—which had their own currencies—owed about $25 million.[5] With so much debt, a national debate began over whether America should have a national bank (one that manages a single national currency) that could assume the states' war debts, that is, be a lender of last resort. Alexander Hamilton, the first secretary of the treasury, successfully argued for such a bank, and the first Bank of the United States operated from 1791 to 1811, when its charter expired. The War of 1812 was funded mainly by borrowing, raising America's foreign debt to $119.2 million in 1815,[6] but, without a central bank, much of this debt was incurred by the states, several of which went bankrupt after the war. Thus, a Second Bank of the United States was chartered in 1816 to standardize America's currency, limit inflation, and manage federal and state debts. President Andrew Jackson was opposed to this bank, believing that it threatened states' rights, and he let the Second Bank's charter expire in 1836.

The First U.S. Bailout

America's first financial crisis surrounded the first Bank of the United States. When the bank opened in December 1791, it took in almost $2.7 million in two months and, flush in reserves, lent credit generously. By March 1792, the bank had little hard currency, producing a panic that led to the first U.S. bailout—authorized by Alexander Hamilton—to restore public confidence in the banking sector.[7]

The current U.S. financial system originated in earlier financial crises—1837, 1857, 1873, 1893, and 1907—that resulted from excessive **speculation** without a national central bank. By 1907, America's banking system was still highly decentralized with 22,000 banks—one for every 4,000 people. In 1907, a run on New York trust companies (private companies offering many of the same services as banks) spread panic that triggered a nationwide run on banks as depositors tried to withdraw their savings, producing a national money shortage. With no public lender to bail out banks, further crisis was only averted by the injection of private sector emergency cash into the economy. These events led to the creation of the Federal Reserve in 1913. The Federal Reserve Board ("the Fed,") uses monetary policies to maintain high employment and stable prices. To ensure it is free from political influence, the Fed receives no funding from Congress. Elected officials and members of the executive branch are prohibited from sitting on its Board of Governors. While the Fed is accountable to Congress, its independence means it does not implement the policy preferences of Congress or the administration. In moments of crisis, it can lend its own currency, Federal Reserve Notes, to meet a bank's shortfall in cash. The Fed also has supervisory powers to ensure that banks comply with banking regulations. America's banking system became more stable after the Fed was established, but crises still occur, and the Fed is in turn extolled and condemned for the effects its policies have on domestic and foreign economies.

The Great Depression

During the 1920s, America became a more influential economic actor globally and began to use its economic clout to advance domestic interests. Before the Great War, America had been a "young debtor" with a poor record of paying debts and wielded little global economic influence. By the war's end, it had become a "mature creditor,"[8] having loaned European governments $10 billion in goods and credits[9] to wage war and provided additional aid for postwar reconstruction. Washington insisted that its wartime allies make good on their debts, causing a diplomatic rift with its allies. Britain and France, like America, were creditors and depended on debt repayment and German reparations for the income to repay America. As reparations were reduced or forgiven, repaying Washington became increasingly difficult, and with their economies in shambles, they needed U.S. goods but lacked sufficient cash for both debt repayment and trade. As financier Otto Kahn remarked, "Having become a creditor nation, we have got now to fit ourselves into the role of a creditor nation. We shall have to make up our minds to be more hospitable to imports."[10]

America's reliance on tariffs to protect domestic industry and generate revenue without regard to foreign economic implications intensified in 1928 to 1933, a period coinciding with the onset of the Great Depression and the height of U.S. isolationism. The Great Depression was a global economic catastrophe that began in America with the crash of the New York Stock Exchange on "Black Tuesday," October 29, 1929. The crash was followed by inflation and bank failures in 1930 and 1931, and the country did not fully recover until World War II stimulated demand for American goods and services.

As the world reeled from the crash, the 1930 Smoot-Hawley tariff imposed the highest tariffs in U.S. history, increasing almost 900 import duties[11] by about 20 percent across all economic sectors. Proponents viewed the tariffs as a domestic measure to protect U.S. agriculture and industry from foreign imports. Foreign governments, however, retaliated by increasing their own tariffs, and depression spread, bringing global trade to a halt. Reflected Thomas Lamont, a partner at J.P. Morgan and a presidential economic adviser, "I almost went down on my knees to beg Herbert Hoover to veto the asinine Hawley-Smoot Tariff. . . . That Act intensified nationalism all over the world."[12] Over 1,000 economists unsuccessfully petitioned Hoover not to sign the bill, but U.S. officials did not care about possible retaliation—only about protecting constituents at home. Thus, during the next two years, U.S. trade fell by 40 percent. The tariff also undermined efforts in the League of Nations (of which the United States was not a member) to stop the global spiral of protectionism and devaluation (**"beggar-thy-neighbor policies"**).[13]

Tariffs were not the only cause of the downward spiral. Before the Great Depression, the world's major economies adhered to the **gold standard**, a system in which currencies were convertible into gold. Since each currency's value was set relative to others, the gold standard ensured stable, predictable exchange rates, which in turn facilitated trade and prevented inflation because governments could only print as much currency as they had gold to back it. The downside was that policymakers were unable to adjust their money supply to manage economic shocks. When the Depression struck, people lost confidence in bank deposits and paper currencies in favor of gold. In 1931, the run on Britain's banks was so great that the country risked running out of gold and thus abandoned the gold standard. Other governments followed. With currencies no longer tied to gold, governments could print money or manipulate interest rates to devalue their currencies, making them cheaper relative to others. Since currency **devaluation** reduced the cost of a country's exports, it aided the domestic economy, but the competitive currency devaluations that ensued as governments abandoned the gold standard were destabilizing, reducing global trade and exacerbating the depression.

In 1933, as the costs of retaliatory tariff and currency policies became apparent, Washington began the shift from unilateralism to negotiating reciprocal trade agreements. According to Secretary of State Cordell Hull, "The appalling repercussions of the 1930 tariff act upon our own domestic prosperity brings home the lesson that in this day and age the tariff is no longer a purely domestic issue" and "slamming the door shut against foreign products, we have found the door shut against our own products."[14] International trade was viewed as crucial to domestic growth and was promoted by trade agreements, beginning with the 1934 Reciprocal Trade Agreements Act (RTAA) that facilitated tariff reductions that were matched by similar concessions by others. Such reductions made it easier for U.S. businesses to expand into foreign markets. Few similar agreements had been reached before, but following the RTAA, Congress gradually extended greater authority to the president to negotiate bilateral trade agreements, and between 1934 and 1945, Washington negotiated reciprocal trade agreements with about 30 countries,[15] substantially expanding international trade.

Postwar Economic Policy

American economic policy became genuinely international after World War II, a tool for U.S. leaders to pursue interests and ideals. European economies had been devastated by the war. By contrast, America's economy—"the arsenal of democracy"—had expanded dramatically. It was the only great power to be enriched by the conflict. By 1945, the United States was the world's leading source of exports, and its gold reserves represented almost two-thirds of the world's total.[16] And foreign aid became a key tool of U.S. foreign policy. American leaders sought to gain access to additional foreign markets for U.S. goods, and U.S. industries had become sufficiently competitive that tariffs were not necessary. America was a hegemon—a dominant power—with the capability and will to exercise leadership in global economic affairs and oversee the establishment of institutions to provide public goods in the form of free trade and monetary stability. These institutions reflected liberal democratic and economic values and were suited to preserving the competitiveness of American industries.

In 1944, forty-four governments met at Bretton Woods, New Hampshire, for the UN Monetary and Financial Conference. From this conference two international economic institutions emerged that became the pillars of globalization—the IMF and the World Bank. There was also an effort to create an International Trade Organization (ITO) that failed owing to congressional concern for U.S. sovereignty. Instead, the GATT, with less authority than the ITO, was established in 1947.

The primary goal at Bretton Woods was to establish an international monetary system to govern global currency relations and prevent the "beggar-thy-neighbor" currency devaluations of the 1930s. Under the new "**gold-exchange standard**," participants agreed to tie (or "peg") the value of their currencies to the U.S. dollar, which had a fixed value of $35 per ounce of gold. It was agreed that, though the value of the dollar would not change, the value of other currencies *relative* to the dollar could fluctuate within narrow limits. The IMF was charged with overseeing this system, and its design reflected American interests. The IMF decision-making structure granted members a voice in proportion to their economic weight, thereby giving Washington effective veto power over important decisions. With this systemic change, other countries began to use U.S. dollars for trade and investment and hold dollars rather than gold in their national reserves to back their own currencies, making the dollar both a "transaction currency" and a "**reserve currency**." To this day, most global trade is conducted in U.S. dollars, making it the world's dominant reserve or "hard currency." The new monetary system gave Washington the unique privilege of borrowing additional hard currency—dollars—with no currency exchange costs, facilitating trade with other countries. It also enabled America to provide security to allies as the Cold War began because Washington could fund its extensive overseas alliances by printing more dollars.

By the late 1960s, however, Washington was spending heavily on the Vietnam War without raising taxes at home or cutting domestic programs. As a result, there were so many dollars in circulation that there was insufficient gold to back them. This inflated the value of the dollar, making it (in theory) less attractive as a reserve currency and making American exports more expensive (and less competitive). Many countries were willing to hold dollars anyway because they were prospering in this system or, in the case of U.S. allies, were willing to pay a price for America's security guarantee. Germany and Japan "were, in effect, paying a tax to support a vital service, just as individuals pay taxes to their own governments to purchase the military forces that protect them."[17] From Washington's perspective, "the international monetary system existed to serve the interests of the United States in maintaining both a healthy domestic economy and a foreign policy calculated to meet its security needs as it alone defined them."[18] By 1970, American allies had become stronger and more independent, and inflation and the dollar appreciation had made U.S. exports less competitive. Thus, President Richard Nixon unilaterally ended the gold-exchange standard, allowing the value of the dollar to fluctuate in response to market forces. The system that followed and remains in place is a **managed float system** in which central banks undertake some monetary policy coordination and buy and sell currencies to promote exchange-rate stability.

With the end of the gold-exchange standard, the IMF's role in monetary affairs began to change accompanied by a rapid expansion in foreign debt in developing countries. The 1973 spike in oil prices increased energy prices, forcing developing countries to borrow from commercial banks to acquire enough cash flow to pay for imported oil. Awash in "petrodollars" (dollars earned from oil sales), banks lent generously to risky clients that invested borrowed money in nontraded goods rather than in export sectors that would produce long-term economic growth. By the end of the 1970s, a series of shocks struck developing countries, especially in Latin America. Interest rates rose sharply in 1979, as Western countries tried to curb **inflation**, making it more costly for developing countries to borrow or repay existing debt. This was accompanied by a second oil price spike that deepened **recession** in industrialized economies, reducing demand for their goods. Developing countries could not earn sufficient foreign exchange to service their debts, and banks tightened lending policies, making it harder for these countries to get additional credit. Thus, the IMF shifted its focus toward assisting developing countries experiencing **balance-of-payments** deficits (payments to other countries exceeding national income). It became an alternate lending source, but unlike commercial banks, it could require that governments implement painful structural economic reforms like deficit reduction to strengthen their economies.

A second objective of Bretton Woods was to foster postwar reconstruction. This task was assigned to the International Bank for Reconstruction and Development (IBRD), commonly known as the World Bank, which provided funds for projects that would fuel economic recovery and growth. Washington helped design decision-making rules to grant paramount influence to wealthy states. With postwar reconstruction completed by the mid-1950s, the World Bank began to focus on economic growth in the less-developed countries outside North America and Europe. Unlike the IMF, which was designed to offer short-term loans to help countries manage financial crises, the World Bank offered medium-to-long-term loans to fund infrastructure that would attract private capital and fuel long-term economic growth.

Over time, the World Bank, with its headquarters in Washington and many American-trained economists, came to be widely viewed as an instrument of U.S. policy. World Bank loans, like those of the IMF, came with strings attached. These reflected the "**Washington consensus**," a term coined in the 1980s reflecting a belief in the superiority of economic reforms that reduced government economic intervention. Known as Structural Adjustment Programs (SAPs), these conditions required austerity measures like budget deficit reduction (including reducing government staff and reducing state pensions), elimination of government subsidies for food and utilities, and wage cuts for public employees. They also required longer-term reforms to "lock in" liberal economic policies and open the recipient's economy to foreign trade and integrate it into the globalizing economy. Structural adjustments involved, for example, downsizing bloated bureaucracies; privatizing state-owned industries; and freeing markets for goods, services, and capital from government control. SAPs became common in the 1980s, especially after that decade's global debt crisis. "Conditionality" elicited anger and frustration in much of the developing world, where adjustments imposed high economic, social, and political costs. Many accused Washington of forcing other governments to implement policies that the United States refused to adopt at home, leaving firms and workers in developing countries more vulnerable to global competition. Advocates of SAPs argued that short-term economic pain was necessary to fuel long-term growth, and the conditions the World Bank imposed provided political cover for weak governments to implement painful but necessary reforms.

By the 1990s, the World Bank had moved away from a "one-size-fits-all" approach to economic development, negotiating conditions that were suitable for particular loan applicants, although structural adjustment to force open recipient economies to global competition remained important. It also began to emphasize poverty reduction strategies and good governance reforms to reduce corruption.

PRESENT: CONTEMPORARY ECONOMIC CHALLENGES

Among the pressing economic issues that defined recent U.S. foreign economic policy were the 2008 financial crisis, trade policy, and emerging economic challengers.

The 2008 Global Financial Crisis

The 2008 global financial crisis established the context in which today's foreign economic policies must be considered. Global finance is an area in which U.S. leadership remains in high demand. Vital U.S. interests are at stake because America's economic health depends on the global economy and the health of global economy depends on America's economy. Policies to stimulate economic growth and job creation at home are examples of unilateralism crafted by Washington to enhance U.S. interests but that have substantial effects abroad. America also continues to rely on multilateral institutions like the Group of 7 (G-7), **Group of 20** (G-20), and IMF to coordinate economic policies with other countries in an interdependent global economy. Since 2008, U.S. interests have trumped values, but values remain important. Post-2008 reforms continued to emphasize liberal economic values, including free-market principles and transparent decision making. While considered inherently valuable, however, Washington believes these values were important for economic recovery and sustained growth.

The Crisis Unfolds The collapse in September 2008 of Lehman Brothers, one of America's largest investment banks, marked the beginning of the crisis—the worst since the Great Depression—but its roots were deeper. In the 1970s, governments worldwide, including America's, began spending beyond their means, even as economies experienced "stagflation" (slow growth alongside inflation). In the 1980s, President Ronald Reagan and British Prime Minister Margaret Thatcher dismantled government regulations in key economic sectors including finance, energy, transportation, and communications to stimulate their economies. As businesses restructured and adopted new productivity-enhancing technologies, America's economy enjoyed high rates of growth, low unemployment, and low inflation, even while much of the world experienced recession. Strong U.S. economic growth continued into the 1990s—"the United States was an economic oasis in a global economic desert."[19]

Simultaneously, economic inequality was growing, and Americans sought more credit to fund their lifestyles. Federal Reserve policies to restore confidence in America's economy following the 9/11 terrorist attacks reduced interest rates for loans to 1 percent in 2003. Credit was readily available at historically low rates, and many Americans bought homes. This created a condition of "debt-fueled growth" in which more money fueled demand—especially in the housing sector. Predatory lenders took advantage of the situation, offering "subprime" adjustable-rate mortgages with little to no down payment to borrowers who did not qualify for traditional mortgages. Lenders often turned around and sold their mortgages to large commercial banks or to government-chartered mortgage companies, such as the Federal National Mortgage Association ("Fannie Mae") and the Federal Home Loan Mortgage Corporation ("Freddie Mac") that held about one half of American mortgages. They in turn sold the loans to investment banks that pooled hundreds or thousands of loans into what were called "low-risk securities." Investors who purchased these mortgage-backed securities earned income from the sum of the monthly mortgage payments, but because so many subprime mortgages were pooled in these securities, they were risky.

The problems in this system did not become apparent as long as housing prices continued to rise as they did after 2003. Increasing real estate prices, however, were unsustainable and the housing "bubble" burst in 2007. Suddenly, American homeowners owed more on their mortgages than their homes were worth. More and more Americans defaulted on their mortgages, and banks stopped lending—to businesses and consumers—fearing that the loans would not be repaid.

In January 2008, America's largest mortgage lender, Countrywide Home Loans Inc., went bankrupt and was bought by Bank of America. In March, Bear Stearns, a Wall Street investment house with a large portfolio of mortgage-backed securities, nearly went bankrupt and was bought by JPMorgan Chase. The Federal Reserve absorbed Bear Stearns's assets and took control of Fannie Mae and Freddie Mac in early September. The crisis came to a boil some days later when the Fed refused to bail out Lehmann Brothers and allowed it to go bankrupt. The Fed and the Treasury Department *did* bail out the nation's biggest insurer, American International Group, after it reported huge losses in credit default swaps (a kind of insurance for mortgage-backed securities). In exchange, the government received almost 80 percent interest in the company. These events showed that big banks and insurers were no longer "too big to fail." Commercial lending froze, and without access to credit, businesses stopped investing and reduced their workforce. There is no single explanation for the financial crisis. Some economists blamed Washington for weak regulations and easy monetary policy, and others blamed the banking sector for predatory practices and corporate greed.

Jump-starting the economy

Brian Fairrington / Cagle Cartoons

The Fed Acts As America's central bank, the Fed played a key role in responding to the crisis, but, owing to the importance of the U.S. economy, the Fed's actions significantly affected the global economy. Central banks like the Fed exist in most countries. Their role is to limit inflation and/or maintain growth. Thus, when there is fear of inflation such banks raise interest rates, thereby reducing the amount of money in circulation. However, when growth slows and unemployment grows, central banks try to stimulate economic growth by reducing interest rates, thereby increasing lending and enlarging the money supply.

The Fed initiated three policies to end the crisis and strengthen America's economy—interest rate adjustments, quantitative easing, and forward guidance. The first, altering the interest rates at which banks borrow, is a standard option for central banks. Higher interest rates make borrowing more costly and therefore discourage additional borrowing. Lower rates encourage borrowing, and cheap credit stimulates growth and employment because demand increases and more workers are needed. After the crisis began, the Fed lowered interest rates, but by 2009, rates were already close to zero and additional cuts were of no value because depositors preferred to hold cash.

Once interest rate reductions had been reduced as far as possible, the Fed adopted other, more innovative policies. One was **quantitative easing** (QE)—a policy of "creating" money electronically which it used to purchase assets like mortgages from commercial banks and other lending institutions. This injected more money into banks, which then had more to lend. The increased supply of money also had the effect of keeping interest rates low.

QE was primarily a domestic policy, but it had a global impact. Because America is the world's largest economy and the Fed issues the principal global reserve currency, its monetary decisions—including increasing the money supply "liquidity"—affect the global financial system. After 2008, the Fed initiated three rounds of quantitative easing: November 2008 to March 2010 (QE1), August 2010 to June 2011 (QE2), and September 2013 to October 2014 (QE3). QE1 was effective in preventing economic meltdown by boosting confidence in Fed policy and fostering growth in America's gross domestic product (GDP). Experts were divided about the impact of subsequent rounds of quantitative easing. In QE2, the Fed bought about $600 billion in "Treasuries" (government bonds—essentially loans to the government). In QE3, it made an open-ended commitment to buy additional assets and maintain interest rates in the 0 to 0.25 percent range. While its advocates viewed the increase in the money supply and low interest rates as necessary to fuel investment, domestic critics viewed it as "the greatest backdoor Wall Street bailout of all time,"[20] claiming that while QE reduced the costs of making loans, Wall Street pocketed the extra cash, and America's economy improved only marginally. By one estimate in 2013, the Fed had spent $4 trillion in return for an additional $40 billion in America's economic output, roughly 0.25 percent of GDP.[21]

The overall impact of QE on America's economy remains contested, but QE2 and QE3 had clear and direct effects on emerging economies overseas where they added significant new capital flows that gave these countries access to vast amounts of credit to finance infrastructure projects and corporate investment and shielded them from the worst results of the global financial crisis. However, this inflow was also destabilizing. Many emerging-market countries did not have the capacity to absorb the excess cash and their currencies were sensitive to perceived shifts in U.S. policies, including an end to asset purchases. In May 2013, when Fed Chair Ben Bernanke announced the Fed *might* slow quantitative easing, the value of currencies in emerging economies fell precipitously. With the end of QE3 in 2014, these economies were left with high debt and the prospect of low growth. The announcement of an end to QE3 also led to appreciation in the value of the dollar. An appreciating dollar makes commodities (raw materials and agricultural products)—traded in dollars—more expensive for other countries, placing additional pressure on emerging economies. With commodity producers compelled to reduce prices in response to the appreciating dollar, economic growth in emerging economies slowed, leaving their governments vulnerable to domestic political instability.

A third instrument available to the Federal Reserve was "forward guidance"—announcements intended to influence markets by signaling future Fed actions. After 2009, the Fed used forward guidance alongside interest rate policy and quantitative easing to boost the economy by reassuring investors that interest rates would remain low, and other central banks including the Bank of Japan, the European Central Bank, and the Bank of England also did so. In 2009, the Fed promised rates would remain low "for an extended time." Later, the message was sharpened. In 2011, the Fed offered a date—"at least until 2013." In late 2012, Fed Chair Bernanke announced that as long as inflation remained below 2.5 percent, the Fed would not raise interest rates until unemployment had fallen below 6.5 percent. Under Janet Yellen, the Fed pursued "qualitative guidance." Rather than offering explicit thresholds, the message promised to focus on "a broad set of labor market conditions,"[22] and in announcing an end to QE3 in October 2014 the Fed promised that interest rates would remain low for a "considerable time."

Although the 2008 crisis originated in America, it was a *global* crisis, and its solution required the aid of global institutions. "In a globalized world, no country can pursue a unilateral international economic policy."[23] America was a leader in global monetary issues and found the key multilateral institutions

Net Capital Flows to Emerging Markets, 1990–2013

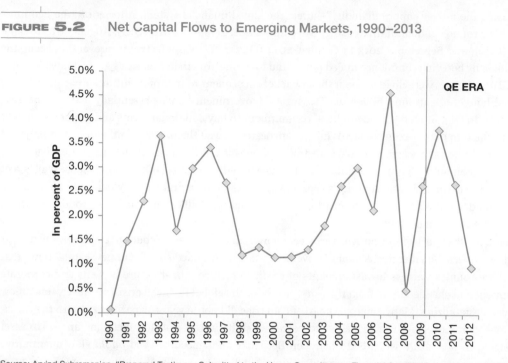

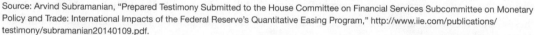

Source: Arvind Subramanian, "Prepared Testimony Submitted to the House Committee on Financial Services Subcommittee on Monetary Policy and Trade: International Impacts of the Federal Reserve's Quantitative Easing Program," http://www.iie.com/publications/testimony/subramanian20140109.pdf.

effective tools for pursuing interests and values. Efforts to repair global finance centered on economic coordination in the G-20, regulatory reform in the Basel Accord on banking reform, and governance reform in the IMF. The institutional efforts described here involved economic coordination and regulation to prevent the errors in the future that caused the 2008 crisis.

The G-20 originated in the 1990s after financial crises in Latin America and Asia when emerging economics including China, India, and Brazil began to demand a greater voice in global economic governance. It reflected dissatisfaction of emerging economies with the G-7, a group of the world's wealthiest countries that was established in the 1970s—Canada, France, Germany, Italy, Japan, Britain, and the United States—that meets annually to coordinate global economic policy and exchange rates. In 1999, the G-20 (G-7 along with middle-income emerging economies) was established "to provide a new mechanism for informal dialogue in the framework of the Bretton Woods institutional system, to broaden the discussion on key economic and financial policy issues among systemically significant economies and promote cooperation to achieve stable and sustainable world economic growth that benefits all."[24] The group, consisting of 20 of the world's largest economies, accounts for about two-thirds of the world's population, 85 percent of global GDP, and 75 percent of world trade.[25] In 2008, the forum was elevated to the level of heads of state to enhance its authority. The first G-20 summit was held in October that year in Washington, D.C.

MAP 5.1 The G-20

> G-20 Members: Argentina, Australia, Brazil, Canada, China, France, Germany, Great Britain, India, Indonesia, Italy, Japan, Mexico, Russia, Saudi Arabia, South Africa, South Korea, Turkey, the United States, and the European Union

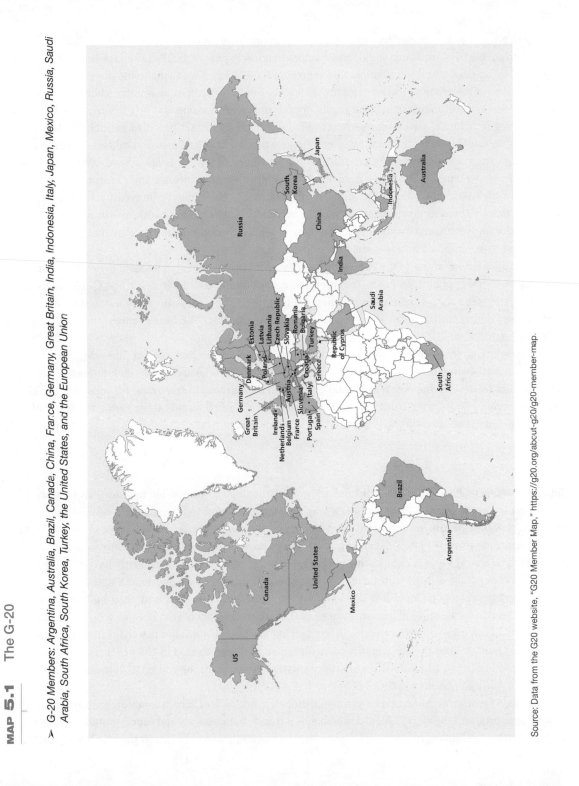

Source: Data from the G20 website, "G20 Member Map," https://g20.org/about-g20/g20-member-map.

The G-20 was active during its initial years. The major economies agreed to increase the IMF's reserves to enable that institution to assist economies in crisis to pursue fiscal stimulus policies domestically, fostering growth and job creation. Such agreement was surprising owing to the diversity of economic policies of the group's members and the preference for austerity in some countries like Germany. The G-20 also agreed to several financial regulatory reforms between 2008 and 2010. Some were to be implemented by national governments—America's 2010 Dodd-Frank Act provided greater regulation of banking in the United States—and by international agencies like the Basel Committee on Banking Supervision. In 2010, members of the Basel Committee signed the Third Basel Accord (Basel III) to enhance the global banking regulatory framework. It required banks to increase their reserve capital in order to absorb losses, improve risk management, and increase transparency while avoiding bankruptcy. Although Basel III was an improvement over the previous regulatory framework, it will not be fully implemented until 2018, and domestic regulations in the United States and elsewhere are more stringent than the yet-to-be-enforced international standards.

The political momentum of the G-20 slowed after 2010, but it remained a useful forum for coordinating economic policies. In 2010, Treasury Secretary Timothy Geithner described G-20 discussions on exchange rates as "critical to bringing about policies that will help create a stronger, more sustainable, and more balanced global economy" and as offering "the best avenue for advancing U.S. interests."[26]

We now turn to trade, an area in which U.S. power and leadership have eroded. In trade relations, there is tension between values and interests—in this case, between free trade and protectionism. Because U.S. leadership has weakened while America's commitment to free trade remains strong, at least in principle, Washington continues working through multilateral forums at the global and regional levels despite domestic pressure to protect U.S. workers and industries.

Trade Policy

Liberal economists favor free trade to achieve economic growth. According to liberal trade theory, trade produces efficiency, which fuels growth. Opening a country's market to foreign goods enhances competition, enabling consumers to benefit from lower prices, greater choice, and higher quality goods. Over time, trade provides jobs, higher wages, and an improved standard of living. Yet protectionism has never gone away, as less competitive industries seek protection and governments have economic objectives other than growth—full employment, national security, labor and health standards, and environmental protection. Moreover, the competition associated with free trade can have negative domestic results, for instance, depressing wages as U.S. laborers compete with cheaper labor overseas. Protectionism can involve tariffs or nontariff barriers like quotas and subsidies that make imports more expensive. **Quotas** limit the amount of a particular good that may be sold in U.S. markets in a given period (usually a year), and **subsidies** are supports (tax breaks, loans, or grants) to domestic firms to make them more competitive globally.

In 2012, America was the second largest merchandise exporter after China, accounting for 8.6 percent of world exports, and the world's biggest merchandise trader, with imports and exports totaling $3.881 trillion.[27] In 2013, China surpassed the United States to become the world's largest trader, with imports and exports totaling $4.159 trillion versus U.S. combined imports and exports of $3.909 trillion.[28] Yet, despite U.S. importance in global trade, trade accounts for only 25 percent of U.S. GDP, a percentage lower than any other developed country except Japan.[29] Foreign trade in goods accounts for only 23 percent of America's economy compared to 46 percent of China's economy.[30]

While most governments accept the wealth-generating impact of free trade in theory, in practice negotiating trade pacts to reduce protectionism is difficult and politicized. Trade agreements have immediate domestic consequences, and domestic actors develop strong positions about agreements. Given the size and diversity of America's domestic economy, there is a relatively small constituency for liberal foreign economic

TABLE **5.1**	The World's Largest Economies
Country	**2014 GDP (Trillion U.S. Dollars)**
United States	$17.5
China	$10.0
Japan	$4.8
Germany	$3.9
France	$2.9
United Kingdom	$2.8
Brazil	$2.2
Italy	$2.2
Russia	$2.1
India	$2.0

Source: CNN.com, http://money.cnn.com/news/economy/world_economies_gdp.

policies. A diverse coalition of Democrats (especially the party's prolabor wing), organized labor, environmentalists, and consumer groups frequently oppose trade agreements. Among their concerns is that free trade agreements (FTAs) will produce domestic job losses as inefficient firms relocate to other countries with lower wages and fewer costly labor standards and environmental and consumer regulations. These groups also worry about environmental pollution and the threats to consumer safety associated with the movement of firms overseas. Thus, trade is a divisive issue in the United States, especially during election years.

Presidents have enjoyed substantial latitude defining trade policy. Congress granted President Bush fast track authority in 2002 to pursue a trade pact with Andean states. Even then, fast track authority was controversial and was not restored after it expired in 2007. Supporters argue that without such authority, known as Trade Promotion Authority, it is impossible for Washington to reach agreements with trading partners that anticipate that Congress will amend any agreement beyond recognition. Ominously, a Democratic filibuster in the Senate and, therefore, the Senate's initial procedural success in blocking consideration of providing the president with fast track trade authority in May 2015 indicated how deep protectionist sentiments of the Democratic Party and its labor union supporters remained. Meanwhile, China was successfully recruiting U.S. allies to join its proposed Asian Infrastructure Investment Bank, and Washington's inability to have fast track authority for negotiating the **Trans-Pacific Partnership** (TPP) threatened to undermine U.S. influence in Asia. However, after the Senate filibuster was narrowly overcome, Congress granted President Obama fast track authority, greatly improving the prospect for approval of the Trans-Pacific and Transatlantic trade agreements.

Free-Trade Multilateralism: From the GATT to the WTO The GATT reflected an era when Washington favored a multilateral trade regime that advanced U.S. interests in free trade and monetary stability during the Cold War. This regime never became a genuinely liberal order, however. Key actors, including Washington, had competing goals that undermined the liberal economic project. Countries continued to practice protectionism for domestic political and social reasons, seeking exemptions from GATT rules and resisting efforts to negotiate reductions in trade barriers. Given the limitations of multilateralism, U.S. policy in the 1980s shifted toward regional trade agreements, and there remains tension in U.S. policy between expanding global trade agreements and pursuing regional and bilateral arrangements. Since the early 1990s, the number of trade pacts increased dramatically and tariffs decreased from a worldwide average of 25 percent in 1980 to below 10 percent in 2009.[31] The variety of trade agreements is consistent with America's commitment to free trade, but more limited arrangements enable Washington to protect domestic economic interests. The first significant regional pact for the United States was NAFTA, negotiated by President George H. W. Bush and signed by President Bill Clinton. Interest in regional and bilateral arrangements grew in the George W. Bush administration, during which time 11 FTAs were negotiated with 16 countries. U.S. interest in additional FTAs waned during President Obama's first term, but trade took on new significance in his second term.

TABLE 5.2   U.S. Trade Agreements

Multilateral Agreements	Began	Status/Date Concluded	Participants
World Trade Organization, Doha Talks	2001	In progress	159 nations
Regional Agreements			
U.S.-EU Transatlantic Trade and Investment Partnership	2013	In progress	
Trans-Pacific Partnership Agreement (TPP)	2009	In progress	11 nations and United States
North American Free Trade Agreement (NAFTA)	1994		United States, Canada, Mexico
FTA of the Americas	1998	Stalled	34 nations
U.S.-South African Customs Union FTA	2002	Stalled	Botswana, Namibia, Lesotho, South Africa, Swaziland, and United States
The Enterprise for ASEAN Initiative	2002		U.S. bilateral agreements with ASEAN members
U.S.-Andean FTA	2003	Stalled	Colombia, Peru, Ecuador, Bolivia, and United States
Central American FTA	2004	2005	Costa Rica, El Salvador, Guatemala, Honduras, Nicaragua, and United States

Multilateral Agreements	Began	Status/Date Concluded	Participants
Bilateral Agreements			
U.S.-Australia FTA		2004	
U.S.-Bahrain FTA		2004	
U.S.-Chile FTA		2003	
U.S.-Morocco FTA		2004	
U.S.-Oman FTA		2004	
U.S.-Peru Trade Promotion Agreement		2009	
U.S.-Singapore FTA		2003	
U.S.-Colombia FTA		2006	
U.S.-South Korea FTA	2006	2010	
U.S.-Panama FTA	2004	2007	
U.S.-Malaysia FTA	2006		Malaysia joined TPP negotiations in 2010
U.S.-Thailand FTA	2004	Suspended after 2006 coup	
U.S.-United Arab Emirates FTA	2004		

Source: James K. Jackson, "Trade Agreements: Impact on the US Economy," CRS Report RL31932, April 10, 2013.

U.S. negotiators sought an FTA at the 1944 Bretton Woods conference, but the Senate never ratified the resulting ITO. Instead, the 1948 GATT became the principal instrument for pursuing multilateral free-trade talks in ensuing decades. Unlike the ITO, the GATT was not an organization but a negotiating forum in which states agreed on rules for reducing barriers to trade in manufactured goods. Like the proposed ITO, the GATT was based on principles advocated by Washington—nondiscrimination (**most-favored nation rule**), general reciprocity (concessions had to be balanced but not necessarily on a product-by-product basis), and domestic safeguards to suspend GATT rules temporarily that might harm domestic industries. The GATT also allowed exceptions to these rules to permit formation of regional trading groups and customs unions. The GATT was "largely a U.S. creation [that] replaced the ITO in practice when congressional resistance jeopardized the proposed trade organization,"[32] and the "political logic of the GATT/WTO is that because liberalization harms certain interests that will inevitably oppose trade liberalization, it is necessary to liberalize in a coordinated way with concession for concession, thus making it easier to defeat protectionists. Once trade barriers have been lowered, a framework of agreements makes it quite difficult to raise them again."[33]

John Ruggie termed the post–World War II trade order "embedded liberalism."[34] Unlike earlier liberalism, embedded liberalism emphasized *both* multilateralism and domestic intervention to achieve economic growth and full employment. Since all countries, including the United States, wished to limit free trade to advance other domestic and foreign objectives, it never became a completely liberal trading system.

Between 1948 and 1994, the GATT sponsored a series of negotiations, or "trade rounds." Until the 1960s, these focused on tariff reductions. Negotiations then expanded to include antidumping measures—preventing export of goods at prices often below production costs to gain market share—and nontariff trade barriers. In the 1970s, protectionism again threatened global trade as several economic shocks—sharply rising oil prices, soaring inflation, increasing unemployment, and declining confidence in the U.S. dollar—heightened calls to protect industries in America and elsewhere. Washington used "voluntary" quotas and subsidies to insulate key industries from global competition, including the automotive, minerals, and transportation sectors. Much of this protectionism sought to slow imports from fast-growing Asian economies, notably Japan and the "East Asian Tigers." In consequence, in the 1980s

TABLE 5.3   GATT/WTO Trade Rounds

Year	Place or Name	Coverage	Countries
1947	Geneva, Switzerland	Tariffs	23
1949	Annecy, France	Tariffs	13
1951	Torquay, England	Tariffs	38
1956	Geneva, Switzerland	Tariffs	26
1960–1961	Dillon Round	Tariffs	26
1964–1967	Kennedy Round	Tariffs and antidumping measures	62
1973–1979	Tokyo Round	Tariffs, nontariff measures, "framework" agreements	102
1986–1994	Uruguay Round	Tariffs, nontariff measures, rules, services, intellectual property, dispute settlement, textiles, agriculture, creation of WTO	123
2001–Present	Doha Round	Tariffs, nontariff measures, agriculture, nonagricultural market access, intellectual property, trade and development, trade and environment, trade facilitation, WTO rules, dispute settlement	160

Source: Data from WTO, "The GATT Years: From Havannah to Marrakesh," http://www.wto.org/english/thewto_e/whatis_e/tif_e/fact4_e.htm; WTO, "The Doha Round," http://www.wto.org/english/tratop_e/dda_e/dda_e.htm.

a "new regionalism" began to spread in which regional groups were created or reformulated to pursue free trade and economic integration.

The Uruguay Round of negotiations (1986-1994) produced extensive trade reform culminating in creation of the WTO. The WTO operates according to the same norms that underpinned the GATT—reciprocity and nondiscrimination. It is a formal organization that promotes and monitors international trade rules and has a dispute settlement mechanism to adjudicate disputes among its 160 members. Unlike other multilateral economic institutions, the WTO was designed to operate according to consensus and reaches decisions slowly. Thus, little progress was achieved in negotiating additional reductions in trade barriers after the WTO's establishment in 1994.

Trade Disputes in the WTO

The WTO trade dispute mechanism often rules against the United States. Washington has been a complainant in 108 cases, a respondent In 124 cases, and a third party in another 125 cases. The EU is second in this regard—a complainant in 95 cases, a respondent in 82 cases, and a third party in 149 cases.[36]

DID YOU KNOW?

The United States, Canada, the EU, and Japan were dominant economic actors globally when the WTO was established, and developing countries enjoyed little influence in the Uruguay Round. Since then, emerging economies have become more influential and use the WTO to pursue their own trade agendas that are often incompatible with U.S. interests. This tension plagued the latest cycle of trade talks, the Doha Round. Meeting in Doha, Qatar, just months after the 9/11 terrorist attacks, WTO members agreed to begin a new series of trade negotiations. U.S. leaders viewed trade talks as a way to achieve political cohesion among the world's governments. This goal was not realized. The Doha Round was ambitious. It sought to level the playing field between developed and developing countries by negotiating reforms to improve market access for agricultural goods, reduce tariff and nontariff trade barriers, liberalize trade in services, enhance the effectiveness of antidumping measures, and improve dispute settlement to foster participation of developing countries in the process. It also sought to negotiate global rules for the "Singapore issues"—trade facilitation, investment, competition, and transparency in government procurement—subjects raised in a 1996 WTO Ministerial Meeting in Singapore.

The Doha talks were acrimonious. The first post-Doha ministerial talks, held in Cancún, Mexico, collapsed in 2003 when developed and developing countries could not agree on reforms in agriculture and tariff policy or which of the "Singapore issues" should be officially included on the Doha agenda. One reason Doha was difficult was that negotiators were trying to agree on many topics and achieve a comprehensive deal. Another reason was that they included sensitive domestic issues, notably, the use of subsidies to protect agricultural producers. The developing world was eager to limit EU and U.S. subsidies for their farmers. Western farmers are efficient and highly subsidized, selling commodities in developing countries at lower prices than local farmers. The EU and United States were reluctant to reduce subsidies to their politically influential farmers, while developing countries would not agree to policies that would make their own farmers even less competitive or make it difficult to protect their farmers in the event of natural or human-made disaster.

Participants almost reached a bargain in 2008, but a dispute between Washington and India and China over liberalizing agricultural trade prevented agreement. In 2013, it again looked like a deal was in sight, with an agreement concluded in Bali, Indonesia, on "trade facilitation" to reduce red tape in customs procedures, cutting costs of trade globally by 10 percent, and potentially adding $1 trillion to the global economy.[36] But agricultural subsidies remained a source of contention, and in the end, India refused to ratify the agreement without an arrangement to allow developing countries to maintain food-subsidy programs that provide food security for their populations.[37] Washington, however, viewed such subsidies as trade-distorting because they would enable these countries to accumulate large agricultural stockpiles and dump surplus commodities on the world market, depressing prices for farmers elsewhere. In November 2014, however, a U.S.-Indian agreement allowing subsidized food stockpiles was reached without fear of legal challenge until a permanent solution was found—the first major global trade deal since the WTO's founding.

CONTROVERSY

The Import-Export Bank

In 2014, debate erupted in Congress over whether to reauthorize an obscure federal agency: the Import-Export Bank ("Ex Im"). Critics called it "Boeing's Bank," accusing it of "crony capitalism" and unfairly subsidizing politically powerful companies like Boeing, General Electric, and Caterpillar. Supporters defended the bank as necessary to keep U.S. businesses competitive globally. The bank, established in 1934 by President Franklin D. Roosevelt as part of the New Deal, was made an independent executive agency by Congress in 1945. It had been reauthorized by Congress sixteen times, always with bipartisan support and little controversy.

The Ex-Im Bank is an export credit agency that provides loans and loan guarantees to foreign buyers of U.S. goods so they can buy more U.S. goods, and it provides U.S. companies with insurance for overseas transactions. Its loans make it easier for U.S. firms to sell goods abroad, and the insurance enables businesses to export goods to new markets overseas where there is higher risk of nonpayment. "Ex-Im is an absolute necessity in order to compete globally against state-funded and state-subsidized companies,"[38] insisted the CEO of Westinghouse. Boeing, the country's largest exporter by value of exports, made a similar argument. In 2013, $8 billion of the $37 billion in purchases financed by the bank went to Boeing clients[39] and, without Ex-Im, company officials feared airlines would turn to its competitor, Airbus, which sells aircraft with the support of European export-credit. Many small U.S. suppliers also rely on Boeing's success, and politicians in states like Washington and Kansas argued that reauthorization was crucial for their local economies. In June 2015 Congress let the bank's charter lapse, but in December reauthorized it through September 2019.

Free Trade in the Americas   While WTO talks languished, Washington aggressively pursued regional trade efforts. NAFTA became the model for all later regional efforts. Examining NAFTA also highlights trends across U.S. trade policy—emphasis on free-trade pacts to achieve economic liberalization and democratization based on a belief that these reinforce each other, a belief (often mistaken) that these trends will support U.S. political interests in a region and that the gradual decline of U.S. power makes Washington less able to dictate the terms of regional pacts.

Free trade is not new in the Americas. In 1854, U.S. officials negotiated with the British North American Colonies, which in 1867 would become independent Canada, a reciprocity treaty, eliminating duties on grains, meat, dairy products, and fish and promoting trade between the two economies until 1866 when protectionist fervor in the United States and anger over British and Canadian actions during America's Civil War led Washington to abrogate the agreement. After a brief attempt to liberalize U.S.-Canadian trade in the mid-1930s, a significant effort occurred in 1965, achieving free trade for motor vehicle manufacturers. It was not until the 1980s that Canada and Mexico sought more comprehensive trade agreements with Washington to avoid growing U.S. protectionist sentiment. In 1988, Washington signed with Canada, its largest trading partner, the Canadian-United States Free Trade Agreement (CUSFTA), to eliminate tariffs and other protectionist measures on goods, services, and foreign direct investment.

NAFTA began with the announcement in 1990 of negotiations for a free-trade area between the United States and Mexico. Canada, fearing it might lose the advantages it had secured in CUSFTA, joined the talks. For Mexico, a deal would promote growth by encouraging imports of goods and capital and lock in market-oriented economic reforms begun after Mexico's debt crisis in 1982 by raising "the political cost of reversing economic reforms and [making] it easier to deflect protectionist demands of industrial and special interest groups."[40] Washington was interested in supporting economic liberalization, gaining access to Mexico's growing market, and sparking progress in the ongoing Uruguay Round. NAFTA also offered insurance if those multilateral talks failed. NAFTA's U.S. advocates argued that an FTA would lead to job growth in America and generate economic growth in Mexico that would reduce illegal immigration into the United States.

After fourteen months, Canadian Prime Minister Brian Mulroney, Mexican President Carlos Salinas, and President George H. W. Bush signed NAFTA in 1992. The agreement eliminated many tariffs but did not achieve free trade in every sector. Mexico continued to operate a state-owned oil company (Pemex), and free trade in agriculture was achieved slowly, especially for politically sensitive commodities like corn, milk, beans, and sugar. In addition to reducing tariffs, NAFTA added protection for **intellectual property** (patents, trademarks, and copyrights) and prohibited nontariff trade barriers such as "local content rules" that require a certain percentage of equipment and services to be produced domestically.

The agreement was politically controversial in the United States and became an issue in the 1992 presidential race between George H. W. Bush and Bill Clinton. Bush argued that NAFTA would create jobs, but opponents, including labor organizations like the AFL-CIO, environmentalists, and consumer rights groups opposed the pact. Labor feared that lower wages in Mexico would induce U.S. firms to relocate there, and those that remained would offer lower wages to U.S. workers to remain competitive. Independent presidential candidate Ross Perot famously argued that NAFTA would create a "giant sucking sound" as jobs drained out of America into Mexico. Environmentalists feared increased pollution as firms moved to Mexico to evade U.S. and Canadian environmental standards, and consumer-rights advocates worried that harmonization of health, safety, and environmental standards would mean lower standards and less consumer protection.

Candidate Bill Clinton did not oppose NAFTA but promised to negotiate two side agreements to mitigate concerns of labor and environmentalists. The 1993 North American Agreement on Labor Cooperation and the North American Agreement on Environmental Cooperation created supranational institutions to hold governments accountable for enforcing their own labor and environmental standards, though the agreements lacked enforcement power. Clinton then lobbied for NAFTA's ratification, arguing it would generate new jobs. NAFTA was ratified by the Senate in November 1993 and entered into force on January 1, 1994. It was the first FTA to include developed and developing countries, treating them as equals. It would serve as a model for later regional negotiations, including the TPP and Transatlantic Trade and Investment Partnership (TTIP) that President Obama sought to complete during his second term.

Two decades later, NAFTA remained controversial. Proponents credited it with substantial increases in trade among North American partners—156 percent in twenty years—and higher incomes. They noted that in 1993 trade in North America was valued at $290 billion and in 2012 was valued at over $1.1 trillion.[41] They argued it had increased intrafirm trade, increased foreign direct investment, created an integrated supply chain, promoted intraregional travel, created two million jobs annually, and led to structural shifts that offer U.S. workers better jobs at lower costs to employers.[42] Critics countered it had achieved none of its early promises. Illegal immigration into the United States persisted, environmental problems remained, income inequality was growing, real wages had seen little growth, and drug trafficking had continued. They pointed to the effect of free trade on farmers, especially Mexican corn producers, and cited stagnant wages and higher food prices—notably the staple tortilla—as contributing to illegal immigration from Mexico. Others argued NAFTA had benefited major corporations and investors at the expense of ordinary Americans. It is difficult to disentangle NAFTA's effects from other global trends—intensifying globalization and the creation of the WTO—occurring at the same time. Owing to these trends, trade was already increasing and was accelerated by Mexico's entry into the GATT (1985) and NAFTA (1994).

Proponents speak of the need to "reinvigorate" NAFTA and pursue deeper North American economic integration. They applaud the inclusion of Canada and Mexico in talks to create a transpacific trade pact and argue they should also be included in transatlantic trade talks. Detractors counter that including Canada and Mexico in broader trade talks will reinforce problems already evident in NAFTA and claim it is time to renegotiate NAFTA to get a better deal for U.S. workers and industry.

While NAFTA was entering into force, the Free Trade Area of the Americas (FTAA) was proposed at the 1994 Summit of the Americas, a meeting of the 34 democratically elected heads of state in the Western Hemisphere. The FTAA would have been a comprehensive FTA among all countries in the hemisphere except authoritarian Cuba, and the same rules regulating trade and finance would have applied to all members. The agreement would have created a regional economy even larger than that of the EU (though it would not have included Europe's political and economic integration) and would have granted the United States equal access to all member markets. Advocates argued the proposed pact would raise living standards across the region, improve working conditions, and lead to stronger environmental protections.[43] Negotiations began in 1998 with the goal of completing negotiations by 2005.

Despite initial enthusiasm for hemispheric free trade, talks moved slowly, and no agreement was reached by 2005. Washington and others were waiting to see what progress would be made in the WTO's Doha Round and, more importantly, Latin American governments failed to unite around a free-trade relationship with Washington. During the period negotiations were underway, left-leaning governments were elected in Venezuela (1999), Chile (2000), Brazil (2003), Argentina (2003), and Uruguay (2005). Venezuelan President Hugo Chávez was especially vocal in his opposition to Washington and free trade. Referring to the FTAA as "an annexationist plan" to extend U.S. control over the region, he described it as "an old project of the imperial eagle that from the beginning has wanted to sink its claws"[44] into Latin America. In 2001, Chávez announced formation of the Bolivarian Alliance for the Americas (ALBA) as an alternative to the FTAA. Other leftist leaders were not as hostile as Chávez but feared that the FTAA would prove a mechanism by which Washington would lock in unfair trade advantages. U.S. negotiators were unwilling to discuss agricultural policy at all in the FTAA because it was being discussed in the WTO, and any agreement reached in the Doha talks would apply to the FTAA. Chile's President Ricardo Lagos summed up the frustrations of Latin American governments: "It is very difficult to promote free trade when . . . the asymmetry favors those who have more and not those who have less."[45]

With the imminent failure of FTAA talks and breakdown of global negotiations in Cancún in 2003, Washington became more interested in pursuing bilateral and regional agreements. What emerged was a "hub and spoke" system of trade groups rather than comprehensive regionalism. The 2004 Central American-Dominican Republic Free Trade Agreement involving the United States, Costa Rica, El Salvador, Guatemala, Honduras, Nicaragua, and the Dominican Republic was born and modeled after NAFTA. Washington also negotiated bilateral agreements with Chile (2003), Panama (2004), Colombia (2006), and Peru (2009).

The Trans-Pacific Partnership (TPP)   The TPP had been under negotiation among Singapore, Chile, New Zealand, and Brunei since 2002. Other countries gradually joined negotiations—Australia, Canada, Japan, Malaysia, Mexico, Peru, and Vietnam—with U.S. participation starting in 2008. In November 2009, President Obama committed himself to the talks, with the goal of "shaping a regional agreement that will have broad-based membership and the high standards worthy of a 21st-century trade agreement."[46] Achieving an agreement would harmonize trade agreements with other U.S. free-trade partners. These included some of America's fastest growing trade partners. As a group, these countries encompassed 800 million people, 40 percent of the world's GDP, and 40 percent of its trade. In 2013, America exported over $622.5 billion in manufactured goods to TPP countries, shipping almost $2 billion in goods to TPP countries every day. By one estimate, the United States would earn over $78 billion a year under the TPP and far more if free trade expanded to include the rest of the Asia-Pacific region.[47]

The draft treaty has 29 chapters including financial services, telecommunications, and food standards. It is more far-reaching than other trade agreements, seeking to liberalize trade in all goods and services and including issues not addressed by other trade agreements, like state-owned enterprises and intellectual property. Its proponents hoped it would eventually eliminate all tariffs and nontariff barriers to trade and investment.

The TPP was part of Washington's "pivot" to Asia (chapter 12). Trade was a central element of the pivot and was described by former Obama national security advisor Tom Donilon as the "centerpiece

TABLE 5.4   Trans-Pacific Partnership Countries (2012)

Country	Total trade with the United States (in billions)	Trade balance with the United States
Australia	$40.7	+
Brunei	$0.2	+
Canada	$616.0	−
Chile	$28.3	+
Japan	$216.4	−
Malaysia	$38.8	−
Mexico	$494.0	−
New Zealand	$6.7	+
Peru	$15.8	+
Singapore	$50.8	+
Vietnam	$24.9	−

Source: Data from *The Washington Post*, "Everything You Need to Know about the Trans Pacific Partnership," Wonk Blog, http://www .washingtonpost.com/blogs/wonkblog/wp/2013/12/11/everything-you-need-to-know-about-the-trans-pacific-partnership.

of our economic rebalancing."[48] But negotiations excluded China, and observers feared the TPP might invite Chinese retaliation.

Although talks were underway for over a decade, progress was slow. Negotiations stalled in 2013 with Japan's insistence on exemptions for rice, wheat, dairy, sugar, beef, and pork and Washington's efforts to get greater access for U.S. corporations in Japan's automotive market. Countries were experiencing "negotiation fatigue,"[49] explained Japan's TPP negotiator.

The agreement faced criticism at home and abroad, including concerns that it was being negotiated "in secret" with Washington not making draft texts available to lawmakers or the public. Secrecy is common in trade talks to ensure negotiators are not pressured during negotiation. Leaked materials, however, elevated concerns about the final document. In November 2013, the website Wikileaks published one of its most controversial chapters, on intellectual property. Although several Democratic senators, law professors, and public interest groups expressed concern about the agreement, proponents argued it would give U.S. companies greater access to some of the world's fastest growing markets, extend and deepen economic liberalism in Asia, and expand U.S. influence in the region. The TPP offered "a secure and lasting foothold for liberal trade, investment, and regulatory principles in the world's most economically promising region, one that might otherwise remain frozen in China's lengthening state capitalist shadow."[50] Initial agreement was finally reached in October 2015 on what was history's largest regional trade pact.

The Transatlantic Trade and Investment Partnership (TTIP) Washington is also pursuing a free trade agreement with Europe. America and Europe have one of the world's largest and most complex economic relationship. The U.S.-EU market accounted for over half of the value of world GDP and about 30 percent of world trade in 2013. Trade in goods and services between the United States and the EU totaled about $2.7 billion a day in 2012, and bilateral direct investment approached $4 trillion that same year.[51] As of 2010, according to Secretary of Commerce Gary Locke, transatlantic foreign direct investment accounted for 14 million jobs in Europe and America. Thus, the United States-European Union High Level Working Group on Jobs and Growth (HLWG) identified "a wide range of potential options for expanding transatlantic trade and investment." These included

- "elimination or reduction of conventional barriers to trade in goods, such as tariffs and tariff-rate quotas;

- elimination, reduction, or prevention of barriers to trade in goods, services, and investment;

- enhanced compatibility of regulations and standards;

- elimination, reduction, or prevention of unnecessary 'behind the border' nontariff barriers to trade in all categories; and

- enhanced cooperation for the development of rules and principles on global issues of common concern and also for the achievement of shared global economic goals."[52]

The HLWG report fostered the opening of U.S.-EU negotiations. The proposed elimination of all tariffs and building the world's largest free-trade area—the TTIP—would raise Europe's GDP by an estimated 0.4 percent and America's by 1 percent. "It's clear," declared the EU trade commissioner, "that the general public is much more interested in this deal than in any other deal before" because "the two biggest economies in the world are speaking to each other."[53] The EU concluded the agreement could bring annual benefits of $159 billion for its 28 members and strengthen their economic influence vis-à-vis rising China. And the benefits would be greater if nontariff trade barriers like import quotas or government-purchasing rules were also reduced or eliminated. Thus, the tariff on European chemical exports to America is only 1.2 percent, while nontariff barriers add 19 percent to their cost.

The TTIP may be too ambitious. The United States and the EU "are the biggest investors in each other's economies. But this very closeness makes progress harder. Easy deals have mostly been done; what is left is complicated. Tariffs are low (below 3% on average, though higher on farm products) but non-tariff barriers abound. Many have to do with consumers, public health, the environment or national security. Governments are not usually elected to compromise on such matters."[54] Thus, the EU has been a vigorous proponent of environmental regulation. The pre-EU European Economic Community adopted its first Environmental Action Program in 1973. Thereafter, the EU legislated the most extensive environmental regulations in the world. In 2005, it implemented a system of emissions trading that produced conflict with other governments and international airlines. The **cap and trade system** it imposed was designed to combat carbon emissions by allocating greenhouse gas allowances to airlines. If an airline produced less greenhouse gas than allowed, it could auction its remaining allowance to other companies. If an airline exceeded its allowance, it would have to purchase allowances for its emissions. In 2011, however,

Congress passed the European Union Emissions Trading Scheme Prohibition Act forbidding airlines from paying into the system, arguing that the EU lacked authority to regulate international travel. Standardization of environmental regulation is likely to be a major issue in negotiating the TTIP.

Although both sides agree that a free-trade zone would enhance their economies, disagreements emerged within and between the two. Many Europeans are concerned that the major role corporations were playing in negotiations threatened environmental and consumer-protection regulations. One issue involves whether corporations could sue countries that do not comply with the treaty. Differences exist between America and Europe on issues from trade in genetically modified foods and hormone-treated beef—both of which many European consumers oppose—to animal rights. Another problem involves French insistence on a "cultural exclusion" for audio-visual services. Hence, a Dutch observer concluded that political leaders "were way more optimistic than they should have been when they got started."[55] Negotiations were also impeded by a shutdown of the U.S. government in 2013 and European anger over a report made public by Edward Snowden that America's National Security Agency had bugged EU offices.

America's Trade Imbalance   Another dimension of trade policy involves the **balance of trade**, that is, the level of imports relative to exports. A country has a trade surplus and earns revenue from trade when the value of its exports exceeds the value of its imports. By contrast, when a country imports more than it exports, it has a trade deficit and accumulates debt. Washington has been running an overall trade deficit since the 1980s, though it maintains a trade surplus in certain bilateral trade relations, with, for example, in 2014 Hong Kong, the Netherlands, the United Arab Emirates, Belgium, Brazil, Australia, Panama, Singapore, and Argentina.[56] In 2013, America's largest bilateral deficit was with China, although the United States also had substantial deficits with Japan, Germany, Mexico, and Canada.[57]

DID YOU KNOW?

The Trade Gap with China

The U.S. trade gap with China hit a record high in September 2014. Imports from China were up nearly 13 percent from the previous month, with much of the increase attributed to Apple's release of the iPhone 6 and iPhone 6 Plus, which are assembled in China (though many of the iPhone's parts are manufactured elsewhere, including America, Taiwan, Japan, and Italy).[58]

America's trade imbalance and its causes and consequences are hotly contested. Some economists associate the trade deficit with high levels of economic growth; that is, when the U.S. economy is thriving U.S. consumers buy more imports. These economists believe trade balances are not harmful and attract foreign investment. Efforts to reduce deficits by suppressing demand, they argue, stunt economic growth. Others view trade deficits as harmful either because they are the consequence of the fact that U.S. companies are uncompetitive globally or because of the historical strength of the U.S. dollar, which

FIGURE 5.3   U.S. Trade in Goods with the World

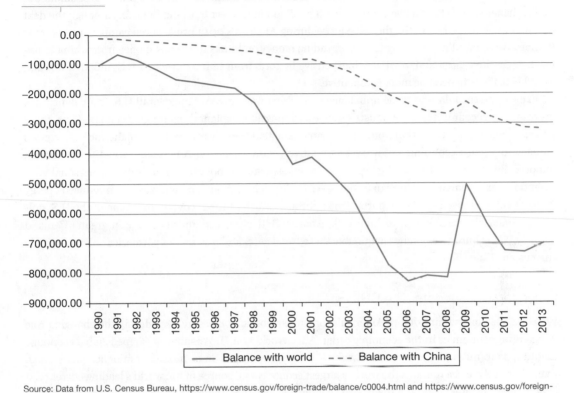

Source: Data from U.S. Census Bureau, https://www.census.gov/foreign-trade/balance/c0004.html and https://www.census.gov/foreign-trade/balance/c5700.html.

Note: Figures are in millions of U.S. dollars, on a nominal basis.

makes U.S. goods and services more expensive for foreign buyers. Trade deficits, they believe, stifle U.S. economic growth.

Many politicians and some economists blame unfair trade and exchange-rate policies of other governments, notably China for U.S. deficits. Presidential candidates have routinely demanded "tougher" trade policies toward China. And many Americans fear China's growing economic influence. Disputes over issues like China's dumping of solar panels have exacerbated trade tensions. Some 61 percent of Americans regard trade deficits as a serious problem, and an even larger percentage regard the loss of jobs to China as serious.[59] Erecting trade barriers to Chinese exports to the United States would, however, shield U.S.-based firms from foreign competition, thereby reducing their global competitiveness.

Almost 80 percent worry about the high level of U.S. debt held by China.[60] As Hillary Clinton declared to Australia's prime minister, "How do you deal toughly with your banker?"[61] That debt consists of U.S. government securities, mainly treasury bonds, purchased by China that constitutes funds China has lent the United States to pay for Chinese imports. If China invested its surplus funds in other countries,

Washington would have to borrow from other sources to pay for imports, probably at higher interest rates. The debt to China constituted about $1.25 trillion of America's total debt in 2014, the largest amount in foreign hands, and U.S. taxpayers paid some $30 billion in interest to China in 2012. Although the debt to China has declined recently, the issue arose during America's 2012 presidential campaign when Mitt Romney declared, "I'm not going to keep spending money on things to borrow money from China to pay for it."[62] On the other hand, relatively inexpensive imports from China have kept U.S. inflation low and forced U.S. firms to become more competitive.

Even while the bilateral trade imbalance with China was growing, the overall U.S. trade deficit has decreased in recent years. Economists offer several possible explanations for this change. First, there was less demand for imports at home at the same time that there was growing demand for U.S. exports abroad. America's economic recovery was relatively slow, reducing Americans' appetite for foreign imports. By contrast, in several emerging economies, which rebounded more quickly, personal consumption—and demand for foreign imports—rose. Second, America's oil and gas boom reduced energy imports and increased energy exports. Third, through much of the recovery, the value of the U.S. dollar remained historically low, making U.S. exports relatively cheap and therefore in greater demand globally.[63] It is hard to say how sustainable these trends are, and it is unlikely America will run a trade surplus any time soon.

Emerging Challengers: The BRICS

We conclude our examination of America's foreign economic policies by considering the changing role of emerging economies in the economic order. After World War II, Washington shaped global economic institutions to reflect its interests and values. Over time, American economic dominance has eroded. Even though America remains the world's largest economy and source of the world's leading currency, it is no longer unchallenged, and the liberal economic values that underpin the global economic order do not always support U.S. economic interests. Washington still exercises substantial influence in economic affairs, but not consistently across all issue areas.

Between 2000 and 2010, the emerging economies grew dramatically, and by 2012 they accounted for 50 percent of world GDP. Among these economies, Brazil, Russia, India, China, and South Africa[64] experienced the most rapid growth from 1993 to 2007, by 6.5 percent annually in India and 10.5 percent annually in China, becoming four of the largest ten national economies in the world. During this period, almost three-quarters of developing countries grew faster than America.[65]

The BRICS' rapid growth has had positive and negative effects globally. Their growth kept global growth from falling even more sharply following the recession in the developed world. Simultaneously, trade imbalances ballooned. America experienced widening trade deficits as U.S. consumers imported more, and some of the BRICS, especially China, accumulated huge trade surpluses as they exported more to the developed world. The BRICS retained these surpluses, accumulating ever-larger dollar reserves that helped them maintain lower exchange rates for their currencies that made their exports less expensive.

The BRICS' impact has not only been economic but has had consequences for social, political, and even military relations. Rapid economic growth meant that more money was available for military spending. Brazil, India, Russia, and especially China (chapter 12) have all planned to increase

FIGURE **5.4** Emerging-Market Share of World GDP

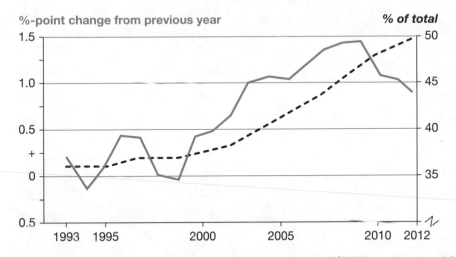

Source: Data from the International Monetary Fund, http://www.economist.com/news/briefing/21582257-most-dramatic-and-disruptive-period-emerging-market-growth-world-has-ever-seen.

Note: Figures are at purchasing-power parity.

their defense budgets in the coming years. The emerging economies also sought greater political influence in global institutions consistent with their economic status. We have already noted how India thwarted the efforts of the WTO to achieve a comprehensive trade deal in 2014. They also wish a larger voice in the IMF. That agency is funded by member governments, and those that contribute the most to the fund also enjoy the most influence. The United States has had a controlling share in the fund, giving it substantial influence in the Board of Governors, the IMF's highest decision-making body. With 16.75 percent of the votes, Washington can veto major policy reforms. By contrast, Brazil, Russia, India, and China combined accounted for only 10.26 percent of the votes in the IMF, while Europe's largest economies—Germany, France, Britain, and Italy—have a combined share of 17.6 percent of the votes. The IMF provides loans on terms requiring policy reforms as well as interest. These reforms reflected U.S. interests and values—"the Washington Consensus"—that recipients frequently found economically and politically painful. Led by China, the BRICS argued for a greater voice in IMF policymaking.

In 2010, the IMF Board of Governors—including the United States—agreed to reforms to increase members' quota subscriptions (the funding provided to the IMF), doubling the fund's resources and shifting more than 6 percent of voting shares to emerging and developing economies. This shift would make China the third largest donor and reduce Western influence. The reforms also would give a greater voice to Brazil and India. Implementation, though, was subject to ratification by IMF members. Because Washington has effective veto power over major IMF decisions, its support was necessary, but as of 2015, Congress had failed to ratify the reform package. Congress did not have to authorize any new money but needed to approve the transfer of funds already allocated to the IMF from one budget line

TABLE 5.5   IMF Vote Reform

	Vote Share (%)	GDP 2013 (millions of U.S. dollars)
United States	16.75	16,800,000
Largest European Economies	17.55	10,962,460
Germany	5.81	3,634,823
France	4.29	2,734,949
Britain	4.29	2,521,381
Italy	3.16	2,071,307
Emerging Economies	10.26	15,459,517
China	3.81	9,240,270
Russia	2.39	2,096,777
India	2.34	1,876,797
Brazil	1.72	2,245,673

Sources: Vote share data from "IMF Members' Quota and Voting Power, and IMF Board of Governors," International Monetary Fund, December 1, 2014, http://www.imf.org/external/np/sec/memdir/members.aspx; GDP data from World Bank, "Gross Domestic Product 2013," World Development Indicators Database, September 22, 2014, http://databank.worldbank.org/data/download/GDP.pdf.

to another. In March 2013, a bipartisan group of former U.S. cabinet officials and legislators called on Congress to implement the IMF reforms. In a letter to then House Speaker John Boehner and Senate Majority Leader Harry Reid, they argued that "by helping to foster the conditions for economic growth, the IMF enhances political stability in volatile regions of the world. . . . Continued support [of the IMF] will ensure the U.S.' ability to leverage its economic development dollars and ensure its on-going influence on the IMF to prioritize areas we deem critical, such as improving governance, privatization, and strengthened financial systems."[66]

With IMF governance reform stalled by Congress, Brazil, Russia, India, China, and South Africa announced their intention in July 2014 to establish the New Development Bank in Shanghai, a developing-country alternative to the IMF and World Bank. Each sponsor agreed to contribute $10 billion for an initial capitalization of $50 billion that would grow to $100 billion. The BRICS fund would be available for members to draw on during balance of payments crises and would fund infrastructure projects in emerging economies. In contrast to existing global institutions, the New Development Bank would ensure that emerging economies control funding decisions. There are challenges to be overcome to get this initiative up and running, not the least of which is the fact that the other BRICS have slower rates of economic growth than China. But, if the new bank gets started, it will pose a significant challenge to the U.S.-led global economic institutions and the dominance of the U.S. dollar.

Announcing the BRICS New Development Bank: Vladimir Putin (Russia), Narendra Modi (India), Dilma Rousseff (Brazil), Xi Jinping (China), and Jacob Zuma (South Africa) at the BRICS 2014 Summit

Nelson Almeida/AFP/Getty Images

China also announced formation of an Asian Infrastructure Development Bank (AIIB), as another rival to the Western-dominated IMF and World Bank and the Asian Development Bank. The AIIB would have available funding amounts similar to the New Development Bank that would be used to fund new infrastructure—roads, ports, railroads—which the growing economies of Asia seek, while affording Beijing increasing economic influence in the region. Washington has opposed this initiative, but by April 2015, 36 countries, including some of America's closest European and Asian allies, had announced they would become members of the AIIB and lend money to it.

FUTURE: FOREIGN ECONOMIC POLICY

Financial and Monetary Policy

As noted above, there are three principle financial and monetary policy options in the pursuit of economic recovery: interest rate reductions, quantitative easing, and forward guidance. Devaluation is an additional option.

Policy Options

a. *Interest rate reductions.* By 2014, at nearly 0 percent, interest rates were about as low as they could possibly go and still stimulate spending. Further reductions are not a viable policy option for America but would probably benefit major European and Asian economies.

b. *Additional quantitative easing.* The policy of creating money to buy assets was abandoned in 2014 after three rounds had achieved success in keeping interest rates and inflation low and stimulating economic growth. The end of QE3 was hailed in some quarters as a welcome signal that economic growth and job creation were sufficiently robust to continue without government support. Others argue that the costs of QE are overstated and that a premature end to quantitative easing will ensure another round— QE4—down the road.

c. *Employ forward guidance.* Supporters of forward guidance believe clearly communicating future monetary policies is an effective tool to lower interest rates and reduce volatility. Fed leaders including Greenspan and Yellen, however, tended to use vague technical jargon—"Fedspeak"— that obscures rather than illuminates. Opaque communications can have dramatic market effects, particularly when they seem to indicate policies like QE will end earlier than expected. Even with clear communication, some believe forward guidance entails long-term risks, particularly if financial markets focus narrowly on certain elements of a central bank's forward guidance, any change in that guidance might prove disruptive.

Trade

There are two central policy options for U.S. policymakers in trade: greater protectionism or greater trade liberalization. Each, however, can take several forms. Is it in America's interest, for instance, to pursue free trade through global institutions or to establish regional free trade?

Policy Options

a. *Increase protectionism, and pursue a policy of economic nationalism.* A protectionist policy would be a difficult course for Washington to follow. First, participation in the WTO strictly limits the restrictions that governments can place on trade. When the WTO allows restrictions, it is to enable governments to protect threatened sectors temporarily—from short-term economic shocks—and not to protect noncompetitive industries over time. Second, the structure of the global economy has evolved since the protectionist era of the 1920s. Today, most global trade is conducted among affiliates of multinational companies, and global supply chains are so highly integrated that even companies that produce for a domestic market rely heavily on imported parts. Such factors mean there would be relatively little support domestically for protectionism, which would impose higher costs on U.S. firms and households.

b. *Continue multilateral efforts to liberalize trade through the WTO.* Washington still works through the WTO to extend trade liberalization into new sectors globally, but the WTO process is slow, especially when politically sensitive sectors, like agriculture, are negotiated. Of late, emerging economies like India have been obstructionist.

c. *Negotiate new regional FTAs.* Given the difficulty in negotiating additions to the multilateral trade regime, Washington has focused on negotiating and extending regional FTAs—notably the TTP and the TTIP. Liberalized trade with Asia and Europe would generate new growth and investment, but significant difficulties remain in negotiating these agreements. Sensitive issues and sectors are under negotiation in both cases, including the status of state-owned enterprises and intellectual property in the TPP and nontariff barriers like health and environmental standards in the TTIP. Progress has also been hampered by public opposition over the secretive process of trade talks and European anger over U.S. surveillance of the EU.

d. *Grant the president fast track or Trade Promotion Authority (TPA).* Negotiation fatigue has also been cited as a reason for stalled progress in regional trade talks. Advocates of TPA contend that permission to negotiate a treaty that Congress must vote up or down without amendments would facilitate negotiations with Europe and Asia. Without TPA, other governments are reluctant to finalize trade deals, recognizing that Congress could amend agreements beyond recognition, forcing additional talks. Democrats, traditionally more suspicious of trade agreements and their impact on U.S. workers, opposed granting President Obama TPA, and as long as they enjoyed a Senate majority, they could prevent reauthorization. After the Republican sweep of Congress in 2014, Obama did receive TPA. And agreement was reached among the United States and eleven other countries on the TPP, involving 40 percent of the world's economy, although the Senate still had to ratify it.

e. *Reduce trade imbalances.* The trade and budget deficits and the debt they produce have been sources of political conflict in recent years. One option is to ignore the trade balance, assuming it will right itself eventually or be offset by greater foreign investment in the United States. Most politicians, however, fear public reaction to trade deficits.

f. *Increase the competitiveness of U.S. industries and labor.* This can involve offering government assistance to domestic industries. However, the WTO restricts national efforts to support industry openly. Washington could improve competitiveness by authorizing the Trade Adjustment Assistance (TAA) to U.S. workers who lose jobs because of foreign competition. First created by the 1962 Trade Expansion Act, TAA offers job placement assistance, income support, education, and retraining to help workers find jobs in new fields. Reauthorized several times since 1974, TAA was most recently reauthorized for another six years in June 2015. Neither Democrats, who would like to see more job retraining and unemployment support, nor Republicans, who believe the program costs too much, view TAA as the ideal solution to improving competitiveness.[67]

g. *Implement tough policies against countries that use unfair trade and exchange-rate policies.* This policy would involve applying pressure to compel countries like China to revalue their currency to reflect its market value as occurred in mid-2015 and end unfair trade policies like predatory pricing ("dumping"). Such a policy is complicated by China's possession of U.S. foreign debt. In addition, U.S. demand for inexpensive Chinese goods keeps American inflation low. If Washington were to "get tough," Beijing might sell surplus dollars, reducing the dollar's value and invest additional funds elsewhere, reducing foreign investment in America and forcing U.S. firms to borrow from other lenders at higher interest rates.

h. *Keep the U.S. dollar weak.* Through much of the recovery, the dollar remained historically weak, making U.S. exports less expensive relative to foreign competitors but also making imports more costly. Perceptions that America's economy was recovering and that the Federal Reserve would increase interest rates have driven up the dollar's value. Higher interest rates will benefit investors, but a stronger dollar makes U.S. exports more expensive relative to foreign competitors, slowing domestic economic growth. With the dollar at its highest level since 2006, the Bank for International Settlements in December 2014 warned that the appreciating dollar could destabilize the global economy, particularly emerging economies, which have international bank loans amounting to $3.1 trillion, mainly in U.S. dollars.[68] Their debt obligations increase as their currencies depreciate relative to the dollar. In 2013, G-20 finance ministers agreed not to engage "directly" in competitive devaluation, but "loose" U.S. monetary policy that could produce such competition because Washington was using monetary policy to advance domestic objectives.

Emerging Economies

American monetary and trade policies have direct impact on emerging economies that demand a greater voice in global economic governance. How should Washington react to the demands of the BRICS?

Policy Options

a. *Do nothing.* Maintain the current decision-making structures in the IMF and the World Bank. These institutions afford enormous influence to the wealthiest countries that contribute the most funding to these agencies. Although IMF members agreed in 2010 to a reform that would increase the contributions of emerging economies and grant them greater voting power, it required U.S. congressional approval. Without such approval, the reform effort stalled, and the BRICS began to turn to alternative institutions like their proposed New Development Bank. If such alternative arrangements gain traction, Washington will lose additional influence in the global monetary and financial regimes.

b. *Reform the global economic institutions.* Accepting the 2010 reform package would offer emerging economies a greater voice in economic governance, and Washington would retain its current share of the vote. To date, Congress has refused to pass the reform measure or transfer funds necessary to meet the new U.S. quota obligation. American intransigence will drive emerging economies away from existing institutions where Washington enjoys great influence to alternative arrangements.

c. *Rely increasingly on informal arrangements like the G-20 that involve emerging economies.* During the financial crisis, Washington coordinated economic policy closely with the G-20 to prevent the crisis from becoming another Great Depression. However, as the crisis subsided, the G-20 itself became less united, complicating Washington's work with the group to coordinate global economic policy.

CONCLUSION: AMERICA AND THE GLOBALIZED ECONOMY

Since becoming a world power, America has had to balance interests and values in foreign economic policy. U.S. interests emphasize economic growth within a stable and highly integrated global and regional economy, while values favor liberal economic policies to achieve these goals. A principled belief in liberal economic policies sometimes may clash with economic interests. When this occurs, interests often dominate, but in global economics that does not require Washington to abandon multilateralism. In financial and monetary policy where U.S. leadership remains strong, officials have considerable latitude in using domestic and foreign policy tools. Washington has relied unilaterally on the Fed, an independent government agency, to maintain low interest rates that promote economic growth, while also using the G-20 and the IMF to coordinate policy globally. In other areas, like trade, where U.S. leadership is weaker and unilateral measures are ineffective, Washington works through the WTO when possible but increasingly focuses on developing regional trade institutions.

The rise of the BRICS poses challenges for U.S. foreign economic policies. As these economies grow, their governments seek greater influence in international economic institutions. Such influence will come at the expense of U.S. influence, and a key challenge for America in the years ahead will be to preserve U.S. leadership while recognizing the changing distribution of economic power and offering a greater voice to the BRICS in economic institutions based on *both* liberal economic and political norms.

DISCUSSION QUESTIONS

1. What evidence is there that the United States is no longer an economic hegemon?

2. How do neoliberal and neomercantilist policies differ? Which do you favor for the United States, and why?

3. Discuss the evolution of America's foreign trade policies over time.

4. What is monetary policy, and what is the Fed's role in shaping such policy? How did the Fed respond to the global financial crisis of 2008?

5. In what ways are America's domestic and foreign trade policies and practices linked?

6. What political and economic differences impede economic cooperation between the G-7 and the BRICS and other emerging economies?

KEY TERMS

balance of payments (p. 135)

balance of trade (p. 154)

beggar-thy-neighbor policies (p. 133)

BRICS (p. 128)

cap and trade system (p. 153)

devaluation (p. 133)

embedded liberalism (p. 146)

emerging economies (p. 128)

"fast track" authority (p. 130)

free trade (p. 128)

gold standard (p. 133)

gold-exchange standard (p. 134)

Group of 20 (p. 136)

inflation (p. 135)

integrated supply chain (p. 150)

intellectual property (p. 149)

managed float system
    (p. 135)

monetary policy (p. 131)

most-favored nation rule (p. 145)

neoliberals (p. 128)

neomercantilists (p. 128)

protectionism (p. 129)

purchasing-power parity
    (p. 157)

quantitative easing (p. 138)

quotas (p. 142)

recession (p. 135)

reserve or "hard" currency
    (p. 134)

speculation (p. 132)

subsidies (p. 142)

tariffs (p. 131)

Transatlantic Trade and
    Investment Partnership
    (TTIP) (p. 150)

Trans-Pacific Partnership
    (TPP) (p. 143)

Washington consensus
    (p. 135)

Sharpen your skill with SAGE edge at **edge.sagepub.com/mansbach**

SAGE edge for Students provides a personalized approach to help you accomplish your coursework goals in an easy-to-use learning environment.

6

Democracy and Human Rights

LEGITIMATE OBJECTIVES OF AMERICAN POLICY?

President Barack Obama signs the Jackson-Vanik Repeal and Sergei Magnitsky Rule of Law Accountability Act in December 2002.

Mandel Ngan/AFP/Getty Images

American values and interests are in constant tension regarding **human rights**. The Declaration of Independence and the Constitution's Bill of Rights showcase U.S. values and the nation's commitment to universal human rights, including democracy, but American foreign policies do not always reflect these values. "Americans don't see it this way, but the country with the most puzzling human rights record in the world is their own."[1] A human rights expert observed that although Washington led efforts to promote the 1948 **Universal Declaration of Human Rights** (UDHR), since then it "has been the chief laggard in translating them into international law."[2] And America has long resisted multilateral tools to advance human rights. It only ratified the 1948 Genocide Convention in 1988, and it took another four years to ratify the 1966 International Covenant on Civil and Political Rights, codifying the civil rights and liberties articulated in the nonbinding UDHR. Between 1948 and 2015, Washington signed eleven multilateral human rights treaties but ratified only six. Indeed, all UN members have ratified the 1990 Convention on the Rights of the Child *except* America and Somalia. U.S. leaders have refused even to *sign* nine human rights treaties dealing with issues like women's and migrants' rights. Some observers argue that Washington does not need to participate in these treaties, because its domestic protections already meet or exceed the standards set by international law. Others insist that if Washington seeks to advance its values it ought to set an example and hold itself accountable under international law to persuade other governments to improve their human rights records.

Another contradiction in U.S. policy involves efforts to hold other governments accountable for human rights abuses. Washington rarely hesitates to criticize major powers like Russia and China, medium powers like Venezuela and Iran, and small states like Myanmar or Cuba, but when advancing human rights conflicts with geostrategic or trade interests, values are often set aside. When strategic imperatives have required cooperation with nondemocratic regimes, Washington has frequently turned a blind eye to human rights, as did the Reagan administration in supporting anticommunist regimes in El Salvador and Guatemala in the 1980s.

This chapter examines why there is tension between values and interests and U.S. efforts to promote democracy and human rights elsewhere and notes how human rights is an issue where Washington's inconsistency (or hypocrisy according to critics) undermines U.S. influence.

SOURCES OF U.S. HUMAN RIGHTS POLICIES

Several trends have long coexisted in U.S. human rights policies, but since America's emergence as a global leader, concern for interests has frequently trumped concern for human rights. Rather than

Timeline

1900

1945–1946 The Nuremberg trials charge Nazi leaders with "crimes against humanity."

1948 UN Universal Declaration of Human Rights

1968 U.S. soldiers are accused of a massacre in My Lai, Vietnam.

1974 The Jackson-Vanik Amendment ties U.S. trade policy to Russian human rights practices.

1900 (Continued)

1994 The Clinton administration refuses to characterize violence in Rwanda as genocide.

promoting the spread of global human rights norms, U.S. policy has favored unilaterally identifying and ending human rights abuses in specific countries and regions.

External sources of U.S. human rights policy include the threat environment, the balance of power, economic interdependence, and the willingness of other governments to respond to external pressure. During the early Cold War, bipolarity eroded U.S. human rights concerns. Washington tended to point to Soviet abuses for political gain, and Moscow reciprocated. Recently, fears of transnational terrorism have frequently overshadowed human rights concerns. Washington is sometimes less critical of human rights abuses by friendly governments, especially when such violations involve counterterrorism. In some cases, America has benefited from these abuses, as in the Central Intelligence Agency's (CIA's) program to turn prisoners over to governments in places like Egypt and Thailand for detainment and interrogation. U.S. officials have also tended to interpret human rights laws in a manner that gives them latitude to pursue, detain, and interrogate terrorist suspects.

Economic factors also influence U.S. emphasis on democracy promotion and human rights. Washington has repeatedly used trade policy to advance human rights. As economies become globalized, however, there are additional opportunities and costs to using trade policy to influence the human rights policies of trade partners. Sanctions against China, for example, also reduce U.S. exports and raise costs for U.S. consumers.

Finally, U.S. leaders are constrained by the resistance of repressive regimes that regard limiting human rights as necessary to their survival or security. China, Russia, Nigeria, Saudi Arabia, and Zimbabwe, for example, resist pressures to implement reforms to protect the civil and political rights of citizens, and efforts to persuade these regimes to implement reforms have limited success.

Congress and the president are significant governmental sources of human rights policy. The executive branch is responsible for articulating a coherent foreign policy, including balancing democracy and human rights with other goals. Human rights treaties require the Senate's advice and consent. Congress has historically pressed for a more robust human rights policy when presidents prioritized other goals, as did the Nixon, Ford, and Reagan administrations. Congressional action in the 1970s reflected societal pressures that, reacting to human rights abuses in the Vietnam War including the killing of civilians by

2000

2000 President Clinton argues China should be admitted to the World Trade Organization (WTO) to encourage human rights reform.

2001 Congress passes the USA Patriot Act.

2002 The Naval base at Guantánamo is repurposed to detain suspected terrorists captured overseas.

2003 It is revealed that U.S. personnel at Abu Ghraib prison (Iraq) committed widespread human rights violations.

2000 (Continued)

2009 President Obama signs an executive order to close the Guantánamo facility within a year.

2013 *The Guardian* leaks documents provided by Edward Snowden revealing widespread surveillance of Americans and foreign leaders by the National Security Agency (NSA).

U.S. soldiers in the village of My Lai in 1968, forced the administration to pay greater attention to human rights. In 1976, Congress established a human rights bureau in the State Department and thereafter required that bureau to report to it annually on human rights standards of countries receiving U.S. aid (and later all governments). That year, Congress also passed the Jackson-Vanik amendment to the 1974 Trade Act, denying Soviet-bloc countries preferential trade status and investment guarantees if they prevented their citizens from emigrating. This legislation pressured Moscow to allow hundreds of thousands of Soviet citizens to emigrate to America and Israel.[3] Congress played a similar role in the 1980s, rejecting President Ronald Reagan's nomination of Ernest Lefever as assistant secretary of state for human rights and humanitarian affairs because Lefever believed America had "no responsibility—and certainly no authority—to promote human rights in other sovereign states."[4]

Societal sources of human rights policy run deeper than public opinion. In some respects, the advancement of human rights has always been part of America's political culture. Political scientist Andrew Moravcik observed that America's "rights culture" involves three dimensions: a deep respect—even reverence—for the Constitution, a partiality for local government institutions linked to popular sovereignty, and a preference for "negative human rights" (individual civil and political liberties that governments may not limit) over "positive human rights" (social and economic rights that governments must provide) in international human rights instruments.[5]

The Bill of Rights, which is an enduring symbol of freedom and liberty to Americans, has also been an obstacle to U.S. participation in multilateral human rights treaties because Washington fears assuming international obligations that might conflict with the rights and powers described in the Constitution. These concerns take several forms. Some opponents of multilateralism fear that in acceding to human rights treaties, Washington may become obligated to protect rights *not* recognized in the Constitution, especially positive economic, social, and cultural rights that have never been central in American political culture. Others worry that such treaties may infringe on the rights of U.S. states to exercise sovereignty over matters like marriage, education, or capital punishment. What such arguments have in common is a view of America as "exceptional," with a legal and a judicial system that is superior to others and that cannot be judged by others' standards.

Individuals have also shaped U.S. human rights policy. Senator John Bricker (R-OH) unsuccessfully fought in the 1950s to amend the Constitution to prohibit ratification of **self-executing treaties**. Bricker argued that a treaty should "become effective in the United States only through legislation which would be valid in the absence of the treaty."[6] Bricker wanted to make it impossible for treaties to limit civil rights and liberties protected by the Bill of Rights: "My purpose in offering this resolution is to bury the so-called Covenant on Human Rights so deep that no one holding high public office will ever dare to attempt its resurrection."[7] Bricker's belief that treaties might supersede the Constitution is still shared by many in Congress.

During the Cold War, John Foster Dulles believed that containing communism was sufficient as human rights policy.[8] In their role as secretary of state, Dulles and later Henry Kissinger viewed human rights through the lens of national interest. "I believe," Kissinger argued, "it is dangerous for us to make the domestic policy of countries around the world a direct objective of U.S. foreign policy"[9] because doing so would damage relations with key allies. President Jimmy Carter, by contrast, was driven by his personal moral code to elevate human rights—at least rhetorically—on his foreign-policy agenda. Presidents

Reagan and Clinton both articulated doctrines of democracy promotion. Reagan's "crusade for freedom" supported anticommunist guerrilla forces fighting communist regimes in Afghanistan, Cambodia, and Nicaragua, and Clinton's doctrine of democratic enlargement integrated human rights and economic policy as it sought expansion of the "world's free community of market democracies."[10]

PAST: DISCERNING TRENDS IN U.S. HUMAN RIGHTS POLICY

Human rights scholar David Forsythe describes three orientations in U.S. human rights policy. The first, enlightenment **cosmopolitanism** (a variant of classical liberalism), emphasizes that universal human rights apply to all without consideration of national origin or characteristics like race, **ethnicity**, or religion. "The revolutionary generation was the most cosmopolitan of any in American history. The revolutionary leaders . . . were not obsessed, as were later generations, with the unique character of America or with separating America from the course of Western civilization. . . . They regarded everyone from different nations as their countrymen and ignored neighborhoods, towns, and countries as 'distinctions too limited for continental minds.'"[11] Jimmy Carter was the only presidential proponent of enlightened cosmopolitanism. For much of American history, it has been nongovernmental organizations (NGOs) and progressive lawyers who advocated universal application of human rights.

A second orientation derives from **American exceptionalism,** a "providential nationalism" that views America as a "city on the hill," with values that are divinely supported and thus not subject to criticism. A third orientation is pragmatism that defines human rights policy on a case-by-case basis, balancing such rights against other interests. Recent U.S. human rights policy has exhibited all three tendencies. As Arthur Schlesinger observed, "Americans have agreed since 1776 that the United States must be the beacon of human rights to an unregenerate world. The question has always been how America is to execute this mission."[12] The question of how to advance its values without compromising interests has been a concern since America's emergence as a superpower after World War II.

Postwar Human Rights Policy

In negotiations to establish a United Nations, Washington supported incorporating only general references to human rights in the UN Charter, short of the binding obligations that small states and NGOs advocated. Americans played a prominent role in drafting the UDHR that became the cornerstone of the human rights regime. In 1946, President Harry Truman appointed Eleanor Roosevelt to represent Washington in establishing the UN Commission on Human Rights that drafted the UDHR. Mrs. Roosevelt was elected chair of both the preparatory body and the Commission, where she worked aggressively to include negative civil and political liberties as well as the social and economic rights sought by other governments. Washington opposed making human rights binding, and the final document remained aspirational. It supported the UDHR in the UN, but it would be many years before the United States signed the International Covenant on Civil and Political Rights that codified the civil and political rights articulated in the UDHR. The United States also signed but did not ratify the International Covenant on Economic, Social, and Cultural Rights. Indeed, Washington

🗝 KEY DOCUMENT
Franklin D. Roosevelt, "Four Freedoms Speech," 1941

In his 1941 State of the Union Address, nearly a year before America would enter World War II, Franklin Roosevelt articulated a cosmopolitan vision of freedom:

"In the future days, which we seek to make secure, we look forward to a world founded upon four essential human freedoms. The first is freedom of speech and expression—everywhere in the world. The second is freedom of every person to worship God in his own way—everywhere in the world. The third is freedom from want—which . . . means economic understandings which will secure to every nation a healthy peacetime life for its inhabitants—everywhere in the world. The fourth is freedom from fear—which . . . means a worldwide reduction of armaments to such a point and in such a thorough fashion that no nation will be in a position to commit an act of physical aggression against any neighbor—anywhere in the world."

Source: Franklin D. Roosevelt, "Four Freedoms Speech," January 1, 1941, http://www.fdrlibrary.marist.edu/pdfs/fftext.pdf.

frequently has signed human rights agreements but has been reluctant to ratify them and when it did so often attached reservations that limited U.S. obligations.

One reason why Washington opposed binding instruments between the 1940s and the 1960s was concern that such obligations would embarrass America owing to domestic race relations. Presidents "were keenly aware that race was an albatross around the neck of U.S. foreign policy."[13] Thus, it would be the 1970s before any serious effort was made to sign or ratify new human rights treaties. The many reservations, understandings, and declarations that accompanied ratification led critics to claim U.S. participation was "specious, meretricious, and hypocritical."[14] Limits on U.S. acceptance of multilateral agreements included refusal to undertake obligations inconsistent with the Constitution or requiring changes to existing law or practice such as the jurisdiction of the International Court of Justice to adjudicate disputes over treaties. Washington also refused treaties that were self-executing—that may be enforced in courts without prior congressional legislation—despite a constitutional provision in Article VI that treaties are the law of the land and hence are self-executing.[15]

The Carter Years After the election of Jimmy Carter in 1976, human rights assumed a central place in U.S. foreign policy. Carter was a vigorous advocate during his first two years in office, denouncing communist as well as friendly governments in Argentina, Iran, South Africa, South Korea, and Rhodesia (Zimbabwe) for human rights violations. But he reserved his strongest criticisms in cases where

Race and U.S. Human Rights Policy

America's civil rights struggles have complicated efforts to foster human rights abroad. Americans contend that "all men are created equal," but reality has not always reflected this. Slavery was only abolished in 1864 with the Thirteenth Amendment to the Constitution, and legally sanctioned discrimination continued until the civil rights movement of the 1950s and 1960s. Many governments, especially those in communist and developing states, accused Washington of hypocrisy in human rights owing to racially motivated domestic violence. They reported the marches, sit-ins, and protests in which African-Americans demanded equal rights, and the race riots that erupted in Newark, Los Angeles, and Detroit. Even Secretary Dulles recognized the impact such events had on America's image. As the battle to desegregate schools began in Little Rock, Arkansas, in 1957, Dulles observed, "This situation [is] ruining our foreign policy. . . . The effect of this in Asia and Africa will be worse for us than [the invasion of] Hungary was for the Russians."[16] Thus, some observers believe the need for a better image abroad was a "critical factor" influencing presidential administrations in that era to pursue civil rights reform.[17]

Today, U.S. racial unrest continues to damage America's global image. The world followed closely when police in separate incidents in New York and Missouri killed two unarmed African-Americans in 2014. In July, Eric Garner died in New York City after a police officer put him in a chokehold while trying to arrest him for selling cigarettes on the street. Several weeks later, Michael Brown, a teenager in Ferguson, Missouri, was shot in an encounter with white police. His death sparked national protests, and in Ferguson riots and looting prompted the governor to declare a state of emergency, impose a curfew, and deploy the National Guard to restore order. Later that year, just days apart, a grand jury in Missouri decided not to indict the police officer who had shot Brown and another grand jury in New York decided not to indict the officer accused of killing Garner.

Both decisions sparked criticism from abroad. A French human rights expert explained that the cases "added to our existing concerns over the longstanding prevalence of racial discrimination faced by African-Americans, particularly in relation to access to justice and discriminatory police practices."[18] Regimes that Washington often criticized for human rights abuses relished an opportunity to reciprocate. China's news agency Xinhua noted, "The Ferguson incident once again demonstrates that even in a country that has for years tried to play the role of an international human rights judge and defender, there is still much room for improvement at home."[19] Russia's foreign ministry was less diplomatic, urging Americans to "pay more attention to restoring order in their own country before imposing their dubious experience on other nations."[20] Even Iran's Ayatollah Khamenei joined the conversation on Twitter: "The day when American nation realize their socioeconomic problems stem from domination of #Israel over their govt, what'll happen? #Ferguson."[21] Amnesty International tweeted what many non-Americans were thinking: "U.S. can't tell other countries to improve their records on policing and peaceful assembly if it won't clear up its own human rights record."[22]

Foreign criticism of America erupted again in April 2015 after riots in Baltimore protesting the death of a 25-year-old African-American, Freddie Gray, who died of a spinal cord injury while in police custody. North Korea's state newspaper accused America of being "the worst tundra of human rights in the world."[23] Russia's state television compared events in Baltimore to pro-Western protests in Ukraine in 2014, accusing President Obama of hypocrisy for having praised Ukrainian protestors for exercising their democratic rights while chastising Baltimore protestors as criminals. Although America is more complex than these regimes were willing to acknowledge, their responses highlighted how U.S. race relations can undermine efforts to pursue human rights abroad.

TABLE 6.1   U.S. Participation in Global and Regional Human Rights Instruments

Human Rights Instrument	Ratification Status	U.S. Status
Convention on the Prevention and Punishment of the Crime of Genocide (1948)	Signature 1948 Ratification/Accession 1988	State Party
International Convention on the Elimination of All Forms of Racial Discrimination (1965)	Signature 1966 Ratification/Accession 1994	State Party
International Covenant on Civil and Political Rights (1966)	Signature 1977 Ratification/Accession 1992	State Party
Optional Protocol to the International Covenant on Civil and Political Rights (1966)	Signature NA Ratification/Accession NA	No Action
Second Optional Protocol to the International Covenant on Civil and Political Rights, Aiming at the Abolition of the Death Penalty (1989)	Signature NA Ratification/Accession NA	No Action
International Covenant on Economic, Social, and Cultural Rights (1966)	Signature 1977 Ratification/Accession NA	Signatory
Optional Protocol to the International Covenant on Economic, Social, and Cultural Rights (2008)	Signature NA Ratification/Accession NA	No Action
American Convention on Human Rights (1969)	Signature 1977 Ratification/Accession NA	Signatory
Convention on the Elimination of All Forms of Discrimination Against Women (1979)	Signature 1980 Ratification/Accession NA	Signatory
Optional Protocol to the Convention on the Elimination of All Forms of Discrimination Against Women (1999)	Signature NA Ratification/Accession NA	No Action
Convention Against Torture and Other Cruel, Inhuman, or Degrading Treatment or Punishment (1984)	Signature 1988 Ratification/Accession 1994	State Party
Optional Protocol to the Convention Against Torture and Other Cruel, Inhuman, or Degrading Treatment or Punishment (2002)	Signature NA Ratification/Accession NA	No Action
Convention on the Rights of the Child (1989)	Signature 1995 Ratification/Accession NA	Signatory
Optional Protocol to the Convention on the Rights of the Child on the Involvement of Children in Armed Conflict (2000)	Signature 2000 Ratification/Accession 2002	State Party
Optional Protocol to the Convention on the Rights of the Child on the Sale of Children, Child Prostitution, and Child Pornography (2000)	Signature 2000 Ratification/Accession 2002	State Party

Human Rights Instrument	Ratification Status	U.S. Status
Optional Protocol to the Convention on the Rights of the Child on a Communications Procedure (2011)	Signature NA Ratification/Accession NA	No Action
International Convention on the Protection of the Rights of All Migrant Workers and Members of Their Families (1990)	Signature NA Ratification/Accession NA	No Action
International Convention for the Protection of All Persons from Enforced Disappearance (2006)	Signature NA Ratification/Accession NA	No Action
Convention on the Rights of Persons with Disabilities (2006)	Signature 2009 Ratification/Accession NA	Signatory
Optional Protocol to the Convention on the Rights of Persons with Disabilities (2008)	Signature NA Ratification/Accession NA	No Action

Source: Adapted from "Status of Ratification of 18 International Human Rights Treaties," Office of the High Commissioner for Human Rights," http://indicators.ohchr.org.

Washington had no major interests at stake, such as Uruguay, Nicaragua, and Chile. "Our policy," claimed Carter, "is based on an historical vision of America's role. . . . Our policy is rooted in our moral values. . . . For too many years, we've been willing to adopt the flawed and erroneous principles and tactics of our adversaries, sometimes abandoning our own values for theirs."[24] Critics charged, however, that Carter pursued human rights at the expense of other interests, and that his policies fostered strategic setbacks such as the Soviet invasion of Afghanistan, Iran's Islamic Revolution, and the revolution of the left-wing Sandinistas in Nicaragua, all in 1979. Later he would reflect, "I did not fully grasp all the ramifications of our new policy."[25]

From Reagan to George W. Bush: U.S. Democracy Promotion from 1980 to 2008 In his first term, President Reagan sought unsuccessfully to reverse Carter's human rights policies, emphasizing quiet diplomacy and strategic and economic interests, especially restoration of U.S. power. Reagan propounded the Kirkpatrick Doctrine (named for Jean Kirkpatrick, who became Reagan's UN ambassador)—that right-wing authoritarian regimes, including several U.S. allies in Latin America, need not be held to the same human rights standards as leftist totalitarian regimes. And several authoritarian regimes that had been sanctioned by the Carter administration, including South Korea, El Salvador, and Haiti, resumed abusing human rights after Reagan's election. Reagan downplayed human rights and sought to resume military aid to authoritarian allies in the developing world, emphasizing "constructive engagement" with them. His administration only elevated human rights under public pressure and used human rights policy to target foes, fearing that pressure on friendly regimes might alienate them without producing change. Elliott Abrams, Reagan's assistant secretary of state for human rights, declared, "it is not enough to ask who is in power and what is he like. We also have to ask what is the alternative, what are the likely prospects for improvement."[26] In Reagan's second term, some advances were made in human rights owing to fear of instability in countries like the Philippines and El Salvador where insurrections challenged U.S.-backed regimes.

Major human rights challenges in the immediate post–Cold War period arose in the former Yugoslavia, China, the Middle East, and Africa, and observers saw an opportunity for the George H. W. Bush administration to focus more than his predecessor on human rights and democratization. Bush, however, continued Reagan's policy of "constructive engagement." This was evident in relations with China, where in June 1989, the army violently suppressed prodemocracy student demonstrators. Bush sought to preserve strong U.S.–Chinese ties. Congress, however, was outraged and sought to impose economic sanctions to punish Beijing for human rights violations. Bush also used military force in defense of human rights to offer humanitarian aid to famine victims in Somalia and justify intervention in Panama in humanitarian terms—to bring Manuel Noriega to trial on drug-trafficking charges. By this time, human rights were becoming institutionalized in the State Department as a legitimate foreign-policy goal, and thus, though Bush did not prioritize human rights, they became a legitimate concern in the State Department.[27]

Little change occurred in the Clinton administration. President Clinton included human rights and democracy promotion as pillars of his foreign policy but was mainly interested in pursuing policies that advanced U.S. strategic and economic interests like free trade. Clinton's emphasis on interests was reflected in his doctrine of democratic enlargement, first articulated in 1993. Democratic enlargement had four components as explained by Anthony Lake, Clinton's national security adviser:

> First, we should strengthen the community of major market democracies—including our own—which constitutes the core from which enlargement is proceeding.
>
> Second, we should help foster and consolidate new democracies and market economies, where possible, especially in states of special significance and opportunity.
>
> Third, we must counter the aggression—and support the liberalization—of states hostile to democracy and markets.
>
> Fourth, we need to pursue our humanitarian agenda not only by providing aid, but also by working to help democracy and market economics take root in regions of greatest humanitarian concern.[28]

Thus, Clinton refused to chastise China about human rights and advocated China's admittance to the WTO, arguing that it would "have a profound impact on human rights and political liberty."[29] In his second term, Clinton began to emphasize intervention abroad to prevent human rights abuses. One area where Clinton advanced human rights was in fostering international tribunals to hold individuals accountable for the worst violations of international **humanitarian law—genocide**, **ethnic cleansing**, and crimes against humanity. Washington was instrumental in creating the International Criminal Tribunal for the Former Yugoslavia and the International Criminal Tribunal for Rwanda. Clinton was slow to sign the 1998 Rome Statute creating the International Criminal Court (ICC), a permanent tribunal to try persons accused of violating humanitarian law, largely owing to opposition from Republicans and those in the armed forces who feared that the court could become politicized and be used to pursue unfounded charges against U.S. citizens, whose constitutional protections (including protection from double jeopardy and the right to confront one's accusers) would be stripped away.

George W. Bush had a mixed human rights record. Human rights were prominent on his foreign-policy agenda. The administration's efforts to reduce HIV/AIDs in Africa increased U.S. funding for that continent by more than 640 percent and dramatically improved Africans' access to testing, counseling, and treatment. In consequence, U.S. approval ratings in Africa soared to unprecedented levels by the end of Bush's second term. After 2001, however, Bush's human rights policies became associated with the global War on Terror, largely because the administration viewed human rights promotion as necessary to defeat terrorism *and* justified human rights violations as necessary to conduct that war. On the former, Bush argued in his 2002 State of the Union address, "America will lead by defending liberty and justice . . . [and] will always stand firm for the nonnegotiable demands of human dignity: the rule of law, limits on the power of the state, respect for women, private property, free speech, equal justice, and religious tolerance."[30] U.S. officials and allies conducting the War on Terror, however, violated many of these rights. Let us examine these policies and why it was difficult for the Obama administration to reverse them.

PRESENT: RECENT CHALLENGES TO DEMOCRACY PROMOTION AND HUMAN RIGHTS

Washington faces two challenges in promoting democracy and human rights abroad, and both involve tradeoffs between advancing values and protecting interests like security and sovereignty. The first involves the choice of tools to foster human rights and democracy. As we have seen, Washington has a mixed record working through multilateral institutions. Institutions like the **UN Human Rights Council** (HRC) or the ICC may share U.S. values in principle but are not always effective or efficient means to spread those values. And working through multilateral channels may conflict with pressing U.S. interests. Thus, Washington often uses tools like diplomacy, trade and aid, and even military force to advance human rights and promote democratization. But such efforts, too, are shaped as much by U.S. interests as by values. The second challenge involves pursuing vital interests in ways that reflect U.S. values. Coping with this challenge proved especially difficult after 2001. Efforts to achieve homeland security produced policies that undermined the civil and political liberties of U.S. citizens and foreigners. Thus, Washington has come under scrutiny at home and abroad for surrendering its values in the effort to fight a war without a clear battlefield or a definite end, against an enemy that is not easily identified.

Promoting Democracy and Human Rights Abroad

The George W. Bush administration refused to participate in multilateral institutions like the HRC and the ICC, opting to act unilaterally after 2001 to pursue human rights and promote democracy. Except in the Middle East, the developing world was largely ignored other than censuring a few persistent human rights violators like Myanmar, Cuba, Sudan, and Zimbabwe and applauding reformers like Indonesia and Liberia. Since the 1970s, much of the work promoting human rights and democracy has been conducted at lower levels of the U.S. foreign-policy establishment, for example, in the State Department, the Agency for International Development, the Treasury Department, and the Defense Department.

President Obama came to office in 2009 promising to end the Bush-era emphasis on unilateralism and elevate the importance of human rights. During his two terms, Washington worked with the HRC and, in a limited way, the ICC. He signed a new human rights treaty, the Convention on the Rights of People with Disabilities, but continued to ignore other near-universal treaties including the Convention on the Elimination of All Forms of Discrimination Against Women and the Convention on the Rights of the Child. Many of Obama's supporters were disappointed by his policy of "principled pragmatism" that emphasized engagement with repressive regimes, arguing that negotiating with countries like China and Iran undermined America's commitment to human rights. The credibility of this commitment was also weakened by continued detention of illegal combatants at Guantánamo, refusal to punish officials accused of torture, the use of drones to kill suspected terrorists, and revelations about NSA wiretapping.

DID YOU KNOW?

Sexual Orientation in U.S. Human Rights Policy

The Obama administration made sexual orientation a signature human rights issue. In 2015, Obama appointed the first Special Envoy for the Human Rights of Lesbian, Gay, Bisexual, and Transgender (LGBT) persons. In announcing the appointment, Secretary of State John Kerry declared that "defending and promoting the human rights of LGBT persons is at the core of our commitment to advancing human rights globally. . . . It's time to assert the equality and dignity of all persons, no matter their sexual orientation or gender identity."[31]

Let us examine U.S. involvement with multilateral institutions—the Human Rights Council and the ICC—and then describe other efforts to advance human rights and democracy.

The United Nations Human Rights Council The HRC was established in 2006 to replace the controversial Commission on Human Rights. The commission, established in 1946 with U.S. leadership, was politicized during the Cold War when Washington and Moscow each used it to condemn the human rights practices of the other. After the Cold War, it remained controversial because countries like Cuba and Sudan, which routinely violated citizens' human rights, used their seats on the commission to shield themselves from criticism. Americans were dissatisfied with the commission, especially after Washington lost reelection to the group in 2002 for the first time since its creation and 2003 after Libya won a seat over U.S. objections.

The commission's limitations were widely recognized, and in 2006, as part of Secretary-General Kofi Annan's efforts at UN reform, the General Assembly voted to replace it with a new body, the 47-member HRC. Washington was one of only four governments to vote against the council, citing concerns that the proposed agency was not strong enough to prevent human rights violators from election to the council or using membership to shield themselves from scrutiny. U.S. officials were skeptical that the HRC would play a "constructive role" in efforts to foster human rights and refused to participate in the first election. During the next two years, the Bush administration remained critical of the HRC for its disproportionate focus on Israel's human rights abuses, the continuing presence of human rights violators on the council, and the tendency to single out—sometimes exclusively—America in reports on topics like poverty and torture.[32]

On entering office, President Obama reversed U.S. policy and, arguing for principled pragmatism, insisted that Washington would have more influence from within the HRC. "Human rights are an essential element of American global foreign policy," Secretary of State Hillary Clinton explained. "With others, we will engage in the work of improving the UN human rights system to advance the vision of the UN Declaration on Human Rights."[33] John Bolton, George W. Bush's UN ambassador and a critic of the UN, countered that participation "legitimizes something that doesn't deserve legitimacy."[34] Washington was elected to two three-year terms on the HRC—2009 and 2012. (States are not eligible for immediate reelection after two consecutive terms.)

Supporters of U.S. involvement credited Washington for building cross-regional coalitions in the council; pursuing resolutions addressing abuses in Iran, Libya, Yemen, and Syria; and making progress on issues like freedom of assembly and association and the rights of LGBT persons. Critics protested that the HRC still has too many repressive regimes among its members, including China, Cuba, and Russia, which sat on the Council for two consecutive terms (2006 to 2012), rotated off for a year, and were promptly reelected for another term (2013 to 2016). One observer argued that these regimes "collude to shield each other from rigorous human rights scrutiny and undermine earnest efforts to promote fundamental human rights and condemn governments that violate these rights."[35]

The ICC   The Obama administration also grew more receptive to the ICC, although it has not made an effort to join the court. The ICC was established in 2002 as a permanent tribunal to try individuals accused of the worst violations of human rights and humanitarian law. Created by the 1998 Rome Statute, the ICC was a response to the inefficiencies of ad hoc international tribunals that had been created to try individuals accused of **war crimes** and **crimes against humanity** in the Balkans and Rwanda. Those tribunals were expensive and operated longer than originally intended. President Clinton had supported the negotiation of the ICC and signed the treaty but had never submitted it to the Senate for ratification. In 2002, President Bush withdrew the U.S. signature and declared that Washington did not intend to become a party to the ICC. Supporters of the court argued that Bush's action damaged U.S. credibility as an advocate of human rights. The Vienna Convention on the Law of Treaties, they pointed out, required that as a signatory Washington would only have been obligated to "refrain from acts which defeat the object and purpose of the treaty," and given the nature of the crimes over which the ICC has jurisdiction, it was unlikely Washington would violate the obligations of a signatory.[36]

There remains substantial U.S. opposition to the ICC. The terms of the treaty, critics claim, leave open the possibility that U.S. citizens may fall under the court's jurisdiction even though America is not a member. This is unlikely. By the Rome Statute, there are limits to the court's jurisdiction, notably that the accused must be a national of an ICC member or a state that accepts the court's jurisdiction, the crime must have occurred on the territory of a member state or a state that accepts the court's jurisdiction, *or* the UN Security Council (in which Washington has a veto) must refer the case to the ICC prosecutor. Moreover, the ICC's jurisdiction is "complementary" to national courts. If a U.S. citizen accused of crimes falling under the ICC's jurisdiction were tried in America, the ICC would lack jurisdiction.

Opponents also argue that the ICC potentially violates U.S. sovereignty by allowing an international tribunal to try U.S. citizens without the legal protections of the Bill of Rights. To ensure that the court would not indict U.S. citizens, the 2002 American Servicemen's Protection Act (ASPA) makes illegal any cooperation with the ICC and bars U.S. military aid to countries unless they agree to shield U.S. troops on their territory from ICC prosecution. After the Rome Statute entered into force, Bush began negotiating agreements with signatories to ensure U.S. citizens in their territory would be protected from ICC prosecution.

In 2009, the Obama administration agreed to participate as an observer in the ICC's governing body. The 2010 National Security Strategy explained that participation was a moral and security imperative. It noted that the United States was "engaging with State Parties to the Rome Statute on issues of concern and is supporting the ICC's prosecution of those cases that advance U.S. interests and values, consistent with the requirements of U.S. law."[37] In 2013, Congress promised rewards for information on ICC fugitives that leads to their transfer to or conviction by the ICC, and U.S. officials helped transfer an indicted African warlord to the court. Thus far, however, Washington has refrained from offering direct support that would violate ASPA.

Given its dislike of existing multilateral institutions, Washington has emphasized unilateral and bilateral efforts to advance democracy and human rights in the Middle East, especially after the 2011 Arab Spring, and elsewhere.

Democracy Promotion in Sudan and South Sudan   U.S. initiatives were crucial to ending a civil war in 2005 in Sudan, then Africa's largest country, and supporting the eventual separation of South Sudan in 2011. Sudan was a complex case, involving multiple conflicts that the Sudanese government chose to conduct and negotiate separately—a civil war between the North and South and another war beginning in 2003 in the Darfur region in Western Sudan. Human rights, foreign aid, democracy promotion, and interventionism intersected in these conflicts as Washington tried to advance its values, while protecting vital interests.

Between independence in 1956 and South Sudan's secession, Sudan was divided between Muslim Arabs in the north, which had come under Arab influence in the 17th century, and Christian and animist Black Africans in the south, where Christian missionaries in the 19th century had converted native populations. These two cultures contained hundreds of ethnic, tribal, and language divisions. However, Sudan's conflicts cannot be attributed solely to ethnic and religious identities. Decolonization, economic conditions, religious and cultural persecution, and environmental factors all played a role.

Sudan briefly became a U.S. ally in the 1970s, following an attempted communist coup against President Gaafar Nimeiry. Nimeiry was no democrat, but Sudan was stable and served as a counterweight to hostile regimes in Libya and Ethiopia. This changed in the 1980s as Islamists became influential and clashed with modernizers. Nimeiry himself embraced political Islam, aligning with Sudan's Muslim Brotherhood. In 1983, his imposition of severe Islamic law alienated allies in Sudan and elsewhere including America. Thus, civil war erupted between Sudan and the Sudan's People's Liberation Movement/Army (SPLM/A) in the south. At issue in this conflict were Nimeiry's efforts to impose Islamic practices on Sudan's diverse peoples, its control over oil revenues although oil reserves were located in the south, and its violent counterinsurgency campaigns that targeted both civilians and rebels. Nimeiry was deposed in 1985, and in 1989, a military coup brought to power President Omar al-Bashir. Sudan soon became a sanctuary for terrorists including Osama bin Laden, Carlos the Jackal, and Abu Nidal.

MAP **6.1**   Sudan and Surrounding Region

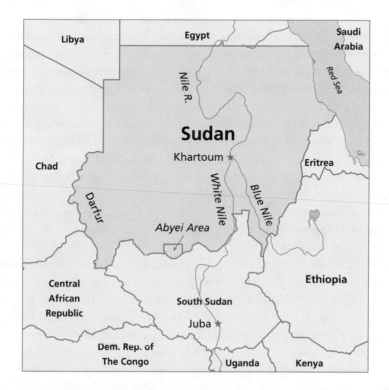

The Clinton administration sought to isolate Sudan, imposing economic sanctions and labeling it a state sponsor of terrorism for its support of al-Qaeda. In 2000, however, U.S. officials did not view transnational terrorism as a direct threat to U.S. interests, and President Bush pursued a strategy of "constructive engagement" to advance human rights and democracy in Sudan. This involved working with Khartoum to end its isolation and negotiate a peace settlement to give the south greater voice in decision making. During the civil war, two million Sudanese had died and four million had been displaced from their homes. The war also intensified the effects of famine originally caused by severe drought. Human rights activists were also deeply troubled by human rights violations, including the systematic enslavement of southern women and children and the extensive use of child soldiers by government forces, their militias, and rebel groups.[38]

American evangelicals, who viewed the conflict, erroneously, as religious, supported Bush's policy. In March 2001, the independent U.S. Commission on International Religious Freedom called Sudan "the world's most violent abuser of the right to freedom of religion and belief"[39] and called on Bush to intervene to end the abuses. Thereafter, Bush appointed a special humanitarian coordinator for Sudan and a special envoy for Sudan's peace process. The president was also actively involved. According to a White

House official, Bush "'could have been the desk officer because he was so engaged on southern Sudan."[40] He regularly met with those lobbying for U.S. involvement and made numerous phone calls to President al-Bashir and Chairman John Garang of the SPLM/A.

The administration's involvement was crucial in achieving a comprehensive peace agreement that paved the way for South Sudan's later secession from Sudan. The agreement granted the south regional autonomy and representation in a unity government and was designed to foster reconciliation or, barring that, peaceful secession. The two sides could not agree on key issues necessary to achieving reconciliation, and in January 2011, South Sudan voted to secede. In July, it became a sovereign state, but unresolved disputes continued to plague relations. Thus, the distribution of oil revenues was never agreed upon. Although South Sudan contains most of Sudan's oil reserves, it is landlocked and must transport oil through Sudan to get it to market. Border disputes also remained, notably over the oil-rich region of Abyei that straddles the two countries. A conflict in Sudan in the neighboring Nuba Mountains region where the government was accused of genocide against ethnic minorities spilled into South Sudan where thousands of people were displaced. South Sudan itself remained unstable. In December 2013, a political crisis unfolded with a power struggle between President Salva Kiir and his vice president that triggered a civil war that pitted the Dinka and Nuer ethnic groups against each other and killed thousands of people and displaced millions by late 2014.[41]

Critics claimed that Obama's policy in the region was unclear and inconsistent and that the administration's diplomacy was too quiet. They argued that Washington had not done enough to isolate Sudan's President Bashir and in South Sudan was unwilling to oppose President Kiir, even as his policies intensified a humanitarian crisis. Instead, Washington encouraged regional solutions. In the case of South Sudan, it allocated $5 million to establish a special court to hold perpetrators to account,[42] $45 million to the UN Refugee Agency to cope with refugees, and asked Kenya to help resolve these conflicts.

Just as progress was being made in negotiations to implement the comprehensive agreement between North and South Sudan, a new conflict in the Darfur region—a territory about the size of France in western Sudan—began attracting international attention. This conflict pitted Arab Muslims against black African Muslims and was more about power sharing and resources than race or ethnicity. The Darfur conflict began in 2003, when two Darfuri rebel movements rebelled against policies that produced political and economic marginalization of the region and Sudan's failure to protect Darfur's inhabitants from attacks by nomads. The Sudanese government responded with military force, including air raids that were frequently followed by ruthless attacks by self-defense militias known as *Janjaweed*. These Arab militias were composed of dislocated herders whom the government recruited and armed. *Janjaweed,* the "devils on horseback,"[43] looted and set fire to villages and killed and raped their inhabitants. Hundreds of villages were destroyed, some 400,000 civilians were killed, and over 2.5 million were displaced.[44] Some of the displaced fled to refugee camps in neighboring Chad while others remained in camps in Darfur as **internally displaced persons**.

Sudan denied supporting the *Janjaweed* and resisted international pressure to end its reign of violence. Frustrated by Sudan's inaction, Washington in 2004 was the first to apply the label genocide to the violence in Darfur. It was also the first time any administration had labeled an ongoing conflict genocidal. Determining genocide is complicated by the need to demonstrate "*intent* to destroy, in whole or in part, a national, ethnical, racial or religious group" (emphasis added).[45] It is also politically fraught by a provision that Contracting Parties to the Genocide Convention *take action* "for the prevention and suppression of acts of genocide."[46] In Rwanda in 1994—where evidence for genocide was clear—the Clinton administration refused to use the "g-word," but by 2004, the State Department's position had evolved. Using the term genocide did not, State Department officials argued, legally obligate Washington to act in Darfur—a key consideration since these same officials recognized the difficulty in demonstrating that violence in Darfur was genocidal in *intent*.

KEY DOCUMENT
"Genocide in Darfur"

A 2004 State Department memo argued that "based on the available facts, a determination that genocide has occurred in Darfur would have no immediate legal—as opposed to moral, political, or policy—consequences for the United States. . . . From a policy perspective, however, a finding of genocide can act as a spur to the international community to take more forceful and immediate actions to respond to ongoing atrocities. Article VIII of the Genocide Convention provides that any Contracting Party 'may call upon the competent organs of the United Nations to take such action under the Charter of the United Nations as they consider appropriate for the prevention and suppression' of genocide and related genocidal acts."

Source: U.S. Department of State, Information Memorandum, "Genocide in Darfur," June 25, 2004, The National Security Archive, http://nsarchive.gwu.edu/NSAEBB/NSAEBB356/20040625_darfur.PDF.

In September 2004, the Security Council established a Commission of Inquiry to determine if genocide was occurring in Darfur. In early 2005, the commission reported that "the crucial element of genocidal intent appears to be missing, at least as far as the central Government authorities are concerned,"[47] but recommended that the council refer the situation to the ICC to investigate serious violations of international humanitarian law. In March 2005, the Security Council referred the Darfur situation to the ICC prosecutor. Washington had lobbied for a hybrid tribunal in Africa but allowed the resolution to pass "because of the need for the international community to work together in order to end the climate of impunity in the Sudan, and because the resolution provided protection from investigation or prosecution for United States nationals and members of the armed forces of non-State parties."[48] In 2009, President Bashir became the first sitting leader indicted by the ICC for war crimes and crimes against humanity. Nevertheless, Bashir remained in power, and the Darfur conflict continued, even escalating, despite a brief effort to bring peace in 2010 to 2011.

Washington's policy toward Darfur was frequently overshadowed by preoccupation with Sudan's north–south conflict and terrorism concerns. Consequently, private individuals and NGOs proved important in sustaining public interest in Darfur. American celebrities have made it their mission to keep the public—and government officials—aware of Sudan's conflicts and other humanitarian crises. To this end, George Clooney, along with actors Don Cheadle, Matt Damon, and Brad Pitt, founded the group Not On Our Watch. These celebrities raised awareness through media appearances, op-eds in national news outlets, and testimony before the Congress and UN meetings, and their influence has been significant. Columnist Nicholas Kristof wrote, "Bono knows G-8 poverty policy issues better than I do. Mia Farrow beat the news media in getting good photographs of the Janjaweed in Darfur. Ashley Judd has been to rural Bihar, India, to learn about sex trafficking. Ben Affleck knows Congo and South Sudan inside out. George Clooney has done more for Darfur than the White House National Security Council. And Angelina Jolie has traveled and visited with refugees and desperate people all over, including three trips to the greater Darfur area, if I remember right. That's two more trips than Condi Rice has made."[49]

Cuba: A New Approach to Democratic Reform   For many years Washington employed unilateral pressures to bring about democratization in Cuba. The regime, in power since 1959, is a dictatorship and persistent violator of human rights. It outlawed virtually all forms of political dissent, and violators were punished with political exile and prison sentences in conditions that Cuban dissidents have described as "subhuman."[50] America's Cuba policy was largely a relic of the Cold War. Since the 1960s, Washington relied almost exclusively on sanctions to force Cuba to introduce democratic reforms until in 2015 President Obama announced a new policy.

U.S. efforts to overthrow Fidel Castro included the unsuccessful 1961 Bay of Pigs invasion. Thereafter, Washington enforced Cuba's economic and diplomatic isolation to foster regime change. Presidents Eisenhower and Kennedy instituted a complete economic **embargo** between 1960 and 1962, outlawing trade with and travel to Cuba after Castro **nationalized** the assets of U.S.-owned companies. Cuba turned toward the USSR and became economically dependent on trade ties with Moscow. President Carter eased restrictions on travel to and spending in Cuba in 1977. But in April 1980, Castro allowed political dissidents to leave the country and 125,000 exiles, many just released from jail and mental hospitals, fled to Florida on overcrowded boats where Cuban-Americans had become a powerful anti-Castro political force. In 1981, President Reagan again tightened the embargo in response to Cuba's support for leftist guerrillas in Central and South America.

Thereafter, Congress pressed for stronger sanctions. In 1992, the Cuban Democracy Act reinstituted a ban that had been lifted in 1975 that prevented subsidiaries of U.S. companies based in third-world countries from trading with Cuba. It also limited Cuba's use of dollars for international transactions and authorized the White House to limit the **remittances** that could be sent to Cuba. The 1996 Helms-Burton Act formalized an embargo on trade and financial transactions that had been in place since the Kennedy administration. It also punished foreign companies that traded with or invested in Cuba, and it enabled Americans who had lost property in Cuba in the 1960s to sue the Cuban government and foreign investors who profited from that property. Bacardi, which relocated to America after its distilling facilities in Cuba were nationalized in 1960, lobbied for the right to litigate, but other governments challenged this as a violation of WTO agreements.

President Clinton was an advocate of limited engagement with Cuba and was reluctant to sign the bill. But after Cuban jets in March 1996 shot down two U.S. planes belonging to an anti-Castro group seeking to help Cuban refugees flee the country, political pressure on Clinton intensified. He signed the bill into law but suspended the lawsuit provision (a practice continued by presidents since). After tensions declined, Clinton signed the Trade Sanctions Reform and Export Enhancements Act that enabled some U.S. producers to sell agricultural commodities and medical supplies to Cuba. George W. Bush initially was open to continuing Clinton's limited engagement, but in the face of Cuban-American pressure, his administration took a hard line toward the country, tightening enforcement of the embargo.

U.S. sanctions against Cuba became controversial after the Cold War. Critics argued that sanctions had not fostered democratization or human rights reform and instead had entrenched the Castro regime. They argued that Washington would acquire greater influence by easing trade and travel restrictions. Governments in Latin America increasingly opposed U.S. policies that isolated Cuba, especially the exclusion of Cuba from regional forums like the Organization of American States (OAS).

Changes in Cuba and America in recent years made it possible for the two countries slowly to begin normalizing relations. In 2008, Raúl Castro, Fidel's brother, became Cuba's president and implemented modest economic reforms, and a new generation of Cuban-Americans became less favorable of Cuba's political isolation and sought to ease restrictions that limited their ability to travel to and send remittances home. Finally, fewer American voters supported the embargo.

In this new climate, President Obama, who campaigned on improving relations with Cuba and who won 35 percent of the Cuban-American vote in Florida in 2008 and 48 percent in 2012, lifted restrictions

U.S. and Cuban delegations in talks to re-establish diplomatic relations, May 2015

AP Photo/Jacquelyn Martin

on family visits to Cuba in 2009, allowing Cuban-Americans to visit Cuba and send gifts and money back to Cuba as long as they were not given to senior government or communist party officials. Obama also eased restrictions on telecommunications companies, allowing them to seek licensing agreements in Cuba so more Cubans could have access to cellphones and satellite television. Then in 2014, Washington negotiated an historic deal with Cuba to restore diplomatic relations. The administration freed three Cuban prisoners imprisoned for spying and in 2015 removed Cuba from the State Department's list of **state sponsors of terrorism**. Cuba released 53 political prisoners, a U.S. contractor arrested in 2009, and a Cuban who had been imprisoned for 20 years for spying for America. The administration then announced it would ease sanctions. In April 2015, Obama and Raúl Castro met at a Summit of the Americas meeting in Panama—the first such meeting attended by Cuba since expulsion from the OAS in 1962.

Critics denounced the agreement, arguing it would do little to improve human rights. Indeed, just weeks after its announcement, Cuba detained 50 activists planning a demonstration in Havana's Revolutionary Square. Declared Senator Marco Rubio (R-FL): "The Castro regime's latest acts of repression against political dissidents in Cuba make a mockery of President Obama's new U.S.-Cuba policy. . . . The fact that the regime continues to violate the human rights of Cubans like this shows that it has even less incentive to change its ways."[51]

Promoting Human Rights in Tibet   U.S. criticism of China's human rights record, which China regards as interference in its domestic affairs, has long been a source of friction. Before the Clinton administration, there had been repeated efforts to link China's human rights record with Beijing's trading privileges. However, after President Clinton renewed China's privileges in 1994 under pressure from U.S. firms, it effectively delinked the two issues, a situation that continues. China's human rights policies in Tibet, however, remain an obstacle to better Sino-U.S. relations.

Tibet, located to the northeast of the Himalayas, is a sovereign territory of China, but the five million ethnic Tibetans are not Han Chinese. They have their own language and practice Tibetan or "Yellow Hat" Buddhism, and their spiritual leader is the Dalai Lama. Since 1950, there have been repeated efforts by Tibetans to gain independence and end state-sanctioned migration of Han Chinese that is eroding Tibetan culture, language, and religion. In 1951, Tibetan leaders signed the "Seventeen Point Agreement" under which Tibet would retain its autonomy and religion. Beijing, however, disregarded the agreement. In 1959, an uprising erupted in Lhasa, Tibet's capital, resulting in thousands of deaths and the flight of the Dalai Lama and many of his followers to India. In 1965, Beijing established the Tibetan Autonomous Region in order to integrate Tibet fully into China.

Confronted by Tibetan unrest, China imposed martial law in the region in 1988. During the following decades, Beijing constructed road and rail links to Tibet to promote Han Chinese migration and urbanize the region. The continuing dilution of Tibetan culture and the growing presence of Chinese migrants climaxed in violent protests in 2008, shortly before the Beijing Olympics. Pro-Tibetan activists tried to disrupt the relay of the Olympic torch from Olympia, Greece, to China. China blamed the Dalai Lama and other Tibetan exiles, and several Tibetans were executed for involvement in the protest. President Bush, facing criticism for attending the Olympics in Beijing, defended his policy: "In the long run, America better remain engaged with China and understand that we can have a cooperative and constructive, yet candid, relationship. . . . It's important to make sure that America is engaged with China, even though we may have some disagreements."[52] Since 2011, Tibetan protests against Chinese repression have involved self-immolation by Buddhist monks, and since 2013, Chinese hackers have targeted the mobile phones of Tibetan and other activists at home and overseas. Beijing also maintains a massive security presence in Tibet, while restricting the movement of Tibetans in the region, increasing control over Buddhist monasteries, and forcibly relocating millions of Tibetans in "New Socialist Villages."[53]

U.S. leaders have repeatedly criticized China's policies in Tibet. In 2011, President Obama, like his predecessors, hosted the Dalai Lama at the White House. Obama declared that while Washington regards Tibet as part of China he supported "the preservation of the unique religious, cultural, and linguistic traditions of Tibet and the Tibetan people throughout the world."[54] Some days later, China's president responded angrily: "We should thoroughly fight against separatist activities by the Dalai clique by firmly relying on all ethnic groups . . . and completely smash any plot to destroy stability in Tibet and jeopardize national unity."[55] After Obama's meeting with the Dalai Lama in 2014, a Chinese government spokesman declared that the event interfered in China's internal affairs and would impair Sino-U.S. relations. Chinese officials were again outraged in 2015 when the Dalai Lama and President Obama attended the National Prayer Breakfast, hosted by Congress. American human rights advocates argue that Washington should use robust diplomacy and trade restrictions to pressure China to end its human rights practices in Tibet.

When Values and Interests Conflict

U.S. human rights policy has always been characterized by contradictions when values and interests collide. In recent years, these contradictions have led to charges at home and abroad that Washington practices a double standard in human rights by engaging in some of the very behavior it condemns elsewhere. These charges became sharper after 9/11 when, in their effort to protect American citizens and territory from transnational terrorism, U.S. officials began to ignore domestic and international law by denying "unlawful combatants" the rights of prisoners of war, using "extraordinary rendition"—apprehending and transferring suspected terrorists without due process to other countries where they could be imprisoned and interrogated—using torture in interrogations, and detaining prisoners in Guantánamo indefinitely without trial.

The security apparatus that evolved after 9/11 also was said to threaten the rights of Americans and individuals overseas, producing questions about how much government surveillance is acceptable in a free society. Such alleged violations not only involve values but also erode U.S. soft power.

Illegal Combatants The treatment of suspected terrorists posed significant challenges for U.S. officials who try to balance the imperatives of security while conforming to democratic values. The Geneva Conventions, the foundational documents of international humanitarian law, distinguish between combatants and civilians, specifying how each is to be treated in the conduct of international and civil wars. Soldiers fighting for another country's army are considered lawful combatants, protected by the Geneva Conventions if taken prisoner. Civilians are noncombatants who are to be protected from harm. Terrorists, who wear no uniform, fight for no recognized authority, and ignore the laws of war, fall into neither category and are considered **illegal combatants**. U.S. officials argue that terrorists fall outside the protections of the Geneva Conventions and do not have prisoner-of-war status and its legal protections. Human rights activists counter that there is no such intermediate status—neither combatant nor civilian—and that even terrorists are protected by international law.[56]

In 2001, President Bush signed an executive directive giving the CIA discretion to detain or kill terrorists wherever they were found, and in the following months the White House legal counsel sought a legal framework under which, without prior approval of the president or the Departments of Justice or State, "illegal combatants" could be held indefinitely without trial in secret locations. In March 2006, in the case of *Hamdan v. Rumsfeld* the Supreme Court ruled that military commissions were not "competent tribunals" to try "enemy combatants," and that their use violated a prisoner's rights under the Third Geneva Convention, which prohibits "the passing of sentences and the carrying out of executions without previous judgment pronounced by a regularly constituted court affording all the judicial guarantees which are recognized as indispensable."[57] The court declared it made no difference that al-Qaeda had not signed the convention because it applied to individuals in "international conflicts" within states that were signatories (e.g., Afghanistan). Thus, even those detained as illegal combatants, many of whom were imprisoned without trial in secret CIA prisons, enjoyed protection under the Geneva Conventions. Thereafter, Congress passed the Military Commissions Act giving the president authority to identify "unlawful enemy combatants" who would not be entitled to prisoner-of-war status or the protection of the Geneva Conventions and authorizing trials by military commissions that had lower evidential standards than civilian courts.

Most of those detained as enemy combatants were not U.S. citizens, but those who were raised additional legal concerns. The Supreme Court ruled in 2004 and 2010 respectively that as U.S. citizens, Yaser Hamdi and José Padilla could not be denied their constitutional rights to an attorney and a prompt and fair trial in an American court. Although the court upheld the president's right to detain citizens as "enemy combatants" during wartime, such prisoners could challenge the merits of their imprisonment before a neutral fact finder. In 2004, Combatant Status Review Tribunals were established to decide whether individuals were "enemy combatants" but were ruled inadequate by the Supreme Court in 2008.

Extraordinary Rendition, "Black Sites," and Targeted Killings After 9/11, many countries participated in the CIA's secret detention and extraordinary rendition programs, allowing the agency to run secret interrogation prisons ("black sites") in countries including Afghanistan, Lithuania, Poland, Morocco, Romania, Thailand, and at the U.S. base at Guantánamo Bay.[58] Canada, Britain, Italy, and Germany were among the countries that cooperated with America's extraordinary rendition. This involved allowing the use of airspace for secret flights and airports for refueling, transporting detainees without legal extradition, and using "enhanced interrogation techniques." Some suspects were initially detained by U.S. agencies, but many were seized by local security personnel at the behest of the CIA or FBI and detained in covert CIA prisons overseas. Both black sites and extraordinary rendition "entailed the abduction and disappearance of detainees, their extra-legal transfer on secret flights to undisclosed locations around the world, followed by their incommunicado detention, interrogation, torture, and abuse,"[59] circumventing U.S. laws that prohibit holding prisoners in secret in an extrajudicial manner. According to a U.S. intelligence officer, the prison system was never part of "a grand strategy" but was instead "very reactive."[60] Nonetheless, these policies undermined America's moral credibility globally.

Among those seized and held in this manner was Khalid Shaikh Muhammad, described as "the principal architect of the 9/11 attacks" in the 9/11 Commission Report, who was captured in Pakistan in 2003 and interned in the Guantánamo detention camp. A number of captives, for instance, German national

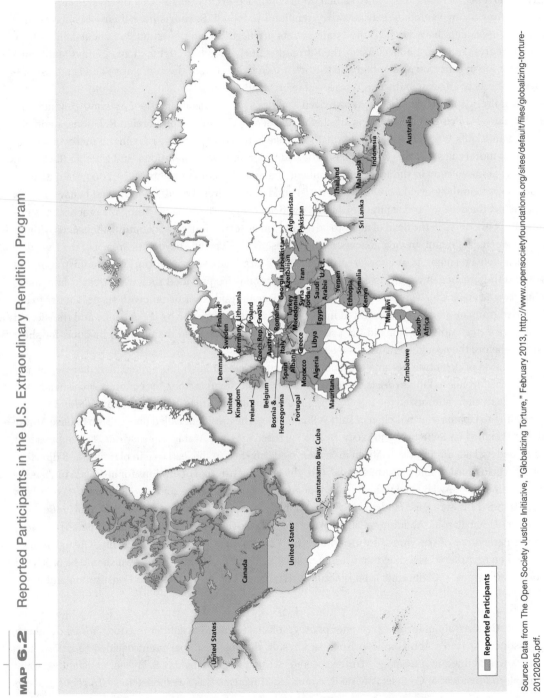

MAP 6.2 Reported Participants in the U.S. Extraordinary Rendition Program

Source: Data from The Open Society Justice Initiative, "Globalizing Torture," February 2013, http://www.opensocietyfoundations.org/sites/default/files/globalizing-torture-20120205.pdf.

Khaled al Masri, who was seized by local authorities in Skopje, Macedonia, were cases of mistaken identity or "erroneous renditions." Masri's detention continued even after the CIA discovered its mistake. Efforts thus far by victims of extraordinary rendition to have U.S. courts hear their cases have failed because presidents have invoked the "state secrets privilege" to stop lawsuits.[61] A few detainees have sought redress in foreign courts. Thus, the European Court of Human Rights in 2013 found Macedonia liable for Masri's arbitrary detention and torture, which it defined as "the cumulative and acute psychological effects of anguish and stress" employed to break his spirit.[62]

After President Bush publicly acknowledged America's secret prisons in 2006, pressure grew at home and in Europe to curb abuses. In hearings before the Senate Committee on Foreign Relations, an official at Human Rights Watch testified that "what's at stake here [is] whether we're going to preserve a set of legal and moral rules that this country has struggled to develop over generations, and whether the United States is going to remain the world's preeminent champion of human rights."[63] In 2007, then Senator Obama wrote in the journal *Foreign Affairs*: "To build a better, freer world, we must first behave in ways that reflect the decency and aspirations of the American people. This means ending the practices of shipping away prisoners in the dead of night to be tortured in far-off countries, of detaining thousands without charge or trial, of maintaining a network of secret prisons to jail people beyond the reach of the law."[64]

Although President Obama ordered the closure of CIA black sites in 2009, the administration did not end the practice of rendition of suspects to other countries provided they were treated humanely. Thus, two Somalis who were Swedish citizens and a Somali resident of Britain with suspected ties to the terrorist group al-Shabab were arrested in Djibouti in 2012, questioned by U.S. agents, and transferred to America to stand trial. Nor did the president prevent the CIA from detaining individuals for short periods before they could be transferred elsewhere.

The issue of detention became less contentious after the administration intensified its campaign of using aerial drones to kill terrorists overseas. Aided by John Brennan, then his counterterrorism adviser, Obama personally authorized the targeted killing of individual terrorists in Pakistan, Somalia, and Yemen. According to Obama's former chief of staff William Daley, the president called his decision to have Anwar al-Awlaki killed on September 30, 2011, by drones based in Saudi Arabia "an easy one."[65] The president described Awlaki, an American citizen in Yemen, as having taken "the lead role in planning and directing the efforts to murder innocent Americans" and "the leader of external operations for al-Qaeda in the Arabian Peninsula."[66] Awlaki had publicly called for attacks against America, and several of the 9/11 hijackers had attended his sermons. He had also "operationally" aided individual terrorists like the "underwear bomber" Umar Farouk Abdulmutallab and overseas attacks including (posthumously) the 2015 attacks on the Paris office of the French satirical magazine *Charlie Hebdo*. Awlaki's citizenship, Obama argued, "should no more serve as a shield than a sniper shooting down on an innocent crowd should be protected from a swat team."[67] Civil rights groups argue such targeted killings violated the Constitution and international law.

Torture Concern about torture grew after photographs taken by a U.S. soldier in 2003 showed the abuse of prisoners at Iraq's Abu Ghraib prison. As a result, the Justice Department decided to review how torture was defined in a 46-page "Torture Memo" written in 2002 by Jay S. Bybee, assistant attorney general, to Presidential Counsel Alberto R. Gonzales. The memo was a response to a CIA request to use "more aggressive" interrogation techniques of terrorist suspects outside the United States and gave the agency what it sought, declaring that to constitute torture, "physical pain must be equivalent in intensity to the pain accompanying serious physical injury, such as organ failure, impairment of bodily function, or even death." Even if the president authorized interrogation that could be defined as torture, "in the circumstances of the current war against al Qaeda and its allies," criminal prosecution under America's antitorture statute would represent "an unconstitutional infringement of the President's authority to conduct war."[68]

A second memo in 2004 disavowed torture but in a footnote reiterated the conclusions reached in 2002. Although coercive interrogation techniques were of dubious value in eliciting useful information, two additional memos in 2005 reaffirmed the methods previously authorized, and a third indicated that interrogation methods that had earlier been authorized did not violate the UN Convention against Torture. Although the Justice Department declared torture to be "abhorrent," Gonzales, Vice President Cheney, and Attorney General Michael Mukasey defended the practice of "waterboarding"—a procedure in which water is forced into a captive's mouth and nose to induce the sensation of drowning—as an acceptable "enhanced interrogation technique." President Bush admitted authorizing waterboarding on three high-level terrorists.[69]

Under public pressure, Congress passed the Detainee Treatment Act in 2005 that followed the interrogation standards set by the Army Field Manual that prohibited violence, intimidation, and torture. Bush threatened to veto the bill because it contained an amendment offered by Senator John McCain (R-AZ) that outlawed "cruel, inhuman and degrading treatment" of suspected terrorists. McCain, who had been tortured as a prisoner of war in North Vietnam, declared: "The image of the United States was very badly harmed by the pictures of prisoner abuse. We have to send a message to the world that we will not ever allow such kind of treatment to be repeated."[70] The president finally signed the bill but issued a "signing statement," declaring he would interpret its language in the context of his constitutional powers as commander in chief. In 2007, the White House agreed to let the CIA resume using several interrogation methods it had used in its secret prisons and said that these were lawful under the Third Geneva Convention, which the Supreme Court had ruled was applicable to the conflict with al-Qaeda, and the 2005 Detainee Treatment Act that barred "cruel, inhuman and degrading treatment" of anyone in U.S. custody, whether within or outside America.

Diverging from the policies of the Bush administration, President Obama in 2009 issued an executive order intended to balance intelligence gathering with the humane treatment of prisoners in U.S. custody in order to ensure compliance with the Geneva Conventions and other relevant treaties. The executive order required that individuals "shall in all circumstances be treated humanely and shall not be subjected to violence to life and person (including murder of all kinds, mutilation, cruel treatment, and torture), nor to outrages upon personal dignity (including humiliating and degrading treatment), whenever such individuals are in the custody or under the effective control of an officer, employee, or other agent of the United States Government or detained within a facility owned, operated, or controlled by a department or agency of the United States."[71]

In 2014, the Senate's Select Subcommittee on Intelligence released a report detailing CIA torture. Among its findings were that the CIA's techniques were brutal and more widespread than the agency had indicated, the agency had misled Congress and the White House, senior officials overruled those who tried to end some of the most brutal interrogation techniques, and such interrogation techniques did not produce information that could not have been acquired by other means. Senator Dianne Feinstein (D-CA), the chair of the Senate committee, described the CIA program as "a stain on our values and our history."[72]

Guantánamo Bay: "Un-American by Any Name"   The facility at Guantánamo Bay has long been a focus for criticism of U.S. policies.[73] In January 2002, the Bush administration established the camp, which consisted of three facilities (one later closed) to detain enemy combatants captured in Afghanistan and elsewhere at a site outside America and therefore not under U.S. legal jurisdiction. Based on the Military Commissions Act, a federal appeals court ruled against lawsuits filed on behalf of Guantánamo detainees who demanded a hearing in an American court where they would enjoy constitutional guarantees. However, in a 5–4 decision, the Supreme Court ruled in 2008 in *Boumediene v. Bush* that Guantánamo detainees were protected by the Constitution and had the right to appeal to civilian courts to challenge their detention. Based on this decision, several prisoners successfully sought their release from Guantánamo, but the bar for winning such cases was raised higher in 2010 when a federal court ruled that government intelligence reports were entitled to a "presumption of regularity" (reputability). The federal appeals court upheld the ruling and the Supreme Court refused to hear further appeals.

In 2004, the International Committee of the Red Cross confirmed the use of torture at Guantánamo. According to former president Jimmy Carter, "American authorities have revealed that, in order to obtain confessions, some of the few being tried (only in military courts) have been tortured by waterboarding

MAP 6.3   Guantánamo Bay, Cuba

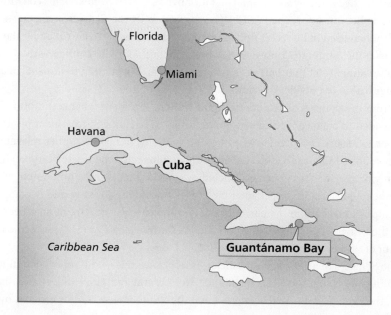

more than 100 times or intimidated with semiautomatic weapons, power drills or threats to sexually assault their mothers."[74] Over the years, the status of Guantánamo has become increasingly controversial. There have been repeated demands it be closed and its prisoners either freed or tried in U.S. courts. In 2009, President Obama suspended the proceedings of the Guantánamo military commission for 120 days, but a military judge denied the order. The president also ordered the facility be closed within the year, declaring, "9/11 was an enormous trauma to our country. The fear and anger that it provoked was understandable, but in some cases, it led us to act contrary to our ideals. We are taking concrete actions to change course. I have unequivocally prohibited the use of torture by the United States, and I have ordered the prison at Guantánamo Bay closed by early next year."[75]

Nevertheless, Guantánamo remained open. Few detainees have been tried, and some remain in detention although the government has no plans to charge them. They remain detained for several reasons. There may be insufficient evidence to hold trials in civilian or military courts; foreign countries may refuse to grant them asylum; and the American public opposes trying detainees in U.S. courts or housing them in maximum-security U.S. prisons where they may radicalize others or plan attacks in America. Two-thirds of Americans opposed closing the Guantánamo camp and moving detainees to U.S. prisons.[76] An effort by the administration to move Guantánamo detainees to a prison in Illinois failed in the face of congressional objections, and in 2011, Congress voted not to permit moving detainees to the United States and to prevent their transfer to countries "unless specified conditions are met" that according to President Obama "would hinder the conduct of delicate negotiations with foreign countries and therefore the effort to conclude detainee transfers in accord with our national security."[77] Thereafter, the president authorized the resumption of military trials that complied with the Geneva Conventions and laws outlawing torture. In 2012, Congress again voted against transferring Guantánamo prisoners to U.S. facilities.

Whether to keep keeping Guantánamo open or not remains controversial. Human rights groups like Amnesty International and Human Rights Watch, organizations like the European Union and the OAS, and leaders of U.S. allies have criticized the Guantánamo internments, while hardliners in America support its continued operation and have thwarted efforts to close the facility. In a letter read before the Senate in 2013, 38 former U.S. military officers argued that Guantánamo "is a betrayal of American values" and a threat to national security: "The prison is a symbol of torture and justice delayed. More than a decade after it opened, Guantánamo remains a recruiting poster for terrorists, which makes us all less safe."[78]

Of the roughly 800 detainees held at the camp, most had been released or sent to other countries by spring 2011, eight had been convicted by military courts (of which three later successfully appealed), and nine had died in custody, including six whose deaths were ruled suicides. In 2013, the administration created a new Pentagon position to facilitate the transfer of the detainees for whom transfer was approved, if they posed no further danger, and named Clifford Sloan, an attorney, as the State Department's special envoy to close the camp. By the time Sloan left the position in late 2014, thirty-nine prisoners had been transferred out of Guantánamo to other countries. In January 2015, another five Yemeni prisoners were released to Estonia and Oman. They were not returned to Yemen because of the civil war in that country and the possibility they might join terrorist groups there. Citing what they considered the administration's "irresponsible release" of detainees, Republican senators threatened to pass legislation to suspend transfers from Guantánamo for two years.[79] Of the remaining 122 detainees, most had been incarcerated for over a decade, twenty were designated for trial or military commissions (including Khalid Sheikh Mohammed, whose proposed trial in New York City triggered stiff resistance), thirty-three were deemed too dangerous to release and designated for indefinite detention without charge or trial, and fifty-seven had been approved for and were awaiting repatriation to their homelands.[80]

The USA Patriot Act, the NSA, and Intelligence Surveillance Nowhere is the tension between interests and values as visible as in the debate regarding how far the government may go in efforts to gather information needed to keep America safe. U.S. surveillance efforts have been criticized for violating the civil and political liberties of Americans and non-U.S. citizens outside the United States. In 2001, the **USA Patriot Act** authorized enhanced surveillance efforts to improve national security, but these efforts have met with repeated criticisms that they violate individual privacy. While the Patriot Act generated controversy at home, it also raised questions globally about U.S. leadership in promoting human rights, particularly when viewed alongside the practices described earlier. Surveillance emerged as a foreign-policy issue in 2013 when National Security Agency (NSA) contractor Edward Snowden leaked documents revealing that U.S. intelligence agencies were not just spying on U.S. citizens but had data collection programs that targeted individuals and leaders around the world. Global opinion polls taken before and after the revelations revealed that people became "significantly less likely to believe the U.S. government respects the personal freedoms of its citizens."[81]

The Patriot Act was passed just six weeks after 9/11. Fourteen of the law's seventeen provisions were permanently renewed in 2006, and Congress renewed the remaining three for an additional four years in 2011. The act reduced restrictions on intelligence gathering by government agencies in America, enabled the government to detain and deport terrorism suspects more easily, and expanded the government's ability to regulate financial transactions. The act allowed the government to use electronic surveillance to gather intelligence about suspected terrorist activities using wiretaps previously only available for investigating other criminal activities; legalized the use of "roving wiretaps" linked to individual suspects rather than phones; permitted the government to obtain a secret court order for suspects' personal and business records including in-store or online purchases, hotel records, and credit and library records; facilitated the sharing of information among law enforcement, defense, and intelligence agencies; and enabled officials to obtain search warrants wherever terrorism-related activity was believed to have occurred. Three sections were especially controversial. Section 215 gave the government access to an individual's personal and business records (the "library provision"). Section 206 legalized "roving wire-taps," and Section 6001 of the 2004 Intelligence Reform and Terrorism Prevention Act authorized the issuance of warrants to investigate foreign "lone wolf" suspects with no known ties to terrorist groups.

Security-conscious hardliners contended these expanded powers enhanced the government's ability to prevent or react swiftly to acts or potential acts of terrorism, but civil liberties advocates argued they infringed individual rights. The American Civil Liberties Union (ACLU) maintained that the Patriot Act gave the government "unchecked power to rifle through individuals' financial records, medical histories, Internet usage, bookstore purchases, library usage, travel patterns, or any other activity that leaves a record."[82] Thus, under the law, government agencies no longer had to produce evidence that suspects were agents of a foreign power or that they believed records were related to criminal activity. In addition, those ordered to surrender such records could not reveal the search to anyone else. Finally, the standard of proof to receive approval for searches was lowered, and judges had no authority to reject applications for searches. These provisions, the ACLU claimed, violated the Constitution's First Amendment guarantee of freedom of speech and the Fourth Amendment's protection from searches and seizures without probable cause or obtaining a warrant.

The debate was fueled in June 2013 when Snowden leaked classified information about the government's surveillance activities to journalists writing for *The Guardian* and *The Washington Post*. Snowden disclosed that the NSA was "collecting the telephone records of tens of millions of Americans" and had required the telecommunications company Verizon to share all of its telephone data. The government was also using an Internet monitoring program called Prism to tap the servers of nine Internet companies—Microsoft, Yahoo, Google, Facebook, PalTalk, AOL, Skype, YouTube, and Apple[83]—to oversee foreigners' email and online postings. By law these companies could not reveal how many data requests from law enforcement authorities were related to national security. In the following weeks, it was revealed that the NSA had over 61,000 hacking operations worldwide and had spied on European Union offices and computer networks in America and Europe, including those of the EU's permanent UN mission in New York. It had also monitored the phones of thirty-eight embassies and missions, including those of friendly countries like France, Italy, Greece, Japan, South Korea, and India, and thirty-five world leaders, including those of German Chancellor Angela Merkel and Brazil's President Dilma Rousseff.[84] Foreign officials and publics were outraged. President Rousseff abruptly canceled her scheduled visit to Washington and declared at the UN General Assembly: "Tampering in such a manner in the lives and affairs of other countries is a breach of international law and, as such, it is an affront to the principles that should otherwise govern relations among countries, especially among friendly nations."[85]

Demonstrators in Brazil hold signs that read "Dilma [Rousseff]: give a welcome to Snowden!" and "Asylum for Snowden now!"

AP Photo/Andre Penner

Many Americans were also appalled by the extent of NSA surveillance and began to advocate greater privacy protection. And as sections 215, 206, and 6001 were about to expire in 2015, a federal appeals court ruled that the Patriot Act did not allow the collection of bulk telephone metadata (records of length, time, and frequency of calls and who calls whom). Then, over the opposition of Senate hardliners, Congress passed the USA Freedom Act ending the NSA's bulk phone data collection. While retaining much of the existing system including roving wiretaps, it created a less intrusive system that leaves metadata in the hands of phone companies like Verizon and AT&T and requires the government to ask a special court for permission for those data. The formerly secret Foreign Intelligence Surveillance Court must declassify earlier decisions. President Obama welcomed and signed the new law, chastising those in Congress who had delayed its passage for several days, and claiming "enactment of this legislation will strengthen civil liberty safeguards and provide greater public confidence in these programs."[86] Nevertheless, Senator Rand Paul (R-KY), then a candidate for the Republican presidential nomination, denounced the president for continuing "to conduct an illegal program," referring to the decision of the federal appeals court that the original data collection program in the Patriot Act was unauthorized. And shortly later it was revealed that, with the president's approval, the NSA had secretly expanded its warrantless surveillance of Americans' international emails to hunt for computer hackers who were criminals but not suspected terrorists.

FUTURE: PROMOTING DEMOCRACY AND HUMAN RIGHTS

Let us examine options for managing these issues. Each policy places a different emphasis on the relative balance of values and interests.

Multilateralism: The HRC and the ICC
Policy Options

a. *Engage multilateral institutions to advance human rights and democracy,* an option involving participation in multilateral institutions like the HRC. A key advantage of membership is that U.S. leaders can shape the rules of these organizations to ensure they operate as intended. Achieving these reforms would be difficult, but joining the multilateral process would visibly commit America to improving human rights globally. Regarding the HRC, this would mean continuing to seek membership, as the rules allow, while working from within for reforms to prevent human rights violators from using membership to shield themselves.

A similar logic recommends joining the ICC, a step Washington is unlikely to take anytime soon. Engaging the ICC, however, might involve supporting its work as a nonmember. The Obama administration has pursued a strategy of selective "positive engagement." In recent years, Washington has supported the court when doing so fosters U.S. interests, a policy that leads to a dual standard that other countries find objectionable. Washington was late in supporting ICC involvement in Sudan and Syria, but in 2011, it assisted in tracking and apprehending Joseph Kony, leader of Uganda's Lord's Resistance Army. Some observers suggest that the United States has been so engaged during the Obama administration that it "has become a *de facto* member."[87]

Pursuing justice through the ICC can produce tradeoffs, as President Obama's Sudan envoy explained: "The decision by the ICC to accuse Sudanese president Omar al-Bashir of genocide will make my mission more difficult and challenging especially if we realize that resolving the crisis in Darfur and South, issues of oil and combating terrorism at a 100 percent, we need Bashir."[88] In addition, Africans—once among the strongest advocates of the ICC and its largest bloc of members—34 of 122—are wary of the institution because the court has pursued more cases in Africa than in all other regions combined. African leaders criticized the ICC as it began prosecuting African politicians like Kenya's President Uhuru Kenyatta.

U.S. officials must consider what unconditional support for the ICC would mean if a U.S. citizen were accused of crimes like torture that fall under its jurisdiction. Even as a nonmember, a supportive United States might experience global pressure to prosecute American leaders who in the future could be accused of such crimes. By some accounts, the ICC is already applying increasing pressure on members by its strategy of "positive complementarity," that is, fostering interest in using national legal systems to prosecute crimes.[89]

b. *Advocate establishing ad hoc tribunals*, which U.S. officials did in 2005 to investigate human rights abuses in Sudan and supported doing in regard to Syria in 2014. Ad hoc tribunals are, however, costly and inefficient in comparison to a single institution with a permanent staff and secure funding. Every ad hoc tribunal requires a new statute giving it legal authority and defining its mandate, its funding source, judges, prosecutor, and trained staff.

Alternatively, Washington could emphasize unilateral tools to advance human rights and complement multilateralism, and in human rights direct pressure may be useful.

Dealing with Specific Human Rights Abuses

When Washington identifies governments that abuse human rights, it has several options.

Policy Options

a. *Ignore human rights abuses in countries like Sudan, Cuba, and China.* This strategy might facilitate pursuing interests like security or trade but would trigger protests by American human rights activists, NGOs like Amnesty International, and governments that look to U.S. leadership. Thus, ignoring human rights abuses in Tibet and treating them as an internal Chinese concern would be viewed as cynical and expedient. The problem becomes how to pressure Beijing without undermining other interests in U.S.-China relations.

b. *Press leaders to initiate human rights and democratic reform.* Engagement poses several dilemmas for Washington. Some pressure may be necessary if America wishes to cooperate with the regime in question to achieve other interests, but it may trigger criticism that the U.S. prioritizes interests over values. Regarding South Sudan, some observers argued that Washington had a responsibility to make peace there a priority because U.S. diplomacy was crucial to achieving South Sudan's independence. But it is unclear how much involvement would be welcome or with whom Washington should work. An African Union report in 2015 held both the country's president and former vice president responsible for "organized massacres and large-scale violence," concluding that both should "be barred from participation in the transitional executive," and blaming America, Britain, and Norway for backing a deal that created a "politically unchallenged armed power in South Sudan."[90]

In the case of Tibet, America's human rights community favors making China pay an economic and political price for human rights abuses. Limiting U.S.-Chinese trade or public denunciation of abuses in Tibet, however, would entail economic costs for U.S. firms against which China would retaliate. And Beijing would treat such policies as violations of China's sovereignty, and they might poison Sino-American relations thereby ending China's cooperation in other issues such as how to deal with North Korea.

A less provocative approach such as endorsing the Dalai Lama as Tibet's spiritual leader might be feasible. Such endorsement, however, must avoid threatening China's dominant position in Tibet. With that crucial caveat, China might be prepared to accept this because the current Dalai Lama is elderly, and Beijing expects to name his successor. A middle path, while delicate, is possible as reflected in the resolution of a brief Sino-American crisis triggered after a blind Chinese dissident, Chen Guangcheng, escaped from house arrest in 2012 and took refuge in America's embassy in Beijing. It appeared that U.S. officials were confronted with a stark choice—either turning Chen over to Chinese officials and infuriating American human rights activists or granting Chen political asylum and infuriating Chinese leaders who were embarrassed by his escape. Negotiations, however, resulted in a compromise by which China allowed Chen to accept an invitation to become a visiting scholar at New York University law school. Thus, Beijing sent Chen where he could do little harm and claimed it as a Chinese decision rather than foreign interference in China's domestic affairs.

c. *Isolate countries economically and politically until they end abusive practices.* Policies of isolation also face the dilemma of balancing values and interests. In the case of Cuba during the Cold War and the following years, values and interests were aligned, and Washington viewed isolation as necessary for both. America isolated Cuba by imposing economic sanctions, ejecting Havana from the OAS, and severing bilateral diplomatic ties. Today, interests and values are no longer closely aligned, and congressional sanctions remain in place even as U.S. diplomats negotiate normalization of relations. This mixed strategy of engagement and isolation is not sustainable in the long run. As more Americans travel to Cuba, it will be increasingly difficult to return to a policy of isolating Havana. Opinion polls in both countries indicate majorities want stronger ties and, after easing executive sanctions, U.S. businesses saw significant opportunities in trading with Cuba.[91]

d. *Employ humanitarian intervention to stop genocide in Darfur and ethnic cleansing in South Sudan.* Given the severity of abuses in the region, some human rights observers advocate **humanitarian intervention**. However, the United States and the international community have had a poor record intervening in support of human rights in Africa, and such intervention is costly. Thus, Washington is unlikely to intervene for humanitarian purposes unless there are important strategic interests at stake.

HUMAN RIGHTS AND NATIONAL SECURITY

The worst practices related to America's War on Terror were products of efforts to enhance U.S. security. Most had ended by 2015, but years after the 9/11 attacks, the U.S. government and public have not had a serious debate about the tradeoffs between security and human rights.

Illegal Combatants

Future wars may look more like the insurgencies in Afghanistan and Iraq and less like the interstate wars that dominated recent centuries and fostered the laws of war. Thus, the question of what legal protections exist for terrorists, guerrillas, and similar "illegal combatants" in U.S. custody remains.

Policy Options

a. *Continue treating illegal combatants as outside the protection the Geneva Conventions.* This option privileges security but would continue to undermine U.S. moral standing and outrage those who argue that America should act in a manner consistent with its values, especially when existing practices fail to discriminate between the innocent and the guilty. Offering due process to detainees is a human right, and mistreating illegal combatants fuels anti-Americanism and provides additional recruits for terrorist groups. Thus, the status quo may be inconsistent with U.S. values *and* security. Advocates of the status quo believe the opposite—that keeping dangerous militants in custody is necessary to ensure they do not participate in future terrorist activities.

b. *Offer illegal combatants the rights afforded in the Geneva Conventions,* an option consistent with U.S. values. This would entail treating detainees as prisoners of war for whom detention is not a punishment but a means to prevent their return to conflict. While in custody, they would be treated humanely and would be repatriated after hostilities end. This option is complicated by the nature of the conflicts in which illegal combatants are involved. Insurgencies are of long duration, and some never completely end, making it difficult to determine when to repatriate detainees. While advocates of this option argue it would enhance America's moral standing, releasing detainees before a conflict ends may enable those individuals to fight again, thereby endangering U.S. security.

But what about those who are already in custody in the Guantánamo detention camp?

c. *Maintain the Guantánamo facility to house those too dangerous to release,* a position advocated by those who prioritize security. They argue there are individuals who are so dangerous they must remain in U.S. custody but kept far from the general population, leaving Guantánamo Bay the only alternative to incarceration.

d. *Close the Guantánamo detention camp.* This option, which would require congressional action, involves repatriating detainees who have been approved to return to their homelands and transferring remaining detainees to prisons in the United States or other countries where they can be charged and tried for their crimes. Those who privilege values favor this option.

Torture

Exactly what constitutes torture is not always clear under U.S. and international law, and there are practical considerations that influence policy choices. Thus, Guantánamo detainees have gone on hunger strikes to protest their confinement. In 2013, as frustration mounted over indefinite detention, 106 detainees embarked on a mass hunger strike, and authorities force-fed some of them through a greased nasal tube, a procedure that, in the words of the president of the American Medical Association, violates the "core ethical values of the medical profession."[92] U.S. officials insisted, however, they were doing what was necessary to keep prisoners alive.

Policy Options

a. *Ban torture outright.* The Obama administration ended the most brutal practices of the War on Terror. "At the very least," argues political scientist Robert Jervis, torture "alienated U.S. allies and gave ammunition to those who opposed Washington's policies, contributing to the belief that the United States was hypocritical in its public defense of liberty and prone to treat Muslims as less than human."[93] Ending torture would help restore America's image and its credibility as a proponent of human rights.

b. *Allow torture to obtain information that cannot otherwise be obtained.* This option is inconsistent with stated American values but may enhance security—though its effectiveness is controversial. Must it result in information to stop an imminent attack or is it "effective" if it produces "a general understanding" about the adversary?[94] Both types of information are valuable. A 2014 poll found that a narrow majority of Americans (53 percent) believed "the use of torture could be often or sometimes justified."[95] Thus, although President Obama has formally banned torture, it could emerge as an option under a new president or in the event of an imminent threat to national security like nuclear terrorism.

c. *Hold accountable those accused of using or authorizing torture.* This is among the most controversial of the options because there are many interpretations of what constitutes torture in U.S. law. Although the CIA's enhanced interrogation techniques—including using sleep deprivation, stress positions, and waterboarding—"certainly count as torture in the ordinary sense of the term,"[96] holding officials accountable might mean prosecuting senior officials like Vice President Cheney and President Bush. The Obama administration has not chosen this option, and it is unlikely that future administrations would do so partly because in the event of another attack on the U.S. homeland, a future president may want to adopt these techniques. This option would produce deep domestic political divisions.

Intelligence Surveillance

The issues to consider in designing intelligence surveillance include whose data and how much should be collected and how transparent the process should be.

Policy Options

a. *Continue to conduct bulk data collection to ensure that intelligence analysts have all the information needed for U.S. security.* This option privileges security interests over values but alienates allies and angers citizens without clearly offering security benefits greater than the costs incurred. Opponents view the strategy as overkill, because the intelligence community does not even have the capability to analyze all of the data it gathers.

b. *Hold U.S. citizens' privacy to a higher standard.* While prioritizing values, this option would be difficult to implement. Owing to the Internet, data are constantly crossing borders. "Advances in technology began permanently blurring the distinctions between domestic and foreign surveillance and between U.S. citizens and foreign nationals."[97] Thus, laws preventing intelligence agencies from gathering data about U.S. citizens at home offer little protection if electronic searches and communications are routed through servers in other countries. Nor would such laws address foreign governments' concerns about NSA data collection.

c. *Work with foreign governments to find a balance that allows U.S. intelligence agencies access to data they require but respects local privacy laws.* This option attempts to balance privacy and security but would likely require U.S. officials to share sensitive data with foreign governments before those governments authorized releasing data about their citizens.

d. *Work with companies that collect data to ensure these are secure but available to officials if needed.* Private companies collect mountains of data when doing business. If they cannot protect customer data from invasive government policies, they lose credibility worldwide. After the Snowden revelations, Apple, for instance, revised its privacy policy to explain how it handles government requests for information and updated its mobile operating system to prevent data being extracted from devices without a personal passcode.[98] Such actions benefit U.S. and foreign consumers but have potential security implications. Personal data are more secure, and privacy is protected, but if the government needs the information it is difficult—and time-consuming—to acquire it.

CONCLUSION: AN INCONSISTENT HUMAN RIGHTS RECORD

There is a perennial tension in U.S. foreign policy between strategic interests and values articulated in foundational documents like the Bill of Rights that emphasize the government's responsibility to protect both civil and political liberties. This tension is evident in decisions regarding where and how to promote human rights and democratic reform and in the policies of the government and the conduct of those acting on its behalf. In deciding when to pursue human rights, Washington has been reluctant to press vigorously when doing so might harm U.S. interests. The case to act regardless of interests must be strong and have influential advocates, and there are few such cases. Foreign policy is rarely formulated to pursue purely altruistic goals.

Equally important is whether U.S. officials practice the values they claim to represent. When they do, America is admired and respected and acquires soft power that enables it to advance its human rights agenda more effectively. When they do not, moral standing is lost, along with the influence it confers.

DISCUSSION QUESTIONS

1. What are the enduring trends in U.S. efforts to advance human rights and democracy abroad? What new challenges exist for U.S. foreign policy in this area?

2. What are the advantages of working through multilateral institutions in pursuing human rights and promoting democracy? What are the limitations?

3. What tools are available to U.S. leaders to influence human rights practices in other countries?

4. Discuss the ways U.S. values and interests clash in dealing with human rights.

5. How should America deal with the issue of "illegal combatants"?

6. When human rights and national security conflict, which should take precedence?

KEY TERMS

American exceptionalism (p. 169)

cosmopolitanism (p. 169)

crimes against humanity (p. 177)

embargo (p. 182)

ethnic cleansing (p. 174)

ethnicity (p. 169)

genocide (p. 174)

human rights (p. 165)

humanitarian intervention (p. 196)

humanitarian law (p. 174)

illegal combatants (p. 185)

internally displaced persons (p. 180)

nationalized (p. 182)

remittances (p. 182)

self-executing treaties (p. 168)

state sponsors of terrorism (p. 184)

UN Human Rights Council (p. 175)

Universal Declaration of Human Rights (p. 165)

USA Patriot Act (p. 192)

war crimes (p. 177)

$SAGE edge™
for CQ Press

Sharpen your skill with SAGE edge at **edge.sagepub.com/mansbach**

SAGE edge for Students provides a personalized approach to help you accomplish your coursework goals in an easy-to-use learning environment.

7

America and the Global South

AID, INTERVENTION, AND NEGLECT

Philippine soldiers
with U.S. aid
packages after
Typhoon Haiyan
(2013)

Bryan Denton/Corbis/AP Images

Washington seeks to balance values and interests in relations with the Global South, and this shapes its choices among strategies of aid, intervention, or neglect. In most cases, U.S. policies incorporate all three strategies to some degree. What varies is their relative balance. The most coercive, intervention, has historically involved military or political involvement to compel governments to accept and act according to U.S. interests. Intervention still occurs, most recently in Afghanistan and Iraq, but it may take other forms, including foreign aid. Foreign aid to support economic development frequently involves conditions requiring political and economic reforms and as such constitutes intervention by giving Washington influence over how a regime governs its people and its economy. Neglect can involve turning a blind eye to certain countries or problems but may involve acknowledging challenges without developing specific or coherent policy responses.

Several themes in the previous chapter are also germane to analysis of U.S. relations with less-developed countries that are collectively termed the Global South. Although there is great diversity among these countries, they experience similar challenges of governance, economic development, crime and violence, inadequate health care, and destabilizing population flows. Alleviating the suffering of peoples in these countries is consistent with human rights and democratic values. In relations with the Global South, Washington has a longstanding interest in encouraging political and economic reform that achieves **human development** and **human security**. Washington also has significant interests in particular countries in the Global South that bear on its relations with other major powers. Thus, the United States seeks to woo less-developed countries like Myanmar, Laos, and Cambodia that are influenced by China and is developing close relations with Vietnam, a country estranged from China. Similarly, America and China both seek greater influence in Central Asia, where Russia views less-developed states, formerly Soviet republics, as within its sphere of influence. In Latin America, Washington seeks better relations with countries that are attracted to China or the leftist policies of Venezuela, and in the Middle East it seeks to improve relations with Egypt after those relations deteriorated during the Arab Spring.

SOURCES OF U.S. AID AND INTERVENTION

Several external factors influence U.S. foreign policy toward the Global South. Bipolarity and the Cold War elevated national security concerns to the top of America's foreign-policy agenda. Washington viewed countries in the "periphery" primarily as potential allies against the Soviet bloc. The Cold War also shaped how countries in the Global South chose to interact with America. In the 1950s, leaders such as India's Jawaharlal Nehru, Egypt's Gamal Abdel Nasser, and Yugoslavia's Josip Broz Tito pursued a

Timeline

1900	1900 (Continued)	2000
1947 Marshall Plan to support Europe's postwar recovery	**1994** U.S. invasion of Haiti	**2000** Millennium Development Goals adopted
1954 Food for Peace Program established	**1994** Mexico's debt crisis	**2002** President Bush establishes an Emergency Plan for AIDS Relief.
1961 U.S. Agency for International Development established	**1997** Asian financial crisis	**2003** Failed states become a key issue in U.S. national security strategy.
1983 U.S. invasion of Grenada		**2003** President Bush launches the Emergency Plan for AIDS Relief.
1989 U.S. invasion of Panama		**2004** Millennium Challenge Account established
		2014 Ebola outbreak in West Africa
		2015 Millennium Development Goals expire.

policy of nonalignment, by which they maintained independent foreign policies and played the United States and USSR off against each other.

Natural and other disasters are another external source of U.S. policy. In 1976, Secretary of State Henry Kissinger declared: "Disaster relief is becoming increasingly a major instrument of our foreign policy."[1] That is also true today. Aid to relieve suffering in the face of disasters has led to a proliferation of governmental and nongovernment aid programs that assume a life of their own and seek the next crisis where they can help. What was once emergency relief mutated into long-term aid programs that become indistinguishable from long-term-development assistance. The willingness of governments to accept this assistance and the conditions attached to it is another external factor. Many Americans like former Senator Jesse Helms (R-NC) express frustration with "pouring money down foreign rat holes."[2] They want to see tangible economic and political improvements in governments like Zimbabwe, Sudan, and Haiti that accept millions of dollars of U.S. aid year after year.

The U.S. Agency for International Development (USAID), created by the 1961 Foreign Assistance Act, is the lead government agency overseeing U.S. development assistance. It is the organization through which most U.S. foreign aid is distributed for health care, human-rights promotion, food security, environmental sustainability, education, and disaster relief. In total, over twenty U.S. government agencies are involved in providing foreign assistance. The Department of the Treasury oversees U.S. contributions to the World Bank and other international development programs. The Department of State has wide-ranging aid responsibilities including administration of "activities dealing with international narcotics control and law enforcement, terrorism, weapons proliferation, democracy promotion, non-UN peacekeeping operations, refugee relief, and voluntary support for a range of international organizations such as UNICEF."[3] The Peace Corps is an autonomous agency that uses volunteers to work on educational, health, and development projects overseas. Since its establishment in 1961, over 220,000 Americans have served in 140 countries.[4] Each agency has its own interests and expertise, and sometimes their aid goals conflict with their other foreign and domestic objectives. The 1954 Food for Peace program, for example, is administered by the Department of Agriculture. It initially viewed food aid as a way to pay midwestern farmers for their grain; however, as we shall see, cheap U.S. food may do more harm than good overseas, but the policy is difficult to change owing to vested societal interests.

Societal groups such as philanthropic NGOs like the Clinton Foundation and the Bill and Melinda Gates Foundation work to tackle the most serious developmental and humanitarian challenges in the Global South. Roman Catholics and mainline Protestant religious groups advocate on behalf of economic and social justice overseas and support incorporating poverty reduction into U.S. development policy, whereas evangelical groups are less supportive of development aid but rally around humanitarian causes.[5] Commercial interests are also influential in the foreign-aid process, especially in supporting "**tied aid**" that requires recipients to purchase goods and services from American farms and companies.

At the individual level, presidents and key members of Congress are influential in shaping U.S. foreign policies toward the Global South. President Richard Nixon was not interested in hemispheric issues at all, except for Cuba.[6] Ronald Reagan was determined to combat communism by any means in Latin America, notably in El Salvador, Nicaragua, and Cuba, and actively practiced intervention there. President George W. Bush emphasized health and failed states, and his aid policies had a great impact in Africa. Senator Helms was an anti-aid crusader who successfully fought in 1973 to prevent U.S. money from going to international family planning organizations that "promoted" abortions.[7] He was even more successful implementing his preferred policies in his role as chair of the Senate Foreign Relations Committee (1995–2001). Celebrities have used their status as a platform to publicize humanitarian and development causes. Irish rock star Bono of U2 fame cofounded ONE, a global antipoverty campaign, and has been credited with pioneering celebrity activism,[8] but many others preceded him. In 1954, the actor Danny Kaye became the first Goodwill Ambassador for UNICEF, the United Nations Children's Fund. Over the years, Audrey Hepburn, Jackie Chan, Orlando Bloom, Katy Perry, and others have used their celebrity to advocate improved health care, education, and security for children worldwide.

PAST: U.S. AID AND INTERVENTION

This chapter focuses on human security and development, although this terminology is relatively new. Human security refers to the protection and well-being of individuals and communities, not nation-states or sovereignty. The concept first appeared in the 1994 UN Human Development Report, which explained "the concept of security has for too long been interpreted narrowly: as security of territory from external aggression, or as protection of national interests in foreign policy or as global security from the threat of a nuclear holocaust. It has been related more to nation-states than to people."[9] Human security exists when people live free from threats of violence, crime, human-rights abuses, poverty, environmental stress, and illness and disease. From this perspective, states are obligated to provide for the security of their citizens and for people elsewhere who face threats to life and well-being. Both protection and development are essential to this enterprise. The surest way to achieve protection is through development but not development as it was often practiced in the West. Macroeconomic policies that focus on restructuring economies and increasing national income ignore people and frequently produce human insecurity. Human development seeks to improve the human condition by achieving higher standards of living, better access to education, and health care. While analytically distinct, protection and development are difficult to separate in practice as we shall see. Although the idea of human security is consistent with U.S. values, achieving it may conflict with U.S. interests.

We now begin by examining U.S. interventions in the Global South, especially in Latin America, where U.S. officials often justified their intervening as support for democracy or human rights. U.S. interests, however, drove many of these events. We then turn to the evolution of U.S. aid policy. Initially managed almost solely for political ends, it was not until the 1970s that officials began to offer development aid that focused on human needs, but it would be some time before human security was the focus of aid.

Intervention

The time period of the late 19th and early 20th centuries was an era of gunboat diplomacy during which Washington intervened frequently in the Americas in what are known as the "Banana Wars" to maintain stability and preserve America's sphere of influence. U.S. intervention in Latin America continued after World War II frequently as part of its Cold War strategy of containing communism.

Nicaragua and Grenada: Freedom and Security President Ronald Reagan authorized interventions in Nicaragua and Grenada to contain communist influence. The Reagan Doctrine, as we saw in the last chapter, was an offensive strategy to recover communist-controlled territories by aiding anticommunist regimes, however distasteful. In Nicaragua, intervention involved military and financial support for anticommunist forces for almost a decade. In Grenada, U.S. intervention took the form of a brief military invasion in 1983.

Washington intervened in Nicaragua in support of anticommunist forces rebelling against a Marxist Sandinista government led by Daniel Ortega. The Sandinistas had ties to the USSR, considered themselves socialist (though not communist), and sought to export socialism to neighboring El Salvador and Guatemala. Reagan believed the Sandinistas threatened the stability of the entire region. He cut off all aid to the regime, redirected it to bolster neighboring regimes, and supported counterrevolutionary Nicaraguan "contras" in Honduras with arms and money. He also authorized the CIA to provide direct support to the contras, including training soldiers and mining Nicaraguan harbors. The contras were corrupt and brutal. As awareness of their abuses grew, Congress began to restrict U.S. aid. Thereafter, in what became known as the Iran-Contra affair, members of the administration, notably National Security Council staff member Oliver North, sought private sources of funding, illegally sold military equipment to Iran[10] in exchange for aid in gaining the release of U.S. hostages in Lebanon, and used the profits to fund the contras.

U.S. attention turned to Grenada, a tiny Caribbean island, in 1979 after leftists believed to be working with Cuba seized power. The new leader, Maurice Bishop, began to strengthen ties with Washington but was overthrown and killed in October 1983 by former leftist allies. Reagan feared Cuban influence in the region and its possible use for ferrying Cuban troops to Angola in Africa. The Organization for Eastern Caribbean states requested U.S. action to "depose the outlaw regime."[11] Within days, Reagan launched an invasion force of 8,000 to "rescue" 800 American students attending medical school in Grenada and restore democratic government. Some observers believed that the invasion was orchestrated to restore the image of American strength after Hezbollah's bombing of U.S. military barracks in Lebanon that killed 241 servicemen just days earlier. The UN General Assembly overwhelmingly condemned the invasion as a violation of international law. Anti-American demonstrations erupted across Latin America, and U.S. diplomatic missions in Ecuador and Bolivia were attacked.[12]

Panama and Colombia: The War on Drugs Cold war concerns were not involved in U.S. intervention in Panama. Manuel Noriega, Panama's military ruler, had been a U.S. ally in opposing communism in the region. By the mid-1980s, it was becoming difficult to ignore his regime's abuses, including his role in the death of a political opponent, sharing intelligence "simultaneously" with Cuba and the United States, selling arms to the M-19 guerrilla group in Colombia, and involvement in money laundering and drug trafficking.[13] Washington used diplomatic pressure and economic sanctions to try removing Noriega from power. A failed coup attempt in October 1989 raised tensions, and at a meeting of the Panamanian legislature on December 15, Noriega declared a state of war with the United States. The next evening, an off-duty U.S. Marine was killed by Panamanian troops, and a Navy lieutenant and his wife who witnessed the shooting were detained and threatened. Within days, 24,000 U.S. troops invaded Panama to oust the regime and take Noriega into custody.

U.S. intervention to combat drug trafficking was focused particularly on Colombia. In this case, intervention was in partnership with the Colombian government. Colombia had experienced decades of internal violence involving the leftist guerrilla groups the Revolutionary Armed Forces of Colombia

(FARC) and the National Liberation Army (ELN) and right-wing paramilitaries coordinated by the United Self-Defense Forces of Colombia (AUC). Violence escalated in the 1990s when cocaine production moved from Bolivia and Peru to Colombia and provided income to fund the violent groups. By 1999, Colombia was experiencing a crisis. The government had lost control of much of its territory, poverty and inequality were growing, and violence was escalating. There were 2,000 terrorist attacks and over 3,000 kidnappings in 1999 alone, and Colombians were "leaving the country in droves."[14] Colombia's President Andrés Pastrana Arango developed Plan Colombia to stop guerrilla violence, combat drug trafficking, and encourage development. Colombia would allocate $4 billion and request $3.5 billion from other governments. Since 90 percent of cocaine smuggled into America came from Colombia, President Clinton argued that instability there was a direct threat to U.S. interests.

In 2000, Congress approved funding to support Colombia's efforts. By 2012, Washington had spent nearly $8 billion, mostly in efforts to suppress the cocaine trade. This included interdiction of drug shipments and coca eradication programs. After 2001, when America commenced its War on Terror, Congress eased restrictions on funding to allow Colombia to use U.S. aid to combat its guerrilla insurgency. Washington considered the FARC, ELN, and AUC as terrorist groups. Congress authorized up to 800 troops and 600 contractors to deploy to Colombia to support its efforts (but not participate in combat).[15] By 2012, the Colombian government had a stronger security presence across the country. The insurgency had eased, and violence had declined. Critics of the plan and U.S. involvement charged it prioritized security over development and even undermined development efforts by extensive use of aerial eradication programs that poisoned soils and nearby crops, a policy Colombia suspended in 2015. It also encouraged human rights abuses by the Colombian army while failing to curtail the drug trade.

Haiti: Humanitarian Intervention? Intervention in Haiti in 1993 marked the beginning of a new era as the first in the Western Hemisphere to be justified as a humanitarian effort. In reality, U.S. goals in the operation were not clear. Between 1957 and 1986, Haiti was governed first by President François "Papa Doc" Duvalier and then by his son Jean-Claude "Baby Doc" Duvalier. Both were brutal dictators and self-described "Presidents for Life" under whose rule journalists, activists, and political opponents were intimidated, tortured, disappeared, and even killed. The Duvaliers and their supporters lived extravagantly while Haiti's economic conditions deteriorated. Haiti began its transition to democracy after protests ousted "Baby Doc" in 1986, but corruption, political instability, and economic inequality persisted. Haiti's first democratically elected president, Jean-Bertrand Aristide, pursued social and political reforms upon entering office in 1991 but alienated the military and the political elites and was ousted in a coup later that year. When diplomatic pressure and economic sanctions failed to persuade the military regime to step down, Clinton threatened invasion and successfully sought a UN Security Council resolution to authorize a U.S.-led force to restore Aristide to office. While U.S. forces were mobilizing, former president Jimmy Carter negotiated an agreement to reinstate Aristide to complete his term. Aristide was reelected president in 2000, after a constitutionally mandated break, but in 2004, protests erupted over claims the 2000 election had been rigged, forcing him to flee again, this time with American intervention to escort him safely out of the country.

Clinton justified intervention in Haiti as necessary to end the deteriorating humanitarian situation that had been identified in the UN resolution and to restore democracy. The U.S. invasion, however, appears to have served U.S. interests as well. U.S. intervention in Haiti offered an opportunity for

Clinton to demonstrate U.S. resolve and leadership in the post–Cold War world after the tragic deaths of U.S. soldiers in Somalia the previous year. Clinton explained: "The United States must protect our interests, to stop the brutal atrocities that threaten tens of thousands of Haitians, to secure our borders, and to preserve stability and promote democracy in our hemisphere and to uphold the reliability of the commitments we make and the commitments others make to us."[16] The invasion also allowed him to retreat from a campaign promise to welcome into America Haitians fleeing instability after over 37,000 had fled by boat.[17]

Military invasions constitute coercive intervention that violates the sovereignty of targeted states. There are other ways to intervene overseas to influence the foreign and domestic policies of other states. Foreign aid is one such tool that is usually consistent with U.S. values and advances U.S. interests in the Global South. Where America sends aid—and where it does not—often indicates U.S. foreign-policy priorities.

Aid

Most governments, including America's, use aid to advance military and strategic interests that may include economic and political stability and improved bilateral relations. During the Cold War, most bilateral aid, even that allocated for development purposes, was intended to support America's interest in combating communism. Some analysts found this "interest" to be a moral obligation consistent with U.S. values. The "obligation to aid nations that resist the economic and military pressure exerted against their national liberties by Communist states," wrote one, "is simply a facet of our general obligation toward the international common good."[18] Recipients used U.S. aid to foster economic development by financing antipoverty initiatives and national infrastructure projects like energy grids, transportation networks, and education and health care systems and, as a result of U.S. conditions for providing aid, to introduce policy reforms that accelerated growth. Governments also provide humanitarian relief, a form of charity that contributes to stabilizing societies and economies in crisis. More than other forms of aid, such relief is considered a moral obligation consistent with U.S. values. Finally, Washington also uses the promise of aid to advance human rights and democracy. If recipients fail to respect their citizens' rights, aid may be withheld.

The effectiveness of aid toward achieving these goals is uneven. When it does so, aid can increase America's soft power—the "ability to attract others by the legitimacy of U.S. policies and the values that underlie them."[19] It may foster human rights and government transparency, health care and education, and higher levels of economic growth. But aid does not always bring success, and sometimes it is harmful. In such cases, poverty deepens and inequality grows, governments become more indebted and corrupt, economic productivity is stifled owing to cheap or free overseas commodities and goods, and societies may become dependent on continuing infusions of aid. Aid can also be "deeply intrusive . . . especially where it aims to affect individual and society customs, traditions, behaviors, and political/institutional shortcomings."[20]

There are a number of explanations for aid inefficiency and ineffectiveness. Aid is commonly subject to the "**principal-agent problem**" that arises when "there is only an indirect and distant relationship" between donors and recipients in low-income countries. Many U.S. actors intervene in the process between the decision to provide aid and its actual distribution, and none may have complete or accurate information about the recipient's needs or aid's effectiveness.[21] The conditions that are attached to aid also can limit effectiveness if they are not appropriate to the circumstances in the recipient country.

The problem is especially challenging because policymakers frequently disagree about the appropriate conditions for national development. Moreover, providing too much aid may be worse than providing too little if it fosters inflation that increases the cost of household staples and stifles local manufacturing and agricultural production.

The Marshall Plan (1947–1949) was a successful example of U.S. development assistance. The plan was designed to help Europe recover from World War II and help its political institutions resist communist influence. Thereafter, the Truman administration began focusing on less developed countries. In 1950, the Point Four Program offered technical assistance to countries in Latin America and Asia to "make available to peace-loving people the benefits of our [U.S.] store of technical knowledge in order to help them realize their aspirations for a better life."[22] Much of Africa and the Middle East remained colony states and therefore not eligible for aid. The 1957 Development Loan Fund (DLF) offered long-term loans to finance large-scale development projects and was welcomed by newly independent countries like India. Each of these programs was undertaken to counter the USSR's efforts to increase its influence in the developing world.

The 1961 Foreign Assistance Act established the USAID to coordinate formerly separate, ad hoc foreign-aid programs, including Point Four and the DLF. The new USAID offered long-term development assistance to countries with democratically elected governments and national development plans. In Africa, Nigeria, Tanzania, and Tunisia were early beneficiaries of USAID assistance. Latin American countries received development aid under America's Alliance for Progress that sought "to promote economic and social reform and democratic governance."[23] The Alliance for Progress represented President John F. Kennedy's effort to limit Cuba's regional influence. Recipients were given responsibility for their own development, but an Inter-American Committee for the Alliance for Progress reviewed national development plans and estimated the aid requirements for each, a process similar to that of the Marshall Plan in Europe.[24] These programs were largely abandoned by the end of the decade owing to concerns that they were not meeting expectations for alleviating poverty and fostering development. In addition, the beginning of U.S.-Soviet détente reduced the strategic objectives of U.S. aid in the Global South.

U.S. national priorities began to shift in the 1970s as America's intervention in Vietnam left fewer resources for development assistance in nonstrategic regions. By mid-decade, aid to southern Africa increased owing to the emergence of Marxist-oriented governments in Angola and Mozambique and civil war in Rhodesia—all threats, U.S. officials believed, to the stability of the region. In Latin America and elsewhere in Africa, development aid declined, but that which was provided was focused less on building economies and more on providing for human needs—food, health, and education. The focus of aid shifted again in the 1980s, with aid levels increasing as Cold War tensions again escalated. During this era, development aid focused on strengthening democracy and legal institutions in countries like El Salvador, Honduras, and Guatemala and introducing macroeconomic reforms such as building free markets, supporting export sectors, and privatization that would reduce communist influence.

The neoliberal economic reforms advanced by the Reagan administration were largely in response to the debt crisis that began in Latin America in 1982. During the 1970s, Latin American countries had borrowed freely from public lenders, including the United States, other governments, the International Monetary Fund (IMF) and World Bank, and commercial banks. They used these loans for large infrastructural projects—roads, water supply, and telecommunications—that did not offer a swift return on investment or for nonrevenue-generating expenses including public expenditures, imports, or bribes to corrupt officials. In 1979, global recession combined with weak export markets, low commodity prices, high interest rates, and high oil prices produced a debt crisis. Governments were unable to earn enough from exports to service existing debts, and commercial banks were unwilling to extend additional credit. In August 1982, Mexico announced it was unable to service its $80 billion debt. The crisis quickly spread across the region and beyond, threatening the global financial system. Commercial banks sought to reschedule loans, and recession intensified in Latin America. The United States was a central player in this crisis and worked with commercial lenders and the IMF to provide emergency funding. Officials had three principal economic objectives in Latin America throughout the crisis: (1) maintain economic growth, (2) provide additional capital, and (3) introduce neoliberal structural reforms such as reducing government spending and balancing budgets to make Latin American countries more attractive to private investors and sustain long-term development.[25] Thus, additional U.S. and multilateral loans to Latin American governments came with conditions that governments adopt structural adjustment policies to integrate their economies into the global market and attract foreign investment. The following decade, a currency crisis in East Asia spread from Thailand to South Korea, then the world's eleventh largest economy, other Asian countries, and then to Russia and Brazil. These countries sought aid from the IMF, the World Bank, and the United States in exchange for commitments to accept structural economic reforms and liberalize trade.

These painful austerity policies known as the Washington consensus generated opposition to U.S. economic policies, and countries in the Global South began to demand new development and aid strategies. In Latin America, leftist populist governments emerged in Venezuela, Bolivia, Chile, Brazil, and Argentina. At the forefront of this movement was Venezuelan President Hugo Chávez, who employed anti-American rhetoric and worked to reduce U.S. influence in the region. Chávez sought closer ties with Russia, China, and Iran and proposed new regional economic arrangements, notably the Bolivarian Alliance for the Americas (ALBA) with Bolivia, Cuba, Ecuador, and Nicaragua and several Caribbean countries. Venezuela and like-minded regimes cooperated in regional forums to encourage poverty reduction and socioeconomic reforms that increased the states' roles in managing their economies. Although there was some progress toward alleviating poverty, until 2014 when oil prices plummeted, democracy and human rights were eroded—especially in Venezuela where following Chávez's death in 2013 President Nicolás Maduro violently suppressed students protesting crime and deteriorating economic conditions.

After the Cold War ended, U.S. foreign aid decreased dramatically, reaching its lowest levels in 1996 and 1997. As overall funding declined, more of what remained was allocated to development and humanitarian needs. U.S. foreign aid spending began to increase again in the late 1990s with calls for debt relief following East Asia's financial crisis and more aid for new democracies and countries facing crisis and possible collapse. Foreign assistance increased still more after September 2001, with efforts to foster development in Iraq and Afghanistan.

Let us now examine contemporary challenges facing Washington in its relations with the Global South as well as its policies of aid and intervention—and sometimes neglect.

PRESENT: CHALLENGES IN THE GLOBAL SOUTH

We begin our discussion of policy challenges facing America in relations with the Global South with the problem of fragile states. Administrations from Clinton to Obama have been preoccupied with the threats such states pose to U.S. security and the welfare of their citizens. We then turn to several

FIGURE **7.1**   Foreign Aid Funding Trends, FY 1977–FY 2010

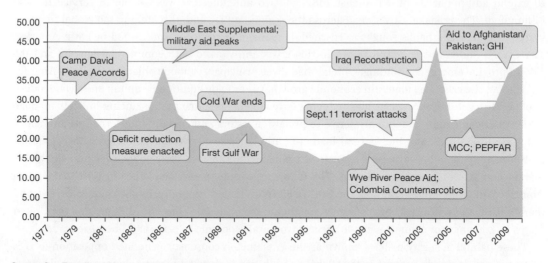

Source: Curt Tarnoff and Marian Leonardo Lawson, "Foreign Aid: An Introduction to U.S. Programs and Policy," CRS Report for Congress, R40213, February 10, 2011, https://www.fas.org/sgp/crs/row/R40213.pdf.

Notes: Figures are U.S. dollars (in billions) spent on aid. MCC = Millennium Challenge Corporation; PEPFAR = President's Emergency Plan for AIDS Relief; GHI = Global Health Initiative.

controversial challenges associated with weak, low-income countries, beginning with U.S. poverty-reduction and development policies. Foreign aid is the principle instrument to achieve these goals, but although Americans want to help those in need they are skeptical about the value of aid. An exception is health aid, which we consider separately. We conclude this section by considering refugees and migrants.

Fragile and Failing States

Fragile and failing states have been significant concerns for U.S. policymakers since the mid-1990s. For much of this time, "the dominant national security narrative in the United States stressed the dangers posed by weak or failing states,"[26] including terrorism, regional instability and conflict, and transnational crime. American liberals also view fragile states as threats to human security because of transnational crime, disease, poverty, and environmental degradation. **Fragile states** are characterized by governments that lack authority over much of their territory and are unable to deliver the services associated with governing including security, rule of law, and economic prosperity. Their inability to meet the basic needs of citizens is accompanied by a loss of legitimacy. In addition, paramilitaries that terrorize populations and bloated, ineffective, and corrupt bureaucracies are associated with fragile states. The most fragile of states, where governments have virtually collapsed, are described as "failing" or "**failed states**."

There is no universally accepted definition of fragile states. One index, created by the Fund for Peace and published annually in the journal *Foreign Policy*, includes 12 indicators: demographic pressures arising from factors like food scarcity and population growth; population displacement including refugees; group grievances that produce violence; migration out of the country; uneven economic development among groups and regions; poverty; state legitimacy; absence of public services like health care, sanitation, and education; protection of human rights; internal conflict and threats to security; conflict among elites; and foreign intervention.[27] Map 7.1 reveals that many of the countries most at risk in 2014 were in the Global South, especially in Africa, and that since the Arab Spring, additional countries in the Middle East and Central Asia, including Pakistan, Syria, Iraq, Afghanistan, and Yemen, have moved closer to eventual failure. Table 7.1 lists the 20 most fragile states included in the index. Fourteen of these are in Africa, five are in the Middle East/Central Asia, and only one (Haiti) is in the Western hemisphere.

U.S. interests and values intersect in the challenge posed by fragile states. U.S. values suggest a desire to see fragile states achieve economic and political stability that will enable them to pursue democracy and economic development. This is also consistent with U.S. interests because fragile states threaten U.S. security by providing terrorists and criminals with safe havens, fueling refugee flows to America and Europe, disrupting trade, and creating crises to which America as a global leader is expected to respond. U.S. policies that advance American values and foster stability and prosperity also reduce terrorism, conflict, crime, and environmental stress. Stabilizing fragile states, however, is a costly and lengthy process, requiring a sustained commitment.

MAP 7.1   The Fund for Peace 2014 Fragile States Index

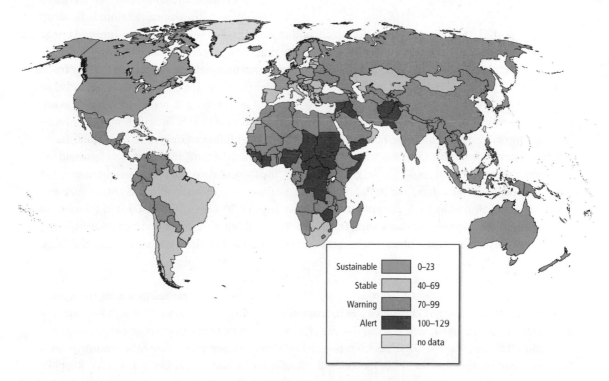

Source: Data from The Fund for Peace, "Fragile States Index: 2014," http://fsi.fundforpeace.org/rankings-2014.

TABLE **7.1**   Most Fragile States (2014)

1. South Sudan	11. Zimbabwe
2. Somalia	12. Guinea
3. Central African Republic	13. Iraq
4. Congo (D.R.)	14. Cote d'Ivoire
5. Sudan	15. Syria
6. Chad	16. Guinea Bissau
7. Afghanistan	17. Nigeria
8. Yemen	18. Kenya
9. Haiti	19. Ethiopia
10. Pakistan	19. Niger (tied)

Source: Data from The Fund for Peace, "Fragile States Index: 2014," http://fsi.fundforpeace.org/rankings-2014.

Unfortunately, U.S. foreign policy tends to be reactive, focusing on the direst situations that pose immediate threats to U.S. interests. Thus, "in any given week, the likelihood that the United States' top leaders will meet to ponder how to fix fragile states is incredibly small. If a weak state's dysfunctions aid and abet more pressing threats, such as possible terrorist attacks, that state will surely get scrutinized; if not, the task of coming up with plausible ways to shore up its stability quickly falls to officials at lower levels."[28]

U.S. officials often frame failing and fragile states as a threat to interests. President Bill Clinton regarded failed states as a threat to stability in regions where America had clear interests and viewed the solution as including nation-building to prevent state failure. "It is far more effective," the 1997 National Security Strategy reported, "to help prevent nations from failing than to rebuild them after an internal crisis; far more beneficial to help people stay in their homes than it is to feed and house them in refugee camps; and far less taxing for relief agencies and international organizations to strengthen the institutions of conflict resolution than to heal ethnic and social divisions that have already exploded in bloodshed."[29] Clinton was strongly criticized in 1994 for not intervening to prevent Rwanda's genocide. George W. Bush also viewed failing states primarily as threats to U.S. interests, and his administration pursued nation-building in Afghanistan and Iraq but failed to intervene in Angola, Haiti, or Sierra Leone where U.S. interests were not threatened. Barack Obama, by contrast, acknowledged the human security threats posed by fragile states that "incubate and spawn infectious disease, illicit weapons and drug smugglers, and destabilizing refugee flows. Too often, failures in governance and endemic corruption hold back the potential of rising regions."[30] Like Clinton, Obama focused on preventing state weakness but, according to some critics, without a coherent or innovative policy.[31]

We now turn to examples of state weakness and consider the U.S. interests and values that were involved.

The Democratic Republic of Congo (DRC)   The DRC is consistently ranked as among the world's most fragile states. Formerly Zaire, civil war in erupted in the DRC in 1997 as a spillover from Rwanda's genocidal conflict. A huge country, about the size of Western Europe with a population of 67 million and over 200 ethnic groups, the DRC has been plagued by violence since then. Nine other countries with their own conflicts border the DRC, including the fragile South Sudan and Central African Republic

🔑 KEY DOCUMENT
The 2015 National Security Strategy

"Build Capacity to Prevent Conflict

Within states, the nexus of weak governance and widespread grievance allows extremism to take root, violent non-state actors to rise up, and conflict to overtake state structures. To meet these challenges, we will continue to work with partners and through multilateral organizations to address the root causes of conflict before they erupt and to contain and resolve them when they do. We prefer to partner with those fragile states that have a genuine political commitment to establishing legitimate governance and providing for their people. The focus of our efforts will be on proven areas of need and impact, such as inclusive politics, enabling effective and equitable service delivery, reforming security and rule of law sectors, combating corruption and organized crime, and promoting economic opportunity, particularly among youth and women. . . .

We will continue to bolster the capacity of the U.N. and regional organizations to help resolve disputes, build resilience to crises and shocks, strengthen governance, end extreme poverty, and increase prosperity, so that fragile states can provide for the basic needs of their citizens and can avoid being vulnerable hosts for extremism and terrorism. . . . We will strengthen the operational capacity of regional organizations like the African Union (AU) and broaden the ranks of capable troop-contributing countries, including through the African Peacekeeping Rapid Response Partnership, which will help African countries rapidly deploy to emerging crises."

Source: The White House, National Security Strategy, February 2015, http://nssarchive.us/national-security-strategy-2015, 10–11.

(CAR). Rebel groups in these conflicts use the DRC as their base. Rwanda and Uganda also fueled conflict by providing military support to rebel groups in the DRC. Conflicting groups also fight over access to valuable resources—diamonds, copper, tin, coltan (a metal ore used in high-tech devices like cell phones, laptops, and medical equipment), timber, and charcoal—and reliance on the profits from such resources to finance conflict has produced a war economy in which elites have a vested economic interest in perpetuating conflict.

Washington does not have a direct security interest in the DRC, but near constant war across the region has produced a humanitarian crisis. The civil war is believed to have resulted in six million deaths, making it one of the world's bloodiest conflicts since World War II and producing massive population displacement. In recent years, some 2.7 million Congolese have been displaced within the country and another 430,000 have fled to neighboring countries. There are also substantial numbers of refugees in the DRC who have fled wars elsewhere, most recently from the CAR.[32] Human-rights abuses occur in this environment, including child soldiers and human trafficking. Poverty and demographic pressures are overwhelming. The DRC is ranked 186 of 187 on the UN's Human Development Index.[33] It has one of the world's highest birth rates and nearly half its population is under the age of 15. Few attend school, and most inhabitants live in extreme poverty, earning below $1.25 a day. Washington has tried to help broker peace agreements and has provided billions of dollars in aid. Recent annual aid packages have included $200 to $300 million in development assistance, $50 to $150 million in emergency humanitarian relief, and a half-billion dollars in contributions to the UN Organization and Stabilization Operation in DRC.[34] U.S.-DRC trade is limited owing to congressional restrictions on U.S. firms trading in conflict minerals central to the DRC's economy.

Zimbabwe Zimbabwe offers another example of extreme state fragility. South Rhodesia declared independence from Britain in 1961, and after racial conflict Zimbabwe gained independence in 1980. By 2003, governed by President Robert Mugabe, Zimbabwe was cited as an example of "how to kill a country,"[35] and in 2005 Condoleezza Rice, then George W. Bush's nominee for secretary of state called it an "outpost of tyranny." In 2014, it ranked 11th on the Fund for Peace's Fragile State Index after ranking 2nd in 2009. Zimbabwe has all the characteristics of states at risk of failure, suffering from demographic pressures, uneven economic development, government illegitimacy, and elite factionalism. Although Zimbabwe has not experienced outright war, it has been plagued by political and economic instability.

Once a prosperous county, by 2000 Zimbabwe was plagued by land seizures, currency crises, and food insecurity. President Mugabe had declared that land disparity—a holdover from colonialism, when the most fertile land was reserved for the white population—was largely responsible for Zimbabwe's economic problems. Mugabe's solution was to seize Zimbabwe's commercial farms and redistribute land among traditional black farmers under communal ownership. By 2005, some 4,000 white owners had fled their farms and most land was redistributed, but to Mugabe's supporters and government officials rather than peasant farmers, fueling grievances.

Land redistribution had disastrous economic consequences. Investors fled, fearing seizure of their assets, and foreign direct investment disappeared. Peasants who resettled on lands confiscated in the land grab were not granted title to the land, and in the first year alone, commercial farmland lost three-quarters of its value. Banks collapsed, and those that remained refused to extend credit to farmers who lacked land titles and therefore collateral that could be used to back loans needed to purchase equipment and supplies. Ripple effects included famine and economic collapse,[36] bringing Zimbabwe to the brink of bankruptcy. Thereafter, inflation rose to 6,000 percent per year, and basic staples like gas, cooking oil, bread, and salt became unavailable. In 2009, Zimbabwe's central bank introduced a Z$100 billion note (one trillion Zimbabwean dollars traded for about US$30) to keep up with hyperinflation. Zimbabwe went through **redenomination** of its dollar several times, limited bank withdrawals, and eventually allowed the use of foreign currencies for domestic transactions.

Washington condemned corrupt electoral practices that enabled Mugabe to maintain power and used targeted sanctions to weaken his regime. The 2001 Zimbabwe Democracy and Economic Recovery Act imposed travel and economic sanctions on the country's officials and business leaders and instructed U.S. representatives in the IMF and World Bank to oppose extending credit to Zimbabwe or considering debt cancellation/reduction. Presidents Bush and Obama issued executive orders to extend sanctions against regime officials, but Washington continued to provide assistance, including health and economic aid, to ease Zimbabwe's humanitarian crisis. This dual policy actually hindered efforts to improve governance and strengthen the state because Zimbabwean officials, secure in the knowledge the United States would not end humanitarian assistance, resisted efforts to introduce reforms.

Haiti Haiti is among the poorest countries in the Western hemisphere and is its most fragile state. It has experienced frequent foreign intervention, economic decline, human flight, elite factionalism, human-rights abuses, and poor public services. The extent of Haiti's fragility was evident in 2010 after an earthquake destroyed most of the capital, Port-au-Prince, and caused 200,000 deaths. Thereafter, a cholera epidemic infected over 665,000 people, of whom 8,183 died.[37] Haiti is especially vulnerable to natural disasters owing to poor infrastructure and extreme poverty. By comparison, in 2010, only 700 people died when a much more powerful earthquake struck Chile, a high-income country. Other governments including America's promised Haiti $9 billion in aid and disaster relief following the earthquake—three times Haiti's annual budget—but Haiti's problems remain formidable. In 2013, three-quarters of Haitians were unemployed or working in the informal economy. There was little foreign investment, and most of those with a college education had left the country. Indeed, a country may not be able to absorb large amounts of aid quickly, and it may foster additional corruption and violence. In Haiti's case, "a combination of endemic corruption, the now non-existent institutional infrastructure, and the large amounts of money flowing into the country all make this the perfect time to commit crime."[38]

Mexico Mexico, a country of great concern to U.S. policymakers, illustrates a different set of challenges. A study in contrasts, it has a booming economy but is plagued by drug-related violence and weak institutions. Since 2006, Mexico's leaders have prioritized reducing drug-related crime and restoring rule of law. President Enrique Peña Nieto continued a policy begun by Felipe Calderón of capturing or killing drug kingpins to "decapitate" and weaken Mexican drug cartels. Such aggressive efforts fostered widespread human-rights violations by Mexico's army and police. The policy was successful in destroying the large Knights Templar, Gulf, and Zeta cartels, but drug-related violence increased dramatically as numerous smaller cartel offshoots fought for control of territory and formed new powerful groups like the Jalisco New Generation cartel.[39] The cartels' influence in society was evident in 2014 when 43 students from a rural teaching college, who were protesting discriminatory funding for their school, were abducted by police, reportedly with the authorization of a local mayor, and handed over to a cartel to be killed. Since the drug war began, over 90,000 Mexicans have died, and inhabitants live in fear, forming vigilante groups known as *autodefensas* to provide security where the local police cannot or will not.[40]

Washington has an interest in preventing violence, drugs, and organized crime from spilling over the border and in having a secure and stable neighbor. It has not sent military advisers to Mexico, as it did in Colombia, to help eradicate drug violence. Instead, the 2007 Mérida Initiative—a bilateral partnership emphasizing shared responsibility—is the primary vehicle for cooperation. Mexico's drug violence is fueled by Americans' demand for heroin, methamphetamine, marijuana, and cocaine. Thus, Washington provides Mexico's federal government with aid to support its efforts to fight organized crime and violence and reform its criminal justice system but also commits the United States to curbing domestic drug demand and gun and currency trafficking to Mexico. For its part, Mexico has invested nearly $80 billion in its security efforts. Although America has been unsuccessful in slowing domestic demand for illicit drugs, it has provided substantial aid. Between 2008 and 2015, Congress appropriated about $2.5 billion in Mérida aid to Mexico, although withholding some of this assistance owing to concerns about human-rights abuses in Mexico's war on drugs.[41]

Administrations from Clinton to Obama have discussed formulating a "failed state" or "fragile state" strategy, but none has successfully done so. This is partly a matter of priorities: officials tend to focus attention and resources on imminent security challenges in a few fragile states like Afghanistan and Iraq. But it is also a product of the complex nature of the problem. Numerous factors contribute to state fragility, and each case is different. Factors like poverty, transnational crime, environmental stress, refugees, and disease can interact to produce weak states that are prone to conflict and instability. Thus, it may be more productive to formulate discrete policies for each challenge, rather than a "fragile-state strategy."

Poverty and Underdevelopment

How much and what kind of assistance to offer governments struggling with poverty and underdevelopment has been a source of controversy. American values support offering assistance to fight poverty, foster long-term development, and relieve humanitarian crises. Many Americans believe it is a moral imperative to relieve suffering and support economic growth. As President Obama noted in 2010, development assistance "is rooted in America's enduring commitment to the dignity and potential of every human being." Obama also acknowledged that aid is a "strategic and economic imperative."[42] In fact, most aid decisions are made to advance interests.

Washington maintains a general interest in the political and economic stability that follows economic growth and development in strategic regions like Latin America and the Middle East. Economic growth and stability open new markets for trade, and development is accompanied by lower levels of crime, violence, and human flight, and higher incomes—all characteristics of strong, stable states. Offering development assistance helps Washington build relationships with people and governments, conferring soft power that makes it easier for Washington to accomplish other policy objectives. Thus, the Bush administration became popular in Africa, as we shall see, for combatting HIV/AIDS. But the United States also sends substantial foreign aid to countries like Afghanistan, Pakistan, and Iraq in which it has geostrategic interests. Aid helps Washington influence these countries and helps their institutions resist extremism and reduce dependence on military power. Finally, domestic constituents benefit from a robust foreign-aid policy that distributes U.S.-produced goods and services.

Understanding Foreign Aid We now examine what aid donors call official development assistance (ODA). The United States defines foreign aid more broadly, as any assistance dispersed to help states pursue economic development, achieve peace and security, or meet humanitarian needs, but it is economic development assistance that is at the center of foreign-aid debates. Such aid is given to stimulate economic growth and private investment and strengthen local institutions. Sometimes military aid may be needed to support this effort. Table 7.2 reveals how the United States classified aid spent in several major aid recipients, offering insights into U.S. priorities in each country.

U.S. funding on foreign aid remains a source of controversy at home and abroad. America is the world's largest donor of development aid, dispensing $32 billion in 2013 and surpassing others by many billions.

TABLE 7.2   U.S. Foreign Assistance by Category (2014)

	Aid Spent (millions)	Peace and Security	Program Management	Economic Development	Health	Democracy, Human Rights, Governance	Humanitarian Assistance	Education and Social Services	Environment
Afghanistan	$1,950.00	7%	13%	20%	8%	19%	3%	15%	16%
Kenya	$736.42	1%	2%	11%	69%	1%	11%	3%	1%
Ethiopia	$677.57	0%	3%	19%	47%	0%	21%	10%	0%
Tanzania	$713.73	0%	3%	28%	58%	1%	1%	6%	4%
Pakistan	$921.61	0%	9%	28%	12%	7%	8%	13%	22%
Jordan	$1,030.00	0%	1%	55%	16%	2%	15%	9%	2%
Iraq	$155.43	2%	10%	19%	10%	57%	1%	0%	—
South Africa	$556.35	0%	0%	2%	96%	0%	0%	1%	0%

Source: Foreign Assistance Worldwide, ForeignAssistance.Gov., http://beta.foreignassistance.gov.

Note: Values for each country may not total 100% due to rounding.

Only when public support for foreign aid was at an all-time low in the mid-1990s did another country (France in 1995; Japan in 1997) provide more aid than America. Washington, however, does not meet the UN target of aid equivalent to 0.7 percent of national income. Although U.S. officials support the UN goal of increasing foreign aid—in fact, U.S. ODA tripled under Bush from $9.95 billion in 2000 to $26.84 billion in 2008—they have rejected meeting quantitative targets. Thus, at 0.19 percent, the world's largest donor is near the bottom of donor countries in terms of aid as a percentage of national income.[43] Hence, critics argue that the world's largest donor and largest economy is not doing what it should to support global development.

Examining aid as a percentage of America's federal budget brings critics' arguments into focus. On average, Americans believe the United States spends somewhere between 25 and 30 percent of its national budget on foreign aid, and most say that is too much. In reality, *less than 1 percent* of the $4 trillion federal budget is devoted to foreign aid. There are still Americans (28 percent) who believe the United States ought to spend less. About a third of the aid budget, $5.3 billion (2014), is devoted to global health. A sixth—$2.7 billion—is spent on economic development, emphasizing infrastructural projects like roads and ports, electrical grids, and telecommunications. Another sixth is spent on humanitarian assistance including refugee support and disaster preparedness and response.[44]

Another controversy involves the balance between bilateral and multilateral assistance. Bilateral aid allows Washington to maintain more control over who receives aid, for what purpose, and under what conditions and allows targeting aid toward actors and issues in which it has strategic interests. Bilateral aid also allows donors to see that their aid is used effectively and enables them to ensure it is being dispersed to less risky recipients and is achieving intended effects. Multilateral aid can mean less control, and so economic development is an area in which Washington seeks significant influence in multilateral organizations.

In 2000, the UN introduced the Millennium Development Goals (MDGs) to be achieved by members by 2015 aided by agencies like the IMF and the World Bank. The MDGs consisted of eight goals described in the Millennium Declaration that was adopted by 198 states including the United States at the Millennium Summit. They were (1) eradicating extreme poverty and hunger; (2) achieving universal primary education; (3) promoting gender equality and empowering women; (4) reducing child mortality; (5) improving maternal health; (6) combatting HIV/AIDS, malaria, and other diseases; (7) ensuring environmental sustainability; and (8) forging global partnerships for development. The goals offered a common vision and framework toward reducing extreme global poverty and included 21 measurable targets to evaluate progress. Philanthropist and former Microsoft CEO Bill Gates described them in 2008 as "the best idea for focusing the world on fighting global poverty that I have ever seen."[45]

U.S. foreign-aid policy was aligned closely with the MDGs, especially its health-related goals. The Bush administration, nevertheless, refused to commit itself publicly to the goals. Although Bush accepted the goals of the Millennium Declaration, he argued that the UN Secretariat had ignored issues of importance to Washington including good governance, democracy, and human rights and had introduced new commitments—notably increasing foreign aid to meet or exceed 0.7 percent of gross national income. Bush identified more closely with the 2002 "Monterey Consensus," a broad-based development agenda that called on developing countries to take responsibility for poverty reduction—including good governance—and that urged rich countries to support their efforts with more open trade and foreign-aid policies.[46] The Bush administration instead introduced the Millennium Challenge Account (MCA) in 2002, a partnered initiative to increase aid by 50 percent over three years to be implemented by the Millennium Challenge Corporation (MCC) that was established in 2004. The MCA was designed to provide $5 billion a year to countries that are "ruling justly, investing in their people, and establishing economic freedom."[47] The idea was to offer incentives for countries to demonstrate they could use aid responsibly and effectively. Eligible countries submitted proposals for funding and negotiated a "compact" with the MCC that articulated benchmarks for measuring success. Congress took two years to establish the program and was slow to approve funds, partly because applicants had to demonstrate they met the requirements for good governance and liberal economic policies. President Obama embraced the MDGs, describing them as "America's goals," but has otherwise largely continued Bush-era development policies, including the MCC.

Washington also participated in multilateral efforts to provide debt relief for poor indebted countries to help them free resources to spend on achieving the MDGs. This could mean forgiving debt entirely or reducing it to sustainable levels. Debt relief remains controversial. Supporters, who see debt relief as merely a part of a broader aid strategy, argue that extreme indebtedness makes it impossible for the poorest countries to invest in economic growth and frightens private investors. Opponents argue it has little impact in poor countries because bad governments will assume additional debts to finance existing policies that redistribute resources to political supporters rather than reinvestment in economic development. Between 1999 and 2002, Washington independently forgave $23.9 billion in foreign debt. It also participated in the joint IMF/World Bank Highly Indebted Poor Country (HIPC) Initiative and Multilateral Debt Relief Initiative that by 2014 had relieved 36 low-income countries of $96 billion in debt.[48]

Global Health and Disease

Global health policy is an important component of U.S. foreign aid. America's global health policy has two main goals—ensuring that people have access to adequate health care as part of a broader development strategy and preventing and treating outbreaks of infectious disease. Such a policy also reflects U.S. humanitarian values. Washington also has an interest in stopping the spread of infectious diseases like avian flu, Middle East Respiratory Syndrome (MERS), West Nile virus, and drug-resistant tuberculosis. Disease outbreaks that begin overseas can reach America quickly in a world in which people, animals, and agricultural goods—and the bacteria and viruses they carry—are transported among countries.

In recent years, a number of outbreaks globally have posed challenges for foreign health policy. MERS, for instance, is a respiratory illness that is difficult to diagnose because it has symptoms associated with common respiratory ailments—fever, cough, and shortness of breath—much like the severe acute respiratory syndrome that spread from China to 37 countries in 2002 to 2003, sickening 8,000 people, of whom over 700 died. The first known case of MERS appeared in Jordan in 2012 and spread across the Middle East, and a small number of infected travelers returned to America and other countries. The 2014 Ebola outbreak in West Africa offered another example of how U.S. foreign health policy is driven by security concerns. Ebola is a viral hemorrhagic disease spread by direct contact with blood and body fluids of a person showing symptoms. It has a 50 percent fatality rate.[49] The origin of the outbreak was traced to Guinea. Within months, the disease spread to Liberia, Sierra Leone, Nigeria, and Senegal, becoming the largest Ebola epidemic since discovery of the disease in 1976. By June 2015, there had been over 15,000 confirmed cases and 11,173 deaths.[50] U.S. officials treated the outbreak as a humanitarian crisis and a security threat with an emphasis on the latter. A 2015 report issued by the

U.S. UN Ambassador Samantha Power visits the Western Africa Emergency Response Center in Freetown, Sierra Leone.

Reuters/Michelle Nichols

Presidential Commission for the Study of Bioethical Issues was critical of America's response, observing that only when faced with the (remote) possibility that the disease would spread to the United States did officials launch a comprehensive strategy to provide humanitarian relief in Africa. "Both justice and prudence demand that we do our part in combating such devastating outbreaks," the report read. "Once we recognize our humanitarian obligations and the ability of infectious diseases to travel in our interconnected world, we cannot choose between the ethical and the prudential."[51]

Disease emerged on the U.S. foreign-policy agenda during the Clinton administration as officials began to understand the severity of the HIV/AIDS pandemic, but it was only late in his second term that Clinton began to emphasize fighting HIV/AIDS. HIV, the human immunodeficiency virus, causes acquired immunodeficiency syndrome (AIDS). It is spread by sexual contact and blood and can be transferred from mother to child during pregnancy, delivery, or breastfeeding. It weakens the immune system so that the body cannot fight other infections. HIV spread worldwide in the 1980s and 1990s, and 90 percent of those infected died.

Sub-Saharan Africa was hardest hit. Some of Clinton's economic policies may actually have impeded efforts to combat HIV/AIDS, especially support for intellectual property protection that would allow pharmaceutical companies to retain patent rights against those trying to produce cheaper AIDS medicines. Clinton's real contribution to global health did not come until after he left office and established the William J. Clinton Foundation, which included the Clinton HIV/AIDS Initiative that became the Clinton Health Initiative in 2010.

George W. Bush emphasized health issues in his foreign policy. His administration took a disease-specific approach, best seen in the 2003 President's Emergency Plan for AIDS Relief (PEPFAR) and the 2005 President's Malaria Initiative. PEPFAR committed $15 billion to AIDS relief between 2003 and 2008 and sought to support a comprehensive approach encompassing prevention, care, and treatment. Owing to PEPFAR, U.S. aid to Africa increased sixfold during the Bush administration—from $1.3 billion to $7.3 billion.[52] Most U.S. funding for AIDS relief continues today. PEPFAR increased access in sub-Saharan Africa, where the AIDS crisis persists, to antiretroviral (ARV) treatments that suppress HIV and decrease death rates. By 2013, 35 million people were living with HIV globally, and the annual rate of new infections was down to 2.1 million, representing a substantial decrease from the previous decade.[53] By the end of Bush's administration, "global health issues—principally HIV/AIDS but also malaria, tuberculosis, neglected tropical diseases, and pandemic influenza preparedness—had achieved unprecedented visibility and the commitment of administration officials at the highest levels, most notably the office of the president."[54]

The Obama administration continued to support these initiatives but also focused attention on other health issues, like child and maternal health and public-private partnerships, with greater emphasis on partnering with multilateral organizations. To this end, Obama fostered the 2009 Global Health Initiative to develop a coherent strategy for advancing health worldwide, but it was shuttered in 2012 and replaced by the State Department's Office of Global Health Diplomacy.

Today's greatest policy challenges, where values and interests clash most, encompass funding levels, funding priorities, and partnerships with multilateral institutions. Washington is the largest donor of global health funding and as we saw earlier, U.S. foreign health assistance comprises a third of the U.S. foreign aid budget. Most health aid goes to HIV/AIDS projects, followed by maternal and child health and malaria.[55] We evaluate arguments for and against increasing funding levels later, but it is worth noting that of all aid priorities, Americans tend to be more supportive of foreign aid that is used to "improve health" in developing countries.[56]

HIV in Sub-Saharan Africa

Of the 35 million people living with HIV in 2013, 24.7 million were in Sub-Saharan Africa. Southern Africa continues to be hit hardest, with nearly 17.9 percent of the population in South Africa, 15 percent in Zimbabwe, and nearly 25 percent in Lesotho living with HIV in 2012.

Source: "UNAIDS Report Shows That 19 Million of the 35 Million People Living with HIV Today Do Not Know That They Have the Virus," UNAIDS, July 16, 2014, http://www.unaids.org/en/resources/presscentre/pressreleaseandstatementarchive/2014/july/20140716prgapreport.

Funding priorities are a second challenge, especially as the HIV/AIDS pandemic evolves. More HIV-infected people are living longer, posing challenges for health funding. Currently, global aid efforts have provided over 13 million people worldwide access to expensive ARV therapy to suppress HIV. In sub-Saharan Africa alone, nearly 90 percent of people living with HIV who know their status are receiving therapy.[57] These expensive treatments must be provided over a person's lifetime. If donors continue to target HIV/AIDS as much as they have in the past in order to fulfill the need to support long-term care, less aid will be available for other health challenges, including preventing and treating infectious diseases like MERS and Ebola and building health infrastructure in low-income countries.

The merits of focusing on crisis response and infrastructure development gained new attention among officials and health advocacy groups as Washington struggled to formulate a coherent response to the West African Ebola outbreak. When Washington rolled out its Ebola response in 2014, it mobilized crisis assistance to care for the infected and contain the spread of the disease quickly. Every agency with a health function contributed in some fashion. USAID provided medical supplies and equipment, information, and training to communities and households; the National Institutes of Health sought an Ebola vaccine; the Centers for Disease Control provided on-the-ground expertise in affected countries; the Defense Department sent "field-deployable" hospitals and personnel protective gear; and the U.S. Africa Command set up staging bases to coordinate relief efforts.[58] Some humanitarian organizations criticized the administration's response as woefully insufficient. Others, who months later saw new Ebola treatment centers sitting empty, argued it was too much. "If they had been built when we needed them, it wouldn't have been too much," declared a Liberian official. "But they were too late."[59] For all of its crisis assistance, some observers argue, the United States is not adequately investing in "functioning health systems"[60] in poor regions. This involves more than investing in health care infrastructure; it also requires investing in good governance, which must be part of a larger development strategy.

Finally, we consider how closely America should cooperate with multilateral institutions to disperse health funding. Most U.S. health assistance is distributed directly to governments in need, allowing U.S. officials to oversee how recipients use aid. Washington also works closely with and is the largest funder of several multilateral organizations like the World Health Organization (WHO) and UNAIDS. America and WHO, the UN agency that coordinates health issues, cooperate in several areas: sharing virus specimens (needed to produce vaccines); disaster and pandemic preparedness; disease surveillance, reporting, and response; general research and development; and stopping the sale of substandard and counterfeit medicines. The United States helped establish and coordinates closely with the Global Fund to Fight

FIGURE 7.2 A Snapshot of U.S. Global Health Funding

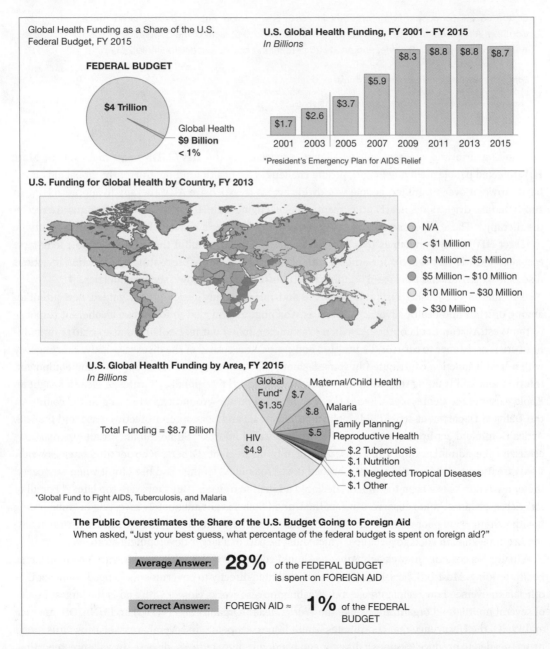

Global Health Funding as a Share of the U.S. Federal Budget, FY 2015

FEDERAL BUDGET

$4 Trillion

Global Health
$9 Billion
< 1%

U.S. Global Health Funding, FY 2001 – FY 2015
In Billions

$1.7 | $2.6 | $3.7 | $5.9 | $8.3 | $8.8 | $8.8 | $8.7
2001 | 2003 | 2005 | 2007 | 2009 | 2011 | 2013 | 2015

*President's Emergency Plan for AIDS Relief

U.S. Funding for Global Health by Country, FY 2013

○ N/A
○ < $1 Million
○ $1 Million – $5 Million
● $5 Million – $10 Million
○ $10 Million – $30 Million
● > $30 Million

U.S. Global Health Funding by Area, FY 2015
In Billions

Global Fund* $1.35
Maternal/Child Health $.7
Malaria $.8
Family Planning/ Reproductive Health $.5
HIV $4.9
$.2 Tuberculosis
$.1 Nutrition
$.1 Neglected Tropical Diseases
$.1 Other

Total Funding = $8.7 Billion

*Global Fund to Fight AIDS, Tuberculosis, and Malaria

The Public Overestimates the Share of the U.S. Budget Going to Foreign Aid
When asked, "Just your best guess, what percentage of the federal budget is spent on foreign aid?"

Average Answer: **28%** of the FEDERAL BUDGET is spent on FOREIGN AID

Correct Answer: FOREIGN AID ≈ **1%** of the FEDERAL BUDGET

Source: Kaiser Family Foundation (http://www.kff.org) analysis. Original data and detailed source information are available at http://kff.org/JAMA_04-23-2014.

Note: Represents funding through the Global Health Initiative (GHI) only.

AIDS, Tuberculosis, and Malaria, a partnership among governments, international organizations, and nongovernmental organizations that raises and distributes funds for preventing and treating these diseases in low- and middle-income countries. Today the Global Fund accounts for half of donor financing for malaria, 80 percent of donor financing for tuberculosis, and a quarter of HIV donor funding.[61]

In theory, multilateral organizations can pool states' contributions to pursue their mandates more effectively, but they may have different health and program management priorities than U.S. officials, which is controversial in Washington because America is such a large donor. One way officials have worked around this criticism is by funding voluntary programs outside the regular budget. Thus, Washington contributes to programs it supports, thereby ensuring the issues it cares about are well funded, but it also undermines global institutions, leaving them less capable of defining their own agendas.

Refugees and Migrants

America is a nation of immigrants, a fact in which many Americans take pride. Nevertheless, immigration poses domestic and foreign policy challenges. America's political culture reflects "The New Colossus," a poem engraved on the pedestal of the Statue of Liberty: "Give me your tired, your poor, your huddled masses yearning to breathe free." America's national identity continues to be shaped by the immigrant origins of its communities and the "melting pot" culture they sustain. Americans and foreigners alike view the United States as a "land of opportunity" where anyone can build a free and prosperous life for themselves and their children. Yet these values conflict with societal interests. Americans fear an influx of immigrants will take away jobs, erode "American" culture, and even undermine national security.

People migrate for many reasons—employment or education opportunities, security from violence, or family ties. Not all migrants move voluntarily. Their homes may be lost in war or natural disaster, or domestic groups or even their own government may threaten their security. In 2015, Amnesty International reported, "we are witnessing the worst refugee crisis of our era, with millions of women, men and children struggling to survive amidst brutal wars, networks of people traffickers and governments who pursue selfish political interests instead of showing basic human compassion."[62] According to the UN refugee agency, there were almost 60 million displaced persons by 2015 including 14 million who were displaced during 2014.[63]

Such refugees seek **asylum**, that is, protection, from their governments. There is a body of international law, rooted in the 1951 Convention on the Status of Refugees and its 1967 Protocol, that defines a "refugee" as someone with a well-founded fear of persecution based on religion, race, nationality, political views, or membership in a particular social group, and who cannot expect protection from his or her government and requires such people be protected from detention or *refoulement* (forcible return).

Congress imposes an annual ceiling on how many refugees may be admitted into the United States. Since 2013, that ceiling has been 70,000 (see Figure 7.3). The legal definition of a refugee was designed to aid those seeking protection, but in reality, since few states are willing to admit everyone claiming persecution, determining whom to admit has involved a political decision. During the Cold War, Washington tended to accept those fleeing persecution by communist governments. As the Cold War ended, more refugees were accepted from Soviet bloc countries, and in the 1990s, those fleeing ethnic cleansing in the Balkans. Today, many refugees come from Asia, the Middle East, and Africa.

America's policy regarding refugees and how it treats those it admits reflects U.S. foreign-policy priorities. Thus, for decades, Washington has been generous to those fleeing communist Cuba. The 1966

FIGURE **7.3**   The Shifting Origins of Refugees to the United States over Time

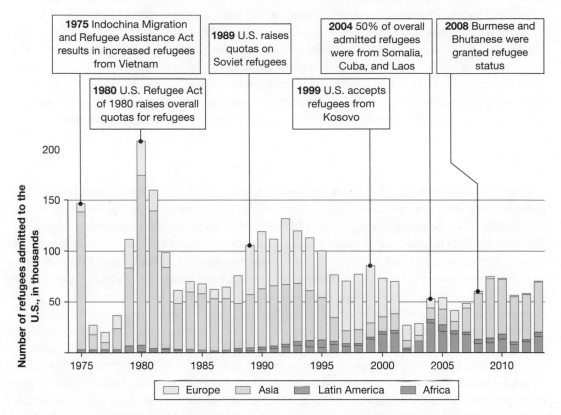

Source: Christopher Inkpen and Ruth Igielnik, "Where Refugees to the U.S. Come From," Pew Research Center, July 28, 2014, http://www.pewresearch.org/fact-tank/2014/07/28/where-refugees-to-the-u-s-come-from.

Cuban Adjustment Act allowed any Cuban entering America to seek permanent residence after one year and thereafter U.S. citizenship. In 1996, as Cuban migration rapidly grew, the law was revised to repatriate Cubans stopped at sea. Haitians, by contrast, have been held to an unusually high standard. The Coast Guard actively interdicts Haitians at sea and detains them until they can be repatriated. America also accepted few refugees from Iraq after 2007 or from Afghanistan. These numbers seem woefully inadequate to some critics who noted that thousands of people in those countries waiting for asylum had worked for U.S. agencies at great risk to themselves and their families. U.S. officials have also been slow to admit refugees from Syria. In the first four years of that country's brutal civil war, only about 700 refugees were accepted by the United States, even as millions fled to crowded camps in Jordan, Lebanon, and Turkey. In December 2014, State Department officials announced plans to accept about 10,000 Syrian refugees a year. However much Americans want to aid Syrian refugees, fears about terrorism weigh heavily in asylum policy. "In the case of Syrian refugees," argues one congressional Republican "our intelligence on the ground is alarmingly slim, making it harder to identify extremists."[64]

In recent years, U.S. efforts to reduce illegal immigration have raised new questions. International law seeks to protect refugees but allows governments to determine whether someone meets this definition. Those seeking entry into America who do not meet the criteria for asylum as defined by federal law may be deported back to their country of origin. A record 409,849 illegal immigrants were deported from the United States in 2012.[65] A 2014 Human Rights Watch report charged that the processes Washington uses to return undocumented aliens to their home countries consistently fails to identify those seeking political asylum. Migrants must prove they have a "credible fear" or "reasonable fear" of returning home. (The "credible" standard applies to first-time asylum seekers and the "reasonable" standard applies to repeat cases.) If a U.S. immigration agent believes a migrant meets the standard, that person meets with an asylum officer who makes an official determination of whether he or she meets the criteria for asylum. Human Rights Watch found that fewer migrants were identified as requesting asylum at the first stage despite fears about returning to their home country.[66]

TABLE 7.3 Countries of Origin of Refugees to America (2014)

Total	69,985
Iraq	19,651
Burma (Myanmar)	14,577
Somalia	9,011
Bhutan	8,316
Dem. Rep. of Congo	4,502
Cuba	4,063
Iran	2,833
Eritrea	1,445
Sudan	1,307
Afghanistan	758

Source: U.S. Department of Health and Human Services, Office of Refugee Resettlement, "Fiscal Year 2014 Refugee Arrivals," February 11, 2015, http://www.acf.hhs.gov/programs/orr/resource/fiscal-year-2014-refugee-arrivals.

Another recent issue raises questions regarding U.S. policy about who ought to be granted refugee status. In Latin America, the nonbinding 1984 Cartagena Declaration enlarged the definition of refugee to include "persons who have fled their country because their lives, safety or freedom have been threatened by generalized violence, foreign aggression, internal conflicts, massive violation of human rights or other circumstances which have seriously disturbed public order."[67] Washington was not a signatory to the declaration and is reluctant to offer asylum to those fleeing violence. This became an issue in 2014 when the number of unaccompanied children apprehended trying to enter the country illegally increased to 60,000 from 13,625 in 2012. The number of families apprehended while seeking to enter America also increased to over 66,000.[68] Some Americans believe that President Obama's June 2012 executive action, Deferred Action for Childhood Arrivals (DACA), created undue expectations among these children and families. DACA granted two-year deportation deferrals and work permits to about 1.7 million undocumented migrants who had entered America before age sixteen and were under thirty at the time of the announcement. Many of these migrants sought to receive asylum from gang and drug-related violence in Guatemala, Honduras, and El Salvador—countries not previously significant sources of illegal immigration. Many of these children and families were placed in crowded detention facilities for months awaiting formal deportation hearings. The UN has urged Washington to treat such children as refugees fleeing conflict and offer them asylum.

FUTURE: BALANCING AID, INTERVENTION, AND NEGLECT

As we have seen, U.S. policy in the Global South has been characterized by aid, intervention, or neglect, and it is difficult for U.S. policymakers to determine if, when, and how to intervene.

Fragile and Failing States

Washington views fragile states primarily through the lens of national security, but U.S. values also emphasize extending humanitarian relief to people who experience human insecurity. Most fragile states confront the security challenges discussed earlier: poverty and economic underdevelopment, crime and violence, destabilizing population flows, and health insecurity.

Policy Options

a. *Develop a comprehensive aid strategy for dealing with fragile and failing states.* On the surface, this seems reasonable since reinforcing political, social, economic, and environmental challenges produces fragile states. But it is the interaction of all of these factors that makes this the most challenging and possibly least realistic of the options. It is difficult to discern complex cause-and-effect relationships among these factors. Are poverty, intergroup grievances, refugee flows, and lack of public services causes or effects of state weakness, or are they both? The recipe is likely to vary from state to state, but even if it were clear where to begin, a comprehensive strategy would require a massive, long-term commitment of support and close coordination among donors and recipients. And it risks creating aid dependence or imposing institutions that ill suit the conditions in recipient countries. Pursuing each challenge independently, however, also threatens to undermine efforts to address linked challenges. In what follows, we take this route and consider policies to address individual challenges.

b. *Intervene in the weakest states to restore order and build effective regimes.* Intervention is more likely when strategic interests are threatened and less so when only values are at stake. Even when Washington identifies an interest worth pursuing, efforts in Afghanistan and Iraq demonstrate that state building is not easy and that it is difficult to justify in an international order based on the sanctity of sovereignty.

c. *Ignore fragile states.* Humanitarian advocates argue that this is the status quo, at least in countries like Sudan, South Sudan, Zimbabwe, Haiti, and Syria where Washington does not have significant strategic interests. However, the United States rarely ignores completely the plight of fragile states because doing so risks intensifying threats to security and human suffering. But sometimes America's response is so modest, critics insist, that it might as well do nothing, or its aid does more harm than good, especially in the weakest states, by empowering entrenched elites and fueling corruption, conflict, and aid dependence. When Washington does not act or acts ineffectively, it opens opportunities for intervention by NGOs and individual advocates.

Poverty and Underdevelopment: Aid or Trade?

Foreign aid is not a panacea, and there are problems associated with how it is used in developing countries. Corruption may ensure that aid rarely is directed to projects or people its donors intended to support. Aid dependencies can emerge in which officials in recipient states have little incentive to invest in infrastructure and institutions that will wean them of aid. Although some Americans oppose foreign aid entirely on the grounds it is ineffective in stimulating growth or strengthening institutions, most believe aid can be effective if it is used wisely.

Policy Options

a. *Reduce U.S. foreign aid and rely on trade policy and private investment.* Those who favor trade over aid argue that more progress can be achieved by use of liberal economic trade policies that encourage private foreign investment. They cite Africa's strong growth of about 5 percent per year since 2000 (higher than any region except emerging Asia), reduced poverty, improved nutrition, and spreading democratization as evidence of the value of trade.[69] These successes do correlate with greater economic liberalization in Africa and increasing demand globally for African commodities like oil. But there are limits to how much liberal trade policies can achieve for Africa. First, African countries must diversify their economies, as some are doing, to sustain economic growth. The poorest countries, however, are unable to finance new infrastructure or social welfare programs to enhance labor productivity without aid. Such programs make these countries more attractive to foreign investors. Second, U.S. trade barriers that support domestic industry flood local markets, reduce prices, and make it difficult for industries or agriculture in the Global South to compete. Such trade barriers are politically difficult to remove. In 2005, when President Bush tried to lower trade barriers to supplement America's $350 million tsunami relief package for Thailand and Sri Lanka, U.S. textile manufacturers and shrimpers were outraged. "We've already been bled white,"[70] argued the textile lobby, and the move would undercut efforts to punish Thailand for illegally dumping shrimp below cost on the U.S. market.

b. *Increase aid to move toward the UN target of 0.7 percent of gross national income.* For those who believe America has a moral responsibility to improve the plight of the poor, there is no excuse for spending so small a percentage of the national budget and income on foreign aid. Investments in foreign aid may prevent the emergence of threats requiring more expensive military intervention later. But not all aid is helpful, and some can be harmful to the societies it is intended to support. Before supporting dramatic increases in spending, it is necessary to ensure aid is appropriate to the goals sought and is used wisely and effectively. Thus, "aid, by itself, has never developed anything, but where it has been allied to good public policy, sound economic management, and a strong determination to battle poverty, it has made an enormous difference in countries like India, Indonesia, and even China."[71]

c. *Reform aid policy and practices that undermine development goals.* Eliminating corruption and inefficiency in aid recipients and finding the proper mix of aid and market access would enhance foreign aid. Some U.S. aid policies, however, place the interests of the donor above the interests of recipients. Food aid illustrates several harmful practices. Most U.S. food distributed as aid is grown in America and sent overseas where the USAID distributes it to private relief organizations. Although this practice generates jobs and income domestically, it dumps cheap or free food in foreign markets where local farmers must cut prices to unprofitable levels to compete. Most "emergency" food aid is not short-term assistance. It depresses local food prices for years, putting farmers out of work. It also leaves the institutions

Kenyans thrashing rice grass to remove the grains

AP Photo/ Khalil Senosi

of recipient states out of the distribution chain, perpetuating state weakness. The Obama administration has proposed spending more *within* the recipient countries to support local farmers and economic and political institutions but has encountered stiff domestic opposition from the farm lobby, the shipping lobby, and private relief groups that work with USAID.[72]

   d. *Support new Sustainable Development Goals (SDGs) to help achieve the MDGs.* As the MDGs expired in 2015, targets for safe drinking water, malaria, and tuberculosis were being achieved. Extreme poverty had been cut in half, although China accounted for most global progress. In Sub-Saharan Africa the reduction in poverty was modest—from 56 percent in 1990 to 48 percent in 2010. Others MDGs, including reducing child and maternal mortality and the number of people living in slum conditions, lagged far behind.

   In the years preceding the expiration of the MDGs, governments, including in the United States, discussed new SDGs to continue the work of the MDGs. By early 2015, an initial draft of SDGs included seventeen new goals, with 169 development targets for 2030. Critics disparaged the draft. In contrast to the MDGs, the proposed SDGs were very specific, very expensive, and so extensive that they communicated "no priorities at all."[73] Supporters countered that they represented all stakeholders: developing countries that prioritized education, health care, job opportunities, and responsive government and developed countries that wanted to see progress in achieving gender equality, human rights, and environmental sustainability.[74]

Health and Disease

Substantial U.S. aid is devoted to health. Consistent with America's humanitarian impulse to aid the suffering, it also serves U.S. interests to prevent the spread of infectious diseases and support healthy, economically productive populations.

Policy Options

a. *Cut health aid and reallocate funding to promote other development goals.* Advocates of this option emphasize that achieving higher levels of development will improve health, but a healthy population is crucial to support development. The two goals are related in a virtuous cycle in which improvements in one reinforce the other. Moreover, health is an area in which foreign aid has been successful and, unlike other aid priorities, receives strong public support.

b. *Continue to rely on bilateral foreign aid to support efforts to fight global diseases like HIV/ AIDS and malaria.* This status quo strategy generates goodwill and improves America's moral standing because health aid has been successful in managing the spread of serious diseases like HIV/AIDS, malaria, and tuberculosis. Like other strategies, however, high levels of aid risk producing aid dependence and offer little incentive for recipients to devote substantial resources to national health care.

c. *Strengthen the capacity of multilateral institutions.* Well-funded multilateral institutions like the WHO and Global Fund are important partners in achieving health goals. Their work has been weakened by states' policies of using voluntary contributions to ensure the programs they favor are well funded. Because Washington is such a major contributor to these organizations, where it designates its contributions and where it does not influences the global health agenda. Allowing these organizations more freedom to set their agendas might enable them to begin to address some of the gaps in global health policy.

d. *Build the capacity of low-income states to provide citizens with improved health care.* This requires health care infrastructure—hospitals and clinics—and greater capacity. Greater capacity requires a stable economy with growth sufficient to allow for long-term planning and budget processes to ensure stable sources of funding, trained staff, and supporting infrastructure like electric, computing, and transportation systems. Thus, this option can only be accomplished in the context of a comprehensive development strategy.

Population Flows: Refugees and Migrants

Tradeoffs between values and interests also exist in refugee and migration policies. U.S. values support offering relief, including permanent relocation, to those fleeing persecution and violence. Moreover, acting according to the principles on which America was founded enhances U.S. soft power. However, many Americans fear that being too generous in accommodating refugees and migrants risks undermining other U.S. interests.

Policy Options

a. *Reduce refugee and asylum policies.* This option is inconsistent with U.S. values and treaty commitments. Reneging on these responsibilities would undermine America's moral standing. Washington is unlikely to discontinue or significantly reduce admitting refugees.

b. *Expand refugee and asylum policies to accept all those fleeing persecution or conflict and to accept additional refugees from areas where America has active military operations.* Such changes would increase U.S. moral standing, but any significant increase in refugees admitted to the United States is unlikely because of the domestic political sensitivity of the issue. It would involve accepting, at least in principle, the Cartagena Declaration that recognizes violence as a legitimate basis for asylum. Washington is unlikely to go this route because it would involve a massive increase in refugees eligible for asylum, especially from Central America, more than the U.S. public would be willing to absorb. It is already difficult to increase caps for refugees from Iraq and Afghanistan owing to fear that extremists might be able to use asylum as a way of entering America.

c. *Continue the existing policy of managing refugee flows into America.* The current policy of placing annual caps on the total number of refugees accepted into America each year and the number accepted from different regions or countries is consistent with the practices of other developed countries. For this reason, Washington is unlikely to increase significantly the number of refugees it admits. Washington does, however, face pressure from domestic and foreign sources to improve its treatment of those waiting to have their status determined, especially those with special skills like engineers or nurses.

d. *Invest in foreign aid policies to foster economic development in countries from where refugees and migrants emigrate.* Advocates of this strategy argue that the best way to reduce refugees and migrants is to improve conditions in source countries. This means ending wars, conflicts, and political oppression and stimulating economic development, thus encompassing all of the strategies discussed here and in the previous chapter.

CONCLUSION: THE VALUE OF A COHERENT POLICY

Designing a coherent foreign policy toward the Global South poses real dilemmas for the United States, as it encompasses many different states, with a wide variety of challenges among them. In fact, U.S. foreign policy toward these states must incorporate all of the issues we cover in the first section of this text—military security, weapons of mass destruction, economic growth and stability, human rights and democracy, and environmental challenges. We have been able to examine some of these challenges here. We have seen that U.S. involvement in much of the Global South has long been characterized by neglect as much as by aid and intervention. As much as Americans believe there is a moral imperative to intervene to help the poor and oppressed, inaction, weak action, or counterproductive action is often the result. This relative neglect occurs because of the presence of competing domestic and foreign policy priorities but also because Americans cannot always agree (with good reason) on the appropriate policy responses for managing the complex and interconnected issues in the Global South.

Human security and development seem to have been elevated to a permanent place on the global agenda. America cannot achieve these goals by itself, but if officials can craft and implement cohesive and effective responses to these challenges that reflect American values they would enhance U.S. leadership and soft power.

DISCUSSION QUESTIONS

1. What are some of the several forms intervention might take? What kind of intervention is most suited for managing each of the challenges discussed in this chapter?

2. What challenges do fragile states pose for America? Should they be viewed as threats to U.S. interests or opportunities, and what policy responses are appropriate?

3. Foreign aid funding levels are an ongoing source of controversy in U.S. politics. Does America give enough foreign aid? Explain your response.

4. Why does global health pose such a challenge for U.S. foreign policymakers? Should Washington focus health funding on combatting infectious disease or building health infrastructure?

5. What tradeoffs between values and interests are involved in the issue of refugees and migrants? Should values or interests take priority?

6. What evidence of aid, intervention, and neglect do you see in other issues described in this chapter? Does any single approach dominate?

KEY TERMS

asylum (p. 223)

failed states (p. 210)

fragile states (p. 210)

human development (p. 202)

human security (p. 202)

principal-agent problem (p. 207)

redenomination (p. 214)

tied aid (p. 203)

⑤SAGE edge™
for CQ Press

Sharpen your skill with SAGE edge at **edge.sagepub.com/mansbach**

SAGE edge for Students provides a personalized approach to help you accomplish your coursework goals in an easy-to-use learning environment.

8

Energy and the Environment

THE LIMITS OF U.S. LEADERSHIP

Demonstrators protest the Keystone pipeline.

AP Photo/Nam Y. Huh

In September 2008, TransCanada filed an application for a cross-border permit to begin work on the Keystone XL pipeline to carry heavy crude oil, known as bitumen, from Alberta's **tar sands** to refineries on the Gulf Coast of Texas. The regulatory review process that followed in Washington was plagued by controversy about the pipeline's environmental effects.

Environmentalists viewed the proposal as a test of the Obama administration's commitment to confronting climate change. In 2012, as NATO heads of state met in Chicago, environmental activists demonstrated outside the Canadian Consulate to protest the proposed pipeline. Some protestors chanted "No pipeline," while others played dead in the street, covered in chocolate syrup representing the oil that the pipeline would carry. Ranchers and farmers in America's Midwest opposed the pipeline, fearing that leaks would kill cattle and poison farmlands. On Earth Day, one group, the Cowboy and Indian Alliance, rode on horseback to the National Mall in Washington, D.C., where members erected teepees, organized a protest, and met with political leaders to raise awareness.

This chapter examines two issues in U.S. foreign policy—energy and the environment. Environmental issues illustrate the problems of managing transboundary natural resources and **collective goods** that offer benefits that must be shared and made available to everyone if they are enjoyed by anyone. Since no one can be deprived of collective goods such as clear air and water or military security if they are available to anyone, there is no incentive for individuals to pay for them because they have a "free ride."

Concerns about air and water pollution, hazardous waste disposal, biodiversity, and climate change pose complex policy problems linked to issues like trade, development, and human rights—and energy. They also raise questions about who should pay to solve these problems. Even though Washington had taken an active role in formulating agreements on endangered species and ozone depletion, it was unwilling to assume leadership in confronting environmental challenges as evidenced by failure to ratify environmental treaties including the Convention on Biological Diversity, the **Stockholm Convention on Persistent Organic Pollutants**, the Basel Convention on Control of Transboundary Movements of Hazardous Wastes and Their Disposal, and the Kyoto Protocol to the UN Framework Convention on Climate Change.

Energy and environment are inseparable. Energy is a foreign-policy issue because America has long relied on foreign sources of oil and is an environmental issue because fossil fuels are a finite resource and are linked to **global warming**. Like other environmental issues, energy policy has an impact on economic development. Oil and gas drive advanced industrial economies and without access to supplies of fuel growth will suffer.

SOURCES OF U.S. ENVIRONMENTAL AND ENERGY POLICIES

Owing to the transnational character of many environmental problems, external factors help shape U.S. environmental policy, thereby linking foreign and domestic politics. Such issues fall under the sovereign control of multiple actors, while others, like climate change and biodiversity, are global, requiring collective management. Such problems have different causes and effects. Rarely are the leading sources of environmental problems those most adversely affected by them. Advanced economies like America's have until recently been principal sources of emissions that contribute to climate change. Governments are driven by competing values in developing solutions. Some favor the "polluter pays" principle that those responsible for environmental damage should be responsible for reversing the damage. Others oppose that principle because past polluters may not be the same as current polluters. Finally, while some seek to limit activities that are potentially harmful to the environment, others insist on waiting until there is undeniable scientific evidence to warrant action.

Policymaking is also complicated by factors beyond government control. Because environmental issues are linked, efforts to address one may exacerbate another. Policymakers rely on science to define and solve environmental problems, but scientists do not always have answers because of the complexity of environmental systems or because proposed solutions have political and moral consequences.

Societal interest groups oppose measures that harm them economically. Coal and manufacturing industries opposed the Kyoto Protocol, and biotechnology companies opposed the Convention on Biological Diversity. Public opinion also plays a role, rallying for or against action. In the 1960s and 1970s, spurred by growing public awareness, Washington led efforts to promote global solutions to environmental problems. By the 1990s, the pendulum had moved in the other direction until Al Gore's 2006 film *An Inconvenient Truth* shifted public sentiment back in favor of government efforts to protect the environment. In 2014, a movement began demanding that universities divest stock in coal companies from their endowment funds, and Stanford was among the first to do so.

Government factors like America's constitutional separation of powers complicate the treaty process, constraining U.S. participation in international agreements like the Kyoto Protocol. Because the president has authority to negotiate treaties, that role is central to understanding U.S. participation in environmental agreements, but a president's ability to enter into agreements is limited by the requirement that the Senate ratify treaties. The federal system also separates federal policymakers from policy implementation, which is often the responsibility of state and local officials.

Individual factors matter. Richard Nixon, who oversaw the establishment of the Environmental Protection Agency (EPA) and signed into law the Clean Water Act (1972) and the Endangered Species Act (1973), was not an environmentalist but a pragmatist who acted to satisfy the public's desire for environmental causes, especially protecting endangered species. Ronald Reagan had little interest in environmental issues, and consistent with his belief in free markets, he rolled back environmental initiatives of his predecessors. Although George W. Bush never viewed himself as anti-environmentalist, he had an uneasy relationship with the environmental movement, and he and members of his administration like Vice President Dick Cheney were connected to the energy industry. By contrast, Barack Obama entered office with an ambitious environmental agenda though the financial crisis, congressional gridlock, and competing domestic priorities proved obstacles to his ambitions.

Timeline

1900

1960 Organization of Petroleum Exporting Countries (OPEC) is formed.

1960–1965 Clean Water, Clean Air, and Solid Waste Acts are passed.

1969 National Environmental Policy Act is passed.

1970 President Nixon creates the Environmental Protection Agency (EPA).

1900 (Continued)

1972 UN Conference on Human Development, Stockholm, Sweden

1973 Endangered Species Act is passed.

1973 First oil crisis and OPEC embargo

1977 Department of Energy is established.

1900 (Continued)

1979 Second oil crisis

1987 Montreal Protocol to reduce ozone depletion

March **1989** *Exxon Valdez* oil spill

1992 UN Conference on Environment and Development

1992 UN Framework Convention on Climate Change

1997 Kyoto Protocol

PAST: CHANGING TRENDS IN U.S. ENVIRONMENTAL LEADERSHIP

For early settlers during the era of "manifest destiny," nature was something to be conquered and civilized. America's bountiful resources identified America as "nature's nation." While Europe had cathedrals and castles, America had majestic mountains and rivers, vast plains, and incomparable forests.[1]

Thomas Jefferson advocated farming practices to increase agricultural productivity, and his promotion of intensive land use and introduction of foreign species are viewed today as environmentally harmful.[2] By contrast, Theodore Roosevelt is recalled as the country's "Conservationist President," having created the Forest Service, 51 Federal Bird Reservations, 4 National Game Preserves, 150 National Forests, and 5 National Parks.[3] In 1908, Roosevelt argued for a sustainable environmental policy. "We have become great because of the lavish use of our resources and we have just reason to be proud of our growth. But the time has come to inquire seriously what will happen when our forests are gone, when the coal, the iron, the oil, and the gas are exhausted, when the soils shall have been still further impoverished and washed into the streams, polluting the rivers, denuding the fields and obstructing navigation."[4]

For much of the 20th century, America was viewed as a global leader in protecting its natural resources. It was the first country to protect natural areas, with the Yosemite Grant (1864). By 1906, over 150 million acres with 20 percent of the nation's standing timber was under federal control. In 1916, Congress established the National Park Service to manage national parks. Washington also took the lead in protecting endangered species. The 1900 Lacey Act criminalized the transport of fish, wildlife, and plants killed in violation of state, federal, tribal, or foreign laws. It was amended in 2008 to extend protection to additional plants and plant products, including illegally harvested timber.[5]

Before 1970, Washington did not have a national environmental policy excepting efforts to manage public lands and limit the trade in protected species. The environment only emerged as a prominent issue in the 1960s. Thereafter, Washington became an environmental leader. In 1970, President Nixon signed the National Environmental Policy Act, establishing a national policy to protect the environment and requiring federal agencies to consider the environmental impact of policies before implementing them. Agencies were also required to release environmental impact assessments to keep the public informed.

2000

2008 TransCanada applies for a permit to build a transboundary oil pipeline.

2009 Copenhagen Climate Conference

2009 EPA announces new vehicle fuel standards.

2012 President Obama denies TransCanada a permit.

2012 TransCanada reapplies for a U.S. permit.

2000 (Continued)

2012 Rio+20 Summit

2013 Kyoto Protocol is extended.

2015 Congress approvers Keystone pipeline; President Obama vetoes the legislation.

Later that year, the United States established the EPA and thereafter implemented ambitious domestic environmental legislation including the 1963 Clean Air Act, the 1970 Endangered Species Act, and the 1972 Clean Water Act. Washington also took the lead in negotiating and implementing related international conservation agreements—the Convention on International Trade in Endangered Species of Wild Fauna and Flora (1973), the Ramsar Convention on Wetlands of International Importance Especially as Waterfowl Habitat (1972), and the moratorium on commercial whaling (1982).[6]

In the 1980s, U.S. environmental leadership waned. Washington failed to agree to multilateral accords including the 1982 Convention on the Law of the Sea that among its provisions sought to protect the marine environment. Nor did it join agreements on the transport of hazardous wastes and toxic chemicals or agreements on biological diversity and climate change. When Washington took the lead in seeking global cooperation, it was often to "internationalize U.S. domestic regulations."[7]

Critics blame this shift on changing ideology. A strong environmental movement in the 1960s and 1970s pushed Presidents Nixon and Gerald Ford to elevate environmental issues on the political agenda.

TABLE 8.1   U.S. Participation in Major Environmental Treaties, 1970–2014

Year	Treaty	Signed	Ratified
1971	Ramsar Convention on Wetlands of International Importance	+	+
1972	Stockholm Declaration	+	+
1972	London Convention on Dumping at Sea	+	+
1972	World Heritage Convention	+	+
1973	Convention on International Trade in Endangered Species	+	+
1974	International Convention for Safety of Life at Sea	+	+
1978	Convention on Prevention of Pollution from Ships	+	+
1979	Convention on Long-Range Transboundary Air Pollution	+	+
1979	Convention on the Conservation of Migratory Species of Wild Animals	–	–
1982	Convention on the Law of the Sea	–	–
1982	Amendments to the Ramsar Convention	+	+
1983	International Tropical Timber Agreement	+	+
1985	Vienna Convention for Protection of the Ozone Layer	+	+
1987	Montreal Protocol on Substances that Deplete the Ozone Layer	+	+

Year	Treaty	Signed	Ratified
1989	Basel Convention on the Transport of Hazardous Wastes	+	−
1991	Convention on Environmental Impact Assessment in a Transboundary Context	+	−
1992	UN Framework Convention on Climate Change	+	+
1992	Convention on Biological Diversity	+	−
1992	Convention on Transboundary Effects of Industrial Accidents	+	−
1994	Convention to Combat Desertification	+	+
1994	International Tropical Timber Agreement	+	+
1997	Kyoto Protocol	+	−
1998	Rotterdam Convention on Prior Informed Consent	+	
1998	Aarhus Convention on Information, Public Participation and Access to Justice	−	−
2000	Cartagena Protocol on Biosafety	−	−
2001	Stockholm Convention on Persistent Organic Pollutants	+	−
2006	International Tropical Timber Agreement	+	+
2013	Minamata Convention on Mercury	+	+

Sources: R. Daniel Kelemen and David Vogel, "Trading Places: The Role of the United States and the European Union in International Environmental Politics," *Comparative Political Studies* 43:4 (2010): 429–430; "Global Treaty on Mercury Pollution Gets Boost from United States," UNEP News Center, November 7, 2013, http://www.unep.org/NewsCentre/default.aspx?DocumentID=2755&ArticleID=9691.

In the 1980s and 1990s, a "wise-use" movement that advocated protecting private property rights and opening the country's remaining natural resources to development emerged. President Reagan was less committed to environmental protection than his predecessor, Jimmy Carter, but he signed the 1987 Montreal Protocol on Substances that Deplete the Ozone Layer. Thus, we also must consider factors other than ideology, including the evolution of environmental threats, the costs of inaction, and the existence of a scientific consensus on problems and solutions.

The global character of environmental challenges raises questions about sovereignty because problems like ozone depletion, climate change, and biodiversity involve **transboundary externalities**— activities in one country that can harm others. Such issues require solutions that must be implemented by international, national, state, and even local governments. Participation in multilateral agreements may entail new taxes, market mechanisms, restrictions on industry, or the use of private property and natural resources in many countries. Proposed environmental solutions may conflict with national objectives like economic growth.

America's political process provides insights into why environmental leadership has varied. The environment is an area in which a majority party in Congress or the party of the president cannot dictate foreign policy outcomes. More than other foreign-policy concerns, environmental policies have local impact. State and local legislation has to conform to international obligations. Thus, international environmental policy may become a heated domestic issue. States like West Virginia that depend on coal mining oppose policies that would harm their economy, even if it means their representatives have to defy the preferences of their political party. Regions that rely on tourism are likely to support the same international agreements. It is difficult for a government to assume leadership on environmental issues when state and local officials are divided. Washington is more likely to lead on international issues that it already regulates domestically and when it can advocate agreements that are consistent with U.S. law and is more likely to resist environmental cooperation that requires new legislation.

Involvement in Multilateral Environmental Regimes

Ozone depletion and climate change are often contrasted as cases of effective and ineffective efforts to achieve global cooperation. While leading efforts to combat ozone depletion, Washington has impeded efforts to manage climate change. Biodiversity is another area in which Washington was involved in negotiating a treaty that closely reflected existing U.S. regulations but that has not been ratified owing to concerns about implementation.

Ozone Depletion **Ozone** is a trace gas, found primarily in the stratosphere. It is essential to life because it absorbs ultraviolet B radiation (UV-B) that harms plants and animals. The ozone layer is vulnerable to erosion by chlorofluorocarbons (CFCs), one of a class of chemicals known as ozone-depleting substances (ODS) including halons, used in firefighting, and methyl bromide, a pesticide. The thinning of the ozone layer directly affects human health because reduced levels of stratospheric ozone make people susceptible to skin cancer, cataracts, blindness, and weakened immune systems. **Ozone depletion** also has indirect effects because it damages crops, livestock, and fisheries. Among the indirect effects is the interference of UV-B rays with the reproductive cycle of phytoplankton. These constitute the bottom of the food chain and absorb more carbon than they release. Thus, destruction of ozone also causes climate change.

Washington took the lead in passing domestic air-quality legislation with the 1955 Air Pollution Control Act and the 1970 Clean Air Act that authorized federal and state governments to develop comprehensive regulations to limit atmospheric emissions. These efforts to regulate air quality had little to do with ozone and were primarily intended to reduce pollution in U.S. industrial cities.

In the 1970s, concern about ozone grew. America was the largest consumer and producer of CFCs, accounting for 35 percent of the world's total,[8] and became a leader in ozone research and diplomacy to limit ODS emissions. Scientific interest in ozone research began after a controversy over the impact of nitrogen emissions from a planned fleet of supersonic transport airplanes. It was discovered that chlorine in the exhaust of the space shuttle was a more dangerous ozone-depleting substance than nitrogen. Thus, the National Aeronautics and Space Administration (NASA) began studying stratospheric ozone, and soon NASA commanded 70 percent of global funding on such research. Also in the early 1970s, chemists at the University of California found that CFCs, with "atmospheric lifetimes" of between 40 to 150 years (the time emissions remain in the atmosphere), were especially damaging to ozone. These long-lasting compounds were pervasive, used in manufacturing aerosol sprays, packing materials, and refrigerants. In the upper atmosphere they are a source of inorganic chlorine that sets off a catalytic reaction that breaks down ozone molecules.[9] Thus, amendments to the Clean Air Act authorized efforts to regulate CFC emissions in 1978, making the United States among the first countries to regulate these chemicals.

The Donora Smog

In 1948, the residents of Donora, Pennsylvania, experienced one of the worst air-pollution disasters in U.S. history. On October 27, the town was blanketed in a yellow cloud of smog. The residents of Donora were no strangers to smog, with steel mills, railroad yards, and a zinc plant nearby. For years they had complained about pollution that "eats the paint off your houses" and killed fish in the Monongahela River.[10] This time, a layer of cold air that had descended the previous night trapped the toxic blend of carbon monoxide, sulfur dioxide, and metal dust. Recalled one town resident, "The smog created a burning sensation in your throat and eyes and nose, but we still thought that was just normal for Donora."[11] By the time the smog cleared, twenty people had died. The disaster led to passage of state and federal regulations—beginning with the 1955 Air Pollution Control Act—to regulate industrial pollution.

DID YOU KNOW?

By the 1980s, evidence had accumulated that industrial chemicals were harming the ozone layer, and a conference on the issue was convened in 1985 in Vienna, Austria. Washington took a leading role at the conference partly because the EPA administrator was convinced action was needed and because the EPA was being sued by a nongovernmental organization, the Natural Resource Defense Council, for failing to implement existing ozone regulations. The final document, the Vienna Convention for the Protection of the Ozone Layer (1985), called for cooperation to monitor ozone and established state responsibility to protect it.

Efforts to control ozone-depleting substances took on new urgency when scientists from the British Antarctic Survey reported a hole in the ozone layer above their research stations. NASA confirmed the presence of the hole and found that it extended over the entire continent. They confirmed that CFCs were responsible, and the consequences of inaction seemed sufficiently great to spur agreement on the Montreal Protocol.

Ozone depletion posed an unusual foreign-policy challenge. According to the State Department's chief negotiator for the Montreal Protocol, "The problem of protecting the stratospheric ozone layer presented an unusual challenge to diplomacy. Military power was irrelevant. Economic might was not decisive either: it did not take great wealth or sophisticated technology to produce large quantities of ozone-depleting chemicals. Traditional notions of sovereignty became questionable because local decisions and activities could affect the well-being of the entire planet. The very nature of ozone depletion meant that no single country or group of countries, however powerful, could effectively solve the problem."[12] Ozone depletion represented a "**global commons**" problem—the actions of a few countries could have global consequences that could not be effectively addressed without everyone's participation.

Smog in Donora, Pennsylvania

PhotoQuest/Getty Images

Although Washington was viewed as a leader in efforts to draft a treaty to phase out ODS, U.S. participation was controversial domestically because as a global-commons issue and an emerging scientific problem, it was difficult to reach agreement on what action was needed. By 1987, evidence for the link between CFCs and ozone depletion had grown, and because the dangers were so great, scientists and policymakers believed that action had to be taken before the certainty of the problem had been established (a norm called the "precautionary principle"). The EPA worked closely with the State Department to craft a negotiating position that included a near-term freeze on using CFCs, a scheduled phase out, and periodic reviews to update findings. Not everyone was convinced of the problem's severity and interagency debate ensued. The Departments of Energy, Commerce, and the Interior opposed a treaty. Interior Secretary Donald Hodel did not understand the issue: "People who don't stand out in the sun—it doesn't affect them."[13] Environmentalists criticized his proposed "personal protection" strategy that relied on hats, sunscreen, and sunglasses rather than government regulation. A lawyer for the Natural Resources Defense Council noted that Hodel's strategy would be ten times as costly as ending the use of ozone-depleting chemicals in a decade because of health problems and lower food production, adding that it was "hard" to get animals to wear hats and sunglasses.

Policymakers relied heavily on experts to formulate a negotiating strategy. What mattered most was that Secretary of State George Schultz supported a multinational treaty. Schultz believed in the environmental and health hazards of ozone-depleting substances and feared the damage to U.S. credibility should Washington withdraw from negotiations after having persuaded other countries to adopt CFC regulations.[14]

Support gradually coalesced around Schultz's position. EPA advocates pushed for precautionary action as did industry, which recognized that the status quo, with Washington having already banned CFCs, placed U.S. CFC producers at a global economic disadvantage that would be overcome by a global treaty.[15] The eventual agreement phased out the most widely used CFCs by 50 percent by 2000, and a later amendment required that these chemicals be completely eliminated. This was a landmark agreement for its universal participation in eliminating ten ozone-depleting substances worldwide. The Montreal Protocol was responsible for repairing the hole in the ozone layer over Antarctica.

After the protocol came into force in 1989, Washington continued to participate in efforts to extend ozone controls, but in the 1990s, the U.S. position on new chemicals hindered, rather than advanced, global efforts. As other governments sought to extend the Montreal Protocol to cover more ozone-depleting substances, Washington resisted phasing out hydrochlorofluorocarbons (HCFCs), a manufactured CFC substitute with less ozone-depleting potential, and the pesticide methyl bromide. Both are potent greenhouse gases used in U.S. industry and agriculture and were eventually phased out under amendments to the Montreal Protocol. In America, the EPA phased out methyl bromide between 1995 and 2005, no longer allowing its production, but even today it grants "critical use" exemptions to agricultural users and others, including golf-course operators who were exempted until November 2014[16] and could use existing stocks of the pesticide if they demonstrated there were "no technically or economically feasible alternatives."[17] HCFCs will not be phased out until 2040.

After the Montreal Protocol eliminated CFCs and HCFCs, countries turned to substitutes, notably hydrofluorocarbons (HFCs) that do not destroy ozone. However, as climate science advanced, it became apparent that these ozone-friendly chemicals—used primarily as refrigerants but also as solvents, aerosols, and ingredients in foams and fire extinguishers—were **greenhouse gases** thousands of times more powerful than carbon dioxide in altering climate. While representing a small fraction of greenhouse gases, their impact was significant, and demand for them was expected to grow as the desire for refrigerators and air conditioners increased in developing countries. Unchecked, HFCs could grow to nearly 20 percent of carbon-dioxide emissions by 2050.[18]

Because these substances posed no threat to ozone, the Montreal Protocol did not regulate them. But some governments, including the Obama administration, argued that increasing HFC usage was a consequence of efforts to limit ODS. Thus, the Montreal Protocol should be employed to limit the resulting damage. Since 2009, Washington has worked with Canada and Mexico to craft amendments to the treaty to reduce this CFC substitute, and in June 2013, Washington and Beijing agreed to cooperate in persuading countries like Brazil and India where demand for HFCs was growing to reduce their use of these chemicals. Unlike the ozone regime, in which Washington was regarded as an early leader, it has been seen as "an obstinate 'postponer'"[19] in reaching a global climate treaty.

Climate Change **Climate change** is the most controversial contemporary global environmental issue. The earth's climate is regulated by the **greenhouse effect,** a natural atmospheric process that keeps the planet habitable. The atmosphere is a protective layer that admits some solar radiation that can be absorbed by the earth. Some radiation is also reflected back into space without reaching the earth's surface. Infrared heat from the warmed earth also radiates outward, but the atmosphere absorbs it before it can escape into space. As the atmosphere warms, so does the earth's surface. While this is a natural phenomenon, human activities emit gases that intensify the greenhouse effect. By burning fossil

fuels, humans emit heat-trapping carbon dioxide in the atmosphere, and other activities like deforestation and agriculture contribute to higher levels of carbon dioxide and other potent greenhouse gases like
methane and the HFCs in the atmosphere where they trap heat. The earth's climate has natural cycles,
fluctuating between ice ages and warm periods. These natural cycles have been attributed to volcanic
activity, warm or cool ocean temperatures, and variations in the amount of sunlight—the presence or
absence of sunspots, for example. But mainstream scientists agree that global warming has accelerated
since the industrial revolution too quickly to be explained by natural processes. Human activities, they
contend, explain rapid warming.

"Anthropogenic" (human) climate change is a challenging foreign-policy problem. It took decades to
form a scientific consensus about the existence of anthropogenic climate change. Climate is complex and,
even now, when scientists employ sophisticated computer models, there remain uncertainties about the
amount and speed of warming and its impact on the environment and our societies. A healthy climate
is a collective good. All countries benefit from the economic activities that produce the emissions contributing to climate change. But a few are disproportionately responsible for emissions though costs are
distributed globally. Thus, there is little incentive for anyone to "pay" to limit global warming.

Countries that produce the most emissions are least likely to experience immediate harm, and it is
difficult to calculate the extent to which environmental damage is due to climate change or other factors
like draining wetlands to build in flood zones or intensive agricultural practices that strip the land and
release acidifying chemicals into waterways. Finally, like most environmental issues, climate change has
to compete with other challenges with more immediate and visible costs. Thus, Senator Lindsey Graham
(R-SC), who had earlier worked on bipartisan climate legislation, no longer viewed climate as a pressing priority in 2014. Speaking of Obama's climate plan, unveiled while Washington was preoccupied by
Russian aggression in Ukraine, Graham protested: "The heat I'm worried about right now is the heat
from the world blowing up. . . . I think we got our priorities a little misplaced here."[20] Many Americans
believe the earth is warming but regard climate change as a low priority.

Early climate research took place in the 19th century, but not until the 1950s did scientists begin to
measure atmospheric carbon dioxide concentrations and their effects systematically. As climate became
a political issue in the 1970s, the debate intensified. Some scientists warned of a warming climate, while
others considered a possible "new ice age." The World Meteorological Organization hosted the First
World Climate Conference in 1979, but it took another decade before climate change became a global

Global Warming or Climate Change?

DID YOU KNOW?

The terms *global warming* and *climate change* are often used interchangeably, but they are not
the same. Global warming refers to the observed increase in the earth's average temperature.
Climate change is the term preferred by scientists because it encompasses the variety of effects
of a changing climate, including increasing global temperatures; changes in rainfall, ice cover,
and global weather patterns (like more frequent and severe heat waves and intense rain and
snow storms); and changes in oceans that are making water warmer and more acidic.

issue. During the 1980s, a scientific consensus began to emerge that human activities were elevating concentrations of gases that intensified the greenhouse effect and warming the planet. Senate hearings were held to examine the issue in 1988, one of the hottest and driest years in decades. One observer remarked that "congressional attitudes about chlorofluorocarbons (CFCs) and carbon dioxide emissions are influenced far more by the fact that the corn in most of Iowa is nowhere near as high as an elephant's eye and that outside the House and Senate chambers it has been stifling hot, than any number of scientific treatises on the subject."[21]

Not everyone agreed that science pointed to human-induced warming, and the senators who scheduled the hearings were criticized for orchestrating them to coincide with the heat. Even so, the public debate in America intensified that year—the same year that the UN Environment Program (UNEP) and the World Meteorological Organization formed the Intergovernmental Panel on Climate Change (IPCC) to review and assess "the current state of knowledge in climate change and its potential environmental and

MAP 8.1   Coal Production by State, 2012

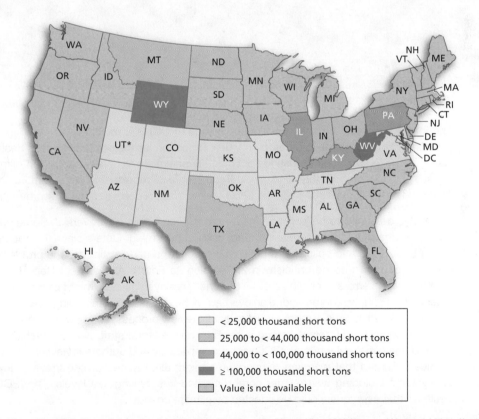

Source: Adapted from U.S. Energy Information Administration, "Rankings: Coal Production, 2013 (thousand short tons)," http://www.eia.gov/state/rankings/?sid=U.S.#/series/48.

socio-economic impacts."[22] IPCC's first report (1990) indicated that gas emissions from human activities were intensifying the greenhouse effect and spurred UN efforts to negotiate a Framework Convention on Climate Change (UNFCCC), to be signed at the 1992 UN Conference on Environment and Development (the Rio Conference, or Earth Summit). President George H. W. Bush, however, was not convinced that human activity contributed to global warming and advocated unilateral market-based responses rather than the binding emissions limits advocated by Europeans, warning that such limits would be economically costly. A study by the Council of Economic Advisers estimated it would cost between $800 billion and $3.6 trillion to cut U.S. carbon emissions by 20 percent by 2100.[23]

Coal-producing states opposed efforts to reduce fossil-fuel dependence, and firms around the country lobbied Congress and the administration to avoid costly emissions reductions. Policymakers were concerned that reducing emissions would increase energy costs, causing a loss of jobs to countries that did not participate in the treaty system or that could comply more easily than the United States. The final UNFCCC document reflected Washington's position by establishing a framework for continuing negotiations but no binding emissions targets.

→ ←   *CONTROVERSY*

The IPCC

The Intergovernmental Panel on Climate Change (IPCC) is a multinational scientific group that assesses climate change in order to provide information for the political process dealing with the issue. The IPCC relies on thousands of volunteer scientists to review and report climate change studies. They contribute their findings to IPCC technical reports that are summarized for policymakers. The 195 governments in the IPCC review these reports and must approve the reports.

The IPCC, designed to be politically neutral, has been highly controversial. Some critics charge it with exaggerating the extent and impact of global warming. Others claim it is too conservative owing to bureaucratic politics and political pressure and underestimates the problem. The IPCC was the focus of intense criticism in 2007 when its Fourth Assessment Report was found to contain serious errors, including a claim that the Himalayan glaciers might disappear by 2035. An independent review recommended an overhaul of the organization, including new governance and management structures, a more robust scientific review process, and new guidelines for reporting potential conflicts of interest among authors, review editors, staff, and leadership. Controversy erupted again in 2014 when an IPCC report compiled by 400 authors reviewing 12,000 scientific studies indicated that warming temperatures might already be causing irreversible damage to ecosystems including warm-water coral reefs and was raising sea levels. The IPCC chairman declared that everyone would be affected by climate change.

Unlike his predecessors, President Bill Clinton was interested in restoring U.S. environmental leadership, and Vice President Al Gore was a vigorous advocate of environmental causes who, as a senator, had participated in the 1988 hearings that launched domestic debate on global warming. Gore was critical of George H. W. Bush's environmental policy, arguing in 1987 that the Bush "administration's decision to censor scientific testimony on the seriousness of the greenhouse effect—and initially to oppose an international convention to begin working out a solution to it—may well mean that the president himself does not yet see the threat clearly."[24] Gore argued that global warming, along with ozone depletion, should be treated as "strategic national-security issues." Clinton placed climate on the national agenda immediately after entering office, proposing a national energy tax to reduce emissions in his 1993 budget. Although both houses of Congress had Democratic majorities, the initiative failed to pass and was replaced with a more politically acceptable gasoline tax.[25] On Earth Day, Clinton declared, "I reaffirm my personal and announce our Nation's commitment to reducing our emissions of greenhouse gases to their 1990 levels by the year 2000."[26] Some months later, he unveiled a Climate Change Action Plan that introduced or expanded over fifty initiatives to reduce U.S. emissions to 1990 levels. The following year, Congress reverted to Republican control and for the rest of his tenure Clinton was unable to gain traction for his climate agenda because Congress sought to cut government spending, including funds for environmental and alternative energy programs.

In 1996 climate talks, Clinton indicated that Washington might consider binding emissions reductions but only if an emissions trading scheme were included that would allow countries with high emissions to trade credits with developing countries. Before the 1997 Kyoto climate talks, the Senate passed the Byrd-Hagel Resolution, expressing its objection to binding emissions reductions and its unwillingness to ratify an agreement that might harm America's economy. Nevertheless, Clinton sent Gore to participate in negotiations, and the treaty that opened for signature in Kyoto contained differential commitments— binding emissions reductions below 1990 levels for wealthy nations but not for developing countries. The treaty allowed some flexibility in meeting targets by mechanisms that allow a country with binding reduction targets to earn emission credits by emissions trading or financing emissions-reduction projects in developing countries. But binding targets were a deal-breaker for many Americans.

Clinton signed the treaty to "lock in" commitments he thought were in the national interest even though he did not send it to the Senate for ratification. Washington continued to participate in climate talks for the rest of Clinton's presidency, arguing for flexibility in achieving reductions, including trading emissions credits and granting countries credits for carbon "sinks" like old growth forests that absorbed and stored carbon dioxide. By the time Clinton left office, the treaty had not entered into force, having failed to meet the threshold of ratification by fifty-five countries responsible for at least 55 percent of total 1990 emissions.

The Kyoto Protocol would not meet this threshold until 2006, and Washington was not a participant. George W. Bush had opposed Kyoto as a presidential candidate, and as president he opposed the treaty and balked at regulating CO_2 emissions through domestic legislation. Bush described the pact as "fatally flawed," citing the need for more "sound science," the unfairness of an agreement that did not require developing countries like China to reduce emissions, and the costs the protocol would entail for U.S. industries and consumers. In 2001, Bush's national security adviser, Condoleezza Rice, informed European diplomats that "Kyoto is dead," and they would "have to find new ways to deal with the problem."[27] Bush's position on Kyoto would not change, though he would come to accept that anthropogenic climate change was occurring, and in 2007 he acknowledged, "We must lead the world to

FIGURE **8.1**   Global Carbon Dioxide Emissions

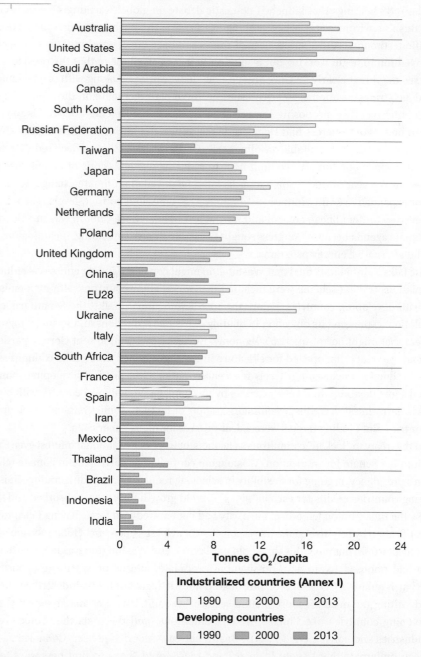

Source: PBL Netherlands Environmental Assessment Agency, "Trends in Global CO_2 Emissions: 2014 Report," p. 11, http://edgar.jrc .ec.europa.eu/news_docs/jrc-2014-trends-in-global-co2-emissions-2014-report-93171.pdf.

produce fewer greenhouse gas emissions, and we must do it in a way that does not undermine economic growth or prevent nations from delivering greater prosperity for their people."[28] Critics insisted Bush did too little to halt climate change and looked to a change in U.S. climate policy with the election of Barack Obama.

Obama highlighted climate change in his campaign, promising to reduce carbon dioxide emissions by 80 percent by 2050 and invest heavily in energy-saving technologies. He argued that climate-related threats to U.S. national security and ecological harm required Americans to assume leadership on energy issues. "This is a security threat, an economic albatross, and a moral challenge of our time."[29] As president, Obama was receptive to environmental regulation, but his effort to reduce emissions was impeded by domestic opposition, the economic crisis, and his decision to prioritize health care reform. In the first year of Obama's presidency, it appeared Washington might again assume environmental leadership. In the summer of 2009, the House passed a bill to create a "cap and trade" system to limit greenhouse gas emissions. The reaction of environmentalists and industry was mixed, but Senate opposition prevented the bill's passage.

The 2009 Copenhagen Climate Conference required leading officials of key nations to reach agreement between the developing and rich countries, and Obama became the first U.S. president to participate personally in climate talks. The president and Secretary of State Hillary Clinton interrupted a private meeting between Chinese Premier Wen Jiabao and leaders of other developing countries. "In the end, after lots of cajoling, debating, and compromising, the leaders in that room fashioned a deal that, while far from perfect, saved the summit from failure and put us on the road to future progress."[30] An agreement was reached to limit global temperature increases to 2 degrees Celsius, allocate $30 billion over three years to help poor countries deal with climate change, and raise $100 billion a year by 2020 to assist them to do so. While the Copenhagen Accord did not set binding emissions reductions, Obama formally associated Washington with the pact and submitted an emissions reductions target of 17 percent below 2005 emissions.[31]

Washington, however, surrendered its environmental leadership after the 2010 midterm elections. Senator-elect Marco Rubio (R-FL) declared, "I don't think there's the scientific evidence to justify it," and Senator-elect Rand Paul (R-KY) said, "I think anyone who makes an absolute conclusion is probably overstating their conclusion."[32] Both became influential members of Congress and opposed Obama's climate policy. Given congressional skepticism, Obama did not attend the 2010 Cancún, Mexico, climate talks, and at the 2011 Durban, South Africa, talks, U.S. negotiators were described as "obstructionist" by other governments for insisting that any legally binding agreement include *both* developed and developing countries. In a letter to Secretary Clinton, environmental groups argued that the U.S. position threatened to impede "the global cooperation so desperately needed to address the threat of climate change."[33]

The Durban conference ended with an agreement to extend the Kyoto Protocol for at least five years in order to continue negotiating to achieve "an agreed outcome with legal force" that would apply to all countries. In 2012, it was agreed to extend Kyoto until 2020. Washington, which was a party to these discussions because of its participation in the UNFCCC, remained outside the Kyoto system, but Obama continued to argue for U.S. leadership in global climate policy and for participation in talks in Paris in 2015 to conclude a legally binding treaty to replace Kyoto. "American influence," he insisted, "is always stronger when we lead by example."[34]

🗝 KEY DOCUMENT
The 2010 U.S. National Security Strategy

President Obama's 2010 National Security Strategy was the first to define climate change as a national-security issue. "The danger from climate change is real, urgent, and severe. The change wrought by a warming planet will lead to new conflicts over refugees and resources; new suffering from drought and famine; catastrophic natural disasters; and the degradation of land across the globe. The United States will therefore confront climate change based upon clear guidance from the science, and in cooperation with all nations—for there is no effective solution to climate change that does not depend upon all nations taking responsibility for their own actions and for the planet we will leave behind."

Source: National Security Strategy, The White House, May 2010, http://www.whitehouse.gov/sites/default/files/rss_viewer/national_security_strategy.pdf.

Owing to domestic opposition to U.S. participation in the Kyoto process because it did not place binding emissions reduction targets for emerging countries like China, Washington and Beijing negotiated a historic bilateral agreement in 2014 to reduce carbon emissions beyond 2020. Like Kyoto, this bilateral agreement placed different obligations on the parties. Washington agreed to cut emissions to 17 percent below 2005 levels by 2020. China promised to reach its peak carbon emissions no later than 2030 and pledged to increase renewable zero-emissions energy to about 20 percent of its energy consumption by 2030. U.S. leaders praised the agreement as an advance in achieving cooperation toward emissions reductions, while critics argued that China was getting a much better deal.

Those who had been disappointed with Obama's failure to pursue a robust climate-change agenda during his first term were encouraged when he highlighted the issue in his 2013 inaugural address: "We will respond to the threat of climate change, knowing that the failure to do so would betray our children and future generations. . . . Some may still deny the overwhelming judgment of science, but none can avoid the devastating impact of raging fires and crippling drought and more powerful storms."[35] In June 2013, he announced an ambitious climate plan to develop new standards to regulate emissions from coal-fired power plants and again promised to keep "the United States of America a leader—a global leader—in the fight against climate change."[36] With Congress unwilling to act, Obama began using executive authority.

Washington's efforts to use the EPA to regulate emissions began in 2009. The transportation sector accounted for 30 percent of U.S. greenhouse gas emissions. Passenger cars and light trucks contributed over 60 percent of those emissions, and freight trucks and buses produced nearly 20 percent.[37] In 2007, the Supreme Court ruled that carbon dioxide was a pollutant subject to EPA regulation under the Clean Air Act, and this ruling opened the way for the agency to regulate emissions. In 2009, the EPA sought a 30 percent reduction in carbon-dioxide emissions from cars and light trucks by 2016 by requiring automakers to improve fuel efficiency from an average of 25 miles per gallon (mpg) to an average of 35.5 mpg. In 2014, Obama ordered higher fuel standards for large trucks. Environmentalists applauded these moves, and companies like FedEx and Waste Management that benefit from lower fuel costs from better mileage expressed support. The American Trucking Association was more cautious, expressing its hope that the government would not impose economic burdens on the trucking industry. Then in 2015, the president used executive authority to allow the EPA to issue a final set of regulations to limit greenhouse gas emissions from power plants and another regulation based on the Clean Water Act called "Waters of the U.S." to limit pollution in rivers, lakes, and wetlands. Opponents argued that the latter regulation violated the rights of property owners and would dampen economic growth.

The transportation sector was not the principal source of U.S. emissions. Power plants accounted for nearly 40 percent of U.S. carbon emissions, especially older, coal-fired plants. In keeping with the president's promises, in 2014 the EPA announced new standards that required existing power stations to reduce CO_2 emissions by 30 percent below 2005 levels by 2030. The EPA indicated it would allow states flexibility in choosing how to meet targets—upgrading plants, switching from coal to natural gas, or promoting renewable energy. If this policy succeeded, advocates claimed, U.S. CO_2 emissions would drop by 12 percent from 2005 levels. "One of the best things we can do for our economy, our health, and our environment," argued Obama, "is to lead the world in producing cleaner, safer energy," and "a low-carbon, clean energy economy can be an engine of growth for decades to come."[38]

Response to this aggressive initiative was mixed. Some environmentalists viewed it as politically courageous "baby steps" that were nonetheless significant and might spur change in other countries. Others argued the plan did not go far enough and that real progress would only occur if cuts in other greenhouse gases were made and if other countries followed Washington's initiative. Opponents claimed that mandated emissions cuts would increase energy costs without contributing to emissions reductions. Some critics thought that lacking congressional legislation, the policy was an abuse of executive authority.

Biodiversity Washington, as we saw, had initially been a leader in multilateral environmental policy but later became an obstacle to multilateralism. One victim was biological diversity (**biodiversity**)—the variety of life on the planet including microorganisms, plants, animals, genes, and ecosystems like rainforests and wetlands. Humans benefit from biodiversity. Diverse ecosystems provide food and clean water and are sources of medicines and biotechnologies. They protect human and natural habitats from natural shocks like hurricanes. Although biodiversity is important, measuring it is difficult. Scientists constantly discover previously unknown species. Of an estimated 3 to 30 million species, scientists have identified about 2 million and monitor about 50,000.[39] These efforts reveal that planetary biodiversity is decreasing even faster than the last mass extinction 65 million years ago. Human behavior in involved in biodiversity loss, which is driven by several factors "in rough order of impact to date: habitat loss, overharvesting, invasive species, pollution, and climate change."[40]

Declining biodiversity is a difficult issue to manage globally. Although some of its effects—like the loss of rainforests that accelerates climate change—are global, the ecosystems that require protection are in sovereign states, and governments do not wish to lose control of their own natural resources to achieve global objectives. Many biodiverse sites are in the developing world where preservation comes at the cost of economic growth.

MAP 8.2   Share of Electricity Generated by Coal

Source: Data from the U.S. Energy Information Administration, "Total Petroleum and Other Liquids Production—2014," http://www.eia
.gov/beta/international.

The main global instrument for protecting biodiversity is the Convention on Biological Diversity (CBD). Negotiations began in 1991, with the goal of a treaty by the 1992 Earth Summit, which led to the adoption of Agenda 21, a wide-ranging blueprint for action to achieve sustainable development globally. In the decade before the Rio Summit, Washington was a leader in efforts to negotiate a treaty to protect endangered habitats and species. Initially, it sought an agreement resembling America's 1973 Endangered Species Act. Early advocacy included both Senate Republicans and Democrats, but as negotiations progressed, the content of the proposed treaty broadened and produced domestic disquiet. Washington's position shifted from support to opposition because of concern for intellectual property rights, sovereignty, and cost (despite establishment of a Global Environment Facility that gave the United States greater control over decisions about allocating environmental funding). These concerns persisted, and today the CBD enjoys nearly universal participation. Only Andorra, the United States, and the Vatican do not participate.

Intellectual property rights constitute the most significant obstacle to U.S. participation. Developing states, including several biodiverse nations, supported a treaty that gave "countries of origin" rights to a share of profits derived from genetic resources found in their territory. This meant that U.S. pharmaceutical and biotechnology firms had to share the profits of new medicines and bioengineered plant seeds with countries from which they acquired the genetic resources to make their discoveries. Thus, when the treaty was opened for signature in 1992, President George H. W. Bush concluded that it was against America's interest to sign the treaty.

U.S. participation in the CBD was also delayed by concerns about sovereignty because the treaty would require Washington to change the Endangered Species Act, which farmers and ranchers believed already placed too many limits on how they could use their land. President Clinton did sign the CBD in 1993 but sent it to the Senate with seven understandings attached. One declared that existing federal, state, and local laws were sufficient to enable implementation of U.S. treaty responsibilities and would not alter the balance of federal and state authority. Although the Senate Foreign Relations Committee supported the treaty subject to the understandings, Republican opposition blocked ratification.

Proponents of participation argued, much as did Clinton in his letter to the Senate, that joining the CBD would not infringe on U.S. sovereignty or require new state or federal legislation because it allowed countries to exercise national control over their environmental resources. Washington could exercise leadership at little cost. "No country possesses an inventory, description, and understanding of its wild-life, habitat networks, and ecological processes greater than the United States. In addition, [it] embodies a tradition of public engagement that leads to greater biodiversity-related protection and enforcement than most countries."[41] Without having ratified the treaty, Washington lacked the influence it would have enjoyed in meeting to discuss how to extend and strengthen the agreement.

The Politics of Energy

The global economy is driven by fossil fuels, especially coal and oil. America has vast coal and natural gas reserves but until recently was dependent on foreign sources of oil. Since much of the world's known oil reserves are in the Middle East, that region has long been a focus of U.S. foreign policy. U.S. reliance on foreign oil made the country hostage to regional political instability, but since the discovery of new energy sources in North America, U.S. policy has shifted to drawing on reserves at home and in Canada and achieving independence from Middle East oil.

The Middle East as a Source of Oil In the decades following the development of the oil industry in the Middle East, a small group of U.S. and European international oil companies called the Seven Sisters—Esso (later Exxon), Gulf, Mobil, Socal (later Chevron), Texaco, Royal Dutch Shell, and British Petroleum—played a dominant role in the production, distribution, and pricing of oil, while paying oil-producing countries only a small royalty. Single companies or corporate partnerships divided up the region, enhancing their bargaining leverage with individual governments and limiting competition with one another. The companies enjoyed the political backing of their home governments.

Inflation during and after World War II reduced the value of the fixed royalties oil companies paid, and in 1945 Venezuela forced companies to pay it 50 percent of their profits. In 1950, Saudi Arabia forced the U.S. consortium Aramco (the Saudi Arabian Oil Company) to accept a 50–50 split of profits under threat of nationalization, and thereafter most oil-producing countries imposed similar agreements. When Iran's government demanded a similar arrangement, British Petroleum refused, and in 1951, Iran sought to nationalize the British-owned Anglo-Iranian Oil Company. Fearful that other oil-rich countries would emulate Iran, the West imposed a global boycott of Iranian oil. A power struggle ensued between

Iran's popular nationalist Prime Minister Mohammad Mosaddeqh and its royal ruler Mohammad Reza Shah Pahlavi. Aided by the CIA and Britain's MI6, Mosaddeqh was deposed in 1953. Iranian oil was again privatized in the National Iranian Oil Company, owned jointly by the Seven Sisters.

The power of the Seven Sisters to set prices was further eroded by the entry of new companies— Amoco, Occidental, and Getty. These cut prices and therefore profits of the larger firms. The latter in turn reduced posted prices (the price they would accept for their oil), which reduced the taxes they paid to oil-producing countries. Lower prices globally also reduced profits from oil production in America, which led to a decline in domestic production. Thus, after 1948, America began to import more oil than it exported. In response, Washington mandated oil import quotas in 1959 to shelter domestic producers from inexpensive imported oil, an action that further diluted the power of the large international oil companies.

To prevent oil companies from further reducing prices and therefore revenues, Iraq hosted a meeting of other oil-producing countries (Iran, Iraq, Kuwait, Saudi Arabia, and Venezuela) that established OPEC in 1960. Other countries joined later: Qatar (1961), Indonesia (1962), Libya (1962), the United Arab Emirates (1967), Algeria (1969), Nigeria (1971), Ecuador (1973), Gabon (1975), and Angola (2007). During the 1960s, OPEC successfully stabilized oil prices although increased production and inflation gradually decreased oil's "real price" (prices adjusted for inflation unlike "nominal prices" that are not adjusted for inflation).

Following the 1967 Six-Day War, Arab producers embargoed oil exports to countries that supported Israel. Although the embargo increased prices, the effort failed after the United States and non-Arab country oil-producers increased production, thereby depriving countries like Saudi Arabia of considerable oil revenue. As a result, OPEC's Arab members formed an Organization of Arab Petroleum Exporting Countries (OAPEC) the following year within OPEC to coordinate their actions. OPEC also increased the posted price of oil and set a minimum tax rate of 55 percent on profits.

By the 1970s, OPEC was able to prevent additional reductions in posted oil prices. In 1970, Libya threatened to seize the oil companies' assets unless they raised the price of Libyan crude and reduced the amount being pumped. The companies' effort to defy Libya collapsed when Occidental Petroleum, the largest oil company in the country, broke ranks after Libya threatened to cut permissible production from 800,000 to 500,000 barrels a day, and Occidental could not obtain sufficient oil from other companies to meet contractual commitments. Libya's success led other oil-producing countries to demand similar increases and, trying to stabilize prices, the companies sought to negotiate with oil-producing governments for a common price.

In ensuing years, several factors produced an upward price spiral—global demand, devaluation of the U.S. dollar, the 1973 Yom Kippur War, and a second Arab oil embargo. In the absence of increasing supply and declining American oil production along with growing U.S. demand, prices moved higher. U.S. dollar devaluations in 1971 and 1973, however, pushed real oil prices in the other direction and diluted profits because purchasers paid for oil in dollars. OPEC members had more dollars, but these were worth less, leading them to demand higher nominal prices as they limited supply by assigning production quotas to members.

Moreover, several Arab oil producers including Algeria and Libya nationalized oil production in 1971, and the nationalizations "demonstrated the extent of the changes in the structure of the system" that made nationalization feasible, and "actions by the more militant producers also served to increase pressure on other regimes to respond in kind."[42] Iraq and Iran followed the Algerian-Libyan example, and in late 1972, Kuwait, Qatar, Saudi Arabia, and the United Arab Emirates reached an agreement to acquire majority ownership of the industry within ten years. Full or majority state control was achieved by the mid-1970s with companies largely limited to managing operations.

Following the Yom Kippur War, Arab states sought to use the oil weapon to force industrialized countries to change their policies toward Israel. OPEC raised its posted oil price by over $2 a barrel, and OAPEC cut production by 5 percent each month to force Israel to withdraw from territories it had occupied in 1967. After the Nixon administration asked Congress for emergency military aid for Israel, Saudi Arabia reduced oil production and placed an embargo on sales to America. Thereafter, a selective oil embargo was imposed on the United States, the Netherlands, and Portugal. Although the transfer of oil among companies permitted non-Arab oil to reach America, spot shortages and gas lines appeared despite rationing, lower speed limits, and abandoning the oil import quota. Between 1970 and 1974, oil's nominal price jumped from $1.21 to $11.00,[43] slowing U.S. economic growth. Politics and economics had combined to boost the price of oil (the first "oil shock"), the profits of oil-producing states, and the costs to oil consumers. "These price increases produced the largest 'peacetime' international transfer of wealth in history"[44] and triggered a global recession in 1974.

Between 1973 and 1980 supplies remained tight, OPEC discipline held, and prices continued to rise. Divisions among producers, however, soon became apparent. Iran sought to raise prices quickly to assure domestic political and social stability, while Saudi Arabia with a smaller population and larger oil reserves preferred lower price increases. In 1979 to 1980, oil prices again shot up. The 1979 Iranian revolution reduced the flow of Iranian oil, and the subsequent Iran-Iraq war heightened concerns about disruption in oil supplies and triggered hikes in both the nominal and real prices of oil. Iran's postrevolutionary regime viewed Washington as an enemy, while the conservative Saudi monarchy regarded Washington as an ally in maintaining regional stability and resisting Iran.

Prices peaked in 1981 after the second "oil shock" and then began to fall owing to economic recession, conservation efforts by consumers, a breakdown of discipline in the OPEC cartel, and resulting overproduction. Non-OPEC oil producers such as Norway, Mexico, Britain, Russia, and Oman began to account for a larger share of production. By April 1994, real oil prices had dropped close to 1973 levels. Declining oil revenues and their political consequences played a role in events leading to Iraq's 1990 invasion of Kuwait. Kuwait sought to pressure Iraq to repay debts it had incurred during Iraq's war with Iran, debts that Saddam Hussein argued were a result of a war it had waged against a "Persian" Shia foe on behalf of the entire "Arab" world. In addition to Kuwait's "ingratitude," Iraq charged that Kuwait was profiting by exceeding its OPEC production quota and pumping more than its share of oil from a disputed oil field that straddled their border. Command of Iraq and Kuwait gave Saddam control of 20 percent of the world's known oil reserves. Worse, occupation of Kuwait had moved Iraq's army to the Saudi border, endangering an additional 25 percent. Although the invasion of Kuwait raised prices, the rise was temporary because Saddam's threat to Saudi Arabia dissipated after a U.S.-led coalition drove Iraq from Kuwait in 1991.

Other factors eroded OPEC's influence. Conflicts among members were exacerbated by oversupply, partly a result of widespread cheating on production quotas. High levels of production were a source of wealth as long as prices remained stable, but excessive supply reduced profits as prices declined. As the leading source of oil, Saudi Arabia played a key role in maintaining OPEC production levels.

TABLE 8.2   Leading Oil Producers and Consumers, 2014

Producers (2014)	
Country	Thousand barrels per day
United States	13,973
Saudi Arabia	11,624
Russia	10,853
China	4,572
Canada	4,383
United Arab Emirates	3,471
Iran	3,375
Iraq	3,371
Brazil	2,950
Mexico	2,812

Consumers (2013)	
Country	Thousand barrels per day
United States	18,961
China	10,480
Japan	4,531
India	3,660
Russia	3,493
Brazil	3,003
Saudi Arabia	2,961
Canada	2,431
Germany	2,403
South Korea	2,324

Source: Data from the U.S. Energy Information Administration, "Total Petroleum and Other Liquids Production—2014," http://www.eia.gov/beta/international.

As prices fell in the 1980s and 1990s, the Saudis increased production to increase market share, keeping prices low until Asia's 1998 financial crisis.

In ensuing years, several factors pushed oil prices upward—OPEC production cuts, a strike in Venezuela that closed down the country's state-owned oil company, America's 2003 invasion of Iraq, and the 2011 civil war in Libya. The crucial factor, however, was surging energy demand in Asia, especially China. In March 2008, the nominal price of oil almost reached $104 a barrel which, adjusted for inflation, exceeded the previous record set during the second "oil shock" in 1980, dropping again only after America's financial crisis became global.

Energy security was a key issue during World War II and also during the Cold War. "Oil provided the point at which foreign policy, international economic considerations, national security, and corporate interests would all converge."[45] After the Cold War, energy politics began to change again.

The Changing Politics of Oil As of 2011, Saudi Arabia and Russia were the world's leading oil producers while the United States remained the world's leading consumer, but change was occurring. Developments in China and America became key factors in oil production and prices. China's average annual growth rate of 10 percent from 2000 to 2011 and its continuing high growth rate were accompanied by rising demand for energy. In a single decade, China's energy consumption rose from half that of America to become the world's largest energy consumer. China's oil consumption surged, making it the world's second largest consumer. By 2011, China imported over half its daily consumption, and domestic production had peaked. China's growing thirst for oil accounted for much of the increase in global demand that year and pushed prices higher. Despite the Great Recession, the real price of oil remained high by historical standards. The demand for oil also increased the geopolitical importance of the Middle East for Beijing, especially since Saudi Arabia is its largest source of oil imports. And China's demand for energy is likely to continue to increase. Per capita energy consumption of the country's 1.3 billion people remains far lower than that of Americans and will rise as the country develops economically. Global energy demand spurred mainly by China and India is predicted to increase by a third by 2035, and China will become the world's leading oil importer by 2017.

Another element in the politics of oil has been the increase in U.S. shale-oil and shale-gas production owing to the introduction of hydraulic fracturing or "fracking"—creating fractures in rock formations by injecting fluid into cracks that allow oil and gas to flow to where it can be extracted. This process became commercially viable in areas like North Dakota's Bakken Shale and Texas's Eagle Ford because of oil's increased price. Between 2008 and 2011, America increased oil production by 14 percent and natural gas production by 10 percent, overtaking Russian energy production in 2013. America's declining reliance on oil imports, declared Henry Kissinger, is "of huge strategic consequence."[46]

The United States became the world's largest oil producer in 2014, and the IEA predicted it could become energy independent and even a net oil exporter by 2030.[47] However, that agency also predicted that, by the mid-2020s, non-OPEC production would begin to decrease. Its director concluded, "We expect the Middle East will come back and be a very important producer and exporter of oil, just because there are huge resources of low-cost light oil."[48] Moreover, Saudi Arabia's Aramco has invested in the Motiva oil refinery, America's largest producer of petroleum products. "The Saudis are securing a home for their heavy crude," declared an analyst. "But there is no question that security is also part of the

FIGURE 8.2   China's Oil Production and Consumption, 1990–2013

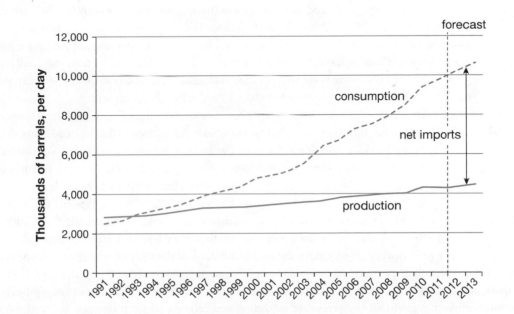

Source: U.S. Energy Information Administration, International Energy Statistics and Short-Term Energy Outlook (August 2012).

equation." Added another: "The Motiva relationship guarantees the Saudis an important but subtle footprint in the United States, and they want to have some negotiating strength when geopolitical issues in the Middle East and elsewhere arise."[49]

Canada and the Keystone Pipeline

U.S. energy policy has increasingly focused on resources closer to home. Canada has the world's third largest proven oil reserves but much of its oil is costly to extract and refine. Its Alberta oil sands are deposits made up of sand, clay, water, and bitumen, a thick semisolid form of petroleum that has the consistency of peanut butter. Of Canada's 179 billion barrels of oil reserves, about 175 billion are located in oil sands. In fact, Canada has oil and gas resources comparable to America's but produces less than half of the U.S. output because it is so costly to produce. But as technological obstacles are overcome, Canada's production capacity will increase dramatically.

At present, Canada lacks adequate infrastructure to transport the oil it extracts to refineries that can process it into gasoline or send it to U.S. ports where it could be sent overseas. To transport this oil to the United States, oil companies must use a pipeline (rail and truck delivery is costlier and highly dangerous) that crosses the U.S.–Canada border, but that requires a presidential permit to be built. Before issuing a permit, the U.S. State Department must consider the project's impact on the "national interest," including its environmental impact.[50]

The United States has issued permits for several major pipelines since 2008. A Canadian company, Enbridge, operates a network that transports oil from Alberta to America's Midwest and eastern Canada. Another Canadian company, TransCanada, operates the Keystone Mainline Pipeline that moves oil from Alberta to refineries in Illinois and Kansas. This pipeline cuts across the Canadian provinces of Saskatchewan and Manitoba, then turns sharply south and cuts through the Dakotas, and finally delivers its oil to storage tanks in Steele City, Nebraska. In 2005, when TransCanada applied for permission to build this pipeline, America was recovering from Hurricanes Katrina and Rita. Katrina shut down natural gas and crude oil production in the Gulf of Mexico, the site of about 25 percent of U.S. crude oil production. Just as oil and natural gas production was beginning to recover, Rita made landfall, closing refineries in Louisiana and Alabama. Thus, for much of September, America lost about a third of its refining capacity.[51]

The Keystone Mainline Pipeline offered the security of an alternate source of crude for inland refineries, and by 2008, TransCanada had received permission to build it. Extensions to that pipeline, since they do not cross international borders, did not require State Department approval and several were added. In early 2011, the Keystone Cushing Extension began to deliver oil to tank farms in Cushing, Oklahoma, and in 2014, the Keystone Gulf Coast pipeline began to deliver crude from Cushing to refineries in Texas.

In September 2008, TransCanada applied for a permit to build the Keystone XL Pipeline that would follow a more direct 1,200-mile route from Alberta's oil sands into Montana, terminating at a hub in Nebraska. The proposed pipeline would have the capacity to deliver 830,000 billion barrels of oil a day and require a 50-foot right-of-way along the route with most of the right-of-way crossing privately owned land. It proved more controversial than the first Keystone pipeline.

In an unusual alliance, environmentalists and landowners were united in opposing the new pipeline. Environmentalists argued that the process of extracting and refining oil from bitumen released more greenhouse emissions than did lighter crudes like that extracted from Bakken Shale. To be transported by

MAP 8.3   Keystone XL Pipeline Map

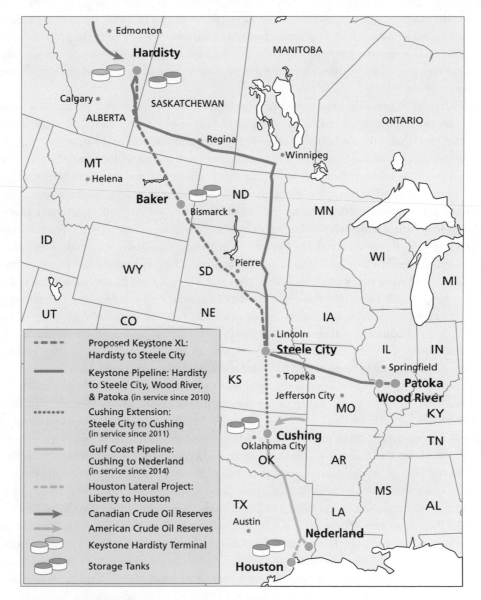

Source: Courtesy of TransCanada, http://keystone-xl.com.

Note: Map is current as of July 7, 2015.

pipeline or rail, bitumen must be separated from the sands in which it is deposited and then diluted—a process called "upgrading"—for transport and processing at refineries designed for lighter crudes. Estimates vary, but the carbon-intensive extraction and processing of bitumen likely produces 14 to 17 percent more greenhouse emissions over the life cycle of the fuel—extraction, transportation, upgrading/refining, distribution of refined fuel, and combustion—than the lighter crude oils presently used in the United States.[52] Estimates that examine only the production and/or extraction phases claim oil sands crude might have greenhouse emissions as much as 81 percent greater than light crudes. Critics of the proposed pipeline, including the EPA, argued that the impact on emissions is greater still, as State Department assessments do not consider the social cost of carbon, a measure that assesses damage to agricultural productivity, human health, and property.[53]

Those who wished to see the Keystone XL pipeline built countered that although bitumen is more carbon-intensive than conventional crudes, the development of the oil sands is inevitable regardless of the pipeline's fate, and that in the absence of new pipelines, the transport of bitumen by other means, including rail, truck, or barge, will increase greenhouse emissions even more. Moreover, they argued, the oil industry is making an effort to reduce carbon emissions through carbon-capture and storage technologies that are expected, when implemented, to capture more than a third of carbon dioxide emissions at mining sites.

Pipeline opponents warned that pipeline leaks would be costly. On this point, environmentalists were united with landowners along the pipeline's proposed route who feared the risk the pipeline posed to crops and livestock. Residents feared the impact on their water supply should a leak contaminate the Ogallala Aquifer (beneath the Great Plains), one of the world's largest aquifers and one that lies close to the surface. And when heavy crude leaks into lakes and rivers, it sinks to the bottom and is difficult to remove. Several spills confirmed this while the State Department was undertaking its environmental review of the first TransCanada application. In one case in 2010, a leak in an Enbridge pipeline spewed 840,000 gallons of bitumen in Michigan's Kalamazoo River. Efforts to clean the river continued into 2014, and some claim it will never be completely cleaned up. In another incident in 2013, residents of Mayflower, Arkansas, had to be evacuated following a spill of 210,000 gallons of bitumen.

Proponents countered that the Keystone XL would employ the newest technologies making it safer than existing pipelines. And without adequate pipeline capacity, developers would transport oil by rail or truck, both of which are just as, if not more, risky than pipelines. Two incidents in 2013 raised awareness about the dangers of transporting oil by rail. In July, a train carrying seventy-two tank cars filled with Bakken light crude derailed in the Quebec town of Lac-Mégantic. Light crude is highly flammable, unlike the heavy crude extracted from Alberta's oil sands, and the explosions that followed leveled the small Quebec town, killing forty-seven people. Several months later, a train carrying light crude derailed and exploded in a rural area in western Alabama. No one was killed, but it is unknown how much of the train's 2.9 million gallons of oil spilled into the swamp or how much of it burned in the explosions that followed the derailment. Oil continued to seep into the wetlands from the rail bed months later.[54] These incidents increased pressure to tighten regulations on tank cars, and both the Canadian and U.S. governments have removed thousands of tank cars from service. Tougher regulations mean higher transportation costs and ultimately higher fuel costs. For these reasons, proponents contend pipelines are the best means of transport.

Finally, proponents cited the economic benefits of pipelines. The addition of new pipelines, including the Keystone XL, would relieve the bottleneck preventing much of Canada's crude from reaching refineries in the Gulf that are designed to process heavy oil. It would also create jobs and offer the United States a reliable fuel source that would reduce America's need for oil from volatile regions (the Middle East and Venezuela), thus enhancing national security. Finally, they contended, if inadequate infrastructure prevented Canada from selling its oil to U.S. buyers, Canada would seek buyers in China and other Asian countries.

In April 2010, the Department of State issued a Draft Environmental Impact Statement and sought public comments. In October, Secretary of State Clinton indicated that the administration was "inclined" to approve the Keystone XL pipeline. Reaction was mixed, with labor unions asking the State Department to approve the project and a number of senators, mayors, and environmental groups expressing concern about the pipeline's impact. A year later, the State Department released a Supplemental Environmental Impact Statement, but it too met with criticism from environmentalists in Congress and in the EPA, who argued that it did not adequately respond to the concerns raised in the original draft statement. The State Department issued a Final Environmental Impact Statement in August, a month after the House of Representatives tried to expedite the process by requiring a decision on the project by November 1, 2011. On November 10, President Obama announced that no decision would be forthcoming until *after* the 2012 presidential election in order to give the administration time to assess alternative routes and further evaluate the project's impact on climate change. Undeterred, the House added a provision to payroll tax legislation, requiring the president to make a decision by February 21, 2012. Then, in January, the president denied TransCanada its presidential permit and signaled that TransCanada should reapply. In May 2012, TransCanada submitted a new application for the project, restarting the State Department's review process.

The following January, in a controversial decision, Nebraska's governor approved the new pipeline route through his state, apparently eliminating one obstacle to the project. In June, in a speech on climate change, Obama declared that the "net effects of the pipeline's impact on our climate will be absolutely critical to determining whether this project is allowed to go forward."[55] And, in January 2014, the State Department released a Final Environmental Impact Statement finding that the pipeline would *not* have a significant impact on climate change. This did not move the debate closer to conclusion. In April, the State Department indefinitely extended its review process following a ruling by a district judge in Nebraska that the governor did not have the constitutional authority to approve the route. With progress toward a decision stalled, both Houses of Congress passed a bill in early 2015 approving construction of the Keystone XL pipeline. Obama vetoed the bill on the grounds it eliminated his presidential authority to make the decision. In November 2015 he rejected the pipeline citing a State Department finding that it was not in the national interest.

FUTURE: ENVIRONMENTAL AND ENERGY ALTERNATIVES

Let us examine America's options for managing these global issues.

Ozone and Climate Change

Efforts to combat either ozone depletion or climate change tend to affect each other—in good and bad ways. Thus, phasing out ozone-depleting CFCs under the Montreal Protocol had unforeseen but positive climate effects, as CFCs are also greenhouse gases. However, some CFC alternatives exacerbate global warming more than carbon dioxide. We begin by examining unilateral, domestic options, as these are likely to be pursued in the near future. Each has potential benefits as well as potential risks. A successful climate strategy will not rely on any single option but will employ several.

Policy Options

a. *Support further research to reduce uncertainties about climate change,* the strategy favored by Presidents George H. W. Bush and George W. Bush. Proponents argue that new technologies and increasing wealth will make it easier for future generations to manage climate change and adapt to changes that do occur. Opponents counter that there is enough evidence to warrant action now, and if we wait it may be too late to avoid catastrophic consequences. There remains uncertainty about what temperature increases will produce a "tipping point" (the highest increase in average global temperatures before climate change becomes devastating and irreversible) and what political, economic, and social effects will follow. Continued research may be beneficial in informing how to mitigate and adapt to climate change.

However, there are policy questions that will not be informed by "stronger science." In regard to climate, most scientists agree that the warming that is occurring today has human causes, but they cannot reliably disentangle the human and natural causes. Many variables are involved, and relationships among them are complex. And even if scientists could agree on the tipping point or on the emissions reductions necessary to prevent it, it remains for society to determine how much climate change is acceptable. Do we only care about climate change once people are directly affected? Are we willing to act as soon as people anywhere are harmed or wait until Americans are affected? And who will pay for taking action? Even once the science is settled there remain political questions to resolve in formulating a policy response.

b. *Adopt market-based approaches to incentivize emissions reductions.* There are currently few economic incentives for industries or consumers to reduce greenhouse emissions. The impacts of these gases are "external costs" that are not built into the price of the goods or services that emit them. Our use of cars and most consumer goods, electricity, the construction of homes, and even our online habits add climate-altering emissions to the atmosphere. If the goods themselves do not produce emissions, their production and distribution do. Market-based approaches try to reduce demand for goods and services by attaching a price to the emissions they produce or the fuel that generates the emissions. This is achieved either by the tax structure or by creating a market for emissions in which companies buy and sell emissions "allowances." The first is a "carbon tax," and the second a "cap and trade" system. Both generate revenues, but their ability to alter consumer behavior is uncertain, particularly if alternate energy sources remain costly. Thus, market mechanisms alone will probably not be sufficient to prevent climate change.

Carbon taxes are levies on carbon emissions or on the fuel that produces them. Proponents argue that taxes would offer an economic incentive to reduce emissions and generate revenue that can be used for other purposes, including deficit reduction or reinvestment in new emission-reduction technologies. A carbon tax is controversial in the United States, where it is politically difficult to pass new taxes of any kind. Some also oppose a carbon tax for the unfair burden they believe it would impose on low-income citizens who must spend much of their income on energy. Even advocates of carbon taxes recognize that the devil is in the details. A carbon tax has been successfully used in Boulder, Colorado, since 2006. In 2012, residents voted to extend the tax, which generates about $1.9 million for the city at a yearly cost of $21 to residents.[56] But Australia, which implemented a national carbon tax in 2012, found it too costly for consumers and business and repealed the tax in 2014.

Cap and trade is a market-based mechanism used successfully in the 1990s in the United States to control the emissions that caused acid rain. The system imposes a "cap" (limit) on emissions, offering companies an emissions allowance, but it does not dictate how they use that allowance. To meet their cap, companies can switch to cleaner fuels like natural gas rather than coal, reduce output, or install technologies ("scrubbers") to collect harmful emissions before they are released. If companies do not reach their limit, they can sell their extra allowance to others—the "trade" in cap and trade. If they exceed their cap, they can buy additional allowances from those willing to sell. The price of allowances is determined by the market: how high the caps are—higher caps mean more and cheaper allowances and lower caps fewer and more expensive allowances—and how costly it is to reduce greenhouse emissions.

Proponents of cap and trade insist it is a flexible system that encourages firms to be innovative in limiting emissions, while opponents claim it is a hidden tax on business that will reduce efficiency and increase consumer costs. The reality is not that simple. How a cap and trade system is designed determines how much innovation is encouraged and at what cost. Which emissions should be capped? How should initial allowances be allocated among industries? Should allowances be given away, sold, or auctioned? The choice will have distributional and equity consequences. How should the initial price of emissions be set? Should there be limits to how high or low prices may go? Some conclude that stability may remove incentives for innovation while others argue that price uncertainty may harm innovation because firms will not invest in new technologies without high returns.[57]

c. *Commit to public investment—subsidies—in the research and development of clean energy such as solar and wind power.* This option removes some of the obstacles to innovation by removing the risk involved in developing new technologies, but it involves dependence on imports from countries like China. As a sole strategy the use of subsidies would be costly and politically controversial.

d. *Adopt an approach that directly regulates pollution levels.* Known as "command and control measures," such approaches place legal limits on pollution levels and may impose requirements on the types of equipment that must be used to reduce pollution. President Obama's 2014 climate proposal involves such a limit on pollution from transportation and power plants. It does not, however, require particular technologies to meet the legal limits. Instead, states may opt to pursue market-based strategies to meet the limits required by federal law. The advantage to a command and control strategy is that it is possible to keep emissions at desired levels. But there can be high compliance costs, particularly if the policy requires industry to adopt certain technologies and sets stringent limits.

e. *Employ geo-engineering to offset global warming.* Geo-engineering uses technology to counteract the warming that is occurring globally and would require global cooperation. It might involve removing carbon dioxide from the air, either by means of expensive scrubbing technologies or by planting trees and stimulating the growth of phytoplankton, effectively creating new carbon sinks. Alternatively, it might involve manipulating the amount of sunlight that is reflected back into the atmosphere—perhaps by injecting particles into the atmosphere that mimic the cooling effect of volcanic eruptions. It is difficult to know how successful they would be. Even if successful, they would probably involve other costs. One of the chemicals under consideration to decrease the earth's reflectiveness is sulfur dioxide, which produces sulfuric acid in the atmosphere that destroys ozone and causes acid rain.[58]

But how might Washington pursue multilateral solutions to climate change?

f. *Return as a full participant to the Kyoto Process.* Washington is a party to the Framework Convention on Climate Change but not the Kyoto Protocol. Many countries would like to see the United States join the Kyoto process and lead negotiations to draft a successor treaty. Without U.S. participation, global negotiations are unlikely to reduce emissions sufficiently to prevent average global temperatures from exceeding the level agreed upon in Copenhagen in 2009. But as long as developing countries are not required to make binding cuts, Washington's position is unlikely to change. China is now the world's largest emitter of greenhouse gases and if not required to limit its emissions, participation in the Kyoto process would place U.S. companies at a competitive disadvantage. U.S. foreign-policy officials insist that any arrangement must hold *all* countries accountable for their greenhouse emissions.

g. *Revise the Montreal Protocol to phase out CFC alternatives that contribute to the greenhouse effect.* The hole in the ozone layer and climate change are distinct problems, so why link policies? As noted earlier, the Montreal Protocol regime (the 1987 protocol and the amendments that have strengthened it) has been successful in phasing out ozone-depleting substances. Because HFCs, the favored CFC alternative, have no ozone-depleting effect, they are not covered by the Montreal regime, but some—including the Obama administration—argue they should be, as they are also powerful greenhouse gases. Employing the Montreal process to phase out HFCs would allow progress on climate change without negotiating a politically unpalatable climate change agreement. It would also be favorable to U.S. commercial interests because American companies no longer manufacture HFCs as competitively as they once did—HFCs are produced more cheaply in Asia—and the United States would be more competitive in manufacturing the new substitutes.

h. *Pursue multilateral discussions to manage climate change in a new negotiating forum.* According to one analysis, U.S. negotiators seem "ready to move beyond the UNFCCC."[59] U.S. officials could seek other forums or create a new one to reach a climate agreement that includes major sources of emissions like China. The way the deal was struck in Copenhagen and bilateral discussions between the United States and China in 2014 in which they agreed to seek a phase out of climate-warming HFCs under the Montreal Protocol suggest that this course may be fruitful. Negotiations among a few powerful countries might offer Washington greater leverage in crafting an agreement that could gain domestic acceptance. However, many countries would not wish such a change because a UN framework gives them a greater voice.

Biodiversity

The United States is one of three countries that have not ratified the Convention on Biodiversity, and it has only two options.

Policy Options

a. *Remain outside of the convention,* a likely preference for the foreseeable future owing to domestic politics. Influential firms in the pharmaceutical and biotechnology industries are opposed to participation because it would increase their costs. Some small firms, farmers, and ranchers fear that ratification would restrict their use of land or other resources. Other supporters of the status quo contend that since the United States is already a leader in conservation efforts, there is no need to ratify the treaty.

b. *Ratify the convention*, which would demonstrate U.S. leadership in environmental issues generally and biological diversity in particular. As a full party to the treaty, Washington would have a stronger voice in the process of reviewing the treaty and in shaping conservation policies elsewhere in the world and greater influence generally in environmental diplomacy.

Oil

Middle East oil has played a major role in U.S. foreign policy, and regional conflicts like Iraq's invasion of Kuwait in 1990 affect the price and availability of oil imported by America. Notwithstanding the rapidly expanding domestic production of oil in America in recent years that has reduced monthly imports, America imported over 300,000 barrels a month in 2013 compared to between 180,000 and 190,000 barrels a month in 1981.[60]

Policy Options

a. *Diversify oil sources by continuing to develop domestic production and importing more oil from Canada.* Technological advances have expanded the known oil reserves in the United States and Canada and made it cost-effective to extract previously inaccessible resources. Thus, energy independence is finally possible, but the infrastructure to deliver oil to refineries for processing is inadequate. One solution would be to expand the existing pipeline network with additional pipelines, including pipelines connecting Canada's oil fields with refineries in the United States. Environmentalists and private landowners over whose property pipelines would travel are opposed, but advocates insist that new technologies are safe and point out that the oil reserves will be exploited one way or another. In the absence of enhanced infrastructure, the options are to transport oil to the United States via rail (a dangerous and expensive alternative) or transport it elsewhere, for instance, to western ports for sale to Asia.

b. *Diversify oil sources but limit domestic production and foreign imports to light crude.* Some of the recently discovered oil is less environmentally friendly than the light crude that most U.S. and Canadian facilities are designed to refine. It contributes more greenhouse emissions and produces greater environmental harm in the event of spills. It also must be transported great distances to refineries capable of processing it.

The impact of growing North American energy production as well as greater energy efficiency and introduction of new sources of renewable energy is likely to be felt globally. The Arab oil weapon will not be available until non-OPEC oil production begins to fall, especially since members have not had individual quotas since 2012, and OPEC is likely to enjoy less global influence. The Saudis, for example, recognize the significance of U.S. shale oil and gas production. A related consequence will be greater U.S. ability to stabilize energy prices during crises in the Middle East and elsewhere. Thus, in the near future Washington will enjoy greater flexibility in its policies toward the region. It may choose to pay less attention to the Middle East or to have the luxury of adopting policies toward the Arab states with less concern about oil.

Whether oil production in the United States and elsewhere combined with energy conservation and renewable energy will stay abreast of global oil consumption in the developing world remains unclear.

Much depends on China and India. One energy analyst notes, "The growing economies of Asia get so much more marginal economic utility out of a gallon of fuel than we do. In a poorer country, you might have a couple guys on a moped, burning one gallon of fuel to get to the market and back. They get so much more economic value out of doing that than a construction worker in the United States gets in his pickup truck burning 5 gallons per day."[61] If he is correct, the oil-rich Arab Middle East will remain an important and contested geopolitical region in coming decades.

c. *Remain committed to the security of the oil-rich Arab states.* For decades, the United States provided security for conservative oil-rich states of the Middle East like Saudi Arabia. Washington already provides them with a security umbrella against Iran. However, those governments were disturbed by Washington's initial embrace of the Arab Spring, its willingness to desert Egypt's President Mubarak, and its failure to take military action against Iran or the Syrian regime (chapter 10).

America's growing domestic gas and oil production reduces but does not eliminate U.S. dependence on Middle East oil. Although Canada (1.2 billion barrels), Venezuela (288 million barrels), and Mexico (307 million barrels) contribute to U.S. oil imports, the Persian Gulf still remains a crucial source. Countries in that region accounted for 684 million barrels imported by America in 2014, of which Saudi Arabia accounted for 426 million.[62]

d. *Reduce Washington's commitment to the security of the oil-rich Arab states.* Even if the United States' need for Middle East oil continued to drop, threats to the security of major oil-producers could have dramatic consequences on energy prices, especially for U.S. allies in Europe and Asia that rely heavily on oil imports. China is on the verge of becoming the world's leading oil importer. Thus, if the United States severed its commitment to the security of the Persian Gulf states, China would be tempted to fill the security vacuum to protect its access to the energy that it requires. Even more dangerous is the possibility that, in the absence of America's security umbrella, Saudi Arabia might feel compelled to acquire its own weapons of mass destruction owing to the threat posed by a potentially nuclear-armed Iran.

CONCLUSION: ENVIRONMENT AND ENERGY ISSUES

This chapter has dealt with environment and energy, issues that are connected but that also have distinctive foreign-policy implications. Environmental issues became a priority for the Obama administration in its second term. The president's announcement of his climate policy in June 2014 was followed by his doubling the size of marine sanctuaries in the Pacific Ocean that will be off-limits to fishing or energy exploration. As a former EPA administrator argues, "These kinds of issues only get elevated if the president puts it high on his priority list."[63] But presidential support is rarely enough. Opponents of Obama's climate policy were quick to challenge it in the courts. While the Supreme Court upheld the EPA's authority to regulate greenhouse emissions from large industrial polluters including power plants and oil refineries, justices faulted the EPA's interpretation of the Clean Air Act, charging the agency with "tailoring" legislation to bureaucratic policy goals by reinterpreting the law.

Environmental issues get political traction when the costs of challenges like climate change are clear and imminent. In June 2014, a bipartisan group of political and economic leaders issued a report assessing the economic risks to America from climate change. The report recommended aggressive action by the business community to adapt to climate change and mitigate its effects by reducing emissions. "I have come to believe that climate change is the existential issue of our age," said Robert Rubin, treasury secretary under Bill Clinton.[64] Other environmental issues are linked to climate change. In addition to ozone depletion and biodiversity loss, deforestation, desertification, and the health of the oceans are both causes and effects of climate change.

America's foreign energy policy has been fairly consistent in seeking access to reliable sources of oil, especially from the Middle East. With the discovery of new recoverable energy sources in the United States and Canada, there is actually a surplus of oil in North America, promising—for a while—greater energy independence. Thus, in June 2014, the Obama administration took steps to allow the export of small amounts of oil after a forty-year ban on such exports if Congress approves. American oil executives sought this change as domestic production surpassed the capacity of domestic refineries. In addition, the Obama administration's decision in May 2015 to allow Shell to drill for oil off Alaska, a major victory for the oil industry, infuriated environmentalists. Nevertheless, the Middle East will remain an important focus for U.S. policymakers.

This new reality of abundant domestic energy resources and the rapid decline in oil prices in 2014 and 2015 benefited U.S. and Chinese consumers but proved economically devastating to producers including Russia, Iran, Venezuela, and Nigeria. It also had implications closer to home. Refineries in Canada like those in America are coping with a surplus of oil, and Canadian companies are eager to have it refined in the United States, where facilities are designed for processing and shipping heavy crude. Domestic concerns about the environmental impact of the Keystone XL Pipeline, however, have stalled the project, angering Canada. "We've never had a worse relationship with the United States," explained the leader of Canada's Liberal Party, "because perhaps our entire continental relationship has been reduced to not just one industry or one company but one single project."[65] The goals of energy independence, environmental conservation, and economic development involve different priorities, and the difficulties in balancing these will continue to infuse policy debate.

DISCUSSION QUESTIONS

1. Should the United States agree to binding limits to American greenhouse gas emissions even if developing countries do not do so?

2. Should the United States agree to a biodiversity agreement that will increase costs for U.S. pharmaceutical and biotechnology industries?

3. Should wealthy countries like the United States provide funds for environmental projects in the developing world?

4. What are the arguments in favor of and against construction of the Keystone XL pipeline?

5. Discuss the pros and cons of imposing a cap and trade system to manage carbon dioxide emissions?

6. How are environmental and energy issues linked?

KEY TERMS

biodiversity (p. 249)

carbon taxes (p. 260)

climate change (p. 241)

collective goods (p. 233)

global commons (p. 239)

global warming (p. 233)

greenhouse effect (p. 241)

greenhouse gases (p. 241)

ozone (p. 238)

ozone depletion (p. 238)

precautionary
   principle (p. 240)

Stockholm Convention on Persistent
   Organic Pollutants (p. 233)

sustainable environmental
   policy (p. 235)

tar sands (p. 232)

transboundary externalities (p. 237)

⑤SAGE edge™
for CQ Press

Sharpen your skill with SAGE edge at **edge.sagepub.com/mansbach**

SAGE edge for Students provides a personalized approach to help you accomplish your coursework goals in an easy-to-use learning environment.

9

America and the Palestinian-Israeli Imbroglio

President Barack
Obama and Israeli
Prime Minister
Benjamin Netanyahu:
worst of friends

Mark Wilson/Getty Images

America has been a staunch friend of Israel since its birth. Americans view Israel as a rare Middle Eastern democracy and an outpost of U.S. values. In addition to sharing democracy, both are economically developed countries with dense economic and social ties. Both stand for human rights (though Israel has violated Palestinian rights) and stress individualism and free-market capitalism. Although sentiment and shared values explain much of the relationship, Israel is a stable, powerful, and valuable geopolitical ally in an unstable and violent region.

SOURCES OF U.S. POLICY TOWARD ISRAEL

External factors were less central in shaping U.S. policy toward Israel in the 1940s and 1950s than in many other issues. America's failure to assist European Jews before World War II and the Holocaust produced guilt and sympathy for the plight of those who survived and for Israel as a small democratic country surrounded by large enemies. By contrast, key government agencies including the Departments of State and Defense argued that a pro-Israeli policy would harm U.S. relations with the oil-rich Arab states.

Individuals were crucial in mobilizing support for Israel in 1948, including President Harry Truman and Supreme Court Justices Louis Brandeis and Felix Frankfurter who were pro-Zionist. "A sentimental attachment to the ancient Hebrews infused the religious upbringing of Harry Truman and Lyndon Johnson, the two presidents who did most to cement American ties with Israel."[1]

Congress, responsive to societal factors like the voting strength of ethnic minorities in key constituencies, was supportive of a pro-Israeli policy. The Israel lobby, as we saw in chapter 1, is a source of controversy. Although there are many groups that seek close U.S.-Israeli ties, they are divided about how to achieve this. Some, for example, Christians United for Israel, want America to back all Israeli policies. Other groups, such as J Street, Americans for Peace Now, the Israel Policy Forum, and the Tikkun Community, while pro-Israeli, argue that Israel should seek to accommodate Palestinian interests. Such groups also provide campaign contributions to U.S. politicians, both Democrats and Republicans, who support Israel. In recent years, contributions from pro-Israeli groups have been directed increasingly to conservative congressional Republicans, unlike earlier decades when liberal congressional Democrats were the major recipients, in part because of perceived criticism of Israeli policies by the Obama administration.

The best-known pro-Israel group is the American Israel Public Affairs Committee (AIPAC), with over 100,000 members, which describes its mission as strengthening "the ties between the United States

Timeline

1900

1948 Founding of Israel and War of Independence

1956 Suez War

1964 PLO established

1967 Six-Day War

1973 Yom Kippur War

1977 Anwar Sadat visits Israel.

1900 (Continued)

1979 Israeli-Egyptian Peace Treaty

1982 Israeli invasion of Lebanon

1987 First intifada

1988 PLO accepts "Two-State" Solution.

1993 Oslo Peace Process

1995 Assassination of Yitzhak Rabin

and its ally Israel."[2] It "empowers pro-Israel activists across all ages, religions and races to be politically engaged and build relationships with members of Congress from both sides of the aisle to promote the U.S.-Israel relationship."[3] U.S. politicians routinely consult with or attend meetings of AIPAC, as did Vice President Joe Biden in 2013 when he assured his audience of U.S. willingness to use force against Iran if it acquired nuclear weapons.

AIPAC avoids being seen as promoting policies unpopular in America. During the 2013 controversy about whether to attack Syria after its use of chemical weapons, AIPAC cautiously lobbied Congress to support President Obama but did not want Israel to be seen as taking sides in America's domestic debate. Nor does the group always get what it wants. Its effort to get Congress to legislate additional sanctions against Iran—opposed by the president in the midst of negotiations with Tehran—narrowly fell short of mobilizing sufficient votes in the Senate to override a presidential veto or to sustain a filibuster as did its effort to defeat the Iran nuclear agreement.

Despite the Israel lobby, U.S. policy toward Israel has repeatedly shifted. Bill Clinton, for instance, pressed "Israel to make far-reaching concessions on the West Bank," while the Bush administration altered U.S. policy and stood by "Israeli Prime Minister Ariel Sharon" as he rejected "all talk of territorial concessions."[4] Pro-Israel groups urge Washington to provide economic and military assistance to Israel, but such aid would probably be forthcoming anyway owing to the convergence in U.S.-Israeli strategic interests.

Following Israel's independence, pro-Israeli sentiment in America was centered among liberal Democrats and labor unions that admired Israel's democracy and the socialist leanings of its leftist political parties and leaders like David Ben-Gurion. The sources of pro-Israeli sentiment shifted after Israel's Labor Party ceded political dominance in 1977 to hardliners in the rightwing Likud Party such as Menachem Begin, Yizthak Shamir, Ariel Sharon, and Benjamin Netanyahu. Increasingly, Israel's American advocates were conservatives associated with evangelical Christianity. Known as "Christian Zionists" and organized in groups like Christians United For Israel, they believe that the return of the Jewish people to Palestine was God's will and a precondition for the second coming of Christ as foretold by the Hebrew prophet Ezekiel. Evangelical leaders like Pat Robertson and Jerry Falwell were pro-Israeli, and at a meeting of evangelicals in 2006 attended by Republican politicians the Rev. John

2000

2000 Second intifada
2003 West Bank reoccupied by Israel
2003 U.S.-sponsored "Roadmap"
2005 Israel Leaves Gaza.
2006 Israel-Hezbollah War
2007 Hamas coup in Gaza
2008–2009 Israel-Hamas War

2000 (Continued)

2012 Gaza War
March **2013** President Obama visits Israel.
2013–2014 Peace talks resume and collapse.
2014 Israel-Hamas War
March **2015** Netanyahu reelected prime minister

Hagee called support for Israel "God's foreign policy."[5] In a 2011 poll, nearly two-thirds of America's evangelical Protestants and conservative Republicans thought that protecting Israel was an important foreign-policy goal.[6]

Some groups oppose Israel's occupation of the West Bank and East Jerusalem. The movement "Boycott, Divestment and Sanctions" has pressured Israel to cease settlement construction and leave the occupied territories. In 2014, the Presbyterian Church (USA) at its general convention narrowly voted to divest three U.S. companies that sold Israel equipment that aided settlement expansion. Following the 2014 Hamas-Israeli war, the boycott movement gained additional steam among Europeans.

In 1964, Egypt and the Arab League—an international organization that includes Palestine—established the Palestinian Liberation Organization (PLO) as an umbrella organization to coordinate Palestinian groups. And after 1967, the PLO became increasingly independent of its Arab patrons and was seen as representative of the Palestinians.

PAST: FROM ISRAEL'S BIRTH TO THE SIX-DAY WAR, 1948–1967

America has been deeply involved in relations between Israelis and Palestinians since the UN recommended Palestine's partition. Since then, American leaders have tried to balance support for Israel's security without alienating the Arab world with reconciling Israeli and Palestinian interests and ending the conflict that divides them.

Israel's Birth

The Middle East reflects nationalist, cultural, and religious passions. Its conflicts are rooted in history, and at their center are Israeli-Palestinian relations. Israel grew out of Zionism, a 19th-century movement in reaction to European anti-Semitism for the return of the Jewish people to their homeland, the biblical Land of Israel.

Jewish settlement in Palestine in the 1930s triggered conflict with Palestinian Arabs. As Jews arrived from Europe, Britain limited Jewish immigration to placate the Arabs whose support Britain sought as World War II loomed. The wartime Holocaust produced global sympathy for Jewish survivors who arrived in Palestine after the war, but the influx triggered additional violence. Faced with communal violence, Britain decided to surrender its mandate and turn the issue over to the UN. On November 29, 1947, the General Assembly voted to partition Palestine into two states, one Jewish and the other Arab. Jewish leaders accepted the plan, but Arab leaders rejected it. As Britain withdrew, Israel declared its independence on May 14, 1948, and five Arab armies invaded the new country. Washington recognized Israel's independence 11 minutes after it was declared.

There followed Israel's triumphal war of independence, with Israel governing three-quarters of Palestine. Jordan controlled East Jerusalem and the West Bank of the River Jordan, and Egypt occupied the Gaza Strip on the Mediterranean coast. The war produced hundreds of thousands of Arab Palestinian refugees who settled in camps in Jordan, Syria, Lebanon, and Gaza, where they became wards of the UN Relief and Works Agency. Some had fled voluntarily while others had been driven out. The establishment of Israel and the flight of Arab Palestinians became known to Palestinians as "al-Nakba," or catastrophe.

KEY DOCUMENT
The Balfour Declaration

In November 1917, British Foreign Secretary Arthur Balfour wrote a letter to Baron Rothschild to be forwarded to Great Britain's Zionist Federation declaring, "His Majesty's government view with favor the establishment in Palestine of a national home for the Jewish people, and will use their best endeavors to facilitate the achievement of this object, it being clearly understood that nothing shall be done which may prejudice the civil and religious rights of existing non-Jewish communities in Palestine, or the rights and political status enjoyed by Jews in any other country." Thus, the Balfour Declaration gave incompatible assurances to Jews and Arabs, legitimating a Jewish homeland in Palestine that Britain administered as a League of Nations mandate.

Source: Modern History Sourcebook, "The Balfour Declaration," http://www.fordham.edu/halsall/mod/balfour.asp.

The Six-Day War and Its Consequences

Israel's triumph in the 1967 Six-Day War against Egypt, Syria, and Jordan transformed the region. Israeli occupation of the Sinai Peninsula, the Gaza Strip, the West Bank, the Golan Heights, and Jerusalem doubled its territory. Thereafter, Washington sought to broker a settlement that would recognize the security claims of Israelis and Palestinian demands for autonomy. Since 2001, Washington has supported establishing an independent Palestinian state. This policy has posed a dilemma for U.S. leaders—how can Washington support Israel while earning the trust of Palestinians and bringing about a "two-state" (Israel and Palestine) solution? At some moments, peace has seemed tantalizingly close, only to prove illusory.

Following the Six-Day War, the UN Security Council unanimously adopted Resolution 242, which shaped later debate about the issue. Resolution 242 was adopted under Chapter VI of the UN Charter, "pacific resolution of disputes," labeling neither Israel nor its Arab neighbors as aggressors. It required adversaries to negotiate its meaning and implementation. Negotiation was needed to establish "a just and lasting peace in the Middle East" to be based on "withdrawal of Israel armed forces from territories occupied" in 1967 and "respect for and acknowledgment of the sovereignty, territorial integrity and political independence of every State in the area and their right to live in peace within secure and recognized boundaries free from threats or acts of force." Israel was expected to trade territories it had conquered in return for peace.

Resolution 242 remained a contested topic owing to the adversaries' divergent interpretations. What constituted "secure and recognized boundaries"? Inasmuch as the Arabs had rejected the UN partition and Israel's boundaries were the outcome of war rather than a peace treaty, those boundaries could be

MAP 9.1   Occupied Territories, Israeli Settlements, and Palestinian
Refugee Camps

considered temporary rather than definitive. Israel also argued that for its boundaries to be "secure" it had to retain some of the occupied territory. Moreover, declaring the "inadmissibility of the acquisition of territory by war" but not requiring Israel to leave *all* "occupied territories," did Resolution 242 imply Israel could retain some of the territories it regarded as necessary for security? Finally, "Palestinians" were not explicitly mentioned in the resolution except for an allusion to "a just settlement of the refugee problem." Did that phrase endorse the right of return to *all* Palestinian refugees or only some? Did a "just" settlement require establishing a sovereign Palestinian state? Such differences would continue to bedevil Israeli-Palestinian relations, but the resolution's ambiguity suited President Lyndon Johnson's desire to allow Israel to retain its conquests until its Arab neighbors were prepared to agree to peace.

The Six-Day War traumatized Palestinians who realized Arab governments were pursuing their own interests. Some years earlier, Yasser Arafat had secretly established al-Fatah (the Movement for the National Liberation of Palestine) with the aims of destroying Israel and establishing a Palestinian state. Fatah began launching attacks against Israel from Gaza, Lebanon, and Jordan in 1965, becoming the leading group in the PLO. Thereafter, Palestinian groups intensified attacks against Israel including the murder of Israeli athletes by Black September at the 1972 Munich Olympics. In 1974, the General

🔑 KEY DOCUMENT
UN Resolution 242

1. *Affirms* that the fulfillment of Charter principles requires the establishment of a just and lasting peace in the Middle East which should include the application of both the following principles:

   (i) Withdrawal of Israel armed forces from territories occupied in the recent conflict;

   (ii) Termination of all claims or states of belligerency and respect for and acknowledgment of the sovereignty, territorial integrity and political independence of every State in the area and their right to live in peace within secure and recognized boundaries free from threats or acts of force;

2. *Affirms further* the necessity

   (a) For guaranteeing freedom of navigation through international waterways in the area;

   (b) For achieving a just settlement of the refugee problem;

   (c) For guaranteeing the territorial inviolability and political independence of every State in the area, through measures including the establishment of demilitarized zones.

Source: UN Security Council, Resolution 242 (November 1967), http://unispal.un.org/unispal.nsf/0/7 D35E1F729DF491C85256EE700686136.

Assembly granted the PLO "observer entity" status, recognizing it as the "representative of the Palestinian people," and the PLO tentatively contemplated negotiating a diplomatic solution while still calling for Israel's destruction. The PLO was seen as a future government for a Palestinian state—the Palestinian Authority (PA)—with a legislature, the Palestinian Legislative Council. Arafat remained PLO chairman and Palestinian president until his death in 2004 and was succeeded by Mahmoud Abbas.

PRESENT: 1967–2015

Over time, events transformed the issue from a territorial dispute between Israel and its Arab neighbors into the effort of Palestinians to end Israel's occupation of territories conquered in 1967 and establish a state. In 1982, Israel invaded Lebanon, which had hosted the PLO after its expulsion from Jordan in 1970, and the PLO's leaders were forced to flee to Tunisia. The PLO was taken by surprise by the first intifada (popular uprising) in 1987 in the West Bank and Gaza. In 1988, Fatah endorsed a two-state solution subject to the right of return for Palestinian refugees and liberation of the occupied territories. Only in 1993 did the PLO recognize Israel and Israel recognize the PLO as representing the Palestinians. In 1996, the PLO deleted those articles in its charter that endorsed armed struggle and the destruction of the Jewish state.

American Policy and the Israeli-Palestinian Peace Process

After failing to recover territory lost to Israel in 1967, Egypt's President Anwar Sadat concluded in 1973 that military action was necessary.

The Yom Kippur War   Egypt and Syria launched a surprise attack against Israel on October 6, 1973, Yom Kippur, the holiest day in the Jewish calendar. After briefly losing part of the Sinai and the Golan Heights, the war ended with a ceasefire after Israel regained the areas it had lost and had driven Egyptian forces back across the Suez Canal, threatening the annihilation of Egypt's Third Army.

Washington viewed the conflict through the prism of America's need for Middle East oil and the credibility of its commitment to Israeli security. The superpowers provided their clients with massive amounts of additional military equipment. U.S. aid to Israel triggered an effort by the Arab members of the Organization of Petroleum Exporting Countries to embargo oil exports to America and its allies, causing a worldwide spike in oil prices (chapter 8). Israel's advance into Egypt heightened tension between the superpowers, leading Washington to raise the level of its nuclear alert. The crisis induced Secretary of State Henry Kissinger to persuade Israel to permit the resupply of Egyptian forces, confirming Sadat's belief in the political benefits of the war, which raised Arab morale and revealed how dependent Israel had become on U.S. political and economic support.

Kissinger **mediated** a ceasefire and a partial Israeli withdrawal from Sinai in January 1974, paving the way for Sadat's dramatic visit to Israel and Egypt's peaceful reacquisition of the entire Sinai. Kissinger's role in the settlement made it clear Washington was the key player in subsequent events. "Sometime in the mid-1970s the term *peace process* began to be widely used to describe the American-led efforts to bring about a negotiated peace between Israel and its Arab neighbors. The phrase stuck, and ever since it has been synonymous with the gradual step-by-step approach to resolving one of the world's most difficult conflicts."[7]

The Peace Process Begins The prospect of Egyptian-Israeli peace persuaded President Jimmy Carter to seek a comprehensive settlement. After visiting Israel, Egypt, and Jordan, Carter convened a multinational meeting in Geneva, Switzerland, to negotiate Israel's withdrawal from the occupied territories, Arab recognition of Israel, and reunification of Jerusalem. However, on November 20, 1977, Sadat transformed regional politics with a three-day visit to Jerusalem, where he was greeted by Israeli Prime Minister Begin and spoke before Israel's parliament. "We really and truly welcome you," declared Sadat, "to live among us in peace and security."[8]

Sadat was less interested in the multilateral Geneva talks than in a bilateral agreement with Israel that would not deal with the Palestinian issue. Carter, who had no advance knowledge of Sadat's visit to Israel, organized a meeting between Sadat and Begin at the presidential retreat at Camp David, Maryland. For Begin, a bilateral meeting was also preferable to an international conference because he would not have to address Israel's occupation of the West Bank. For Sadat, a meeting offered the prospect of Western economic aid, American friendship, and the return of the Sinai Peninsula. The Camp David meeting lasted thirteen days, climaxing with an agreement on September 17, 1978—Framework for Peace in the Middle East (the "Camp David Accords"). The accords became possible when Begin agreed to allow Israel's parliament to decide the fate of Israeli settlements in Sinai, and Carter postponed his effort to resolve the status of the West Bank.

The Camp David Accords consisted of two agreements. The first committed participants to negotiate about providing "full autonomy" and a "self-governing authority" for Palestinians in Gaza and the West Bank leading to a withdrawal of Israeli troops. The second sketched out terms for a 1979 Egyptian-Israeli peace treaty. Under the treaty, Egypt formally recognized Israel, limited its military presence in Sinai, and gave Israel access to the Suez Canal and Red Sea in return for withdrawal of Israel's armed forces and settlers from Sinai. Washington agreed to provide economic and military aid to both countries. Begin and Sadat were awarded a Nobel Peace Prize, and the treaty has remained in effect since. The two countries exchanged ambassadors in 1980, and Egypt began to sell oil to Israel. The treaty was unpopular in the Arab world, and Egypt was expelled from the Arab League and not readmitted for a decade.

Although a step toward peace, the Camp David Accords had little impact on Israeli-Palestinian relations. In 1988, Jordan surrendered its claim to the West Bank and Jerusalem, leaving the Palestinians to negotiate directly with Israel. After defeating Iraq and liberating Kuwait in 1991, U.S. influence seemed unchallenged in the Middle East, and Washington concluded it could resolve the Israel-Palestinian issue.

From Madrid to Oslo President George H. W. Bush and Secretary of State James Baker were determined to press Israel to surrender the occupied territories in return for peace. To this end, they organized a multilateral conference in Madrid, Spain. Initially, Israel, led by Prime Minister Yitzhak Shamir, who had succeeded Begin, resisted until Baker threatened to withhold U.S. loan guarantees to resettle Russian Jewish immigrants in Israel. The threat mobilized pro-Israeli domestic groups and aroused fierce debate in America. It became a sore point in U.S.-Israeli relations when the Bush administration linked the loan request to Israel's willingness to cease settlement expansion, and Congress refused to overrule the president. The loan dispute played a role in the 1992 electoral victory of Yitzhak Rabin, who was committed to ending settlement expansion. Thereafter Congress agreed to the loan guarantees.

The Madrid conference was the first direct negotiation between Israel and its adversaries, except Egypt. "To much pomp and publicity, the peace conference opened on October 30, 1991, in the Spanish capital. Millions around the world delighted to the sight of Israeli and Arab leaders gathered in the rococo Royal Palace (from which a portrait of Charles V massacring Moors had been hastily removed) and seated around the same ornate table."[9] Despite the animosity of the participants, U.S. representatives managed to get agreement on a two-tier framework of bilateral and multilateral negotiations on several issues. Bilateral talks between Israelis and Palestinians were based on a proposed two-step process—interim Palestinian self-government followed by permanent status talks.

Israel, however, refused to budge regarding the occupied territories, while the Palestinians continued to demand establishment of a Palestinian state in those areas. Nor could Syria and Israel bridge their disagreement over Israeli occupation of the Golan Heights. Owing to such differences, negotiations concerning issues like refugees and economic development proved fruitless. By 1994, it was clear the talks had failed. Baker later described the conference as "a rich tale of determination, false starts, personal and political courage, blind alleys, perseverance, misjudgments, lost tempers, endless negotiations, scores of creative compromises, and both good faith and bad."[10] Although the Madrid talks continued fitfully in public, secret **back-channel** meetings between Palestinians and Israelis were occurring in Oslo, Norway.

The Oslo Accords and Camp David Summits   On September 13, 1993, Rabin and Arafat signed the Declaration of Principles on Interim Self-Government Arrangements at the White House. Along with Israeli Foreign Minister Shimon Peres, Rabin would receive a 1994 Nobel Peace Prize. Standing next to President Clinton, Arafat declared, "We must realize the prophecy of Isaiah, that the cry of violence shall no more be heard in your land, nor wrack nor ruin within your borders." Rabin replied, "Let me say to you, the Palestinians, we are destined to live together on the same soil in the same land," and "we say to you today, in a loud and clear voice: enough of blood and tears. Enough!"[11]

The Declaration of Principles was followed in 1994 by an Israeli-Jordanian peace treaty mediated by Clinton, and the two countries normalized their relations. Thereafter, an interim agreement concerning steps to carry out the Oslo Accords was signed in September 1995. It recognized the PLO as the legitimate representative of the Palestinians, established a self-governing Palestinian Authority (PA) in the West Bank, and a "mutual commitment to act, in accordance with this agreement, immediately, efficiently and effectively against acts or threats of terrorism, violence or incitement, whether committed by Palestinians or Israelis."[12] The West Bank was divided into three areas—Area A where the PA enjoyed full civil and security control, Area B under Palestinian civil control and joint Palestinian-Israeli security control, and Area C encompassing strategically sensitive locations remaining under Israeli control. Article 31 declared: "Neither side shall initiate or take any step that will change the status of the West Bank and the Gaza Strip pending the outcome of the permanent status negotiations."[13] The Palestinians believed Article 31 required cessation of Israeli settlement construction. In October 1998, the two parties signed the Wye River Memorandum in the company of President Clinton in which they agreed to take additional steps toward carrying out the interim agreement. The Oslo Accords and the interim agreement marked a high point in the peace process. In ensuing years, the PLO formally recognized Israel while the PA took control of local government and internal security in Gaza and major West Bank cities with Ramallah as its administrative capital. Self-government was supposed to last five years, after which a permanent agreement would take effect.

Although the Oslo Accords focused on security issues, economic cooperation and development were important if the Palestinians were to embrace peace. Thus, the accords called for economic cooperation and development for the region as well as multilateral economic assistance for the Palestinians involving America, the European Union (EU), and other donors. By 1997, foreign aid accounted for about 15 percent of the Palestinians' gross national product, and the Clinton administration hoped for dramatic economic improvement and an inflow of private investment after a final status agreement was reached.

The Oslo Accords, however, triggered the assassination of Prime Minister Rabin in November 1995 and eroded Palestinian support for Arafat. The peace process ground to a halt, and planning for economic development ended after Israeli elections in 1996 returned to power a hardline coalition led by the Likud Party with Netanyahu as prime minister. Terrorism continued, and a wave of Palestinian suicide attacks took place before Israel's election.

Although Rabin and his successors slowed expansion of Israeli settlements at the request of Secretary of State Madeleine Albright, expansion of existing settlements continued. Elections in 1999 saw the victory of Labor Party leader Ehud Barak, who continued expanding existing settlements to the dismay of Arafat, who regarded the policy as contrary to the spirit of the Oslo Accords and Article 31 of the Interim Agreement and prejudicial to a final territorial settlement.

The closest that Israelis and Palestinians came to a final agreement owed much to President Clinton's efforts at summit conferences with Barak and Arafat at Camp David in 2000. Under terms proposed by Clinton and accepted by Israel, the Palestinians would receive all of Gaza and most of the West Bank except for a small area that was the site of heavily populated Jewish settlement blocs in exchange for which an equivalent area in Israel would be added to Gaza. Arab neighborhoods in Jerusalem would be turned over to the Palestinians, and both sides would declare the city their capital.

Talks between Barak and Arafat at Taba, Egypt, in early 2001 were a last-ditch effort to reach agreement. Negotiators agreed that Resolution 242 would be the basis for borders between Israel and a Palestinian state. Israel demanded sovereignty over settlement blocs containing 80 percent of Jewish residents in the West Bank and Gaza, which comprised about 6 percent of these territories, in return for territorial compensation elsewhere. At a White House meeting in December 2000, Clinton proposed the parameters for a territorial swap in which between 94 and 96 percent of the West Bank territory should constitute a Palestinian state. "The land annexed by Israel should be compensated by a land swap of 1 to 3 percent"[14] that would minimize annexed areas and the number of Palestinians affected.

However, disagreement persisted over the extent of Israel's "security settlements," and talks ended owing to an imminent Israeli election that brought to power a hardline coalition led by Ariel Sharon. In the end, Arafat, whom Clinton blamed for the failed outcome, balked, rejecting the most generous terms for a settlement offered until then by an Israeli leader. Under pressure from Clinton, whose presidency was ending, Arafat and Barak had come close to a final status agreement.

The Second Intifada Complicating negotiations was the onset of the second intifada in September 2000 during which 3,000 Palestinians and 1,000 Israelis died. The failure of negotiations and continued Israeli settlement expansion had heightened tension, but violence was triggered when Sharon, then a candidate to become Israel's prime minister, escorted by 1,000 police officers provocatively visited Jerusalem's Temple Mount, the site of the Dome of the Rock and the al-Aqsa Mosque, on September 28. The two sites were holy to both Muslims and Jews. Sharon declared that the area would remain under Israel's control and that he merely wished to pray at the Temple Mount.

Israeli wall surrounding the Shuafat refugee camp in East Jerusalem

Ahmad Gharablia/AFP/Getty Images

The ensuing car bombs, riots, kidnappings, rocket attacks from Gaza, and suicide attacks in Israeli cities were regarded by Israelis as terrorist acts and by Palestinians as justifiable national resistance. In response, Israeli forces demolished the homes of families of suicide bombers, reoccupied West Bank towns, used airstrikes, and resorted to mass arrests and targeted killings of foes including Hamas leader Sheikh Ahmed Yassin. Matters deteriorated after the failure of the Taba meeting. Violence took place in West Bank cities like Jenin and Bethlehem and continued until 2005, dooming any prospect for a settlement. The second intifada and the suicide bombings in Israel triggered its decision to build a security barrier along the West Bank running over 400 miles. Opponents of the barrier contended it was illegal under international law because it enclosed and therefore annexed Palestinian lands, a position upheld in a 2004 advisory opinion of the International Court of Justice.

The "Roadmap" and Its Failure The peace process came to a halt, and Israel refused negotiations proposed by the Arab League in 2002. A "roadmap" for peace leading to a Palestinian state was proposed by Washington, the EU, and the UN after the appointment of Mahmoud Abbas as PA Prime Minister in 2003 and after America and Israel refused to deal with Arafat any longer because of his continued association with violent elements in the PLO. Arafat had been besieged in Ramallah by Israeli troops, where he remained isolated until his death in 2004.

The roadmap involved a series of reciprocal steps—the first an end to Palestinian violence followed by a cessation of Israel's settlement construction, and, if all went well, the establishment of a democratic Palestinian state, which President George H. W. Bush sought to achieve by 2005. Bush, Sharon, and Abbas met in Aqaba, Jordan, in 2003, but the ceasefire that was declared proved temporary. In early 2004, Prime Minister Sharon announced that Israeli settlements in Gaza would be dismantled followed by a unilateral withdrawal of Israeli troops. Despite settler protests, Israel's disengagement took place in

August 2005, creating a power vacuum Hamas would later fill. At a summit at Sharm el-Sheikh, Egypt, in February 2005 attended by Jordan's King Abdullah and Egypt's President Hosni Mubarak, Sharon publicly committed Israel to the establishment of a Palestinian state, and Abbas called for an end to the intifada. Owing to a resumption of Palestinian violence and Israeli retaliation, however, the parties were unable to continue the process, and Israel continued to construct its barrier on the West Bank.

The Geneva Accord

DID YOU KNOW

An effort to achieve peace took place at an *unofficial* conference that brought prominent Israeli and Palestinian politicians to Geneva in 2003. The negotiators went beyond the incremental road-map and sought a comprehensive "final status" agreement to resolve the issues of Jerusalem and Jewish settlements in the occupied territories and the return of Palestinian refugees to their homes. Negotiation produced a nonbinding Draft Permanent Status Agreement that called for a two-state solution in which each recognized the legitimacy of the other's right to exist and territorial boundaries that would give Palestinians much of Gaza and the West Bank. Both would have their capitals in their areas of Jerusalem. Israel would "be responsible for resettling the Israelis residing in Palestinian sovereign territory outside this territory."

Source: OPT: Geneva Initiative—Draft Permanent Status Agreement, October 12, 2003, http://reliefweb.int/report/israel/opt-geneva-initiative-draft-permanent-status-agreement.

Efforts to revive the peace process were complicated by the emergence of two extremist groups—Hamas, an offshoot of Egypt's Muslim Brotherhood, and Hezbollah, a Shia Islamic group aided by Iran. Neither recognized Israel's right to exist. Both threatened Israeli security and were designated terrorist groups by America and the EU (until the EU's General Court removed this designation of Hamas in late 2014).

Hamas ("Islamic Resistance Movement")

Sheikh Yassin founded Hamas in 1987 during the first intifada, drawing support from Palestinians who regarded Arafat and the PLO as authoritarian, corrupt, and ineffective. Advocating Israel's destruction, Hamas sought to establish an *Islamic* Palestinian state. Its 1988 covenant committed it to "raise the banner of Allah over every inch of Palestine" (Article 6) and rejected "so-called peaceful solutions and international conferences" that contradicted "the principles of the Islamic Resistance Movement" (Article 13).[15] Hamas's military wing was responsible for guerrilla attacks and many suicide bombings in Israel during the second intifada. Hamas opposed the Oslo Accords and repeatedly sought to undermine the peace process.

In 2006, Hamas won an electoral majority in the Palestinian legislature. Following violent clashes with Fatah, it seized power in Gaza in June 2007 while Fatah retained control of the West Bank. This led to a division of Palestinian territory and continued tension between the two groups. Thereafter, Israel and Egypt isolated Gaza, and America cut off aid to Gaza's Palestinians. Since Hamas took control of Gaza, its relations with Israel have seesawed between spasms of violence and uneasy ceasefires. Periodic

Hamas, Hezbollah, and Iran

Cartoons by Barry, Creative Commons Attribution-ShareAlike 2.0 Generic (CC BY-SA 2.0)

efforts to mediate the rift among the Palestinians failed, and rockets fired by Gaza militants led Israel to blockade the territory and destroy the tunnels built to smuggle in weapons. Israel's blockade produced an economic and humanitarian crisis in Gaza that led to a crisis with Turkey in 2010 after nine Turks who were trying to break the blockade died in a skirmish with Israeli soldiers who boarded their vessel.

After the Gaza coup d'état, prospects for peace grew increasingly remote. The Palestinian schism complicated negotiations for establishing a single Palestinian state. Neither America nor Israel was prepared to negotiate with a "terrorist" group. Intermittent rocket fire from Gaza followed by Israeli retaliation continued between 2005 and 2008 when Egypt mediated a ceasefire. Following Hamas's kidnapping of an Israeli soldier, Israel invaded Gaza and launched airstrikes against Hamas in December 2008 ("Operation Cast Lead") to suppress rocket fire from Gaza and destroy Hamas's stockpiles of weapons. The soldier, Gilad Shalit, remained a hostage from 2006 until 2011 when he was exchanged for over 1,000 Palestinians imprisoned by Israel. Three weeks after its incursion, Israel withdrew from Gaza, leaving Hamas in power. Episodic violence continued, and after several Egyptian soldiers were killed in 2012 near Gaza's border, Egyptian security forces halted the movement of goods through tunnels linking Gaza to Egypt, squeezing Gaza's fragile economy.

An effort to bridge the Palestinian schism in 2011 led Hamas to agree that its resistance would be peaceful, but the group failed to suppress violent militants from other Palestinian factions. After Iranian-supplied missiles were fired from Gaza, some with the range to reach Tel Aviv and Jerusalem, Israel renewed intensive bombing of Hamas in 2012, while using its U.S.-financed mobile Iron Dome anti-missile system. Israel seemed about to invade Gaza again when Secretary of State Hillary Clinton rushed back from

Southeast Asia and, aided by Egypt's President Mohamed Morsi, persuaded Israel to desist. The Egyptian revolution (chapter 10) that brought Morsi to power in 2012 had strengthened Hamas because Egypt's Islamic government sympathized with its aims, but Morsi's overthrow a year later again isolated the group. By late 2013 Hamas was bankrupt.

The third and bloodiest Israeli-Hamas war erupted in 2014. Three Israeli teenagers were kidnapped and murdered on the West Bank by members of Hamas, and a Palestinian teenager was murdered in retaliation. Netanyahu declared that the events showed that Israel would have to maintain a long-term presence in the West Bank. Hamas resumed missile attacks, and Netanyahu under domestic political pressure retaliated with airstrikes and sent soldiers again into Gaza ("Operation Protective Edge") to

Israel's Iron Dome anti-missile system

Jack Guez/AFP/Getty Images

end missile attacks and close down tunnels through which Hamas was infiltrating militants into Israel.

After several abortive ceasefires, an open-ended and vaguely worded ceasefire was reached. Neither side had achieved its objectives. Hamas sought to end Israel's blockade of Gaza, its political isolation, and its financial woes, but with hostile regimes in Egypt and Syria it remained isolated. "In all the other invasions and assaults on Gaza," wrote a Palestinian analyst, "there was at least some government that would come out and talk about how what Israel was doing was illegal and show some support. This time around, there's been nothing."[16] Israel sought to disarm Hamas, destroying its arsenal of rockets and the tunnels it had built into Israel. In this it was only partly successful, and Hamas had grown more popular in Gaza.

In a repeat of earlier wars with Hamas, there were numerous Palestinian civilian casualties prompting Amnesty International to accuse Israel of war crimes and straining U.S.–Israeli relations. "This is the most sustained period of antagonism in the relationship," declared a former U.S. ambassador to Israel. "I don't know how the relationship recovers as long as you have this president and this prime minister."[17] With American public opinion and Congress supporting Israel's military operation and Arab governments remaining silent, the Obama administration had little influence over Israel. Protests in sympathy with Gaza's residents took place in Europe as well as eruptions of ugly anti-Semitic incidents. Israel's sense of insecurity had deepened, and domestic fissures had reopened.

If Hamas threatened Israel's southwestern border, the paramilitary group Hezbollah, located in southern Lebanon on Israel's northern border, which both Washington and the EU regard as a terrorist organization, posed as great a threat owing to links with Iran and its global reach—reflected in the group's bombing of a Jewish synagogue in Argentina in 1994.

Hezbollah ("Party of God")

Lebanon's population is a religious and ethnic mosaic. Its Muslim majority is divided into Sunni, Shia, and Druze communities, and its Christians include Maronites, Greek Orthodox, and Greek Catholics. Lebanon also hosts a large Palestinian refugee population. To minimize communal conflict, Lebanon's constitution reserves parliamentary seats for different sects. The country's president must be a Maronite Christian, its prime minister a Sunni Muslim, and the Speaker of parliament a Shia Muslim.

These communities view one another with suspicion and have their own political parties, territorial fiefs, and paramilitary militias. Between 1975 and 1990, the country descended into bloody sectarian war. Syria intervened in 1976 and dominated Lebanese politics until 2005 when it was linked to several assassinations including that of a former Lebanese prime minister. Israel invaded Lebanon in 1978 and in 1982 seeking to set up a security zone in south Lebanon. Its 1982 intervention climaxed with a siege of Lebanon's capital, Beirut, the massacre of Palestinians in two refugee camps by Israeli-supported Christian militias, and the PLO's expulsion from the country. Israel withdrew from most of Lebanon in 1985, retaining a buffer zone in the south. These events prepared the ground for Hezbollah's emergence.

Hezbollah attracted support from Lebanon's Shia population and championed the Palestinian cause. It became a major actor after Iran's 1979 Islamic revolution and Israel's 1982 invasion of Lebanon. Following the invasion, U.S. Marines entered Lebanon as part of a multinational force sent to oversee the PLO's withdrawal to Tunisia. In April, Hezbollah car-bombed America's embassy in Beirut and in October launched devastating suicide attacks against U.S. and French troops in the city. The remaining American Marines left in 1983. Hezbollah remained aligned with Syria and Iran and sought to drive Israel from Lebanon. During the 1980s, the group attacked Israel, kidnapped Westerners, and, during Lebanon's civil war, consolidated its influence among Lebanon's Shiites.

The Beirut Marine Barracks Bombing

Hezbollah's suicide bombing of the Marine barracks in Beirut, Lebanon, on October 23, 1983, resulted in the largest one-day loss of Marine lives since the World War II Battle of Iwo Jima.

Following Lebanon's civil war, Hezbollah continued attacking Israeli soldiers until Israel withdrew from Lebanon in 2000. Claiming responsibility for ending the Israeli presence, Hezbollah leader Hassan Nasrallah acquired unrivaled popularity in Lebanon's Shia community. Thereafter, Hezbollah's dependence on Iran grew as it harassed Israeli forces in cross-border raids. It also funded itself from the South American cocaine trade and drug smuggling in West Africa, laundering funds using Lebanese money-exchange houses to move millions of dollars in drug profits through America's banks. "Hezbollah is operating like a major drug cartel,"[18] declared an agent for America's Drug Enforcement Agency. According to a law-enforcement agent, "They operate like the Gambinos [a New York crime family] on steroids."[19]

Following Hezbollah's abduction of two Israeli soldiers in July 2006 to barter for the release of Lebanese imprisoned by Israel, Israel launched a major assault against the group, resulting in over 1,000 Lebanese deaths and destruction of large areas of Beirut. In retaliation, Hezbollah fired Iranian rockets at Israeli cities resulting in 55 Israeli deaths.[20] A UN-brokered truce took effect in August, and Security Council Resolution 1701 provided for peacekeepers in southern Lebanon and required Hezbollah to disarm. Hezbollah refused to do so, and, owing to its resistance against Israel's incursion, was acclaimed in much of the Arab world. Hezbollah was rearmed by Iran, adding sophisticated Iranian missiles to its arsenal. It continued to act as Iran's proxy, a role reflected in attacks against Israeli citizens overseas.

Hezbollah sought to use its prestige to cement its influence in Lebanon. After clashes with Lebanon's armed forces and opposition to Lebanon's government, the group emerged as the country's leading power broker—a state within the state—with a capacity to veto government action. In 2009, Hezbollah entered the government. With the onset of Syria's civil war in 2011, Hezbollah faced the prospect that Iran's ally, the regime of Bashar al-Assad, might be overthrown. Thus, it intervened to aid Assad, alienating Sunni Muslims in Syria and Lebanon and muddying its reputation as a foe of Israel (chapter 11).

Israel avoided involvement in Syria's civil war, but its leaders were dismayed by American reluctance to respond militarily to Assad's use of chemical weapons, believing that Iran would conclude that U.S. threats against its acquiring nuclear weapons were not credible. Israel also made it clear it would not permit the transfer of sophisticated weapons from Syria to Hezbollah, attacking Syrian convoys and storage facilities to prevent Hezbollah from acquiring "game changing" weapons like surface-to-sea missiles, surface-to-air missiles, and Iranian mobile surface-to-surface missiles. These attacks were part of Israel's continuing conflict with Iran and Hezbollah rather than efforts to alter the outcome of Syria's civil war.

Israel and Iran's "Existential Threat"

Although we dealt with Iran's effort to acquire nuclear weapons earlier, it merits additional discussion here because of Israel's concern that such weapons would pose an existential threat to the Jewish state. Israel sought to blunt Iran's nuclear ambitions by assassinating prominent scientists involved in Iran's nuclear program and, with American cooperation, launching a cyberattack in 2010 to infiltrate the computer system at Iran's Natanz facility. Iran's election in 2013 of President Hassan Rouhani to succeed the hardline Mahmoud Ahmadinejad and Rouhani's overtures to the West raised Israeli suspicions that his "moderation" was an effort to delay matters while progressing toward acquiring weapons of mass destruction (WMD).

Although America and Israel agree that Iran should not be permitted to acquire nuclear weapons, they differ over if and when military action would be needed. Michael Oren, formerly Israeli ambassador to Washington, explained, "America's clock is large and slow, and our clock is small and fast. And what we have is this dialogue between clocks."[21] Netanyahu laid out Israel's perspective: "Our clocks are ticking at a different pace. We're closer than the United States, we're more vulnerable, and therefore we'll have to address this question of whether to stop Iran before the United States does."[22] Whereas

Netanyahu predicted that Iran would overcome most impediments to building a nuclear weapon by the spring or summer of 2013, President Obama claimed that it would take Iran a year or two to reach that objective, time for negotiations to avoid war. Thereafter Netanyahu argued that Rouhani was engaged in "media spin in order to keep the centrifuges spinning" and called Iran's new president a "wolf in sheep's clothing."[23]

Although both America and Israel repeatedly threatened to use military force to prevent Iran from acquiring weapons of mass destruction, given different clocks, there were differences between the two governments about *when* a **preventive attack** should be launched, with Israel seeking to attack before Iran's nuclear program proceeded further and the Obama administration prepared to wait and see if sanctions and diplomacy would be sufficient. Netanyahu demanded Iran meet four conditions: cease enriching uranium, remove enriched uranium from the country, close its nuclear fuel processing plant at Fordo near Qum, and renounce plutonium reprocessing. The interim agreement with Iran violated Israel's demand that Iran dismantle its nuclear program. One U.S. official pointed out that Netanyahu "will be satisfied with nothing less than the dismantlement of every scrap of the Iranian nuclear infrastructure," and "we'd love that too—but there's no way that's going to happen at this point in the negotiation. And for us, the goal is to make sure that we are putting limits and constraints on the program, and ensuring that if the Iranians decided to race for a bomb, we would know in time to react."[24]

During his visit to Israel in March 2013, Obama encouraged Israelis to be patient and let sanctions work. "The Iranian government," he argued, "is now under more pressure than ever before, and that pressure is increasing. It is isolated. Its economy is in a dire condition. Its leadership is divided." He voiced his belief that "peace is far more preferable to war, and the inevitable costs—and unintended consequences—that would come with it." If Iran persisted in developing nuclear weapons despite diplomatic efforts, Washington retained the option of using force. "Iran must know this time is not unlimited. And I have made the position of the United States of America clear: Iran must not get a nuclear weapon."[25] Such comments seemed to placate Netanyahu during his visit to Washington in September 2013, but, according to an American expert on Iran, "should the Iranians offer something that the West finds attractive, and that the Israelis have problems with, then the rubber meets the road."[26]

Washington's agreement to cancel a military strike after Syria's use of poison gas in 2013 was seen by Israelis as reducing the credibility of America's commitment to use force against Iran if that country acquired WMD. To reassure Israel, President Obama declared that Iran's nuclear program was a "far larger issue" for America than Syria's use of chemical weapons. What Iran should recognize from the Syrian case is that "a credible threat of force, combined with a rigorous diplomatic effort"[27] would make a deal possible. U.S. diplomat Dennis Ross explained the relationship between U.S. policy toward Syria and Iran pithily: "These two situations are deeply intertwined. If the Syrians are forced to give up their weapons, it will make a difference to the Iranian calculation," enhancing the prospects for a peaceful outcome to the Iranian issues. "If the Syrians can drag this out and give up just a little," he added, "that will send a very different message to the supreme leader [Ayatollah Khamenei]."[28]

Despite differences with Israel over Iran, the Obama administration still harbored hopes for fruitful Israeli-Palestinian negotiations. Frustrated in efforts to achieve statehood through negotiation, however, the PLO sought UN status as a sovereign state in 2011. The Obama administration opposed the effort, and it failed when the Security Council was unable to assemble the minimum of 9 of 15 votes necessary to pass a resolution. Even had it done so, America's veto would have prevented the resolution's passage. In late

Benjamin Netanyahu and the Iran Deal

In his speech to Congress, Prime Minister Netanyahu inveighed against what he called a "bad deal" between Washington and Tehran that would allow Iran to retain a capability to restart its effort to develop nuclear weapons. The Obama administration and many Democratic members of Congress, forty-nine of whom boycotted the speech, regarded Netanyahu's acceptance of the invitation from Speaker John Boehner to speak as divisive interference in U.S. domestic politics and an effort to improve his own domestic standing only weeks before Israeli elections. President Obama defended the P5+1-Iranian framework agreement of March 2015 as "a once in a lifetime opportunity" and "our best bet" to curb Iran's nuclear weapons program. He also reassured Israelis by adding, "if anybody messes with Israel, America will be there."

Source: Peter Baker, "President Obama Calls Preliminary Iran Nuclear Deal 'Our Best Bet,'" *New York Times*, April 5, 2015, http://www.nytimes.com/2015/04/06/world/middleeast/obama-strongly-defends-iran-nuclear-deal.html?_r=0.

November 2012, a majority of states in the General Assembly agreed to admit the PLO as a nonmember observer state, a status enjoyed by the Vatican. As such, the PLO could participate in assembly debates and would find it easier to enter other UN agencies. Although pleased with a symbolic victory that showed that most countries supported its statehood, the PLO insisted it would continue seeking UN recognition as a sovereign state. Thereafter, in Israel's 2013 elections, Netanyahu's electoral bloc, though remaining the largest in parliament, fared poorly. Netanyahu's coalition included rightwing parties that were even more hardline than Likud. However, although Israelis and Palestinians disagreed on many issues, many on both sides wanted President Obama "to play a larger role in resolving the Israeli-Palestinian stalemate."[29]

The Kerry Round of Negotiations

Thus, Israel succumbed to pressure from Secretary of State Kerry in 2013 to reopen negotiations with the Palestinians. As a Middle East expert observed, Kerry had "gotten them into the pool. Right now they're in the very shallow end, and they're going to have to swim in deeper waters—and they can be treacherous. It's still an achievement that he's gotten them into the pool."[30] Kerry followed up with several trips to the Middle East, engaging in shuttle diplomacy between Palestinian and Israeli leaders. He had previously also proposed a plan to encourage private investment in the West Bank to reduce Palestinian unemployment and increase the West Bank's gross domestic product by 50 percent within three years. For its part, the PLO, nearing bankruptcy, was pressed by the Americans and the Arab League to reopen talks with Israel. Referring to Abbas and Netanyahu, Kerry commented, "Both leaders have demonstrated a willingness to make difficult decisions that have been instrumental in getting to this point."[31]

Resumption of talks in August began on a sour note. A condition set by the PLO to resume talks had been the release of imprisoned Palestinians. Israel met the condition, but minimally, by initially releasing only 26 prisoners. Israel also announced shortly before the talks began that it was building additional housing units in East Jerusalem and adding settlements on the West Bank eligible for government subsidies. Settlement construction announced earlier, if completed, would virtually sever East Jerusalem from the West Bank. Netanyahu, an observer noted, "is like a man who, while negotiating the division of a pizza, continues to eat it."[32]

As in earlier efforts, even agreement over principles was elusive, and, as negotiations approached their end in April 2014, the effort collapsed. Although Abbas conceded that Israeli soldiers could remain in the West Bank for as long as five years and a U.S.-led NATO force could remain in a Palestinian state indefinitely, Kerry no longer sought to achieve a comprehensive settlement but limited his objective to a vague "framework agreement" of principles that Israel's defense minister harshly criticized. Other events contributing to a deteriorating atmosphere included Israel's failure to release a fourth group of Palestinian prisoners until Abbas agreed to extend negotiations beyond the deadline. The PLO denied that extending negotiations was linked to prisoner release and applied to join several international organizations as a step toward sovereign recognition, thereby violating an agreement not to take such action as long as negotiations continued. Israel responded by halting the transfer of taxes it collected for the PA, bringing the PA close to bankruptcy.

The next step in this hostile tit-for-tat was a threat by Abbas to disband the PA and leave Israel responsible for maintaining West Bank security. Simultaneously, the PLO and Hamas resumed negotiations to unify the Palestinian movement, and Netanyahu suspended negotiations, declaring that Abbas could "have peace with Israel or a pact with Hamas—he can't have both."[33] Having decided that negotiations were going nowhere, Abbas sought to reinvigorate the Palestinian movement and regain control of Gaza, while Hamas wished to end its isolation. Abbas "had shut down," declared an American official. "His experience in the last nine months, of settlements gone wild has just, I think, convinced him that he doesn't have a partner."[34] A further meeting between Abbas and Israel's lead negotiator failed to overcome the breach caused by PLO-Hamas negotiations, and Abbas formed a new government that included ministers from Gaza. The new government papered over the PLO-Hamas differences, while giving Netanyahu an excuse to end the talks.

Secretary Kerry declared that both sides shared the blame for the breakdown of talks but pointed to Israel's announcement of additional apartment construction in Jerusalem as the final straw. "Poof," he said, "that was sort of the moment,"[35] a remark that drew angry responses from Israeli officials. Kerry further angered Israel when he compared it to pre-1993 South Africa, declaring that Israel risked becoming an "apartheid state."[36] Washington declared a "pause" in its efforts to reconcile the adversaries.

With a breakdown of negotiations and Abbas's effort to woo Hamas, it seemed little would change. But after formation of a Palestinian cabinet consisting of nonpolitical experts and Abbas's promise that it would adhere to his policy of nonviolence and follow earlier Israeli-Palestinian agreements, Israel's leaders were in for a shock. Instead of refusing to deal with a Palestinian government that Hamas supported, the Obama administration said it was prepared to work with that government because no Hamas members were in the cabinet. "With what we know now," declared a State Department spokesman, "we will work with this government."[37] "We're not naïve," commented a U.S. official. "We understand that this could be Hamas's nose under the tent, that it could lead Hamas to get a foothold in the West Bank, that terrorist cells could spring up in the West Bank again under a looser regime. So we're watching all of that very carefully to ensure that it doesn't happen."[38] Pro-Israeli members of Congress were outraged, and Israel swiftly approved yet more settlement expansion in the West Bank and Jerusalem.

Thereafter, Israeli-Palestinian relations rapidly deteriorated. Another Israeli-Hamas war erupted. The cycle of violence resumed. America's mediator between Israel and the Palestinians, Martin Indyk, sadly noted, "It's the distrust between the leaders and between the people that holds us up and makes it difficult" after "20 years of distrust."[39]

FUTURE: DISPUTED ISSUES

"There is no such thing as benign neglect when it comes to the Middle East,"[40] declared a Middle East analyst. Washington still seeks to assure Israel's security, while, in Obama's words, not turning "our backs on the legitimate Palestinian aspiration for dignity, opportunity, and a state of their own."[41]

Achieving a settlement remains hostage to Israeli and Palestinian hardliners. Cautious intelligence and military officials enjoy a uniquely influential role in Israeli policymaking, and settlers in the occupied territories oppose efforts to make them leave. In 1994, an Israeli extremist undermined the peace process when he murdered 29 Muslim worshippers in a mosque at the Cave of the Patriarchs in the city

The Wailing Wall and al-Aqsa

Mahfouz Abu Turk/Apaimages/APA Images

of Hebron. Israel's Prime Minister Rabin was assassinated in 1995 by an Israeli student angered by the possible surrender of some of the occupied territories. Egypt's President Sadat was assassinated in 1981 by members of an Islamic group led by a radical Egyptian military officer who were infuriated by Sadat's visit to Jerusalem and subsequent peace treaty with Israel. Extremism thus begets extremism.

Israel wants its foes to recognize its sovereign legitimacy as a Jewish state with secure borders and Jerusalem as its capital. Most Palestinians seek an independent state consisting of Gaza and the West Bank with Jerusalem as its capital and the right of return for Palestinian refugees and their descendants. Each side demands control of their religion's holy sites in Jerusalem—for Jews, the "Wailing Wall" (or Western Wall) that formed part of the enclosure of Herod's temple near the most sacred area of the ancient First and Second Temples of Jerusalem at which Jews gather for prayer, and for Muslims, the al-Aqsa Mosque (the "Noble Sanctuary"), the destination of the Prophet's Night Journey from Mecca on a spirit horse. In 2014, Jewish groups ascended the Temple Mount, site of both al-Aqsa and the ancient Jewish temple, and Israel's closure of al-Aqsa for several days triggered violent Palestinian demonstrations. What Muslims regard as provocative, Jews see as the right to pray at their holiest site.

Two States or One?

A central issue is whether both parties will accept two sovereign states living side by side and what their boundaries should be. This solution was endorsed by the Arab League in 2002 and is premised on the principle of "land-for-peace." In 2013, the Arab League softened the terms of its original plan, endorsing Clinton's proposal for Israel and the Palestinians to swap land rather than reinstate the precise pre-1967 boundaries. Israel lives in a dangerous neighborhood, and security concerns are paramount: "The PowerPoint maps that Israeli military briefers use for Sinai, Gaza, Lebanon, and Syria today consist of multicolored circles, and inside each are clusters of different armed groups . . . with nonstate actors, armed with rockets, dressed as civilians and nested among civilians on four out of its five borders."[42]

Most Israelis favor a two-state solution but not within pre-1967 borders. Israeli prime ministers including Ariel Sharon and Ehud Olmert recognized that Israel might become a segregated state if it did not surrender the occupied territories. The Palestinians refused to accept Prime Minister Netanyahu's demand that they recognize Israel as a *Jewish* state because it undermined their "right of return." Netanyahu had endorsed a two-state solution in 2009 at Bar-Ilan, which he repeated in 2014 when noting he remained committed "to a vision of peace of two states."[43] During Israel's 2015 election campaign, however, Netanyahu abruptly declared he would not agree to a two-state solution while prime minister. Then after his reelection he again changed course: "I never retracted my speech in Bar-Ilan University six years ago calling for a demilitarized state that recognizes the Jewish state. What has changed is the reality."[44] An angry President Obama, nevertheless, hinted that Washington might have to rethink its policy toward Israel. "We take him at his word that it wouldn't happen during his prime ministership, and so that's why we've got to evaluate what other options are available to make sure we don't see a chaotic situation in the region."[45]

Palestinians, too, disagree on the issue, the PLO having agreed to two states and Hamas remaining ambiguous. Hamas's 1988 charter called for eliminating Israel and establishing a single Islamic state. In 2006, however, the group's legislative program noted that the question of whether to recognize Israel could be put to a vote by the Palestinian people. That year, Ismail Haniyeh, Hamas's prime minister in Gaza, spoke of the possibility of a long-term truce with Israel, perhaps lasting twenty years, and a "temporary two-state solution"[46] if Israel left the territories it had occupied in 1967.

Policy Options

a. *Back Israeli hardliners who advocate a one-state solution.* Although hardline Israelis oppose an independent Palestinian state and some are members of a "Greater Israel Caucus" that regards the West Bank as forever part of Israel, few American politicians would support them because it would mark a dramatic reversal of U.S. policy. Nevertheless, there are variations of this option. For some, a one-state solution implies that West Bank Palestinians should either move across the River Jordan or that Jordan should again exercise authority in the West Bank as it had before 1967. However, Jordan has formally surrendered its claim to the West Bank and Jerusalem, and its leaders suspect the loyalty of Palestinian refugees who remain in their country.

A more benign one-state vision is promoted by Israeli writer Daniel Gavron, who suggests "that Israeli and the Palestinian territories can be merged into a dynamic, multi-ethnic, culturally rich nation with new forms of co-existence between its different constituents."[47] But even if Palestinians and Israelis agreed to a single democratic state, it would dilute Israel's Jewish identity and lead to a Palestinian majority.

b. *Pressure Israel to accept a two-state solution.* "Negotiations will be necessary," declared President Obama, "but there is little secret about where they must lead—two states for two peoples."[48] On several occasions, Palestinians and Israelis have come close to achieving this outcome, but differences regarding settlements, boundaries, and the status of Jerusalem have stymied a final agreement. Land swaps might overcome the problem, and expanding the boundaries of Jerusalem to accommodate a Palestinian capital, combined with internationalization of the city's holy sites would move the two sides closer to agreement. It would be necessary to negotiate with a united Palestinian movement, end Gaza's isolation, and improve the economic well-being of its inhabitants.

c. *Support the status quo in which Israel shares borders with autonomous but nonsovereign Palestinian communities in Gaza and Areas A and B of the West Bank.* Although this situation has existed for years, Palestinians always assumed it was an interim condition on the road to independence. If that prospect disappeared, it would likely lead to renewed violence—a third intifada—in which Palestinians again resorted to violent protests and terrorism, and Israel would become increasingly besieged and isolated. Indeed, Abbas declared in 2015 that the PLO was no longer bound by the Oslo Accords, owing to Israeli violations of the agreement.

Settlements

Israeli settlements in the occupied territories and the "right of return" for Palestinian refugees are emotional issues for Israeli settlers and Palestinians. Israel's settlers seek to fulfill the promise of Zionism throughout biblical Israel including ancient Judea and Samaria (the West Bank). Palestinians contend that settlements

Israel's Maale Adumim settlement near Jerusalem

Ammar Awad/Reuters/Corbis

encroach on their land and involve illegal Israeli efforts to create "facts on the ground" in anticipation of negotiation over territorial boundaries and the return of Palestinians to their former homes. Even as Israeli-Palestinian talks resumed in 2013, Israel's government announced plans to add 1,500 apartments to a settlement in East Jerusalem and to construct 20,000 new apartments in West Bank settlements. Kerry criticized the announcement, asking, "If you say you're working for peace and a Palestine that is a whole Palestine that belongs to the people who live there, how can you say, 'We're planning to build in the place that will eventually be Palestine'? It sends a message that somehow, perhaps, you're not really serious."[49] By 2013, in the area of the West Bank designated Area C where Israel retained military control, there were over 300,000 Jewish settlers in 100 settlements (some of which had existed before 1948) and about 200,000 more in areas annexed by Israel in East Jerusalem. Indeed, some Israeli hardliners publicly suggest that Israel annex all of Area C.

Policy Options

a. *Pressure Israel to cease expanding existing settlements or establishing new ones* that are regarded by the UN and the International Court of Justice as illegal. Previous U.S. presidents including Carter and Reagan expressed concern about settlement expansion, and in his 2009 speech in Cairo, President Obama unequivocally stated: "Israelis must acknowledge that just as Israel's right to exist cannot be denied, neither can Palestine's. The United States does not accept the legitimacy of continued Israeli settlements. This construction violates previous agreements and undermines efforts to achieve peace. It is time for these settlements to stop."[50] Four years later, he declared, "Israelis must recognize that continued settlement activity is counterproductive to the cause of peace, and that an independent Palestine must be viable—that real borders will have to be drawn."[51] The EU has tried to pressure Israel by refusing to give the same preferential status to imports from the occupied territories that it gives to goods produced within Israel. In 2014, Sweden became the first European state to recognize a Palestinian state despite Israeli protests, and the Vatican announced in May 2015 it would also do so. In addition, the British, Irish, Spanish, French, and EU parliaments followed with non-binding votes recognizing an independent Palestine. Although Washington has leverage with Israel, pressuring Israel to cease settlement expansion or forcing Israel to withdraw from settlements as a confidence measure would produce intense opposition in Israel and among Israel's American supporters. If Israel refused to give way and Washington failed to impose sanctions, it would stoke further anti-Americanism among Muslims.

b. *Encourage and help finance intensive Jewish settlement in Israel's Negev Desert*, which some have suggested be given to the Palestinians in return for West Bank settlements. Although this could be a bargaining chip, it probably would not be sufficient to resolve the overall problem because it would not satisfy the aspirations of Israel's religious nationalists. Even if it slowed the expansion of West Bank settlements, it would not persuade existing Jewish settlers to give up their homes and would produce friction between Israelis and the Bedouin Arabs who already live in the Negev.

c. *Pressure Israel to abandon most of its settlements on the West Bank while permitting it to retain those vital to its security*, especially the larger settlements located near its 1967 border (the Green Line) in which 60 percent of Israeli settlers in the West Bank live. In a letter to Prime Minister Sharon in 2004, President George W. Bush, after endorsing Sharon's "vision of two states living side by side in peace and security as the key to peace," seemed willing to let Israel unilaterally annex major settlement blocs. "As part of a final peace settlement," wrote Bush, "Israel must have secure and recognized borders, which should emerge from negotiations between the parties in accordance with UNSC Resolutions 242 and 338. In light of new realities on the ground, including already existing major Israeli population centers, it is unrealistic to expect that the outcome of final status negotiations will be a full and complete return to the armistice lines of 1949, and all previous efforts to negotiate a two-state solution have reached the same conclusion."[52]

These large settlements near the Green Line, which have been the sites of most recent settlement expansion, involve about 2 percent of the West Bank. Israel could compensate the Palestinians by swapping land elsewhere in exchange for them. President Clinton proposed this idea in December 2000, and the Arab League has endorsed it. America could encourage such swaps by providing financial aid to cover the costs to Israel in moving settlers as well as development funds for Palestinians displaced by the remaining settlements.

Refugees

Another impediment to a final settlement is the status of displaced Palestinian refugees. The Palestinian demand for the "right of return" is linked to the belief that Israel is not prepared to accept a two-state solution and that refugees have no option but to resettle in Israel. Given their number—almost five million including descendants of those who left Israel—Palestinians, along with the 670,000 Arabs living in Israel, would swamp the country's six million Jewish citizens.

Policy Options

a. *Press Israel to grant all Palestinian refugees the right of return.* Some Palestinians demand the right of all Palestinians to return to Israel. For most Israelis and their American supporters this would be unacceptable because Israel would no longer be a Jewish state. American leaders and moderate Palestinians recognize this option is unrealistic.

b. *Support Israel's sovereign right to refuse any right of return.* Although most Palestinians recognize that Israel will refuse to grant all Palestinian refugees the right of return and Washington will not force Israel to do so, it would be difficult to get Palestinians to surrender the *principle* of returning to their former homes. To do so would further divide the Palestinian movement and render a final settlement virtually impossible.

c. *Seek a compromise by which Palestinians would enjoy a "symbolic" right of return*, an option widely discussed among American, Israeli, and Palestinian negotiators. It would entail the return of relatively few Palestinians thereby upholding the *principle* but not to the extent of endangering Israel's status as a Jewish state. In 2008, Abbas was apparently prepared to accept the return of between 40,000 and 60,000 refugees over a period of years. Stephen Hadley, President George W. Bush's national security adviser, recalled, "Our reading was that there was a deal to be done on [the refugee issue]."[53] Abbas also declared that he had given up "his" right of return, an admission widely criticized by Palestinians. But he expressed clearly what he wanted in exchange. "Palestine now for me is '67 borders, with East Jerusalem as its capital,"[54] that is, a compromise on the right of return must involve two states.

Hamas and Gaza

When Prime Minister Sharon announced that Israel would withdraw from Gaza, he expected that the PA in Ramallah on the West Bank would administer the area while Israel controlled Gaza's borders, coastline, and airspace. The decision would also show, he believed, that Israel was committed to a peaceful settlement. Hamas's takeover of Gaza undermined Sharon's vision and intensified the split between Hamas and the Fatah-dominated PA, and violence continued between Hamas and Israel. Despite the formation of a unity government by Fatah and Hamas, their schism has not been bridged. Until it is, there will be no single entity to represent all Palestinians with which Israel can negotiate.

Policy Options

a. *Refuse to recognize Hamas,* which America has declared to be a terrorist group. Hamas still advocates violence against Israel and refuses to recognize Israel's right to exist. Although Washington's non-recognition of Hamas enjoys popular support in Israel and America, it precludes negotiation with a single Palestinian entity. Possibly an agreement could be reached with the PA in the West Bank to establish a "rump" state that would legally encompass Gaza but from which Gaza would remain independent until Hamas was ousted or was persuaded to join the Fatah-dominated PA.

b. *Seek to reconcile Hamas and Fatah.* Despite signing a reconciliation agreement in 2011, the two groups remained divided, with Hamas initially opposing Abbas's effort to gain UN recognition of a Palestinian state. Forming a single legitimate Palestinian entity would advance the peace process because Israel would have a negotiating "partner." However, Hamas is loathed by Israel, and the PLO-Hamas unity talks in 2014 were the excuse Israel used to end negotiations with Abbas. America is not trusted by Hamas, and efforts by Arab countries have failed to persuade the group to moderate its policies.

c. *Negotiate with Hamas,* which might reduce its hostility toward America, and would be possible only if Hamas rejected violence and recognized Israel's right to exist. Such negotiations, unless secret, would be vigorously opposed by Israel, America's pro-Israeli groups, and members of Congress. It would also make American leaders vulnerable to accusations of pandering to "terrorists."

Iran and Israel

U.S.-Israeli differences over the Iranian threat hang heavily over the Israeli-Palestinian peace process. Israel demanded that Iran renounce *any capability* to make a weapon while the Obama administration sought to prevent Tehran from *obtaining* a nuclear weapon, while allowing Tehran to retain capabilities that could later allow it to construct such a weapon. Negotiations with Iran on the nuclear issue were perceived by some Israelis as raising questions about the reliability of Washington's commitment to Israel's security, while Washington regarded Israel's position as unattainable short of a war which at best would delay Iran's progress toward making a nuclear weapon.

Policy Options

a. *Publicly declare there will be no strike against Iran unless Iran reneges on the agreement.* American leaders are in no hurry to attack Iran, especially after Iran's President Rouhani initiated negotiations with Washington. Although a senior U.S. official argued that U.S.-Israeli differences over Iran merely involved a manageable "tactical disagreement," Aaron David Miller concluded, "When the U.S. and Israel are at fundamental odds, it weakens U.S. power in the region and sends very bad signals to America's other allies."[55] Negotiations with Iran were time-consuming, and some viewed them as a delaying tactic to enable Iran to "go nuclear." Israeli anxiety will increase over time, and American hardliners and domestic supporters of Israel are likely to increase pressure on Washington to act before it becomes too late.

b. *Plan a joint attack that reflects Israel's "red line,"* a policy that would appease domestic groups that want Washington to move quickly and allow Israel and America to coordinate preparations for an attack, increasing the prospect it would succeed in degrading Iran's ability to go nuclear. However, it would also foreclose a peaceful solution, encourage Iran to restart preparations for acquiring nuclear weapons, and prove domestically divisive as congressional "hawks" and "doves" argued about the policy's merits.

c. *Let Israel go it alone.* Washington could let Israel unilaterally try to eliminate the Iranian nuclear program and could facilitate Israel's success by providing stealth aircraft, air refueling tankers, and advanced "bunker buster" bombs, 30,000-pound "Massive Ordnance Penetrators" that could penetrate Iran's Fordo nuclear enrichment complex, which is buried under a mountain. "Hopefully we never have to use it," declared a senior U.S. official. "But if we had to, it would work."[56] Even with such weapons, Israel might not have the ability to do the job by itself, and the result would be disastrous—a regional war with Iran developing nuclear weapons as quickly as possible and pro-Israeli groups accusing Washington of having betrayed its ally. In the end, Washington might have no choice but to join the conflict to assure the security of Israel and America's Arab friends in the Persian Gulf. The U.S.-Iranian deal confronted Netanyahu with a dilemma because Israel's justification for attacking would be weakened if U.S.-Iranian relations continue to improve.

Netanyahu's demand that Iran be forbidden any enrichment of nuclear fuel was "aimed to ensure that no deal is struck at all" because "Netanyahu and much of Israel's security establishment viewed the status quo—ever increasing sanctions that cripple Iran's economy, combined with the ever-present threat of war—as preferable to any realistic diplomatic deal."[57] If a resolution of the Iranian nuclear issue is part of a broader agreement "to end Iran's isolation on the condition that it shifts its behavior, it could divorce Iran's ideological and strategic impulses," then "Iran would have compelling incentives to disentangle itself from anti-Israeli hostilities."[58]

d. *Coordinate an attack with Israel* that would offer the prospect of achieving its military objective. Since a joint attack probably would take place later than a unilateral Israeli strike, Iran would be closer to its objective of acquiring nuclear weapons, but economic sanctions and diplomatic negotiations would have been permitted to run their course. However, a joint attack would set off a destabilizing conflict in the Persian Gulf and elsewhere in the Middle East.

e. *Let Iran acquire nuclear weapons.* Washington might conclude that an attack would not succeed and that Iran could be deterred from using nuclear weapons by the threat of nuclear retaliation. It would be difficult to persuade Israel to agree to this outcome and would trigger a domestic firestorm on the part of those who would describe it as betrayal of a close ally. It would also produce a decline of the credibility of American commitments in the Middle East and Asia.

Economic and Resource Issues

A final set of issues involves regional economic development and the distribution of resources between Israel and the Palestinians. Israel is an economically developed state, ranking high on global indices of economic competitiveness and capability to exploit the opportunities offered by new technologies. Its citizens have a per capita gross domestic product (GDP) of over $32,000. America and Israel have had a free trade agreement since 1985, and America is Israel's largest single trading partner. Each has large direct investments in the other, especially in high-tech manufacturing, and American and Israeli firms collaborate in commercial and military research and development. In addition, Washington provides Israel with over $3 billion in military assistance each year.

By contrast, per capita Palestinian GDP in 2012 was under $1,700. Gaza's unemployment rate in 2013 was almost 28 percent and the West Bank's 17 percent. U.S.-Palestinian trade was negligible. The PA depends on foreign funding to pay its bills, and Palestinians are among the world's largest per capita recipients of foreign aid. "From FY2008 to the present, annual regular-year U.S. bilateral assistance to the West Bank and Gaza Strip has averaged around $500 million, including annual averages of approximately $200 million in direct budgetary assistance and $100 million in non-lethal security assistance for the PA in the West Bank."[59] Both adversaries would benefit economically from a peace settlement.

Israel and the PA have several resource conflicts. One involves deposits of natural gas in the eastern Mediterranean off Israel and Gaza. Offshore gas promises to make Israel energy independent, and a partnership between U.S. and Israeli firms to develop gas fields off Israel's coast will allow Israel to export gas to Jordan and the PA, which could improve relations with Israel. The Palestinians and Lebanese contend, however, that these reserves are located in their economic zones. In 1994, the PA was ceded a 20-mile maritime zone off Gaza's coast, but five years later, Britain's BG Group obtained rights to develop Gaza's offshore gas reserves that would be provided to the Palestinians if Israel retains "full security control" of the sea off Gaza.

Another issue involves the scarce water resources in the West Bank. Israel retains control of the Jordan River basin and most of the West Bank's underground aquifers. According to a Palestinian human rights group, the 500,000 Israeli settlers in the West Bank and Jerusalem use six times the amount of water used by the area's 2.6 million Palestinians and have prevented Palestinian development of additional water resources.[60] In 2013, a modest agreement was reached among Israel, Jordan, and the PLO to enable construction of desalination plants using hydroelectric power in Aqaba, Jordan, to pump water from the Red Sea to the Dead Sea. Israel also agreed to supply additional water to the West Bank and to Jordan.

Policy Options

a. *Support the status quo* in which Washington funnels aid to the PA to keep it afloat and maintain security in the West Bank, while backing Israel's control of regional energy and water resources. This cautious policy, while promising stability in the short run, will not advance the peace process and does little to prod Israel to negotiate seriously with the Palestinians on economic and resource issues.

b. *Provide development assistance to the Palestinians.* The Obama administration has pushed a plan to encourage investment in the West Bank. U.S. investment and aid would afford Washington with additional leverage with the Palestinians that would help persuade them to renew negotiations with Israel. However, it is at best a means to maintain the peace process on life support and would do little to resolve resource disputes unless it included investment aimed at helping Palestinians develop existing water and energy sources.

c. *Encourage Israeli-Palestinian economic cooperation and resource redistribution along with American investment in and aid to the region.* This is the most ambitious of Washington's options and could be an incentive for a final settlement. But it would make sense only in conjunction with resolving other issues such as creating a Palestinian state and ceasing Israeli settlements construction. The investment and aid would be directed toward enlarging the region's overall economic pie and expanding regional water and energy resources to facilitate a redistribution that would benefit Palestinians while minimizing what Israel would have to surrender. Thus, U.S. investment in advanced desalination facilities like those that use a reverse osmosis process and in exploitation of energy sources in the eastern Mediterranean would increase overall regional resources, creating conditions in which both sides could benefit.

CONCLUSION: IS PEACE POSSIBLE?

Although the regional status quo has evolved, the clash between religions and nationalities persists. The future became even cloudier after the angry breakdown of Israeli-Palestinian negotiations in April 2014. Speaking to the UN in September 2014, Palestinian President Abbas declared it was impossible "to return to the cycle of negotiations that failed to deal with the substance of the matter and the fundamental question"[61] and demanded that the UN set a time limit to Israeli's presence in the West Bank. An effort by the PLO to get a binding Security Council resolution demanding an Israeli withdrawal from the occupied territories was blocked. Thereafter, the PLO applied for admission to the International Criminal Court. Washington then threatened to cut off financial assistance to the Palestinians, and Israel withheld tax revenues it collects for the PA that are vital for it to provide public services.

A two-state solution had little backing in Netanyahu's cabinet although it enjoyed support among a majority of Israelis. Netanyahu could cobble together a parliamentary majority with the Labor Party as well as smaller groups favoring two states if he left Likud as Sharon had done to found a new centrist party. Instead, he accelerated settlement expansion and demanded military control of the Jordan Valley on the West Bank. His demand that Palestinians acknowledge Israel as a "Jewish state" implied Palestinian refugees would have to surrender the "right of return" prior to a comprehensive settlement.

Israelis crave security in an insecure and changing region. "What we have to understand," declared Israel's former national security adviser, "[it] is going to be changed—to what, I don't know," but the result of the Arab Spring "means that we will be encircled by an area which will be no man's land at the end of the day." And this requires a strategy of "Wait and keep the castle."[62] Among Israeli concerns, the most important were the growing role of Islamic extremists, American indecisiveness about Syria and Iran, and Iran's progress toward acquiring nuclear weapons.

Although Israel remained a Middle East superpower, its position was complicated by events in Egypt and Syria. In some ways, it was in a stronger position, at least in the short term. Among these changes was the emergence of new governments in Egypt where President Mubarak had been briefly replaced by a government dominated by the Muslim Brotherhood, which was in turn overthrown by the army. Although the Brotherhood had honored the Egyptian-Israeli peace treaty, it did not provide Israel the security it had enjoyed under Mubarak, who loathed Islamists and refused to aid Hamas. Israel was pleased by the army coup that ousted the Brotherhood government, sensing it would be more secure with Egypt's anti-Islamist military leaders who viewed Hamas as a militant arm of the Brotherhood.

Neighboring Syria was riven by civil war. The Assad regime, though Israel's enemy, had avoided direct confrontation over the Golan Heights and maintained stability along its border with Israel. If it collapses, there was a risk of Islamic extremists creating havoc along that border. Syria's chaotic condition creates the additional prospect of that country's stockpiles of advanced weapons falling into the hands of extremists or Israel's nemesis, Hezbollah. Events in Syria and Egypt had reduced the prospect of a conventional interstate war but increased the threat to Israel posed by Hamas, Hezbollah, and radical jihadists.

President Obama sought to make progress in resolving the Israeli-Palestinian stalemate during his first term, thereby reducing Muslim animosity toward America. In Cairo in 2009, the president had said, "Too many tears have flowed. Too much blood has been shed. All of us have a responsibility to work for the day when the mothers of Israelis and Palestinians can see their children grow up without fear; when the Holy Land of three great faiths is the place of peace that God intended it to be; when Jerusalem is a secure and lasting home for Jews and Christians and Muslims, and a place for all of the children of Abraham to mingle peacefully together as in the story of Isra, when Moses, Jesus, and Mohammed (peace be upon them) joined in prayer."[63] And in Israel in 2014, he warned that if "Palestinians come to believe that the possibility of a contiguous, sovereign Palestinian state is no longer within reach, then our ability to manage the international fallout is going to be limited."[64]

Washington, however, made little headway in breaking the deadlock. Obama did not visit Israel until his second term and was dealing with an Israeli leader who, having agreed to a two-state solution, had done little to accomplish it. By the time of his reelection, Obama was disliked by many Israelis and was no longer trusted by Palestinians for whom little had changed. The president had no desire to get mired in the Middle East quagmire but could not ignore the region. Former U.S. Middle East envoy Dennis Ross is pessimistic: "Most Israelis and Palestinians today simply don't believe that peace is possible." On the one hand, "Israelis feel that their withdrawal from territory (like southern Lebanon and the Gaza Strip) has not brought peace and security; instead it has produced only violence"; on the other, "Palestinians discount what Israelis say about two states and believe instead that the Israelis will never accept Palestinian independence,"[65] a belief fostered by expansion of Israeli settlements.

In the face of such pessimism, President Obama spoke of the virtues of Israeli-Palestinian peace to a group of young Israelis during his visit. "I believe that Israel is rooted not just in history and tradition but also in a simple and profound idea: the idea that people deserve to be free in a land of their own." Peace, he argued, was crucial for Israel's security, "the only path to true security." "And given the march of technology, the only way to truly protect the Israeli people is through the absence of war—because no wall is high enough, and no Iron Dome is strong enough, to stop every enemy from inflicting harm." Then he added: "But the Palestinian people's right to self-determination and justice must also be recognized. Put yourself in their shoes—look at the world through their eyes. It is not fair that a Palestinian child cannot grow up in a state of her own, and lives with the presence of a foreign army that controls the movements of her parents every single day. It is not just when settler violence against Palestinians goes unpunished. It is not right to prevent Palestinians from farming their lands; to restrict a student's ability to move around the West Bank; or to displace Palestinian families from their home. Neither occupation nor expulsion is the answer. Just as Israelis built a state in their homeland, Palestinians have a right to be a free people in their own land."[66] In the same vein, Secretary Kerry alluded to the example of Nelson Mandela, who had brought peace to South Africa: "The naysayers are wrong to call peace in this region an impossible goal," adding, "It always seems impossible until it is done."[67]

DISCUSSION QUESTIONS

1. Should American peacekeeping troops be sent to the Middle East to separate Palestinians and Israelis?

2. What U.S. policy toward the Palestinian question would best serve American foreign-policy interests?

3. Should Washington exert pressure on Israel to extend settlements in the occupied territories? What form could such pressure take?

4. Should the United States impose its vision of a peaceful settlement on Israel and the Palestinians?

5. In what ways do domestic factors affect U.S. policy in the Middle East?

6. Should the United States enter into a formal alliance with Israel to guarantee its security from Iran and a Palestinian state?

KEY TERMS

back channel (p. 276)

coup d'état (p. 280)

mediation (p. 274)

preventive attack (p. 284)

Zionism (p. 270)

$SAGE edge™
for CQ Press

Sharpen your skill with SAGE edge at **edge.sagepub.com/mansbach**

SAGE edge for Students provides a personalized approach to help you accomplish your coursework goals in an easy-to-use learning environment.

Arab Spring or Arab Winter?

Daryl Cagle, CagleCartoons.com

Dangers of the Arab Spring

America's relations with the Arab world that stretches from Morocco on the Atlantic Ocean to the Sultanate of Oman at the mouth of the Persian Gulf had emphasized stability and **expediency** rather than values until the "Arab Spring." U.S. policy aimed to maintain secure sources of oil, support conservative pro-American leaders in the Persian Gulf, limit Soviet influence in the region, contain aggressive foes like Saddam Hussein and Shia Iran, and assure Israel's security. As the Arab Spring swept across the region in 2011, Washington came to believe that liberal values were the wave of the future. America supported democratic transitions because they reflected U.S. ideals *and* would secure U.S. influence against anti-Americanism among democratic regimes angered by prior American support for hated dictators.

The acme of the Arab Spring was a revolution in Egypt that overthrew its pro-American president. It marked the moment when U.S. policy shifted from unquestioning support of authoritarian leaders

MAP 10.1   The Present-day Middle East and North Africa

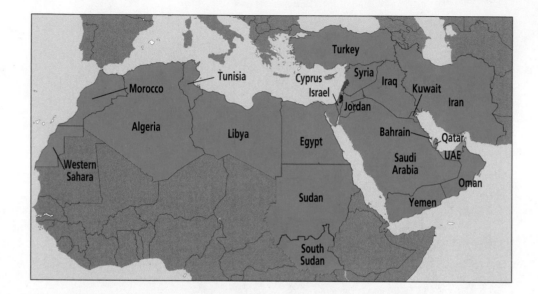

to a nuanced policy of encouraging democratic reform. History, however, plays tricks. Writing in 2012, two political scientists had presciently noted that "there is a considerable risk of war in states that are starting to democratize and that lack the coherent political institutions needed to make democracy function, such as an effective state, the rule of law, organized parties that compete in fair elections, and professional news media."[1] Thus, after an Islamist group, Egypt's Muslim Brotherhood, assumed

Timeline

2000

December **2010** Mohamed Bouazizi immolates himself.

January **2011** Tunisian dictator Zine El Abidine Ben Ali flees.

February **2011** Egyptian President Mubarak resigns, and Libyan insurgency begins.

March **2011** Insurrection against Syrian President Bashar al-Assad begins; NATO warplanes bomb Libyan military targets.

2000 (Continued)

October **2011** Libyan dictator Muammar Qaddafi is killed.

June **2012** Islamist Mohamed Morsi wins Egypt's presidential runoff.

September **2012** U.S. ambassador to Libya is killed in Benghazi.

December **2012** Egypt confirms a controversial new constitution.

office, it too proved to be illiberal and was overthrown a year later by Egypt's army. In reaction, Washington began abandoning its support for regime change in favor of accommodating friendly governments of whatever hue.

The shift in American foreign policy toward fostering democracy in the Arab world had begun in 2009 with an eagerly anticipated speech, "A New Beginning," delivered by newly elected President Barack Obama at Cairo's Al-Azhar University. In his address, the president sought to reverse anti-American views among Muslims, praising their democratic aspirations and contributions to culture, religion, and civilization. He also indicated a change in U.S. policy—from supporting dictatorial regimes in the Middle East toward supporting a transition to democracy.

SOURCES OF U.S. POLICY TOWARD THE ARAB WORLD

External factors include significant geopolitical interests in the Arab world—its strategic location as a bridge between Europe and Africa, the Suez Canal linking the Mediterranean Sea and Indian Ocean, the region's oil resources, the penetration of foes like the USSR, America's friendship with Israel, the spread of Islamic extremism, and instability caused by regional wars. Security issues raised by geopolitical concerns made government agencies like the Department of Defense advocates of assuring stability in the Arab world. The CIA, however, was caught by surprise by the Arab Spring.

Several of the issues raised by the Arab Spring divided U.S. decision makers. U.S. military leaders consonant with their roles were reluctant to become involved in Libya's insurrection or Syria's civil war lest America become mired in unwinnable conflicts. By contrast, those wishing to see Western values spread supported greater involvement. Congressional leaders like Senators John McCain (R-AZ) and Lindsey Graham (R-SC) pressed for greater engagement, as did then–Secretary of State Hillary Clinton, who advocated a no-fly zone over Libya. Within the Obama administration, Secretary of State John Kerry and then–Secretary of Defense Chuck Hagel advocated using force against Assad. Kerry and UN Ambassador Samantha Power also urged additional U.S. military support for Syrian insurgents.

2000 (Continued)

May **2013** Hezbollah fighters enter Syria.

July **2013** General Abdul Fatah al-Sisi deposes President Morsi.

August–September **2013** Syrian army uses poison gas to kill civilians; America and Russia pressure Syria to surrender chemical weapons.

2000 (Continued)

January **2014** Geneva II Conference on Syria opens; Egypt adopts a new constitution.

June **2014** Assad is reelected Syria's president; General Sisi is elected Egypt's president.

October **2015** Russia intervenes militarily in Syria.

⚿ KEY DOCUMENT
President Barack Obama's Speech in Cairo

"We meet at a time of tension between the United States and Muslims around the world—tension rooted in historical forces that go beyond any current policy debate. . . . The attacks of September 11th, 2001, and the continued efforts of these extremists to engage in violence against civilians has led some in my country to view Islam as inevitably hostile not only to America and Western countries but also to human rights. . . . I have come here to seek a new beginning between the United States and Muslims around the world; one based upon mutual interest and mutual respect; and one based upon the truth that America and Islam are not exclusive, and need not be in competition. . . . I do have an unyielding belief that all people yearn for certain things: the ability to speak your mind and have a say in how you are governed; confidence in the rule of law and the equal administration of justice; government that is transparent and doesn't steal from the people. . . . No matter where it takes hold, government of the people and by the people sets a single standard for all who hold power: you must maintain your power through consent, not coercion; you must respect the rights of minorities, and participate with a spirit of tolerance and compromise; you must place the interests of your people and the legitimate workings of the political process above your party."

Source: Excerpted from "Text: Obama's Speech in Cairo," *New York Times*, June 4, 2009, http://www
.nytimes.com/2009/06/04/us/politics/04obama.text
.html?pagewanted=all.

Individual factors mattered. President Obama's preference in Libya was to lead "from behind"[2] and let America's allies get in front, and the president's reluctance to become involved in Syria reflected what he believed he had learned from America's wars in Iraq and Afghanistan. Instinctively averse to "isms," Obama's definition of leadership reflected his belief that American power was declining.

Societal factors also played a role in policy toward the Arab world, though not uniformly. In the cases of Libya and Syria, Obama was aware of the reluctance of a war-weary public to get bogged down in new conflicts. Oil companies like ExxonMobil and Chevron lobbied against policies that destabilized oil-rich regimes. The Arab-American population in America though small—about 0.5 percent of America's population—is concentrated in New York City, Detroit, and Los Angeles. It is a heterogeneous group marked by cultural and religious diversity and does not yet enjoy political influence equal to that of other national groups like Greek- or Jewish-Americans. The principal Arab advocacy groups are the American-Arab Anti-Discrimination Committee and the Arab American Institute.

PAST: BEFORE THE ARAB SPRING

American involvement in the Arab world is recent compared to Europe's. Contemporary Arab states were born in the partition of the Ottoman Empire after World War I.

The Arabs: World War I and After

Encouraged by Britain and aided by T. E. Lawrence (Lawrence of Arabia), Hussein bin Ali, head of the Hashemite clan, and his sons Feisal, Abdullah, and Zeid launched a revolt against the Ottomans by the Arabs of western Arabia (the Hejaz) based on their belief that the Arabs could establish a homeland stretching from Syria to Yemen governed by Islamic law. By 1917, the revolt had driven the Ottomans from much of the region. In 1916, however, Britain and France signed a secret treaty negotiated by Sir Mark Sykes and François Georges-Picot that divided the Arab world between them. Britain would receive southern Iraq, Transjordan (the land east of the River Jordan in what is now

MAP 10.2 1916 Sykes-Picot Middle East Partition

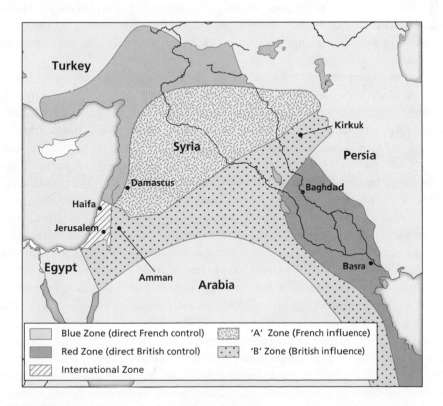

Source: Reprinted by permission of CQ Press, an imprint of SAGE Publications.

Jordan), and Palestine (the land west of the River Jordan, encompassing contemporary Israel, Gaza, and the West Bank), and France would acquire Lebanon, Syria, southeastern Turkey, and northern Iraq. A confederation of Arab states or a single Arab state divided into French and British spheres of influence would be established.

DID YOU KNOW ?

Turkey's Atatürk

Mustafa Kemal, who transformed Ottoman Turkey into a secular republic in 1923, was given the surname Atatürk, "Father of the Turks."

The agreement conflicted with promises made by Sir Henry McMahon, British High Commissioner in Egypt, who had written Hussein, "Great Britain is prepared to recognize and support the independence of the Arabs in all the regions within the limits demanded by the Sharif of Mecca [Hussein]."[3] Lawrence and Prince Feisal attended the 1919 Versailles Conference to plead the Arab cause in the name of Woodrow Wilson's principle of national self-determination, but the European powers were not willing to repudiate their agreement.

The Sykes-Picot Agreement was confirmed in 1922 when the League of Nations authorized the victorious allies to administer former Ottoman territories as "mandates" (colonies being prepared for independence) under which the Ottoman provinces of Iraq, Syria, Lebanon, and Palestine would be governed by British and French administrators. Britain would administer Mesopotamia (Iraq), Transjordan, and Palestine, while Syria and Lebanon became French mandates.

In 1917, Hussein declared himself king of the Hejaz but was deprived of his prize by the Saudis, a rival Arab clan. The Hejaz was conquered by Abd al-Aziz ibn Saud in 1924–1925 and, in 1932, was united with the Nejd to form Saudi Arabia, an absolute monarchy based on the principles of Wahhabism, a conservative branch of Sunni Islam. In 1920, Feisal was declared king of Greater Syria but went into exile after France occupied that country from which it later carved Lebanon. The following year, Britain chose Feisal to rule the new oil-rich country of Iraq and his brother Abdullah to rule Jordan. Anti-British resentment in Iraq sparked an insurrection that Britain suppressed, and Iraq was granted formal independence in 1930. Feisal's son succeeded him in 1933 but was killed by rebellious military officers in 1958. Lebanon became independent in 1943, and Syria followed in 1946.

"It was an era in which Middle Eastern countries and frontiers were fabricated in Europe," and Iraq and Jordan "were British inventions, lines drawn on an empty map by British politicians after the First World War; while the boundaries of Saudi Arabia, Kuwait, and Iraq were established by a British civil servant in 1922, and frontiers between Moslems and Christians were drawn by France in Syria-Lebanon and by Russia on the borders of Armenia and Soviet Azerbaijan."[4]

The Cold War and the Arab World

America's Cold War objectives in the Arab world were access to oil and preventing Soviet penetration. Oil's importance lay in the fact that it was replacing coal as the principal fuel for naval vessels in the early 20th century, and it became the economic lifeblood of Saudi Arabia, Iraq, Iran, Algeria, Libya, and Kuwait.

Soviet involvement in the Arab world was part of its global competition with America. Moscow aided communist movements and established naval facilities in Aden and Socotra in South Yemen and Tartus in Syria to balance U.S. military assets in the region's 'Northern Tier"—Greece, Turkey, and Iran—while avoiding direct confrontation with Washington. Moscow enjoyed warm relations with Arab nationalist leaders in Egypt, Syria, Libya, and Iraq, exploiting their enmity toward Israel and providing economic and military aid. Soviet strategy "was primarily a manipulation of local forces to the detriment of Western positions" and "exploited the new dynamic Arab **nationalism** and its distrust of the West."[5] America feared Soviet influence in a region it regarded as vital to its security. With U.S. encouragement, Britain, Iraq, Turkey, Iran, and Pakistan in 1955 established the Baghdad Pact to contain the USSR. Although it did not join the alliance partly to avoid offending Egypt's President Gamal Abdel Nasser who opposed it, America concluded bilateral treaties with its members.

Nasser was a catalyst for U.S.–Soviet competition. He assumed power in Egypt in 1954, transforming Egypt into a one-party secular socialist republic and fostering **pan-Arab nationalism.** He was a foe of European colonialism and conservative Arab monarchies and a prominent figure in the **non-aligned movement**, and he sought to energize the country's economy by building a dam at Aswan to irrigate the Nile valley. Nasser played off Moscow against Washington. His massive purchase of Soviet arms in 1955 from Czechoslovakia, then a Soviet satellite, brought the Cold War into the heart of the Arab world.

The Czech arms deal helped persuade the Eisenhower administration to offer in 1955 to fund the Aswan Dam, an offer it had already been considering. Nasser's continued dalliance with Moscow caused Washington to withdraw its offer the following year. "Eisenhower and [Secretary of State John Foster] Dulles had reached the limits of their patience with Nasser: he was undermining the Baghdad Pact, he had impeded an Arab-Israel settlement, he had invited Soviet influence into the Middle East, and in May he had even recognized the People's Republic of China."[6] Moscow stepped in to fund the dam, and Nasser nationalized the Suez Canal, seizing an opportunity to burnish his anticolonial reputation and make a profit as well. The 1956 Suez War ensued (chapter 13), and its real winner was Nasser, "who kept the canal, humiliated the colonialists, and balanced Cold War superpowers against one another, while securing his position as undisputed leader of Arab nationalism."[7]

Only months after Egypt's purchase of Soviet weapons, Syria did the same. Washington concluded that Syria, like Egypt, was becoming part of a pro-Soviet regional bloc. Its government copied Nasser's anticolonialism, pan-Arab nationalism, and socialist policies, and with Egypt, Syria formed the short-lived United Arab Republic (1958–1961). Thereafter, U.S.-Soviet regional competition intensified as Moscow exploited Arab nationalism. Moscow supported regimes that sought to alter the region's political complexion, especially those opposed to oil-rich monarchies allied with the West. Faced by growing Soviet influence, President Eisenhower announced the Eisenhower Doctrine in January 1957, promising military and/or economic aid to protect the security and independence of Middle Eastern countries endangered by communist aggression.

In 1957, a crisis erupted in Jordan after King Hussein discovered a plot by pro-Nasser army officers. Aided by loyal Bedouins, the coup was averted, and Syrian troops who had moved toward Jordan's border turned back. During the summer, Syria's economic, political, and military cooperation with Moscow deepened, further alarming Washington. A meeting at which Nasser sought to persuade America's ambassador that neither Egypt nor Syria would become Soviet satellites failed to calm U.S. fears, and Turkey, a NATO ally, massed troops along Syria's border. America, however, decided against intervening owing to the risk of involving Turkey, Jordan, and Iraq and the possibility of a U.S.-Soviet confrontation. "From this point onwards, it was apparent that Western policy in the Middle East based on the Eisenhower Doctrine had come to a dead end, as conservative pro-Western Arab regimes were sitting on a powder-keg of popular sentiment"[8] owing to the popularity of Nasser's pan-Arabism. Nevertheless, Washington sent troops to Lebanon to maintain stability in 1958 when the country's president asked for help to resist an effort by pro-Nasser elements to overthrow the government. The action had the dual purpose of supporting Lebanon's independence and signaling America's resolve to protect its regional interests.

U.S. concern about the security of Persian Gulf oil grew as Moscow cultivated close relations with Iraq after that country's 1958 revolution. In 1972, Moscow and Baghdad signed a Treaty of Friendship and Cooperation, and Iraq increased arms purchases from the USSR. Iraq's Saddam Hussein became a fixture in the "rejectionist front" of those who wanted no compromise with Israel. He also sought to undermine Iran's post-1979 Islamic regime, a policy that led to the 1980-1988 Iran-Iraq War.

In the early 1970s, the Nixon Doctrine that stressed helping allies help themselves replaced the Eisenhower Doctrine with its emphasis on U.S. intervention. Originally applied late in the Vietnam War after Washington sought to reduce its military presence, President Richard Nixon explained the policy as furnishing "military and economic assistance when requested in accordance with our treaty commitments" but looking "to the nation directly threatened to assume the primary responsibility of providing the manpower for its defense."[9] In the Middle East, the Nixon Doctrine involved strengthening allies like Iran and Saudi Arabia as barriers to Soviet influence.

President Jimmy Carter was deeply concerned with brokering an Arab-Israeli settlement, but two events pushed his administration in other directions. The first was the 1979 Iranian revolution and seizure of the American embassy in Tehran that preoccupied the administration for the rest of its time in office. The second was the Soviet invasion of Afghanistan. The first shifted the administration's focus to the danger posed by Iran's transformation into an American adversary, and the second intensified U.S. fears of Soviet expansion toward the Persian Gulf. In 1980, the president articulated a Carter Doctrine: "An attempt by any outside force to gain control of the Persian Gulf region will be regarded as an assault on the vital interests of the United States of America, and such an assault will be repelled by any means necessary, including military force."[10]

In Egypt, Moscow staunchly supported Nasser until his death in 1970 and his successor Anwar Sadat with whom the USSR signed a treaty of friendship. Although the USSR backed Egypt during its 1973 war with Israel, Sadat had already asked Moscow to end its military presence in Egypt owing to the onset of U.S.-Soviet détente. Sadat's shift away from Moscow came as a "complete surprise" to Secretary of State Henry Kissinger.[11] Sadat wrote, "the Soviet Union had planned to provide us with just enough [assistance] to meet our most immediate needs and at the same time maintain its role as our guardian and ensure its presence in the region."[12] Deciding Washington could provide greater help in dealing with Israel than Moscow, he canceled the Egyptian-Soviet treaty in 1976 and began improving relations with America and Israel, climaxing in his historic visit to Jerusalem. After Sadat's assassination in 1981, Vice President Hosni Mubarak replaced him. Mubarak could be trusted to maintain peace with Israel, oppose Syria and post-revolutionary Iran, and repress domestic Islamism, and Washington backed him until his overthrow in 2011.

After the Cold War, U.S. preoccupation with Soviet penetration of the Middle East ebbed, as did the attraction in the region of pan-Arab nationalism. An alternative was political Islam—movements seeking to govern their societies in accordance with Islamic law and custom.

Political Islam

Political Islam encompasses the views of both fundamentalists who believe in the literal truth of their holy book, the Koran, and the writings and practices of the Prophet Muhammad and those who merely wish to be governed according to Islamic religious law.

The Aims of Political Islam Islamists expect rulers to govern subjects according to Islamic precepts and the laws revealed by "the one true God." "From the very opening of the Quran, and the plea that the Lord of the universe show the faithful the straight path to the assurance that He has made of Muslims 'a balanced nation that [they] may be witnesses to people' and on the promise that He will bring victory to those who enter His religion, the close link between Islam and power is evident."[13] Islamists "seek the Islamic reform of society and state" with the goal of "a moral community governed by *Shari'a*, or Islamic law."[14]

Western governments part from political Islam on issues like gender equality, the separation of church and state, freedom of religion, and the primacy of secular law. Some critics question the commitment of Islamists to democratic principles. The source of this concern is tension between the supremacy of law based on religious belief and the rights of citizens and their elected representatives to decide freely what laws and policies they wish.

Placing religion at the center of political life is not uniquely Islamic. No distinction was made between religious and secular obligations in medieval Europe. Most American colonies were founded on the basis of religious scripture. It was only after the American and French Revolutions that secular rule and individual rights triumphed in the West.

We now turn to those who shaped political Islam and the evolution of the Muslim Brotherhood, a group that played a major role in the Arab Spring.

Political Islam and the Muslim Brotherhood Recent decades have witnessed a revival of political Islam that owed much to two figures—Abul A'la Maududi and Hasan al-Banna. Maududi, born in British India, sought to restore the status of Islam in India that had existed before Britain's conquest of the Muslim Moghul Empire. In his view, jihad did not mean violence but exertion of "one's utmost endeavor in promoting a cause,"[15] that is, establishing an Islamic state. Maududi disapproved of democratic institutions, arguing that Islamic law must govern Muslims who should not pursue "Westernization." He "produced an all-inclusive worldview, an internally consistent ideological perspective" that "shaped the concept of the 'Islamic state'"[16] and concluded that this could be achieved by evolution rather than revolution.

Another important contributor was Hasan al-Banna, a schoolteacher who founded the Muslim Brotherhood in Ismailia, Egypt, in 1928 and has been called the "founding father of modern Islamic fundamentalism."[17] Banna denounced British colonialism and Western culture that he viewed as having corrupted Islamic civilization. Secular mores, he claimed, had eroded Islamic values, and he opposed secular trends in Islamic countries like Turkey. Instead, Banna sought to transform Egypt into an Islamic state based on the Koran and the Prophet's teachings, and the Brotherhood's slogan became "Islam is the solution." The return to an earlier and purer Islam would reverse Islam's decline. For him, Islam "was the final arbiter in politics as well as religion, in the things of the market place as well as in those of the state."[18]

Banna was "more nearly a charismatic orator/preacher and a gifted organizer than a creative and consistent thinker"[19] than Maududi. Although the Brotherhood retained its Egyptian roots, it reflected Banna's belief that the Islamic community transcended national boundaries. Achieving his objectives, he argued, demanded patience and could only be achieved by the propagation of the Brotherhood's ideas in a process of evolution, not revolution. Although generally opposing violence as counterproductive, he thought it justifiable if government repression were severe or if victory were within the Brotherhood's grasp. Thus, the Brotherhood formed an armed militia, the Special Apparatus.

As the Brotherhood spread across Egypt, Banna built a complex organization of branches headed by an administrative board linked to the Brotherhood's Cairo center. The group's headquarters established specialized departments for propaganda, education, labor, social services, and relations with non-Egyptian Muslims. In the 1930s, the Brotherhood established branches across the region. It was the first successful Islamic mass movement to contest secular beliefs and demand a return to the puritanical version of the distant past in which Islamic law governed society. In addition to its pan-Islamic appeal, its charities and social institutions enhanced the Brotherhood's popularity. Although Banna conceived the Brotherhood as "an all-embracing organization, transcending political parties, indeed making them unnecessary," he was a pragmatist who "was not averse to playing by the prevailing political rules" when the group could "thereby gain in strength."[20]

Banna remained the Brotherhood's leader until his assassination in 1949. His successor, Hasan al-Hudaybi, recognized that the Brotherhood had to eschew violence and join the political process if it were to survive official repression and remain faithful to Banna's philosophy. Hudaybi was willing to support the military officers who overthrew Egypt's King Farouk in 1952, and the Brotherhood was prepared to forgo pursuit of a global caliphate in favor of Islamic democracy in Egypt. However, the group was alienated by the government's failure to promulgate a constitution that enshrined democracy *and* Islamic law. In 1954, it organized demonstrations, and a member of the Special Apparatus tried to assassinate Nasser.

The Brotherhood's subsequent repression radicalized some of its members, notably Sayyid Qutb. Qutb believed that those who repressed the Brotherhood were not true Muslims and should be targets of violent jihad. His views were repudiated by the Brotherhood, and Hudaybi declared that only God could declare a person's faith. "Within the Brotherhood, Hudaybi's tolerant view—in line with al-Banna's founding vision—prevailed, cementing the group's moderate vocation" while Qutb, "who breathed his last on Nasser's gallows in 1966 went on to become the prophet and martyr of jihad." In the following years, the Brotherhood "followed the path of toleration and eventually came to find democracy compatible with its notion of slow **Islamization**," and it depended "on winning hearts and minds through gradual and peaceful Islamization" even if that required allying with secular politicians. It had become a collection of national groups that "reject global jihad while embracing elections and other features of democracy."[21] Those who adhered to Qutb's views left the Brotherhood and became militant jihadists.

The Brotherhood established a party base, running "independent" candidates for parliament. As its number of elected representatives grew, it became Egypt's largest opposition bloc, winning seats as independents despite being officially banned. It viewed "the election campaign as an ideal apparatus for promulgating the message of Islam as a solution."[22] In 2010 parliamentary elections, the Brotherhood's participation was blunted by government harassment after which the Brotherhood advocated "a non-partisan Islamic system."[23]

As the Arab Spring spread, some observers concluded that historian Bernard Lewis was right in arguing that Islamist groups viewed democracy as a temporary expedient to gain power, after which they would suppress democratic institutions. "For Islamists, democracy, expressing the will of the people, is the road to power, but it is a one-way road, on which there is no return, no rejection of the sovereignty of God, as exercised through His chosen representatives. Their electoral policy has been classically summarized as 'One man (men only), one vote, once.'"[24]

PRESENT: STIRRINGS OF SPRING

On December 17, 2010, Mohamed Bouazizi, a Tunisian vegetable peddler, immolated himself after a policewoman who slapped him seized his cart. That event inspired protests across the Arab world. "Tunisia shared many properties with its neighbors—high unemployment, a corrupt regime, a frustrated public, and more information about the regime from outside the country. Wikileaks turned out to be somewhat of a trigger, as Tunisians learned that their regime was considered to be more corrupt than they had expected."[25]

At the time, most Arab states were authoritarian,[26] but Bouazizi's death triggered revolutionary protests across the region, toppling dictatorships in Tunisia, Egypt, Libya, and Yemen. The contagion even threatened conservative regimes like Saudi Arabia's whose rulers hastened to grant political concessions and increase public spending to mollify citizens. Everywhere, people spread their message that the "people demand the fall of the regime." It appeared that the Arab world would follow the path of the Soviet bloc in ridding itself of tyrants and achieving "people power."

Information and communication technologies and social media facilitated the spread of democratic aspirations. Protesters "were middle-class educated, and underemployed, relatively leaderless and technology-savvy youth," and "digital media appeared to have an important role in the ignition of social protest, the cascade of inspiring images and stories of success across the countries of the region, and the peculiar organizational form that Arab Spring uprisings had." These "technologies provide the entry points for young activists to explore democratic alternatives," allowing "for political discourse and even direct interventions with state policy, and coordinating mechanisms that supports synchronized social movements through marches, protests, and other forms of collective action."[27] **Social media** were less vulnerable to censorship by dictatorships than other forms of communication, and mobile phones played a key role in coordinating activities of regime opponents. Google even adjusted its speak2tweet technology to evade interference from the Egyptian and Syrian governments.

As demonstrations spread, governments wrote constitutions with two common elements to meet protesters' demands—"they generally detailed the aspirations of the state, for example, to be part of the Arab *Umma* [community] and uphold the principles of Islam" and "tended to be laden with strong guarantees for civil and political rights."[28] The combination of secular rights and Islamic principles produced tensions. Within a year, significant change had transformed the region. Three countries (Libya, Egypt, and Morocco) were no longer regarded as authoritarian, and events in Libya and Egypt had illustrated how "young and restless populations" could overthrow "long-serving, geriatric leaders."[29]

Thereafter, counterrevolution engulfed Egypt, civil war convulsed Syria and Libya, and democratic reform virtually ceased. What began as a springtime of optimism and change was transformed into instability and violence. Islamists discovered that deposing authoritarian leaders was easier than governing. Change did not prevent leaders from being corrupt, and assuming power was insufficient to solve complex economic, political, and social challenges.

The Arab Spring had bloomed in contexts ill prepared for democratic change and failed to improve people's lives by providing economic opportunity. Arab countries remained fragmented and densely populated, with poor education systems and little water. Syria's civil war was partly a result of the regime's failure to cope with a drought that devastated the country's farmers and herders. Such conditions threatened to revive the fortunes of authoritarian leaders and Islamic extremists and reopened contested questions about the relationship between military and civilian rule and the role of religion in politics. These issues fueled conflicts between Shia and Sunni Muslims and secular politicians and Islamists.

The transformation that began in Tunisia altered the region's political landscape. Violence engulfed Libya, Egypt, and Syria, and their future still preoccupies American policymakers. What follows traces these momentous events and examines U.S. policies toward them.

Tunisia

After weeks of protests, President Zine al-Abine Ben Ali, in power since 1987, resigned in early 2011 amid Tunisia's "Jasmine Revolution," the first of the region's strongmen to fall victim to the Arab Spring. Some 300 Tunisians had been killed during protests against corruption, economic decline, and authoritarianism. In 2011, multiparty democratic elections were held for a Constituent Assembly to draft a new constitution. "Just as many Tunisian citizens protested peacefully in streets and squares to claim their rights," declared President Obama, "today they stood in lines and cast their votes to determine their own future."[30] The moderate Islamic Ennahda ("Renaissance") Movement won a plurality and formed a coalition government. Inspired by Egypt's Muslim Brotherhood, the party had been banned in 1992 and only legalized in 2011. Although Ennahda remained moderate, its popularity raised suspicions in Tunisia regarding Islamism like those that later appeared elsewhere in the region.

Although Tunisia was democratized, economic and social conditions improved little. After Ben Ali's ouster, Tunisia's economy continued to spiral downward. Unrest culminated in protests, and members of militias attacked demonstrators. Militant Muslims also grew more influential, and paradoxically, Tunisians' relative freedom and high education led many of its young people to join the terrorist group Islamic State of Iraq and Syria (ISIS). Ennahda's leaders continued to profess moderation, and its leader declared, "We don't believe the state has the right to impose its views on what people wear, eat or drink."[31]

Matters further deteriorated when a leading secular politician, Chokri Belaid, who had accused Ennahda of failing to resist hardline Islamists, was assassinated in 2013. Thousands attended his funeral, and a general strike was declared. In May, violence followed the government's ban of a meeting of the militant group Ansar al-Sharia (Tunisia). Influenced by events in Egypt, secular groups organized opposition to Tunisia's ruling Islamists. In July, an assassin using the same gun that had killed Belaid, murdered another opposition leader, triggering the resignation of opposition members in parliament.

Tunisia's transition from authoritarian to democratic rule was rocky. Extremists with weapons from neighboring Libya or returning from Syria threatened the country's security. Fear of Islamism remained high partly because Tunisia was the most secular society in the Arab world, and Ennahda trailed a secular party, Nidaa Tounes (Call for Tunisia) in parliamentary and presidential elections in late 2014. Nevertheless, Ennahda scrupulously adhered to its commitment to inclusive rule, negotiating in good faith with secular parties. Tunisia's new constitution was a liberal contrast to its predecessor, reflecting a balance between religious and secular principles with Islam as the country's religion within a pluralistic civil society. In Tunisia, an Islamist party had proved its commitment to democracy, but, if Tunisia's evolution from authoritarian to democratic rule was difficult, what took place in neighboring Libya was worse.

Libya

During much of Muammar Qaddafi's longtime dictatorship, U.S.-Libyan relations were hostile. Qaddafi's links to international terrorism in the 1970s led to labeling Libya a state sponsor of terrorism. Libya's link to an attack on American servicemen in Berlin triggered a U.S. bombing raid on Tripoli in 1986, and Qaddafi's responsibility for the 1988 bombing of Pan Am Flight 103 over Lockerbie, Scotland, made him an international pariah. Libyan efforts to acquire weapons of mass destruction (WMD) also alienated America. However, after Qaddafi turned over two individuals in 1999 to be tried for the Pan Am bombing, U.S.-Libyan hostility began to wane. The Libyan dictator cut ties to terrorists, agreed to compensate victims of the Pan Am bombing, and renounced efforts to acquire WMD. America renewed diplomatic relations with Libya in 2004.

In 2011, violent demonstrations erupted in Benghazi in eastern Libya. It was home to anti-Qaddafi tribal groups and, although the center of the country's oil-producing region, was the country's poorest region. Benghazi's demonstrators were met with violence, and security forces were driven from the city. Within days, Libya's third largest city, Misrata, had fallen to rebels and was then besieged by Qaddafi's troops. Airstrikes against demonstrators and the use of snipers and artillery triggered a national insurrection starting in eastern Libya and spreading westward to its capital, Tripoli. Qaddafi dismissed opponents as "cockroaches" and "rats," declaring, "All my people love me," a remark that America's UN ambassador called "delusional."[32] Rebels included middle-class professionals, deserters from Libya's army, and radical Islamists. The government tried to shut down Internet and cellphone services, but cellphone videos continued to be uploaded on YouTube. A national council of Qaddafi's foes was organized and declared it would draft a democratic constitution, ensure political pluralism, guarantee human and civil rights, and prepare for free elections.

The UN Security Council imposed economic sanctions on Libyan leaders and called for an investigation into attacks against Libyan citizens. The prosecutor of the International Criminal Court (ICC) accused the regime of war crimes, and the ICC issued an arrest warrant for Qaddafi. After the regime sent armed columns toward Benghazi threatening a massacre, the Security Council authorized a no-fly zone and humanitarian intervention. The Council based its decision on the doctrine of the **Responsibility to Protect (R2P),** a norm first articulated in a 2001 report of the International Commission on Intervention and State Sovereignty permitting humanitarian intervention to protect civilians.

NATO then authorized airstrikes against Qaddafi's forces around Benghazi and enforced the no-fly zone (chapter 13). U.S. and British cruise missile strikes began NATO's "Operation Odyssey Dawn." "I want the American people to know that the use of force is not our first choice and it's not a choice I make lightly," declared President Obama. "But we cannot stand idly by when a tyrant tells his people that there will be no mercy."[33] By August 2011, the tide had turned as rebels advanced westward toward Tripoli. Qaddafi fled and was caught and killed in Sirte, his home city.

Restoring order proved difficult owing to regional rivalries, the autonomy of Libyan cities, feeble government bureaucracies, and the influence of Islamic extremists. Armed militias established during the civil war refused to demobilize. Arms looted from regime stockpiles fell into the hands of extremists. In late 2013, Libya's oil industry came to a halt owing to protests and strikes. Oil terminals and ports were blockaded for months, crippling the country's economy. Libya's prime minister warned oil tankers against dealing with militias, but the government lacked the resources to carry out his orders. One militia tried to ship oil on its own until a U.S. Navy SEAL team seized the tanker near Cyprus.

Terrorists murdered Ambassador Christopher Stevens and three other Americans at a house near the U.S. Consulate in Benghazi on September 11, 2012, an event Hillary Clinton described as her "biggest regret" as secretary of state.[34] Washington initially thought the attack was triggered by Muslim anger at a film produced in America that insulted the Prophet. In a speech at the UN, President Obama described the film as "crude and disgusting" and "an insult not only to Muslims, but to America as well." He observed, however, that the Constitution protected the right to free, even hateful, speech but noted, "Muslims have suffered the most at the hands of extremism."[35] When it turned out the attack had been carried out by the al-Qaeda-linked group Ansar al-Sharia (Libya) on the anniversary of 9/11, Republicans charged the administration with covering up the facts and providing inadequate protection for its diplomats. Witnesses claimed that the group's leader, Ahmed Abu Khattala, had led the attack. The presence of terrorists in Libya led Washington to launch a raid, seizing a member of al-Qaeda connected with the 1998 bombings of U.S. embassies in East Africa but failing to capture Khattala. In 2014, however, Khattala was spirited out of Libya by U.S. commandos and indicted for murder in America.

Libya experienced intensified violence after Qaddafi's death. Extremists attacked Sufi shrines, and tribal fighting continued. These events revealed divisions within the Supreme Security Committee, a force established by the transitional council with militiamen who retained their local identities. Militias formed to fight Qaddafi repeatedly clashed with one another and engaged in gunrunning and drug trafficking. Efforts to dismantle militias while using them for security produced regional warlords, and Prime Minister Ali Zeidan and his successor Abdullah-al Thinni requested foreign assistance to end the violence.

Zeidan enjoyed the support of Libya's liberal and secular elements but not that of Islamists who viewed him and his supporters as "remnants" of the Qaddafi regime. In February 2014 elections for a committee to draft a new constitution triggered violence by Islamists, and rioters stormed parliament as frustration with the country's slow political transition boiled over. An anti-Islamist militia led by former general Khalifa Haftar attacked parliament again in May. Violence raged in Benghazi between Haftar's forces and Islamists, and Haftar attracted support from Libya's anti-Islamists.

Libya was becoming a failed state, fueling the flight of refugees across the Mediterranean toward Europe. Violence erupted between militias from Zintan and Misrata for control of Tripoli and its airport. What began "as localized clashes between rogue brigades for control of Tripoli International Airport" became "an all-out battle for control of the entire capital," and set "the stage for a countrywide showdown between the anti-Islamist and Islamist blocs."[36] Two governments competed for control, one in Bayda in eastern Libya with former members of parliament allied with Haftar and aided by Egypt and the United Arab Emirates and the other, Islamist-led, in Tripoli supported by Turkey and Qatar. Amid the violence, U.S. diplomats, protected by warplanes, were evacuated to Tunisia.

Egypt

For three decades, Egypt's President Mubarak was an American ally, reinforcing his status by stoking fears of Islamic extremism and abiding by Egypt's peace treaty with Israel. Mubarak was an ideal partner for Washington as long as America focused on regional stability. The Arab Spring reached Egypt in early 2011 when demonstrators gathered to protest unemployment, corruption, and dictatorship. As in Tunisia, the trigger was a single incident—the death of a young man after a beating by police. Within days, Facebook, YouTube, Twitter, and cellphones spread the story, and eighteen days later Mubarak was forced from office.

Revolution January 25 was a "day of rage" as demonstrators gathered in Cairo and other cities, using social media to coordinate their actions. Mubarak dismissed his cabinet, while declaring he would meet protesters' concerns but refused to resign. "At the beginning of 2011, the Obama administration faced a dilemma in Egypt. President Hosni Mubarak had been a faithful ally and a pillar of stability in the Middle East," but once the "protests began in earnest, it was clear that history was passing the regime by. The foremost policy challenge in Washington was how to embrace change while maintaining order."[37]

President Obama phoned Mubarak, pressing him to act quickly. Afterward, Obama declared, "I just spoke to him after his speech and told him he has a responsibility to give meaning to those words, to take

Protesters in Cairo's Tahrir ("Martyr") Square

Khaled Elfiqi/epa/Corbis

concrete steps and actions that deliver on that promise."[38] Washington had decided to support reform. The next day Mubarak announced he would not run for reelection but would not step aside. Obama responded that "we have spoken out on behalf of the need for change" and it was his "belief that an orderly transition must be meaningful, it must be peaceful, and it must begin now."[39] The next day, Internet service was restored, and violence exploded between Mubarak's supporters and protesters. "The region is being battered by a perfect storm of powerful trends," declared Secretary Clinton. "This is what has driven demonstrators into the streets of Tunis, Cairo, and cities throughout the region. The status quo is simply not sustainable."[40] On February 11, Mubarak resigned. The army assumed power, committing itself to changing Egypt's constitution and electing a new government. The turmoil took an immediate toll on Egypt's economy as its tourism industry collapsed, foreign currency reserves plummeted, and unemployment soared.

The Islamic Interregnum Parliamentary elections gave the Muslim Brotherhood's Freedom and Justice Party 40 percent of the vote, giving it about half the seats in parliament's lower house and 90 percent of the seats in the upper house. As the election of a new president approached, Egypt's military leaders consolidated their influence, shutting down parliament and claiming the right to issue laws even after a new president took office. U.S.-educated Mohamed Morsi of the Brotherhood was narrowly elected in June 2012, promising "stability, security, justice and prosperity." Once in power, the Brotherhood faced the task of balancing the wishes of its religiously conservative Islamic base with the aspirations of the liberal and secular sectors that, while unhappy with corruption and economic malaise under Mubarak, remained wary of Islamists.

President Morsi set out to reduce the army's influence. He fired Egypt's defense minister to gain support from a younger generation of officers including American-trained General Abdel Fattah al-Sisi. Morsi then recalled the elected parliament that the generals had dissolved and nullified the army's claim to make laws. He also extended his authority over state institutions, notably the judicial system that was still staffed by Mubarak-era judges, ending judicial review, giving himself authority to issue laws until a new constitution took effect, and proclaiming that no court could dismiss the assembly writing the new constitution.

Thus began a train of events leading to Morsi's overthrow. The president's arbitrary actions brought thousands of protesters back into the streets of Cairo with the same slogan they had voiced about Mubarak—"The people want the fall of the regime." In December, Morsi's supporters physically prevented the country's Supreme Constitutional Court from ruling on the legitimacy of the Constituent Assembly that was writing the new constitution, and Morsi appointed new provincial governors, including several members of the Brotherhood and one who was associated with a terrorist group that had murdered 58 tourists in 1997. Thomas Friedman likened the latter's appointment to "Chicago appointing a crony of Al Capone to lead its tourism bureau."[41]

President Morsi's efforts to stifle dissent produced concern about his commitment to democracy, prompting the former director of the UN International Atomic Energy Agency and Nobel Peace Prize recipient Mohamed ElBaradei, to tweet, "Morsi today usurped all state powers & appointed himself Egypt's new pharaoh."[42] The draft of a new constitution was adopted over the objections of secular parties and approved by only a fifth of eligible voters in a referendum in which fewer than a third of voters cast ballots. The Brotherhood-inspired constitution declared Islam to be Egypt's religion and extended

Islamic law by ambiguous commitments to "preserve the true nature of the Egyptian family" and pro-tect "ethics and morals and public order."[43] Although the new constitution strengthened parliament and added human-rights guarantees, critics argued it did not adequately protect freedom of expression and religion nor meet secularist demands for separation of church and state. The constitution and Morsi's concentration of power stoked fears of an emerging dictatorship.

The sequence of events culminating in Morsi's removal predated his election. When Mubarak was ousted, Egypt's military leaders "set a dangerous precedent. Claiming 'revolutionary legitimacy,' the army said that, until the new constitution was written, the rules of the game were whatever the army said they were—even if the army changed its mind. When Morsi was elected before the constitution was written, he claimed the same power."[44] Morsi was only doing what the generals had done.

Despite loans from Qatar, Saudi Arabia, Turkey, and Libya, Egypt's economy was in free fall. Fuel shortages, lack of hard currency, disappearing foreign investment, increasing crime, and declining tour-ism produced a crisis. Negotiations for an International Monetary Fund loan were suspended owing to Egypt's failure to introduce reforms, notably reducing public subsidies on staples like food and oil. Attacks on anti-Morsi demonstrators led a State Department spokeswoman to voice concern about police brutality. Even as the Brotherhood tightened its control by placing supporters in government jobs, secret meetings were being held between Morsi's opponents and military leaders. The country's "deep state"—the professional bureaucrats and military, police, and intelligence apparatus—had turned against the president.

Counterrevolution   Repeatedly Washington counseled Morsi to be more inclusive, but Washington had little influence as it tried to avoid publicly criticizing the elected government. As Morsi's hold on power weakened, President Obama told him, "The United States is committed to the democratic process in Egypt and does not support any single party or group."[45] Even as U.S. officials became disillusioned with Morsi, they found a silver lining, repeating that the Brotherhood was a moderate group but failing to see it was not creating conditions for genuine democracy.

In December 2012, the Egyptian army warned it would intervene to prevent Egypt from "sliding into a dark tunnel of conflict, internal fighting, civil war, sectarian discord and the collapse of state institu-tions."[46] In June 2013, massive demonstrations organized by the Tamarod ("Rebellion"), a grassroots movement that had collected 22 million signatures demanding Morsi's resignation and nullification of the 2012 constitution, protested the Brotherhood's growing power and its exclusion of dissident voices. Morsi's foes declared that June 30 should be his final day in office, and on July 1, Egypt's military leaders gave him an ultimatum—the president had forty-eight hours to meet popular demands or they would intervene. When Morsi refused, Egypt's army carried out its threat two days later. A year after becoming Egypt's president, Morsi was ousted. Declaring that Egypt was descending into chaos, General Sisi suspended its constitution and named the president of Egypt's Supreme Constitutional Court as interim president until elections could be held. The swift end of fuel shortages, reappearance of police on the streets, and reaffirmation of privileges making the armed forces independent of civilian oversight indicated that Egypt's "deep state" had indeed subverted the government.

The ouster of President Morsi produced a wave of nationalist enthusiasm among the Brotherhood's secular opponents. The Brotherhood's leaders were arrested, and its media outlets were shuttered. In August, after promising to disperse pro-Brotherhood demonstrators peacefully, the security services, using armored vehicles and snipers, killed over 500. Morsi's trial for incitement of murder began in late 2013, and he was charged with conspiring with foreign groups including Hamas and Hezbollah to commit terrorism. He was convicted and sentenced to twenty years imprisonment and later to death for allegedly participating in a mass prison break that took place during in 2011. The Brotherhood was declared a terrorist group and dissolved, and its assets were confiscated. America found itself a helpless bystander as the Brotherhood was swept from power. President Obama warned Egypt's new leaders, "While we want to sustain our relationship with Egypt, our traditional cooperation cannot continue as usual when civilians are being killed and rights are being rolled back."[47]

The Obama administration, which had unsuccessfully advised Egypt's military leaders not to over-throw Morsi, refused to call the coup d'état a "coup," because under U.S. law that required terminating America's military and economic aid to Egypt. Egypt's military leaders argued it was not a coup but a popular uprising, and Secretary Kerry echoed this: "The military was asked to intervene by millions and millions of people" and had been "restoring democracy."[48] A former U.S. official concluded, "The law by its terms dictates one thing, and sensible policy dictates that we don't do that."[49] The Obama administration had chosen pragmatism over idealism. According to a senior administration official, "What was driving this decision was what's in the best interest of the United States going forward and how can we have the most leverage to promote our interests in a very volatile situation."[50]

President Obama expressed concern at the actions of Egypt's military leaders, and the administration showed its disapproval by temporarily delaying the delivery of jet fighters, freezing delivery of military hardware, and canceling military exercises with the Egyptian army. Some members of the Senate sought to reconsider military aid to Egypt. "I'm not prepared to sign off on the delivery of additional aid for the Egyptian military," declared Senator Patrick Leahy (D-VT). "I'm not prepared to do that until we see convincing evidence the government is committed to the rule of law."[51] The regime's opponents concluded that America had supported the Islamists, while Islamists believed America favored the coup. As Obama admitted, "We've been blamed by supporters of Morsi. We've been blamed by the other side, as if we are supporters of Morsi."[52]

Although the removal of Morsi and the repression of the Brotherhood slowed the Arab Spring, its bloodiest casualty was Syria. There, the government's violent response to protests triggered civil war pitting President Bashar al-Assad and his Alawite (a branch of Shia Islam) followers against a Sunni insurgency. The conflict generated disagreement in Washington about whether America should get involved and, if so, to what extent.

Syria

The first protests for democratic reform occurred in the city of Daraa in mid-March 2011. In April, the regime began to use ground forces supported by tanks, aircraft, helicopter gunships, and a paramilitary militia against opponents. The first armed resistance by regime foes from the country's Sunni majority was a local rising near the Turkish border. Thereafter began what became a flood of almost 17 million Syrians of a total population of 23 million (2015) driven from their homes,[53] many to other countries whose governments became outspoken foes of Assad.

The Civil War Intensifies America and the European Union imposed sanctions on Syria in May as its army intensified its use of force to crush the insurrection. In Syria, several former military officers established the Free Syrian Army, and Syria's Sunni prime minister defected to the rebels. At this point, U.S. leaders and intelligence agencies believed Assad's regime would not survive, and President Obama declared, "The future of Syria must be determined by its people, but President Bashar al-Assad is standing in their way. For the sake of the Syrian people, the time has come for President Assad to step aside."[54]

Russia and China vetoed UN resolutions condemning Assad, fearing that they might be used to bring about regime change much as NATO had used a UN resolution to justify intervening in Libya. The UN approved a milder statement in support of a nonbinding peace plan drafted by former UN Secretary-General Kofi Annan, but Syrian forces continued to use heavy weapons in urban areas leading to UN condemnation.

International Links As Syria's civil war intensified, members of the international community began to take sides. Iran and Russia remained Assad's strongest supporters, and the Lebanese-based Shia group Hezbollah, an Iranian proxy, intervened to assist Assad to prevent the overthrow of Iran's Arab ally. Iranian leaders viewed the Syrian civil war as part of a larger regional struggle between Shia Iran and Sunni Saudi Arabia and their allies, providing billions in aid to Assad and members of the Quds Force, an elite arm of Iran's Revolutionary Guard Corps. Declared Secretary Kerry, "Believe me, the bad actors, regrettably, have no shortage of their ability to get arms—from Iran, Hezbollah, from Russia, unfortunately."[55] Iraq's Shia government, while not openly taking sides, allowed the transit of Iranian arms shipments to Syria despite American protests. A U.S. official noted, "The abuse of airspace by Iran continues to be a concern."[56]

Assad's foes included Turkey's Prime Minister (later President) Recep Tayyip Erdoğan, who having followed a policy of "zero problems with neighbors" before Syria's civil war opposed Assad's brutal use of force. Syrian-Turkish tension was fueled by incidents along their border including the downing of a Turkish jet in international airspace leading Erdoğan to threaten to invoke NATO's Article 5 that requires alliance partners to come to the aid of a member under attack. NATO did deploy Patriot antimissile batteries in southern Turkey. Other incidents included the explosion of car bombs in a Turkish border town and the downing of a Syrian helicopter in Turkish airspace.

Assad foes also included Jordan, Saudi Arabia, Bahrain, and Kuwait, countries ruled by conservative Sunni monarchs fearful of the spread of instability and encirclement by Shia Iran and its allies. Despite U.S. warnings that weapons could end up in the hands of Sunni extremists, Qatar and other Persian Gulf states shipped arms to Syrian rebels, trying to weaken the link between Iran and Syria but also reflecting frustration with American reluctance to arm the insurgents. The rebels, however, received few arms capable of neutralizing the government's tanks and airpower. Insurgent groups competed for loot and weapons, and fighters joined the better-armed groups, including those led by militant extremists.

Despite escalating violence, the Obama administration was reluctant to aid Assad's foes lest America become embroiled in the civil war. A senior U.S. official who had told supporters of Syria's rebels that "all options are on the table" recalled, "But as I was mouthing the words, I began to wonder if I was doing the right thing." A senior Pentagon official admitted, "Nobody could figure out what to do."[57] At a meeting in October 2012, Secretary of Defense Leon Panetta, Secretary Clinton, and CIA director David Petraeus argued for arming the rebels. Clinton recalled that "Petraeus and I argued that there was a big difference between Qatar and Saudi Arabia dumping weapons into the country and the United States responsibly training and equipping a non-extremist rebel force," but the "president's inclination was to stay the present course and not take the significant further course of arming rebels."[58] In February 2013, the administration announced it would provide humanitarian aid to rebels, leading an opponent of the Assad regime to comment acidly, "Nonlethal assistance—blankets and cellphones—do not topple a regime."[59] By mid-2013, the tide had turned in favor of Assad owing to Hezbollah's intervention, and the rebels' deteriorating situation sharpened debate in Washington about whether to intervene actively.

American Intervention? In June 2013, Secretary Kerry informed President Obama that Assad's forces had used chemical weapons (CW) against civilians, and that if America failed to "impose consequences," the Syrian regime would view it as a "green light for continued CW use."[60] His prediction was borne out when the regime used poison gas on August 21, killing numerous civilians and ignoring the president's earlier warning that "a red line for us is we start seeing a whole bunch of chemical weapons moving around or being utilized."[61] According to a U.S. official, "The idea was to put a chill into the Assad regime without actually trapping the president into any predetermined action." According to another, "what the president said in August was unscripted,"[62] and his remark caught aides by surprise.

The president's threat probably perplexed the actors in the Syrian drama rather than clarifying U.S. policy. "By threatening 'enormous consequences,'" Obama seemed to be saying that "the first chemical attack would bring the Americans running in, guns blazing."[63] Having committed himself, the president's **credibility** was at issue, and he decided to launch airstrikes against Syrian forces. Obama declared, "The world set a red line when governments representing 98 percent of the world's population said the use of chemical weapons are abhorrent and passed a treaty forbidding their use even when countries are engaged in war."[64] But after Britain's Parliament rejected a motion to join America, Obama overruled his advisers and decided to seek congressional authorization for a strike. It was a gamble the president would likely lose if the issue were to be put to a vote.

A Russian proposal to destroy Syria's chemical weapons allowed Obama to escape the dilemma (chapter 4). The president's defenders attributed Russia's proposal and Assad's willingness to go along, as well as an accompanying push to hold a peace conference, to the president's threat. But the episode also reflected presidential indecision. Presidential adviser Benjamin Rhodes described the dilemma: "We need to be realistic about our ability to dictate events in Syria. In the absence of any good options, people have lifted up military support for the opposition as a silver bullet, but it has to be seen as a tactic—not a strategy."[65]

Finally, in June 2013, President Obama secretly endorsed a CIA plan to provide small arms to Assad's foes, and a year later he requested $500 million from Congress to "train and equip vetted elements of the Syrian opposition to help defend the Syrian people, stabilize areas under opposition control, facilitate the provision of essential services, counter terrorist threats, and promote conditions for a negotiated settlement."[66] The plan was abandoned a year later. Indeed, an internal CIA study found that covert aid to insurgents usually failed without the presence of American advisers.[67] In September 2014, responding to the threat of ISIS, Obama authorized additional U.S. aid and dispatched about 400 troops to train and arm 5,000 moderate Sunni rebels a year.

A Divided Opposition As the Syrian civil war ground on, Assad's foes were unable to form a coherent front. Divisions persisted between opposition politicians residing outside Syria and militant groups fighting within the country. Another schism emerged between moderates and radical jihadists, and a third pitted jihadists against one another.

The Syrian National Council (SNC) was formed in 2011 by a coalition of antigovernment exiles in Istanbul, Turkey. It was an umbrella coalition of groups of different views that promised to transform Syria into a democratic and pluralistic civil state. But it proved ineffective and quarrelsome and was viewed with suspicion by those concerned by its Islamist links. In September 2013, eleven of Syria's strongest rebel brigades including militant and moderate fighters announced their rejection of the SNC and its leaders living outside Syria.

Thereafter several groups established the National Coalition for Syrian Revolutionary and Opposition Forces with members from inside and outside Syria who hoped their moderate Islamist organization would gain international recognition, administer rebel-controlled areas, and plan for a post-Assad democracy. The National Coalition swiftly acquired support from America, the EU, and members of the Gulf Cooperation Council (Saudi Arabia, Kuwait, the United Arab Emirates, Qatar, Bahrain, and Oman). But the National Coalition, too, proved fractious, was inadequately financed, and was unable to exert authority over the armed rebels, especially jihadist groups. Within Syria, the Supreme Military Council of the Free Syrian Army remained the titular leader of the insurrection but actually enjoyed little authority over the disparate rebel brigades. Some of its units were nonideological while others were regional, and the Military Council grew increasingly dysfunctional and factionalized.

Although secular moderates initially led the insurrection, Islamic groups increasingly challenged the Free Syrian Army's authority. Jaish al-Islam (Army of Islam)—an umbrella organization of eleven moderate Islamist groups—sought to exclude jihadists linked to al-Qaeda, but the Syrian Islamic Front, a coalition of hardline Islamic groups, included many of the insurrection's most effective fighters. The fighting ability of Sunni extremists made them favored recipients of financial aid from Arab donors. Fund-raisers using social media were especially effective in soliciting contributions. Using suicide tactics against government forces and operating across the country, jihadists also fought among themselves as well as with non-Islamist rebels. "For all practical purposes," concluded a former State Department official, "the moderate armed opposition that the administration really wanted to support—although in a hesitant and halfhearted way—is now on the sidelines."[68] American support for the exiled opposition and the Free Syrian Army proved unsuccessful, and conflicts among Assad's foes helped keep him in power. "Syria today," wrote General Martin Dempsey, chairman of the Joint Chiefs of Staff, "is not about choosing between two sides but rather about choosing one among many sides," and "the side we choose must be ready to promote their interests and ours when the balance shifts in their favor. Today they are not."[69]

Assad Hangs On Two years of indecision took their toll. Had Washington acted decisively to arm and support the anti-Assad insurrection in 2011 or 2012, the regime might have been swiftly overthrown. Rebel fighters steadily gained ground, and the government was forced to employ crude "barrel bombs" and Russian-supplied missiles against rebel-held areas. Beginning in the spring of 2013, regime forces began to push insurgents from strategic positions they had occupied. Hezbollah's intervention proved decisive in the regime's victory in the struggle for the strategic towns of Qusayr, which opened a corridor between Damascus and western and northern Syria, and Yabrud, near the Lebanese border. In April 2014, President Assad announced he was winning his "war on terror" and would run again for president, a move intended to preclude discussion of a transitional government. The regime's recovery dimmed hopes for an early end to civil war, exacerbated conflicts among Assad's foes, and dimmed prospects for peace talks in Geneva, Switzerland.

Washington's initial position had been that Assad should play no role in Syria's political future, but Russia rejected this as predetermining the outcome of negotiations and sent military advisers to aid him. Ryan Crocker, a former U.S. ambassador, concluded that America's determination to oust Assad in advance of negotiations was surreal. "'Assad must go.' Well Assad isn't going to go."[70] After a week of wrangling, the Geneva conference adjourned with its only positive result the fact that both sides were in the same room. A second round of talks was equally fruitless. Syria's government denounced its foes as "terrorists" and refused to discuss their demands for a political transition.

With Hezbollah's intervention and the regime's enemies divided, the opportunity to depose Assad quickly had passed. The growing influence of radical Islamists made critics of Assad less certain his overthrow was desirable because it seemed to support his claim that if he were overthrown, extremists would replace him. Also, American refusal to adopt a robust policy against Assad had angered some of Washington's regional allies. Declared a former U.S. official, "We spent so much damn time navel gazing, and that's the tragedy of it."[71] Nevertheless, although by 2015 Washington had begun to contemplate that Assad might remain, the resurgence of regime foes and the reduction in the numbers of Syrian soldiers owing to casualties and desertions had made the regime increasingly vulnerable and dependent on Hezbollah. Thus, in October 2015 Russia intervened with air, ground, and naval forces to aid Assad.

FUTURE: AN ARAB WINTER?

Egypt

Egypt has long been at the center of Arab political life. Its treaty with Israel remained a rare success in the Arab-Israeli peace process, and its defection from the Soviet embrace during the Cold War was a decisive event. The Egyptian revolution that overthrew Mubarak was the high point of the Arab Spring, and some observers consider the Brotherhood's demise its nadir and the beginning of an Arab Winter.

While the military crushed the Brotherhood, 38 percent of Egypt's voters went to the polls and 98 percent of them voted in favor of a military-backed constitution in what Secretary Kerry described as a "polarized political environment."[72] The new constitution obliged the government to fight terrorism, and the powers it granted its leaders "invite limitless interpretations and ensure that arbitrary and exceptional security measures remain the norm in Egypt."[73] Washington's attitude to the tumultuous events in Egypt was ambiguous, reflecting a desire to foster democracy with a preference for political stability and uncertainty about whether empowering political Islam augured a democratic future or an intolerant theocracy. The absence of clarity in U.S. policy reduced American influence in Egypt and alienated both sides in its political conflicts.

After Mubarak's ouster, Washington chose to engage the Muslim Brotherhood. Concern that an Islamist government would jeopardize regional stability by adopting anti-Israeli policies or encouraging Islamic extremism proved exaggerated. With American encouragement, President Morsi helped broker a ceasefire between Israel and Hamas in 2012, dealt harshly with jihadi extremists in the Sinai Peninsula, and condemned Assad's "oppressive regime." One U.S. official even said of the Brotherhood, "They sound like Republicans half the time."[74] Nevertheless, after the army coup, a former American official explained, "If you said to people you can cast a secret ballot on whether to turn back the clock and have Morsi in power again, I don't think very many people in Washington would turn back that clock."[75]

General Sisi easily won Egypt's presidential election in May 2014. During his campaign, he made it clear he would be a strong president but that his government would be inclusive. Secretary Kerry, visiting Cairo, announced a resumption of U.S. aid to Egypt. Whether Sisi will succeed depends on his ability to end corruption, provide security, and improve Egypt's economy. Sisi, however, had no clear economic or political agenda, and growing extremist violence may produce overreaction by the army. Although Egypt's security apparatus backs the regime, its popularity may ebb as the alleged threat posed by the Brotherhood wanes and, like its predecessors, it, too, may become corrupt and authoritarian.

Policy Options   America's options are fraught with uncertainty about whether Washington can affect what happens in Egypt. Declared a former U.S. official, "Anything they do that is dramatic puts the United States in the middle of a story that we really don't want to be in the middle of."[76]

a.   *Focus on democratization and press Egypt to establish an inclusive democratic system.* Egypt's military rulers laid out a "roadmap" for the country—an interim government, elections, an amended constitution, and establishment of a reconciliation commission. Following Morsi's overthrow, Deputy Secretary of State William Burns scolded Egypt's military leaders. "If representatives of some of the largest parties in Egypt are detained or excluded, how are dialogue and participation possible?"[77] Egypt, however, has sources of financial aid in the Arab world and could realign itself politically with Russia. Israel, too, supports the military regime. Moreover, Morsi's ouster reflected genuine unhappiness of a substantial segment of Egyptian society with his incompetence, authoritarianism, and Islamic inclinations. Polls reflected a marked increase in Egyptian optimism after Mubarak's ouster and an equally significant decline in the country's mood two years later.[78]

Pressuring President Sisi would strain Cairo's military cooperation with America, notably fly-over rights across Egypt for conducting counterterrorist strikes and fast-track transit for U.S. naval vessels through the Suez Canal. "We need them for the Suez Canal, we need them for the peace treaty with Israel, we need them for the overflights, and we need them for the continued fight against violent extremists who are as much of a threat to Egypt's transition to democracy as they are to American interests,"[79] argued General James Mattis, former head of the U.S. Central Command. American pressure would also exacerbate relations with allies like Saudi Arabia that detest political Islam.

b.   *Let events run their course,* which has the advantage of avoiding blame for what happens but may allow matters to further deteriorate in a country that is critical to U.S. interests. Civil war between Islamists and Egypt's army similar to that which wracked Algeria in the early 1990s is one possibility. Radicalization of Egypt's Islamists is taking place, and the prospect of a radical Islamic government is the worst possible outcome for America.

c.   *Engage Egypt's military leaders, encouraging them to pursue liberal political and economic policies.* The resumption of U.S. military aid to Egypt may presage such a policy. One analyst sees promise in engagement, arguing that General Sisi resembles President Nasser before he turned to the USSR. "The challenge for both the United States and Sisi will be to recalibrate their expectations of the relationship so that they focus narrowly on the enduring overlap in strategic interests." America "needs a strong Egypt upon which to anchor its drifting policy in the region, while Sisi needs arms and money to fend off domestic challengers."[80] Sisi, however, mixes nationalism and Islam and, like Nasser, may be willing to switch horses in midstream. Although Washington tried to work with President Morsi, relations deteriorated after Egyptian-Iranian relations began to warm and mobs attacked America's embassy. Morsi's failure to criticize those who had attacked the embassy prompted an angry phone call from Obama.

Engagement requires Washington to encourage an inclusive Egyptian government and economic reform to reduce unemployment, promote growth, and reduce corruption. To encourage reform, America might foster investment in and trade with Egypt, provide expertise and economic aid, and forgive Egyptian debts to America. The objective of such actions would not be democratization as an end in itself but political stability.

Syria

Syria's civil war presented Washington with a quandary. Should America sit back and leave Assad in power, or should it support the insurgency? And if America aided the insurgency, how could it ensure that moderates rather than extremists would triumph? Between 2011 and 2015, the carnage in Syria had exceeded 220,000 dead, including 76,000 in 2014 alone, and the Assad regime was starving pro-rebel communities and impeding efforts to get humanitarian aid to civilians. The UN estimated that 6,000 Syrians were fleeing the country *every* day. Of the 4 million registered Syrian refugees who had fled to Lebanon, Turkey, and Jordan by April 2015,[81] over 1.2 million had fled to Lebanon alone,[82] equal to almost a third of its population, which had the "highest per capita concentration of refugees worldwide."[83] Over 1.7 million were registered in Turkey,[84] including 180,000 from the Syrian Kurdish city of Kobani besieged by ISIS, and refugees were streaming into Europe.

In March 2015, Washington pledged an additional $508 million in relief assistance for Syrian civilians and refugees, having provided $3.7 billion in humanitarian aid since 2011.[85] The UN Human Rights Council condemned the regime's human rights abuses, but China and Russia vetoed a resolution to allow the ICC to investigate war crimes. Frustrated by difficulty in getting the regime to distribute humanitarian aid, America sought to bypass the regime. Secretary Kerry declared, "It's not getting to people. It's going through one gate, one entryway, and it's going through Damascus and/or controlled by the Assad regime. That's unacceptable."[86] Finally, in June 2014, the Security Council unanimously authorized emergency aid without prior approval by the regime, and this began a month later.

Syria had fragmented into small sectarian ghettoes—Alawite, Sunni, and Kurdish. The conflict had spilled into Lebanon and Iraq. Israel feared instability on its Syrian border; America's allies were angry about U.S. passivity in the face of Assad's brutality; and Russia had intervened militarily. A former State Department official noted, "There is a lot of confusion and lack of clarity amongst U.S. allies in the Middle East regarding Washington's true intentions and ultimate objectives," and there is widespread concern "shared by many U.S. allies that the United States' primary objectives when it comes to Iran, Egypt or Syria are to avoid serious confrontation."[87]

Policy options were narrowed by the growing strength of Islamic extremists that worked to Assad's advantage by giving substance to the narrative that his foes were "terrorists." A former State Department adviser summarized America's dilemma. "Some of the more extremist opposition is very scary from an American perspective, and that presents us with all sorts of problems."[88] Syria, concluded Hillary Clinton, was a "wicked problem" and what makes such problems "wicked" "is that every option seems worse than the next."[89] According to a former adviser, the decision not to use force after Assad's use of poison gas "was when things really started to go bad."[90] "A year later, the world is witnessing the Hydra-headed worst-case scenario in which Assad is stronger," and "Assad's most dangerous radicalized opponents, now called the Islamic State, have also gained considerable ground."[91]

Policy Options

a. *Arm the Syrian opposition while negotiating to end the civil war and empower a government without Assad.* The Obama administration tentatively adopted this option but may have done so too late. Russia and Iran continued to support the Assad regime, and it proved difficult to ensure that arms would be given only to moderate insurgents. President Obama's September 2014 decision to bomb the Islamic State in Syria as well as Iraq raised fears that Assad would be the major beneficiary.

b. *Negotiate an end to the conflict that leaves Assad in power.* Press Secretary Jay Carney observed: "While there are shifts in momentum on the battlefield, Bashar al-Assad, in our view, will never rule all of Syria again."[92] By mid-2015, Assad was under increasing military pressure but retained power. Even if he only controlled part of Syria, it would be a victory of sorts. Moreover, polls showed that, although Syria's neighbors still wished him to surrender power, majorities elsewhere were fearful of a jihadist victory and opposed Western military aid to his foes.[93] Indeed, many Syrians found it difficult to understand how Washington could fight ISIS while refusing to intervene against the regime that they regarded as a more deadly foe.

If Syria's civil war conflict were likely to end with jihadists in power or controlling large areas of Syria (and Iraq), Washington might prefer Assad. That choice would reduce tensions between America and Russia and Iran but alienate Israel and Sunni Arabs who fear a Shia axis as well as human-rights groups and Congress who are appalled by the regime's atrocities. American allies were already angered by Washington's failure to carry out airstrikes after the regime's use of chemical weapons. Turkey had encouraged U.S. strikes and felt betrayed, and Saudi leaders were furious at America's support for President Morsi. It would also be difficult to persuade anti-Assad militants to negotiate with the regime. Leaving Assad in power would be seen domestically and abroad as reflecting Washington's failure to act as a global leader.

c. *Use force to depose Assad,* ending the caution shown by the Obama administration to date but without ensuring the winning side would include those preferred by Washington. Owing to war weariness after Iraq and Afghanistan, U.S. public opinion and Congress would probably oppose this course that might lead to a U.S.-Russia confrontation. Still, one analyst concluded, "absent the credible application of force against the Syrian regime, a negotiated transition leading to Mr. Assad's departure is not going to happen."[94] Indeed it may prove impossible to resolve the issue peacefully without including Iran in negotiations.

CONCLUSION: ARAB SPRING OR ARAB WINTER?

Much has happened in the tumultuous years since Mohamed Bouazizi's suicide lit a spark that spread like wildfire across the Arab world. Most Arab states had been governed by authoritarian families or clan-based political parties legitimated by powerless parliaments. Oil wealth had permitted conservative regimes to purchase citizens' docility. After the Arab Spring began, dictators everywhere including China trembled.

A few years later, democracy in the Arab world was in retreat. Political violence afflicted Bahrain, Egypt, Iraq, Libya, Syria, Tunisia, and Yemen, and despite the spread of democratic aspirations, national circumstances produced disparate outcomes in different countries and exacerbated sectarian conflict everywhere. Libya, having rid itself of Qaddafi's tyranny, remained in the grip of violent militias, and Iraq was afflicted by sectarian violence to an extent not seen since the withdrawal of American troops.

The Islamic political parties that won elections during the Arab Spring discovered that governing is difficult. Secular elites remained suspicious even of moderate Islamists. The Muslim Brotherhood's effort to Islamize Egyptian society, its incompetence in coping with economic and social challenges, its monopolization of political power, and its unwillingness to compromise produced a backlash. Its experience revealed the growing resistance of secular Arabs to Islamism. And with failure of moderate Islamists like the Muslim Brotherhood either to gain or retain influence in the region, Islamic extremists, who reject democratic norms, became more powerful. The terrorist group and putative "caliphate" ISIS expressed the view of the extremists when it declared that Islamists must choose "the ammunition boxes over the ballot boxes."[95]

ISIS revealed how the Arab Spring produced chaos in much of the region and how nonstate groups—militias, religious sects, and terrorists—became competitors of states in the Islamic world for individuals' identities and loyalties. Not only are many of these states artificial creations of European imperialism but "the region's insecure, control-obsessed governments—sometimes dominated by minorities—have failed to integrate citizens within an inclusive sense of nationhood."[96] Several of these states were engulfed by civil war while others were plagued by sectarian and ethnic violence. Transnational identities and loyalties including Sunni, Shia, Christian, and Kurdish are subdivided into myriad subgroups reflecting regional and tribal affiliations, moderate or extremist belief systems, and Islamic or secular leanings.

Washington had chosen interests over ideals, but America cannot ignore the region. "The problem is that history teaches that the Middle East doesn't like being ignored. Through soaring energy prices, or the scourge of terrorism, or some other calamity, it has a habit of insinuating itself onto the American agenda."[97] America's options reflected the limits of its influence and the difficulty, perhaps the impossibility, of achieving stability while satisfying the democratic aspirations of the region's growing populations. Little had changed in the Arab world in previous decades, even as democratization had spread to Latin America and Eastern Europe. "The demise of Middle Eastern authoritarianism may come eventually. But there is little reason to think that day is near, and even less reason to think that the United States can significantly increase its chances of happening."[98] Referring to Egypt, Benjamin Rhodes noted, "The president made a decision to side with democratic change," but "we made it clear that it is not our place to dictate the outcomes in any given country."[99] Washington had no clear strategy for achieving both stability and democracy, and in an era of declining U.S. hegemony the Arab world was less amenable to American influence.

The problems of the Arab world stem from the difficulty in establishing liberal democracy where it had never previously existed. The region can no longer rely on the support for democratization that President Obama promised in 2009. As the president's national security adviser Susan Rice noted, "We can't just be consumed 24/7 by one region, important as it is."[100] The Arab Spring was forced to take a back seat to the Israel-Palestinian dispute and Iran's nuclear ambitions. Despite the Arab Spring, Arab societies remained economically and socially backward, caught between authoritarian and corrupt leaders and Islamic fanatics in states with artificial borders. American policy, at least initially, had represented what Samuel Johnson famously called "the triumph of hope over experience." The story of the Arab Spring is not over, and the aspirations of those who thronged the centers of Cairo and Tripoli a few years ago remain. The countries that experienced revolutionary changes may flourish in coming years, and those in turmoil may become stable and prosper.

DISCUSSION QUESTIONS

1. Should America support popular aspirations in Arab societies, possibly empowering Islamists, or should it maintain ties with friendly authoritarian regimes?

2. Should America try to restore order in response to the chaos that engulfed Syria, Libya, and Egypt, or should it let events run their course?

3. Should America seek regime change in the Arab world?

4. What interests does the United States have in the Arab world since becoming virtually self-sufficient in oil and gas production?

5. How are U.S. relations with Iran linked to relations with Sunni Arab states like Saudi Arabia?

6. Despite setbacks, will the Arab Spring ultimately succeed in democratizing Arab societies?

KEY TERMS

credibility (p. 318)

expediency (p. 299)

Islamization (p. 308)

nationalism (p. 305)

nonaligned movement (p. 305)

pan-Arab nationalism (p. 305)

political Islam (p. 307)

Responsibility to Protect (R2P) (p. 311)

secular (p. 304)

social media (p. 309)

⑤SAGE edge™
for CQ Press

Sharpen your skill with SAGE edge at **edge.sagepub.com/mansbach**

SAGE edge for Students provides a personalized approach to help you accomplish your coursework goals in an easy-to-use learning environment.

11

America and Radical Islam

The death of Osama
bin Laden

Spencer Platt/Getty Images

The hijacking of American aircraft and attacks of September 11, 2001, on New York's World Trade Center and the Pentagon near Washington, D.C., changed U.S. foreign policy with dramatic suddenness. America's foe challenged not only American security and its presence in the Middle East but also its basic values—democracy, secularism, capitalism, and modernity. The end of the Cold War had produced uncertainty about American objectives in what President George H. W. Bush termed "the new world order" characterized by the spread of liberal values worldwide. Francis Fukuyama wrote of "the end of history," featuring "the ultimate triumph of Western liberal democracy," "an unabashed victory of economic and political liberalism," and the "triumph of the West, of the Western *idea*."[1]

For four decades the USSR—the "Red Menace"—had provided a focus for U.S policy, and it had disappeared. Islamic extremism—the "Green Menace"—became a substitute after 9/11. Bin Laden was the face of terrorism that Americans knew and associated with the War on Terror. After 9/11 America seemed more vulnerable than at any time since the Cold War. The attacks revealed that terrorists had global reach and were prepared to use indiscriminate violence. The challenge of asymmetric warfare forced Washington to rethink its national security strategy to include proactive force to combat terrorism. It triggered U.S. intervention in Afghanistan in 2001, leading to the longest war in American history. Islamic terrorism was cited as a reason for intervention in Iraq in 2003, and fear of terrorism led to reorganizing America's government.

SOURCES OF U.S. POLICY TOWARD TERRORISM

U.S. policies toward terrorism were largely shaped by external factors, notably attacks on Americans and U.S. interests. No president could have failed to respond to those attacks, but the sources of specific actions taken by Presidents Bush and Obama—the invasion of and military decisions about Afghanistan and Iraq and strikes against terrorist groups—were complex and changing.

Government factors, notably bureaucratic disagreement, repeatedly entered decisions dealing with the War on Terror. Thus, government bureaucracies altered their views about whether Saddam Hussein had weapons of mass destruction (WMD) and were divided over the 2007 to 2008 "surge" of troops to Iraq. The CIA and other agencies initially supported the view that Iraq had WMD, but in time, analysts altered their views. Government agencies were divided over what policies to follow after occupying Baghdad did not end the Iraq war that was becoming a civil war pitting Shias, Sunnis, and Kurds against one another.

Agencies' views also diverged concerning Afghanistan after initial unanimity about invading after the Taliban refused to surrender bin Laden. Fissures appeared in the administration and Congress about the wisdom of focusing on Iraq at the cost of investing more in Afghanistan. Democratic opponents of the war preferred ending the Iraq war and focusing on Afghanistan, while Republicans rallied behind President Bush and advocated security and surveillance domestically as well as overseas.

President Obama was determined to end the Iraq war, and U.S. forces began to withdraw in 2009, completing the process in 2011. The administration, however, was divided over a troop surge in Afghanistan requested by General David Petraeus, then head of U.S. Central Command, who had designed the earlier Iraq surge. According to Secretary of State Hillary Clinton, "The president welcomed a full range of opinions and invited contrary points of view. And I thought it was a very healthy experience because people took him up on it. And one thing we didn't want—to have a decision made and then have somebody say, 'Oh, by the way.' No, come forward now or forever hold your peace."[2] Siding with Petraeus and General Stanley McCrystal, Commander of U.S. Forces Afghanistan, were Clinton, Secretary of Defense Robert Gates, and General Michael Mullen, chairman of the Joint Chiefs of Staff. Opposed were Vice President Joe Biden, Special Representative to Afghanistan Richard Holbrooke, and Ambassador to Afghanistan Karl Eikenberry. Holbrooke, in particular, argued for negotiations with the Taliban and believed the administration was too preoccupied with domestic politics to design a clear strategy.

After three months of debate, Obama decided to send additional troops. One critic viewed the decision as a compromise driven by domestic forces. The "policy that emerged from the reassessment of strategy in 2009—increasing troop levels through the summer of 2011 and withdrawing at the end of 2014—was worse than either of the proposed options," allowing NATO forces "to fight the insurgency" but placing time limits that "kept the fighting from producing enduring political results." Thus, "only in southern Afghanistan and northwest Pakistan are there adherents to al-Qaeda's radical ideology less than a day's drive from the world's least secure [Pakistan's] nuclear arsenal."[3]

In a different context, Hillary Clinton recalled how she and Leon Panetta, then CIA director, collaborated in designing a counterterrorism strategy for President Obama. "Some of the White House national security staff supported our plan, but others were concerned. They wanted to be sure State wasn't trying to usurp the White House's role as the primary coordinator of activity across the various agencies" in combatting "extremist propaganda."[4] This incident reflected Secretary Gates's criticism of the centralization of decision making in the administration. "The controlling nature of the Obama White House and the NSS staff [National Security Council staff] took micromanagement and operational meddling to a new level."[5]

The impact of role was evident when Panetta defended his agency against charges of "poor tradecraft" after several agents were killed by a suicide bomber in Afghanistan. "The CIA cannot speak publicly about its major victories—the plots foiled, the terrorists neutralized. In the past year, we have done exceptionally heavy damage to al-Qaeda and its associates."[6] John Brennan as CIA director warned the Obama administration that extremists in Syria's civil war could threaten America. "We are concerned about the use of Syrian territory by the al-Qaeda organization to recruit individuals and develop the capability to be able not just to carry out attacks inside of Syria but also to use Syria as a launching pad"[7] for attacks against America.

Societal factors also had an impact on the War on Terror. In 2011, 75 percent of Americans polled approved of withdrawal from Iraq, including 96 percent of Democrats—a decision some observers later concluded produced a power vacuum that allowed ISIS to seize large areas of Iraq in 2014.[8] After ISIS decapitated two American journalists in August, however, a large majority of Americans regarded the group as a serious threat to U.S. interests and supported airstrikes in Iraq and Syria.[9]

In earlier administrations, public opinion data "apparently played little role in *policy decisions*, but they helped shape *how issues were* framed in what was a relentless effort to gain public support for the administration's policies on Iraq." President Bush believed "his own instincts provided a better

Timeline

1900

1979 Soviet invasion of Afghanistan

1988 Establishment of al-Qaeda ("the Base") in Afghanistan

1992 Al-Qaeda involved in deaths of U.S. soldiers in Somalia

1993 Bombing in basement of the World Trade Center

1900 (Continued)

1996 Bombing of a U.S. military facility in Saudi Arabia

1998 Bombing of U.S. embassies in Kenya and Tanzania; Bin Laden calls upon Muslims to kill Americans; U.S. cruise missile attacks against terrorist camps in Afghanistan and Sudan

2000

2000 Al-Qaeda attacks the USS *Cole* off Aden, Yemen.

September 11, **2001** Al-Qaeda airplane hijackers attack New York and Washington.

2001–2014 War in Afghanistan

2002 Suicide bombings in Bali, Indonesia

2004 CIA drone attacks against Islamic militants in Pakistan begin guide to the public mood."[10] The Bush administration mounted a campaign to prepare public opinion for intervening in Iraq. America's public supported the initial intervention because the administration had framed the issue "as a central part of the post-9/11 'global war on terrorism.'"[11] The war's popularity peaked in March 2003 after President Bush triumphantly declared an end to combat operations, but revelations about abuse of prisoners by U.S. personnel at Iraq's Abu Ghraib prison in 2004 and an upsurge in sectarian violence in 2006 intensified public opposition. Support increased after the surge of troops in Iraq in 2006 and then leveled off with a majority concluding that U.S. intervention had been a mistake.[12]

Corporate interests sought to profit from the War on Terror. Responding to congressional debate about how illegal migration from Mexico threatened America's homeland security, defense corporations competed to provide expensive "solutions." Seeing an opportunity to profit from fighting terrorism in an era of declining budgets, military contractors including Raytheon, Lockheed Martin, and General Dynamics competed to secure a Homeland Security Department contract for radar and long-range camera systems to strengthen border security, while Northrop Grumman offered an automatic tracking device mounted on aerial drones, and General Atomics, a manufacturer of drones, sought to double the number available for border surveillance. In the words of an economist, "There are only so many missile systems and Apache attack helicopters you can sell. This push toward border security fits very well with the need to create an ongoing stream of revenue."[13]

The views of individuals in the Bush administration, especially "neoconservatives," were central to the decision to intervene in Iraq. Influential "neocons" including Vice President Dick Cheney, Defense Secretary Donald Rumsfeld, and Deputy Secretary of Defense Paul Wolfowitz argued that global politics was a conflict between good and evil, military power was a key policy tool, and America's unique post–Cold War status should be used to promote democracy globally. In his second inaugural address, Bush declared, "It is the policy of the United States to seek and support the growth of democratic movements and institutions in every nation and culture, with the ultimate goal of ending tyranny in our world."[14] This powerful speech that Bush called his "freedom speech" included the words "freedom, free, liberty" forty-nine times.[15]

2000 (Continued)

July **2005** Bomb attacks on London's transport system

2009 Nigerian citizen tries to destroy a U.S. flight by igniting explosives; Al-Qaeda established in the Arabian Peninsula.

2010 Car bomb discovered in New York's Times Square

May **2011** Osama bin Laden killed

2012 Somalia's al-Shabab joins al-Qaeda.

2012–2013 Islamist extremists seize power in northern Mali; French intervene.

2000 (Continued)

April **2013** Boston Marathon bombings

August **2013** Closure of U.S. embassies and global travel alert owing to a terrorist threat

2013–2014 Islamic State of Iraq and Syria (ISIS) declares a caliphate.

2014 U.S.-led coalition initiates air war against ISIS in Iraq and Syria.

April **2015** Al-Qaeda in the Arab Peninsula occupies parts of southern Yemen.

FIGURE 11.1   Public Opinion and the Iraq War

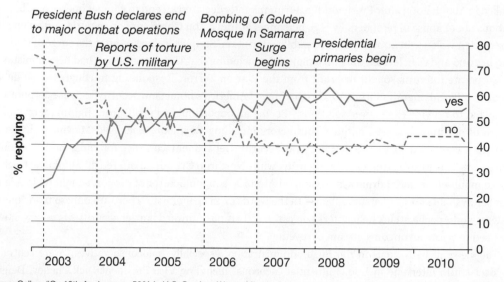

THE ISLAMIC PAST

Islam dates back to the 7th century CE when the Prophet Muhammad claimed to have heard the words of God (Allah), which he revealed to the world in the Koran, Islam's holy scripture.

The Caliphate

During the centuries after Islam's emergence, the **caliphate**—an Islamic empire ruled by those ("caliphs") who succeeded the prophet—conquered the Middle East, North Africa, Persia, Armenia, and Spain. Muslims regard the epoch of the Prophet and his four successors ("caliphs") as a "golden age of pure Islam." Islam's greatest political, military, and cultural achievements took place during the Umayyad dynasty (661–750 CE) in Damascus and the Abbasid dynasty (750–1258 CE) in Baghdad. The Mongols sacked Baghdad in 1258, and the Caliphate split into rival communities. Although the Ottoman Empire's last sultan was Islam's last caliph, in reality, "the caliphate is a political or religious idea whose relevance has waxed and waned according to circumstance," and "by conflating the nineteenth-century Ottoman royal family with these caliphs from a millennium ago or more, Western pundits and nostalgic Muslim thinkers alike have built up a narrative of the caliphate as an enduring institution, central to Islam and Islamic thought between the seventh and twentieth centuries."[16]

There are some 1.6 billion Muslims worldwide, 23 percent of the world's population.[17] Most live in a band of states in the southern hemisphere stretching across Africa and the Middle East to South

MAP 11.1   The Umayyad Caliphate

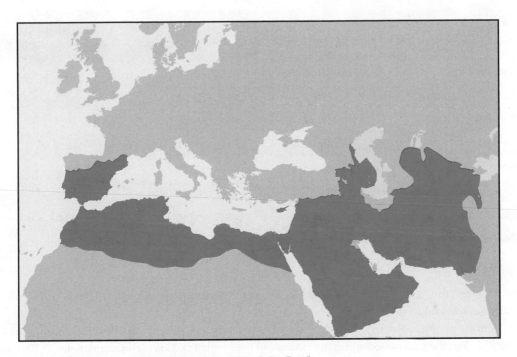

Source: Data from *The Times Concise Atlas of World History* (HarperCollins Travel).

Asia, but their numbers in Europe, America, and sub-Saharan Africa are growing rapidly. The world Islamic community, however, is not united. In addition to divisions between religious moderates and extremists and Islamists and secularists, it consists of Shias and Sunnis, who frequently engage in sectarian violence. These sects emerged after the death of Muhammad. Those who believe Muhammad's son-in-law Ali was his legitimate successor and caliphs should be direct descendants of Ali and Fatima (Muhammad's daughter) took the name Shiat Ali ("partisans of Ali"). Sunni Muslims do not insist that caliphs be descended from Muhammad and believe that Muslims can select their leaders.

Although political Islamists wish to be governed by religious precepts, most work within existing political systems to promote Islamic law, and few are extremists who use violence to impose Islamic principles. Islamic extremists have reappeared periodically for centuries. Thus, the "Assassins," members of a Shia sect, were medieval terrorists who murdered Sunni leaders in Persia.

Jihadism

"Jihadism" refers to a commitment to impose a "pure" version of Islam by those seeking to follow the practices and beliefs of Muhammad's lifetime. Many are Salafi Muslims, "who idealize the period of Muhammad and his Companions as an uncorrupted time for the religious community"

TABLE 11.1   World Muslim Populations by Region

	Estimated 2010 Muslim Population	Estimated 2010 Total Population	Percentage of Population That Is Muslim
Asia-Pacific	985,530,000	4,054,990,000	24.3 %
Middle East-North Africa	317,070,000	341,020,000	93.0
Sub-Saharan Africa	248,110,000	822,720,000	30.2
Europe	43,490,000	742,550,000	5.9
North America	3,480,000	344,530,000	1.0
Latin America-Caribbean	840,000	590,080,000	0.1
World Total	**1,598,510,000**	**6,895,890,000**	**23.2**

Source: Pew Research Center's Forum on Religion & Public Life, Global Religious Landscapes, December 2012, p. 22, http://www.pewforum.org/files/2014/01/global-religion-full.pdf.

and who demand "a return to the practices of the early generations before un-Islamic innovations (*bida*) were introduced."[18]

There are several meanings of jihad, an obligation of Muslims "to struggle (the literal meaning of the word *jihad*) on the path of God and in the example of the Prophet and his early Companions."[19] Jihad can be violent or nonviolent. Violent jihad—the "lesser jihad"—entails waging holy war against unbelievers and apostates (*takfir*) who have renounced "genuine" Islam. Those who adopt this meaning believe that Islamic "warriors" are martyred and will go to paradise in the afterlife. Nonviolent jihad—the "greater jihad"—is "more difficult and more important"[20] and involves personal struggle against evil desires and doing what is right.

Salafi jihadists[21] like Osama bin Laden constitute less than 1 percent of all Muslims[22] and view the world as divided between the House of Islam and the House of War. They seek to overthrow secular governments and moderate Islamic governments (the "near enemy"). Some seek to attack the West (the "far enemy"), especially America and Israel (the "Zionist-Crusader alliance"), and regard killing civilians, including fellow Muslims, permissible, especially the Shia whom they consider infidels ("nonbelievers").

Muslims had declared jihads against enemies for centuries before bin Laden's 1998 "Jihad against Jews and Crusaders." Muhammad declared the first against Arab foes in Mecca in 622 CE, and jihad has been associated with efforts to spread Islam and subdue foreign enemies. Among those who promulgated jihad as holy war was Egyptian scholar Sayyid Qutb (chapter 10). Qutb, who studied in America in the 1940s, was a prolific writer. He assailed Muslim leaders who did not follow Islamic law, comparing them to pre-Islamic Arabs who were "ignorant pagans" against whom jihad should be waged and who were apostates subject to death. True Muslims, he believed, should use violence to impose Islamic values on infidels. Qutb's followers argued that any "government not ruling solely by Sharia is apostate; democracy is not just a mistaken tactic but also an unforgivable sin, because it gives humans sovereignty over Allah."[23]

MAP **11.2** Major Muslim Communities

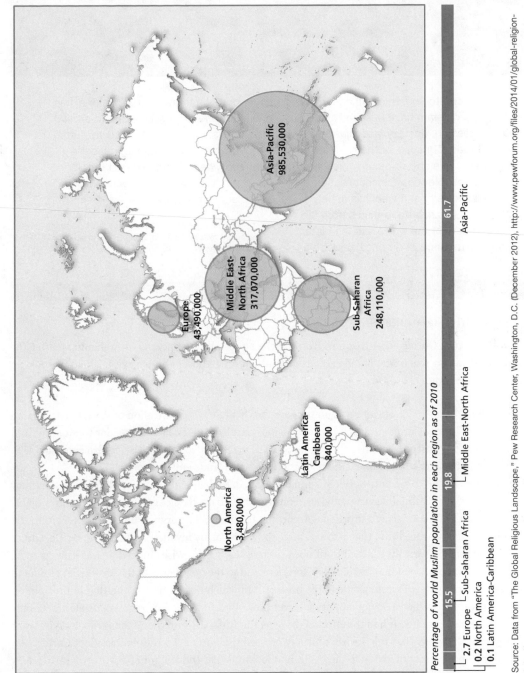

North America
3,480,000

Europe
43,490,000

Middle East-
North Africa
317,070,000

Asia-Pacific
985,530,000

Sub-Saharan
Africa
248,110,000

Latin America-
Caribbean
840,000

Percentage of world Muslim population in each region as of 2010

15.5	19.8	61.7

2.7 Europe └ Sub-Saharan Africa └ Middle East-North Africa   Asia-Pacific

0.2 North America

0.1 Latin America-Caribbean

Source: Data from "The Global Religious Landscape," Pew Research Center, Washington, D.C. (December 2012), http://www.pewforum.org/files/2014/01/global-religion-full.pdf.

Note: Population estimates are rounded to the ten thousands. Percentages are calculated from unrounded numbers. Percentages may not add to 100 due to rounding.

🔑 KEY DOCUMENT

Osama bin Laden, "Declaration of Jihad" (August 23, 1996)

"It is no secret to you, my brothers, that the people of Islam have been afflicted with oppression, hostility, and injustice by the Judeo-Christian alliance and its supporters. This shows our enemies' belief that Muslims' blood is the cheapest and that their property and wealth is merely loot. . . . All this has happened before the eyes and ears of the world, but the blatant imperial arrogance of America, under the cover of the immoral United Nations, has prevented the dispossessed from arming themselves. . . . Men of the radiant future of our *umma* of Muhammad, raise the banner of *jihad* up high against the Judeo-American alliance that has occupied the holy places of Islam."

Source: Osama bin Laden, "Declaration of Jihad," in Bruce Lawrence, ed., *Messages to the World: The Statements of Osama bin Laden* (New York, NY: Verso, 2005), 25, 29.

Radical Islam and Afghanistan

The revolution that Qutb sought began in Egypt in the 1940s and reappeared in Afghanistan after the 1979 Soviet invasion when Muslim guerrillas—**mujahideen** ("those who engage in jihad")—took up arms against the invader.

The Soviet Invasion The Soviet invasion triggered fears of Soviet penetration of the oil-rich Persian Gulf. President Jimmy Carter condemned the invasion, recalled America's ambassador to Moscow, and asked the Senate to postpone deliberation of the SALT II arms control treaty. Carter also cancelled U.S. participation in the Moscow summer Olympics and imposed a trade embargo on the USSR.

Washington sought to aid anti-Soviet Muslim militants in Afghanistan. In a 1998 interview, Zbigniew Brzezinski, Carter's national security adviser, confirmed a claim that covert CIA aid to the mujahideen had begun before Moscow's invasion. "According to the official version of history, CIA aid to the Mujahadeen began during 1980, that is to say, after the Soviet army invaded Afghanistan, 24 December 1979. But the reality, secretly guarded until now, is completely otherwise. Indeed, it was July 3, 1979, that President Carter signed the first directive for secret aid to the opponents of the pro-Soviet regime in Kabul. And that very day, I wrote a note to the president in which I explained to him that in my opinion this aid was going to induce a Soviet military intervention." Brzezinski had no regrets: "That secret operation was an excellent idea. It had the effect of drawing the Russians into the Afghan trap and you want me to regret it? The day that the Soviets officially crossed the border, I wrote to President Carter. 'We now have the opportunity of giving to the USSR its Vietnam War.' Indeed, for almost 10 years, Moscow had to carry on a war unsupportable by the government, a conflict that brought about the demoralization and finally the breakup of the Soviet empire."[24]

Under Ronald Reagan, covert aid continued to flow to Islamic fighters in Afghanistan. A CIA program used Saudi and American funds to purchase arms for anti-Soviet guerrillas. After Moscow withdrew its troops in 1989, violence continued, and civil war erupted in 1992 after the collapse of the communist government. In the absence of a functioning government, Afghanistan dissolved into disparate territories controlled by competing warlords.

The Taliban ("Students of Islamic Knowledge Movement") Devout Muslim religious students established the Taliban, many educated in a strict version of Islam in Pakistani refugee camps. They sought to end Afghanistan's civil war and coalesced into a movement led by Mullah Mohammed Omar. The Taliban's ability to restore order made it popular, and, after entering Kabul in 1996, it established an Islamic emirate. The Taliban "were a *pathogenic* force whose view of the world conspicuously omitted the pragmatic moderation of tribal and religious codes in Afghan society."[25] By 1998, most of Afghanistan was in Taliban hands, and the new rulers imposed an intolerant version of Islamic law that included public executions, severing limbs as punishment, requiring men to grow beards, and banning television, the Internet, films, singing, and musical instruments. Women had to cover themselves from head to toe, could no longer go to school, and could not leave home unaccompanied by a male relative.

The Origins and Evolution of Al-Qaeda

The Saudi Osama bin Laden, the Egyptian Ayman al-Zawahiri, and the Palestinian Abdullah Azzam established al-Qaeda in the summer of 1989 among Muslim participants in the Afghan resistance—"Arab Afghans." Azzam, who argued that Muslims were obliged to wage jihad to liberate Muslim lands from foreign occupation, deeply influenced bin Laden. Azzam also believed that Muslims should not kill one another and advocated focusing the group's effort on liberating Palestine, while Zawahiri sought the overthrow of insufficiently Islamic Arab governments. In this, bin Laden followed Zawahiri.

The group evolved a seven-stage strategy. The first was to "awaken" Muslims and the second to enlarge al-Qaeda. The third and fourth stages included attacking Israel and organizing local and regional jihadists to acquire power in Arab countries. During the fifth and six phases, al-Qaeda would declare a universal caliphate, which would declare war on nonbelievers. With America overextended globally, the final stage would be "definitive victory."[26]

Aided by wealthy Saudis and a "Bureau of Services" that recruited followers, al-Qaeda operated from Sudan from 1989 to 1996. Bin Laden issued a *fatwa* (legal opinion) decrying U.S. involvement in Somalia and was possibly involved in the deaths of Army Rangers in Mogadishu in 1993. Al-Qaeda also had links with Ramzi Ahmed Yousef, who planted a bomb in the parking garage of New York's World Trade Center in 1993 that injured 1,000 people and forced the evacuation of 50,000 others. Two years later, al-Qaeda was responsible for a car bombing outside a U.S. training facility in Riyadh, Saudi Arabia. These incidents focused international attention on Sudan, which forced bin Laden and his followers to return to Afghanistan and where he declared jihad against America and Israel: The "crimes and sins committed by the Americans are a clear declaration of war on God, his messenger, and Muslims," and the "ruling to kill the Americans and their allies—civilians and military—is an individual duty for every Muslim who can do it in any country in which it is possible to do it."[27]

Al-Qaeda's attacks on U.S. embassies in Kenya and Tanzania in August 1998 killed over 200 people, and President Clinton ordered cruise missile strikes against an al-Qaeda training site in Afghanistan and a chemical plant in Sudan believed to be producing nerve gas. "Countries that persistently host terrorists," declared Clinton, "have no right to be safe havens."[28] Then on October 12, 2000, a small boat carrying explosives rammed the destroyer USS *Cole* then anchored off the Yemeni port of Aden, ripping open its hull and killing seventeen sailors. Al-Qaeda operatives were also involved in other plots, including Ramzi Yousef's 1995 unsuccessful plan to place time bombs on commercial planes flying over the Pacific and the 2005 bombing of three hotels in Amman, Jordan, frequented by Americans.

In 1986, the CIA established a Counterterrorist Center, and ten years later formed a unit to learn more about bin Laden and capture or kill him. The "Bin Laden Issue Station" headed by CIA analyst Michael Scheuer "was the first to target an individual rather than a country."[29] The Clinton administration was aware that al-Qaeda was targeting America and intensively sought him. "There was never a terrorist group," said Scheuer, "which we knew more about in terms of goals, organization, method of operation, personnel than al-Qaeda. And that was not only true in 2001, but by the summer of 1998, we had accumulated an extraordinary array of information about this group and about its intentions."[30]

PRESENT: THE WAR ON TERROR

9/11 triggered the War on Terror. It shocked America, auguring a violent future punctuated by terrorism at home and abroad. A joint resolution of Congress, "Authorization for the Use of Military Force"

The World Trade Towers, September 11, 2001

AP Photo/Carmen Taylor

(AUMF), was passed on September 18: "The President is authorized to use all necessary and appropriate force against those nations, organizations, or persons he determines planned, authorized, committed or aided" the 9/11 attacks, "or harbored such organizations or persons, in order to prevent any future acts of international terrorism against the United States by such nations, organizations or persons."[31]

President George W. Bush described America's response in a speech at West Point. "You graduate from this academy in a time of war, taking your place in an American military that is powerful and is honorable," but "our war on terror is only begun."[32] The War on Terror would remain U.S. policy for twelve years until President Barack Obama declared it had ended. Even then, although al-Qaeda had been weakened, terrorism continued.

Afghanistan

After the Taliban refused to hand over bin Laden, Washington launched "Operation Enduring Freedom" in Afghanistan in support of the Taliban's foes in the Northern Alliance that included ethnic Uzbeks, Tajiks, and Hazaras, beginning the longest war in U.S. history. After the Taliban's defeat, Hamid Karzai, a Pashtun, like members of the Taliban, was selected to head an Afghan Interim Administration and was confirmed at a council of warlords in Kabul in 2002. In 2004 and 2009, Karzai was elected Afghanistan's president, and the UN Security Council established a NATO-led International Security Assistance Force (ISAF).

Efforts to capture bin Laden proved frustrating. U.S. forces tracked the fugitives to Tora Bora, a series of mountain caves near Pakistan, destroying al-Qaeda training camps but always a step behind the terrorists until the trail grew cold. "He's either dug in some tunnel, or he's alive," declared Secretary Rumsfeld of bin Laden. "And if he's alive, he's either in Afghanistan or he isn't. And it does not matter; we'll find him one day."[33]

Although the Taliban was driven from power, it reestablished itself in remote regions of Afghanistan. With its political leadership in Pakistan and aided by other mujahideen, including the criminal Haqqani Network, the Taliban began a campaign of guerrilla warfare—targeted assassinations, suicide bombings, and roadside "improvised explosive devices." In 2004, the Bush administration began using CIA-controlled drones to attack militant strongholds in Afghanistan and Pakistan. While quietly allowing Washington to launch strikes from Pakistani bases, Pakistan's government loudly protested what it claimed was a violation of its sovereignty. The Obama administration accelerated drone strikes because they reduced U.S. casualties and attacked militant sanctuaries while limiting America's military "footprint."

Despite an increase in ISAF troop strength in Afghanistan to 140,000 (including 101,000 Americans) NATO efforts to pacify the country were only partly successful. President Obama promised to withdraw most U.S. troops by the end of 2014—a massive undertaking, involving removal of 28,000 vehicles and 40,000 shipping containers of equipment along guerrilla-infested roads.[34] In mid-2013, NATO handed over security for all of Afghanistan to the Afghans, ending a process that increased Afghan security forces from 40,000 to 350,000. ISAF commander General Joseph Andersen expressed concern because "we are in less places," but the "Taliban is just as challenged with strategy, leadership and resources, which causes them to be less effective as well."[35] ISAF formally ended combat missions in late 2014, but the administration left a residual force to train and advise Afghan soldiers and provide specialized assistance to Afghans if needed.

Efforts to negotiate with the Taliban also began. The Taliban opened an office in Doha, Qatar, where direct U.S.-Taliban talks began. Declared Obama, "This is an important first step towards reconciliation,"

MAP 11.3 Ethnic Groups in Afghanistan

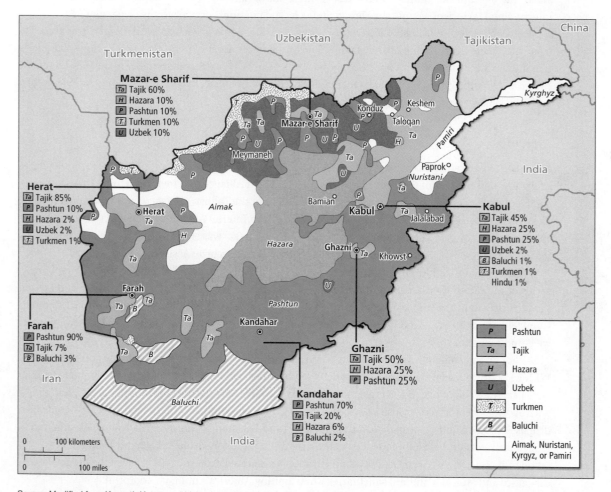

Source: Modified from Kenneth Katzman, "Afghanistan: Post-Taliban Governance, Security, and U.S. Policy," Congressional Research Service, April 27, 2015, https://fas.org/sgp/crs/row/RL30588.pdf, p. 78.

but "we anticipate there will be lots of bumps in the road."[36] Among those "bumps" were U.S. demands that the Taliban sever links with al-Qaeda, join an inclusive Afghan Grand Assembly, renounce violence, and respect the constitutional inclusion of women's rights. The Taliban insisted on complete withdrawal of foreign forces from Afghanistan before any agreement.

President Karzai's belief that Washington would marginalize him to achieve its aims made the road still bumpier. He refused to participate in talks with the Taliban involving America because the group called itself the Islamic Emirate of Afghanistan. After Karzai's objection, the Taliban shuttered its office and "suspended" talks (though these resumed in 2015). Plans to leave a residual U.S. force in Afghanistan were complicated by Karzai's suspicion that Washington would make a deal with the Taliban and Pakistan behind his back. After lengthy negotiations, Karzai and Washington reached an agreement to allow between 8,000 and 12,000 troops to remain after 2014. The administration agreed to give Afghan authorities a voice in how and when Americans could attack the Taliban and whether U.S. forces could conduct unannounced raids on Afghan homes. In speaking to Afghanistan's council of elders, however, Karzai declared he was not prepared to sign a status of forces agreement giving remaining U.S. troops immunity from prosecution in Afghan courts, a prerequisite for letting troops remain after 2014. U.S.-Afghan relations became so strained over Afghan demands that Washington began considering a "zero option"—the removal of *all* troops. But the Obama administration was reluctant to do so. Karzai's refusal to sign the agreement led one U.S. official to observe, "I don't know if I would call it bluffing. But it looks like that's what we were doing, and now it looks like Karzai is calling us out," adding "if we want a deal, we're going to have to wait."[37]

Afghanistan's fragile security would have been endangered if the zero option had been chosen. A former Pentagon official concluded, "If we withdraw, and the international community withdraws its aid, you will see the potential for the Afghan government to collapse, the insurgency to gain momentum and territory, take over eastern Afghanistan, re-creating a safe haven for terrorist elements that still harbor an anti-U.S. agenda. After all of this effort and all of this sacrifice and all of this progress, you're back to a safe haven for terrorists?"[38] After a contested presidential election, Secretary of State John Kerry persuaded the candidates to share power. Ashraf Ghani became president and the loser, his prime minister. Ghani signed the status of forces agreement, but it remained to be seen whether Afghanistan would relapse into chaotic violence, as did Iraq after American forces withdrew. The capability of Afghanistan's security forces was limited, and the prospect that all U.S. forces would be withdrawn by 2016 reduced incentives for the Taliban to reach a settlement. We now examine America's two wars with Iraq, the first ending in the triumph of a U.S.-led coalition while the second ended without accomplishing its aims.

Iraq

Saddam Hussein's invasion of Kuwait triggered the first Iraq war. The second, begun after 9/11, was described by the administration as part of the War on Terror.

The Persian Gulf War (1990–1991)   America's 2003 intervention in Iraq had roots in a conflict that erupted after Iraq's 1990 invasion of neighboring Kuwait. In response to the invasion and the threat posed to Saudi Arabia, President George H. W. Bush organized an international coalition to liberate Kuwait. The war began with a bombing campaign, followed by an overwhelming ground assault ("Operation Desert Storm"). Bin Laden cited Saudi Arabia's decision to allow U.S. forces to use its territory—the "land of the two mosques"[39]—as one reason for declaring jihad against America.

After Iraq was driven from Kuwait, America ceased operations, leaving Saddam Hussein in power but imposing UN-approved measures on Baghdad. No-fly zones were enforced to protect Kurds in northern Iraq and Shias in the south. A UN Special Commission was established to enforce Security Council Resolution 687, requiring destruction of Iraq's WMD programs. Iraqi-American relations remained vexed during the following decade. Friction persisted between Iraq and UNSCOM about access to Iraqi military facilities. Washington's claim that Saddam was hiding WMD was a principal reason for invading Iraq in 2003 (chapter 4).

The Second Iraq War (2003–2011) On March 20, 2003, America launched "Operation Iraqi Freedom." The war evolved in two phases. The first, a conventional conflict, began with airstrikes followed by the advance of Anglo-American forces northward from Kuwait. U.S. forces secured Baghdad, and British forces seized Basra, Iraq's second largest city. On May 1 aboard the aircraft carrier USS *Abraham Lincoln*, President Bush, standing before a banner that read "Mission Accomplished," declared, "Major combat operations in Iraq have ended. In the Battle of Iraq, the United States and our allies have prevailed."[40] Saddam was captured, tried in an Iraqi court for crimes against humanity, and then executed.

By the end of the war's first phase, Iraq was in shambles. Electricity and clean water were unavailable, and its economy was in ruins. U.S. efforts to establish a democratic government were stymied by divisions among Iraq's Sunnis, Shias, and Kurds, and, following the disbanding of Iraq's army and security forces by the Coalition Provisional Authority, Iraq was engulfed by sectarian war.

Iraq elected a permanent government in 2006, and rebuilding its security forces began. After 2010, Iraq's government was dominated by Nuri al-Maliki and his Shia allies at the expense of the country's Sunni and Kurdish minorities. The Kurds remained autonomous, continuing to export oil despite claims from the central government that only it could authorize sales. (A compromise was reached in late 2014.) The war entered a new phase in which Sunni elements of Saddam's regime and jihadists began an insurgency centered in the "Sunni Triangle" (a region northwest of Baghdad dominated by Sunni Muslims) against coalition troops.

A 2006 National Intelligence Estimate reported the war was "breeding a deep resentment of U.S. involvement in the Muslim world."[41] U.S. casualties increased with the onset of irregular war but

President George W. Bush aboard the USS *Abraham Lincoln* announcing victory in Iraq

AP Photo/J. Scott Applewhite

decreased after America's 2007 troop surge and the emergence of Sunni tribal militias (the "Awakening movement") to protect their communities. Civilian deaths plummeted from nearly 4,000 a month in late 2006 to 500 a month in 2007. Failure to reach a U.S.-Iraqi Status of Forces Agreement assuring that remaining U.S. soldiers would not be subject to Iraqi law meant that no U.S. forces remained after 2011.

One justification for America's 2003 invasion was that Saddam Hussein had links to al-Qaeda. In a 2009 television interview, President Bush declared: "Well, first of all, I do think Iraq is a central front in the War on Terror and so does Osama bin Laden."[42]

Iraq and Al-Qaeda: A Connection?   Although President Bush framed America's intervention in Iraq as part of the War on Terror, there was little evidence that Saddam had ties with al-Qaeda. Nevertheless, Vice President Cheney declared, "there is a pattern of relationships going back many years. And in terms of exchanges and in terms of people, we've had recently since the operations in Afghanistan—we've seen al-Qaeda members operating physically in Iraq and off the territory of Iraq."[43] The president argued, "The danger is, is that al-Qaeda becomes an extension of Saddam's madness and his hatred, and his capacity to extend weapons of mass destruction around the world. Both of them need to be dealt with. The War on Terror, you can't distinguish between al-Qaeda and Saddam when you talk about the War on Terror."[44]

The allegation of an al-Qaeda-Iraq link was fostered by a report that Secretary Rumsfeld had Undersecretary of Defense Douglas Feith write for CIA Director George Tenet in 2002. Feith used bits of raw intelligence to make the case that he was asked to make. Thus bureaucratic politics played a key role in justifying the Iraq war. Former CIA analyst Paul Pillar contended the "administration used intelligence not to inform decision-making, but to justify a decision already made."[45] A Pentagon report concluded that no link existed, and the CIA noted, "the reporting provides no conclusive signs of cooperation on specific terrorist operations,"[46] a conclusion reaffirmed in 2008 by the Senate Select Committee on Intelligence. According to the 9/11 Commission: "President Bush had wondered immediately after the attack whether Saddam Hussein's regime might have had a hand in it" but was told "only some anecdotal evidence linked Iraq to al-Qaeda."[47]

London's International Institute of Strategic Studies concluded that the occupation of Iraq, far from reducing terrorism, became "a potent global recruitment pretext"[48] for al-Qaeda. A national intelligence officer described U.S.-occupied Iraq as "a training ground, a recruitment ground, the opportunity for enhancing technical skills," creating "the likelihood that some of the jihadists who are not killed there will, in a sense, go home, wherever home is, and will therefore disperse to various other countries."[49] Sectarian violence again erupted in Iraq with almost 9,000 deaths in 2013, and Iraq's Shia-dominated government increasingly came under Iran's influence. Secretary of Defense Panetta wrote after leaving office, "It was clear to me—and many others—that withdrawing all our forces would endanger the fragile stability then barely holding Iraq together."[50]

Islamic Extremism after 9/11

The War on Terror eroded al-Qaeda's capability to finance, arm, and train local cells to launch complex attacks and climaxed with the death of Osama bin Laden. In the dead of night, May 2, 2011, Navy SEALs avenged 9/11. Flying from Afghanistan in two stealth helicopters, Team 6 raided a compound in Abbottabad, Pakistan, broke through several walls to gain entry, and shot bin Laden. Bin Laden, who had been sought for years in the mountains of Afghanistan and Pakistan, had been living in a compound near a Pakistani military base. After U.S. intelligence intercepted a phone call to an al-Qaeda courier and placed the compound under surveillance, he was located. Less than an hour after the raid began, the team left with bin Laden's body, as well as documents, computer hard drives, and memory sticks, and returned to Afghanistan. Bin Laden was buried at sea.

Pakistan's government was not informed of the raid. President Obama explained, "I didn't tell most people here in the White House. I didn't tell my own family. It was that important for us to maintain operational security. If I'm not revealing to some of my closest aides what we're doing, then I sure as heck am not going to be revealing it to folks who I don't know."[51] There were suspicions that Pakistan's Inter-Services Intelligence agency knew where bin Laden was living but had not shared the information with Washington. Pakistan's air force scrambled fighter aircraft after its airspace was violated, which turned back only after U.S. officials informed Pakistan that an operation was underway against "a high value target." The operation was carefully planned, but the president gave his approval believing that "this was still a 55/45 situation." He described waiting for the outcome of the raid as the longest forty minutes of his life and declared "we got him"[52] on learning it had been successful. Hillary Clinton describes how a crowd outside the White House began to wave American flags and chant "USA! USA!" "Most had been children when al-Qaeda had attacked America on 9/11. They had grown up in the shadow of the War on Terror; it had been part of their consciousness for as long as they could remember. Now they were expressing the emotional release our entire country felt after so many years waiting for justice."[53]

The war in Afghanistan and some 383 U.S. drone strikes in Pakistan between 2004 and 2015[54] eliminated many al-Qaeda leaders and foot soldiers, isolating the group in areas of Pakistan beyond the control of that country's government. Evidence found in bin Laden's compound suggested that the 2005 bombing of London's transport system was "the last successful operation Osama bin Laden oversaw."[55] Shortly after bin Laden's death, Secretary Panetta confidently asserted that America was "within reach of strategically defeating" al-Qaeda, and by eliminating its surviving leaders in Pakistan, Somalia, and Yemen, "we can really cripple al-Qaeda as a threat to this country."[56] Panetta was too optimistic because al-Qaeda "was never a mass movement; it was always meant to be a vanguard. So even with the first generation of leaders largely gone, it's very difficult to declare the movement dead."[57]

Increasingly jihadist terrorism was carried out by autonomous "franchises." These frequently had local objectives, seeking power in their own countries or regions rather than striking America, "the far enemy." Terrorist acts were also carried out by individuals living in non-Islamic societies who were inspired by jihadist propaganda or angered by what they viewed as persecution of Muslims elsewhere. "Al-Qaeda," declared one analyst, "is a portable ideology that is entirely fleshed out, with its own symbols and ways of mobilizing people and money to the cause."[58] There was no longer one al-Qaeda but several regional jihadist groups.

The emergence of regional groups reflected declining cohesion among jihadists. "Like any sprawling organization, al-Qaeda has seen its fair share of bureaucratic infighting. But the squabbling has reached fever pitch since Ayman al-Zawahiri began his tenure as head of the organization."[59] "The organizational challenge in precisely calibrating violence stems from the fact that political and ideological leaders, or the principals, must delegate certain duties—such as planning attacks, soliciting funds, and recruiting—to middle-men or low-level operatives, their agents. Such delegation is problematic as agents in terrorist organizations often see the world differently than their leaders and tend to disagree with them on both how best to serve the cause and how to carry out specific missions."[60] Violent groups emerged in unstable regions in

Asia, the Arabian Peninsula, North Africa, and elsewhere. "The problem we face today," declared an intelligence analyst, "is there are probably more al-Qaeda cells than there have ever been before because of the chaos that's followed the Arab Spring."[61]

Regional Terrorists

Al-Qaeda affiliates emerged in countries where central authority was weak, such as Pakistan, Somalia, Yemen, and Mali, or in Nigeria, Iraq, and Syria where governments were incompetent. A State Department report concluded, "2013 saw the rise of increasingly aggressive and autonomous AQ affiliates and like-minded groups in the Middle East who took advantage of the weak governance and instability in the region to broaden and deepen their operations."[62] Among the best known acts of such groups were bomb attacks on commuter trains in Madrid, Spain (2004), and the bombing of trains on the London Underground (2005).

Regional terrorism forced Washington to alter its counterterrorist strategy. While still concerned about homeland security, U.S. officials became increasingly worried about attacks on overseas targets and increasingly relied on indigenous proxies, providing them with training, intelligence, reconnaissance, and logistics. In 2014, President Obama asked Congress for $5 billion for a Counterterrorism Partnership Fund, using a strategy "that matches this diffuse threat; one that expands our reach without sending forces that stretch our military too thin, or stir up local resentments."[63]

Al-Qaeda in the Arabian Peninsula (AQAP) Al-Qaeda in the Arabian Peninsula was established in Saudi Arabia in 2003 by a former bin Laden aide, merging in 2009 with Yemeni jihadists. It organized an insurrection in southern Yemen after violence erupted there in 2011 and developed links with al-Shabab, a jihadist group in Somalia. Although its operations were largely directed against Yemeni installations, AQAP also sought to attack U.S. targets. With bomb-maker Ibrahim Hassan Asiri, AQAP had a capacity to build bombs without metal parts that could pass airport security. It was responsible for a 2009 attempt to blow up a Detroit-bound jetliner by "underwear bomber" Umar Farouk Abdulmutallab, a 2010 plot involving bombs hidden in desktop printer cartridges, and another underwear bomb plot in 2012.[64] Two brothers responsible for killing twelve people in Paris in 2015 had been trained and/or influenced by AQAP.

The widespread closure of American embassies and consulates in August 2013 and an accompanying travel alert were triggered by an intelligence intercept about an AQAP plan linked to its bomb-making skill. Communications intercepted from al-Qaeda revealed what intelligence officials described as among the most serious plots against U.S. interests since 9/11. A later alert of an AQAP plot led Attorney General Eric Holder to note, "That's a deadly combination, where you have people who have the technical know-how along with the people who have this kind of fervor to give their lives in support of a cause that is directed at the United States and directed at its allies."[65] Washington took an active role in helping Yemen cope with AQAP, trying to eliminate its leaders with repeated drone strikes, including one that killed al-Qaeda's top operative in Yemen, a suspect in the bombing of the USS *Cole*, and Kamal Derwish, the first American citizen killed in the drone campaign. Civil war in Yemen, however, forced Washington to withdraw its military personnel in 2015, and AQAP took advantage of the violence to occupy areas in southern Yemen and seize an oil terminal and stores of arms.

Al-Shabab Somalia became a failed state in the 1990s. U.S. intervention (1992–1994) failed to end a civil war that began after the Cold War, and Somalia proved fertile soil for jihadists, many of whom had fought in Afghanistan. Al-Shabab ("The Youth") occupied southern Somalia in 2006 and sought to establish an Islamic emirate. After Ethiopia intervened, Shabab was routed but continued to wage guerrilla warfare. By 2009, it controlled half of Somalia and "was the only self-proclaimed al-Qaeda ally controlling large territories."[66] The group created havoc even after a UN African Union Mission in Somalia (AMISCOM) with troops from Uganda, Burundi, and Kenya drove it from Somalia's capital in 2011. The next year, Shabab pledged loyalty to al-Qaeda.

American officials feared that Somalia could become a sanctuary for terrorists. Radicalized Somali immigrants in the West provided Shabab with potential overseas allies. Somali-Americans were recruited to join it after 2007, some of whom, it was feared, might return to America to carry out attacks.

The Battle of Mogadishu

The film *Black Hawk Down* depicts the true story of a desperate battle in Mogadishu fought by outnumbered Army Rangers.

U.S. Special Operations and airstrikes, one of which killed Shabab's leader Ahmed Abdi Godane in 2014, aided AMISCOM. After meeting with Somalia's president in 2013, Secretary Clinton applauded "the extraordinary partnership between the leaders and people of Somalia, with international supporters" that had driven Shabab "from Mogadishu and every other major city in Somalia."[67]Although weakened, Shabab continued financing itself by illegally exporting charcoal for smoking tobacco and carried out deadly suicide bombings and attacks against targets in countries participating in AMISCOM like Uganda and Kenya, including Kenya's Westgate mall and Garissa University. Nevertheless, "with continuing losses on the battlefield, a new AMISCON offensive, shrinking finances, and now the death of their charismatic leader,"[68] Shabab was weakened.

Al-Qaeda in the Land of the Islamic Maghreb (AQIM) and Its Offshoots AQIM had roots in the Armed Islamic Group, which led an insurgency against Algeria's government in the 1990s. In 1998, a faction split off to form the Salafist Group for Call and Combat that in 2006 declared its union with al-Qaeda, renaming itself al-Qaeda in the Islamic Maghreb. Thereafter it undertook to attack Western interests and establish Islamic governments across North Africa.

AQIM moved south to North Africa's Sahel region, attacking convoys of oil workers and diplomats. It attacked UN offices in Algiers and the Israeli embassy in Mauritania, using suicide bombers and forging links with suspected terrorists in Europe. AQIM relied for funding on drug smuggling and ransom payments from European governments to free kidnapped citizens.

MAP 11.4   Islamic Militant Groups and Their Areas of Influence in Africa

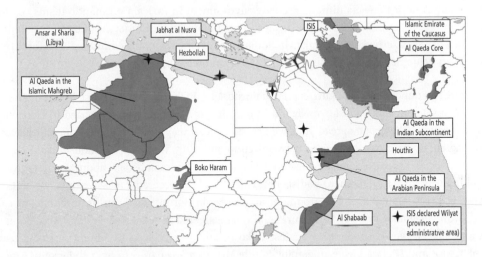

Source: Adapted from the Institute for the Study of War.

In the ensuing chaos in Mali after military officers seized power in 2012, AQIM, with looted arms from Libya, occupied northern Mali and imposed a harsh version of Islamic law. As AQIM moved south toward Bamako, Mali's capital, it triggered a UN-approved intervention by France, Mali's former colonial ruler. The French forced AQIM to flee into the mountains along Algeria's border. Although Washington did not participate in the Mali conflict, it aided France by providing transport to airlift troops and supplies and intelligence gathered by surveillance drones. America also sent a team to train soldiers from African countries sending peacekeepers to Mali.

Algerian Mokhtar Belmokhtar, AQIM's former military commander, formed his own "Masked Men Brigade" with the aid of Libya's Ansar al-Sharia. The State Department described Belmokhtar's group as "the greatest near-term threat to U.S. and Western interests."[69] In 2013, Belmokhtar attacked an energy production facility operated by Britain's BP, Norway's Statoil, and Algeria's Sonatrach in southern Algeria after Algeria allowed France to use its airspace. The attackers took foreign employees hostage, and when Algerian troops retook the facility, 38 hostages including 3 Americans died.

Washington was less concerned that AQIM posed an immediate threat to America's homeland than by its potential for aiding other terrorists by providing a sanctuary in North Africa's thinly populated areas. Referring to AQIM and its possible role in the 2012 attack on America's consulate in Libya, Hillary Clinton observed, "With a larger safe haven and increased freedom to maneuver, terrorists are seeking to extend their reach and their networks in multiple directions. And they are working with other violent extremists to undermine the democratic transitions under way in North Africa, as we tragically saw in Benghazi."[70] Clinton warned that anarchy in Libya after Qaddafi's death had opened a "Pandora's box of weapons": "There's no doubt that the Algerian terrorists had weapons from Libya. There's no doubt that the Malian remnants of al-Qaeda in the Islamic Maghreb has weapons from Libya." She forecast that North Africa could pose problems like those in Afghanistan: "This is going to be a very serious ongoing threat because if you look at the size of northern Mali, if you look at the topography, it's not only desert, it's caves–[it] sounds reminiscent."[71] With few military assets in this region, America faced a difficult security environment in Africa. Commando teams conducted antiterrorist raids in Somalia and Libya. Drones from Djibouti, site of America's Combined Joint Task Force-Horn of Africa, attacked extremists in Somalia and Yemen, and the combined task force trained soldiers from Ethiopia, Niger, Djibouti, and Kenya in counterterrorism.

Boko Haram   Founded in Maiduguri, capital of Borno state, in 2002, Boko Haram ("Western Education Is Sacrilegious") sought to transform Nigeria into an Islamic state and was opposed to elections and secular education. The group spread violence across West Africa, murdering government officials and kidnapping children across the region. Between 2009 and 2015, it massacred thousands of Nigerians including 2,000 in the town of Baga. It also took women and children hostage, abducting 300 girls from a school in 2014, an act even other jihadists denounced, which triggered a massive unsuccessful search involving U.S. reconnaissance. The group declared areas in Borno as a "Muslim territory" or caliphate and swore allegiance to ISIS. At U.S. urging, five endangered countries—Nigeria, Benin, Cameroon, Chad, and Niger—started cooperating against Boko Haram. The African Union authorized a regional force of 7,500, and Nigeria began to employ South African mercenaries to fight the group. America's undersecretary of defense for intelligence described Boko Haram as similar to ISIS two years earlier.

Indiscriminate reprisals by Nigeria's army were a source of recruitment for Boko Haram, and Secretary Kerry warned that human-rights violations by Nigerian forces were encouraging extremism. Although Washington saw Nigeria as a bulwark against Islamic extremism, trust was lacking between the two. U.S. officials were reluctant to share intelligence because Boko Haram informants had penetrated Nigerian security agencies. Although Boko Haram mainly targeted Nigerians, a congressional report declared that its links with other terrorist groups had led to intelligence reports concerning its intent to attack other African targets and the U.S. homeland.[72]

Asian Jihadists   Jemaah Islamiyah ("Islamic Congregation"), a group that sought to establish an Islamic state in Southeast Asia, was responsible for violence in the Philippines and Indonesia, notably the 2002 bombing of two Bali nightclubs that took the lives of many Australians and Britons. It also took credit for suicide bombings at the Marriott and Ritz-Carlton hotels and outside the Australian embassy in Indonesia's capital, Jakarta. Thereafter, many of the group's leaders were arrested, and U.S. military advisers began aiding security forces in the Philippines and Indonesia.

In South Asia, Pakistan's Jaish-e-Mohammed ("The Army of Muhammad") declared war on America. Another Pakistani group, Laskar-e-Taiba ("Army of the Righteous"), carried out widely publicized terrorist attacks on India's parliament building in New Delhi (2001), commuter trains in Mumbai (2006) that killed over 180, and again in Mumbai (2008) that killed 160. In 2014, al-Qaeda leader Zawahiri announced the establishment of Qaedat al-Jihad ("Bases of Jihad") in the Indian subcontinent, making it al-Qaeda's fifth branch, others being North Africa, East Africa, Yemen, and Syria.

Al-Qaeda in Iraq   Al-Qaeda in Iraq was established by Abu Musab al-Zarqawi. Although Zarqawi declared allegiance to al-Qaeda, in 2005 bin Laden questioned Zarqawi's strategy of attacking Shia holy sites. The purging of Sunnis from Iraq's government and army increased Zarqawi's pool of followers. Zarqawi, who died in a 2006 U.S. airstrike, developed "a four-pronged strategy to defeat the American-led coalition"—attack America's coalition partners, Iraqi security forces, aid workers and civilian contractors, and ignite a Shia-Sunni civil war.[73] After 2011, al-Qaeda in Iraq remained dangerous, and by 2014 sectarian violence reached levels not seen since the Iraq war.

The Islamic State of Iraq and Syria Al-Qaeda in Iraq sent volunteers to aid Syrian jihadists in 2013, and its successor, ISIS, became the world's most disruptive terrorist group. America offered a reward of $10 million for information about the group's leader, Abu Bakr al-Baghdadi, who, according to a Pentagon official, "was a street thug when we picked him up in 2004." It was hard to imagine he would "become head of ISIS."[74] In Syria, al-Qaeda in Iraq also established the al-Nusra Front, another jihadist group.

In April, Baghdadi announced a merger of al-Qaeda in Iraq and the Nusra Front. Al-Qaeda leader Zawahiri, however, denied a merger had occurred, condemning the group for killing fellow jihadists and disobeying him by operating in Syria. Unlike the Nusra Front, which sought to attract Syrians, ISIS attacked other anti-Assad rebels and imposed harsh Islamic law in towns it captured. Its occupation of large swaths of territory in Syria and Iraq and its literal interpretation of early Islamic customs attracted thousands of jihadists from around the world including America. About 1,000 additional recruits entered Syria and Iraq each month, some of whom may return home. According to an observer, "It is clear that the first and second generation that started al-Qaeda, most of them are supporting Zawahiri, but the new generation is more radical and closer to ISIS."[75] Zawahiri recognized this, taping a call for unity among jihadists, denouncing the killing of fellow Muslims and encouraging attacks on the West—the opposite of what ISIS was doing.

From its stronghold in the Syrian city of Raqqa, ISIS extended operations back into Iraq. By early 2014, it had seized much of Iraq's Sunni region. In June, it drove Iraq's army from Mosul, a city of a million, continued to Tikrit, and occupied Iraq's largest oil refinery. Hundreds of thousands of Iraqis were displaced as ISIS moved deeper into Iraq. "I never thought it was just a Syrian problem," observed Hillary Clinton. "I thought it was a regional problem. I could not have predicted, however, the extent to which ISIS could be effective in seizing cities in Iraq and trying to erase boundaries to create an Islamic state."[76]

ISIS had spent the previous years in Iraq "breaking senior leaders out of prison and re-establishing a professional command and control structure; expanding operational reach, including into Syria; and exploiting rising Sunni discontent" with Iraq's Shia-dominated government, "thereby encouraging sectarianism."[77] It had developed a sophisticated administrative structure and harnessed technologies including Twitter and online videos. Although Washington had spent billions to train and equip Iraq's army, it collapsed swiftly as Sunni soldiers deserted in large numbers, and several army divisions fled in disorder. Thereafter, ISIS advanced toward Baghdad, seized Iraq's border crossings with Syria and Jordan, occupied Kurdish towns in northern Iraq, fought Lebanese troops, and temporarily seized Iraq's largest dam. Its fighters massacred Shia soldiers, videotaping their atrocities. Responding to ISIS's invasion, Iraq's leading Shia cleric, Grand Ayatollah Ali Sistani, called upon his followers to defend their country, including non-Shia communities, and Shia militias heeded his call.

Iraq requested aid, but President Obama conditioned U.S. help on Prime Minister Maliki's empowerment of Sunnis and Kurds. "There is no military solution that will solve Iraq's problems," declared the White House press secretary, "which is why we've been urgently pressing Iraq's leaders across the political spectrum to govern in a nonsectarian manner, to promote stability and unity among Iraq's diverse populations, to address the legitimate grievances of Iraq's Sunni, Kurd and Shia communities, and build and invest in the capacity of Iraq's security forces."[78] Obama dispatched military advisers while U.S. diplomats sought to replace Maliki. Maliki finally acceded, and in August 2014, Haider al-Abadi became Iraq's prime minister with U.S., Iranian, and Saudi approval.

After leveling a berm on the Syrian-Iraqi border, ISIS declared itself the State of the Islamic Caliphate—with Baghdadi as caliph—consisting of areas it controlled in both countries. "Now that there is an actual caliphate with a caliph," noted an analyst, "a lot of Muslims are going to have to talk about what that means, and there is going to be some sympathy."[79] In declaring a caliphate, ISIS surpassed al-Qaeda, presenting itself as the leader of global jihadism and acquiring adherents in Afghanistan, Algeria, Egypt, and especially Libya, which by mid-2015 was virtually a failed state. In extending its influence in Libya, ISIS directly threatened Europe just across the Mediterranean because its followers might seek to hide among the many thousands of migrants fleeing North Africa to Italy.

After ISIS routed Kurdish fighters, threatening a massacre of Yazidi refugees and the safety of U.S. diplomats in Erbil, Iraq's Kurdish capital, Obama authorized limited airstrikes. "I know that many of you are rightly concerned about any American action in Iraq, even limited strikes like these," the president declared. "As commander in chief, I will not allow the United States to be dragged into fighting another war in Iraq."[80] Thereafter ISIS beheaded two Americans, triggering public outrage in America.

With bipartisan approval, Washington extended airstrikes against ISIS to Syria, agreed to aid moderate Syrian insurgents, and assembled an anti-ISIS coalition of Western allies and Arab states. Describing ISIS as a "cancer," the president promised the coalition would "take the fight to" the terrorists "who are unique in their brutality" and "degrade and ultimately destroy"[81] ISIS. Initial attacks included carrier- and land-based jets and cruise missiles, followed by attacks on Syrian oil facilities, a source of ISIS funding from sales on black markets in Turkey, Iraq, and Syria. Simultaneously, U.S. airstrikes targeted another shadowy organization, the al-Qaeda-affiliated "Khorasan Group" that was planning terrorist attacks against America. In Turkey, America's Military Operations Command began aiding moderate Sunni foes of ISIS (though with limited success owing to the difficulty in recruiting such moderates). Thereafter, President Obama authorized sending 1,500 additional troops to Iraq and requested $5 billion from Congress for military operations against ISIS, including funding to train and reequip Iraq's army. Defending his policies, Obama upped the ante in December 2014, declaring, "Our coalition isn't just going to degrade this barbarous terrorist organization, we're going to destroy it."[82]

Critics pointed to Obama's reluctance to get involved in Syria earlier as responsible for ISIS. "The failure to help build up a credible fighting force of the people who were the originators of the protests against Assad—there were Islamists, there were secularists, there was everything in the middle—the failure to do that left a big vacuum, which the jihadists have now filled,"[83] said Hillary Clinton. Ambassador Ryan Crocker argued, "We need to start talking to the Assad regime again" because "bad as Assad is, he is not as bad as the jihadis who would take over in his absence."[84]

ISIS's foes found it difficult to cooperate against what Secretary Kerry described as "an ambitious, avowed, genocidal, territorial-grabbing, caliphate-desiring, quasi state with an irregular army."[85] America and Iran were at odds over Syria; Iran, Qatar, and Saudi Arabia were engaged in a proxy war in Syria; Kurds sought autonomy; and Turkey, though paying lip service to fighting ISIS, seemed more interested in limiting Kurdish autonomy and stood by as ISIS massacred Syrian Kurds across its border.

The violence engulfing Iraq and Syria also intensified concern about the danger posed by individual "lone wolf" terrorists. Westerners who journeyed to the Middle East to wage jihad could infiltrate their societies more easily than foreign terrorists and return home to continue their struggle.

"Lone Wolves" Jihadist groups encourage individuals to carry out solo attacks against the West. The Internet and social media are potent tools for spreading jihadist propaganda to radicalize and recruit individuals. Jihadist online sites and publications like *Inspire*, an English-language magazine published by an American jihadist, spread anti-American propaganda and provide information about how to make and use bombs.

The bombs planted by two Chechen brothers at the 2013 Boston Marathon were assembled from readily available items like pressure cookers, nails, and gunpowder from fireworks, probably based on information in the jihadi internet manual "Lone Mujahid Pocketbook." Thus, President Obama declared, "one of the dangers that we now face are self-radicalized individuals who are already here in the United States" whose attacks are "difficult to prevent."[86] Examples included Nidal Hasan, a U.S. Muslim of Palestinian descent, who murdered thirteen soldiers at Fort Hood, Texas (2009); Faisal Shahzad, a naturalized citizen, who unsuccessfully sought to set off a car bomb in New York's Times Square (2010); Ahmed Abassi, a Tunisian accused of plotting to establish a cell for terrorist acts (2013); and Usaamah Abdullah Rahim, an advocate of ISIS who was shot by police after they learned he planned to behead police officers in Boston.

Some young Muslims living in the West lack a clear self-identity, feeling neither at home in their parents' adopted country nor members of the society from which their families emigrated. Al-Qaeda, noted a former CIA psychiatrist, makes "a particular effort to recruit lonely people who are looking for a cause." Such "lone wolves" are "angry kids with a veneer of ideology that's about skin-deep"[87] who find a cause like the Syrian civil war that legitimizes their anger.

A toxic combination of violent jihadists and a civil war awash with arms made Syria a national-security threat owing to U.S. and European jihadists who joined the insurgency. "Syria," declared the director of America's National Counterterrorist Center, "has become really the predominant jihadist battlefield in the world." He was concerned about those with Western passports "returning as part of really a global jihadist movement to Western Europe and, potentially, to the United States."[88] ISIS used Syria to identify individuals to recruit, then radicalize them, and train them to become future terrorists in the West. America's FBI director revealed that tracking Americans returning from Syria had become a priority, and America's attorney general urged Europeans to adopt laws like America's to prevent terrorists from traveling to Syria. Washington also urged Turkey to close its border to foreign jihadists heading to Syria. The danger posed by "lone wolves" remains a major concern for homeland security.

Homeland Security

The War on Terror was an asymmetric conflict in which conventional military operations were inadequate to deal with terrorist violence. It involved new strategies, a massive reorganization of America's security and intelligence agencies, passage of new security legislation, implementation of new rules for identifying, detaining, and interrogating enemy combatants, and "extrajudicial" killing of terrorist suspects, often by unmanned drones.

The Department of Homeland Security In 2002, Congress established the cabinet-level Department of Homeland Security. It was the most extensive reorganization of the government's executive branch since consolidation of the military services in a single Defense Department and establishment of the Central Intelligence Agency in the 1940s after the onset of the Cold War. The new department sought to unify agencies involved in protecting American security to avoid intelligence gaps that had prevented officials from thwarting the 9/11 attacks. Homeland Security has 240,000 employees and a budget of almost $60 billion (FY 2014). Its tasks encompass fostering cyber-security, improving aviation security, preventing illegal immigration, developing new technologies to enhance security, and coordinating federal antiterrorist efforts with local and state authorities.

Consolidated in the new department were the Secret Service, the Coast Guard, Customs and Border Protection, Immigration and Customs Enforcement, the Federal Emergency Management Agency, and the Transportation Security Agency familiar to Americans screened at airports. The new department brought together agencies from executive departments including Agriculture, Commerce, Justice, Health and Human Services, Treasury, Energy, Transportation, and Defense.

The Director of National Intelligence 9/11 caught America by surprise. Thus, on the advice of the 9/11 Commission, Congress passed the Intelligence Reform and Terrorist Prevention Act (IRTPA) in 2004. IRTPA placed the country's intelligence community under the Office of a Director of National Intelligence. There is a National Counterterrorism Center in the Directorate of National Intelligence with a database of 20,800 Americans suspected of links to terrorist groups like AQAP and 47,000 (including 800 Americans) on a no-fly list. In total, over a million people were listed in the Center's terrorism database, of whom 680,000 were on "watch lists" requiring extra attention when traveling.[89]

The CIA director had previously coordinated national intelligence. Under the new arrangement, the CIA along with other intelligence agencies—the National Security Agency (NSA), the Defense Intelligence Agency, the FBI, and the State Department's Bureau of Intelligence and Research—with a budget of almost $50 billion report to the Director of National Intelligence (DNI). The DNI briefs the president, the National Security Council, and the Homeland Security Council on intelligence issues. Although the reform enjoyed some success, the DNI still lacks sufficient authority over agencies he oversees, especially the NSA and the military intelligence services in the Defense Department.

In addition to facilitating cooperation in collecting and disseminating information, the reorganization involved developing new intelligence-gathering technologies. These included "Intellipedia" (2005) consisting of online wikis with information available to intelligence analysts and "Analytic Space" (2008), a common online workspace with access to the databases of different intelligence agencies. Information-technology expert Andrew McAfee quotes an NSA analyst: "Before Intellipedia, contacting other agencies was done cautiously, and only through official channels. . . . After nearly two years of involvement with Intellipedia, however, this has changed," and "I do know who I can go to when I need to find something out."[90]

FUTURE: IS THE WAR ON TERROR OVER?

In a speech at the National Defense University in 2013, President Obama recalled, "With the collapse of the Berlin Wall, a new dawn of democracy took hold abroad, and a decade of peace and prosperity arrived at home. For a moment, it seemed the 21st century would be a tranquil time. Then, on September 11th, 2001, we

FIGURE **11.2** Department of Homeland Security

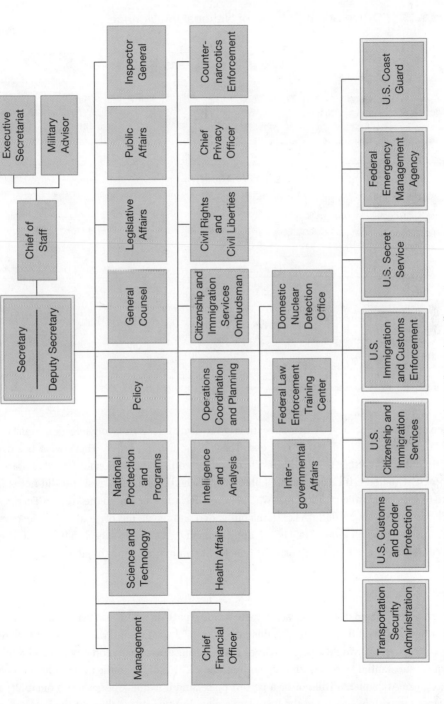

FIGURE 11.3   Office of the Director of National Intelligence

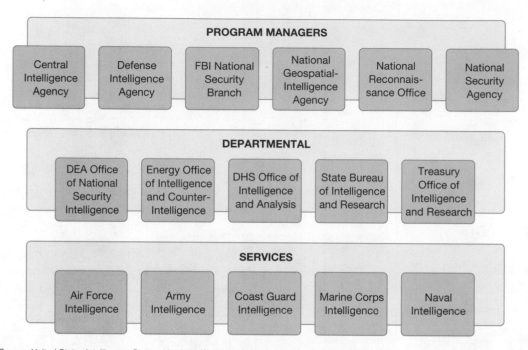

PROGRAM MANAGERS

| Central Intelligence Agency | Defense Intelligence Agency | FBI National Security Branch | National Geospatial-Intelligence Agency | National Reconnaissance Office | National Security Agency |

DEPARTMENTAL

| DEA Office of National Security Intelligence | Energy Office of Intelligence and Counter-Intelligence | DHS Office of Intelligence and Analysis | State Bureau of Intelligence and Research | Treasury Office of Intelligence and Research |

SERVICES

| Air Force Intelligence | Army Intelligence | Coast Guard Intelligence | Marine Corps Intelligence | Naval Intelligence |

Source: United States Intelligence Community, http://www.intelligence.gov/mission/structure.html.

were shaken out of complacency." "Our systematic effort to dismantle terrorist organizations must continue," he added. "But this war, like all wars, must end. That's what history advises. That's what our democracy demands."[91] The president then asked Congress to repeal the 2001 Authorization for Use of Military Force.

The speech attracted criticism from civil libertarians who thought the president did not sufficiently restrict the use of drones and political foes who believed declaring an end to the War on Terror was premature. The president responded, "Ask Osama bin Laden and the 22 out of 30 al-Qaeda leaders who've been taken off the field whether I engage in appeasement."[92] Obama's speech heralded few changes, aiming to continue America's counterterrorist policies and minimizing the threat at home and abroad.

Afghanistan and Pakistan

Although President Obama declared it was "time to turn the page on a decade in which so much of our foreign policy was focused on the wars in Afghanistan and Iraq,"[93] what would transpire afterward remained unclear. Some U.S. troops would remain in Afghanistan because, as a Pentagon report concluded, Afghan forces "require substantial training, advising and assistance."[94] Looking to the future, Obama noted, "We have to recognize Afghanistan will not be a perfect place, and it is not America's responsibility to make it one."[95] Most Americans supported the president's plan, but two-thirds thought the war had not been worth the cost.[96] Washington fears that Afghanistan could again become a terrorist haven.

American-Pakistani relations are crucial for Afghanistan's future. Pakistan did not embrace the War on Terror enthusiastically. It failed to prevent insurgents from gaining sanctuary in border areas and demanded an end to drone strikes to appease domestic anger. In 2011 to 2012 Pakistan closed U.S. supply routes after a strike mistakenly killed Pakistani soldiers. "Pakistanis tend to think of the United States as a bully," wrote Pakistan's former ambassador to America, and Americans believe "Pakistan has taken American dollars with a smile, even as it covertly developed nuclear weapons in the 1980s, passed nuclear secrets to others in the 1990s, and supported Islamist militant groups more recently."[97]

Policy Options

a. *Provide Afghanistan with reduced military support until a ceasefire is reached with the Taliban and provide financial aid to Kabul.* Continued aid would not transform Afghanistan into a prosperous democratic society and might foster corruption and ethnic rivalry but would give the country additional time to achieve stability. Afghanistan's future is, however, tied to what happens in Pakistan.

b. *Cease cooperating with Pakistan because U.S. and Pakistani objectives in Afghanistan are antithetical.* Washington seeks a solution that pacifies Afghanistan while Pakistan seeks Afghan leaders who are friendly to Islamabad. Thus, it is difficult to imagine that stability is possible unless Pakistan is satisfied with the outcome.

c. *Try to make the relationship work,* because Pakistan still needs U.S. aid, and both countries seek a stable Afghanistan, though for different reasons. Pakistan's government has no wish to see the Taliban control Afghanistan if it aids Pakistani jihadists even though it had reasons to support the Taliban in the past. Washington is reluctant to end strikes in Pakistan at a time when its presence in Central Asia is declining. Allowing Pakistan to choose America's drone targets would reduce U.S.-Pakistani tension but prove cumbersome.

Al-Qaeda and Its Affiliates

Bin Laden's death eroded al-Qaeda's attraction. Its leaders inspire others, but al-Qaeda no longer enjoys the influence it had. The terrorist danger has become more diffuse. U.S. counterterrorist operations are directed at jihadists in Yemen, North Africa, Nigeria, and the Middle East, which is witnessing a proliferation of jihadists spawned by the Arab Spring. Finally, in Europe and North America angry "lone wolves" have gone overseas to join extremists or have plotted violence at home.

Policy Options American options for dealing with the remnants of al-Qaeda and its regional sympathizers must reflect local differences and the different threats they pose to U.S. interests.

a. *Station Special Operations forces and drones where they can respond quickly to terrorist threats,* thereby reducing the global terrorist threat and strengthening friendly governments. This entails a commitment of resources in an era of declining budgets and domestic war weariness and risks spreading U.S. forces thinly but would preclude large-scale conventional military commitments.

b. *Calibrate American involvement to fit different threats.* Americans are probably at greatest risk from disaffected individuals at home, a principal reason for domestic surveillance. AQAP, too, threatens America's homeland, while ISIS's establishment of a transnational caliphate is seen as a growing danger.

c. *Rely on allies and regional friends.* NATO's role in Afghanistan lent legitimacy to that conflict. Providing arms and training to local security forces involves a light American "footprint" in the developing world that will arouse less domestic and foreign opposition than large-scale intervention. ISIS, however, poses a unique threat.

The Islamic State of Iraq and Syria

Iraq remained unstable after America's withdrawal, while civil war in Syria provided new opportunities for ISIS. As Ambassador Crocker noted, in the absence of American involvement, northern Iraq risked becoming "a de facto al-Qaeda state," and "that's completely terrifying."[98] ISIS's advance triggered U.S. airstrikes and a call by President Obama for a coalition to join the struggle against ISIS.

Policy Options

a. *Ignore events in Iraq and Syria.* Although the U.S. public was averse to seeing significant ground forces committed to Iraq or Syria, the atrocities committed by ISIS forced Washington to act. Although it may be tempting for America to turn its back on Baghdad and Obama was reluctant to get involved in Syria, ISIS threatened to ignite a regional war between Sunni and Shia Muslims.

b. *Intervene unconditionally against ISIS.* Public opinion and Congress would oppose large-scale intervention in Iraq or Syria. Thus, the president promised, "We're not going to allow ourselves to be dragged back into a situation in which, while we're there, we're keeping a lid on things."[99] However, airstrikes without Iraqi and Syrian ground forces will not defeat ISIS, though they may halt its advance.

c. *Cooperate with Iran against ISIS.* Iran has much to lose if ISIS dominates Iraq and Syria. Iraq is a conduit of Iranian arms to President Assad and potentially part of an Iranian-led Shia coalition. As an ally of Iraq's Shia leaders, Iran began flying military equipment to Baghdad. Iran's president promised to protect Shia sacred sites, and the commander of Iran's elite Quds Force of the Revolutionary Guards advised Iraqi leaders and mobilized Shia militias fighting ISIS on the ground.

American public opinion and congressional leaders with ties to Israel would resist openly cooperating with Israel's enemy, especially in light of U.S.-Iranian disagreement over Syria's future. Nevertheless, while not admitting they were cooperating, America tacitly coordinated with the anti-ISIS efforts of Iran, which conducted airstrikes in a buffer zone it established in Iraq, and President Obama wrote a secret letter to Iran's supreme leader offering conditions for cooperation against ISIS.

d. *Engage in limited intervention in Iraq and Syria.* U.S. airstrikes combined with Special Operations and advisers to begin rebuilding Iraq's army and train moderate Syrian insurgents in Saudi Arabia may repel ISIS's advance. Washington, however, must avoid appearing anti-Sunni and without Sunni allies on the ground will not defeat ISIS. Following coalition airstrikes, Kurds, Shia militias, and some Sunni tribes joined the fight against ISIS, which could no longer concentrate fighters in large groups. ISIS remained resilient, however, and after several setbacks including the loss of Tikrit, it seized Ramadi in Iraq and additional Syrian territory. As a result, in mid-2015, President Obama agreed to send an additional 450 military advisers while still refusing to let them operate beyond their base to identify targets for coalition airstrikes.

"Lone Wolves"

"Lone wolves" pose a difficult challenge. Domestic and foreign surveillance provides valuable intelligence, but the challenge has grown as Western jihadists return from Iraq and Syria. "ISIS's stunning battlefield victories lent the organization credibility and enhanced its allure for the small but important Western community of young radicals it seeks to court,"[100] and we "can expect that Westerners currently in Iraq and Syria will continue to commit atrocities abroad and will come home and attempt some kind of terrorist plot."[101]

Policy Options The State Department advised Americans not to travel to Iraq unless it is "essential" and leave Syria as soon as possible. It is not illegal for Americans to travel to these countries, nor is it illegal for them to fight in another country's army unless they are fighting America. It is, however, illegal for Americans to fight for a "foreign terrorist organization." Those who do may be charged with "providing material support to terrorists," "providing material support or resources to designated terrorist organizations," "conspiracies to engage in violence against people or property overseas," "terrorist attacks against United States nationals," or "receiving military-type training from a foreign terrorist organization."[102]

   a. *Prevent travel to Iraq or Syria.* American jihadist sympathizers become more dangerous if persuaded by radical clerics or jihadist propaganda to travel overseas to join violent extremists. Merely criminalizing travel to Iraq, Syria, or other terrorist sites is likely to have limited impact. Individuals wanting to travel to these countries have little difficulty doing so, especially via Turkey. Sharing data with Turkey about potential American jihadists would be valuable. Even more effective would be mobilizing Western Muslim clerics and parents to dissuade potential jihadists from joining extremist groups.

   The government can use informants and surveillance to identify individuals who are in contact with extremist groups or have expressed a desire to aid them. A number of Americans from across the country including six Somali-Americans have been arrested for attempting to provide material support to a foreign terrorist organization in Syria or Iraq.

   b. *Try to capture or kill Americans fighting for a foreign terrorist group.* If Americans who have joined terrorist groups fail to return home, Washington could try to locate and capture them or even kill them. Anwar al-Awlaki, an American employed by AQAP, was the victim of a targeted U.S. drone strike in Yemen in 2011 after a two-year manhunt. Awlaki had been in contact with the Fort Hood gunman and had helped prepare Abdulmutallab for his effort to bomb an airliner. Although Awlaki had not been tried, the administration justified his death because he had fought for al-Qaeda and was an "imminent threat" to U.S. security. An alternative to assassination involves the capture and rendition of American jihadists (chapter 6).

c. *Counter jihadist propaganda.* "The Internet has had as great an impact on Holy War, Inc."[103] Thus, the online Global Islamic Media Front advised viewers to attack Spain just a few months before the 2004 bombings in Madrid, and *Inspire* provided a hit list of anti-Muslim Westerners before the murderous 2015 attack on the Paris office of the satiric newspaper *Charlie Hebdo* and a plot to kill police in Belgium. On the anniversary of the 9/11 attacks in 2013, Zawahiri released an audio speech on the Internet calling on individual Muslims to launch attacks on American territory.

To counter jihadi media, the State Department's Center for Strategic Counterterrorism Communications began a program in 2013 to discourage potential English-speaking jihadists on English-language websites and social media like Facebook, YouTube, and Twitter. Referring to jihadi sites, the center's coordinator noted, "They were setting the narrative and had a free shot at the audience for radicalizing people."[104] The undersecretary of state for public diplomacy described meeting Arab officials to establish "a communicational coalition, a messaging coalition, to complement what's going on the ground."[105]

d. *Maintain surveillance on citizens returning from Iraq or Syria.* Surveillance of social media like Facebook and Twitter can identify some of those who have returned from war zones and provide information about friends and sympathizers. It may also facilitate providing returnees with counseling to prevent their carrying out terrorist acts and reintegrating them into society. The necessary surveillance, however, raises the controversial issue of government invasion of individual privacy.

The War on Terror

Although President Obama declared an end to the War on Terror, the conflict against terrorism did not cease. Indeed, having declared an end to the War on Terror, the president reversed course later: "We can't erase every trace of evil from the world and small groups of killers have the capacity to do great harm. That was the case before 9/11, and that remains true today. And that's why we must remain vigilant as threats emerge."[106] Having asked that the 2001 AUMF be rescinded, Obama used it to authorize extending America's fight against ISIS to Syria, a claim contested by those in Congress like Senators Tim Kaine (D-VA) and Chris Murphy (D-CT) who demanded congressional approval for the action. Thereafter, the president agreed to seek specific congressional authorization for America's campaign against ISIS. In the absence of either a UN Security Council resolution or a request from Syria's government, Secretary Kerry invoked the right of hot pursuit for strikes in Syria to avoid charges of violating Syrian sovereignty. This did not persuade some of America's European allies to go beyond aiding Iraq, which unlike Syria had requested military assistance. Syria offered to help fight ISIS while condemning U.S. "aggression." For Washington, the dilemma is how to fight ISIS without appearing to aid Assad and his ally, Iran, and how to prevent Iran and Russia from continuing to aid him.

Efforts to enhance homeland security continue as do special operations and drone strikes. Although President Obama declared that drone strikes would be used only "against terrorists who pose a continuing and imminent threat to the American people, and when there are no other governments capable of effectively addressing the threat,"[107] a State Department spokeswoman flatly stated, "In no way would we ever deprive ourselves of a tool to fight a threat if it arises."[108]

Policy Options

a. *Transform the "war" into a "police action" against global criminals.* Such a change would encourage a more multilateral and nuanced approach toward terrorism and mute concerns among America's friends about U.S. policies toward jihadi groups. It would appear less hostile to Islam and attract support among Muslins at home and abroad.

Such a change would have legal implications related to the rights of terrorist suspects and drone strikes. It would meet with approval from human-rights advocates but invite criticism from hardliners as being weak on terrorism. Thus, it might prove divisive domestically while being viewed by extremists as an invitation to intensify efforts against other governments because such efforts would not violate U.S. law.

b. *Continue acting as though the conflict were still a war,* responding robustly to threats domestic *and* overseas much as before. With the end of the Iraq and Afghan wars, the new status quo is less expensive and intrusive and enjoys more support from a war-weary public than would larger military operations. Washington is endeavoring to avoid the appearance of major commitments even in confronting ISIS.

CONCLUSION: HAVE WE WON?

On 9/11, terrorist violence was suddenly elevated to the top of America's foreign-policy agenda. American leaders used military force in Iraq and Afghanistan and implemented bureaucratic and legal reforms at home to thwart potential terrorists. These policies came at great financial and human cost, and their results remain unclear. Did they reduce the threat of terrorism or produce new jihadists determined to attack America?

Osama bin Laden is dead and al-Qaeda is weakened, but terrorism remains. The souring of the Arab Spring brought new recruits to al-Qaeda's affiliates, and ISIS has established a transnational caliphate. In 2013, there were 10,000 terrorist incidents involving 18,000 deaths. Over 60 percent of these incidents occurred in five countries—Iraq, Afghanistan, Pakistan, Nigeria, and Syria.[109] In November 2014 alone, jihadists killed 5,000 people in 664 attacks in fourteen countries around the world.[110] The threat of terrorism is probably impossible to eliminate completely and will remain an American foreign-policy concern in one form or another for the foreseeable future.

DISCUSSION QUESTIONS

1. How should the United States deal with the problem of "lone wolf" terrorists?

2. Should the United States intervene more fully in the fight against ISIS? Should it withdraw completely, or is the present policy of airstrikes sufficient?

3. Which is more dangerous, al-Qaeda or ISIS?

4. Should the United States have withdrawn from Iraq in 2009? Should it withdraw from Afghanistan in 2016 as planned?

5. What is meant by "jihadism," and how does it differ from political Islam?

6. What role did the Arab Spring play in the spread of jihadist groups?

KEY TERMS

caliphate (p. 330)   jihadism (p. 331)   mujahideen (p. 334)

for CQ Press

Sharpen your skill with SAGE edge at **edge.sagepub.com/mansbach**

SAGE edge for Students provides a personalized approach to help you accomplish your coursework goals in an easy-to-use learning environment.

The United States and China

ENGAGEMENT OR CONTAINMENT?

CWS / CARTOON ARTS INTERNATIONAL www.cartoonweb.com

Rising China versus America

CORRIGAN, Toronto Star/Cartoon Arts International/The New York Times Syndicate

American policy toward China involves conflicting objectives. Washington sees growing Chinese military and political power as threatening Asian security and U.S. hegemony globally. Washington regards China's economic growth as mutually beneficial but also views China as challenging American values ranging from free-market capitalism to human rights and democracy. Increasingly, when security interests and the desire to see China adopt Western values have conflicted, interests have trumped values. In 2014, with President Obama due to visit China a month later, throngs of prodemocracy demonstrators occupied the streets of Hong Kong. Should Washington have protested human rights violations, risking deterioration of Sino-American cooperation? "We have principles and values that we want to promote, but we're not looking to inject the United States into the middle of this,"[1] said a senior American official. The tension between interests and values was evident in President Obama's meeting with China's President Xi Jinping at the Asia-Pacific Economic Cooperation (APEC) meeting in November 2014. The primacy of interests was reflected in agreements to avert confrontations between planes and warships off China's coast, environmental cooperation, reduction in China's tariffs on information technologies, and China's subsequent warning against "Western values" in textbooks. Obama barely alluded to values, noting that democracy demonstrations in Hong Kong were a Chinese domestic matter.

In 2012, President Xi became the country's most powerful leader since Mao Zedong. Xi will govern China for a decade. His vision of China's role in the world and restoring its greatness may determine whether China and America can cooperate. Will Beijing behave aggressively toward America and its Asian partners, or will it cooperate with Washington? How should U.S. leaders respond to China's new leaders, with the hand of friendship or an iron gauntlet? The answers are crucial because the two countries are the most powerful in the world economically, politically, and militarily. In several speeches, Xi referred to *The China Dream*, the title of a book that argued that China should surpass America as the world's leading military power. Perhaps Xi's "dream" was only an appeal to Chinese nationalism

Timeline

1900

October **1949** Mao Zedong establishes the People's Republic of China.

1950–1953 Korean War

1954 First Taiwan crisis

1959 Tibetan revolt

1964 China joins the nuclear club.

1966 China's Cultural Revolution begins.

1969 Sino-Soviet border conflict

1900 (Continued)

February **1972** Nixon visits China.

1978 Deng Xiaoping succeeds Mao and initiates economic reforms.

January **1979** America and China establish formal diplomatic relations.

June **1989** Tiananmen Square massacre

1999 NATO bombs China's Embassy in Belgrade.

to reinforce his authority, but on one occasion he declared, "In the China-U.S. relationship, we have enormous shared interests, but of course, unavoidably we have some differences."[2]

"China's rise as a great power is beyond dispute," observed former U.S. diplomat Zalmay Khalilzad. "Its economic growth and potential, its current and future military capacity, the size of its territory and population, all make it likely that China will be a key player in the international scene during the coming century." Khalilzad then asked whether America should follow a strategy of "engagement" or "containment" toward China, answering, "The best strategic option must accomplish three things: preserve the hope inherent in engagement policy while deterring China from becoming hostile and hedging against the possibility that a strong China might challenge U.S. interests. Such a strategy could be called 'congagement.'"[3]

This strategy may confuse Beijing about U.S. intentions. American leaders simultaneously speak of cooperating with Beijing while warning of the need to curb China's ambitions. U.S. leaders have not made up their minds about whether they should engage Beijing and encourage democracy in China or fear that rise and contain China's aspirations. A 2012 U.S. intelligence report concluded that the best outcome would be a political partnership between the two but that a dangerous crisis might be needed to make them cooperate.[4] China's leaders seem convinced that America's aim is containment and that America will not peacefully concede its post–Cold War hegemony. Nevertheless, Xi used the 2014 APEC meeting to soften his rhetoric about China's interests and exhort the role of "soft power" in China's policies.

The conviction that Washington seeks to contain China's rise may explain why President Xi, who spoke of a "great revival of the Chinese nation" as his "Chinese Dream," established a national security committee like America's National Security Council to deal with foreign policy and domestic security. Xi made his first foreign visit after becoming president to Moscow, emphasizing Sino-Russian friendship and the Shanghai Cooperation Organization (China, Kazakhstan, Kyrgyzstan, Russia, Tajikistan, and Uzbekistan) possibly to balance U.S. power. Although America was never mentioned by name by either Xi or his host, Russia's President Vladimir Putin, both resent U.S. power. In Asia, China seeks to become what America became in the Western hemisphere after the Monroe Doctrine.

Will China become a superpower? "China is setting itself up as an autocratic superpower without any interference from the usual counterweights which might otherwise submit its world conquest to international scrutiny,"[5] declare two analysts. By contrast, China specialist David Shambaugh concludes that "China has a very long way to go before it becomes—if it *ever* becomes—a true global power"; China's "global power is beset by multiple weaknesses—not the least of which are domestic." "China remains a lonely power, lacking close friends and possessing no allies."[6] China's economic rise does not easily translate into political influence, and as the frequency of protests in China grows, the country's regime may have to confront a domestic crisis as serious as the 1989 prodemocracy demonstrations that led to the Tiananmen Square massacre.

SOURCES OF AMERICAN POLICY TOWARD CHINA

Various factors influenced America's hostility toward Beijing until the 1970s. External factors included Mao Zedong's defeat of the U.S.-supported regime of Chiang Kai-shek in 1949 and the Korean War that began a year later. Thereafter, Washington guaranteed the security of the island of Taiwan to which

MAP **12.1**   Coastal China and Taiwan

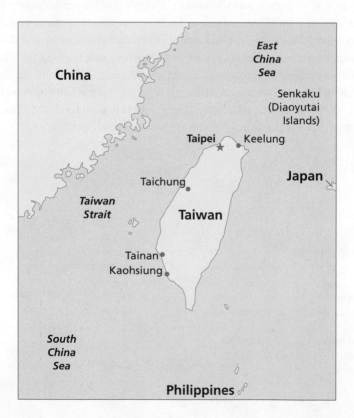

Chiang and his supporters had fled after Mao's triumph on the mainland. Beijing regards Taiwan as a renegade province that must be reunited with the mainland and views U.S. efforts on Taiwan's behalf as interference in China's domestic affairs and an affront to Chinese sovereignty.

Government factors also played a role in American efforts to contain China during the Cold War. Fear of communist expansionism in Asia, especially after the Korean War began, meant there were few bureaucratic opponents to America's military containment of communist China in the Truman and Eisenhower administrations. The impact of the "domino theory"—the belief that if a noncommunist country fell under communist domination, its neighbors would fall like a row of dominos—in the State Department was apparent in comments made by Undersecretary of State Christian Herter during the 1958 Taiwan crisis: "Though the communist emphasis in recent months has been more on subversion and penetration through economic, political, and psychological channels, force has been their principal instrument of expansion in Asia. Therefore their present resort to force must be looked at not alone in the light of Taiwan and the offshore islands, but also in the real possibility of its extension to these new nations of Southeast Asia as well as Korea."[7]

Herter was fulfilling his role as a high-ranking State Department official. And the growing influence of hardline anticommunists in both parties in Congress, many of whom had backed Chiang, translated into support for increased defense expenditures and efforts to undermine Mao's regime. Many in America's foreign-policy establishment viewed Chinese communism as an extension of Soviet **totalitarianism** and part of an international communist conspiracy.

Hardline congressional views reflected societal factors including fear of communism and the influence of the "China lobby." The China lobby consisted of influential individuals who sought to influence America to aid Chiang's effort first to remain in power and later to return to the mainland. Among its leaders were publisher Henry Luce and the businessman Alfred Kohlberg, who founded the American China Policy Association whose actions and views reflected the potency of individual factors.

As civil war engulfed China after 1945, the China lobby sought to persuade Americans that it was imperative to aid Chiang, whom Washington had supported during World War II. Members of the group enjoyed close ties to Chiang's representatives in America and their registered lobbyist and founder of the pro-fascist American Rock Party, William J. Goodwin. After Mao seized power, the China Lobby sought to apportion blame among those in public service whom they regarded as procommunist. Aided by congressional allies such as Senators Joseph McCarthy (R-WI), Pat McCarran (D-NV), and William Knowland (R-CA) and Representative Walter Judd (R-MI), they labeled American diplomats like Owen Lattimore and John Service, both China specialists, who had predicted that Mao would defeat Chiang, as traitors who had hastened the "fall of China." Redbaiter McCarthy publicly labeled Lattimore a "top Soviet spy."[8]

PAST: FROM HOSTILITY TO ENGAGEMENT

Following World War II, American objectives in Asia focused on containing the USSR and China and providing security for Japan, South Korea, and Taiwan. Mao's xenophobic views of the West stemmed partly from China's historical experience. For thousands of years, China's empire—the Middle Kingdom— had been the most populous and richest polity in the world and regarded foreigners as "barbarians." In the 17th century, China's population began to increase, but the country failed to compensate for its demographic explosion by industrialization as had Europe, America, and Japan. Consequently, in the 19th century, the European powers and Japan penetrated deeply into Imperial China and extracted trade and political concessions that undermined Chinese sovereignty. U.S. Secretary of State John Hay's Open Door policy (1899) to force China to trade equally with Western powers and Western repression of China's Boxer Rebellion (1900) fostered anti-Western memories in China. The 1911 Wuchang Uprising started the Xinhai Revolution, leading to the end of the Qing Dynasty and the establishment of the Republic of China under President Sun Yat-Sen. Thereafter, an era of warlords, political disintegration, and further foreign encroachment began.

In the 1920s, two political movements emerged in China: the Kuomintang (Nationalists) and the Communist Party. They collaborated until 1927 when the Kuomintang, led by Chiang, attacked the communists. Despite his initial victory, Chiang proved unable to cope with regional warlords, runaway inflation, or the communists who survived by retreating to remote regions of the country and waging guerrilla warfare. In 1931, Manchuria was invaded by Japan, and further Japanese aggression forced the Kuomintang and the communists into an uneasy alliance that ended with Japan's defeat in 1945 and civil war between Mao and Chiang.

Following Mao's triumph, he established the People's Republic of China (PRC) in 1949, which joined the Soviet bloc. Washington refused to recognize the new government and for decades regarded Chiang's partisans as the legitimate rulers of the Republic of China. Since Mao's victory, U.S.-Chinese relations have passed through several phases as the political climate between the two countries evolved.

Cold War

China's revolution owed little to Moscow, which had discouraged Mao from seeking power in the 1930s and 1940s and provided little aid to China's communists after World War II. Americans, however, viewed Mao's victory as providing the USSR with an Asian ally in the Cold War.

U.S.-Chinese relations were further poisoned after Mao sent hundreds of thousands of "volunteers" into Korea in November 1950 some months after North Korea had invaded South Korea. China had not been involved at the war's outset but entered the conflict after UN (largely U.S.) forces advanced toward the Yalu River, Korea's boundary with China, and seemed poised to invade China. The war ended any possibility that the Truman administration might recognize China's communist government.

U.S.-Chinese relations remained frozen for two decades after the Korean War. Washington sought to extend containment, originally a policy of resisting Soviet expansion in Europe (chapter 14), to Asia. It assumed that Beijing was aggressive and expansionist, willing to sponsor "wars of national liberation" against pro-Western governments, as in Vietnam in the 1950s and 1960s and, albeit cautiously, in the Philippines, Malaysia, Thailand, and Indonesia. Containment lay behind U.S. security guarantees to Japan, Taiwan, Pakistan, and the Philippines and from 1954 to 1977 in the Southeast Asia Treaty Organization whose members included Australia, France, New Zealand, Pakistan, the Philippines, Thailand, the United Kingdom, and the United States. Not until the mid-1960s did American policy toward China begin to change.

Declining Sino-American Hostility

Among the factors that initiated rethinking in Washington about relations with China was recognition that the Soviet bloc was not a monolithic entity run from Moscow. Despite apparent unity, Soviet and Chinese communists were repeatedly at odds. In the 1920s, the dispatch of Soviet advisers to aid the Chinese Communist Party (CCP) had led to its conflict with Chiang. Stalin and Mao disagreed about how to foster a revolution in China, with Stalin arguing that revolution depended on the urban working class as Marx and Lenin had argued. Mao, however, sought to mobilize China's peasant masses for a revolutionary war in the countryside. Mao also ignored Stalin's advice to cooperate with Chiang in fighting Japan during World War II. And after the war's end, Moscow concluded a Treaty of Friendship and Alliance with Chiang's regime.

With Mao's victory, Moscow concluded a similar Treaty of Friendship and Alliance with Mao's regime and provided China with loans and advisers, and China's intervention in Korea papered over differences between the two. After Stalin's death in 1953, however, Mao began to view himself as the preeminent leader of the international communist movement, taking issue with Nikita Khrushchev's 1956 denunciation of Stalin's purges of fellow communists and his "cult of personality." Khrushchev also declared that "peaceful coexistence" with the capitalist West was possible, a position in conflict with Mao's policy of aiding national liberation movements in the developing world. Mao regarded such deviations from Stalinist orthodoxy as heretical. Khrushchev also refused to aid China in developing nuclear weapons or take Beijing's side in its 1962 border dispute with India. In 1960 and 1961, the ideological differences between the Soviet and Chinese communists became public, and the following year, Mao criticized Khrushchev for backing down during the Cuban missile crisis.

Mao also deviated from Soviet emphasis on developing heavy industry as the engine of economic development and in 1958 adopted a radical but disastrous policy—the Great Leap Forward—that organized peasants into regimented agricultural communes and made them establish local industries. The result was economic chaos and widespread famine, and the policy was abandoned in 1960. Even more radical was China's Great Proletarian Cultural Revolution (1966–1976) to impose Mao's personal control over and ideological orthodoxy within the CCP and purge China's intellectual and governing elites. Mao's young "Red Guards" even attacked the Soviet embassy in Beijing, and Mao's radicalism isolated China internationally.

As Soviet-Chinese relations worsened, U.S. policymakers considered how they could take advantage of the split, especially as they sought ways to end the Vietnam War. Mao, in turn, had come to see Moscow as a greater threat to China than Washington. The first evidence of a thaw in Sino-American relations came in April 1971 when a U.S. ping-pong team was invited to visit the PRC. "Ping-pong diplomacy" climaxed at a banquet given by China's Premier Zhou Enlai, who told his guests that "a new chapter in the relations of the American and Chinese people"[9] was opening. America responded by normalizing trade relations with China. Then, in July 1971, Henry Kissinger, then President Richard Nixon's national security adviser, secretly flew to Beijing to prepare for a visit by the president.

Nixon in China

An opera, *Nixon in China*, inspired by the president's visit, was composed in 1987 by John C. Adams and Alice Goodman.

Nixon arrived in China in February 1972, a visit he described as a "week that changed the world." Thereafter, Washington broke diplomatic relations with Taiwan, leaving the American Institute in Taiwan to represent the U.S. informally, and in October the PRC was awarded China's UN seat. The climax of the visit was the Joint Communiqué of the United States of America and the People's Republic of China, known as the Shanghai Communiqué.

The Communiqué dealt with several topics including differences over the Vietnam War, the interests of both countries in Asia, the need for coexistence between their different political and economic systems, and the value of mutual trade. The key clauses involved the status of Taiwan. America acknowledged but did not formally support Beijing's position that Taiwan was a Chinese province and that there was only one China, the PRC, and only one Chinese government. Taiwan's future, it declared, was an internal Chinese matter that should be settled peacefully, and America would withdraw its military presence on the island. In 2003, in a meeting with China's premier, President George W. Bush reaffirmed American support for a "one China" policy, declaring, "We oppose any unilateral decision by either China or Taiwan to change the status quo."[10] Notwithstanding periodic crises, the Communiqué remains the basis of U.S.-Chinese policy toward Taiwan to this day.

Individual factors played a key role in the shift in U.S. policy toward China. Kissinger's pragmatism and negotiating skills were crucial. Equally important was the change in Nixon's view of the world. Having been a hardline anticommunist during much of his career, he had become a pragmatist. Observers declared that "only Nixon could go to China" by which they meant that only someone with the reputation of being an outspoken anticommunist could have persuaded the American public and Congress to make such a dramatic foreign-policy shift. And only Mao and Zhou Enlai could have arranged the visit.

Societal change also helped enable America to adopt a softer line toward Beijing. Once it became clear that Chiang was no longer a threat to Beijing and that with the Sino-Soviet schism the threat of "monolithic communism" had ended, the influence of the China lobby waned. Americans had become disillusioned with the Vietnam War and were prepared to accept compromise with both China and the USSR to reduce global tensions. Finally, the lure of a huge market in China for U.S. goods persuaded America's business community to support improved relations with Beijing.

The end of the Cultural Revolution ended the most radical phase in the PRC's history and Beijing's self-imposed isolation. In 1975 Chiang died, and a year later, so did Mao. After an unsuccessful effort was made to continue Mao's policies by the "gang of four"—a radical faction including Mao's wife, Jiang

🔑 KEY DOCUMENT
The Shanghai Communiqué

- The Chinese side reaffirmed its position: the Taiwan question is the crucial question obstructing the normalization of relations between China and the United States; the Government of the People's Republic of China is the sole legal government of China; Taiwan is a province of China which has long been returned to the motherland; the liberation of Taiwan is China's internal affair in which no other country has the right to interfere; and all U.S. forces and military installations must be withdrawn from Taiwan. The Chinese Government firmly opposes any activities which aim at the creation of "one China, one Taiwan," "one China, two governments," "two Chinas," an "independent Taiwan," or advocate that "the status of Taiwan remains to be determined."

- The U.S. side declared: The United States acknowledges that all Chinese on either side of the Taiwan Strait maintain there is but one China and that Taiwan is a part of China. The United States Government does not challenge that position. It reaffirms its interest in a peaceful settlement of the Taiwan question by the Chinese themselves. With this prospect in mind, it affirms the ultimate objective of the withdrawal of all U.S. forces and military installations from Taiwan. In the meantime, it will progressively reduce its forces and military installations on Taiwan as the tension in the area diminishes.

Source: "Shanghai Communiqué," Taiwan Documents Project, February 28, 1972, http://www.taiwandocuments.org/communique01.htm.

Qing–Deng Xiaoping emerged as China's paramount leader in the late 1970s. Deng, who had opposed Mao's radical economic policies and had been purged during the Cultural Revolution, remained China's leader until his death in 1997. Unlike Mao, Deng believed in the importance of material incentives, and he made profit and loss responsible for economic decisions and fostered technology to increase productivity, thereby introducing elements of American capitalism in China. While advocating liberal economic principles, however, Deng never considered taking the reformist political path followed by Mikhail Gorbachev in Russia, and he played a decisive role in crushing China's democracy movement by sending tanks against student protesters in Tiananmen Square in June 1989.

The end of the Cold War ended the strategic reason for U.S. efforts to encourage closer Sino-American relations, and that relationship again became a major issue in American politics. "China's political system elicits opposition from human rights organizations; its population-control policies anger the anti-abortion movement; its repression of churches offends American Christians; its inexpensive exports trigger demands for protection from organized labor; its reliance on coal and massive dams for energy

Richard Nixon meets
Mao Zedong

AFP/Getty Images

upsets environmental groups; and its rampant piracy and counterfeiting infuriate the film, software, and pharmaceutical industries."[11] The Tiananmen Square massacre set the stage for the next phase in U.S.-Chinese relations. China had set a course of economic growth with a modified market system while perpetuating the CCP's power. Deng's policies had created the conditions for his country's emergence as a global power.

PRESENT: PARTNERS OR ADVERSARIES?

China's rise is indisputable, and Beijing's leaders are increasingly confident of their ability to defend the country's interests. At the same time, "Obama came into office as avowedly 'the first Pacific president,' convinced that George W. Bush's administration had paid too little attention to Asian regional issues and that the United States should enhance its traditional level of engagement there."[12] Secretary of State Hillary Clinton argued that America "had come to a 'pivot point'" in Asia.[13] Thereafter, the Obama administration announced a "Pacific pivot," a rebalancing toward Asia. Beijing saw the pivot as an effort to contain China's ambitions in an era when the role of Marxism had waned and the CCP's authority depended on economic growth, ending rampant corruption, and fomenting nationalism and anti-Americanism.

Chinese demonstrators in Tiananmen Square hold aloft the "Goddess of Democracy" statue in front of Mao's tomb.

Peter Charlesworth/LightRocket via Getty Images

America's "Pivot to the Pacific"

In late 2011 and early 2012, after changing China specialists in the State Department and National Security Council, the Obama administration announced steps to redirect foreign-policy resources to the Pacific in reaction to China's growing power in Asia. Secretary of Defense Robert Gates declared, "The United States and Asia will only become more inextricably linked over the course of this century," and this fact make a strong case "for sustaining our commitments to allies while maintaining a robust military engagement and deterrent posture across the Pacific Rim."[14] In November 2011, President Obama noted, "as a Pacific nation, the United States will play a larger and long-term role in shaping this region and its future, by upholding core principles and in close partnership with our allies and friends."[15] National Security Adviser Tom Donilon later explained: "It was clear that there was an imbalance in the projection and focus of U.S. power. It was the President's judgment that we were over-weighted in some areas and regions, including our military actions in the Middle East. At the same time, we were underweighted in other regions, such as the Asia-Pacific."[16]

The pivot was a continuation of U.S. policies to maintain stability in East and Southeast Asia. China's policies had exacerbated regional tensions and threatened America's regional friends and allies, and Asia was emerging as an important American economic partner. U.S. troops were already present in South Korea and Japan as well as aboard naval vessels. Chinese tactics had made America a crucial source of security for much of Asia.

After the president's announcement, Washington initiated several steps to carry out the pivot. A contingent of 2,500 Marines landed in Darwin, Australia, in April 2012 for training exercises, and naval exercises with Vietnam were conducted in 2011 and 2012. In July 2013, Vietnam's president visited Washington, where he and Obama agreed to strengthen economic and military links. The first of a new generation of U.S. shallow-draft littoral combat ships was deployed to Singapore in 2013, where they could support allies in their disputes with China. Some months later, an additional U.S. army battalion was sent to South Korea. America also arranged to preposition military equipment in and rotate forces through the Philippines, signed a ten-year agreement for access to that country's naval and air bases, agreed to provide it with maritime security assistance, and conducted joint exercises with the Philippine navy. The United States also initiated surveillance flights from Malaysia over the South China Sea despite Beijing's request that Washington halt "close-in" aerial and naval surveillance of China. Finally, the Defense Department indicated that the U.S. Navy would suffer smaller budget cuts than the other services in recognition of China's naval buildup.

Washington decided it was necessary to increase America's political role in Southeast as well as East Asia. One step was improvement in U.S. relations with Myanmar (Burma) as that country moved to democratize its political system. America also joined the East Asia Summit, a group of eighteen countries including China and Russia that meets annually following the Association of Southeast Asian Nations (ASEAN) meeting. After 2010, Washington also intensified efforts to expand the Trans-Pacific Economic Partnership (established in 2005 by Brunei, Chile, New Zealand, and Singapore) into an extensive free trade area embracing Japan and made Asia central to Obama's National Export Initiative, the goal of which was to double American exports.

The pivot reflected China's emergence as a great power and the prospect that Beijing might use its military, economic, and political clout to bully neighbors. "The core message: America is going to play a leadership role in Asia for decades to come."[17] But Beijing viewed the pivot as a hostile effort to limit its "rise." Chinese leaders found it difficult to make sense of U.S. foreign-policy aims amid the partisan clamor in Congress and the differing objectives of U.S. interest groups. Like American leaders, Chinese leaders must take account of bureaucratic and interest group struggles, and passivity in the face of America's pivot might rouse conflict with the country's military leaders and with incensed nationalists, groups that President Xi sought to make his political allies.

Some observers interpret Chinese objectives as defensive and believe that China is preoccupied with four threatening "concentric rings"—the "territory that China administers or claims"; the "14 adjacent countries" that include past foes such as India, Japan, Russia, South Korea, and Vietnam; "the six distinct geopolitical regions that surround China: Northeast Asia, Oceania, continental Southeast Asia, South Asia, and Central Asia"; and "the world far beyond China's immediate neighborhood"[18] that the country needs for trade and raw materials. Thus, when President Xi visited Kazakhstan, a growing source of China's oil, as part of its "marching westward" policy, he spoke of a "strategic partnership with central Asian countries,"[19] a formula that placed China in competition with both Russia and America in that region. Russia's political influence in Central Asia was matched by China's economic clout as the biggest trading partner of all the region's major countries except Uzbekistan, while America's presence in Central Asia was declining as the Afghan war wound down.

Although America is a key source of China's economic growth and technological knowhow, Beijing points out that Washington has deployed military forces around China (including a powerful naval presence in the East and South China Seas), refused to abandon Taiwan, and repeatedly scolded Beijing for human-rights abuses in Tibet and Xinjiang and for its trade and monetary practices. Thus, China's leaders concluded that "as China rises, the United States will resist"[20] ceding its status as a regional power.

Rising China: A New Global Bipolarity?

China's pride in having overcome foreign humiliation has been accompanied by growing assertiveness. The 2008 Beijing Olympics, China's influence in neighboring states like Laos, and its successful test of antisatellite weapons were viewed as reflecting the restoration of China's historical status as a great civilization. Thus, there began to emerge a world with two power centers (bipolarity) as had been the case during the Cold War.

Economic Rise China practices state capitalism—"where states play visible and significant roles in markets"[21]—and this system has been an engine for growth. In 2007, America's economy was four times larger than China's. Five years later, America's economy was only twice the size of China's. Following three decades of rapid growth during which the size of its economy as measured by nominal gross domestic product surpassed those of France, Britain, and Germany, China passed Japan in 2010 to become the world's second largest economy.

The World Bank in late April 2014, however, switched to purchasing power parity (PPP) to calculate gross national product (GNP), and this calculation suggested that China was poised to become the world's largest economy in 2014.[22] Western experts, however, have criticized the PPP referent as potentially misleading. Martin Wolf and David Pilling write: "It is possible to debate whether the newly revised numbers are right. The answer is they are reasonable. A more important question is what do they mean. What they do not mean is that China is already the world's greatest economic power."[23] Wolf and Pilling go on to observe that China is still in many respects a poor country in which purchasing power per head is relatively low, and since China invests close to half of its output, per capita consumption is lower than macro statistics might suggest.

For decades, China's economy grew annually by an average of 10 percent, outstripping other major countries and becoming ninety times larger than when Deng Xiaoping initiated reforms in 1978. During this period, China became the world's largest exporter and second largest importer and overtook America as the world's largest automobile market. Rapid growth made China an insatiable consumer of raw materials for which it scoured the world and invested heavily in authoritarian societies like Sudan that are pariahs in the West. History suggests, however, that past growth rates do not predict the future. Referring to China and India, two leading economists observed, "The single most robust fact about growth rates" is "strong reversion to the mean,"[24] that is, the average, which is a significantly lower global rate of growth. Indeed, recent estimates reflect a significant slowing of China's growth rate as exports declined and domestic investments have soured.

China's growth has been uneven and has produced widespread corruption and domestic food safety and environmental problems. Although Beijing pays lip service to communism, the gap between rich and poor grew so dramatically that inequality became greater than in any country outside of sub-Saharan Africa. Although 300 million Chinese emerged from poverty, its per capita gross domestic product (PPP) ranked 121st globally ($9,600 est. 2013) compared to America, which ranked 14th ($52,800 est. 2013).[25]

Rural China remains poor, and many of the country's 250 million migrant workers left rural communities to work in urban areas where they reside illegally. Millions of migrants are squatters in cities where they lack legal protection and are exploited as cheap labor, and growing demands for social benefits such medical care, education, and an end to pollution threaten China's social and political stability. The gap between China's wealthy coastal regions and less prosperous interior threatens political stability and places pressure on Beijing to maintain high growth.

Exports, aided by government subsidies that kept the costs of domestic industries low, drove China's economic growth. Between 1979 and 2014, U.S.-China trade increased from $5 to $592 billion.[26] In 2012, America's trade deficit with China was over $315 billion, accounting for almost half of America's trade deficit. U.S. exports to China increased fivefold after 2001 when China joined the World Trade Organization (WTO). Chinese exports to America include cellphones, computers, video equipment, and toys, while U.S. exports to China include soybeans, airplanes, automobiles, and semiconductors.

Overseas investment increased Beijing's global economic leverage. Beijing is investing billions on infrastructure in a "New Silk Road" to trade by sea and land with Europe and gain influence in countries like Pakistan. Chinese citizens who save money receive little interest, and China's government uses their savings to invest in oil pipelines in Myanmar, Turkmenistan, and South Sudan and an enormous hydroelectric-producing dam in Sudan. China has also invested heavily in America, and China's State Administration for Foreign Exchange, which manages the country's foreign exchange holdings, opened a New York office to invest in real estate and other U.S. assets.

Although such investment is mutually beneficial, some observers believe it gives Beijing economic influence that could harm American national security. Thus, in 2005, Washington barred the China National Offshore Oil Corporation's (CNOOC) purchase of UNOCOL, an American oil company, and in 2013, CNOOC was only permitted to buy the Canadian oil firm Nexen on condition that it surrender operating control of Nexen's assets in the Gulf of Mexico. A House Intelligence Committee panel described Huawei Technologies as a "national security threat," concerned that acquisition of U.S. telecommunications firms by Chinese corporations would allow them to install equipment to conduct espionage. It was later revealed that America's National Security Agency had hacked into Huawei's headquarters to learn whether it was linked to China's People's Liberation Army (PLA) and whether the PLA could access telephone and computer networks of countries that purchased equipment from Huawei.

As controversial as CNOOC's and Huawei's investments was a decision by Virginia-based Smithfield Foods, a large U.S. pork producer, to sell itself to China's Shuanhui International in the largest Chinese corporate acquisition in America to date (2013). Critics are concerned about the safety of Chinese food products and also cite the possibility that China could export Smithfield's pork back to China, thereby causing a pork shortage in America.

Are these concerns warranted? Agricultural products account for a quarter of U.S. exports to China and could rise significantly if not hindered by U.S. regulations. Some economists argue that America should follow its own free-market principles. The Smithfield sale was important because as a specialist in mergers and acquisitions suggests, "I'm sure all Chinese companies are watching this deal closely. If it goes through, it might start to change the perspective that the U.S. is not open for business to the Chinese."[27]

Chinese holdings of U.S. bonds—which underwrite America's budget deficit—have kept the value of its currency, the renminbi, low relative to the U.S. dollar. This keeps the price of Chinese exports to America low, enabling China to export more to the United States than if the renminbi's value were higher. American politicians charged China with currency manipulation—intentionally keeping the renminbi's value artificially low. This, they argued, cost Americans jobs and encouraged U.S. firms to move to China. Beijing viewed such charges as efforts to curb Chinese exports, thereby increasing China's domestic unemployment. In recent years, however, China has gradually allowed its currency to appreciate in relation to the dollar. China seeks to transform the renminbi into a reserve or hard currency like the U.S. dollar, but until its currency is accepted globally this will prove difficult. The recent devaluation of the renminbi may reflect an effort by China to let the market determine the currency's value at a time of declining economic growth.

Another issue is offshoring—the practice of moving operations overseas. As the world increasingly globalized, China became a major destination for U.S. firms seeking to remain globally competitive. U.S. companies sought to reduce labor costs (including wages and benefits), reduce tax burdens, and avoid costly environmental regulations in order to compete with foreign firms. Many American firms were also outsourcing (subcontracted) work to Chinese suppliers. China was identified in 2012 as among the five most favorable destinations for outsourcing based on cost competitiveness, resources and skills, and business and economic environment.[28]

Over time, other countries have begun to attract industries not only from the West but also from China. A shrinking population of working-age Chinese and rising wages have increased costs in China and encouraged firms to move elsewhere like India and the Philippines where costs remain low. And as costs have been reduced in America by trimming corporate health and pension obligations and the availability of new energy sources, some firms are returning home.

Growing wealth enabled China to afford rapid military modernization. For China's neighbors, economic power seemed more benign than military power.

Military Rise   China's military modernization "caught the world by surprise and unprepared."[29] The process was not easy owing to the influence of the commanders in the PLA who tried to resist shifting strategic and budgetary emphases toward air and naval forces to project military power into the Western Pacific. "Forces for inertia are making real military reforms more difficult," argues political scientist Andrew Scobell. "You've got a lot of fiefdoms and there's the strong disproportionate influence and power of the ground forces."[30]

China's military modernization was partly accomplished by espionage and acquiring "dual-use technologies from Europe, Israel, Russia and elsewhere that enabled the PRC to avoid costly research and development and rapidly advanced military technology." One target of Chinese cyber-espionage was American drone technology, which can be used in Beijing's maritime quarrels with its neighbors. Beijing successfully flew a stealth drone for the first time in November 2013 and was preparing a manned moon mission. Beijing "has near top-of-the-line fighter jets in substantial numbers; she possesses a robust ballistic missile capacity that includes stage separation and multiple independently targeted re-entry vehicle (MIRV) technologies that have been acquired from the West by irregular means, as well as anti-satellite and growing space warfare capabilities."[31]

China's naval capabilities grew rapidly after Beijing shifted its focus from threats on land to those at sea. President Hu Jintao in 2004 spoke of China's "Malacca dilemma"[32] because most of the country's oil passed through the Strait of Malacca and the South China Sea. In 2012, sea trials were held on China's first aircraft carrier, which had been refitted after its purchase from Russia. "Her submarine fleet is growing, and along with her aircraft, they regularly violate the territorial air and sea space of such neighbors as Korea and Japan. Perhaps half a dozen aircraft carriers are on the drawing boards."[33] China's growing military capability was apparent in sales of sophisticated arms to countries like Argentina and Pakistan, and Beijing has had few scruples about selling arms to just about any regime, however unsavory, that can pay.

China's cyber capability is not limited to espionage but also threatens America's computer-dependent infrastructure. Thus, in mid-2015, Chinese hackers apparently breached the U.S. Office of Personnel Management, thereby accessing the data for 21.5 million current and former federal employees and job applicants. Beijing's cyber-capabilities could launch a surprise attack against U.S. command, control, communications, intelligence, surveillance, and reconnaissance facilities. "These capabilities," declared Director of National Intelligence James Clapper, "put all sectors of our country at risk—from government and private networks to critical infrastructures."[34] President Obama alluded to China when he declared in his 2013 State of the Union Address, "we know foreign countries and companies swipe our corporate secrets," and "now our enemies are also seeking the ability to sabotage our power grid, our financial institutions and our air traffic control systems."[35] The president raised the issue in a phone conversation with President Xi in March 2013, and Secretary of the Treasury Jacob Lew again raised it that month in Beijing. "The United States has substantial and growing concerns about the threat to U.S. economic and national security posed by cyber-intrusions, including the theft of commercial information," declared Press Secretary Jay Carney, and Washington had raised this concern "at the highest levels" with China.[36]

A U.S. defense official concluded that America was engaged in an "asymmetrical digital war with China,"[37] and the Obama administration considered action ranging from trade sanctions and diplomatic pressure to offensive and defensive cyber countermeasures if China did not cease cyber-espionage. "After several years of making very little progress to improve behavior," declared a former State Department Internet-policy adviser, "it's reasonable to throw out what you've done in the past and use new instruments to try to get them to behave responsibly."[38] Washington has explained to China's leaders its doctrine for countering cyberattacks, hoping China would reciprocate, but so far Beijing has not done so. While visiting Beijing, Secretary of State John Kerry reached an agreement with China's leaders to establish a "cyber working group" to establish a code of cyber-conduct, but China ended cyber-cooperation after America accused five Chinese military officers of cyber-espionage.

The 2012 Department of Defense (DOD) report to Congress on China emphasized the increase in Beijing's defense budget. China ranks second behind America in defense spending. In 2013, China's defense budget increased by 10.7 percent, in 2014 by 12.2 percent, and in 2015 by 10 percent. Nevertheless, as of 2015, America's military budget was over four times larger than China's and exceeded the *combined* total of the eight next largest military budgets (including China's).[39]

The DOD report concluded that Beijing was "pursuing a long-term, comprehensive military modernization program designed to improve the capacity of China's armed forces to fight and win 'local wars under conditions of **informatization**,' or high-intensity, information-centric regional military operations of short duration." Such modernization is "an essential component of their strategy to take advantage of what they perceive to be a 'window of strategic opportunity' to advance China's national development" during a period of sustained economic growth. "At the same time, Chinese leaders seek to maintain peace and stability along their country's periphery, expand their diplomatic influence to facilitate access to markets, capital, and resources, [and] avoid direct confrontation with America and other countries. This strategy has led to an expansion of China's presence in regions all over the world, creating new and expanding economic and diplomatic interests."[40] Beijing also sought to extend its soft power by establishing 100 "Confucius Institutes" at U.S. universities to teach Mandarin.

The Carnegie Endowment concluded that China's military capability in Asia was nearing America's. One of its authors asked, "Can the United States continue with business as usual in the western Pacific, or must it start thinking of alternative ways to reassure the region about security?"[41] Is China's growing military power intended for aggressive purposes like seizing Taiwan or cowing neighbors like Japan and Vietnam? Chinese leaders insist theirs is a peaceful rise, pointing out that America remains the world's leading nuclear power, the U.S. Pacific Command is the largest of six such regional commands with some 180 naval vessels and 1,900 aircraft, and such forces are augmented by alliances with Australia, Japan, New Zealand, the Philippines, and South Korea.[42]

Owing to Beijing's sensitivity to what President Xi described as "core interests," analysts have tried to understand what those interests are, and U.S. military leaders have sought a dialogue with their Chinese counterparts. Former Australian Prime Minister Kevin Rudd concluded that China's interests include "maintaining the territorial integrity of the country (including countering separatist movements and defending offshore maritime claims)," "ensuring China's energy security," "modernizing China's military and more robustly asserting China's foreign policy interests, and enhancing China's status as a great power."[43]

Beijing's territorial claims have provoked tensions between China and its Asian neighbors. Its leaders emphasize that foreign penetration in previous centuries came from the sea. They perceive their country as encircled by U.S. allies including Taiwan, Japan, and the Philippines that constitute "the first island chain," separating the mainland from the Pacific Ocean. And they believe that U.S. interference in these disputes encourages regional resistance to China's claims. According to an adviser to President Obama, China thinks its regional claims are "in response to our efforts to contain them, but our analysis is that it's really their effort to push our presence further out into the Pacific" to "the second island chain."[44]

China's Territorial Claims

According to political scientist Christopher Joyner, a challenge to China's territorial claims is seen by China as a challenge to its sovereignty. "Any concession is seen as appeasement, with adverse implications both for domestic politics and foreign relations. The point is reinforced by the realization that nationalism and sovereignty remain the strongest political cement holding the 'ideologically bankrupt' Chinese Communist Party together in the post-Cold War Era."[45]

Taiwan   Washington viewed the core of the Shanghai Communiqué as Beijing's commitment to a "peaceful settlement of the Taiwan question." By contrast, China contends that the Shanghai Communiqué was a transitional arrangement that President Nixon had agreed would lead to Taiwan's eventual unification with the mainland. Although Washington terminated its defense treaty with Taiwan in 1979, the Taiwan

Relations Act passed by Congress made U.S.-Chinese diplomatic relations contingent on Beijing's behavior and contained a commitment to defend Taiwan if China used force to regain its "renegade province." Washington argued that arms sales to Taiwan were permissible because China's coastal military buildup opposite Taiwan suggested it might use military coercion. China claimed its buildup was peaceful because it deterred Taiwan from declaring independence and that U.S. arms sales violated China's sovereignty, threatened its security, and belied America's commitment to "one China."

Although Washington agreed in 1982 to reduce arms sales to Taiwan, the U.S. thereafter found ways to evade the commitment until 2001 when President George W. Bush agreed to the sale of an arms package that included antisubmarine patrol aircraft, missile destroyers, and assistance in purchasing submarines. Washington had previously refused Taiwanese requests for submarines because they were regarded as having offensive capability. Beijing regarded the 2001 deal as violating the 1982 agreement.

KEY DOCUMENT
The Taiwan Relations Act

It is the policy of the United States—

(1) to preserve and promote extensive, close, and friendly commercial, cultural, and other relations between the people of the United States and the people on Taiwan, as well as the people on the China mainland and all other peoples of the Western Pacific area;

(2) to declare that peace and stability in the area are in the political, security, and economic interests of the United States, and are matters of international concern;

(3) to make clear that the United States decision to establish diplomatic relations with the People's Republic of China rests upon the expectation that the future of Taiwan will be determined by peaceful means;

(4) to consider any effort to determine the future of Taiwan by other than peaceful means, including by boycotts or embargoes, a threat to the peace and security of the Western Pacific area and of grave concern to the United States;

(5) to provide Taiwan with arms of a defensive character; and

(6) to maintain the capacity of the United States to resist any resort to force or other forms of coercion that would jeopardize the security, or the social or economic system, of the people on Taiwan.

Source: "Taiwan Relations Act U.S. Code Chapter 48 Sections 3301-3316," April 10, 1979, http://www.taiwandocuments.org/tra01.htm.

Washington remained cautious about arms sales. As of 2013, America had not provided the assistance promised to help Taiwan acquire submarines and in the face of Chinese pressure in 2011, turned down Taiwan's request for F-16C/D aircraft to replace older aircraft. Nevertheless, Chinese officials expressed "strong indignation" about what they regarded as "grave interference" in China's domestic affairs that would encourage pro-independence Taiwanese. The Obama administration's decision in 2014 to sell $6.4 billion in arms to Taiwan, including antimissile systems, led Beijing to threaten economic reprisals and temporarily cease military exchanges with America.

U.S. efforts to restrain China's ambitions in other maritime zones—the South China Sea, the Indian Ocean, and the East China Sea—have also raised tension. Although Washington declared its neutrality in these disputes, its "interference" was resented by Beijing. Secretary Clinton used the 2010 ASEAN Regional Forum meeting to articulate Washington's interests in freedom of navigation in the South China Sea and keeping the sea-lanes open to all countries while offering assistance to achieve a peaceful resolution to such disputes.

South China Sea One quarrel involves conflicting claims over the 310,000-square-mile South China Sea that, according to geological studies, is the site of large-scale oil and gas reserves and rich fisheries. The area is also seen by Beijing as a geopolitical issue owing to American naval power, Vietnam's regional ambitions, and China's dependence on imported oil from the Middle East.

The issue has important implications for Washington's role in Asia. As the world's leading naval power, America requires free movement in the South China Sea to project that power into East and Southeast Asia and protect its Asian allies and control passage from the Middle East and Indian Ocean into the Pacific. China's control of the South China Sea, through which passes half the world's commercial shipping, would give it an ability to close the two maritime chokepoints into East and Southeast Asia—the narrow Taiwan Straits in the north and the even narrower Strait of Malacca to the south. Along these strategic sea-lanes moves much of East Asia's exports and imports including oil from the Middle East.

At the heart of the dispute are the Spratly and Paracel Islands, many of which are semisubmerged islets and shoals, and their adjacent economic zones. In 1992, Beijing enacted a Law on the Territorial Sea and the Contiguous Zone that declared the Spratlys and Paracels to be Chinese territories. China is geographically farther from the disputed islands than other claimants, and China's claim is challenged by the Philippines, Malaysia, Vietnam, Taiwan, Singapore, and Brunei. Beijing's claim rests on historical rights based on discovery and occupation dating back to the Han dynasty in the third century CE and arises from a view of authority over people to a ruler rather than the linear boundaries of the territory. Occupation would strengthen claims of sovereign ownership. Although few of these islands can support permanent human settlements, their ownership "can serve as legal base points for states to project claims of exclusive jurisdiction over waters and resources in the South China Sea."[46]

Although Beijing has opposed multilateral negotiations involving ASEAN, China did agree in 2013 to work with ASEAN toward establishing a legally binding Code of Conduct concerning the dispute. Secretary Kerry expressed America's position on a stop in Brunei. "A finalized code of conduct, in which all abide by a common set of rules and standards, is something that will benefit the entire Asia-Pacific community of nations—and beyond."[47] Beijing, however, regards its territorial claims as nonnegotiable and has opposed the involvement of international institutions like the International Court of Justice or the International Tribunal on the Law of the Sea. Instead, it insisted on bilateral negotiations with claimants because it could exert more influence one-on-one. Multilateral negotiations might be interpreted as willingness to compromise its claims. Beijing also sought to formalize its claims under the 1982 Convention on the Law of the Seas (which Washington has not ratified). Under the convention, sovereignty over an island allows a state to establish a 12-mile territorial sea and a 200-mile exclusive economic zone around that island.

China's assertiveness in the South China Sea deepened after President Xi assumed office. In 2012, the Chinese province of Hainan, which administers Beijing's policies in the South China Sea, enacted regulations to permit China's coast guard to intercept foreign vessels engaging in undefined "illegal activities." Chinese authorities went further in early 2014 demanding that all vessels fishing in the South China Sea obtain China's permission. A maritime confrontation occurred in 2014 after China moved a giant oil rig and over 100 ships near the Vietnamese coast and announced it planned to send a second rig. China also began to use sand to enlarge several reefs in the Spratlys and built an aircraft runway on Fiery Cross Reef in steps toward building permanent facilities. In effect, Beijing was unilaterally asserting control of these islands and preparing them to host air and naval forces. ASEAN responded bluntly to these unilateral efforts that it described as undermining regional "peace, security, and stability." Thus, China specialist Bonnie Glaser concludes, "China is currently following a deliberate policy of bullying and intimidating its smaller neighbors into recognizing its sovereignty over large swathes of the sea—and the United States must communicate that such behavior is unacceptable."[48] She adds that American policy must take account of the paradox that "China's neighbors seek greater U.S. economic, diplomatic and military involvement in the region as a counterbalance to China's growing power—but at the same time, every country in the region desires a close relationship with Beijing."[49] Thus, they urge Washington to resist Chinese pressure while avoiding a serious confrontation.

Secretary Clinton in 2010 called for "a collaborative diplomatic process by all claimants for resolving the various territorial disputes without coercion."[50] American policy remained restrained even after a Chinese warship cut across the bow of a U.S. cruiser, an action described by then Secretary of Defense Chuck Hagel that "could be a trigger or a spark that could set off some eventual miscalculation."[51] At the 2012 ASEAN summit, President Obama asked China to resolve its territorial dispute peacefully and permit freedom of navigation.

India and the Indian Ocean "Stretching from the Indian subcontinent to the western shores of the Americas," noted Hillary Clinton, "the region spans two oceans—the Pacific and the Indian—that are increasingly linked by shipping and strategy," and "is home to several of our key allies and important emerging powers like China, India, and Indonesia."[52] The Pentagon has assessed how American forces can provide security not just for East and Southeast Asia, but also for the Indian Ocean, and India plays a growing role in U.S. calculations. Described by President Obama as an "indispensable partner," India is viewed by Washington as critical in balancing China in Asia.

Improved U.S.-Indian relations were made possible by the 2008 Civilian Nuclear Agreement regarding cooperation in developing peaceful uses of nuclear energy. Previously, the relationship had been obstructed by U.S. sanctions resulting from India's development of nuclear weapons and its refusal to sign the Nuclear

MAP 12.2   The South China Sea

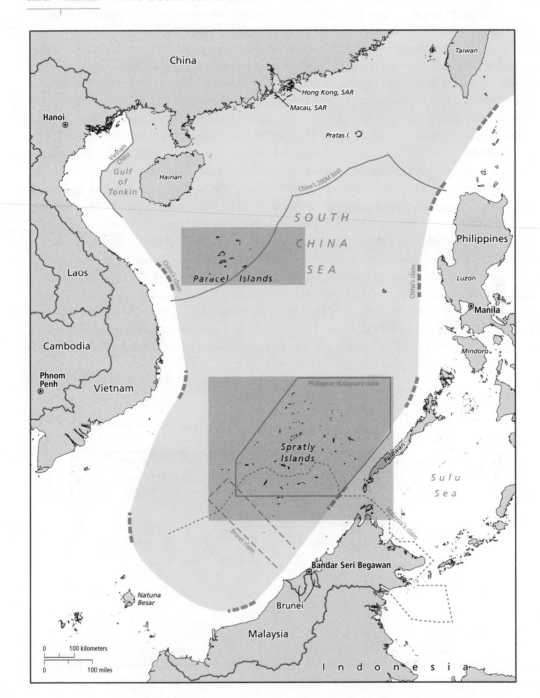

Nonproliferation Treaty. The agreement opened the door to bilateral political and military coordination and was a strategic bet that India would act to balance China. One consequence was initiating an annual U.S.-India Strategic Dialogue in 2010. The dialogue deals with issues ranging from strategic cooperation, energy, and trade to science, technology, and health. In 2012, Japan joined the dialogue. During Obama's visit to India in 2015, agreement was reached on reducing greenhouse gases, joint military hardware production, and evading liability issues linked to American sales of nuclear reactors to India.

India has remained suspicious of China, to which it lost territory during a brief war in 1962. In 2013, tension between the two intensified after cross-border incidents after which India claimed a Chinese incursion into the Ladakh section in Kashmir, along their Himalayan border. Although China and India intensified economic cooperation after Narandra Modi became India's prime minister in 2014, and China wishes to minimize friction with India because of disputes with other neighbors, border issues as well as the presence of Tibet's exile movement in India remained obstacles to relations between the two.

China has long been allied with Pakistan, India's regional foe, and assisted Pakistan to develop nuclear weapons and ballistic missiles. China has also invested in Afghanistan, a country in which both India and Pakistan seek to increase their influence as America's military presence diminishes. India's concern about China's ambitions increased as Beijing's presence in the Indian Ocean grew. Of special concern was China's development and management of Pakistan's port of Gwadar on the Arabian Sea along the route of oil tankers coming from the Persian Gulf and Beijing's investments in port facilities in Sri Lanka, Myanmar, and Bangladesh, all neighbors of India. In addition to providing China with facilities for shipping goods through the Strait of Malacca, some Indians believe these facilities constitute a "string of pearls" strategy to encircle their country. China has also increased its military presence along India's northern border. All this led India to rethink its strategy toward its neighbors and its policy relations with America.

MAP 12.3   China's "String of Pearls"

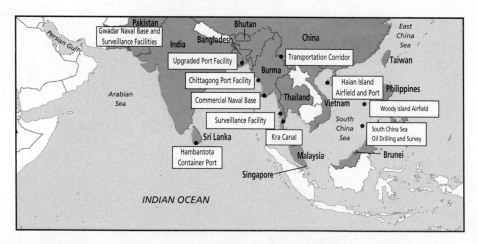

Source: http://kuldeepsinghchouhan.blogspot.com/2010/07/china-string-of-pearls-strategy.html.

India has also increased its military capabilities in recent years. It has more than 1.3 million men in its armed forces and a nuclear capability with long-range missiles able to target China's population centers. In 2011, India became the world's largest weapons importer, had constructed additional airbases close to China, and developed naval forces (including nuclear-powered submarines and aircraft carriers) in its rivalry with China in the Indian Ocean. It also provided military training to Vietnam and Malaysia and, like America, had become more involved politically with ASEAN and ASEAN-sponsored multilateral meetings. India's growing attention to China and its growing military capability were welcomed by Washington.

China's presence in the Indian Ocean is strategically linked to China's dispute over the Senkaku (Japanese)/Diaoyu (Chinese) Islands. Beijing's assertive maritime policy in this region, like that in the South China Sea, has risks, including mobilizing opposition in East, South, and Southeast Asia to contain its ambitions.

Senkaku/Diaoyu Dispute The eight uninhabited Senkaku/Diaoyu Islands in the East China Sea, like the islands in the South China Sea, are astride busy sea-lanes amid rich fishing and natural resources. Japan claims the islands because they had been uninhabited before Japan annexed them in 1895. After World War II, the islands were administered along with Okinawa by America, which returned them to Japan in 1972 (a decision Chinese observers regarded as intentionally hostile). By contrast, China claims ancient ownership of the area as fishing grounds administered by its province of Taiwan and contends that when the 1951 San Francisco Treaty returned Taiwan to China, the Senkaku/Diaoyu Islands should also have been returned.

Senkaku/Diaoyu
Islands

Reuters/Kyodo

Sino-Japanese rivalry in East Asia dates back to the 19th century. Japan's modernization during the Meiji era (1868–1912) undermined China's dominance in Asia. Anti-Japanese feelings in China run high owing to Japan's invasion of China and the atrocities committed there during World War II.

Japan hosts American military bases under their 1951 Mutual Security Treaty and 1954 Mutual Defense Assistance Agreement. Notwithstanding U.S. insistence that it takes no position concerning the sovereignty of the disputed islands and then–Secretary of Defense Leon Panetta's advice to Japan not to escalate the dispute, Panetta publicly informed China's leaders in 2012 that Washington was committed to defending the Senkaku/Diaoyu Islands in accordance with the 1951 treaty. This commitment was reaffirmed unanimously by the Senate a month later and by President Obama during a visit to Japan in April 2014. In response, Beijing declared it was "deeply concerned" by reports that U.S.–Japanese consultations included contingency planning to defend the islands. Thus, a Chinese attempt to occupy the islands by force might trigger a Sino-American military confrontation.

Adding fuel to the fire, Chinese commentators began to question Japan's sovereignty over Okinawa, a strategic island in the Ryukyu chain with over a million Japanese citizens. With American troops based there, Okinawa plays a key role in the U.S.-Japanese alliance. Tokyo and Washington revised their alliance in 2013, agreeing to build a new missile-defense radar system in Japan, deploy U.S. drones in Japan, and cooperate against possible cyberattacks. "Our bilateral defense cooperation," declared Secretary Hagel, "including America's commitment to the security of Japan, is a critical component of our overall relationship and to the Obama administration's rebalance to Asia-Pacific."[53]

In Japan, China's aggressive behavior concerning the islands, along with North Korean hostility, increased public sentiment for increasing the country's military capabilities. Japanese leaders chafed at the limits imposed during America's postwar occupation by Article 9 of their constitution under which "the Japanese people forever renounce war as a sovereign right of the nation and the threat or use of force as means of settling international disputes." Postwar Japan was limited to self-defense forces that until 1992 were forbidden to operate overseas and thereafter were only permitted to participate in international peacekeeping and relief operations. In July 2014, Japanese Prime Minister Shinzo Abe announced his government's reinterpretation of the constitution to allow Japan's armed forces to aid friendly countries under attack, including interception of North Korean missiles aimed at America, a position he reiterated in a speech to Congress in 2015 and approved by Japan's parliament later that year.

Tension rose after Tokyo's governor offered in 2012 to purchase the tiny islands from the family that owned them. After Japanese nationalists unfurled flags on one of the islands, anti-Japanese demonstrations erupted across China against what Chinese nationalists regarded as a revival of Japanese militarism. The Japanese government purchased three of the islands, an action followed by Chinese provocations— visits by Chinese patrol ships to the islands, intrusions into Japanese airspace by Chinese jet fighters, and China's placement of buoys in 2013 near the islands to facilitate a geological survey as part of a program "to safeguard its maritime rights and interests." Some days later, Japanese nationalists and Chinese coast guard vessels converged on the islands, and Chinese ships remained off the islands for over a day. "China," declared its minister of defense, "has indisputable sovereignty over the Diaoyu Islands," and would make "no compromise, no concession, no treaty"[54] in matters of territorial sovereignty, using military force to safeguard its claims, if necessary.

Tokyo increased its naval presence in the region and, to China's annoyance, signed an agreement with Taiwan to fish near the disputed islands. Prime Minister Abe threatened to remove forcibly any Chinese who landed on the islands. Japan also announced plans to build an army base by 2016 on an island nearby and threatened to shoot down Chinese reconnaissance drones overflying Japanese territory after one flew near the Senkakus. Beijing declared it would regard such action as an act of war.

Political scientist Ian Bremmer fears the "possibility of a mistake where someone gets killed is going up" because both countries "are scrambling their fighters in the East China Sea every day," and "the aftermath of a mistake will have both countries actively mistrusting the intentions of each other without a mechanism to really talk to each other and without the Americans acting as an interlocutor."[55] Such a risk was heightened when China announced its establishment of an air defense identification zone (ADIZ) over much of the East China Sea in November 2013. The new zone overlapped Japan's existing air defense zone including the Senkaku/Diaoyu islands, and Beijing asserted that foreign aircraft flying through the zone had to report flight plans to China and identify themselves. Although other maritime countries including America have similar zones, they do not apply to aircraft passing through those zones as opposed to entering their airspace whereas China demanded that *all* aircraft in its zone abide by its rules.

Japan's foreign minister rejected China's ADIZ, and Washington flew two unarmed B-52 bombers from Guam in the ADIZ in defiance of China's claim. According to the Pentagon, the bombers were sent as "a demonstration of long-established international rights to freedom of navigation and transit through international airspace,"[56] reaffirming Washington's commitment to Japan's security. Some days later, Washington and Tokyo accused Beijing of scrambling jet fighters after identifying two U.S. surveillance planes and ten Japanese planes in the ADIZ. A Chinese government spokesman sought to mute criticism of China's ADIZ. "The Air Defense Identification Zone does not equal territorial airspace, and is not an expansion of a country's territorial airspace."[57] Some months later, Japan reported that Chinese military jets had provocatively played chicken with Japanese reconnaissance aircraft in their overlapping air defense identification zones, an action repeated with a U.S. reconnaissance plane in 2014.

Risks of miscalculation may be reduced by a naval code of conduct in the Pacific agreed to by twenty countries including America, China, and Japan in April 2014. A Chinese analyst contended that the new rules would help governments "effectively manage and control maritime crises, reduce misjudgments, and avoid incidents of mutual interference and collisions when on the high seas,"[58] although it remained unclear how the code would be implemented.

Visiting Japan shortly after China had announced its ADIZ, Vice President Joe Biden declared that Washington was "deeply concerned" about China's action that he described as an effort to "unilaterally change the status quo in the East China Sea" that "raised regional tensions and increased the risk of accidents and miscalculation."[59] Biden then visited Beijing, where he and President Xi tried to play down the issue while conceding that differences existed. In effect, Biden simultaneously sought to reassure Japan of continued U.S. support and persuade China that America's pivot to Asia would continue, while tacitly accepting that Beijing would not retract its claim to an air defense zone. According to China specialist Kenneth Lieberthal, Biden's objective was "to make China a central focus of the pivot without making China the bull's-eye."[60] Sino-Japanese tension eased, however, in late 2014, when the two

MAP 12.4   Overlapping Chinese and Japanese Air Defense Identification Zones

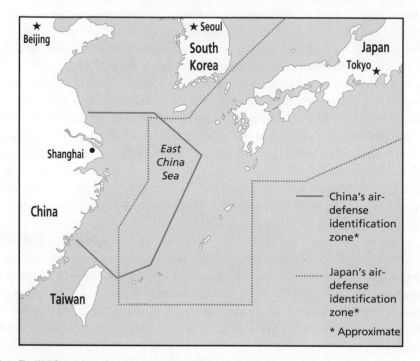

Source: Data from *The Wall Street Journal*.

countries agreed to disagree over the sovereignty of the Senkaku/Diaoyu islands, and Prime Minister Abe and President Xi had a brief meeting.

FUTURE: BALANCING COOPERATION AND CONFLICT

China's Economic Rise

China is an increasingly significant factor in determining American prosperity, and America remains necessary for China's economic growth.

Policy Options

    a. *Design policies assuming economic cooperation between Washington and Beijing benefits both.* "On the economic front" wrote Hillary Clinton, "the United States and China need to work together to ensure strong, sustained, and balanced future global growth. In the aftermath of the global financial crisis, America and China worked effectively through the G-20 to help pull the global economy back from the brink," and "U.S. firms want fair opportunities to export to China's growing markets, which can be important sources of jobs here in the United States, as well as assurances that the $50 billion of American capital invested in China will create a strong foundation for new market and investment opportunities that will support global competitiveness."[61]

Although America and China have economic differences, their economies are interdependent. The two countries can enjoy mutual benefits if they agree to an open and nondiscriminatory trading system, avoid barriers to trade, and create mechanisms to resolve differences. This option would not require Washington to ignore illegal Chinese economic practices or legal actions like levying fines against companies like GlaxoSmithKline and Johnson & Johnson, but it implies that negotiations about such practices be done quietly to encourage China to revise its policies. Despite disagreements, America and China successfully negotiated an agreement in 2014 that Secretary of the Treasury Lew had called "the first time China has agreed to negotiate a bilateral investment treaty, to include all sectors and stages of investment with another country."[62]

Persuading China to alter its economic policies, however, is not easy, especially with interest groups pressuring both governments. American exporters have bridled at Chinese subsidies for domestic companies and at China's refusal to export "rare earth metals" like lithium over which it enjoys a near monopoly but that are essential for technologies like batteries for electric cars. Americans will not cooperate with China if they believe that Beijing is manipulating the value of its currency to encourage exports or if they conclude that China is forcing U.S. firms to share proprietary information with Chinese companies or, worse, are stealing that information. Cooperation will be difficult if China's officials continue to criticize U.S. companies like Apple and impose unjustified regulations on them.

And Beijing will not cooperate if Washington threatens trade sanctions against China for refusing to appreciate its currency as fast as America wishes, if it uses accusations of Chinese human-rights violations to threaten trade relations, or if it acts to limit China's direct foreign investment in America. Both countries would benefit if China rebalances U.S.-Chinese trade by reorienting its economy toward domestic consumption and domestic-led growth and relies less on exports as China's Prime Minister Li Keqiang has promised.

b.   *Make no effort to rectify Chinese economic practices that Washington views as discriminatory or illegal.* Economic appeasement would produce a powerful domestic political backlash among U.S. firms and labor unions that seek to compete with Chinese firms, along with politicians who are expected to defend the interests of their constituents. Such neglect might also encourage China to perpetuate existing unfair practices and encourage it to adopt additional practices that discriminate against U.S. trade and investment.

c.   *Press China to follow "fair" economic practices.* A third option—one that enjoys popularity among Americans—would be to pressure China openly to move rapidly to adopt U.S. demands that Beijing (1) let its currency float freely and revalue quickly, (2) end intellectual piracy and crack down on Chinese firms engaging in the practice, (3) allow foreign firms to invest freely in Chinese government projects, (4) remove requirements that U.S. firms share innovative technologies with Chinese firms as a condition for operating in China, (5) limit Chinese foreign direct investment in America, and (6) end cyber-espionage. Washington has brought several complaints about China's trade practices to the WTO and won cases relating to China's tariffs on American cars and its embargo on exporting rare earth metals, while China won a case against Washington's tariffs on imports of Chinese steel products and solar panels.

However, this approach risks arousing Chinese nationalism and forcing China's leaders to refuse all demands made on them. China enjoys sufficient economic clout that it could resist what it regarded as unwarranted interference in its domestic affairs. China's dollar holdings and purchases of U.S. government securities give it the means to erode America's financial position. The economic friction produced by a hardline policy and the threat it would be perceived to pose to China could also have significant political consequences, strengthening the influence of China's hawks and their position on territorial claims and defense spending, policies that would appeal to domestic nationalist sentiment.

China's rise has created a paradox that is described as "cool war," which "aims to capture two different, mutually contradictory historical developments that are taking place simultaneously. A classic struggle for power is unfolding at the same time as economic cooperation is becoming deeper and more fundamental."[63]

China's Military Rise

China's military rise has created anxieties in Asia. Although China remains less powerful militarily than America, its growing capabilities have created concern in Washington that U.S. economic interests in the Pacific and the security of its regional friends may be endangered in the near future. America's pivot provided Washington with alternative options because it was at once a symbol of the importance America attaches to the region and a step toward balancing Chinese power.

Policy Options

a. *Match China's military rise unilaterally by deploying additional naval and air forces in Asia.* Such unilateralism has drawbacks. First, it entails additional defense expenditures at a time of budgetary stringency or requires the withdrawal of military capabilities from other regions. Alluding to growing U.S. tensions with Russia, analyst Minxin Pei argued, "If the U.S.-Russia relationship goes downhill, the Chinese will get a much easier ride," and America "cannot afford to be tough on both Russia and China at the same time."[64] China can play America and Russia off against each other, much as Nixon played off China against the USSR in the Cold War. American public opinion would oppose sending large-scale forces to Asia, especially so soon after U.S. forces have left Iraq and Afghanistan, and the deployment of U.S. forces sufficient to balance China in Asia would be seen by Beijing as a threat to its security and could prove toxic to Sino-American relations.

b. *Assist America's regional friends and deploy only forces sufficient to serve as a visible commitment to their security.* Such forces require few additional permanent facilities in Asia and would be unlikely to be seen as threatening. Warming American-Indian relations, security treaties with Japan, the Philippines, and South Korea, and periodic military maneuvers with these countries reflect such commitments. This option also enhances U.S. influence in Japan and Tokyo's ability to assuage Japanese nationalism.

c. *Reduce existing American military forces in Asia.* Such a shift would trigger opposition in Congress and in the executive branch. A retreat might also whet China's ambitions and doubtlessly frighten America's regional friends faced with an invidious choice between capitulating to China's territorial claims or developing their own forces, including nuclear weapons, to deter China's regional ambitions. More positively, U.S. withdrawal might induce cooperation between South Korea and Japan if they had to face threats from China and North Korea by themselves.

Territorial Issues

Taiwan America walks a fine line between continued protection of and aid to Taiwan and its desire not to alienate Beijing. China, too, has cautiously dealt with the issue. Although Beijing has honored its pledge not to use force in seeking to reintegrate Taiwan, its leaders will brook no effort by Taiwan to become independent, and such an effort would trigger China's use of military force. In 2005, the PRC passed an "Anti-Secession Law": "In the event that the 'Taiwan independence' secessionist forces should act under any name or by any means to cause the fact of Taiwan's secession from China, or that major incidents entailing Taiwan's secession from China should occur, or that possibilities for a peaceful reunification should be completely exhausted, the state shall employ non-peaceful means and other necessary measures to protect China's sovereignty and territorial integrity."[65]

Policy Options

a. *Reverse America's "one China" policy and support Taiwanese independence.* Although there is some support for this among American conservatives, such a policy would probably trigger a confrontation with Beijing and the prospect of a war that would destroy any possibility of Sino-American engagement. Such a confrontation occurred in 1995. Taiwan's President Lee Teng-hui had spoken of "two Chinas," one of which was the "Republic of China on Taiwan." Beijing made its anger clear by conducting missile tests in the East China Sea and deploying additional military forces on the coast facing Taiwan.

America responded by dispatching two aircraft carrier battle groups to Taiwan, signaling the U.S. commitment to the island. Secretary of Defense William Perry asserted that "while the Chinese are a great military power, the premier—the strongest—military power in the Western Pacific is the United States,"[66] but U.S. naval forces remained *outside* the Taiwan Strait although able to intervene if necessary. When another pro-independence candidate was elected Taiwan's president in 2000, China accelerated its deployment of missiles opposite Taiwan.

b. *Regard Taiwan as a Chinese province but guarantee the island against the PRC's use of force.* Protecting Taiwan is the rationale for U.S. arms sales to the island. Such sales in the future, if seen as threatening by Beijing or as unduly prolonging Taiwanese autonomy, might be met by Chinese sanctions against U.S. companies involved in such sales as well as less cooperation on issues involving North Korea, Syria, and Iran. Even more dangerous would be if China retaliated by resuming sales of nuclear or missile-related technologies to North Korea, Pakistan, and Iran or if China sold massive quantities of its U.S. securities (a threat made in 2011). Any of these would trigger a deterioration of U.S.-Chinese relations from which both countries would suffer.

c. *Cease providing arms and abandon Taiwan,* a course that would placate Beijing. However, it would be viewed by China and America's Asian allies as reflecting U.S. weakness and cause America's friends to accommodate Beijing. It would also produce a political firestorm at home among congressional hawks in both political parties.

South China and East China Seas: Between Rocks and Hard Places China has abrasively asserted territorial claims in the South China and East China Seas. The first has produced friction and occasional violence with neighbors in Southeast Asia, and the second increased tensions with Japan. Chinese claims involve issues of military security and commercial advantage. To date, U.S. policy has been to walk a fine line between appearing as a neutral party with interests in maintaining freedom of navigation and providing support to its Asian friends and allies to resist Chinese bullying.

Policy Options

a. *Continue its current policy of calculated ambiguity,* simultaneously opposing China's efforts to bully its neighbors while claiming to be a neutral onlooker in their disputes. This is a difficult policy to carry out and risks miscalculation by Washington or Beijing that could produce dangerous political and/ or military confrontations. According to a former undersecretary of state, "It's going to have to be very deft and subtle in its implementation because there's going to be a pushback from the Chinese."[67] If mutually understood, however, the policy has the advantage of allowing both countries to satisfy domestic pressure groups while tacitly cooperating. For it to succeed, China need not surrender its claims but merely avoid the use of military force in resolving them, and America must make certain it understands the limits China will accept in U.S. support of its friends. America's aim would be to seek a resolution to the disputes or at least China's willingness to abide by international law in dealing with them.

b. *Act vigorously in supporting the claims of Vietnam, the Philippines, and Japan,* a course that would require significant American forces and a willingness to make clear commitments that, if unfulfilled, would undermine American credibility. Thus, in October 2014, Washington partly lifted its embargo on sending arms to Vietnam to aid Hanoi to resist China's maritime claims. It was as a step toward building a U.S.-Vietnamese partnership to oppose China's ambitions in the South China Sea. Such commitments might produce precisely the sort of confrontation with China they are meant to prevent. China would also be tempted to retaliate economically against U.S. interests and refuse to cooperate with Washington on other issues. For domestic reasons, including the influence of the People's Liberation Army and the country's vocal nationalists, any Chinese leader would find it difficult to capitulate in the face of American threats to the country's "core" interests.

c. *Concede the validity of China's territorial claims.* Such a policy would be regarded as supine by domestic hardliners, and its advocates would be labeled "appeasers." This option would undermine America's interests in freedom of navigation in a region increasingly crucial to U.S. prosperity. In the absence of a U.S. presence, the stability of the political order in the Pacific would be undermined. Taiwan as well as Japan, Vietnam, South Korea, and the Philippines would either have to capitulate to China's bullying or in the cases of Japan and South Korea possibly have to acquire nuclear weapons, a decision that would heighten regional tensions and perhaps even end in a nuclear exchange.

CONCLUSION: CONTAINMENT OR ENGAGEMENT?

On assuming office, President Obama sought to improve Sino-American relations and identify issues over which the two countries could cooperate. Other alternatives were to intensify strategic competition with China, a fiscally unpalatable and dangerous course, or leave the relationship unchanged, an equally unpalatable approach that would permit crises and other events to determine the future. The administration recognized that China had become a global power and that America could not simply impose its policies, a pragmatic recognition reinforced by the effects of America's financial crisis. Thus in a 2011 global survey, "in 15 of 22 nations, the balance of opinion is that China either will replace or already has replaced the United States as the world's leading superpower."[68]

The president's objective was only partly realized. China's approval rating in America plummeted, while negative views of the United States among the Chinese rose dramatically.[69] By the end of Obama's first term and the emergence of Xi Jinping as China's president, although Washington and Beijing remained divided, there had been progress. Although China still refuses to punish North Korea so vigorously that it would cause that regime's collapse, it has moved closer to the U.S. position of cajoling North Korea to surrender its nuclear weapons. On a visit to South Korea in 2014, President Xi reiterated his support for denuclearization of "the Korean peninsula." Finally, although Washington and Beijing still argue about economic issues like the value of China's currency, trade relations flourish.

In June 2013, President Xi and President Obama had an informal "shirtsleeves summit" in California. Historically, war has frequently erupted between hegemons and challengers, but in what political scientist Joseph Nye called "the most important meeting between an American president and a Chinese leader in 40 years, since Nixon and Mao,"[70] the two discussed issues ranging from Asia's maritime disputes to cyber-security and economic relations in an effort to bring about what President Xi called "a new type of great-power relationship."[71] "That means," observed National Security Advisor Susan Rice, "managing inevitable competition while forging deeper cooperation on issues where our interests converge."[72] President Obama said they had made "terrific" progress, and their two days of meetings were described by a U.S. official as "unique, positive and constructive."[73] They made progress over denuclearizing Korea and cooperating to reduce carbon emissions but failed to resolve mutual cyber-insecurity, arms sales to Taiwan, or disputes in the South China and East China Seas. Nevertheless, in July 2014 Xi declared that a confrontation with America would be a disaster.

"Trust remains in short supply. With no immediate threat to its security (beyond the unpredictability of North Korea) and America the only potential long-term threat, China continues a rapid military build-up," while America "remains committed, rhetorically, at least, to its strategic pivot to Asia. This reassures allies alarmed by China's rise, but looks less like a 21st-century 'new model' relationship, than a very old-fashioned 19th-century sort of strategic rivalry."[74] Washington perceives China as a bully, seeking regional hegemony at the expense of U.S. allies.

America's Asian pivot was impeded by crises in the Middle East and Europe. On a visit to South Korea, Secretary of Defense Hagel observed, "Because of what else is going on in the United States and the world, it's important that we spend some time out here."[75] And a former U.S. diplomat argued, "The president has been pulled in too many directions, and I don't think he's developed the relationships that would show a qualitatively different U.S. approach to the region."[76] Having cancelled two

Presidents Xi
and Obama and
"shirtsleeves"
diplomacy

Reuters/Kevin Lamarque

earlier journeys to Asia because of domestic crises, President Obama returned to the region in April 2014, where he denied that Washington sought to contain China even while visiting four countries that felt threatened by Beijing.

China and America are interdependent. Each can harm or help the other, and each is affected by the other's policies. Washington seeks to encourage cooperation with China while nudging it to behave responsibly. Whether the relationship will be one of conflict or collaboration remains unclear. As Hillary Clinton carefully phrased it, "We all know that fears and misperceptions linger on both sides of the Pacific. Some in our country see China's progress as a threat to the United States; some in China worry that America seeks to constrain China's growth. We reject both those views. The fact is that a thriving America is good for China and a thriving China is good for America."[77] It thus becomes necessary "to reduce the malign role played by misperception" that can arise "from one side either perceiving a threat where none is intended or failing to believe in the credibility of the other side's intent to defend its interests."[78]

DISCUSSION QUESTIONS

1. Should U.S. policy toward China emphasize engagement or containment?

2. Should America fear China's rise?

3. Should values or interests be emphasized in U.S. policies toward China?

4. Describe and discuss President Obama's "pivot" to Asia.

5. What action should Washington take in response to Chinese cyber-espionage?

6. What positions should Washington take regarding China's territorial claims in Asia?

KEY TERMS

cult of personality (p. 365)

currency manipulation (p. 373)

dual-use technologies (p. 373)

informatization (p. 374)

national liberation movements (p. 365)

offshoring (p. 373)

outsourcing (p. 373)

peaceful coexistence (p. 365)

totalitarianism (p. 363)

$SAGE edge™
for CQ Press

Sharpen your skill with SAGE edge at **edge.sagepub.com/mansbach**

SAGE edge for Students provides a personalized approach to help you accomplish your coursework goals in an easy-to-use learning environment.

13

America, Europe, and NATO

A CHANGING PARTNERSHIP

President Obama
and Chancellor
Merkel discuss
sanctioning Russia.

T.J. Kirkpatrick/Bloomberg via Getty Images

America's close relations with Europe reflect a transatlantic community of shared democratic ideals and common geopolitical interests. The Cold War involved both a challenge to Western ideals and security, but security took precedence during that conflict. The end of the Cold War removed the security threat, and American dominance was such that promotion of Western values infused both U.S. and European policies. With no enemy in Europe, NATO policies beyond Europe and the eastward expansion of NATO and the European Union (EU) were efforts to reshape the world in the image of the West, part of a strategic relationship with Russia based on shared values. That expansion collided with the power of resurgent Russia under President Vladimir Putin, who regarded Western influence as a threat to Russian interests.

In focusing on U.S.-European issues, keep two things in mind. The first is the "German question"—how to deal with Europe's most powerful state without it becoming a regional hegemon or a source of conflict—which has preoccupied Europeans, Americans, and Russians since the late 19th century. Despite Germany's defeat in two world wars, it is again Europe's economic powerhouse and political arbiter. Second, despite the process of European integration that produced the EU, Britain, though an EU member, retains a bilateral "special relationship" (a term coined by Winston Churchill) with America that dates back to the early 20th century that has led to mutual intimacy enjoyed by no other countries.

SOURCES OF U.S. POLICY TOWARD EUROPE

External political factors have included making common cause with Britain and France against common foes in two world wars and the Cold War as well as common interests with overseas European settler nations including Canada, Australia, and New Zealand. As a group, the EU is America's leading trading partner and has been a key destination since the 1860s of U.S. **foreign direct investment**, the recipient of over half of such investment in 2012.[1] Americans and Europeans are members of and interact in many international organizations including the North Atlantic Treaty Organization (NATO), the G-7, the Organisation for Economic Co-operation and Development (OECD), and the Organization for Security and Cooperation in Europe (OSCE). Americans and Europeans also play prominent roles in nongovernmental organizations like Amnesty International and Greenpeace.

Events in 19th-century Europe like the Irish famine and anti-Jewish pogroms in Russia as well as poverty and political repression triggered waves of immigrants to America, many of whom were welcomed to New York harbor by the Statue of Liberty (a gift of the French people). Many were attracted by America's democratic government, and, as most countries in Europe became democracies, the ties that bound America and Europe deepened. The percentage of European countries defined as "free" is the highest of any region in the world (24 of 25).[2] Increasingly, informal and formal interaction among Europeans and Americans deepened transatlantic links, producing economic interdependence and cooperative policies. And democracy and economic interdependence are two factors that foster durably peaceful relations.[3]

America was founded by Europeans and until recently was a predominantly European society. Along with democratic values, shared commitments to capitalism, consumerism, and individualism infuse European and American societies. These are reinforced by Christian traditions, Protestant and Catholic, exported from Europe to America. The descendants of Scots and English reside in New England and the Southeast; those of Scandinavians and Germans live in America's Midwest, while descendants of Italians, Irish, and European Jewish immigrants populate urban America. Family ties among relatives living on both sides of the Atlantic remain strong.

Individual experiences including intermarriage, tourism, and education reinforce transatlantic bonds. Britain, Italy, Spain, and France are the four leading destinations for U.S. students studying abroad. Scientific exchanges and professional groups transmit ideas back and forth across the Atlantic. Recipients of Britain's Rhodes and Marshall Scholarships return to America as Anglophiles. Rhodes recipients have included President Bill Clinton, Deputy Secretary of State Strobe Talbott, Secretary of Labor Robert Reich, Supreme NATO Commander General Wesley Clark, Director of National Intelligence Dennis Blair, and Senators Bill Bradley (D-NJ), Larry Pressler (R-SD), David Boren (D-OK), Russ

Feingold (D-WI), and J. William Fulbright (D-AR). Fulbright was so impressed by his experience in Britain that he sponsored the Fulbright program to foster the exchange of American and foreign scholars. U.S. recipients of Marshall Scholarships included the journalists Thomas Friedman and Jeffrey Gettleman, former president of both Wellesley College and Duke University Nannerl Keohane, and Harvard foreign-policy scholar Graham Allison.

DID YOU KNOW?

Winston Churchill

Winston Churchill had a British father and an American mother.

PAST: THE NEW WORLD AND THE OLD

U.S.-European relations extend back to America's birth. America's Revolutionary War was won with French assistance. Britain invaded America and burned Washington, D.C., in 1812 and influenced America to declare the Monroe Doctrine in 1823. America rescued Europe in two world wars, intervening in World War I in 1917 and joining Britain in World War II after Japan attacked Pearl Harbor in December 1941.

As World War II drew to a close, Europe was divided by what Winston Churchill famously called an "Iron Curtain" between the democratic West and the Soviet-dominated East. The next chapter discusses the sources of American policy during the Cold War. Here, we examine the impact of the Cold War in Europe and its role in forging a transatlantic partnership.

Timeline

1900

1945 Yalta Conference

1947 Truman Doctrine

1948 Berlin blockade

1949 NATO formed

1990–1991 Cold War ends.

1992–1999 Fragmentation of Yugoslavia

1997 The Czech Republic, Hungary, and Poland join NATO.

2000

2004 Bulgaria, Romania, Slovakia, Slovenia, Estonia, Latvia, and Lithuania join NATO.

2009 Albania and Croatia join NATO.

2014–2015 NATO-Russian confrontation over Ukraine

MAP **13.1**   Immigration to America

➤ *Countries are defined by their modern-day boundaries. Russia and the former USSR countries are combined in this analysis. Birthplace is self-reported by respondents. Sample size in North Carolina is too small to analyze in 1910. Based on Pew Research Center tabulations of the 2013 American Community Survey and 1910 Census.*

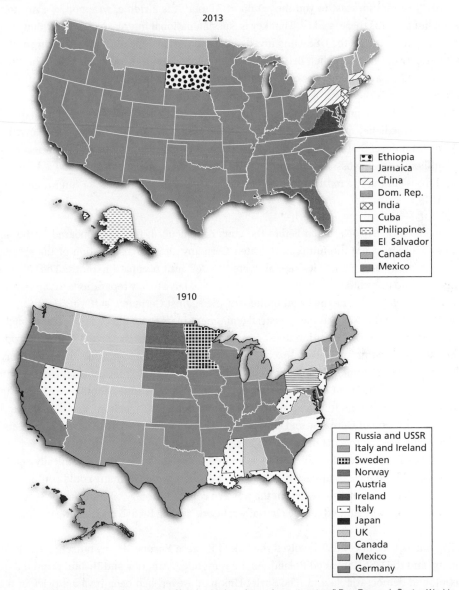

2013

Ethiopia
Jamaica
China
Dom. Rep.
India
Cuba
Philippines
El Salvador
Canada
Mexico

1910

Russia and USSR
Italy and Ireland
Sweden
Norway
Austria
Ireland
Italy
Japan
UK
Canada
Mexico
Germany

Source: "From Germany to Mexico: How America's source of immigrants has changed over a century," Pew Research Center, Washington, D.C. (October 2015), http://www.pewresearch.org/fact-tank/2015/10/07/a-shift-from-germany-to-mexico-for-americas-immigrants/.

Europe and the Cold War

The Cold War had its roots in World War II when Nazi aggression required British, Russian, and American cooperation to mobilize their wartime capabilities. After the defeat of Germany, differences in Western and Soviet values *and* interests combined to end the wartime alliance.

The "Grand Alliance" In a radio broadcast shortly after war began in 1939, Winston Churchill declared, "I cannot forecast to you the action of Russia. It is a riddle, wrapped in a mystery, inside an enigma; but perhaps there is a key. That key is Russian national interest."[4] After Germany broke its 1939 nonaggression pact with the USSR and invaded the country on June 22, 1941, initiating a titanic struggle between the two, Churchill, then Britain's prime minister, vowed to aid the USSR. "The Russian danger is . . . our danger, and the danger of the United States, just as the cause of any Russian fighting for his hearth and home is the cause of free men and free peoples in every quarter of the globe."[5]

Britain, the USSR, and America constituted a "Grand Alliance" that defeated Germany. The alliance was one of expediency and survived because of the common threat posed by Germany. In the 1930s, Soviet dictator Josef Stalin concluded that Britain and France were appeasing the Nazis in order to foster a conflict between Russia and Germany. His suspicions deepened after Western delays in opening a "second front" in Europe until June 1944 despite promises of an earlier invasion to relieve the pressure on the USSR.

The Division of Europe Even before the guns had silenced, fissures appeared in the alliance. Two sources of discord were the future of defeated Germany and the distribution of the spoils among the victors. Germany and Berlin, its capital, were divided into occupation zones. The allies agreed that Germany would be treated as a single economic unit and have to pay reparations to the victors, especially the USSR, which had borne the brunt of the struggle against Germany, suffering 20 million deaths. The Soviet Union would receive all the industrial equipment in its zone, plus one-quarter of such equipment in the Western zones on condition that no reparation be taken from current German production until the country had sufficient foreign-exchange reserves to purchase needed imports. Moscow moved swiftly to remove equipment from its zone without informing its partners of what was being taken, while refusing to permit shipment of agricultural goods to the Western zones. Stalin sought to obtain as much as possible in reparations to hasten the USSR's economic reconstruction. The immediate results were freezing the division of Germany and eliminating Western influence in the Soviet zone. This divergence in allied objectives led to a deterioration of East-West relations.

The United States and Britain were determined that their zones be economically self-sufficient so that they would not have to underwrite Germany's economy and Germany could contribute to Europe's recovery. To hasten economic revival in the western zones, Secretary of State James Byrnes proposed in July 1946 that they be unified. France initially refused, but the British and American zones were unified in 1947.

A second source of conflict involved the fate of Eastern Europe. At the outset of World War II, both Germany and the USSR invaded Poland. As the war ended, America and Britain desired a united, independent, and democratic Poland. The Soviet Union, however, had been invaded twice in the 20th century through Poland by Germany, and Stalin was determined to shut the invasion corridor. Moscow also sought to ensure that Eastern Europe would be governed by regimes friendly to its interests. Thus, Moscow established a provisional government of communist Poles in the city of Lublin, excluding the London government-in-exile recognized by the United States and Britain.

At the Yalta Conference in February 1945, the wartime allies tried to salvage a compromise regarding Poland. It was agreed that a coalition government would be formed by merging the Lublin and London groups followed by "free and unfettered elections," though any Polish government would have to be "friendly" to Moscow. Stalin believed that no noncommunist government could meet this test. Subsequent elections in Poland were rigged, and noncommunist leaders were arrested or exiled. This pattern was repeated elsewhere in Soviet-occupied Eastern Europe. Moscow insisted on forming coalition governments representing "antifascist" political parties, and noncommunist politicians in these countries were accused of having collaborated with the Nazis. The Red Army was the instrument for transforming Eastern Europe into "people's democracies" without a proletarian revolution.

There was little Washington could do to halt this process short of fighting another war. For war-weary publics in Europe and North America such an undertaking, especially against a recent ally, was unthinkable. Indeed, at Yalta, President Franklin D. Roosevelt promised Stalin that U.S. troops would be out of Europe within two years after the war. Western protests achieved little except to convince Stalin that America and Britain sought "capitalist encirclement" of the USSR.

Czechoslovakia was the last to succumb. The most Westernized and democratic country in Eastern Europe, it was the victim of a Soviet-inspired coup in February 1948. The murder of Jan Masaryk, Czech foreign minister and son of the country's founder, outraged the West, emphasizing what Americans regarded as the tragic outcome of their postwar expectations. There was considerable Western sympathy for Czechoslovakia because that country had been betrayed by Britain and France whose policy of "appeasement" peaked in the 1938 Munich agreement by which the country had been dismembered.

The Onset of Cold War in Europe Germany was the key to European security owing to its strategic location and economic potential. The Council of Ministers in 1946 to 1947 made little progress toward bridging the gap between Western and Soviet perceptions of the German issue. By spring 1947, France was prepared to merge its zone with the British and American zones, while the USSR integrated its zone into the Soviet bloc. American leaders regarded developments in Eastern Europe and Germany as evidence of Soviet expansionism.

In February 1947, the British government notified Washington that an economic crisis made it unable to continue assisting Greece or Turkey to resist communist subversion and Soviet pressure. America's response was prompt. In a speech to Congress in March 1947, President Harry Truman announced the Truman Doctrine under which America offered assistance not only to Greece and Turkey but to *all* countries threatened by communism. The Truman Doctrine opened a new phase in U.S. foreign policy during which commitments became global, aiming to combat communism wherever it appeared. "Containment," defined by U.S. diplomat George F. Kennan as resistance to expanding Soviet power "by the adroit and vigilant application of counterforce at a series of constantly shifting geographical and political points" that would lead to "the breakup or the gradual mellowing of Soviet power,"[6] was extended in the Truman Doctrine to include the spread of American values globally.

MAP 13.2   Divided Germany

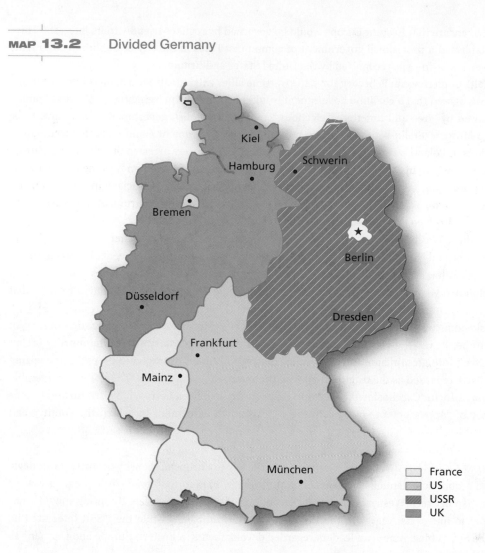

Kiel

Hamburg   Schwerin

Bremen

Berlin ★

Düsseldorf

Dresden

Frankfurt

Mainz

München

☐ France
▦ US
▨ USSR
▓ UK

The Marshall Plan followed, involving massive American loans and grants and, in a first step toward European integration, requiring joint planning by recipients to ensure optimum use of U.S. aid. In his speech at Harvard on June 5, 1947, Secretary of State George Marshall declared, "It is logical that the United States should do whatever it is able to do to assist in the return of normal economic health in the world, without which there can be no political stability and no assured peace. Our policy is directed not against any country or doctrine but against hunger, poverty, desperation and chaos. Its purpose should be the revival of a working economy in the world so as to permit the emergence of political and social conditions in which free institutions can exist."[7]

In consolidating his sphere of influence in Eastern Europe, Stalin imposed ideological and political conformity on the Soviet bloc. By late 1946, he had begun to emphasize the polarization of Europe and

🔑 KEY DOCUMENT

The Truman Doctrine
President Truman's Address to Congress, March 14, 1947

The Truman Doctrine

The United States has received from the Greek Government an urgent appeal for financial and economic assistance. . . .

The very existence of the Greek state is today threatened by the terrorist activities of several thousand armed men, led by Communists, who defy the government's authority at a number of points, particularly along the northern boundaries. . . .

At the present moment in world history nearly every nation must choose between alternative ways of life. . . .

One way of life is based upon the will of the majority, and is distinguished by free institutions, representative government, free elections, guarantees of individual liberty, freedom of speech and religion, and freedom from political oppression.

The second way of life is based upon the will of a minority forcibly imposed upon the majority. It relies upon terror and oppression, a controlled press and radio, fixed elections, and the suppression of personal freedoms.

I believe that it must be the policy of the United States to support free peoples who are resisting attempted subjugation by armed minorities or by outside pressures. . . .

Source: "President Harry S. Truman's Address before a Joint Session of Congress, March 12, 1947," The Avalon Project, http://avalon.law.yale.edu/20th_century/trudoc.asp.

---

the world more generally into two economic systems—capitalist and socialist. To bind other national communist parties to the Communist Party of the Soviet Union (CPSU), Moscow organized the Communist Information Bureau in 1947 with representatives from the CPSU, the ruling communist parties of Eastern Europe, and the Italian and French communist parties.

The most dangerous Cold War issue in Europe involved Berlin. Located deep in the Soviet zone of Germany, Berlin's four zones were governed by military commanders of the occupying powers. Western unification of their three zones of Germany had triggered vigorous protests from Moscow, and the U.S. military commander in Germany, General Lucius Clay, was uneasy: "I pointed out that I had no confirming intelligence of a positive nature, but that I did sense a change in the Soviet position which portended some Soviet action in Germany. I did not predict what course this action would take, though I did state that I was no longer adhering to my previous position that war was impossible."[8]

Following the introduction of a currency reform in Germany's Western zones and Berlin, Stalin acted. The USSR interrupted and then blockaded road, rail, and river traffic into the city in violation of existing agreements. Thus began the "Berlin blockade." America and its allies were faced with the unenviable choice of backing down or using force. This dilemma was overcome, however, by ingenuity and improvisation. By the spring of 1949, an Anglo-American airlift was ferrying up to 13,000 tons of supplies to Berlin each day. As neither side wished to initiate hostilities, a stalemate ensued. Although the blockade was broken, Berlin would remain divided until the end of the Cold War. In the meantime, two governments had emerged in Germany as a whole. In May 1949, West Germany—the Federal Republic of Germany—was established, and in October East Germany—the German Democratic Republic—was declared an independent state.

America's commitment to defend Western Europe and preserve an independent West Berlin was summarized by Clay: "When Berlin falls, western Germany will be next. . . . If we withdraw our position in Europe is threatened. If America does not understand this now, does not know that the issue is cast, then it never will and communism will run rampant."[9] President John Kennedy reaffirmed this commitment when in Berlin in 1963 he declared, "Ich bin ein Berliner!" ("I am a Berliner!")

The Soviet threat in Europe led to establishing a military "shield" behind which West European economic recovery could occur. Recognition of the need for a military presence led to the Anglo-French Treaty of Dunkirk in 1947. A year later, Holland, Belgium, and Luxembourg joined France and Britain in signing the Brussels Pact. A week later, the Berlin blockade began. In this hostile climate, the Senate adopted a bipartisan resolution sponsored by Arthur Vandenberg (R-MI), declaring U.S. willingness to enter into joint military arrangements with the countries of Western Europe, and subsequent negotiations led to the birth of NATO on April 4, 1949.

The North Atlantic Treaty Organization (NATO)

NATO was established to make a potential aggressor recognize that America—with its nuclear capability—was committed to defending Western Europe. The United States would consider an attack on Europe as an attack on itself. NATO's first secretary-general, the alliance's highest ranking civilian, Lord Ismay, said its objectives were "to keep the Russians out, the Americans in, and the Germans down."[10] By Article 5, the signatories agreed that "an armed attack against one or more of them in Europe or North America shall be considered an attack against them all" and "if such an armed attack occurs, each of them, in exercise of the right of individual or collective self-defense recognized by Article 51 of the UN Charter, will assist the Party or Parties so attacked by taking forthwith, individually and in concert with the other Parties, such action as it deems necessary, including the use of armed force, to restore and maintain the security of the North Atlantic area."[11] The only time Article 5 has been invoked was after 9/11 although security cooperation proved unnecessary. Article 4 requiring that members consult was invoked by Turkey on three occasions—in 2003 regarding the war in Iraq and twice in 2012 after Syrian violations of Turkey's borders.

NATO's original members were Belgium, Canada, Denmark, France, Iceland, Italy, Luxembourg, the Netherlands, Norway, Portugal, Britain, and the United States. Since then, NATO has been repeatedly enlarged. Turkey and Greece joined in 1952. West Germany was added in 1955, spurring the Soviet establishment of the Warsaw Treaty Organization. Spain joined in 1982. As a peacetime alliance intended to deter a potential foe rather than defend against or plan an attack, NATO was unprecedented. The treaty was more than a vague agreement and included permanent institutions to meet its objectives. In April

1951, the Supreme Headquarters Allied Powers in Europe (SHAPE) was established in Rocquencourt, France, to integrate NATO planning, and General Dwight Eisenhower was named NATO's first Supreme Allied Commander, a position always occupied by an American. Congress also passed the Mutual Assistance Defense Act, providing military assistance to member countries.

NATO was based on four assumptions. First, the Soviet Union entertained ambitions to invade Western Europe. Second, the countries of Western Europe would be unable to defend themselves for the foreseeable future. Third, Soviet leaders were rational politicians who could be deterred by American nuclear weapons. And, fourth, North America was invulnerable to Soviet attack.

NATO strategy relied on the ability of American bombers to deliver a retaliatory nuclear strike against Soviet cities in the event of a Soviet invasion. This was a "first-strike" nuclear policy. This strategy was attractive because America enjoyed a monopoly of strategic nuclear power until 1949. It was also relatively inexpensive because it did not require large land forces and would not divert scarce resources from Europe's economic recovery. The threat of nuclear retaliation seemed sufficient to *prevent* a Soviet attack and so spare Europe the ravages of another war. As these conditions changed, however, these assumptions became less tenable.

NATO: The Early Years   NATO viewed North Korea's invasion of South Korea in June 1950 as a Soviet-inspired probe of U.S. commitments and a prelude to possible invasion of Western Europe. The Korean War demonstrated that America's nuclear arsenal was insufficient to prevent conventional wars. Until then, NATO had been a political alliance with a unilateral American military commitment. Shortly before the war, National Security Council Paper 68 (NSC-68) had predicted that Moscow would increase its nuclear capability and recommended "the rapid building up of the political, economic, and military strength of the free world." NATO adopted a "forward strategy," calling for Europe's defense to begin at the Elbe River, which separated East and West Germany, rather than at the Rhine River further west as originally planned.

A forward strategy required conventional military forces to withstand the Red Army. As long as U.S. troops were only intended to make the nuclear threat credible, a small U.S. conventional presence made sense. Once Moscow had acquired a nuclear capability, an American decision to use nuclear weapons risked dangerous escalation. The forward strategy called for the allies to stop a Soviet advance at the Elbe, serving as NATO's shield while nuclear forces would serve as its sword.

NATO's new strategy called for Europeans to bear the major conventional burden while America wielded the nuclear sword. Large-scale rearmament, however, entailed sacrifices, limiting Europe's economic recovery. European security was a collective good for all NATO members, and each sought to minimize its costs in providing it. One solution was to rearm West Germany, spreading costs and reducing them for others. West Germany's industrial base and strategic location made its defense imperative, and it seemed logical to call on Germans to contribute to achieving that aim.

What seemed logical proved difficult. The problem was how to involve Germany in Europe's defense without rousing the anxieties of other Europeans so soon after World War II. After several unsuccessful proposals, Germany was admitted to the Brussels Pact, renamed the Western European Union, which was then incorporated into NATO. West Germany agreed not to acquire weapons of mass destruction (WMD), and its contribution to the alliance provided additional manpower for Europe's defense.

Friction in NATO By the mid-1950s, fear of Soviet aggression had ebbed. After Stalin's death in 1953 and a ceasefire ended hostilities in Korea that year, East-West relations thawed. In 1955, a treaty was signed to reunify Austria as a neutral country. The following year witnessed growing friction between Washington and its allies owing to crises in Egypt and Hungary that revealed the allies' diverging interests. While America regarded containing the USSR as its chief foreign-policy objective, France and Britain remained preoccupied with their empires. France was struggling to retain Algeria, while British reluctance to participate fully in Europe's movement toward economic integration arose partly from continued involvement in the British Commonwealth, a global association of former British colonies.

Egypt had been a British protectorate between 1882 and Egyptian independence in 1936. In 1954, Britain agreed to a phased withdrawal from the Suez Canal to be completed by mid-1956, and Egyptian President Gamal Abdel Nasser agreed to Anglo-French supervision of the canal's operation until 1969. The agreement stipulated that British troops could return in the event the canal was threatened by another country. In July 1956, Nasser nationalized the Suez Canal (chapter 10). "This in turn alarmed the British and French, who, without consulting Washington, hatched a plot with the Israelis to have them attack the canal, thereby giving London and Paris the right to 'protect' it—the real intention was to depose Nasser altogether."[12]

The Suez War coincided with the Hungarian Revolution against Soviet occupation and was a disaster that "almost broke up the NATO alliance."[13] The Anglo-French plan had depended on rapid execution, but Britain and France failed to land troops in Egypt until *after* the Egyptians had blocked the canal. In the meantime, America joined the USSR in calling for a ceasefire. To President Eisenhower, who was in the midst of a reelection campaign and had not been informed of the Anglo-French plan, the invasion seemed a revival of European imperialism and a threat to Western relations with the Arab world that would also turn world attention from the brutal Soviet repression of revolution in Hungary. Threatening economic sanctions, he demanded that Britain and France withdraw from the canal. "The real winner, though, was Nasser, who kept the canal, humiliated the colonialists, and balanced Cold War superpowers against one another, while securing his position as undisputed leader of Arab nationalism."[14]

These events endangered NATO unity. NATO had initially been regarded by members as providing a "superior good," a benefit valued so highly—deterring Soviet aggression—that they were willing to forgo other interests to obtain it. The British and French felt betrayed by America and concluded that Washington would not subordinate its objectives to its allies' interests. The overwhelming common interest that had led to NATO's establishment was no longer sufficient to ensure cohesion, a development that became evident after Charles de Gaulle became president of France in 1959.

De Gaulle, Gaullism, and NATO Since his leadership of the Free French movement during World War II, Charles de Gaulle's primary objective had been to restore French grandeur, that is, regain the independence and pride that France had enjoyed before its disastrous defeat in 1940. De Gaulle articulated not only French but European nationalism as well. He hoped to alter NATO to ensure Europe's interests.

Until the 1960s, Gaullist aspirations remained dormant owing to Europe's weakness and the Soviet threat. As these conditions changed, however, contradictions in the alliance emerged. De Gaulle and Washington agreed that for Europe to regain influence, it was necessary to guarantee its security. But whereas Americans believed Europe's security depended on an institutionalized alliance in which America's commitment was beyond doubt, de Gaulle concluded that mutual interest in an independent Europe was itself sufficient to guarantee U.S. support in the event of war. Gaullists viewed the American-dominated alliance system as a hindrance to French pursuit of vital interests. The Suez affair seemed to confirm this.

Gaullists argued that it was natural that a superpower separated by thousands of miles of ocean from Europe had interests that would diverge from those of smaller countries located near the Soviet bloc. Soviet-American détente after 1962, Moscow's growing nuclear capability, and U.S. preoccupation with Cuba and Vietnam, both non-European concerns, convinced de Gaulle that America might sacrifice Europe's interests in pursuit of its own.

An opportunity for France to pursue an independent policy arose after changes in U.S. strategy were proposed by President Kennedy and Secretary of Defense Robert McNamara. By 1960, U.S. cities had become vulnerable because Soviet deployment of intercontinental ballistic missiles (ICBMs) had laid the American heartland open to nuclear retaliation. The development of second-strike weapons (able to survive an enemy's first strike) by both superpowers made a U.S. nuclear first strike in the event of a Soviet conventional invasion unwise and unlikely.

Although America and its European partners sought to deter a Soviet attack on Europe, questions were raised about how to achieve this following the end of America's nuclear monopoly. Kennedy and McNamara concluded that it was increasingly "incredible" for the United States to use a nuclear threat to deter a Soviet conventional incursion in Europe because a first strike would trigger retaliation against America's homeland. Washington tried to persuade its allies to substitute a strategy of conventional defense for the existing strategy of depending entirely on nuclear deterrence. "It is time," argued McNamara, "for the maps to change by which policy is charted and justified. The old ones which assured a U.S. nuclear monopoly . . . and a Communist monopoly of ground combat strength are too far removed from reality to serve as even rough guides."[15] America sought to develop an array of military capabilities, including larger conventional forces, to meet potential Soviet actions ranging from minor incursions to all-out nuclear war. By strengthening conventional capability, Washington sought to challenge Soviet conventional dominance. To avoid nuclear warfare through miscalculation and strengthen the credibility of its commitment to Europe, America prepared to respond in kind to Soviet aggression below the nuclear threshold. Only if it appeared that Europe was on the verge of being overrun would Washington resort to its nuclear sword.

This strategy, "flexible response," depended on three conditions. First, NATO would retain centralized command and control of nuclear weapons. Thus, Washington argued to keep strategic nuclear weapons under ultimate U.S. control so that no "premature" recourse to them could occur that would trigger World War III. Second, Europeans should contribute more to their own defense. Finally, Soviet planners would adopt a similar strategy.

"Flexible response" played into de Gaulle's hands. Europeans feared that relying on conventional defense would have no greater deterrent value than in the past. Should it fail, America's allies would find themselves engaged in a conventional war. Americans might be cheered at the prospect of defending Europe without risking their homeland, but this had little appeal to Europeans. Efforts to match Soviet firepower by deploying tactical nuclear weapons seemed even less desirable. Battlefield nuclear weapons would provide Moscow with additional advantages because Western Europe was geographically smaller and more densely populated than Eastern Europe and the USSR. What would be a "limited" war for America would be "unlimited" for Europe.

De Gaulle questioned whether America would remain committed to Europe's defense in a crisis in which U.S. resort to nuclear weapons would invite retaliatory destruction of its cities. If Europeans were uncertain of U.S. intentions, was it wise to leave their destiny in American hands? For France, de Gaulle believed, the only way to secure political independence *and* military security was to develop its own nuclear force. U.S. leaders argued that such a force would be too small to deter the USSR, undermine "flexible response," and encourage additional nuclear proliferation.

An independent French nuclear force would make it difficult for Washington to impose its strategic preference on NATO because a French threat to use nuclear weapons in response to Soviet aggression would leave America no choice but to come to Europe's aid, a decision that Washington might otherwise be reluctant to make. Thus, in acquiring nuclear weapons, de Gaulle sought to exert French influence over the superpowers in matters affecting France and Europeans more generally. France would no longer be helpless as it had been in the 1956 Suez crisis, and its interests would be protected by its military independence. In 1966, de Gaulle ordered non-French allied forces to leave France. Although France remained in NATO, it ceased participating in NATO's military command structure until rejoining it in 2009.

Further Divisions   Events after the Suez fiasco fueled Europe's fears about American-Soviet cooperation at its expense. America did nothing in response to the construction of the Berlin Wall in August 1961. U.S. inaction fueled a belief that Washington was less interested in German reunification than in European stability and, therefore, would not help Germans realize their principal national objective. The 1975 Helsinki Accords reinforced this perception by declaring the inviolability of the post–World War II frontiers in Europe including the division of Germany.

The 1962 Cuban missile crisis also seemed to confirm de Gaulle's views because it seemed that America was willing to drag Europeans into war over an issue that did not directly involve them. During the crisis, President Kennedy sent former secretary of state Dean Acheson to speak with European leaders. When Acheson met de Gaulle, the latter asked, "Are you consulting or informing me?"[16] As de Gaulle expected, the answer was that Acheson had come to inform, not consult him. Between the mid-1960s and 1970s decisions on issues like the Vietnam War were made by Presidents Johnson and Nixon with little consultation with NATO allies.

By 1972, reasons for European members to support an alliance that limited their options yet involved costs seemed less compelling. If America's commitment was genuine, U.S. protection would be forthcoming even without NATO, and growing Soviet nuclear capability aroused fears that America's nuclear umbrella might not be available even with the alliance. Finally, fear of a Soviet attack in Europe had receded, especially after West Germany initiated a policy of *Ostpolitik* ("East policy") involving reconciliation with East Germany and easing East-West tensions.

During the late 1970s and early 1980s, the Cold War heated up again. The USSR invaded Afghanistan and deployed a formidable array of new missiles. Europeans were particularly disturbed by Soviet deployment of mobile intermediate-range SS-20 ballistic missiles. These weapons were seen as an effort to achieve

Presidents
Gorbachev and
Reagan sign the INF
Treaty.

AFP/Getty Images

nuclear superiority in Europe, thereby enabling Moscow to blackmail Europeans in a crisis under conditions in which U.S.-Soviet strategic nuclear parity would make Washington reluctant to use its ICBMs, precisely the problem that de Gaulle had raised.

America's NATO allies urged the United States to deploy similar forces in Europe to reassure them by linking intermediate and strategic nuclear systems in a seamless deterrent. However, many Europeans, fearful of the prospect of a nuclear war in Europe, joined antinuclear "peace movements" to demonstrate against deployment of new U.S. missiles in Europe. On the verge of U.S. deployment of Pershing II intermediate-range missiles and ground-launched cruise missiles in the face of mass protests, Washington and Moscow signed the Intermediate-Range Nuclear Forces Treaty (INF) in December 1987 requiring them to destroy all intermediate-range ballistic and cruise missiles (chapter, 3).

After Presidents Reagan and Gorbachev signed the INF treaty, the Cold War wound down. In 1990, a Soviet-NATO agreement specified mutual troop reductions in Europe. In 1990, after the Berlin Wall was toppled, West German Chancellor Helmut Kohl persuaded Soviet leader Mikhail Gorbachev to drop his objections to German reunification, and Germany was reunified in October. NATO's survival attested to its adaptability and the persistence of friendship and common values among its members.

PRESENT: NATO'S CHANGING MISSION

Contacts between Russia and NATO intensified after the Cold War, leading to changes in Europe's security architecture. In 1994, NATO established a Partnership for Peace to foster trust with Soviet successor states (including Russia) and former members of the Warsaw Pact. The Partnership "was established as an expression of a joint conviction that stability and security in the Euro-Atlantic area can be achieved only through cooperation and common action," and those that joined committed themselves "to the preservation of democratic societies, their freedom from coercion and intimidation, and the maintenance of the principles of international law."[17]

Russia and NATO signed the Founding Act on Mutual Relations, Cooperation, and Security in 1997, stating they were no longer enemies and would cooperate to assure peace in Europe. "The NATO-Russia Founding Act we have just signed," declared President Clinton, "joins a great nation and history's most successful alliance in common cause for a long-sought but never before realized goal—a peaceful, democratic, undivided Europe."[18] Russia did not object to NATO expansion to include former Soviet-bloc countries provided the alliance did not deploy nuclear weapons or permanently station troops on the territory of new member states.[19] A 2002 NATO summit established the NATO-Russia Council as the official diplomatic link between the alliance and Russia charged with implementing the Founding Act.[20]

NATO also became involved in exporting Western values to Europe's periphery, the Balkans. In doing so, it aroused Moscow's misgivings about the spread of Western influence in a region close to Russia in which it had once enjoyed considerable influence.

U.S.–European Cooperation in the Balkans

Until the end of the Cold War, NATO had focused on defending member states in Western Europe. In the Balkans, however, civil war precipitated by the collapse of the Yugoslav Federation produced instability on Europe's southern flank. During the Cold War, Yugoslavia had been governed by a communist regime headed by Josip Broz Tito until his death in 1980. Tito had remained uniquely independent of Soviet control and maintained the federation of the country's six republics—Bosnia-Herzegovina, Croatia, Macedonia, Montenegro, Serbia, and Slovenia. In addition, Serbia contained two autonomous provinces, one of which, Kosovo, was largely inhabited by ethnic Albanians. In 1987, Slobodan Milošević assumed power in Serbia and two years later became president of Yugoslavia. Although a communist, Milošević recognized that he could acquire popularity as a Serb nationalist, and his efforts to suppress agitation among Kosovo's Albanians found favor with his fellow Serbs.

Like a contagion, nationalism spread to Yugoslavia's other principal nationalities. Slovenians and Croatians declared independence in June 1991 despite Serbia's efforts to prevent them from doing so. The Serb and Croatian communities had a toxic history of hatred arising from a bloody conflict in World War II between a Nazi-backed Croatian fascist movement and its Serbian foes. Europeans were initially divided about Yugoslavia's collapse. "German, Austrian and Italian political leaders, for example, were generally more sympathetic to the views advanced by the governments of Slovenia and Croatia for a confederation of sovereign states, whereas Serbian advocacy of a remodeled federation—though not necessarily according to the highly centralized perspectives of Milošević—were received more sympathetically in London and Paris."[21] Russia supported the Serb position, while President George H. W. Bush regarded the conflict as primarily Europe's responsibility.

In 1992, Bosnia, too, declared independence, and in April, America and the EU recognized Croatian and Bosnian independence. The Bosnian population included Catholic Croatians (17 percent), Orthodox Serbians (31 percent), and those who had become Muslim (44 percent) in earlier centuries when the

Ottoman Turks had governed them. Bosnian Serbs were determined to retain power and link the region to Serbia to form a "greater Serbia." Muslims and Croatians were driven from their Bosnian communities by "ethnic cleansing," and Bosnia became the scene of two conflicts—Bosnian Serbs versus Bosnian Croatians and Bosnian Serbs versus Bosnian Muslims. Milošević's Serbian government aided Bosnian Serbs, and Bosnian Croatians were supported by independent Croatia. War divided the region into three de facto ethnic "states," and before it ended, it cost some 250,000 lives.

In response to the violence, the UN dispatched the UN Protective Force (UNPROFOR) in mid-1992 and imposed an arms embargo on the region. In early 1993, the UN and EU endorsed an Anglo-American peace plan for Bosnia, and the Security Council established the International Criminal Tribunal for the former Yugoslavia (ICTY). The Clinton administration abandoned the policy of its predecessor and began airdropping food to besieged Muslim enclaves, and in March, the UN authorized an American-enforced no-fly zone in Bosnia. Following rejection of the peace plan by Bosnia's Serbs, the UN declared the besieged Muslim communities in Sarajevo, Bihac, Tuzla, Srebrenica, Zepa, and Gorazde to be "safe areas" with protection for humanitarian convoys.

During America's 1992 presidential campaign, Bill Clinton had criticized President Bush's inaction and had advocated lifting the arms embargo and launching airstrikes against the Bosnian Serbs. After his election, the administration sought to carry out these proposals, but America's NATO allies were divided, with those providing UN peacekeepers fearing for their safety. America's military leaders also opposed intervention. Nevertheless, the UN authorized the use of NATO airpower to help UNPROFOR protect Muslim safe areas. A NATO airstrike in April 1994 following the death of a UN peacekeeper led Bosnian Serb forces to take peacekeepers hostage to prevent additional air attacks.

Hostilities continued in 1994 although cooperation between Bosnian Croatians and Muslims began to alter the military balance in Bosnia. Divisions among the Western allies ended after July 1995 when a small Dutch peacekeeping contingent failed to prevent Bosnian Serbs from killing 7,000 Bosnian Muslims in Srebrenica, the worst massacre in Europe since World War II. In August, after a mortar attack on Sarajevo, NATO began "Operation Deliberate Force," a series of air and ground assaults on Serb positions. Military pressure combined with the diplomatic efforts of Assistant Secretary of State Richard Holbrooke led Milošević to open negotiations at Wright-Patterson Air Force Base outside Dayton, Ohio. These produced the Dayton Accords among the presidents of Bosnia, Croatia, and Serbia, recognizing a single federated Bosnian state with two parts—a Serbian Republika Srpska and a Croatian and Muslim region, the Federation of Bosnia and Herzegovina. "American leadership," declared President Clinton, "created a chance to build a peace and stop the suffering."[22]

The accords authorized a NATO-led Implementation Force (IFOR) to enforce the agreement. IFOR remained until late 1996 when it was transformed into a smaller NATO-led Stabilization Force (SFOR) with a mandate to enforce peace and bring war criminals to justice. SFOR was replaced in 2004 by the still smaller European Union EUFOR Althea force, which still remains in Bosnia.

The Dayton Accords did not, however, pacify the Balkans. In 1989, Serbia abruptly ended Kosovo's autonomy, triggering resistance by the area's majority population of ethnic Albanians. Violence intensified in 1998 between Albanian separatists in the Kosovo Liberation Army and Serbian security forces. For Serbs, Kosovo was a focus of nationalist fervor, recalling the Battle of Kosovo in 1389 in which the Ottoman Turks had destroyed an outnumbered Serbian army.

As violence mounted in Kosovo, NATO sought the restoration of peace in the province and stability in neighboring Albania and Macedonia. Efforts to end Serbia's violent repression of Kosovo's Albanians failed, and the Security Council called for a ceasefire while NATO prepared for possible airstrikes. With UN approval, the OSCE authorized a small observer force in Kosovo. Violence erupted again in early 1999; Serbian military repression increased; and the OCSE observers left. Efforts by Ambassador Holbrooke to persuade Milošević to desist were unsuccessful, and in March, NATO commenced a bombing campaign ("Operation Allied Force") against Serbian targets, which lasted seventy-seven days and forced the withdrawal of Serbian forces from Kosovo. Russian and Chinese vetoes made it necessary for NATO to act without Security Council authorization.

While recognizing Serbian "sovereignty and territorial integrity," the Security Council agreed to send peacekeepers to "establish an international civil presence in Kosovo in order to provide an interim admin- istration for Kosovo under which the people of Kosovo can enjoy substantial autonomy within the Federal Republic of Yugoslavia."[23] Initially, some 50,000 troops from over thirty countries constituted the NATO-led Kosovo Force. In 2008, despite Serbian and Russian opposition, Kosovo declared its independence and was subsequently recognized by over 100 states. In 2013, Serbia and Kosovo reached an Agreement on Normal- ization to improve their relations in order to accelerate the integration of the Western Balkans with Europe.

In October 2000, having resigned as president of what remained of Yugoslavia [Serbia and Montene- gro[24]], Milošević was extradited to the ICTY in The Hague, Netherlands, to face charges of war crimes in Bosnia. The trial lasted five years with Milošević acting as his own defense attorney, but before a verdict could be reached, he died of a heart attack.

Following the Cold War, observers questioned NATO's continued existence, asserting that the alli- ance's original goal of protecting Europe from Soviet power was no longer relevant. Thus, NATO sought new missions beyond Europe that promised to advance the liberal values of democracy, human rights, and peace. The alliance reflected these values and enjoyed the advantage of being able to act when an institution like the UN Security Council could not do so.

"Out-of-Area" Operations

Thus, NATO turned to "out-of-area" challenges. In the Middle East, the Arab Spring posed new problems for America and its allies. Instability there triggered a flood of refugees to Europe and threatened the flow of Middle East oil. Of particular concern was the outbreak of civil wars in Libya located across the Mediterranean south of Europe and Syria (chapter 10) on the eastern shore of the Mediterranean south of Turkey, a NATO member. The alliance also provided logistical assistance for disaster relief in Pakistan and the African Union's peacekeeping operations in Darfur, Sudan, and Somalia.

Libya As civil war engulfed Libya, American and European leaders condemned the authoritarianism of Muammar Qaddafi's regime and the violence it used against civilians (chapter 10). President Obama declared that the "suffering and bloodshed" was "outrageous" and "unacceptable."[25] In response to regime brutality, British, French, and American aircraft, with Security Council approval, imposed an arms embargo and a no-fly zone over northern Libya, provided rebels with military and nonmilitary aid, and carried out airstrikes against Libyan ground forces. (Russia would later complain that it assented to the Security Council resolution without realizing that the West would overthrow the regime.) U.S.-European intervention in the conflict indicated that NATO was prepared to foster human rights even at the cost of stability.

Syria   America's European allies also joined Washington in assailing the regime of Bashar al-Assad in Syria for its brutal repression of domestic foes (chapter 10). France, Britain, and the EU joined America in recognizing the anti-Assad National Coalition for Syrian Revolutionary and Opposition Forces but were reluctant to send significant aid to regime opponents. This reluctance was attributable to several factors—the prospect of extremists gaining power, fear of a domestic backlash from publics averse to involvement in another war, fear of escalating tensions between the West and Russia which backed Assad, and uncertainty about whether rebel forces could defeat the regime.

After the regime used chemical weapons in 2013 against its own citizens, France was prepared to join America in a military strike against Syria when Washington and Moscow brokered a deal by which Syria would rid itself of those weapons (chapter 4). The British government, too, was prepared to join the attack until its parliament vetoed London's participation. Europe's interest in Syria stemmed partly from the wave of Syrian refugees to Greece and Italy and the possible return to Europe of radicalized Muslim citizens who had fought in Syria. The EU and several of its members also participated in an unsuccessful peace conference regarding Syria in 2014.

Iran   Following America's imposition of sanctions on Iran for seeking to acquire nuclear weapons in 2010, the EU authorized its own sanctions. The EU barred additional investment in Iran, the export of technology to Iran's energy industry, and credit guarantees for trade. It also severed links with Iranian banks and froze assets of Iranian firms. "Many observers were surprised at how far these latest EU measures went, observing that they send a strong signal and bring U.S. and European sanctions policy on Iran into a broad alignment."[26] Unlike Washington, however, the EU did not embargo Iranian oil until 2012.

America, China, and Russia joined the "EU 3" (France, Britain, and Germany) in 2006 in proposing negotiations with Iran about its nuclear program. The group, called the P5+1 (the five permanent members of the Security Council plus Germany), began negotiations with Iranian diplomats in 2013 (chapter 4). France proved the most demanding of the countries negotiating with Iran but joined the others in supporting the July 2015 agreement with Iran.

Afghanistan   America's European allies contributed significantly to the Afghanistan war that began after 9/11. The International Security Assistance Force (ISAF) was established to aid the Afghan Transitional Authority and the UN Assistance Mission that were seeking to construct a post-Taliban government for Afghanistan "guided by the principle of reinforcing Afghan sovereignty, leadership and ownership."[27]

Command of ISAF passed to NATO in 2003 during which the Taliban launched a wave of suicide bombings, car bombings, and guerrilla attacks, especially along Afghanistan's border with Pakistan. ISAF expanded its operations to contested regions in the country's western and southern regions in 2006 and assumed command over all military operations in Afghanistan in October.

As of 2014, forty-eight countries were contributing to ISAF, including NATO members and NATO partners. Of the 51,000 ISAF troops, donors ranged from America (33,500) and Britain (5,200) to

Malaysia and New Zealand (2 each). Other contributors included Germany, Italy, Poland, Romania, Georgia, Spain, Australia, and Turkey, and Australia, Japan, and South Korea pledged significant financial contributions to improve Afghanistan's security forces and the country's socioeconomic capacity. These pledges reflected NATO's growing interest in Asia and followed a Joint Political Declaration between NATO and Australia, the first of its kind with a partner nation.

After Washington announced the planned withdrawal of most of its troops, other coalition members began to downsize their contributions, and ISAF's mission came to an end in late 2014. The transition toward letting Afghan security forces take over NATO operations had begun in 2011. By mid-2013, Afghan forces had assumed responsibility for the security of most of the country. Concern remained about how Afghanistan would fare after ISAF's departure. Intelligence concerning the Taliban concluded that "though it might not be able to pursue a monopoly of power after NATO's departure, it can consolidate footholds in the south and east,"[28] but the Afghan endgame remained unclear.

Counterterrorism With agreements to share intelligence, America and Europe worked closely to prevent terrorist attacks after 9/11. Located closer than America to terrorist hubs in the Middle East, South Asia, and Africa, with growing Muslim populations that included militant minorities, and within reach of refugee flows, Europe has been at risk of terrorism in recent decades. There were bloody terrorist attacks on public transportation systems in Spain and Britain in 2004 and 2005, and terrorist cells were discovered in Britain, France, Germany, Spain, Italy, and Bosnia.

NATO's "Operation Active Endeavour" was established after 9/11 as a maritime surveillance effort to detect, deter, and protect Europe from terrorist infiltration in the Mediterranean by monitoring, patrolling, escorting, and even boarding vessels. In 2010, NATO established an Emerging Security Challenges Division to cope with terrorism as well as cyber-security, proliferation of WMD, and energy security. The following year, NATO adopted a new cyber-defense policy and an action plan to bolster the cyber-defenses of members and agreed in 2014 that a cyberattack on any member would be regarded as an attack on all. The 2012 establishment of a Communications and Information Agency brought all NATO networks under central protection, and a Computer Incident Response Capability became operational in 2013. NATO also established an Intelligence Liaison Unit to improve the flow of information about terrorist threats.

America's counterterrorist policies produced tension with its allies because European laws are stricter regarding individual privacy. Many Europeans viewed the collection of personal data by America's National Security Agency as a violation of individual rights. German leaders were especially critical of those activities (though several European intelligence agencies had cooperated with the NSA and/or had conducted surveillance activities). Edward Snowden's revelation that the NSA had tapped German Chancellor Merkel's cellphone was especially controversial, and the effort to conclude a German-American intelligence sharing agreement before her visit to Washington in May 2014 failed although Washington assured Merkel that the NSA would no longer eavesdrop on her conversations. German anger was also fueled by revelations about two spy cases involving Germans recruited by the CIA and the CIA's refusal to respond to German inquiries. Germany expelled the CIA station chief from the country. Shortly thereafter President Obama and Chancellor Merkel opened a dialogue to foster intelligence cooperation.

Washington faced a dilemma. "What's more important?" asked NSA director General Keith Alexander. "Partnering with countries may be more important than collecting on them,"[29] especially when faced by the cyber-espionage of adversaries. A former U.S. ambassador to Germany admitted he did not understand why the NSA would spy on Germans. "It was unbelievably stupid," he said, "for no gain."[30]

Europeans also learned that the CIA had used secret prisons in Eastern Europe to detain suspected terrorists without trial. In one instance, the CIA station chief in Milan, Italy, along with 23 U.S. employees were convicted in absentia for kidnapping an Egyptian cleric suspected of terrorism in 2003 and spiriting him to Egypt for interrogation before releasing him in 2007. In an interview with an Italian newspaper, the former station chief, Robert Seldon Lady, admitted, "Of course it was an illegal operation. But that's our job. We're at war against terrorism."[31]

NATO Expansion

NATO expansion was initially not a major issue, but in time Russian leaders viewed it as intruding into a region they still regarded as their sphere of interest. Former Soviet leader Mikhail Gorbachev recalled that during negotiations on German reunification, Secretary of State James Baker had promised that if Moscow accepted NATO membership for reunified Germany, "NATO will not expand one inch east."[32] "The Americans," he declared "promised that NATO wouldn't move beyond the boundaries of Germany after the Cold War, but now half of central and eastern Europe are members, so what happened to their promises? It shows they cannot be trusted."[33] In fact, "formerly secret documents from 1989 and 1990" demonstrated that "there was never a formal deal as Russia alleges—but U.S. and West German officials briefly implied that such a deal might be on the table," and the "dispute over this sequence of events has distorted relations between Washington and Moscow ever since."[34]

East Germany joined NATO as part of united Germany in 1990. The former Soviet Balkan Republics—Lithuania, Latvia, and Estonia—joined in 2004 despite Russian opposition. Former Soviet clients and members of the Soviet-led Warsaw Pact also became members—the Czech Republic, Hungary, and Poland in 1997 and Bulgaria, Romania, and Slovakia in 2004. Albania entered in 2009, and two former Yugoslav republics, Slovenia (2004) and Croatia (2009), extended the alliance into the Balkans.

Conditions for NATO membership are set forth in Article 10 of the North Atlantic Treaty. Any European country may be invited to join subject to unanimous agreement of current members. Post–Cold War accession to NATO was governed by the Membership Action Plan (MAP) in which NATO receives information concerning the political and technical progress of prospective members toward meeting criteria necessary for an official invitation. The program was based on the experience of the early post–Cold War NATO additions and has been the vehicle of accession of other members since. Criteria are willingness and ability to conform to principles like democracy and individual liberty. Candidates are expected "to settle their international disputes by peaceful means; to demonstrate commitment to the rule of law and human rights; to settle ethnic disputes or external territorial disputes including irredentist claims or internal jurisdictional disputes by peaceful means in accordance with OSCE principles and to pursue good neighborly relations; to establish appropriate democratic and civilian control of their armed forces; to refrain from the threat or use of force in any manner inconsistent with the purposes of the UN; to contribute to the development of peaceful and friendly international relations by strengthening their free

MAP **13.3**   NATO Expansion in Europe

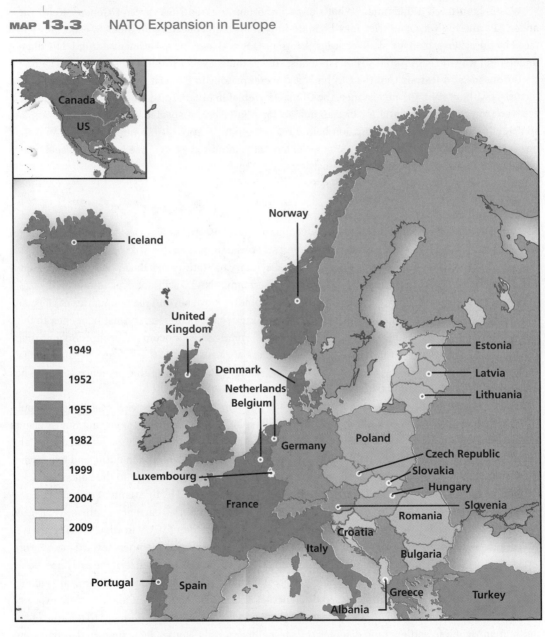

Source: Data from NATO, http://www.nato.int/cps/en/natolive/topics_52044.htm.

institutions and by promoting stability and well-being; and to continue fully to support and be engaged in the Euro-Atlantic Partnership Council and the Partnership for Peace to show a commitment to promoting stability and well-being by economic liberty, social justice, and environmental responsibility."[35]

By 2014, there were three countries with MAPs—Montenegro, Bosnia, and Macedonia. In addition to MAPs there are Individual Partnership Action Plans (IPAPs) that describe reforms in countries with "the political will and ability to deepen their relationship with NATO." Eventual NATO membership is not a requirement for IPAPs, and of those states with such plans, several former Soviet republics including Armenia, Azerbaijan, Kazakhstan, and Moldova have stated they do not intend to join.

At NATO's 2008 summit, President George W. Bush sought to offer Ukraine and Georgia MAPs, declaring, "It would send a signal throughout the region that these two nations are, and will remain, sovereign and independent states."[36] Neither, however, received an invitation. In 2004, Georgia was the first country to agree to an IPAP, but war with Russia in 2008 convinced several NATO members that Georgia and Ukraine were politically unstable and that inviting them to join the alliance would enrage Russia. President Putin, who had been invited to the summit, threatened to boycott it if MAP invitations were extended to the two countries.

Let us now examine events leading to Ukraine's decision to tilt toward Europe, the overthrow of its pro-Russian president, and NATO's reaction. Russian aims of enhancing its security and restoring its power, including its annexation of Crimea, are treated in chapter 14.

NATO and Ukraine

Ukraine abuts Russia. Most western Ukrainians speak Ukrainian and are pro-European, while many eastern Ukrainians speak Russian as their first language and are pro-Russian. Ukraine seemed eager to sign an EU association agreement at a meeting in Vilnius, Lithuania, in November 2013. Such agreements, part of the EU's Eastern Partnership program, establish a framework for bilateral relations with the EU that provide for liberalization of trade between them and may lead to EU membership.

Moscow tried to dissuade Ukraine from accepting this agreement, coercing Kiev by imposing costly restrictions on trade between the two countries and warning Ukraine that signing the association political and free trade agreements would be "suicidal."[37] The EU Enlargement Commissioner declared that such threats against states seeking links with the EU were "unacceptable."[38] Moscow wanted Ukraine to join the Eurasian Economic Union, established by Russia, Armenia, Belarus, Kazakhstan, and Kyrgyzstan (but not Ukraine) in December 2014. Although Putin lauded the group as a potential rival of the EU, it will likely remain relatively minor economically, especially without Ukraine. Even with Ukraine's addition, the group would be economically marginal compared to the EU. Putin's pressure on Ukraine was driven by geopolitical concerns—preventing Western encroachment and giving Moscow dominant influence in central Europe. "For its part, Moscow seeks not political change in the region but domination. That means it must frame Ukraine's future as a zero-sum game with the EU."[39]

In 2013, Putin visited Ukraine's capital, Kiev, to commemorate the 1,025th anniversary of events that brought Christianity to Ukraine and Russia, emphasizing the two countries' common history. Thereafter, the threat of trade sanctions—Russia is the recipient of one-quarter of Ukrainian exports—and Putin's offer to lend a "brotherly" country $15 billion by purchasing Ukrainian euro bonds and reducing the price of natural gas exports to Ukraine persuaded Ukrainian President Viktor Yanukovich to turn down the EU agreement, attributing his change of heart to conditions set by the International Monetary Fund (IMF) for lending funds to his country. The IMF had criticized Ukraine's budget deficit and had recommended economic reforms, including reducing fiscal and external account deficits and eliminating energy subsidies.

Following Ukraine's refusal to go forward with EU negotiations, Sweden's foreign minister tweeted, "Ukraine government suddenly bows deeply to the Kremlin. Politics of brutal pressure evidently works."[40] Although Yanukovich also resisted joining the Eurasian Union, his eastward turn left pro-European Ukrainians in the country's western region aghast and triggered demonstrations in Kiev and elsewhere in western Ukraine.

The agreement was an important EU initiative. "The union," wrote a European scholar, "has major strategic and economic interests at stake: strategically, the EU strives to create a benign environment for itself by spreading its model of rule of law and transparency to its periphery. And inducing Russia to respect the sovereignty [of Ukraine] would finally cement the post-Cold War European order."[41] Without Ukraine, the Eastern Partnership program was at risk. "Everyone thought the Eastern Partnership was just another flabby European project," observed a Russia expert. "But once a country signs up, it is in Weight Watchers and, if they follow the regimen, they change. Russia realized this and did not like it."[42] For the EU, Ukraine's decision to capitulate to Soviet pressure was a serious setback. Ukraine's refusal to sign the agreements was not, however, viewed by European leaders as permanent. European Council President Herman Van Rompuy declared, "The offer is still there and we know time is on our side."[43] To counter Russia's offer of funding to help Ukraine avoid bankruptcy, the United States and the EU put together their own financial package.

DID YOU KNOW?

Iceland and NATO

Although an active member of NATO, Iceland has not had a standing army since 1869.

The Ukrainian government's resort to force against pro-European demonstrators increased their number until hundreds of thousands occupied Maidan Square (later nicknamed "Euromaidan" or Europe Square) in central Kiev in December 2013 and into the following months despite freezing temperatures. Protesters denounced President Yanukovich and Prime Minister Mykola Azarov, who in the wake of demonstrations had used emergency powers to limit freedom of assembly and speech.

The protest effort to force Yanukovich and his government to reverse their turn eastward found support among the country's opposition parties, reflecting their rejection of a closer association with Russia and a desire to be accepted by Europe's democratic societies. As protests continued, ever more Ukrainians demanded the resignation of the country's government and president. Sporadic violence continued and, in late February 2014, exploded as special police and shadowy government supporters massacred over 100 demonstrators (described by Ukrainians as "the Heavenly Hundred"). President Obama, who noted, "We hold the Ukrainian government primarily responsible,"[44] condemned the resort to deadly force, and Secretary Kerry criticized the Ukrainian police's use of force against demonstrators as "disgusting": "As church bells ring tonight amidst the smoke in the streets of Kiev, the United States stands with the people of Ukraine. They deserve better." Kerry also skipped a planned visit to Ukraine and instead visited Moldova because, according to an American official, "we wanted to send a very strong signal of support for those countries that have moved forward with the EU because of what it might mean to their commitment to reform."[45]

Thereafter a compromise mediated by the foreign ministers of Germany, France, and Poland between Yanukovich and opposition leaders seemed to be reached. By its terms, Ukraine's 2004 constitution would be restored, parliament's power would be increased and the president's reduced, and Yanukovich would remain president until December 2014. Russia, however, which had participated in mediating the agreement, refused to endorse it.

The deal failed to placate the demonstrators who regarded the country's politicians as incompetent and corrupt, and one of their "defense units" demanded that Yanukovich resign. Ukraine's parliament then impeached the president, who fled Kiev. From Russia, Yanukovich issued a statement defiantly declaring he was still president and denouncing the new government as a group of "right-wing thugs."

Another Ukrainian revolution had taken place as demonstrators sought to bring about changes that the 2004 Orange Revolution (chapter 14) had failed to achieve. The new revolution was against a bankrupt state riddled by corruption and injustice that had failed its citizens. Ukraine's per capita gross domestic product (GDP) was only a third of Russia's. Its debts and budget deficit were enormous, and by 2014, the country had virtually exhausted its foreign-exchange reserves, and the value of its currency was

Ukrainians protest in Central Kiev.

AP Photo/Sergei Grits

in free fall. Ukraine's pro-Russian eastern and southern regions were also its most impoverished areas (though even in those regions a majority opposed giving Russia the right to use force in Ukraine),[46] and the country remained vulnerable to Russian economic blackmail. Additionally, the defense industries of the two countries were interdependent—a legacy from the Soviet period—and both countries would suffer if ties were severed.

After deposing Yanukovich, reform was in the air in Kiev. Despite the continued presence of old-style politicians, Ukraine adopted economic and political reforms as part of a "reanimation package," partly to satisfy IMF conditions for a loan and partly owing to pressure from America and the EU. Petro Poroshenko, a pro-European billionaire tycoon, was elected Ukraine's president in May 2014 despite continued violence in the east. Poroshenko then signed the EU association agreement on June 27, 2014, declaring, "The signature of this agreement signifies new investment, new rules without corruption and new markets, the biggest market in the world."[47]

FUTURE: NATO REINVENTED

American concern about European security and Russian power waned after the Cold War. NATO cooperation continued, but America's military presence in Europe declined as NATO became an instrument to spread Western values globally and deal with challenges elsewhere.

Out-of-Area Operations

After the Cold War, NATO increasingly turned its attention away, deterring Russia to out-of-area issues. Challenges to Western interests in the Middle East and Asia seemed an answer to NATO's search for a new mission and offered opportunities to extend democracy, human rights, prosperity, and stability to developing societies while combatting threats like terrorism and drug trafficking.

Policy Options

a. *Cease out-of-area missions and reinforce NATO in Europe.* The Ukraine crisis was a reminder that Europe's security remained NATO's principal mission and that the alliance's eastward expansion required additional forces to reassure the Baltic states, Poland, and other former Eastern Bloc members faced with Russia's assertive policies.

Moreover, the results of NATO's out-of-area efforts were modest. Qaddafi's overthrow and the protection of Libyan civilians initially appeared successful. Thereafter, however, Libya descended into chaos. French intervention initially chased Islamic militants from Mali, but they remained a threat across North Africa. The Afghan conflict was unresolved even as America and NATO prepared to withdraw. The Taliban renewed its attacks, and disunity threatened the Afghan government. Finally, despite European-American cooperation, President Assad tenaciously retained power in Syria.

b. *Continue out-of-area missions* to meet continued threats to Western interests beyond Europe. Europe still depends heavily on Persian Gulf oil and faces unprecedented waves of refugees from Syria, Libya, and elsewhere in Africa and Asia. American and European trade with Asia has grown rapidly and is essential to Western prosperity. Such factors suggest that NATO cannot isolate itself from politics and events beyond Europe and must defend Western interests elsewhere in the world.

U.S.-European Cooperation in the Balkans

With Yugoslavia's collapse and the conflicts among and within its successor states, America and its European allies intervened to bring peace to Bosnia and Kosovo.

Policy Options

a.   *Maintain EUFOR.* EUFOR deploys Liaison and Observation Teams of Austrian, Hungarian, and Turkish troops paid for by the EU in Bosnia to prevent communal violence and build state institutions. Its premature withdrawal would threaten a resumption of violence. EUFOR controls the confrontations that occur from time to time among Serbs, Croatians, and Bosnian Muslims, and the vacuum left by its withdrawal would tempt Serbia and Croatia to renew their competitive meddling in Bosnia.

b.   *Admit Bosnia to the EU* to foster its stability and integrate it economically into Europe. The economic benefits of EU membership would dampen communal hostility in time and foster greater unity between the Republika Srpska and the Federation of Bosnia and Herzegovina. Were Bosnia left out of the EU, economic isolation might intensify suspicion and competition among its national communities.

NATO Expansion

Russia had initially worked closely with NATO, supporting ISAF by allowing land transit of nonmilitary equipment to Afghanistan across Russian territory and cooperating in counter-narcotics programs, counterterrorism, nuclear nonproliferation, and suppression of piracy. Moscow had opened a diplomatic mission to NATO, and Russian military officers were invited to NATO headquarters. This changed abruptly with the Ukraine crisis. Russia's militant reaction to NATO expansion heightened security concerns in the West and recognition that NATO need to return to its original mission. In April 2014, NATO suspended all cooperation with Russia. The Balkans, Bosnia, Montenegro, and Macedonia have completed preparations to enter NATO, but the status of Ukraine remained unresolved.

NATO and Ukraine

The Ukraine crisis stemmed from the eastward expansion of NATO and Kiev's desire to tilt westward. Moscow was determined that Ukraine should remain in its sphere of influence. The crisis was a wake-up call for America and Europe. The security of Europe that they had taken for granted after the Cold War again seemed endangered.

Policy Options

a.   *NATO renews its military commitment in Europe.* After the Cold War, most of America's allies failed to meet NATO's agreed goal of spending 2 percent of gross domestic product on defense, and "no longer have the strength to conduct and sustain even medium-sized military operations."[48] Several

NATO members cut defense budgets by up to 40 percent in real terms. In speaking to the European Council in 2013, NATO's secretary-general declared he was "concerned that if Europe is unwilling, or unable, to play its full part in international crisis management, others will fill the vacuum. And we will reduce our ability to protect our values and defend our interests." He continued, "Unless we recommit to our own defense, we risk seeing America disengage—and Europe and America drift apart."[49] Even worse, a mid-2015 poll indicated that large numbers of Germans, French, and Italians had become reluctant to aid allies like Estonia if attacked by Russia.[50]

America's military presence in Europe had declined as Washington sought to deal with problems elsewhere until the Ukraine crisis when Europe again became the site of a NATO-Russian confrontation. After Russia annexed Crimea, Vice President Joe Biden hurried to Europe to reaffirm America's commitment to NATO's eastern members, and President Obama noted, "As NATO allies, we have a solemn commitment to our collective defense, and we will uphold this commitment."[51] The president also spoke of the credibility of U.S. commitments. "Casual indifference would ignore the lessons that are written in the cemeteries of this Continent. It would allow the old way of doing things to gain a foothold in this young century. And that message would be heard, not just in Europe but in Asia and the Americas, in Africa and the Middle East."[52] But would NATO act if Russia entered eastern Ukraine? "Putin has just given NATO something to do," observed one analyst, "but the question is whether NATO is up to it."[53]

NATO's failure to reassure its eastern members would almost certainly split the alliance. Its Baltic members and non-NATO Sweden and Finland feared that they might be Russia's next victims, comparing Moscow's threats to protect "threatened" Russians in neighboring countries to Hitler's demands for Czechoslovakia's Sudetenland to "protect" its German minority. Ivo Daalder, U.S. ambassador to NATO between 2009 and 2013, observed, "Those allies that joined NATO in the last two decades did so fundamentally because they wanted to be under the security blanket provided by the United States and NATO."[54] To reassure them, NATO's secretary-general declared, "NATO will protect every ally and defend against any threat against our fundamental security."[55]

Although U.S. military aircraft were sent to Poland and the Baltic states, a show of force would be dangerous. Russia enjoys immense military advantages near its borders where NATO is weakest, and Obama's proposal for $1 billion for a "European reassurance initiative" would provide only a modest increment in U.S. forces in Europe. It may be too late to guarantee Ukraine's territorial sovereignty, and doing so would entail a commitment NATO could not keep, further eroding its credibility. Thus, Chancellor Angela Merkel made it clear that, as stated in the 1997 NATO-Russian accord, NATO would not permanently deploy troops in countries bordering Russia or ship arms to Ukraine. Instead, NATO began to form a rapid-reaction force staffed by rotating NATO members with prepositioned equipment that could move eastward, thus reassuring NATO's Baltic members while not violating the 1997 agreement.

A robust NATO would require not only a greater U.S. presence but also German leadership. Although Chancellor Merkel was Europe's most powerful leader, she initially encouraged negotiations with Moscow to reduce tensions, but as Putin continued to behave aggressively, she charged him with trampling "with his feet on international law."[56] Her predecessor, Gerhard Schröder, had pursued a "strategic partnership" with Russia, and he defended Putin's policy toward Ukraine, in his words, as resulting from "fears about being encircled."[57] Merkel, increasingly angered by Russian aggressive policies, called Schröder's comments "shameful,"[58] adding, "if Russia continues on its course of the past weeks, it will not only be a catastrophe for Ukraine," but "would also cause massive damage to Russia, economically and politically."[59]

b. *Press Europe to impose additional economic sanctions.* "It's particularly important for the United States to bring Europe along," declared a former U.S. official. "To the extent that the United States tries to put economic pressure on Russian industry, they won't feel the impact as much as they would if we had Europe standing with us."[60] The prospect that Washington might increase sanctions while Europe did not concerned America's business community. "Unilateral sanctions by the United States end up with other countries and their industries filling the void,"[61] warned an official of America's National Association of Manufacturers. European companies, however, depend more heavily than do U.S. firms on trade with Russia, and they, too, were uneasy about imposing sanctions. An executive in a German chemical company warned that sanctions "would not just hurt Russia, but also Germany and Europe as a whole."[62]

The EU still depends on Russia's natural gas. When Russia's Gazprom ceased supplying Ukraine with gas after an upsurge in fighting in 2014, claiming it had not been paid for previous purchases, the company warned Europe that it, too, might experience a reduction in the gas routed through Ukraine. In April 2015, Gazprom warned the EU that if it insisted on an equal gas price for all members, it would mean higher prices, and the EU responded by charging Gazprom with violating Europe's antitrust regulations by raising prices and eliminating competition. "What gives Vladimir Putin his power and control," declared Senator Ron Johnson (R-WI), "is his oil and gas reserves and West and Eastern Europe's dependence on them," adding, "We need to break up his stranglehold on energy supplies."[63]

European sanctions harm Russia more than American sanctions owing to the higher level of Russo-European economic interdependence. The EU accounts for 41 percent of Russia's trade. Over half of Russia's budget depends on energy exports to Europe, and Europe has begun to diversify its energy sources, insisting on market-based pricing of gas rather than long-term contracts. In time, America, Qatar, and Norway can provide alternative energy sources, and Europeans are still negotiating for construction of the Trans-Caspian Gas Pipeline to move gas through Georgia and Turkey, thereby avoiding Russia. Russia and Iran view that proposal as illegal owing to agreements requiring that all countries bordering the Caspian Sea permit the project.

Differential access to energy poses another problem. Germany gets natural gas directly from Russia via the Nord Stream pipeline. Western Europe has easier access to pipeline gas than Eastern Europe, much of which is landlocked and lacks access to liquefied natural gas delivered by sea. An integrated network of pipes is needed to allow gas to be moved to and from countries where it is available to those in need. Pipelines already link some European countries. Germany can send gas to Italy, Poland, and the Czech Republic, but the Baltic countries and Bulgaria depend entirely on Russian gas. Hungary, Slovakia, and Poland can reroute gas to Ukraine ("reverse flow") but were reluctant to do so, fearing Russian retaliation. Following the September 2014 ceasefire in Ukraine, Moscow agreed to a European-mediated proposal for continuing gas exports to Ukraine. However, its proposal for a pipeline—South Stream—to send gas directly to Bulgaria, increasing Russian influence in that country and its neighbors and avoiding Ukraine, was scrapped owing to EU opposition.

FIGURE 13.1   Major EU Recipients of Russian Gas Transiting Ukraine

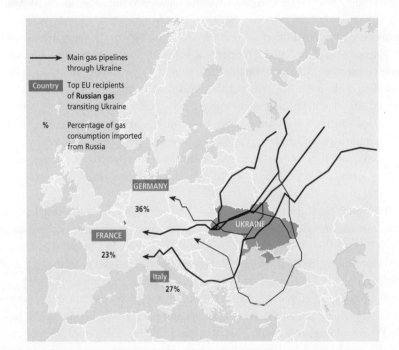

Source: Modified from Business Insider, http://www.businessinsider.com/heres-one-economic-reason-russias-invasion-of-crimea-pulls-in-europe-2014-3.

Europe is divided over the extent of sanctions and how to divide the costs associated with them. Western energy companies could lose investments in Russia, and the 6,000 German companies involved in selling to Russia might lose markets. Europe's annual trade with Russia is $450 billion, and 300,000 German jobs depend on exports to Russia. Europeans rely heavily on Russian natural gas. Britain's financial sector profits from investments by wealthy Russians in everything from bonds and property to private schools for Russian children, and France sells arms to Moscow. Thus, America and Britain called for a halt in French delivery of two assault ships built for Russia, while France called for freezing Russian assets in Britain, preferring these sanctions to sacrificing the jobs of French shipbuilders, although President François Hollande ultimately suspended their delivery.

Following the downing of a Malaysian airliner by pro-Russian separatists in July 2014 (chapter 14), however, European sentiment shifted toward America's robust sanctions policy. After conferring with President Obama, EU leaders agreed to close capital markets to Russian state banks and embargo new weapons and oil-drilling technology. Closing capital markets threatened to cut investment and lending to Russia, and the technology embargo threatened Russian ability to increase oil production by accessing shale and deep sea oil reserves. Russia promptly responded by embargoing EU food imports, valued at $15.8 billion. The EU further expanded sanctions against Russia, especially its financial and energy sectors, in September 2014 although a ceasefire had been declared in Ukraine. The new sanctions, which could be lifted if the ceasefire held, indicated that Europe's perception of Russia had come closer to America's. The shift in German sentiment was particularly striking, with a poll indicating that 70 percent approved of harsher sanctions while only 15 percent viewed Russia as a dependable partner.[64] Thus, Chancellor Merkel warned that sanctions would be reduced only if Russia accepted a permanent solution to the Ukraine crisis. Continued Russian violations of the ceasefire led President Obama to support additional sanctions and provide military aid to Ukraine legislated by Congress in December 2014 even though these policies threatened to divide Washington and its European allies.

c. *Admit Ukraine to NATO.* Ukrainian President Leonid Kuchma in 2002 publicly declared he wanted Ukraine to join NATO and the EU. Ukraine applied for a NATO MAP in 2008 but was rebuffed after Russia objected to what its leaders described as a threat to their country. Kiev abandoned efforts to join NATO after President Yanukovich's election. After intensified Russian intervention in Ukraine, the country's prime minister and president declared that Kiev would again seek NATO membership, and Ukraine officially abandoned its nonaligned status.

An invitation to Ukraine to join NATO would divide NATO between hardliners and members fearful of worsening NATO's confrontation with Russia. If Ukraine were offered NATO membership, Russia would make the country's eastern region ungovernable or even occupy that area. Although President Obama indicated that Ukraine would not be admitted to NATO, domestic hardliners and some NATO eastern members advocate this option.

d. *Aid Ukraine economically.* Providing Ukraine, a nearly bankrupt country, with economic assistance is a promising option. Thus, the IMF approved its long-delayed loan to Kiev of $18 billion while the EU committed $15 billion (equal to Russia's earlier offer). America added $1 billion in loan guarantees, and Germany pledged $690 million. The IMF added an additional $17.5 billion to its original package some months later.

Ukraine was vulnerable to Moscow's economic leverage as well as its military power. In March 2014, Russia's state-owned energy company raised the price of natural gas sold to Ukraine significantly. If Ukraine's economy continues to deteriorate, its government will become increasingly unpopular and vulnerable to Russian influence.

e. *Compromise with Russia to neutralize Ukraine as a buffer and encourage Ukraine to allow its eastern region greater autonomy.* This policy would appear a capitulation to Russian demands, a show of weakness that deprived Ukraine of the sovereign right to decide for itself. There is no reason that Ukraine should choose between East and West or that NATO or Russia should enjoy exclusive influence in Ukraine. To the extent that some Ukrainians prefer to look in one or the other direction, letting them do so, however, would reduce Moscow's insecurity and the likelihood of Russian aggression.

f. *NATO stands aside.* Some argue that Ukraine is not sufficiently important to merit a NATO-Russian confrontation. Others argue that Russian intervention, if unchecked, will invite Moscow to exert greater pressure on Ukraine and NATO's eastern members. The retired chief of NATO's military command concluded, "The odds of reversing what happened in Crimea are very low, so I think the focus needs to shift to ensuring there is no further encroachment into Ukrainian territory," but "for NATO to do nothing is the most dangerous course."[65]

CONCLUSION: NATO REDUX

Transatlantic relations remain vital. Although U.S.-European misunderstandings occurred about issues like America's 2003 invasion of Iraq, the alliance remained solid while emphasizing the spread of Western values beyond North America and Europe but neglecting NATO military power in Europe.

In addition to close political and military ties, Americans and Europeans have enjoyed a stable economic partnership. The G-7, a central pillar of the global economy, includes America, Britain, France, Germany, and Italy. Recent years have proved economically challenging for the EU. Its members were hard hit by the global economic crisis and recovered more slowly than the United States. Several members of the EU's Eurozone (countries in which the euro serves as the common currency)—Cyprus, Portugal, Ireland, Italy, and Greece—neared sovereign default on loans, requiring IMF and EU aid to stay afloat. In return, they were forced to impose painful austerity policies on citizens, many of whom became disenchanted with the EU itself.

Trade and investment remain central to the transatlantic relationship, with trade in goods and services totaling $1 trillion annually and bilateral direct investment approaching $4 trillion. America and the EU accounted for almost half of world GDP and 30 percent of world trade in 2013. Massive trade and investment are credited with promoting growth and job creation in America and Europe. Thus, in 2013, President Obama announced his intention to pursue negotiations on a free trade agreement with the EU—the Transatlantic Trade and Investment Partnership (chapter 5).

After the Cold War, NATO and the EU moved eastward to encompass most of the USSR's former satellites and several former Soviet republics, and it proved a source of friction with Russia. Europe's center of gravity also shifted. Whereas previously the Franco-German relationship constituted Europe's political core, "these days, the real action happens further east." The confrontation over Ukraine revealed that "the Franco-German engine has been replaced by a Russo-German one: as the European Union moves eastward, settling its future borders and borderlands, it is Germany and Russia that will decide who is in and who is out—and under what terms." And "the battle for Ukraine has become a battle over the shape that this Russo-German Europe will take."[66] America will have a less central role in this contest than in past years, and Germany is crucial to restraining Russia owing to their economic interdependence.

The confrontation over Ukraine reminded members of NATO of its original purpose—assuring European security by pooling Western power. NATO still seeks to extend its influence to Asia and the Middle East, but resources are scarce, and the Russian bear has begun to growl again. Perhaps this is a temporary aberration. Americans and Europeans had believed that the rules governing relations with Russia had changed, but President Putin seemed bent on revising the post–Cold War order in Europe. A former U.S. official called the crisis "an earthquake, and not a 4-point earthquake" which ended post–Cold War hopes: "Europe whole and free? Well, it's a Europe free-for-all. And we don't know how to react to it."[67] The next chapter examines the situation from Russia's perspective.

DISCUSSION QUESTIONS

1. Did NATO's eastward expansion cause the Ukraine crisis by threatening Russian security?

2. How should NATO respond to Russia's aggressive policies toward Ukraine?

3. Should NATO continue trying to expand Western values to regions outside of Europe?

4. Should the United States shift its foreign-policy focus back to Europe from Asia and the Middle East?

5. How should NATO and the United States react to the apparent vulnerability of Estonia, Lithuania, and Latvia, all NATO members, located near Russia and with large Russian populations?

6. Should Ukraine be admitted to NATO?

KEY TERMS

foreign direct investment (p. 393)   NATO (p. 400)

⑤SAGE edge™
for CQ Press

Sharpen your skill with SAGE edge at edge.sagepub.com/mansbach

SAGE edge for Students provides a personalized approach to help you accomplish your coursework goals in an easy-to-use learning environment.

14

America and Russia

VALUES VERSUS POWER

Reset button

AP Photo/Fabrice Coffrini

We now examine the evolution of U.S.-Russian relations. During the Cold War, U.S. policy reflected security concerns about Soviet expansionism and preoccupation with Western values in capitalism's ideological struggle with communism. After the Cold War, America sought to spread liberal values to Eastern Europe and Russia, but Vladimir Putin's authoritarianism, nationalism, and refusal to accept his country's post–Cold War status produced a clash of values with Washington. As the remaining superpower, Washington failed to recognize that Moscow loathed the eastward movement of NATO and the EU, regarding them as threats to its interests.

PAST: A BIPOLAR WORLD

Some date the Cold War's onset from Western intervention against the Bolsheviks in 1917 to 1918, while others date it from mutual suspicion after World War II. During the Cold War, the Soviet Union was the "other" superpower in a bipolar world. Washington and Moscow, allies during World War II, emerged from the war as dominant actors in global politics.

THE COLD WAR AND THE SOURCES OF AMERICAN POLICY

Thirteen Days

The 1962 Cuban missile crisis lasted for thirteen days. *Thirteen Days* became the title of Robert Kennedy's memoir of the crisis and a 2000 film starring Kevin Costner that re-created the crisis.

DID YOU KNOW?

U.S. policy toward the USSR during the Cold War reflected a complex set of factors. External factors included the bipolar distribution of power such that the USSR posed the only danger to America, especially after 1949 when it became the second member of the "nuclear club." As Europe's colonial empires declined, Washington and Moscow competed to fill resulting power vacuums in the developing world as well as in Europe. Geography played a role in other ways as well. Although the superpowers tacitly agreed not to meddle in its foe's sphere of interest, two anomalies remained—Cuba and Berlin—the former a communist state 90 miles from Florida and the latter located behind the iron curtain. Both became flashpoints for crises that threatened U.S.-Soviet hot war.

Soviet behavior in Eastern Europe and its zone of Germany, whether driven by expansionist aims or insecurity, was aggressive. Agreements at the Yalta and Potsdam Conferences concerning these regions were violated by Moscow (chapter 13). In Asia, too, events boded ill as revolution in China brought a communist regime to power and North Korea's invasion of South Korea triggered a bloody conflict that lasted three years.

American responses included establishing NATO, reorganizing its defense and intelligence establishments, providing allies with economic aid, and providing a commitment—the Truman Doctrine—to assist democracies to resist communist expansion. Government factors helped implement these policies. The military services fought for higher budgets, and defense spending soared from $9.1 billion in 1948 to $52.8 billion in 1953. Leaders of key foreign-policy bureaucracies in the Truman administration like Secretaries of State James Byrnes, George Marshall (later secretary of defense), and Dean Acheson fulfilled their departmental role by planning and implementing a vigorous response to Soviet actions.

In 1946, Republicans regained control of Congress for the first time since 1930. Bipartisanship flourished as both parties in the Senate supported internationalist policies like the Marshall Plan and cooperated with the Truman administration in designing policies to resist the expansion of Soviet communism. Some Republicans, notably Congressman Richard Nixon and Senator Joe McCarthy, argued that communists and communist sympathizers had infiltrated U.S. bureaucracies like the State Department and the Foreign Service as well as U.S. interest groups and industries. Such charges became virulent after the "loss of China," making it difficult for members of Congress to advocate compromise with the Soviet Union. For much of the Cold War, Republicans benefited electorally by characterizing Democrats as less defense-minded and more conciliatory toward the USSR. Political candidates from both parties sought to appear "tough" toward the USSR.

Societal factors reinforced the anti-Soviet rhetoric of politicians. The Truman administration persuaded Americans of the need for a stronger defense and for policies designed to contain Soviet expansionism. Throughout the Cold War, public attitudes toward the USSR hardened during periods of high threat or when it appeared the Soviet Union was becoming stronger relative to America. Thus, after the Korean War, almost 89 percent of Americans held "unfavorable" views of the USSR, and, after Soviet repression of the Hungarian Revolution in 1956, over 86 percent of Americans viewed the USSR "unfavorably." By contrast, when U.S.-Soviet tensions eased in the 1970s during the era of "détente," attitudes of the U.S. public toward the USSR became less unfavorable (43 percent in May 1972 and 30 percent in July 1973). However, after the 1979 Soviet invasion of Afghanistan, "unfavorable" U.S. attitudes jumped to 73 percent.[1] Summing up these changes, one observer concluded, "The change in Soviet-American relations can be charted in American public opinion as clearly as in official diplomatic announcements and news stories."[2]

Communities of Eastern Europeans in Chicago, Buffalo, Cleveland, New York, and Cuban émigrés in Miami (after Fidel Castro took power in Cuba) were strongly anticommunist. These communities formed influential interest groups that mobilized politicians and public opinion against the USSR. Among the most active was the Polish American Congress (PAC), founded in Buffalo in 1944. The PAC opposed the wartime agreements with the USSR regarding Eastern Europe, advocated establishing Radio Free

Timeline

1900	2000	2000 (Continued)
1991 Dissolution of the USSR	**2000–2008** Putin Russia's president	August **2008** Russo-Georgian War
1992 Kazakhstan, Ukraine, and Belarus agree to ship nuclear weapons to Russia; Nunn-Lugar program approved.	June **2001** Bush-Putin summit	March **2009** Russo-U.S. agreement to "reset" relations
1993 START II Treaty	**2003** Strategic Offensive Reductions Treaty	April **2010** New START Treaty
1999 U.S.-Russian disagreement over Kosovo	**2003** "Rose Revolution" in Georgia	November **2010** NATO approves missile-defense system.
December **1999** Yeltsin resigns.	**2004-2005** Ukraine's "Orange Revolution"	**2011** Phase 1 European missile defense system begun
	2008–2012 Medvedev Russia's president	**2012** Putin reelected Russian president

An early Cold War confrontation: The Berlin airlift

The Granger Collection, New York

Europe to broadcast to the "captive nations" in the Soviet bloc, held Stalin responsible for the murder of Polish officers during World War II, and opposed concessions to Moscow. A similar role was later played by the Cuban-American National Foundation.

2000 (Continued)

May **2012** NATO missile defense becomes operational.

June **2012** Putin-Obama summit

August **2012** Russia joins the WTO.

October **2012** Russia ends Nunn-Lugar program.

March **2013** U.S. cancels final phase of European missile defense.

August **2013** Obama cancels summit with Putin after Edward Snowden's defection.

March **2014** Russia annexes Crimea; America and EU impose economic sanctions.

2000 (Continued)

2014 Separatists seek to secede from Ukraine; Ukrainian army battles separatists; Russian intervention intensifies.

July **2014** Flight MH17 destroyed by Ukrainian separatists

September **2014** Unsuccessful Ukrainian ceasefire

February **2015** Second Ukrainian ceasefire

KEY DOCUMENT
Churchill's "Iron Curtain" Speech

"From Stettin in the Baltic to Trieste in the Adriatic an iron curtain has descended across the Continent. Behind that line lie all the capitals of the ancient states of Central and Eastern Europe. Warsaw, Berlin, Prague, Vienna, Budapest, Belgrade, Bucharest and Sofia, all these famous cities and the populations around them lie in what I must call the Soviet sphere, and all are subject in one form or another, not only to Soviet influence but to a very high and, in some cases, increasing measure of control from Moscow."

Source: Modern History Sourcebook: Winston S. Churchill: "Iron Curtain Speech," March 5, 1946, http://www.fordham .edu/halsall/mod/churchill-iron.asp.

Individual leaders with strong personal beliefs also helped mobilize Americans against the USSR. Winston Churchill, a long-time foe of communism, believed the Cold War had been caused by the failure to "strangle Bolshevism at birth"[3] in 1917 and popularized the term *Iron Curtain* in a speech at Westminster College in Fulton, Missouri, in March 1946.

President Truman, too, was suspicious of Soviet motives and was influenced by his prior experience. On hearing of North Korea's invasion of South Korea, he drew an analogy from the 1930s: "In my generation this was not the first occasion when the strong had attacked the weak. I remembered how each time that the democracies failed to act it had encouraged the aggressors to keep going ahead. Communism was acting in Korea just as Hitler, Mussolini and the Japanese had acted ten, fifteen and twenty years earlier. . . . If this was allowed to go unchallenged it would mean a third world war, just as similar incidents had brought on a second world war."[4] By contrast, former Vice President Henry Wallace, a third-party candidate for president in 1948, advocated friendship with USSR. In a letter to Truman in 1946, he declared that "the world has changed and that today there can be no 'one world' unless the United States and Russia can find some way of living together."[5]

Soviet leaders were also crucial in the Cold War's evolution. Soviet dictator Joseph Stalin was paranoid and suspected that he was surrounded by foes at home and abroad. In February 1946, he declared that war was an inevitable byproduct of capitalism. Nikita Khrushchev, who denounced Stalin in 1956 and declared that East-West coexistence was possible, was a risk taker, as evidenced by the secret delivery of nuclear missiles to Cuba in 1962. That decision brought the superpowers to the brink of nuclear war, a seminal event that transformed the Cold War. Khrushchev and John Kennedy recognized a common interest in avoiding nuclear disaster and began negotiating confidence-building and arms-control agreements to reduce tension.

Few Russians had a greater individual impact than Mikhail Gorbachev, who played a key role in ending the Cold War after becoming General-Secretary of the Soviet communist party in 1985. Gorbachev recognized that Moscow could no longer afford overseas commitments it had made during the Cold War or the arms race with America. Thus, he initiated political and economic reform (*perestroika*) at home and unilaterally acted to reduce Soviet-American hostility. The "Polish Pope" John Paul II also played a unique role in ending the Cold War. In 1979, John Paul returned to his native land in a journey described as a "psychological earthquake, an opportunity for mass political catharsis."[6] He spoke of "solidarity" in a speech in Warsaw and encouraged Poland's worker movement, Solidarity. Solidarity in turn helped convince Gorbachev of the need for reform. "Here is the specific chain of causation that goes from the election of the Polish pope in 1978 to the end of communism, and hence of the end of the cold war, in 1989."[7]

The Cold War Ends

Domestic factors helped persuade Washington to accept Gorbachev's initiatives. In the early 1980s, the Nuclear Freeze Movement emerged in America. Supported by congressional liberals, the movement opposed increases in arms expenditures during the last years of the Carter administration (1979–1980) and President Reagan's first term (1980–1984). The group reflected public fear of war following the Senate's failure to ratify the SALT II arms control agreement after Moscow's invasion of Afghanistan. The movement was an umbrella coalition of 130 organizations established to persuade the superpowers to "adopt a mutual freeze on the testing, production, and deployment of nuclear weapons"[8] and delivery systems. In June 1982, the Freeze Movement mobilized a million people in New York City to lobby the superpowers and the UN. Despite the Reagan administration's opposition, voters in nine of ten U.S. states that held referendums on the freeze resolution voted in favor of it. It was the largest referendum on a single issue in U.S. history. Favored by some 70 percent of the public, the resolution was endorsed by the House of Representatives and was supported by the Democratic candidates for president in 1984 and numerous city governments and state legislatures.

The end of the Cold War began when Hungary allowed East Germans to flee to Austria in March 1989, and Moscow declined to halt the exodus. In June, Poland held free elections. In November, the Berlin Wall came down, and shortly afterward Gorbachev and President George H. W. Bush declared an end to the conflict at a summit in Malta. Within a year, the Soviet communist party had surrendered power. President Bush supported Gorbachev until his ouster, although the Central Intelligence Agency (CIA) and the Departments of State and Defense concluded that Boris Yeltsin, president of the Russian Federation, would become Russia's new leader. At Yeltsin's urging, the USSR was dissolved on December 8, 1991. Former Soviet republics—Estonia, Lithuania, Latvia, Ukraine, and Belarus in Europe; Georgia, Armenia, and Azerbaijan in the Caucasus; and Kyrgyzstan, Uzbekistan, Kazakhstan, Tajikistan, and Turkmenistan in Central Asia—became sovereign states. Russia, too, became independent, and Yeltsin established the Commonwealth of Independent States, a loose grouping of twelve of the fifteen newly independent countries.

U.S. contacts with the newly independent countries rapidly multiplied. The Baltic and Eastern European countries joined EU and NATO. Most of the new Central Asian countries retained their former communist leaders; others fell to quarreling, while several were rent by civil strife. Russia still regarded Eastern Europe as having special importance for its national security, and many Russians continued to live in Russia's "near abroad."

Some observers viewed the end of the Cold War and the dissolution of the USSR as the results of hardline foreign policies pursued by the Reagan administration—higher defense budgets and support for Soviet foes in Afghanistan and Angola. An alternative explanation was that the Soviet collapse was due to internal factors. Gorbachev's "dramatic reduction of Soviet subsidies for states in the Eastern bloc, his withdrawal of support for old-line Warsaw Pact regimes, and perestroika created totally new political dynamics in Eastern Europe and led to the largely peaceful disintegration of various communist regimes and the weakening of Moscow's influence in the region. Ronald Reagan contributed to this process by increasing the pressure on the Kremlin, but it was Gorbachev, not the White House, who ended the Soviet empire."[9]

The end of the Cold War replaced the hostility of previous decades with a "normal" relationship. Russia remained a nuclear power, though economically and politically weaker than the USSR. Although the Cold War was over, questions remained. What would happen to Moscow's 27,000 nuclear weapons? Would Russia permit the post-Soviet states to remain independent? How would Washington redefine its interests in a world without a "red menace"? Even before the USSR's dissolution was completed, it appeared that an era of cooperative U.S.-Russian relations had begun.

PRESENT: FROM COOPERATION TO CONFLICT

The immediate post–Cold War period proved a brief honeymoon. With Russian and U.S. support, the UN Security Council condemned Iraq's 1990 invasion of Kuwait and adopted Resolution 678, authorizing

MAP 14.1   Successor States of the USSR

Source: Data from The World Bank, "Transition: The First Ten Years: Analysis and Lessons for Eastern Europe and the Former Soviet Union," 2002, http://siteresources.worldbank.org/ECAEXT/Resources/complete.pdf.

Note: Ukraine, Kazakhstan, and Belarus are nuclear weapons free.

UN members to use force if Iraq did not comply with previous UN resolutions. This was the first time since 1950 that the Security Council was able to invoke Chapter 7 of its Charter ("Action with Respect to Threats to the Peace, Breaches of the Peace and Acts of Aggression").

The Russian-American "Honeymoon"

Encouraged by Presidents George H. W. Bush and Bill Clinton, Russia adopted reforms to transform Russia's centrally planned economy into a market economy. This effort triggered runaway inflation and economic contraction. Washington also sought to nudge Russia toward democracy. The Reagan and George H. W. Bush administrations "understood the dangers of a crumbling superpower and managed the Soviet Union's decline with an impressive combination of empathy and toughness,"[10] while failing to recognize the implications of its imploding economy.

The Clinton administration, Russian specialist Dimitri Simes believes, was too eager to help Yeltsin, expecting Russia to accept "the United States' definition of Russia's national interests." Clinton was so taken with Russia's president that he commented, "Yeltsin drunk is better than most of the alternatives sober."[11] Clinton employed "the spinach treatment," pressing Russia to adopt policies that "Washington deemed healthy, no matter how unappetizing these policies seemed in Moscow."[12] One analyst writes of "the overbearing and ultimately counterproductive tone that Washington and its allies took toward Moscow throughout the 1990s, which reinforced Russian insecurity and would later help to justify the reactionary and standoffish strain in Russia's Putin-era foreign policy."[13]

Ultimately, Russia's political institutions proved incapable of instituting the changes pushed by reformers. Durable political institutions, including political parties, were not established. Despite democratic forms, Russia's political institutions remained in the hands of small coteries frequently acting illegally in their own economic and political interests, especially after Putin took power. Corruption was widespread, and Russia only partly transformed its economy, selling valuable assets inexpensively to Yeltsin's and then Putin's friends, while ensuring that major economic sectors remained under state control.

Strains in Russo-American Relations

Several factors boded ill for democracy in Russia and Russo-American cooperation. Among these were the decline of Russia's economy, the limits placed on U.S. investment in Russia, and Yeltsin's erratic behavior including shelling Russia's parliament with tanks in 1993 and invading Chechnya to prevent it seceding from the Russian Federation.

Chechnya After the Soviet collapse, the republic of Chechnya in the Russian Caucasus sought independence. In 1994, Russian troops entered Chechnya to end its secession. The first Chechen war lasted until 1996 and was accompanied by human rights abuses that damaged U.S.-Russian relations. Chechnya continued to resist, and militants in neighboring Russian territories aided Muslim Chechen insurgents. In 1999, war resumed, leading to the leveling of much of Chechnya's capital, Grozny. Chechen's militants resorted to terrorism in Russia, occupying a Moscow theater (2002) that led to the death of 100 hostages, attacking the Moscow subway (2004), and occupying a school in Beslan (2004) in the North Caucasus that led to over 300 deaths including many children.

Enter Putin In September 1999, Yeltsin appointed a former Soviet intelligence officer, Vladimir Putin, as prime minister. After seventeen years in the intelligence service, including a lengthy period in East Germany, Putin had retired as a KGB lieutenant-colonel. In 1998, Yeltsin appointed Putin director of the Federal Security Service and later secretary of Russia's Security Council. Putin's organization of a ruthless offensive against the rebellious Chechens earned him public attention. "Everyone saw in him what he or she wanted: the loyal statist, the clean-cut modernizing reformer, the sober and disciplined KGB man."[14] In 2001, President George W. Bush met Putin at a summit in Slovenia. "I looked the man in the eye," declared Bush. "I found him to be very straightforward and trustworthy and we had a very good dialogue. I was able to get a sense of his soul."[15]

In December 1999, Yeltsin resigned, appointing Putin Russia's acting president. In 2000 and 2004, Putin won election as president, and many of his appointees were former members of the Soviet security services. Putin's popularity rested on a popular desire for political and economic stability after the tumultuous Yeltsin years. The belief that post-Soviet Russia would embrace Western values proved chimerical, and Russia's new elite inherited the privileges previously enjoyed by the Soviet elite.

American leaders believed Russia would join a U.S.-dominated world, featuring market capitalism, democratic norms, and respect for human rights. In adopting domestic reform, Moscow, it was hoped, would become responsive to popular pressures. Events soon after the Cold War indicated that Russia would align its foreign policies closer to those of the West on issues like weapons of mass destruction (WMD) proliferation and trade.

By the time Putin became Russia's president, U.S.-Russian relations had cooled. On some issues, cooperation continued, while others, like the entry of the Baltic republics into NATO, generated tension. The "reset" was a pragmatic effort to renew cooperation after U.S.-Russian relations had deteriorated between 2007 and 2009, and Presidents Obama and Dmitry Medvedev agreed in London to a "fresh start." (Medvedev was elected Russia's president in 2008 because Putin could legally serve only two consecutive four-year terms.) In March 2009, in Geneva, Switzerland, Secretary of State Hillary Clinton presented Russian Foreign Minister Sergei Lavrov with a red button that read "Reset" in English and "Peregruzka" in Russian. Clinton declared that the button "represents what President Obama and Vice President Biden and I have been saying and that is 'We want to reset our relationship.' And so we will do it together." She then asked Lavrov: "We worked hard to get the right Russian word. Do you think we got it?" Lavrov replied: "You got it wrong. This says 'peregruzka,' which means overcharged," adding, "We won't let you do that to us."[16] The correct Russian word was "perezagruzka." Medvedev later described the next three years as "the best period in U.S.-Russia relations in history."[17]

Security Cooperation

Terrorism and Afghanistan Russo-American relations improved after 9/11 as Putin offered to aid U.S. efforts against al-Qaeda and the Afghan Taliban. Moscow regarded Islamic extremism as a threat to the stability of its Muslim republics in the North Caucasus—Chechnya, Ingushetia, and Dagestan—and to its neighbors in Central Asia. Russia agreed to U.S. bases in Kyrgyzstan and Uzbekistan to support America's presence in Afghanistan. Concerned by U.S. influence in Central Asia, however, Moscow changed its mind and persuaded Uzbekistan to close America's base there in 2005, but, despite efforts to get Kyrgyzstan to do the same, the Manas "transit center" remained open to U.S. troops until 2014. In 2009, the insecurity of Pakistan's overland supply routes for NATO forces in Afghanistan led to establishing the Northern Distribution Network, a series of commercially based logistical arrangements that facilitated supplying NATO forces through Russia.[18] Cooperation in counterterrorism, though inconsistent, continued, and Moscow provided Washington with information about a visit to Dagestan by one of two brothers involved in the 2013 Boston Marathon bombing.

Arms Control Washington and Moscow also cooperated on arms control following the Cold War. There was concern about Soviet nuclear weapons remaining in post-Soviet states and the insecurity of Moscow's immense nuclear stockpile. Washington feared that nuclear material might fall in the hands of "rogue" governments or terrorists or that underpaid Russian scientists might sell their knowledge to such countries or groups. In 1992, Kazakhstan, Ukraine, and Belarus agreed to send their Soviet-era nuclear weapons to Russia, and in 1993 America and Russia signed the Strategic Arms Reduction Treaty (START II) under which both would reduce their strategic nuclear warheads to 3,000 to 3,500 by 2003. They also agreed to eliminate land-based missiles with multiple warheads. The treaty was ratified by the Senate in 1996 but not by Russia's legislature until 2000. In 2002, however, Russia withdrew from the treaty in response to America's abrogation of the 1972 antiballistic missile (ABM) treaty. The two did agree in 2003 to a Strategic Offensive Reductions Treaty (SORT), limiting the strategic warheads each deployed to 1,700 to 2,200, but it would remain in force only until 2013 unless another agreement was reached.

To enhance the security of Russia's WMD, Senators Sam Nunn (D-GA) and Richard Lugar (R-IN) cosponsored the Cooperative Threat Reduction Program in 1992 that "aimed at reducing the threat posed by terrorist organizations or proliferant states seeking to acquire weapons of mass destruction (WMD) expertise, material, and equipment."[19] The program provided funds and expertise to decommission stockpiles of WMD in post-Soviet states and helped employ Russian scientists and create joint ventures with Russian firms willing to shift from weapons production to other endeavors.

The two countries also cooperated in disposing of plutonium from Russia's nuclear warheads by processing it to generate electricity in nuclear reactors. Following the Cold War, America and Russia had more weapons-grade plutonium and enriched uranium than they needed. In 1994, they agreed that Russia would shut down three plutonium-producing nuclear reactors by 2000. America had previously shut down all such reactors, and Russia followed suit at most of its reactors. In September 2000, the two countries signed the Plutonium Management and Disposition Agreement, committing each to dispose of thirty-four metric tons of excess plutonium, enough to produce 17,000 nuclear weapons, and Washington provided $400 million to help Russia eliminate surplus plutonium. Russia failed to meet the deadline, but in 2010 the two countries updated their commitment, and Russia agreed to close the last of its plutonium-producing reactors by 2018.

In October 2012, Russia announced it would not renew Nunn-Lugar, an action that reflected Moscow's opposition to U.S. plans for missile defense in Europe and concern about provisions in the Nunn-Lugar agreement that shielded Americans from legal liability for accidents associated with the program. This did not mean the end of U.S.-Russian nonproliferation cooperation. Another agreement

FIGURE **14.1**   The Nunn-Lugar Scorecard

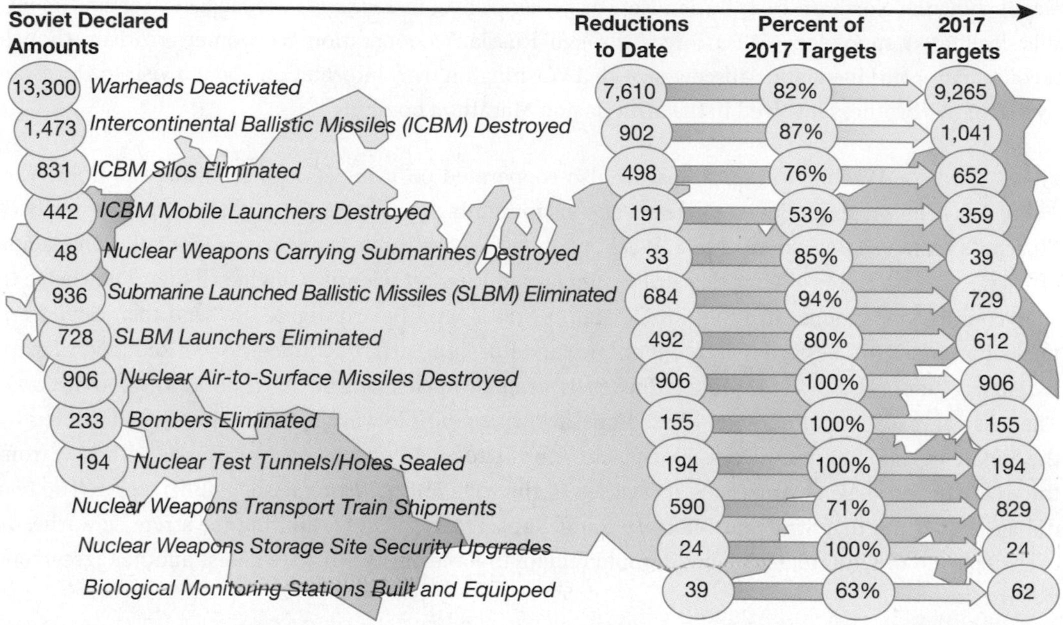

Soviet Declared Amounts		Reductions to Date	Percent of 2017 Targets	2017 Targets
13,300	Warheads Deactivated	7,610	82%	9,265
1,473	Intercontinental Ballistic Missiles (ICBM) Destroyed	902	87%	1,041
831	ICBM Silos Eliminated	498	76%	652
442	ICBM Mobile Launchers Destroyed	191	53%	359
48	Nuclear Weapons Carrying Submarines Destroyed	33	85%	39
936	Submarine Launched Ballistic Missiles (SLBM) Eliminated	684	94%	729
728	SLBM Launchers Eliminated	492	80%	612
906	Nuclear Air-to-Surface Missiles Destroyed	906	100%	906
233	Bombers Eliminated	155	100%	155
194	Nuclear Test Tunnels/Holes Sealed	194	100%	194
	Nuclear Weapons Transport Train Shipments	590	71%	829
	Nuclear Weapons Storage Site Security Upgrades	24	100%	24
	Biological Monitoring Stations Built and Equipped	39	63%	62

Source: http://lugar.senate.gov/nunnlugar/scorecard.html.

was reached just before the 2013 expiration of Nunn-Lugar defining less ambitious arrangements under the 2003 Multilateral Nuclear Environmental Program. America continued its nuclear security–related work but was no longer involved in dismantling Russian missiles, bombers, and chemical weapons.[20] But as U.S.-Russian tension increased in 2014, Moscow ended Russo-American cooperation in securing nuclear materials in Russia.

The most significant U.S.-Russian arms agreement was the 2010 New START Treaty— the successor to SORT. Under New START the two countries agreed to reduce strategic nuclear weapons to 1,550 deployed nuclear warheads and 700 strategic delivery vehicles (missiles, bombers, and submarines) within seven years. Each was limited to 800 nondeployed delivery systems. This was the high point of the reset. In June 2013, President Obama proposed additional bilateral reductions to limit both countries to 1,000 deployed strategic warheads. His proposal, however, met with criticism from congressional conservatives who demanded modernization of America's arsenal before additional cuts, and Secretary of State John Kerry angered Republicans by suggesting that reductions could be achieved by informal agreement that would not require Senate ratification. Advocates of nuclear disarmament also criticized the proposal, noting that reducing "deployed" warheads and putting them in storage did not actually eliminate warheads. As U.S.-Russian relations worsened in 2013 to 2014, Moscow indicated it was not interested in additional cuts.

There were other arms-control disagreements. In 2007, Russia suspended the 1990 Conventional Armed Forces in Europe treaty that limited the numbers and territorial location of troops because of Western insistence that Russia remove all its troops from Georgia and Moldova. In 2008, Washington claimed that Russia had violated the landmark 1987 Intermediate-Range Nuclear Forces Treaty by testing a new ground-launched cruise missile. At the same time, dangerous aerial and naval incidents involving Russia and the West proliferated in Europe.

America, Russia, and the Middle East: Eroding Cooperation

We noted earlier how NATO altered its focus after the Cold War to "out-of-area" challenges. Although not threatening Russia directly, Moscow viewed Washington's efforts to extend its values to other regions, especially the Middle East, as arrogant unilateralism.

The Arab Spring Initial Russian reaction to revolutionary stirrings in the Arab world was cautious. Moscow was concerned about foreign intervention in the region. "Internationally, Russia could lose major arms contracts and significant investments in energy resources, following regime changes in these states." Moscow also considered "the Middle East a neighboring region" and was "concerned about U.S. and NATO unilateralism" as well as the growing influence of Islamic extremism, raising "fears in Moscow that such revolutions could be repeated in the restive North Caucasus and Central Asia."[21]

Libya For decades, Libya's Muammar Qaddafi had been a source of hard currency for arms purchases from Russia. Moscow was also an investor in Libyan oilfields—sources of supplemental energy exports to Europe that Russian production could not satisfy. A month after Libya's civil war erupted in 2011 (chapter 10), the Security Council authorized "all necessary measures" to protect Libyan civilians from government violence. Having not vetoed the UN authorization, Moscow felt deceived when NATO helped overthrow Qaddafi and denounced the way NATO had interpreted the UN resolution, declaring NATO intervention violated the principle of state sovereignty. Putin used events in Libya to justify higher defense spending and argued that NATO intervention had exacerbated conditions in Libya. The president of Moscow's Institute of the Middle East compared Western intervention to Soviet expansionism during the Cold War: "You are the Soviet Union now, guys, and you pay the price. You are trying to distribute democracy the way we tried to distribute socialism. You do it the Western way. They hate both."[22] The Libyan experience turned Russia's leaders against "regime change," and Putin argued that America wanted to repeat these mistakes in Syria.

Syria Close Syrian-Russian relations dated back to the 1950s. Under President Hafez al-Assad and his son, Bashar, Syria became Moscow's staunchest Arab ally. Syria was a major destination for Russian arms sales, and Russian arms industries had "contracts worth at least $3 billion"[23] with Syria. As in Libya, Russia had investments in Syria's oil industry, and Russia's only naval facility in the Mediterranean was located in Syria. Syria was also a conduit for Russian arms to Hezbollah and Hamas. Moscow declared the arms it sent Syria did not violate the UN arms embargo imposed during Syria's civil war because they involved deals reached before that embargo. Secretary Kerry responded, "Whether it's an old contract or not, it has a profoundly negative impact on the balance of interests and the stability of the region, and it does put Israel at risk."[24]

Moscow sought to support Assad as civil war engulfed Syria. Washington's aims were more ambiguous. It sought to prevent the conflict from spilling into neighboring states and urged Assad's removal to weaken Iran's influence in the region while preventing extremists from taking power. Believing it had been deceived in Libya, Moscow repeatedly blocked U.S. efforts to topple Assad, declaring they violated Syrian sovereignty. Former CIA director and Secretary of Defense Robert Gates noted, "The Russians felt they had been played for suckers on Libya. They felt there had been a bait and switch. I said at the time we would pay hell ever getting them to cooperate in the future."[25] Unlike Moscow's response to Libya, Russia used its Security Council veto to protect its Syrian client.

After Assad used poison gas against civilians in August 2013, President Obama threatened to use force, eliciting an irate response from President Putin: "In accordance with applicable international law, the authorization of the use of force against a sovereign state can only be given by the Security Council of the United Nations. Any other reasons, or methods, to justify the use of force against an independent and sovereign state are unacceptable and cannot be qualified as anything other than aggression."[26]

When Washington appeared ready to launch a punitive strike, Putin proposed that Syria place its chemical weapons under international control. The following day, President Obama delayed a congressional vote on using force to see if an agreement brokered by Russia could be arranged. The deal had been suggested earlier by Secretary Kerry who, when asked what Assad could do to avoid a U.S. attack, had answered, "He could turn over every single bit of his chemical weapons to the international community in the next week. Turn it over, all of it, without delay, and allow a full and total accounting for that."[27] Putin "was thus able to take credit as the United States and others scrambled to spin the situation in their favor" and was "the real winner of this particular round of the Syrian conflict."[28] After intense negotiations, Washington and Moscow reached a deal—"Framework for Elimination of Syrian Chemical Weapons"—by which Syria would become the 190th member of the Chemical Weapons Convention, and its chemical arsenal would be removed and destroyed. A U.S. official described as "head spinning"[29] the sudden shift in the Syrian situation combined with overtures for negotiations from Iran's new president.

President Obama's critics charged that his reluctance to use force against Assad fostered perceptions of weakness in U.S. foreign policy that contributed to Putin's later aggressive actions toward Ukraine. "This is the ultimate result of a feckless foreign policy," declared Senator John McCain (R-AZ), and Senator Mitch McConnell (R-KY) added, "The president has eroded American credibility in the world."[30] A diplomat argued, "In the Great Game scheme of things Syria gives Russia leverage on the West as payback for meddling in Ukraine, its backyard and most important geopolitical stake."[31]

Efforts to overcome U.S.-Russian differences over Assad's fate during subsequent meetings between Presidents Obama and Putin and Secretary Clinton and Foreign Minister Lavrov proved fruitless. Despite rhetoric favoring a negotiated solution, Moscow steadfastly argued that Assad's replacement could not be a precondition for negotiations, as Washington demanded, and continued providing Assad with advisers and arms. Assad remained dependent on Russia and Iran for political support, funding, and arms.

By late 2012, however, Russian diplomats began to consider the possibility that Assad might not survive, and Moscow might be faced either by a pro-Western regime or, worse, Islamic militants. There were indications that Putin might be seeking a compromise when he said, "We are not concerned about the fate of Assad's regime. We understand what is going on there and that the family has held power for 40 years. We are worried about a different thing—what next? We simply don't want the current opposition, having become the authorities, to start fighting the people who are the current authorities." He added, "Our position is not to keep Assad and his regime in power at any cost."[32] By spring 2013, Washington, too, had softened its position, recognizing that Assad's regime was no longer in imminent danger of collapsing, and in May 2015, Secretary Kerry journeyed to Russia for conversations with Putin about resolving the Syrian impasse. These talks were viewed by Russian observers as a diplomatic victory for Putin. Thereafter, Russia intervened in Syria militarily to aid Assad.

Iran   U.S. and Russian leaders cooperated to try to prevent Iran from acquiring nuclear weapons. Moscow's proposal that Iranian uranium be enriched in Russia and provided to Iran when needed to fuel Iranian nuclear reactors gained traction during negotiations. Russia had constructed Iran's first nuclear reactor at Bushehr on those terms, and Moscow offered to sell additional nuclear reactors to Iran on similar conditions.

Moscow, however, never fully agreed with the United States about the extent to which Iran posed a threat, the reason given by Washington for missile defense in Europe. Before negotiations began in 2013 between Iran and the P5+1 (chapter 4), Russia's deputy foreign minister took issue with America: "We believe a long-term settlement should be based on the recognition of Iran's unconditional right to develop its civilian nuclear program, including the right to enrich uranium"[33] under the supervision of the IAEA. By contrast, Washington and its allies argued that Iran should accept restrictions on enriching uranium before a deal could be reached. As U.S.-Russian tension over Ukraine intensified in 2014, cooperation over Iran became difficult, and Russia and Iran pursued a deal for exporting Russian electricity and constructing power plants in Iran. Shortly after an initial framework agreement was signed in March 2015, Moscow removed its ban on selling advanced antiballistic missiles to Iran, a decision that infuriated America and Israel.

U.S. policies in Europe also produced friction. If NATO's policies in the Middle East irritated Moscow, its role in the Balkans seemed a more direct challenge.

Western Intervention in the Balkans

War erupted among Yugoslavia's national communities in 1992 (chapter 13). Yugoslavia's disintegration began as NATO was seeking a new post–Cold War mission, and Russia was emerging from the USSR's disintegration. For the rest of the decade, Russia's attitude toward NATO's role in the Balkan wars was ambivalent.

Moscow supported UN resolutions to end Serbian aggression in Bosnia in 1992, recognizing Bosnia's independence and approving UN sanctions against Serbia. However, the policy of Russian Foreign Minister Andrei Kozyrev was condemned by nationalists who accused their government of betraying Russia's "historic ally" Serbia in return for Western economic aid. Under domestic pressure, Kozyrev backpedaled and demanded an end to sanctions on Serbia. Moscow also opposed the Clinton administration's decision to use air power against Bosnian Serbs to aid the UN Protective Force (UNPROFOR). Use of NATO airpower in 1993 elicited additional Russian objections. Moscow, however, used its influence with Slobodan Milošević to persuade him to negotiate an end to the conflict and provided peacekeepers for the Implementation Force (IFOR) commanded by a Russian general who was the deputy to IFOR's NATO commander.

The Security Council did not authorize NATO's 1999 Kosovo operation. Thus, Moscow vociferously opposed airstrikes against Serbia, viewing them as violating Serbian sovereignty and part of "NATO's drive for unilateral security in Europe."[34] NATO's Kosovo operation was undertaken with little regard to Russian objections, and when then Russian Prime Minister Yevgeny Primakov, in midflight to Washington for talks, learned that the bombing campaign had begun, he ordered the plane to turn back to Moscow, dramatizing Russia's objections.

"Most Russians," Simes concludes, "were prepared to accept NATO enlargement as an unhappy but unthreatening development—until the 1999 Kosovo crisis. When NATO went to war against Serbia, despite strong Russian objections and without approval from the UN Security Council, the Russian elite and the Russian people quickly came to the conclusion that they had been profoundly misled and that NATO remained directed against them. Great powers—particularly great powers in decline—do not appreciate such demonstrations of their irrelevance."[35]

Russia and NATO Enlargement

The reason for NATO enlargement in the 1990s was not a threat from the East but a desire to spread Western values across Europe. In 2002, American public opinion even supported inviting Russia to join NATO,[36] but Washington did little to foster Russian entry into the alliance. Referring to Russia as "NATO's final frontier," Charles Kupchan argued that the West was "making a historic mistake in treating Russia as a strategic pariah."[37] Instead, Moscow joined the Shanghai Cooperation Organization in 2001 composed of China, Russia, Kazakhstan, Kyrgyzstan, Tajikistan, and Uzbekistan. Such Sino-Russian links reflected a common aversion to American hegemony and potential opportunities for trade.

Both Georgia and Ukraine experienced "color revolutions" that prompted them to seek NATO admission, and Ukrainian soldiers joined U.S. forces in Iraq after 2003. After President George W. Bush advocated inviting Ukraine and Georgia to join NATO, Putin, who had been invited to the 2008 NATO summit, threatened to boycott the meeting if invitations were extended to them. The prodemocracy revolutions in Georgia and Ukraine raised Russo-American tensions. Both countries were strategically situated near Russia, and Ukraine hosted Russia's Black Sea fleet in Crimea.

The "Color Revolutions" Georgia was the site of the "Rose Revolution" (so called because its supporters brought roses with them to Georgia's parliament). Mikheil Saakashvili, a Columbia Law School graduate, was elected Georgia's president after a bloodless coup in 2003. He introduced market-oriented economic principles, supported democratic reforms, and sought to reestablish Georgia's control over the provinces of South Ossetia and Abkhazia, whose 1990 secession from Georgia had been aided by Russia.

In a 1991 referendum, Abkhazia elected to remain part of the USSR. After the USSR's disintegration, Abkhaz leaders had sought a federation in which Georgians and Abkhazians would share power. Georgia refused and in 1992 tried to impose its authority on the province by force. Russia responded by defending the Abkhazians. A 1994 treaty allowed 3,000 peacekeepers (mainly Russian) to oversee a ceasefire, and a 2014 treaty gave Russia control of Abkhazia's foreign and security policies. Violence also flared in South

Ossetia in 1991 to 1992. After a Russian-mediated ceasefire, South Ossetia remained independent. After another war (2004), Georgia took control of Georgian-populated areas in South Ossetia.

Saakashvili's efforts to regain Georgia's "lost" provinces and take his country into NATO earned the animosity of Russia's leaders who saw him as part of a U.S. effort to reduce Moscow's regional influence. Washington advised Saakashvili to temper his anti-Russian rhetoric, but he overplayed his hand by invading South Ossetia in August 2008. The operation was a fiasco. Russia intervened and supported South Ossetian and Abhazian independence. Declared President Medvedev, "In accordance with the Constitution and the federal laws, as President of the Russian Federation it is my duty to protect the lives and dignity of Russian citizens wherever they may be."[38]

Washington provided verbal support for Georgia and suspended the NATO-Russia Council after the war but did little more. A subsequent EU report blamed Georgia for the war. Russian leaders rejected U.S. protests against Moscow's intervention, reasoning that Washington had supported the independence of Serbia's province of Kosovo. Why, they argued, should Russia not do the same in Georgia? Russian leaders also made it clear they wanted Saakashvili's removal, and after Georgia's defeat many Georgians agreed. Allegations of corruption and authoritarianism contributed to his electoral defeat in 2012.

Although NATO had accepted Georgia's Individual Partnership Action Plan (IPAP) in 2006, and a 2008 referendum indicated popular support for joining NATO, its members turned down the country's request for a Membership Action Plan (MAP) in 2014, offering only a vague cooperation "package." The 2008 Russo-Georgian war and the later Ukraine crisis suggested that Georgian admission to NATO would infuriate Russia, and in May 2014, President Obama indicated there were no plans to admit Georgia or Ukraine to NATO. Georgia's relations with Russia remained tense after their war and Russia's support for the independence of Abkhazia and South Ossetia.

Some have viewed Washington's passivity toward Russian support for independent Abkhazia and South Ossetia as emboldening President Putin to annex Crimea in 2014. Critics also claim that Obama's willingness to compromise on America's proposed European missile-defense system constituted appeasement. From Moscow's perspective, however, the missile-defense system was another reason to resist America's eastward thrust.

Missile Defense The George W. Bush administration believed that Iran's nuclear ambitions posed dangers to America and its allies that required missile defense. In 2001, Washington declared that the Cold War doctrine of "mutual assured destruction" was obsolete and then abrogated the ABM treaty, straining relations with its NATO allies and Russia. Radar sites for the proposed missile-defense system ("Ground-based Midcourse Defense") were to be deployed in America, Britain, and the Czech Republic and interceptor sites in Poland. Europeans were divided over the proposal for several reasons. The system was under U.S. not NATO command; it failed to cover southeastern Europe; and it was oriented toward intercepting Iranian intercontinental ballistic missiles (ICBMs) targeting America rather than shorter-range missiles aimed at Europe.

Russian leaders denounced the proposed system, arguing it violated the NATO-Russia Founding Act prohibiting permanent military deployments in former Warsaw Pact countries. Moscow also claimed it would undermine Russian security by eroding Russia's ability to retaliate against a U.S. attack, especially if the system were later expanded. Washington responded that the proposed system was too small to be of value against Russia's numerous nuclear weapons and was only intended to provide protection from third parties, notably Iran.

Initially Putin sought a compromise involving a joint NATO-Russian mobile ABM. In 2007, Moscow offered to give NATO access to information from radar sites in Gabala, Azerbaijan (leased by Russia after the Soviet collapse), and Krasnodar Krai, Russia, rendering radar sites in Eastern Europe unnecessary and establishing a joint Russian-NATO system. But his proposed compromise could not protect all of Europe.

Candidate Obama had opposed missile defense as expensive and untested. As president, he announced that America would for go radar sites in Europe but was forced to retreat in the face of charges by members of Congress that he was capitulating to Russia. Poland and the Czech Republic were embarrassed because they had agreed to America's proposal despite strong domestic opposition. Washington then announced a new proposal—the U.S.-European Phased Adaptive Approach (EPAA) located in Europe

🔑 KEY DOCUMENT
The Phases of the Proposed NATO Missile Defense

Phase 1 (2011 timeframe)—Addresses regional ballistic missile threats to our European Allies and our deployed personnel and their families by deploying a land-based AN/TPY-2 radar and existing Aegis BMD-capable ships equipped with proven SM-3 Block IA interceptors. . . .

Phase 2 (2015 timeframe)—After appropriate testing, we will deploy a more capable version of the SM-3 interceptor (Block IB). We will also add a land-based SM-3 ballistic missile defense interceptor site, which Romania has agreed to host, in order to expand the defended area against short- and medium-range missile threats. . . .

Phase 3 (2018 timeframe)—After development and testing are complete,

we will deploy a more advanced SM-3 interceptor (Block IIA) and add a second land-based SM-3 site, which Poland agreed to host in October 2009, to counter short-, medium-, and intermediate-range missile threats. . . .

Phase 4 (2020 timeframe)—After development and testing are complete, we will deploy the SM-3 Block IIB interceptor to enhance our ability to counter medium- and intermediate-range missiles and potential future ICBM threats to the United States from the Middle East.

Source: U.S. Department of State, United States European Phased Adaptive Approach, May 3, 2011, http://www.state .gov/t/avc/rls/162447.htm.

and at sea to provide coverage for all of NATO but limited to protection from shorter-range missiles. It would be implemented in four phases. "Each phase would add new capabilities to the overall system," and "it was precisely this adaptability that worried Moscow."[39]

At its 2010 summit, NATO approved the revised proposal, which elicited fewer Russian objectives than the earlier proposal for fixed-missile defense in the Czech Republic and Poland. Obama justified the proposal to Moscow as a way to reduce Senate opposition to the New START treaty. Initially, it appeared Moscow was prepared to accept the revised proposal. Russia was invited to participate in the system by sharing its radars and Western intelligence, and the NATO-Russia Council began to regard missile defense as a potential focus for NATO-Russian cooperation.

Russia's envoy to NATO suggested a joint missile-defense system, integrating Russia within it. This would make Russian missile-defense forces responsible for protecting some areas of Europe, a condition unacceptable to NATO. Instead, NATO proposed two separate systems that would share information. The Russians then demanded a binding agreement that the system could not be used against Russian nuclear forces and would not develop a future anti-ICBM capability. However, the Senate's Resolution of Advice and Consent to Ratification of the New START treaty explicitly prohibited legal limitations on missile defense without its consent. Russian leaders remained wary partly owing to conflicting statements by U.S. officials about the purpose and scope of the project and argued that Iran lacked the missiles the system was designed to intercept.

American unwillingness to guarantee that the missile-defense system would not undermine Russia's deterrent reflected the impact of U.S. domestic politics on a president who did not wish to be criticized as weak. Russian defense officials opposed the U.S. plan and tested a new ICBM designed to overcome the EPAA. As Moscow examined the EPAA, its concern grew because "Phase 3 entailed deployment of interceptors along Russia's borders in Poland" and "Phase 4 was explicitly designed to intercept ICBMs, which formed the backbone of Russia's strategic deterrent." Thus, "Moscow feared that, even if the Obama administration was committed to working with Russia to find a common position, once the EPAA was in place a future U.S. administration could use it as a platform for building a larger, more capable system that would pose a threat to Russian ICBMs."[40] Washington's refusal to provide Moscow with the guarantee it sought left Russia angry and suspicious.

Ukraine Ukraine was the most important of the post-Soviet states because of its size and strategic location on the Black Sea and Russia's western border and was thus wooed by both Washington and Moscow. Its first president, Leonid Kravchuk, was unable to end the precipitous decline in his nation's economy. His successor, Leonid Kuchma, was pro-Russian. Pro-Russian Viktor Yanukovich won Ukraine's 2004 presidential election, but EU observers, decrying electoral fraud, claimed his opponent Viktor Yushchenko was the winner. The Internet helped mobilize large-scale demonstrations that triggered Ukraine's "Orange Revolution" (so called because of the orange-colored shirts worn by protesters). A second election further divided the country. Yanukovich drew support from ethnic Russians in southeastern Ukraine, while those living in western Ukraine who favored closer relations with the EU and NATO supported Yushchenko. Yushchenko triumphed, aided by financial aid from Washington to nongovernmental groups that backed him.

MAP 14.2   Distribution of Ethnic Russians in Ukraine

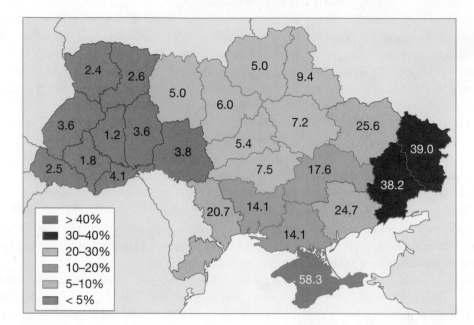

Source: Data from the All-Ukranian Population Census 2001, http://2001.ukrcensus.gov.ua/eng/results/general/nationality.

Dissension within Ukraine's leadership along with the global economic crisis, however, eroded Yushchenko's popularity. Yanukovich thus won a rematch in 2010 and reoriented his country toward Moscow. It appeared in 2009 that Ukraine was on a path toward NATO membership, but with Yanukovich's election the issue of NATO membership was closed for the time being. As noted earlier, President Putin dissuaded Yanukovich from accepting the EU's Eastern Partnership, beginning a chain of events that climaxed in the most dangerous confrontation between Russia and the West since the Cold War. Yanukovich's overthrow threatened to push Western influence to Russia's border, a nightmare for Putin and his aspirations to restore Russia's influence in the former Soviet republics.

Putin's reaction was swift, sending troops into the Ukrainian region of Crimea in March 2014 and sponsoring a pseudo-referendum about whether Crimea wished to secede from Ukraine and join Russia. Putin declared that Western support of Kosovo's independence was a precedent for Crimean secession from Ukraine. Unlike Crimea, however, Kosovo became a sovereign state. Russian intimidation made the outcome of the referendum meaningless, and the referendum did not offer voters the alternative of remaining part of Ukraine. Finally, it ignored both the 1975 Final Act of the Conference on Security and Cooperation in Europe, which guaranteed the "inviolability of borders" in Europe, and the 1994 Budapest Memorandum on Security Assurance for Ukraine in which Moscow guaranteed Ukrainian sovereignty.

🔑 KEY DOCUMENT
1994 Budapest Memorandum

1. The Russian Federation, the United Kingdom of Great Britain and Northern Ireland and the United States of America reaffirm their commitment to Ukraine, in accordance with the principles of the Final Act of the Conference on Security and Cooperation in Europe, to respect the independence and sovereignty and the existing borders of Ukraine;

2. The Russian Federation, the United Kingdom of Great Britain and Northern Ireland and the United States of America reaffirm their obligation to refrain from the threat or use of force against the territorial integrity or political independence of Ukraine. . . . [41]

Source: "Budapest Memorandums on Security Assurances, 1994," Council on Foreign Relations, December 5, 1994, http://www.cfr.org/arms-control-disarmament-and-nonproliferation/budapest-memorandums-security-assurances-1994/p32484.

Moscow claimed that 97 percent of Crimeans voted to secede from Ukraine and join Russia, leading America's UN ambassador, Samantha Power, to comment acidly, "I missed the day in school where self-determination was defined as Russia-determination."[42] After annexing Crimea, Putin declared that it had "always been an integral part of Russia in the hearts and minds of people." Claiming he had acted to protect Crimea from "Russophobes and neo-Nazis," he recalled the humiliating collapse of the USSR: "Millions of Russians went to bed in one country and woke up abroad. Overnight, they were minorities in the former Soviet republics, and the Russian people became one of the biggest—if not the biggest— divided nation in the world." The West "cheated us again and again, made decisions behind our back, presenting us with completed facts. That's the way it was with the expansion of NATO in the east, with the deployment of military infrastructure at our borders" but its support for Yanukovich's ouster had crossed "a red line."[43]

Following an intense propaganda campaign reminiscent of the Cold War, Moscow conducted military maneuvers on Ukraine's border, fostered pro-Russian demonstrations in southeastern Ukraine, and demanded that Kiev adopt a federal system to give pro-Russians greater autonomy. Moscow sent heavy weapons into Ukraine and alarmed Ukrainian leaders by conducting additional military maneuvers. U.S. and European leaders responded by isolating Russia politically. Washington suspended an agreement to exchange Russian and American nuclear scientists and cooperate in designing a planetary asteroid defense. The West also suspended Moscow's membership in the G-8 economic group (the G-7 plus Russia), cancelling a G-8 summit planned for Sochi, Russia, and NATO-Russian cooperation. "It is not appropriate to invade a country and at the end of a barrel of a gun dictate what you are trying to achieve," declared Secretary Kerry.[44]

The West then imposed economic sanctions on Russian government officials and banks, freezing their assets in America and Europe. Even modest sanctions produced concern in Russian banking and business circles. Although Russia's currency reserves and low debt allowed it to buy time, its economy was stagnating. "It's a catastrophe for Ukraine and for Russia," observed a Russian scholar. "The problem is that quite a few people in Russia don't understand the consequences. They believe the country is strong and can do whatever it wants to do."[45]

Responding to criticism that he had been naïve, President Obama argued: "The fact that Russia felt compelled to go in militarily and lay bare these violations of international law indicates less influence, not more." Russia was a "problem" and "regional power" but not America's "No. 1 national security threat."[46] "We're making it clear that there are consequences for their actions," he declared. "We'll continue to make clear to Russia that further provocations will achieve nothing except to further isolate Russia and diminish its place in the world."[47]

Russian pressure persisted. Even as Moscow denied involvement, masked soldiers without identifying insignia, known as "Green Men," organized protests, occupied official buildings, and distributed weapons to Ukrainian separatists. One uniformed man admitted he was a "lieutenant colonel of the Russian Army,"[48] and Moscow sought to cover up the burial of Russian soldiers killed in Ukraine. Putin demanded Ukraine cease efforts to reimpose its authority on the country's southeastern region, leading Secretary Kerry to describe Russia's actions as "an illegal and illegitimate effort to destabilize a sovereign state" and "a contrived pretest for military intervention, just as we saw in Crimea."[49]

"It's hard to fathom that groups of armed men sprang forward from the population in eastern Ukraine and systematically began to occupy government facilities," wrote NATO commander General Philip Breedlove. "What is happening in eastern Ukraine is a military operation that is well planned and organized, and we assess that it is being carried out at the direction of Russia."[50] A former U.S. counterintelligence

MAP **14.3**   Crimea

officer described Russia's tactics as "special war"—"an amalgam of espionage, subversion, even forms of terrorism to attain political ends without going to war in any conventional sense."[51]

Russian media referred to Ukrainian separatists as "supporters of federalization,"[52] a euphemism for those who wished to secede from the country or establish a system in which they could veto Ukrainian policies. Ukraine's leaders discussed the possibility of a more federal structure for the country, but its prime minister called Russia's desire to federalize Ukraine a ploy to place pro-Russian governors in power to impede Ukrainian policies.

Russian leaders publicly discussed the prospect of civil war, contending that Ukraine's Russophone population was suffering abuse, a claim rejected in a UN report. Putin also announced that Russia's parliament had given him the "right to use armed forces in Ukraine." "The question," he declared, "is to ensure the rights and interests of the Russian southeast. It's new Russia. Kharkiv, Lugansk, Donetsk, Odessa were not part of Ukraine in czarist times, they were transferred in 1920. Why? God knows."[53] The same day, Kerry and Foreign Minister Lavrov agreed on steps to de-escalate tension: "All sides must refrain from any violence, intimidation or provocative action," and "All illegal armed groups must be disarmed; all illegally seized buildings must be returned to legitimate owners; all illegally occupied streets, squares and other public places in Ukrainian cities and towns must be vacated."[54]

The agreement was stillborn. Russian military maneuvers near Ukraine continued, and Moscow's support for separatist elements intensified. In city after city—Slovyanka, Luhansk, and Donetsk—Ukrainian security forces were unable to dislodge pro-Russian militias. In May 2014, pro-Russian militias held illegal and unsupervised referendums in cities in southeast Ukraine. America, the EU, and Ukraine's government denounced these as illegal, and, although events in Ukraine increased President Putin's domestic popularity, most Ukrainians, including Russian speakers, favored a united country within its existing borders.[55] In the eastern region of Donetsk, only 5 percent sought independence and only 27 percent wanted to become Russian.[56] Moscow further escalated its pressure by increasing the price of gas exports to Ukraine a third higher than it had previously offered, claiming it was owed payment for previous sales and demanding to be paid in advance for new deliveries. Implicit was a warning that Russia might cut off energy exports to Ukraine as it had in 2006 and 2009.

Responding to Russia's failure to abide by the Kerry-Lavrov agreement, America and the EU announced new sanctions against Ukrainian separatists and individual Russians including Igor Sechin, an associate of Putin and chief executive of Rosneft, Russia's state-owned oil company. Other Russian banks and companies including several involved in oil and gas construction were also placed on the sanctions list. President Obama described the sanctions as "the next stage in a calibrated effort to change Russia's behavior."[57]

Washington sought to work with the EU in designing sanctions, but even after they were imposed, Western oil firms continued investing in Russia, and several including ExxonMobil, BP, and Total of France signed contracts to explore for shale oil in Russia, expand Russia's offshore oil drilling, and build a liquefied natural gas plant for exports to Asia. "My message to Russia is simple," declared Total's chief executive, "it is business as usual."[58]

The prospect of a Russian invasion receded in May 2014, after Putin advised postponing referendums in eastern Ukraine, welcomed Ukraine's presidential election, and endorsed a Ukrainian national dialogue. "We are interested that on our western borders we have peace and calm in Ukraine. We are today working with the people in power, and after the election we will work with the newly elected structure."[59] Russia also reduced its price for natural gas after Ukraine paid a down payment on what it owed. Nevertheless, Washington remained cautious. "We believe the situation continues to be a crisis," declared a senior adviser. "There are people dying on a regular basis in eastern and southern Ukraine, given the violence perpetrated and initiated by separatist factions there. So by no means are we out of the woods on Ukraine."[60]

Petro Poroshenko won Ukraine's presidential election, promising to pursue European values and end corruption. In Donetsk, only 2 percent of those registered cast votes, and separatist resistance continued. Following the election, Poroshenko proposed a unilateral ceasefire, and Putin asked Russia's parliament to rescind its authorization to use force in Ukraine.

President Obama, nevertheless, warned Putin that Russia faced new sanctions if it continued undermining Ukraine. "What we're focused here on is not just the words of the Russian president, though we welcome them," declared the White House press secretary. "What we're focused on are the actions."[61] Putin's shift from confrontation may have been due to economic sanctions, diplomatic isolation, and NATO's revival, or, as NATO's secretary-general thought, Putin was playing a "double game" and his shift was "pure tactics."[62] Moscow was "creating facts on the ground" with the goal of building "structural guarantees against Ukraine's potential NATO accession."[63] In doing so, however, Moscow lost control over the separatists. The rebel movements remained uncoordinated despite the presence of Russian commanders and appeared unwilling to heed Putin's effort to restrain them.

The ceasefire was short-lived, and Poroshenko renewed Ukraine's military effort to reoccupy its eastern region. As government forces advanced, Putin again warned that Russia might intervene. Then, on July 17, 2014, a sophisticated Russian Buk missile launcher manned by separatists trained by Russians destroyed Malaysian Airlines flight MH17, killing 298 people, an event "unambiguously terrifying and unforgivable."[64] A half-hour later, a separatist leader was overheard informing a Russian intelligence officer that "we have shot down a plane."[65] Thereafter, Russia prevented a UN investigation of the incident.

As Ukrainian forces encircled pro-Russian militias in August, Russia's intervention escalated, forcing Ukraine's army to retreat. Putin bragged: "If I wanted to I could take Kiev in two weeks." He also discussed opening negotiations about "the statehood of Ukraine's southeast,"[66] that is, the self-proclaimed republics in Donetsk and Luhansk. Within days, Poroshenko agreed to a ceasefire (Minsk I) on terms proposed by Putin including a buffer zone at the Russo-Ukrainian border, the disbanding of militias, Ukraine's protection of the Russian language, and political decentralization. In October, pro-European political parties won elections to Ukraine's parliament though few votes were cast in pro-Russian areas. Moscow then backed the plan of separatists to hold local elections earlier than had been agreed upon in September by the government and separatists.

As in Georgia, the ceasefire in Ukraine produced a "frozen conflict" in which political issues remained unresolved. Russia continued aiding Ukrainian separatists by resupplying them with arms and providing "volunteers." On-and-off hostilities between Ukraine and separatists persisted including fighting for the Donetsk airport. Thus, some U.S. officials proposed sending arms and advisers to Ukraine despite opposition from Europeans, notably Chancellor Merkel. Then, in February 2015, another ceasefire was declared (Minsk II) similar to that reached earlier. Whether Putin had achieved what he sought—annexing Crimea, destabilizing Ukraine, fostering the country's decentralization, and increasing his domestic popularity—or whether he wished to avoid additional sanctions and the costs of overt military intervention was unclear.

Economic Issues and Human Rights

Confrontation over Ukraine and imposition of sanctions on Russia make it apparent that economic issues were difficult to isolate from political and security matters. When the "reset" began, Russia's foreign minister pointed to economic relations as a potentially fruitful area of cooperation. Russia is the world's sixth largest economy and, until overtaken by America, was the world's leading energy producer. Unlike U.S. links with Europe and China, however, U.S.-Russian economic ties were limited, accounting for just 3 percent of America's total foreign investment and about one-half of 1 percent of U.S. exports in 2012. Much of that investment was in Russia's energy sector, which was of declining interest to American investors owing to the growth in U.S. energy production. Despite their leaders' promise to modernize Russia's business practices and improve the investment climate, complex Russian regulations and Moscow's meddling in Western corporations trying to invest or export limited modernization. In turn, Western criticism of Russia's human rights record lessened Russian interest in Western investment and trade.

Nevertheless, PepsiCo invested $1 billion in Russia, employing some 40,000, and Boeing invested $7 billion that it planned to increase to $27 billion by 2021. Russia also sought to attract U.S. venture capital to build a high-tech center and reduce dependence on energy exports. Moscow was especially interested in developing its eastern territories, and Putin noted in 2013 that like America, Russia would pivot toward Asia. Moscow began to participate in the annual Asia-Pacific Economic Cooperation forum that it hosted in Vladivostok in 2012, and Rosneft arranged to increase oil exports to China while Russia's state gas company, Gazprom, decided to build a natural gas terminal to increase energy exports to Japan and a pipeline for gas to China to replace European markets.

Human rights concerns also intruded following irregularities in Russia's 2011 legislative elections and the "arranged" reelection of Putin as Russia's president in 2012. Both triggered anti-Putin demonstrations in Moscow. Russian fears of political chaos and foreign foes reinforced Putin's domestic support, and he demonized America to deflect domestic unrest. After Secretary Clinton criticized Russia's 2011 election as "flawed," Putin accused her of "sending signals" to his Russian adversaries, blaming America for encouraging antigovernment protests. Putin also sent the U.S. Agency for International Development packing in September 2012. USAID had contributed almost $3 billion in foreign aid to Russia in previous decades, but Putin claimed that political motives influenced how it distributed the funding. Moscow also clamped down on foreign-funded nongovernmental organizations, especially those advocating democracy and human rights, making them register as "foreign agents" and claiming they interfered in Russia's domestic affairs. Russian authorities raided the Moscow office of Amnesty International and took legal action against a Russian group for engaging in "political activities" after it had hosted an American diplomat.

U.S. support enabled Russia to join the World Trade Organization (WTO) in 2012, the last major state to do so. By entering the WTO, Russia was entitled to "permanent normal trade relations status" with other members. Thus, in December 2012, Congress ended Cold War restrictions on trade with Russia, including the Jackson-Vanik amendment. While ending trade restrictions, however, Congress denounced Russian human rights abuses. "The Obama administration," declared Senator Orrin Hatch

(R-UT), "has not articulated a clear and coherent strategy regarding Russia. Instead, they ask Congress to simply pass permanent normal trade relations and remove Russia from long-standing human rights law, while ignoring Russia's rampant corruption, theft of U.S. intellectual property, poor human rights record and adversarial foreign policies."[67]

President Obama did not want human rights conditions attached to the trade bill, but Congress imposed sanctions on individuals linked to the imprisonment and death of Russian lawyer Sergei Magnitsky. Magnitsky, representing the London-based Hermitage Capital Management fund, had claimed that Russian tax officials were corrupt. He was subsequently arrested for tax evasion and died of "pancreatitis." Human rights groups concluded he had been beaten in prison and denied medical care. Under the "Magnitsky Act" Washington froze the assets of and refused visas to eighteen Russians involved in abusing human rights, triggering a tit-for-tat sequence. Russian leaders retaliated by banning eighteen prominent Americans from visiting or investing in Russia. They also banned the adoption of Russian orphans by Americans, erected barriers to U.S. meat imports, and claimed that America's 2012 election had been marked by irregularities. Finally, a Russian judge acquitted the only official to be tried for Magnitsky's death in prison.

Moscow's prosecution of prominent activists like Alexei Navalny, an anticorruption blogger, also raised concern about human rights. After Navalny's imprisonment for protesting Putin's 2012 inauguration, Amnesty International declared him a "prisoner of conscience." Other human rights issues included the mysterious deaths of writer Alexander Litvinenko, journalist Anna Politovskaya, human rights activist Galina Starovoitova, and anti-Putin activist Boris Nemtsov. Russia also imprisoned the former owners of Russia's Yukos oil company and members of the Russian band Pussy Riot who had shouted "Mother Mary please drive Putin away" in a Moscow cathedral. Shortly before the 2014 Winter Olympic Games in Sochi, President Putin signed into law a homophobic bill, prompting President Obama to declare he had "no patience for countries that try to treat gays or lesbians or transgendered persons in ways that intimidate them or are harmful to them."[68] After Moscow passed laws to prevent public demonstrations, the White House called on Moscow "to ensure that the universal human rights and fundamental freedoms of all its citizens, including the freedoms of speech and assembly, are protected and respected."[69]

FUTURE: CHURCHILL'S "RIDDLE WRAPPED IN A MYSTERY INSIDE AN ENIGMA"

Although America and Russia had divergent interests that made it unlikely they would become close friends, the immediate post–Cold War era revealed there were some areas where cooperation was possible.

Syria and Iran

In the case of Syria, cooperation proved difficult, but both countries sought to limit Iran's WMD program.

Policy Options

a. *Pursue American unilateralism in Syria.* Washington could feel compelled to intervene in Syria's civil war for humanitarian reasons, to prevent the spread of violence to neighboring states, or if Islamic extremists threatened to take power. Russia opposed foreign intervention in Syria, and Putin might use U.S. intervention in Syria to justify overt aggression in Ukraine. Moreover, after lengthy wars in Iraq and Afghanistan, unilateral U.S. involvement in Syria's civil war would provoke domestic opposition and congressional resistance and Pentagon reluctance owing to budget and manpower constraints.

An opportunity to invoke NATO solidarity arose with Syrian aircraft entering Turkish airspace, but NATO showed no appetite for intervening. Another opportunity arose after Syria used chemical weapons against civilians, but Obama failed to carry out his threat to use force, instead choosing to join Russia in persuading Assad to surrender chemical weapons.

b.   *Pursue Russo-American cooperation in Syria and Iran.* Despite differences over Assad's future, the removal of Syria's chemical weapons illustrated that Moscow and Washington could cooperate if their interests converged. Washington has also moved closer to Moscow's position that Assad's future should be left to the outcome of negotiations. One possibility is collaborating to promote a moderate successor to Assad. Moscow fears the instability caused by Islamist or democratic ideas. Moscow and Washington both wish to contain Islamic extremism, which might spread to Russia's Muslim regions or in post-Soviet Central Asia. Russia's 2015 military intervention in Syria to aid Assad was partly justified by such concerns.

Both Moscow and Washington fear the destabilizing impact of an Israeli attack if Iran appears determined to "go nuclear." If America were drawn into such a conflict, Moscow would view it as another instance of U.S. "adventurism" near Russia's borders.

Syrian President Assad: caught between Washington and Moscow

RJ Matson, CagleCartoons.com

Missile Defense

For Russia, Washington's unwillingness to abandon plans for an antimissile system in Europe remained a nettlesome issue in relations with America. The administration enjoyed greater flexibility regarding missile defense after the Senate ratified the New START treaty, and President Putin indicated his willingness to negotiate additional arms reductions if a solution could be found to differences about missile defense. Missile defense might become an area of U.S.-Russian cooperation, but there are points of contention that must be resolved first.

Policy Options

a. *Give up the idea of missile defense.* If Washington is prepared to destroy Iran's nuclear capability if that country acquires WMD, why is a missile defense in Europe necessary? The first phase of the system was completed in 2011 with deployment of U.S. naval vessels with interceptors in the Mediterranean. Cancelling the entire project would be difficult considering the resources already invested, the sense of betrayal by allies that had approved the EPAA, and the charges of appeasement that would be directed at the administration by political foes. Moreover, Washington cannot give Moscow a guarantee that the system would not undermine Russia's deterrence strategy because of the Senate's prohibition in the New Start Treaty.

b. *Accept Russian offers of a unified system, including Russian and Azeri radars.* Even without the legal guarantee Russia seeks, there are possibilities for U.S.-Russian cooperation, including a jointly operated radar in Russia, sharing early-warning information, transparency limits on numbers of interceptors, joint missile-defense exercises, and joint threat assessments. Whatever the arrangements, the key would be to include Russia in missile defense.

c. *Eliminate EPAA's phase 4.* Altering the plan without a plausible excuse would lead to charges of presidential weakness and domestic partisan conflict. North Korea's nuclear and missile tests and its threat to attack America, however, provided the Obama administration with an excuse to cancel the final phase of the EPAA. In March 2013, Washington announced it had canceled this phase to save money and would deploy additional missile interceptors at Fort Greely, Alaska, to enhance missile defense against North Korea. Moscow had indicated that its major concern was the fourth phase of European missile defense. Nevertheless, to preclude domestic controversy, a Pentagon spokesman insisted that the "missile defense decisions Secretary [Chuck] Hagel announced were in no way about Russia."[70]

Ukraine

Missile defense became entangled with Russian objections to NATO expansion. Russian pressure on Ukraine aimed to thwart U.S. and European efforts to draw that country westward. Was the Ukraine crisis Russia's fault, as most Americans believe? Political scientist John Mearsheimer, who had earlier urged Ukraine to retain nuclear weapons after the USSR disintegrated, argues that American blindness to Russian interests and Washington's effort to export liberal values were responsible for the crisis rather than Russian aggressiveness. "The taproot of the trouble is NATO enlargement, the central element of a larger strategy to move Ukraine out of Russia's orbit and integrate it into the West. At the same time, the EU's expansion eastward and the West's backing of the prodemocracy movement in Ukraine—beginning with the Orange Revolution in 2004—were critical elements, too. Since the mid-1990s, Russian leaders have adamantly opposed NATO enlargement, and in recent years, they have made it clear that they would not stand by while their strategically important neighbor turned into a Western bastion." For Putin, the overthrow of Yanukovich "was the final straw."[71]

Unlike Mearsheimer, Russian specialist Jeffrey Mankoff argues that Russian policy toward Ukraine "is at once a replay and an escalation of tactics that the Kremlin has used in recent decades to maintain its influence across the domains of the former Soviet Union" by supporting "breakaway ethnic regions" in Moldova, Georgia, and Azerbaijan. "Moscow's meddling has created so-called frozen conflicts in these states. In which the splinter territories remain beyond the control of the central governments and the local de facto authorities enjoy Russian protection and influence."[72] For this reason Alexander Motyl, a Russian specialist, concludes that "Kennan's case for containing Russia makes just as much sense now"[73] as it did during the Cold War, especially to reassure NATO's Baltic members.

Policy Options

a. *Threaten force.* It would be difficult for Washington to threaten force to undo Russia's annexation of Crimea. The threat would not be credible owing to Moscow's regional military superiority and the growing quality of Russian forces as reflected in "hybrid warfare" of irregular forces, cyberattacks, "volunteers," and propaganda against Ukraine and its support for right- and leftwing extremist parties in the EU. Russia's defense budget grew from $29 billion in 2000 to $81 billion in 2015[74] owing to what Putin termed "methodical attempts to undermine the strategic balance"[75] reflected in NATO's eastward expansion and America's missile-defense system. Arming Ukraine might lead to additional Russian escalation.

Following the Cold War, U.S. troop strength in Europe declined from 400,000 to 67,000. Declared a military analyst, "The limited ground forces in Europe are not designed to suddenly project power against Russia in a number of days."[76] The symbolic U.S. ground commitment in the Baltic region and NATO's proposed rapid-response force and military exercises in western Ukraine provided reassurance but would not stop Moscow if it again resorted to hybrid warfare. Poland argued that Russia's behavior made the 1997 guarantee of not stationing NATO troops in the east obsolete, but other NATO members remain skittish about a military presence that might provoke Russia. U.S. military intervention would risk a crisis that could spiral out of control. Thus, President Obama declared: "We are not going to be getting into a military excursion in Ukraine," and "I think even the Ukrainians would acknowledge that for us to engage Russia militarily would not be appropriate and wouldn't be good for Ukraine either."[77]

b. *Accept Russia's annexation of Crimea and negotiate Ukraine's future.* President Obama proceeded cautiously during the Crimean crisis. While imposing sanctions, he argued, "we can calibrate our response based on whether Russia chooses to escalate or de-escalate the situation."[78] The September 2014 ceasefire in Ukraine "on terms favorable"[79] to Putin made a peaceful resolution to the crisis possible. Thereafter, Ukraine agreed to grant the Donetsk and Luhansk regions a special status including Russian as an official language, election to local councils, and funding for economic development. Russian support for Ukrainian separatists, however, did not cease, and additional talks were held in Minsk, Belarus, in February 2015, resulting in another ceasefire.

c. *Ratchet up economic sanctions.* A former State Department official warned, "Until Putin and his circle pay a real price for their actions—and I think the U.S. and E.U. can impose such a price—the Kremlin won't see a reason to stop."[80] Several rounds of sanctions hurt Russia's economy by barring investment in its energy and defense sectors and targeting Russian banks. America's growing energy production may provide an alternative source for Europe. Increased U.S. energy production, notably shale oil and gas, had reduced world energy prices, dramatically cutting Moscow's export earnings and the value of its currency. As a former energy official on the National Security Council noted, "In World War II, we were the arsenal of democracy. I think we're going to become the arsenal of energy."[81]

Sanctions alone were unlikely to reverse Russia's annexation of Crimea. Although the U.S. public supported sanctions, American firms like McDonalds, Visa, MasterCard, Hearst, and Walt Disney were victims of Russian retaliation. Washington was also concerned lest sanctions make cooperation with Moscow on other issues impossible and produce friction with the EU for which economic costs of reduced trade with Moscow were more painful than for America.

Economic Relations and Human Rights

Economic relations cannot be isolated from other issues, and U.S. businesses were concerned that human rights disputes and trade sanctions would sour U.S.-Russian trade.

Policy Options

a. *Decouple trade and human rights.* The conditions attached to the "Magnitsky Act" harmed U.S.-Russian relations. Russian hardliners viewed the legislation as American interference in Russia's domestic politics that excused Moscow's nationalist impulses. The problem, however, lay in domestic U.S. politics.

b. *Joint ventures in energy.* Since the Cold War, Russia has relied on energy exports for economic growth, and Western firms have technology needed to reverse Russia's diminishing reserves of accessible oil and gas. Russia's energy industry was privatized after the USSR's collapse, but Putin's government ousted the "oligarchs," transferring their assets to state-owned firms run by Putin's friends. Today, two state companies, Rosneft and Gazprom, monopolize Russia's energy production.

Deals with Moscow are risky. In 2006, Russia forced Shell to sell offshore oil assets to Gazprom after it had spent $20 billion on the project. British oil giant BP established a joint venture, TNK-BP, in 2003, the largest foreign investment in Russia to that time, but in 2008, Russian police raided the offices of BP and TNK-BP and forced the British chief executive of TNK-BP to flee the country. In 2011, BP signed an agreement with Rosneft to develop Russia's Arctic oil resources, but that arrangement collapsed under political pressure. BP was forced to sell its 50 percent stake in TNK-BP to Rosneft in 2012. Shortly after, Rosneft purchased the remainder of TNK-BP from a group of Russian billionaires. Rosneft then turned to ExxonMobil to help explore for Arctic oil after the company agreed to give Rosneft assets elsewhere in the world, aiding it to diversify internationally. Such ventures, if successful, may improve U.S.-Russian economic relations.

CONCLUSION: DID THE "RESET" SUCCEED?

Putin remained a mystery to American leaders. "The West," according to an American analyst, "has focused on the notion that Putin is a pragmatic realist who will cooperate with us whenever there are sufficient common interests. We let that belief overshadow his stated goal of revising a post–Cold War settlement in which Moscow lost control over significant territory and watched as the West expanded its domain."[82] Dennis Blair, former director of national intelligence, declared bluntly that U.S. presidents "should think of dictators like they think of domestic politicians of the other party, opponents who smile on occasion when it suits their purposes, and cooperate when it is to their advantage, but who are at heart trying to push the U.S. out of power, will kneecap the United States if they get the chance and will only go along if the U.S. has more power than they."[83]

Putin reflects "a long tradition of Russian imperial conservatism" which combines authoritarianism with a belief that Russia is threatened by Western materialism. His ideology stresses that "Russia was a unique civilization with its own path and historical mission" and predicts "the eventual downfall of the West."[84] Its effort to create a Eurasian Union was characterized by Secretary Clinton as an attempt to "re-Sovietize" these regions.[85]

Although Russian President Dmitry Medvedev enjoyed a warm relationship with President Obama, Putin and Obama were not personally close. Unlike Medvedev, Putin did not enthuse about democratic reform, human rights, market economics, or the rule of law. He wanted Russia to recover the political

Meeting of Presidents Vladimir Putin and Barack Obama

Jason Reed/Reuters/Corbis

and economic status enjoyed by the USSR. "He's about lost power, lost glory," declared Robert Gates. "It will be very difficult to make headway as long as he's there."[86]

Obama was Moscow's preferred candidate in America's 2012 presidential election. To Moscow, Mitt Romney seemed a recycled neoconservative likely to follow George W. Bush's unilateralism. Obama's offhand remark to Medvedev that he would enjoy greater "flexibility" in dealing with missile defense after the 2012 election led critics to call the president too accommodating in foreign policy. Perhaps Moscow also believed this was the case. "Russians," wrote political scientist Ariel Cohen, "characterized the current U.S. president as a well-meaning leader who is somewhat weak and naive. While Russians view past Republican presidents as hard-nosed realists, they had their share of troubles with well-meaning Democrats. Kennedy had his Cuban missile crisis; Carter, Russia's Afghanistan invasion; and Obama, his 'reset' policy. Every time the Russians perceived a weakness in a Democrat president, they made a move—even though later they may have come to regret it."[87]

The "reset" benefited America—assisting NATO in Afghanistan and achieving the New START Treaty, which reduced U.S. defense costs while allowing Washington to modernize its nuclear arsenal. Russia also joined America in negotiating with Iran and trying to persuade North Korea to for go its nuclear ambitions. Although Moscow persisted in opposing intervention in Syria, Washington, too, had reasons to avoid intervening, and the Russo-American agreement regarding Syrian chemical weapons allowed President Obama to avoid attacking Syria and gave Putin a political victory. Thus, "whereas the United States, as a global superpower, needs Russia's help in addressing many issues, Russia needs the United States for relatively little."[88]

Moscow, too, benefited from the reset, especially the agreement to reduce nuclear warheads because economic woes made it difficult for Moscow to maintain its nuclear arsenal. America also supported Russian entry in the WTO with favorable conditions for Russian industry. But the reset did not get Russia all it sought. Although Washington revised its initial missile-defense plan and retreated from deploying that system's final phase, it did not cancel the project.

After Putin's reelection as Russia's president in 2012, relations worsened owing to differences over Syria, missile defense, and Ukraine. Moscow's willingness to grant asylum to Edward Snowden after he fled America with classified material about NSA surveillance programs strained relations to the point that Obama cancelled a scheduled summit meeting with Putin, and America withdrew from the civil society working group, a bilateral panel established as part of the reset.

Russia still seeks recognition of a sphere of interest in Eastern Europe. It seeks to be treated as an equal rather than as a has-been superpower, and its criticisms of American policies allow the leadership to profit from Russian nationalism and resentment at the collapse of the USSR. "Western policies have certainly created an environment where the Russian elite can readily portray the nation as isolated, victimized and threatened, even if the Kremlin exploits this environment opportunistically." Thus, "Russia oscillates between more cooperative and truculent positions, motivated by its desire to be a sovereign, semi-detached but equally respected part of Europe, with the need to play to the gallery at home being paramount."[89]

Both countries are nuclear powers, and mutual trust is critical. Complex and difficult issues remain: NATO's role in Eastern Europe, Afghanistan after American withdrawal, Iran, and Syria. "The low-hanging fruit has already been picked, so [cooperation] will be less substantial than before."[90] Trust was hardly evident after Russia's annexation of Crimea. Putin's position reflected "a worldview fairly widely shared among the Russian political elite, who believe that the West is out to get them," and the West "instigated the [Ukrainian] revolution to bring the country into the Western orbit despite its natural propensity to ally with Russia."[91]

The U.S. public mirrored Putin's suspicions about America. A March 2014 poll revealed Americans who viewed Russia as a "very serious threat" had risen from 11 to 29 percent in less than two years. "That's a 25-percentage point increase since 2012 and represents the highest number on that question since the break-up of the Soviet Union."[92] In addition, 68 percent had an "unfavorable" view of Putin, and a large majority favored imposing economic sanctions on Russia. As Moscow continued meddling in Ukraine, Americans and Europeans held increasingly "unfavorable" views of Russia.[93]

Did Russia's annexation of Crimea mark the beginning of a new cold war? Probably not, but, as Secretary Kerry insisted, the fact that Russia has interests in Ukraine "doesn't legitimize just taking what you want because you want it or because you're angry about the end of the Cold War or the end of the Soviet Union, or whatever it is."[94] What Crimea's annexation portended was a more confrontational future between the two and greater difficulty in cooperating at least until the Putin era in Russia ends.

An alternative possibility—originally conceived shortly after the Cold War—would be to revive the prospects for Russian economic growth and political respectability that would accompany Russia's integration into Europe. Washington's willingness to pursue this course would likely reinforce Russia's self-identity as a "normal" state and possible partner. "The good news is that on matters that are genuinely of mutual interest, Russia is ready to deal,"[95] or, at least, so it seemed until the Ukrainian crisis.

The bad news is that owing to Ukraine, U.S.-Russian cooperation on other issues became more difficult. The question of whether the Ukrainian crisis is an anomaly or the beginning of an extended era of U.S.-Russian hostility remains. Should Washington beef up its presence in Europe as it did during the Cold War and renounce the 1997 Founding Act and the 2002 NATO-Russia Council? Whatever the answers, as a former U.S. ambassador to Russia observed, "anybody who suggests we are going to disengage and let them just stew just doesn't get it. We have to deal with them."[96]

DISCUSSION QUESTIONS

1. Is there any way to persuade Moscow to return Crimea to Ukraine?

2. Is a new U.S.-Russian cold war emerging?

3. Should the United States continue to deploy a new missile defense system in Europe?

4. On what issues is U.S.-Russian cooperation most likely to prosper?

5. How should Washington deal with "frozen conflicts" such as those in Georgia and Ukraine?

6. Who or what was responsible for the original Cold War?

KEY TERMS

détente (p. 426)   frozen conflict (p. 446)

for CQ Press

Sharpen your skill with SAGE edge at **edge.sagepub.com/mansbach**

SAGE edge for Students provides a personalized approach to help you accomplish your coursework goals in an easy-to-use learning environment.

15

Conclusion

AMERICA, A WARY HEGEMON

President Obama at the West Point Commencement in May 2014, emphasizing the role of America's global leadership

Official White House Photo/Pete Souza

This text has described the trends characterizing American foreign policy in the past and present as well as future alternatives. Although President Obama campaigned as a liberal, he showed more concern for realist power and security mixed with a desire to spread liberal values. He shifted from the unilateralism of the Bush years to greater multilateralism in areas ranging from military security and the environment to concluding large-scale regional trade agreements with Asia and Europe.

Recognizing America's declining economic and political status *relative* to other major states, Obama proved cautious in using force. He used new military technologies and strategies such as drones, cyberwarfare, and Special Forces to manage complex threats cost-effectively without placing large numbers of troops in harm's way in light of public weariness with the long wars in Afghanistan and Iraq and pressures at home to reduce the budget deficit and husband available resources.

Obama also showed willingness to negotiate with foes like Iran and use multilateral processes to deal with weapons of mass destruction (WMD) threats in Syria, Iran, and North Korea. His effort to pivot to Asia and engage and contain "rising" China was undermined by Russian aggressiveness in Ukraine, sectarian strife in the Middle East, and the proliferation of dangerous terrorist groups like ISIS. The administration's effort to mediate a settlement in the Israeli-Palestinian dispute failed, while negotiations with Iran offered optimism for future relations with Tehran.

THE EVOLUTION OF AMERICAN FOREIGN POLICY BEFORE THE COLD WAR

American foreign policy underwent a dramatic shift in the 20th century after the country had already become an economic superpower. Presidents like Theodore Roosevelt and Woodrow Wilson declared their desire that America participate to a greater extent throughout the world. World War I precipitated an expansion of American interests owing to U.S. sympathy for the cause of democracy and the European balance of power. America had already become democracy's arsenal when German submarines and

Isolationism

October 1, 1941, Dr. Seuss Political Cartoons. Special Collection & Archives, UC San Diego Library

inept diplomacy brought the United States into the war in 1917. Following the war, Americans rejected the Versailles Treaty and the League of Nations and sought, as in earlier centuries, to avoid military entanglement in Europe or Asia (though not the Western Hemisphere).

American public opinion accepted what Wilson's successor, Warren Harding, advocated in Boston in May 1920: "America's present need is not heroics, but healing; not nostrums, but normalcy; not revolution, but restoration; not agitation, but adjustment; not surgery, but serenity; not the dramatic, but the dispassionate; not experiment, but equipoise; not submergence in internationality, but sustainment in triumphant nationality."[1] Americans sought to avoid involvement overseas—a desire heightened by the Great Depression—because they believed those conflicts did not affect their core interests. Instead, others were urged to emulate America's example. Although President Franklin Roosevelt had tried to persuade Americans that their fates were linked to those in Europe who were fighting Nazi tyranny, isolationism only ended after Japan bombed Pearl Harbor on December 7, 1941, bringing America into World War II.

The world changed in myriad ways after the emergence of America as a superpower in World War II. The war persuaded Americans and their leaders that they had global responsibilities, and that without their active participation in world affairs democracy and global order could not be secured. Hence, America joined the UN, sought to restore the devastated economies of Europe and Asia, and, as the Cold War with the USSR and its allies deepened, became increasingly committed to the security of those believed to be endangered by Moscow and infected by its ideology. America's grand strategy as articulated by diplomat George Kennan was "that of a long-term, patient but firm and vigilant containment of Russian expansive tendencies" in the form of "the adroit and vigilant application of counterforce at a series of constantly shifting geographical and political points, corresponding to the shifts and maneuvers of Soviet policy" that will, in the end, "promote tendencies which must eventually find their outlet in either the breakup or the gradual mellowing of Soviet power."[2]

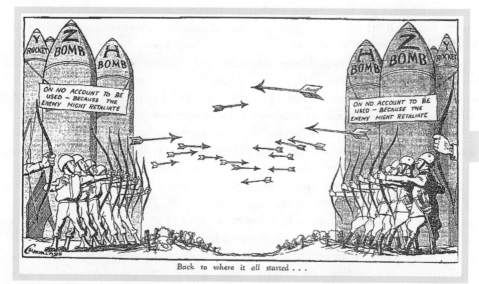

Back to where it all started . . .

The Cold War

American leaders militarized Kennan's version of containment, and military commitments to a host of allies around the world played a role in their strategy. America remained protected by two great oceans, and its remoteness from Europe and Asia reassured those who sought American protection that the United States would remain a "benign" hegemon rather than an acquisitive imperialist power. "This new American grand strategy for the postwar world," concludes political scientist Robert Kagan, "could not have been a more radical departure from 'normalcy'" because it involved "the promotion of a liberal world order that would defend not only America's interests but those of many other nations as well."[3] In the end, Kennan proved correct, and the American-led "free world" won the Cold War, and the USSR finally collapsed.

AFTER THE COLD WAR

With the end of the Cold War, the United States appeared to stand alone as the unchallenged hegemon in a global system in which globalization had made people interdependent economically, politically, and culturally. The proliferation of nongovernmental groups advocating solutions to collective problems like global warming has fostered global civil society and promised global governance of a variety of issue areas. Under American hegemony, an open global economy flourished as barriers to trade and investment were reduced, corporations became increasingly transnational, and international economic organizations such as the World Bank, the World Trade Organization, and the International Monetary Fund were established to maintain economic order. American leadership produced the United Nations and other international agencies to maintain peace and cope with challenges to human security and well-being.

After the Cold War, with American encouragement, democracy spread to the developing world and the countries of the former Soviet bloc. Concern for human rights deepened, and even authoritarian regimes felt it necessary to pay lip service to this concern. All this led optimists like G. John Ikenberry to conclude that "the liberal principles that Washington has pushed enjoy near-universal appeal, because they have tended to be a good fit with the modernizing forces of economic growth and social advancement" while Washington's chief foes "aren't just up against the United States; they would also have to contend with the most globally organized and deeply entrenched order the world has ever seen, one that is dominated by states that are liberal, capitalist, and democratic."[4]

There is, however, a darker side to world affairs that is reflected in the views of Kagan, who argues that the liberal order was created by and continues to depend on the **power** and determination of America.[5] Although he believes that the United States is not in decline, other observers are persuaded that America is growing ever less dominant relative to countries like China and Russia and is less able to maintain order and control outcomes around the world. Nevertheless, public fear of American decline combined with the multiple foreign-policy crises of the Obama years ensured that foreign policy would be a central concern during the nominating process and subsequent 2016 presidential election.

With the passage of time since the Cold War, however, the erosion of American hegemony, and the emergence of an increasingly multipolar world, America has retreated from its one-time role as the world's policeman. "America," argues political scientist William Martel, "does not have a coherent, functioning grand strategy" as it did during the Cold War when "containment" guided America's foreign policy. "Without one, the nation, its leaders, and people will experience a sense of drift and confusion.

How do we know what is important, what threatens our interests, when we should act, and what instruments of power should we use? According to Ralph Waldo Emerson, 'A foolish consistency is the hobgoblin of little minds, adored by little statesmen and philosophers and divines,' but, a coherent grand strategy provides the United States with an overarching sense of purpose in its international affairs. It helps to build domestic support and provide international clarity for its foreign policies."[6] What is happening according to political scientist Randall Schweller is a transition from "an age of order to an age of entropy,"[7] that is, disorder.

Can a global leader exercise hegemony "from behind"? Kagan thinks not: "The United States, in short, was the 'indispensable nation,' as Bill Clinton would proclaim—indispensable, that is, to the liberal world order,"[8] and it is hard to imagine that the "indispensable nation" can lead "from behind." Power—both hard and soft—is crucial to leadership, yet in recent years, American power has declined in a relative sense economically and (to a lesser extent) militarily, and U.S. strategy has relied more heavily on local proxies trained and armed by America. Although this approach reflects American public opinion, it has not always achieved what Washington sought, whether in Russian aggressiveness in Ukraine or in the rapid collapse of Iraq's army in 2014. Kagan criticizes the Obama foreign-policy establishment and the generation it represents when he writes of a "sense of futility" that followed the country's financial crisis and reflects what one scholar calls the "Iraq syndrome,"[9] the fear that America could be dragged into another Middle East civil war. "Senior White House officials," writes Kagan, "especially the younger ones, look at problems like the struggle in Syria and believe that there is little if anything the United State can do. This is the lesson of their generation, the lesson of Iraq and Afghanistan: that America has neither the power nor the understanding nor the skill to fix problems in the world." And he adds that this "is also escapism"[10] because such officials including the president may not appreciate what is at stake and how quickly the liberal global order could disappear. Responding to such criticism, Obama's final National Security Strategy included ninety-four references to American leadership.

Contemporary Foreign-Policy Challenges

In the absence of a clear ends and means strategy, allies in Asia, Europe, and the Middle East became concerned about America's commitment to their security and the credibility of its deterrence of China, Russia, and Iran. The administration of George W. Bush had been widely regarded by allies as well as domestic foes as overly eager to use military force in fighting the War on Terror after 9/11 and in the effort to spread democracy and foster regime change in Afghanistan and the Middle East. However, it is frequently forgotten that prior to 9/11 President Bush had tried to limit America's overseas commitments including humanitarian interventions in which the Clinton administration had become involved, for example, in Bosnia. America, declared diplomat Richard Haass, would become a "reluctant sheriff,"[11] involving itself only when local powers could not maintain peace. But neither the War on Terror nor the invasions of Afghanistan and Iraq constituted a coherent global strategy, nor did America's allies see them as such. Instead, as Kagan suggests, "the rest of the world saw the United States not as a global leader seeking the global good but as an angry Leviathan narrowly focused on destroying those who had attacked it," and "the only thing worse than a self-absorbed hegemon is an incompetent self-absorbed hegemon."[12]

President Obama assumed office committed to ending the "bad" war in Iraq and pacifying and reforming Afghanistan in a "good" war. In neither case did Washington realize its objectives. Iraq is in the midst of a sectarian war between Shia and Sunni Muslims with little to show after a decade of U.S. intervention. Afghanistan is still threatened by the Taliban-led insurrection against a government installed by America and may descend into civil war among ethnic groups and warlords after all American troops leave that might allow al-Qaeda militants to return to their Afghan sanctuaries. The president reluctantly contributed airpower to assist America's European allies in protecting Libyans from Muammar al-Qaddafi. Qaddafi was overthrown, but America's ambassador was murdered in the violent chaos that followed and continues in Libya.

Unlike President George W. Bush, President Obama became convinced that America should resort to military force sparingly and only when vital interests were at stake. In a 2009 speech at West Point, he announced plans to beef up American forces in Afghanistan, while in a later speech there in 2014 he declared, "You are the first class to graduate since 9/11 who may not be sent into combat in Iraq or Afghanistan."[13] He observed, "Since World War Two, some of our most costly mistakes came not from our restraint, but from our willingness to rush into military adventures without thinking through the consequences,"[14] contending that unless critical interests were at stake, "the threshold for military action must be higher."[15] Obama's position reflected American public opinion, at least unless events somewhere posed such a threat. "I would betray my duty to you, and to the country we love,"

Is America's lead waning?

© Chappatte in The International New York Times - www.globecartoon.com

the president continued, "if I sent you into harm's way simply because I saw a problem somewhere in the world that needed to be fixed or because I was worried about critics who think military intervention is the only way for America to avoid looking weak."[16]

Thus, the president declared an end to the War on Terror while continuing to use drones and Special Forces against terrorists in Pakistan, Yemen, Somalia, Libya, Iraq, and Syria and putting forward a plan to fund counterterrorist partnerships with countries under threat from terrorist groups. Nevertheless, ISIS seized large areas in Syria and Iraq over which their governments had lost control. The president also sought to end human-rights abuses associated with the War on Terror by closing the internment camp at Guantánamo, Cuba (which remained open owing to congressional opposition to housing prisoners in America), and ending policies like extraordinary rendition of suspected terrorists, but American efforts to end massive human-rights violations in Syria, Egypt, South Sudan, and North Korea have been minimal.

It was President Obama's misfortune that he was simultaneously confronted with challenges in Ukraine, Iraq, Syria, Israel, and elsewhere that made a coherent strategy virtually impossible to design and drove his domestic foreign-policy rating to new lows. While imposing sanctions on Russia over Ukraine, he sought to cooperate with Moscow on arms control and negotiations with North Korea and Iran. While differing with Shia Iran over the future of Syria and negotiating a framework agreement to curb Iran's nuclear ambitions, he was finding common ground with Tehran over ISIS even as he sought a coalition against ISIS consisting of Sunni states and opponents of Syria's President Assad. Simultaneously, the president sought to reassure Israel while condemning its war in Gaza and seeking a two-state solution and an end to settlement expansion. A former Obama adviser admitted, "You name it, the world is aflame. Foreign policy is always complicated. We always have a mix of complicated interests. That's not unusual. What's unusual is there's this outbreak of violence and instability everywhere."[17] Let us briefly examine some of Obama's policies in a disorderly world.

Having "pivoted" to Asia in response to China's growing strength and aggressiveness, Washington largely failed to convince Beijing that it did not seek to contain China while thwarting Chinese territorial ambitions in the Sea of Japan and the East and South China Seas. With only a modest increment in military forces in Asia, Washington's scolding China and its maritime ambitions irritated Beijing while not persuading America's friends that its commitments were credible. Indeed, it is difficult to imagine that Washington would become embroiled in a major military confrontation with China over uninhabited islets and sandbars unless the security of Japan, South Korea, or Taiwan was in imminent danger, especially in light of other challenges in the Middle East and Europe. Nevertheless, with tensions high a conflict might start by accident, or America's Asian allies might trigger a conflict in which Washington did not wish to become involved but felt it had no alternative but to do so.

Having removed most U.S. forces from Europe and cut back plans for European missile defense, America was poorly prepared to respond to Russian intervention in Ukraine and its annexation of Crimea. The former head of Saudi intelligence observed, "While the wolf is eating the sheep, there is no shepherd to come to the rescue."[18] Few Americans wanted to see U.S. troops in Ukraine, but the modest economic sanctions imposed by Washington and its European allies did not prevent Russia and Russian "volunteers" from continuing to aid those in Ukraine seeking to "federalize" the country or secede from it. As described by French analyst François Heibourg, "Mr. Putin does not do frontal attacks, he does judo"[19] that is sufficiently subtle that it does not justify a major Western response. Although Washington would probably respond militarily if Russia invaded a NATO country, a former U.S. defense official commented, "I would worry that it would be late. Not too late, but late, and that would send a message round the world."[20]

The death of Osama bin Laden during a raid by U.S. Navy Seals was probably President Obama's most memorable foreign-policy triumph until the 2015 agreement with Iran. Nevertheless, in the Middle East, too, recent American policy has seemed irresolute, a vivid contrast to the militancy of the Bush administration and its "neoconservatives." Having threatened to use force against Syria's President al-Assad if he employed chemical weapons, the Obama administration backed off in return for a deal with Assad brokered by Russia for destroying Syria's remaining chemical weapons. At the same time, Washington while initially refusing to aid Assad's foes ultimately began to contribute non-lethal aid and weapons covertly to Syria's Sunni opposition but only after Assad was in the driver's seat again aided by Russia, Iran, and Hezbollah, with the opposition involved in its own civil war, and without fear of overt American intervention. Only after ISIS made the region tremble did Washington agree to help train "moderate" Sunni rebels. President Obama had previously dismissed the claim that aid to "what was essentially an opposition made up of former doctors, farmers, pharmacists and so forth" would have made a difference in Syria as "a fantasy."[21] "The concern is," declared former Obama defense secretary Leon Panetta, "the president's defining what America's role in the world is in the 21st century hasn't happened."[22]

Elsewhere, having supported the overthrow of a military regime in Egypt by the Muslim Brotherhood in the name of democracy, Washington said little about the new government's antidemocratic policies and even less after that government was ousted in a military coup. There were claims that America had supported the coup against Egypt's Islamist government as well as claims that Washington had tried to prevent it. In either case, President Sisi's military government paid little attention to U.S. advice.

In failing to carry out its threat against Assad, supporting an Islamic government in Egypt, and negotiating with Iran over that country's nuclear program, Washington incensed its long-term ally, Saudi Arabia, and intensified Israeli suspicion of American motives. Relations between Israel and the United States had been close during Bush's presidency but began to sour after President Obama took office and urged Israel to stop building settlements in the occupied territories and show flexibility in negotiating with the Palestinians. A new round of peace negotiations prompted by Secretary of State John Kerry yielded little and collapsed in mutual recriminations exacerbated by Washington's willingness to consider dealing with a Palestinian government after Hamas and the PLO had agreed to unify their movement. Shortly thereafter, a third Israel-Hamas war erupted.

America's passivity during Syria's civil war and Egypt's turmoil also enhanced Islamic extremists in the Middle East and North Africa, and the region has become the "chief cauldron of contemporary disorder."[23] If America's 2003 intervention in Iraq had radicalized Muslims, Washington's indecisiveness mobilized al-Qaeda affiliates around the world. In the meantime, Iraq had descended into renewed sectarian violence with a Shia government that had grown more dependent on Iran as it grew less dependent on America, which had installed it in the first place.

Washington also entered into negotiations and completed a preliminary agreement with Iran in March 2015 to curb that country's nuclear ambitions—an outcome that raised profound concern in Israel and in America's conservative Sunni allies including Saudi Arabia, Jordan, Egypt, and the United Arab Emirates—even while Iran continued to provide arms, fighters, and funding to Syria's President Assad and supported the Shia Houthis in Yemen. Notwithstanding the March agreement, further progress faced domestic opposition in America and Iran, and important details remained unresolved until the final agreement was reached several weeks later than expected in July 2015. Meanwhile, Iran remained on the threshold of building a nuclear weapon even as North Korea continued its nuclear tests and moved toward deploying long-range missiles.

What Next?

When President Obama accepted the Nobel Peace Prize early in his first term, he admitted, "We must begin by acknowledging the hard truth: We will not eradicate violent conflict in our lifetimes. There will be times when nations—acting individually or in concert—will find the use of force not only necessary but morally justified." And he touched upon the dilemma he would face in the following years: "So part of our challenge is reconciling these two seemingly irreconcilable truths—that war is sometimes necessary, and war at some level is an expression of human folly."[24] It was that dilemma that became manifest in Europe, East Asia, the Middle East, and Central Asia where countries questioned American commitments and, in so doing, posed threats to the post–Cold War international order. The president's caution was apparent when he defended his foreign-policy legacy by asking "Why is it that everybody is so eager to use military force after we've just gone through a decade of war at enormous cost to our troops and to our budget. And what is it exactly that these critics think would have been accomplished?" And he expressed what may someday be called the Obama doctrine with a baseball analogy. "You hit singles, you hit doubles; every once in a while we may be able to hit a home run. But we steadily advance the interests of the American people and our partnership with folks around the world."[25] Obama's policy of restraint was reasoned and thoughtful but led a former national security official in his administration to conclude rather tersely and pointedly, "We're seeing the 'light footprint' run out of gas."[26]

In the *Aeneid* (Book vi. ll. 851 ff.), written after Augustus became emperor of Rome, the poet Virgil challenges his countrymen: "Roman, be this thy care—these thine arts—to bear dominion over the nations and to impose the law of peace, to spare the humbled and to war down the proud!" Kagan would have Americans follow the arduous task Virgil set for Romans. What he fears is that, in the face of economic crisis, renewed assertiveness by foes, and setbacks overseas, American foreign policy reveals that "Americans would like a world order that was essentially self-regulating and self-sustaining" because it "is the answer to the conundrum of power and interest that so bedevils them—how to create a world conducive to American ideals and interests without requiring the costly and morally complex exercise of American power."[27]

President Obama's answer to Kagan could well have been his comment that "apparently people have forgotten that America, as the most powerful country on earth, still does not control everything around the world."[28] "Indeed, with U.S. hegemony waning but no successor waiting to pick up the baton, the likeliest future is one in which the current international system gives way to a disorderly one with a larger number of power centers acting with increasing autonomy, paying less heed to U.S. interests and preferences. This will cause new problems even as it makes existing ones more difficult to solve. In short, the post–Cold War order is unraveling, and while not perfect, it will be missed."[29]

KEY TERM

power (p. 460)

for CQ Press

Sharpen your skill with SAGE edge at **edge.sagepub.com/mansbach**

SAGE edge for Students provides a personalized approach to help you accomplish your coursework goals in an easy-to-use learning environment.

Glossary

affiliation: A close link to a group or organization.

alliance: A group of countries joined together to enhance their security.

American exceptionalism: The special character of the United States as a uniquely free nation based on democratic ideals and personal liberty.

arms control: Any international control or limitation of the development, testing, production, deployment, or use of weapons based on the premise that certain weapons are particularly destabilizing and dangerous.

asylum: Protection granted by another government to refugees offering them protection from persecution in their home country.

asymmetric warfare: Warfare in which opposing groups or nations have unequal military resources, and the weaker opponent uses unconventional weapons and tactics as terrorism to exploit the vulnerabilities of the enemy.

attitudes: Relatively enduring organization of beliefs, feelings, intentions, and expectations of individuals or groups.

authoritarian government: Enforcing strict obedience to authority at the expense of personal freedom.

autonomy: Freedom from external control or influence.

back channel: A secret, unofficial, or informal channel of communication as used in politics or diplomacy.

balance of payments: The record of all economic transactions between the residents of a country—individuals, firms, and government—and the rest of the world.

balance of power: A foreign policy aimed at preventing any state(s) from gaining a preponderance of power in relation to its rivals.

balance of trade: The difference between the values of exports and imports of a country, said to be favorable or unfavorable, as exports are greater or less than imports.

beggar-thy-neighbor policies: Policies by which a country attempts to remedy its economic problems by means such as currency devaluation and higher tariffs that exacerbate the economic problems of other countries.

bilateralism: A foreign policy of cooperation between two states.

biodiversity: The variety of life forms in the world or in a particular habitat or ecosystem.

bipolarity: An international system characterized by two dominant states or blocs of states.

BRICS: An acronym standing for Brazil, Russia, India, China, and South Africa, a group of countries that have newly advanced economic development.

bureaucracy: A large group of appointed officials who are involved in running a government.

Bush Doctrine: A policy that America could launch preemptive attacks to defend itself from terrorists and countries that supported terrorists in order to prevent possible attacks before they occurred and that promoting democracy—by force if necessary—was central to U.S. security strategy.

caliphate: An Islamic empire ruled by those ("caliphs") who succeeded the prophet Muhammad.

cap and trade system: A market-based approach to controlling pollution that allows corporations or governments to trade emissions allowances under an overall cap, or limit, on those emissions.

capability: An actor's assets that allow it to exert influence over others.

carbon taxes: Levies on carbon emissions or on the fuel that produces them.

checks and balances: A system in which the different branches of government have powers that affect and control the other parts so that no branch can become dominant.

climate change: A change in global or regional climate patterns, in particular a change apparent from the mid to late 20th century onward and attributed largely to the increased levels of atmospheric carbon dioxide produced by the use of fossil fuels.

Clinton Doctrine: A policy by which the United States would forcefully intervene to prevent human rights abuses, with or without the authority of the UN Security Council.

collective good: Benefits such as military security or clean air from which individuals cannot be excluded and, as a result, for which beneficiaries have no incentive to pay.

Concert of Europe: The Concert of Europe, also known as the Congress System, established after the era of Napoleon and the French Revolution by the old great powers of Europe, involved meeting from time to time in an international conference to find solutions to solve issues that threatened Europe's peace and stability.

containment: U.S. foreign policy to halt the spread of communism in the Cold War by applying economic, diplomatic, and ultimately military pressure on the USSR.

cosmopolitanism: The idea that all human beings, regardless of their political affiliation, are (or can and should be) citizens in a single community.

coup d'état: The sudden and illegal seizure of a government.

credibility: The quality of being convincing or believable, especially of commitments and threats.

crimes against humanity: Crimes, including genocide, directed against a large group because of religion, ethnicity, country of origin, or other reason unconnected with any individual's responsibility for having committed a criminal act.

cult of personality: Adulation of a living national leader or public figure.

currency manipulation: Intentionally keeping the value of a particular currency artificially low or high.

cyberattack: Use of information systems to exploit, disrupt, or destroy an enemy's military or civilian computer networks.

cyber-espionage: Hacking computer systems in order to spy on an adversary or steal political and commercial secrets from governments and corporations.

cyber-security: Technologies, processes, and practices designed to protect networks, computers, programs, and data from attack, damage, or unauthorized access.

decolonization: The release of a country or territory from political control by another country.

democracy: Political system based on the right of all citizens to participate in government, often by electing representatives.

democratic peace theory: Theory that democracies do not fight wars with one another.

détente: The easing of hostility.

deterrence: A strategy intended to dissuade an adversary from taking an action not yet started by threatening to retaliate with military force.

devaluation: Reducing the value of a currency relative to other currencies to increase exports.

dictatorship: Form of government in which a ruler exercises absolute power.

disarmament: The reduction or abolition of a country's military forces and armaments based on the premise that armaments cause war.

disengagement: A policy to cease interacting with another country or other countries.

domino theory: A theory that if one country is taken over by an expansionist neighbor, others nearby will also fall like a row of dominos.

dual-use technologies: Technologies normally used for civilian purposes but which may have military applications.

economic development: Sustained actions of policymakers that promote a population's standard of living.

embargo: An official ban on trade or other commercial activity with a particular country.

embedded liberalism: A post–World War II combination of multilateral free trade internationally and government intervention to provide welfare to citizens domestically.

emerging economies: Countries with economies that are progressing toward becoming advanced, as shown by some liquidity in local debt and equity markets and the existence of some form of market exchange and regulatory body.

engagement: A policy of interacting with other countries.

ethnic cleansing: A euphemism for rendering an area ethnically homogeneous by murder or expulsion from a territory of people from a particular ethnic background.

ethnicity: A group, often based on common ancestry, whose members identify with one another owing to a shared culture, religion, or language.

ethnocentrism: Belief in the superiority of one's own ethnic group or culture.

expediency: The quality of being convenient and practical despite possibly being improper or immoral.

external factors: Events or conditions outside a state that influence its policymakers.

failed states: States whose governments have virtually collapsed.

fast track authority: A congressional resolution that gives the president authority to negotiate trade agreements and requires Congress to vote on such agreements within ninety days without amending them.

first-strike capability: The capability to attack first and destroy an enemy's ability to retaliate.

Fissile Material Cut-Off Treaty: A ban proposed by President Bill Clinton in 1993 to stop production of materials capable of sustaining an explosive fission chain reaction.

foreign direct investment: Overseas investment in physical resources such as buildings and machinery.

foreign policy: Sum of an actor's goals and purposive actions in global politics.

fragile states: States with governments that lack authority over much of their territory and are unable to deliver the services associated with governing and that suffer a loss of legitimacy.

free-market capitalism: A system of economics that minimizes government intervention and maximizes the role of markets.

free trade: International trade left to its natural course without tariffs, quotas, or other government-imposed restrictions.

frozen conflict: A conflict in which violence has ended, but there has been no progress toward a settlement.

genocide: Deliberate and systematic destruction of an ethnic, racial, or cultural group.

geostrategy: A combination of geopolitical and strategic factors characterizing a particular geographic region.

global commons: The Earth's shared natural resources such as the oceans, the atmosphere, and outer space.

global warming: (See greenhouse effect).

Global Zero: A world with no nuclear weapons.

globalization: Processes that produce worldwide interconnectedness and interdependence and facilitate the movement of persons, things, and ideas across sovereign boundaries.

gold-exchange standard: A monetary system in one country in which currency is maintained at a par with that of another country that is on the gold standard.

gold standard: Monetary system in which the unit of currency is equal in value and exchangeable for a specified amount of gold.

government factors: Attributes of a government or regime that influence its foreign policy.

government or bureaucratic politics model: A model of decision making in which foreign policy is the result of competition and negotiation among different bureaucracies and interest groups with different interests and perspectives.

grand strategy: Comprehensive, long-term plan of essential actions by which a country plans to achieve its major objectives.

greenhouse effect: The result of greenhouse gases trapping heat in the atmosphere described as "global warming" or the observed increase in the earth's average temperature.

greenhouse gas: A gas such as carbon dioxide, methane, or nitrous oxide that is believed to produce global warming.

Group of 20 (G-20): The G-7 along with middle-income emerging economies like China, India, and Brazil.

habeas corpus: A legal action by means of which detainees can seek relief from unlawful imprisonment.

hard power: Power based on coercion and/or rewards.

hegemon: The leading or commanding country in an international system.

highly enriched uranium (HEU): Weapons-grade uranium enriched to 90 percent U-235.

human development: A development process that prioritizes improving the living conditions of people.

human rights: Basic rights that individuals enjoy by virtue of their humanness that can be neither created nor abused by governments.

human security: The process of protecting people from threats to their lives and well-being, including threats from terrorism, crime, poverty, environmental degradation, and economic and political exploitation.

humanitarian: Seeking to promote human welfare.

humanitarian intervention: The use of military force against a state when the aim of that action is ending human-rights violations being perpetrated by the targeted state.

humanitarian law: A set of rules which seek, for humanitarian reasons, to limit the effects of armed conflict.

ideals: Ideas or standards of perfection or excellence.

identities: Characteristics that individuals believe define themselves and that, when shared, define a group and its interests.

ideology: Doctrinaire body of ideas that reflects the beliefs of a political group and fosters particular policies.

illegal combatants: Fighters (including terrorists) who wear no uniform, fight for no recognized authority, and ignore the laws of war.

incrementalism: Changing gradually in small steps.

independence: Freedom from the influence of others.

individual factors: Attributes of particular individuals that influence their foreign-policy decisions or actions.

individualism: A belief that the needs of each person are more important than the needs of the whole society or group.

inflation: A general increase in prices and fall in the purchasing value of money.

informatization: The upgrading of a system through application of information technology.

insider attack: An attack on a soldier by a fellow soldier or the soldier of an ally.

instrumental: Helping or causing something to happen or be done.

integrated supply chain: A close alignment and coordination within a supply chain (inputs required to produce a product), consisting of all parties involved in fulfilling a purchase, including raw materials, manufacturing, transporting completed items, and support services.

intellectual property: A work or invention that is the result of creativity, such as a book, film, or design, to which the author owns rights and may apply for a patent, copyright, or trademark.

intercontinental ballistic missile (ICBM): A ballistic missile with a range greater than 5,500 kilometers.

interdependence: Relationship in which two or more actors are sensitive and vulnerable to one another's behavior.

interest group: A group that tries to influence the policies of government in a way that advances their own interests.

internally displaced person: Someone forced to flee his or her home but who remains within his or her country's borders.

international crisis: A threatening situation that arises unexpectedly and requires a rapid decision before the situation deteriorates.

internationalism: A foreign policy or practice of involvement in world affairs.

interventionism: Unsolicited interference by one state in the affairs of another.

Islamization: Transforming a secular state into one governed by Islamic law and practices.

isolationism: A policy of abstaining from political or economic relations with other countries.

jihadism: The belief that waging a holy war on behalf of Islam is a religious duty.

legitimacy: Accepted as right and proper.

liberal interventionist: Policymaker who seeks to spread freedom and democracy and believes outside intervention can do so aided by international law and organizations.

liberalist: An analyst or a practitioner who takes an optimistic approach to foreign policy that assumes the importance of values, the perfectibility of humankind, and the utility of democracy, international organization, and economic interdependence in maintaining peace.

managed float system: Monetary system in which the value of a currency against other currencies is determined by supply and demand that is partly a consequence of government and bank coordinated currency purchases and sales.

Manichean worldview: The belief that the world reflects the duality of "good" versus "evil."

Manifest Destiny: The belief that the United States not only could but was destined to stretch from coast to coast.

mediation: The attempt to settle a dispute through participation of a third party (mediator) who attempts to identify points of agreement and make those in conflict reach an agreement.

military-industrial complex: A combination of defense industries, members of Congress, and the Pentagon that cooperate to encourage higher U.S. defense expenditures.

monetary policy: The actions of a central bank that determine the size and rate of growth of the money supply, which in turn affects interest rates. As the money supply grows, interest rates decline, and as it decreases, interest rates rise.

most-favored nation rule: Requirement for countries to treat one another equally in trade relations.

mujahideen: Those who engage in Jihad. Often used specifically to refer to Islamist guerrilla fighters who organized after the 1979 Soviet invasion of Afghanistan.

multilateralism: A foreign policy based on cooperating with other countries.

multiple, independently targetable reentry vehicle (MIRV): A ballistic missile payload containing several warheads, each capable of being aimed to hit a different target.

mutual assured destruction (MAD): A situation in which rivals possess second-strike forces, thereby assuring if either launched a nuclear first strike the other would retaliate, assuring the destruction of both.

national interest: The idea that a state has a set of goals that will collectively benefit its citizens.

national liberation movement: A revolutionary movement that seeks the national independence of a country that had been a colony.

nationalism: A community based on common cultural characteristics that binds a population and often produces a desire for national independence or autonomy.

nationalistic: Belief in the superiority of one's own country over others.

nationalize: To bring under the ownership or control of a state, as industries and land.

neoconservatives: Policymakers who advocate the assertive promotion of democracy and national interest in foreign policy including resort to force.

neo-isolationist: Contemporary isolationist.

neoliberalism: Economic doctrine based on minimum government interference and reliance on free markets.

neomercantilism: A contemporary version of the theory of mercantilism emphasizing economic protectionism and commercial policies as means of increasing domestic income and employment.

neutrality: A policy of being impartial or not allied with any party in an armed conflict.

New Deal: A series of domestic welfare programs enacted in the United States in the 1930s in response to the Great Depression.

new sovereignists: Those who wish the United States to resist incorporating international norms or joining multilateral agreements and international institutions because they believe such actions limit American sovereignty and lack constitutional legitimacy.

no-fly zone: Air space off-limits to the air force of a particular country.

nonaligned movement: A group of mainly less developed countries that were not members of either the Soviet or American alliance system in the Cold War.

nongovernmental organization (NGO): An organization that is neither a part of a government nor a conventional for-profit business. NGOs are usually organized around specific issues and perform a variety of functions including advocacy, humanitarian assistance, and policy analysis and expertise.

noninterventionism: A foreign policy based on noninterference or involvement in other states.

nonpolarity: A international system with no centers of power.

norm: A principle of right action for members of a group and serving to guide, control, or regulate behavior.

North Atlantic Treaty Organization (NATO): An alliance established in 1949 to make a potential aggressor recognize that America, with its nuclear capability, was committed to defending Western Europe.

Nuclear Nonproliferation Treaty (NPT): A treaty signed by President Lyndon Johnson in 1968 that created two categories of states, nuclear-weapons states (NWS) and nonnuclear-weapons states (NNWS), with rules for each to prevent the proliferation of nuclear weapons.

offshoring: The corporate practice of moving business operations overseas.

opinion leader: An individual whose opinions by virtue of specialized knowledge or profession are highly regarded by others and that influence their views.

organizational process model: A model of decision making in which large "semi-feudal" bureaucracies use a repertoire of standard operating procedures when dealing with routine and recurring situations.

outsourcing: Subcontracting work to suppliers overseas.

ozone: A form of oxygen that in the upper atmosphere absorbs ultraviolet rays, thereby preventing them from reaching the surface of the earth.

ozone depletion: Destruction of the upper atmospheric layer of ozone gas, caused by substances formed from the breakdown of chemicals such as chlorofluorocarbon, chlorofluoromethane, or halon used in aerosol cans, plastic foams, refrigerants, and certain solvents.

P5+1 Group: The five permanent members of the UN Security Council—China, France, Russia, Britain, and America—plus Germany.

Pan-Arab nationalism: Desire to form a single nation-state of the Arabs in the Middle East.

peace dividend: Funds that a government originally planned to spend on its military that become available for other purposes after a war ends.

peaceful coexistence: Policy of peace between nations of widely differing political systems and ideologies, especially between communist and noncommunist countries.

pluralism: A condition where multiple people, groups, or entities share political power.

political culture: Attitudes, beliefs, and values that shape a society's perspectives and behavior.

political Islam (Islamism): A set of ideologies holding that Islam should guide social and political as well as personal life.

power: The ability to influence others to do what an actor wishes them to do.

power politics: Foreign policy based on the use of military or economic power to influence the actions and decisions of other countries.

power vacuum: An area that strong states do not control but that they fear others might control.

pragmatist: One who adopts a practical, matter-of-fact way of approaching or assessing situations or solving problems.

precautionary principle: A norm calling for action to be taken before the certainty of a problem has been established.

preemptive war: War initiated to gain an advantage over an enemy that itself is about to attack.

preventive attack: An attack to destroy the potential threat of the targeted party.

principal-agent problem: When a principal hires an agent to perform specific duties that are in the best interest of the principal but may be costly or not in the best interests of the agent, resulting in conflicts of interest and moral hazard issues.

proliferation: The spread of conventional weapons, weapons of mass destruction, or weapons-applicable materials and technologies to countries or actors that did not previously have such weapons, materials, or capabilities. It can also refer to a country or actor increasing its arsenal of conventional or WMD capabilities.

Proliferation Security Initiative (PSI): A commitment outlined by President George H. W. Bush in 2003 to take action to interdict weapons shipments, disrupt proliferation networks, and shut down the front companies that support them.

propaganda: Information, frequently of a misleading nature, used to promote a particular political cause or point of view.

protectionism: The practice of shielding a country's domestic industries from foreign competition by taxing imports.

public opinion: The collective opinion of many people on some issue, or policy, especially as a guide to action.

purchasing power parity (PPP): The number of units of a country's currency required to buy the same amount of goods and services in the domestic market as a U.S. dollar would buy in the United States.

quantitative easing: The policy of a central bank that infuses a predetermined quantity of money into the economy by buying financial assets from commercial banks and private entities.

quotas: Protectionist measures that limit the amount of imports to a country.

rally-round-the-flag effect: Propensity for public opinion to support the government in moments of crisis or the onset of war.

rational actor model: A model of decision making in which foreign-policy decisions are believed to result from the choices of unitary actors based on cost-benefit assessment of alternative options.

rationality: Acting to achieve one's interests by examining the relative costs and benefits of all alternatives.

realist: Foreign-policy analysts and practitioners whose approach to foreign policy assumes that states seek power and security and that their interests and policies are determined by the distribution of power

recession: A reduction in a country's GDP for at least two consecutive quarters.

redenomination: The process of a central bank officially changing the value of banknotes or coins and reissuing currency for circulation, usually after a period of high inflation.

remittance: Funds sent by those working overseas to their home country, usually to their families.

reserve or "hard" currency: A foreign currency like the U.S. dollar, the value of which is believed to be stable and is held by central banks and other major financial institutions to pay off international debt obligations.

Responsibility to Protect (R2P): A norm that states forfeit aspects of their sovereignty when they fail to protect their populations from atrocities and human rights violations.

retrencher: A policymaker who seeks to limit America's foreign commitments to vital interests.

role factors: Aspects of the function that officials assume in government that influence a country's foreign policy.

rule of law: The principle that people and institutions are subject to and accountable to law that is fairly applied and enforced.

sanctions: Penalties applied unilaterally by one country (or multilaterally, by several countries) on another country (or group of countries) that may include trade barriers and restrictions on financial transactions.

second-strike capability: A capability of absorbing an enemy nuclear attack while retaining the capability to retaliate.

sectarian violence: Violence among adherents of different religions, ethnicities, or ideologies.

secularism: The principle that religion should not determine public policy or serve as the basis of law.

security: The condition of being protected or safe from harm.

self-executing treaties: Treaties that can be enforced without prior legislation by Congress.

separation of powers: A system in which the branches of government (executive, legislative, judicial) have separate and unique powers that the others cannot impinge upon.

shaper: A policymaker who seeks to increase America's role in fostering international rules and agreements.

signature strikes: Unmanned drone attacks based not on who the targets are but on whether they are exhibiting suspicious patterns of behavior thought to be "signatures" of terrorists.

social media: Websites and applications that enable users to create and share content or to participate in social networking.

socialization: The process by which individuals acquire the knowledge, language, social skills, and values required for integration into a community.

societal factors: Characteristics of a country's community and the groups in that community that influence the country's foreign policy.

soft power: Power based on culture and reputation that shapes the preferences of others.

sovereignty: Status of states as legal equals under international law, according to which they are supreme within their boundaries and subject to no higher external authority.

speculation: Trading in an asset or making a financial transaction that has a risk of losing most or all of the initial outlay, in expectation of a substantial gain.

sphere of influence: An area over which one country enjoys dominant influence.

standard operating procedures: Established routines that bureaucracies follow to carry out recurring tasks.

state sponsors of terrorism: Countries determined by the secretary of state to have repeatedly provided support for acts of international terrorism that are subject to sanctions including a ban on defense exports and sales, controls over exports of dual use items, and miscellaneous financial restrictions.

state-centric: Model of global politics in which sovereign states are the source of most important activities and the focus of most scholars and practitioners.

Stockholm Convention on Persistent Organic Pollutants (2001): A multilateral treaty to eliminate or restrict the production and use of persistent organic pollutants used as pesticides, solvents, pharmaceuticals, and industrial chemicals.

subsidies: Protectionist measures that provide government aid to firms to make them more competitive globally.

sustainable environmental policy: An environmental policy that manages the rates of renewable resource harvest, pollution creation, and nonrenewable resource depletion to conserve environmental resources and support human society indefinitely.

tactical nuclear weapons: Nuclear weapons that are designed to be used on battlefields and that are limited in range and/or size.

tar sands: A combination of clay, sand, water, and bitumen, a heavy black viscous oil.

targeted strikes: Unmanned drone attacks aimed at specific terrorists or terrorist groups.

tariff: A tax imposed on imported goods and services.

terrorism: The unlawful use of force and violence against persons or property to intimidate or coerce a government, the civilian population, or any segment thereof, in furtherance of political or social objectives.

tied aid: Grants of aid that require recipients to purchase goods and services from American farms and companies.

totalitarianism: A political system in which rulers control all aspect of society.

Transatlantic Trade and Investment Partnership (TTIP): A proposed agreement between the European Union and the United States to remove or reduce barriers to trade and foreign investment.

transboundary externalities: Environmental activities in one country that can harm others.

transnational: Crossing national frontiers and involving social groups and nongovernmental actors.

Trans-Pacific Partnership (TPP): A proposed trade agreement between twelve Pacific Rim countries seeking to lower trade barriers such as tariffs, establish a common framework for intellectual property, enforce standards for labor law and environmental law, and establish an investor-state dispute settlement mechanism.

two-level games: When negotiating agreements with other states, a country's leaders must take account of the demands of actors at both the domestic and international levels.

UN Human Rights Council: The main intergovernmental body within the United Nations system made up of forty-seven states and responsible for the promotion and protection of human rights worldwide.

UN Monitoring, Verification and Inspection Commission: A body created through the UN Security Council tasked between 1999 and 2007 with disarming Iraq of its weapons of mass destruction and operating a system of ongoing monitoring and verification to check Iraq's compliance with its obligations not to reacquire the same weapons banned by the Security Council.

unilateralism: A foreign policy or practice of conducting foreign affairs with minimal consultation or cooperation with other countries.

unipolar moment: The period immediately after the Cold War when America was a uniquely dominant state in global politics.

unipolarity: International system dominated by a single center of power.

Universal Declaration of Human Rights: A declaration adopted by the United Nations General Assembly in 1948 that expresses the set of rights to which all human beings are inherently entitled.

USA Patriot Act: A law authorized by congress in 2001 to enhance surveillance efforts to improve national security.

values: Important and lasting beliefs or ideals shared by the members of a culture about what is good or bad and desirable or undesirable.

war crimes: Crimes committed against an enemy, prisoners of war, or subjects in wartime that violate international agreements.

Washington consensus: The neoliberal belief that countries suffering economic distress should follow policies based on austerity, free-market reforms, and minimal government intervention in the economy.

weapons of mass destruction (WMD): Nuclear, biological, and chemical weapons that can kill large numbers of people indiscriminately.

Zionism: An international movement originally for the establishment of a Jewish national or religious community in Palestine and later for the support of modern Israel.

Notes

INTRODUCTION

1. Cited in Mark Landler, "Obama Signals a Shift from Military Might to Diplomacy," *New York Times,* November 25, 2013, http://www.nytimes.com/2013/11/26/world/middleeast/longer-term-deal-with-iran.html.

2. Cited in David E. Sanger, "For Obama, an Evolving Doctrine on Foreign Policy," *New York Times,* September 24, 2013, http://www.nytimes.com/2013/09/25/world/middleeast/obamas-evolving-doctrine.html.

3. Cited in Thomas L. Friedman, "Foreign Policy by Whisper and Nudge," *New York Times,* August 24, 2013, http://www.nytimes.com/2013/08/25/opinion/sunday/friedman-foreign-policy-by-whisper-and-nudge.html?pagewanted=all.

4. Graham T. Allison and Phillip Zelikow, *Essence of Decision: Explaining the Cuban Missile Crisis*, 2nd ed. (New York, NY: Longman, 1999), 4–5.

5. Ibid., 5–6.

6. Ibid., 6.

CHAPTER 1

1. Hillary Rodham Clinton, "Leading through Civilian Power: Redefining American Diplomacy and Development," *Foreign Affairs* 89:6 (November/December 2010): 15.

2. This typology is derived from James N. Rosenau, "Pre-Theories and Theories of Foreign Policy," in R. Barry Farrell, ed., *Approaches to Comparative and International Politics* (Evanston, IL: Northwestern University Press, 1966), 27–92.

3. Gideon Rachman, "American Decline: This Time It's Real," *Foreign Policy* 184 (January/February 2011): 63, 59.

4. Joseph S. Nye, Jr., "The Future of American Power: Dominance and Decline in Perspective," *Foreign Affairs* 89:6 (November/December 2010): 3, 12.

5. Office of the Press Secretary (8 May 2009). "Briefing by White House Press Secretary Robert Gibbs." http://www.whitehouse.gov/the_press_office/Briefing-by-White-House-Press-Secretary-Robert-Gibbs-5-8-09.

6. Jared P. Cole, "The Political Question Doctrine: Justiciability and the Separation of Powers," *Congressional Reference Service,* December 23, 2014, https://www.fas.org/sgp/crs/misc/R43834.pdf.

7. Kimi Lynn King and James Meernik, "The Supreme Court and the Powers of the Executive: The Adjudication of Foreign Policy," *Political Research Quarterly* 52:4 (December 1999): 818.

8. Roger Hilsman, *To Move a Nation* (Garden City, NY: Doubleday, 1967): 5.

9. Graham Allison and Philip Zelikow, *Essence of Decision*, 2nd ed. (New York, NY: Longman, 1999), 143.

10. Cited in Peter Baker, "How Obama Came to Plan for 'Surge' in Afghanistan," *New York Times,* December 5, 2009, http://www.nytimes.com/2009/12/06/world/asia/06reconstruct.html?pagewanted=all.

11. Cited in Richard E. Neustadt, *Presidential Power and the Modern Presidents* (New York, NY: Free Press, 1990), 10. Emphasis in original.

12. Ibid., 37.

13. Warner R. Schilling, "The Politics of National Defense: Fiscal 1950," in Schilling, Paul Hammond, and Glenn Snyder, eds., *Strategy, Politics, and Defense Budgets* (New York, NY: Columbia University Press, 1962), 230.

14. Eisenhower's Farewell Address to the Nation, January 17, 1961, http://mcadams.posc.mu.edu/ike.htm.

15. Alexis de Tocqueville, *Democracy in America,* ed. J. P. Mayer, trans. George Lawrence (New York, NY: Anchor Books, 1969), 228–229.

16. Alexander Hamilton, "Speech on the Constitutional Convention on a Plan of Government," in Morton J. Frisch, ed., *Selected Writings and Speeches of Alexander Hamilton* (Washington, DC: American Enterprise Institute, 1985), 108.

17. Gabriel Almond, *The American People and Foreign Policy* (New York, NY: Praeger, 1960), 53.

18. George F. Kennan, *American Diplomacy: Expanded Edition* (Chicago, IL: University of Chicago Press, 1984), 66.

19. "A World of Troubles" and "Arms and the Men," *The Economist*, October 6, 2012, 15, 18.

20. Chris Cillizza, "Winner and Losers from Election 2012," *Washington Post,* November 7, 2012, http://www.washingtonpost.com/blogs/the-fix/wp/2012/11/07/winners-and-losers-from-election-2012.

21. Niccolò Machiavelli, *The Prince*, trans. Luigi Ricci (New York, NY: Mentor Books, 1952), 93.

22. William R. Caspary, "The 'Mood Theory': A Study of Public Opinion and Foreign Policy," *American Political Science Review* 64:2 (June 1970): 546. Emphasis in original.

23. Almond, *The American People and Foreign Policy*, 5.

24. John J. Mearsheimer and Stephen M. Walt, *The Israel Lobby and U.S. Foreign Policy* (New York, NY: Farrar, Straus, and Giroux 2007), 5, 6.

25. Aaron Friedberg, "An Uncivilized Argument," *Foreign Policy* 155 (July/August 2006): 59.

26. Dennis Ross, "The Mind-Set Matters," in ibid., 61.

27. Shlomo Ben-Ami, "The Complex Truth," in ibid., 62, 63.

28. Cited in Tony Judt, "A Lobby, Not a Conspiracy," *New York Times,* April 19, 2006, http://www.nytimes.com/2006/04/19/opinion/19judt.html?pagewanted=1&_r=1&ei=5087&en=2706f771ea2e35aa&ex=1145592000.

29. George F. Kennan, *Memoirs 1925–1950* (Boston, MA: Little, Brown, 1967), 53.

30. Robert D. Putnam, "Diplomacy and Domestic Politics: The Logic of Two-Level Games," *International Organization* 42:3 (Summer 1988): 434.

31. Jane Mayer, "Covert Operations," *The New Yorker*, August 30, 2010, http://www.newyorker.com/magazine/2010/08/30/covert-operations?currentPage=all.

32. Robert J. Art, *The TFX Decision, McNamara and the Military* (Boston, MA: Little Brown, 1968), 166.

33. George W. Bush, "Graduation Speech at West Point," June 1, 2002, *Voices of Democracy,* http://vod.academicwebpages.com/bush-graduation-speech-speech-text.

34. Steve Smith, "Policy Preferences and Bureaucratic Position: The Case of the American Hostage Rescue Mission," *International Affairs* 61:1 (Winter 1984): 24.

35. Harold D. Lasswell, *Psychopathology and Politics* (Chicago, IL: University of Chicago Press, 1930), 75.

36. Harold D. Lasswell, *Power and Personality* (New York, NY: W.W. Norton, 1948), 120.

37. Garry Wills, *Nixon Agonistes: The Crisis of the Self-Made Man* (New York, NY: Houghton Mifflin, 2002), 412.

38. Alexander L. George and Juliette L. George, *Woodrow Wilson and Colonel House: A Personality Study* (New York, NY: Dover, 1964), 11. Emphasis in original.

39. John G. Stoessinger, *Crusaders and Pragamatists* (New York, NY: W. W. Norton, 1985), 27, 289, 290.

40. Cited in Ron Suskind, "Faith, Certainty and the Presidency of George W. Bush," *New York Times Magazine,* October 17, 2004, http://www.nytimes.com/2004/10/17/magazine/17BUSH.html.

41. Ole R. Holsti, "The 'Operational Code' Approach to the Study of Political Leaders: John Foster Dulles' Philosophical and Instrumental Beliefs," *Canadian Journal of Political Science* 3:1 (March 1970): 130.

42. David Rothkopf, "National Insecurity," *Foreign Policy* 204 (September/October 2014): 49.

43. Cited in Michael D. Shear, "With Foreign Leaders, Obama Keeps It Mostly Business," *New York Times*, March 10, 2015, http://www.nytimes.com/2015/03/11/us/politics/with-foreign-leaders-obama-keeps-it-mostly-business.html.

44. Cited in Peter Baker, "In Book, Panetta Recounts Frustration with Obama," *New York Times,* October 6, 2014, http://www.nytimes.com/2014/10/07/world/middleeast/ex-defense-secretary-panetta-tells-of-frustrations-with-obama.html.

45. Arthur M. Schlesinger, Jr., *The Coming of the New Deal* (New York, NY: Houghton Mifflin, 1958), 502, 527–528.

46. Cited in Scott Shane, "Petraeus's Quieter Style at C.I.A. Leaves Void on Libya Furor," *New York Times,* November 2, 2012, http://www.nytimes.com/2012/11/03/world/africa/petraeuss-lower-profile-at-cia-leaves-void-in-benghazi-furor.html.

47. Arnold Rogow, *James Forrestal: A Study of Personality, Politics, and Policy* (New York, NY: Macmillan, 1963), 351.

CHAPTER 2

1. Barack H. Obama, "Nobel Lecture: A Just and Lasting Peace," December 10, 2009, http://www.nobelprize.org/nobel_prizes/peace/laureates/2009/obama-lecture_en.html.

2. Chris Good, "Obama Stresses Multilateralism in Announcing Libya Strikes," *The Atlantic,* March 19, 2011, http://www.theatlantic.com/politics/archive/2011/03/obama-stresses-multilateralism-in-announcing-libya-strikes/72738.

3. B. Liddell Hart, *Strategy* (New York, NY: Praeger, 1967), 333–372.

4. Paul Kennedy, "Grand Strategies in War and Peace: Towards a Broader Definition," in *Grand Strategies in War and Peace*, ed. Paul Kennedy (New Haven, CT: Yale University Press, 1992), 5.

5. Hal Brands, "The Promise and Pitfalls of Grand Strategy," Strategic Studies Institute External Research Associates Program Monograph, August 2012, 4, http://www.strategicstudiesinstitute.army.mil/pubs/display.cfm?pubid=1121.

6. William C. Martel, "America's Dangerous Drift," *The Diplomat*, February 25, 2013, http://thediplomat.com/2013/02/25/americas-dangerous-drift.

7. Manfred Jonas, "Isolationism," in Alexander DeConde, ed., *Encyclopedia of American Foreign Policy* (New York, NY: Charles Scribner's Sons, 1978), 496.

8. Robert J. Art, *A Grand Strategy for America* (Ithaca, NY: Cornell University Press, 2003), 173.

9. Andrew Johnstone, "Isolationism and Internationalism in American Foreign Relations," *Journal of Transatlantic Studies* 9:1 (2011): 11.

10. George C. Herring, *From Colony to Superpower: US Foreign Relations since 1776*, vol. 12 (New York, NY: Oxford University Press, 2008), 1.

11. John Lewis Gaddis, *Surprise, Security and the American Experience* (Cambridge, MA: Harvard University Press, 2004), 24.

12. Jonas, "Isolationism," 498.

13. Johnstone, "Isolationism and Internationalism in American Foreign Relations," 13.

14. Glenn Hastedt, *Encyclopedia of American Foreign Policy* (New York, NY: Facts on File, 2004), 325–326.

15. David C. Hendrickson, *Union, Nation, or Empire: The American Debate over International Relations 1789–1941* (Lawrence: University Press of Kansas, 2009), 6.

16. J. Simon Rofe and John Thompson, "'Internationalists in Isolationist Times'—Theodore and Franklin Roosevelt and a Rooseveltian Maxim," *Journal of Transatlantic Studies* 9:1 (2011), 47.

17. David M. Malone and Yuen Foong Khong, "Unilateralism and US Foreign Policy," in Malone and Khong, eds., *U.S. Foreign Policy: International Perspectives* (Boulder, CO: Lynne Rienner, 2003), 3.

18. Robert O. Keohane, "Multilateralism: An Agenda for Research," *International Journal*, 45:4 (Autumn 1990): 731.

19. John Ruggie, "Multilateralism: The Anatomy of an Institution," *International Organization*, 46:3 (Summer 1992): 571, 572.

20. Malone and Khong, "Unilateralism and US Foreign Policy," 3.

21. Will Inboden, "Two Parties, Two Approaches to Multilateralism," *Foreign Policy*, May 31, 2012, http://shadow.foreignpolicy.com/posts/2012/05/31/two_parties_two_approaches_to_multilateralism.

22. Ibid.

23. Ibid.

24. Joshua W. Busby, Jonathan Monten, Jordan Tama, and William Inboden, "Congress Is Already Post-Partisan," *Foreign Affairs,* January 28, 2013, http://www.foreignaffairs.com/articles/138791/joshua-w-busby-jonathan-monten-jordan-tama-and-william-inboden/congress-is-already-post-partisan.

25. Doris A. Graber, "Intervention and Nonintervention," in DeConde, ed., *Encyclopedia of American Foreign Policy*, 482.

26. Ibid., 483.

27. Ronald E. Powaski, *Toward an Entangling Alliance: American Isolationism, Internationalism, and Europe, 1901–1950* (New York, NY: Greenwood Press, 1991), xi.

28. A. Kalaitzidis and G.W. Streich, *U.S. Foreign Policy: A Documentary Resource Guide.* (Santa Barbara, CA: Greenwood, 2011), xix.

29. "Monroe Doctrine; December 2, 1823," The Avalon Project, http://avalon.law.yale.edu/19th_century/monroe.asp.

30. Walter A. McDougall, *Promised Land, Crusader State: The American Encounter with the World since 1776* (New York, NY: Houghton Mifflin, 1997), 57.

31. See also, Hendrickson, *Union, Nation or Empire,* 278.

32. Jerald A. Combs, *The History of American Foreign Policy,* 3rd. ed. (Armonk, NY: M.E. Sharpe, 2008), 57–58.

33. Herring, *From Colony to Superpower*, 180.

34. Ibid., 182.

35. Cited in ibid., 207.

36. Rofe and Thompson, "'Internationalists in Isolationist Times,'" 48.

37. "Transcript of Theodore Roosevelt's Corollary to the Monroe Doctrine," http://www.ourdocuments.gov/doc.php?doc=56&page=transcript.

38. Cited in Carlos F. Diaz-Alejandro, "Direct Investment in Latin America," in Charles P. Kindleberger, ed., *The International Corporation* (Cambridge, MA: MIT Press, 1970), 320.

39. Rofe and Thompson, "'Internationalists in Isolationist Times,'" 48.

40. Herring, *From Colony to Superpower*, 406.

41. Justus D. Doenecke, "American Internationalism, 1939–1941," *The Journal of Libertarian Studies*, 1:3–4 (Summer/Fall 1982): 201, http://mises.org/journals/jls/6_3/6_3_1.pdf.

42. Gerald P. Nye, "Is Neutrality Possible for America?" in John N. Andrews and Carl A. Marsden, eds., *Tomorrow in the Making* (New York, NY: Whittlesey House, 1939), https://www.mtholyoke.edu/acad/intrel/interwar/nye.htm.

43. "Most Back Cuts Overall—but Not to the Military," *ABC News*, March 6, 2013, http://abcnews.go.com/blogs/politics/2013/03/most-back-cuts-overall-but-not-to-the-military/.

44. "Franklin D. Roosevelt: Proposal for Lend-Lease," http://www.britannica.com/presidents/article-9116959.

45. Henry R. Luce, "The American Century," *Life Magazine,* February 1941, http://www.informationclearinghouse.info/article6139.htm.

46. James M. Lindsay, "George W. Bush, Barack Obama and the Future of US Global Leadership," *International Affairs* 87:4 (2011).

47. Cited in John Dumbrell, "Unilateralism and 'America First'? President George W. Bush's Foreign Policy," *Political Quarterly* 73:3 (July 2002): 284.

48. Michael Hirsh, "Bush and the World," *Foreign Affairs,* September/October 2002, http://www.foreignaffairs.com/articles/58244/michael-hirsh/bush-and-the-world.

49. George H. W. Bush, Address to the Nation on the Invasion of Iraq, January 16, 1991, http://millercenter.org/scripps/archive/speeches/detail/3428.

50. William J. Clinton, *National Security Strategy of the United States, 1994–1995: Engagement and Enlargement* (Washington, DC: Potomac Books, 1994), 5.

51. Michael T. Klare, "The Clinton Doctrine", *The Nation,* April 1, 1999, http://www.thenation.com/article/clinton-doctrine#.

52. Francine Kiefer, "Clinton 'Doctrine': Is It Substance or Spin?" *Christian Science Monitor,* June 28, 1999, http://www.csmonitor.com/1999/0628/p2s1.html.

53. "To Paris, U.S. Looks Like a 'Hyperpower,'" *New York Times*, February 5, 1999, http://www.nytimes.com/1999/02/05/news/05iht-france.t_0.html.

54. Lindsay, "George W. Bush, Barack Obama and the Future of US Global Leadership," 769.

55. Cited in ibid.

56. Inaugural Address by George W. Bush, published January 20, 2005, *New York Times,* http://www.nytimes.com/2005/01/20/politics/20BUSH-TEXT.html.

57. Melvyn P. Leffler, "Bush's Foreign Policy," *Foreign Policy* 144 (September/October 2004): 22.

58. James M. Lindsay, "Rally 'Round the Flag," *Brookings Daily War Report,* The Brookings Institution, March 25, 2003, http://www.brookings.edu/research/opinions/2003/03/25iraq-lindsay.

59. James Kitfield, "Can Mitt Romney Recover the Soul of Republican Foreign Policy?" *The Atlantic*, August 27, 2012, http://www.theatlantic.com/international/archive/2012/08/can-mitt-romney-recover-the-soul-of-republican-foreign-policy/261602.

60. Barack Obama, "Renewing American Leadership," *Foreign Affairs* 86:4 (July/August 2007): 2–4.

61. Lindsay, "George W. Bush, Barack Obama and the Future of U.S. Global Leadership," 773.

62. Ryan Lizza, "The Consequentialist: How the Arab Spring Remade Obama's Foreign Policy," *The New Yorker*, May 2, 2011, http://www.newyorker.com/reporting/2011/05/02/110502fa_fact_lizza.

63. "The Nobel Peace Prize 2009 Press Release," Nobelprize.org (October 9, 2009), http://www.nobelprize.org/nobel_prizes/peace/laureates/2009/press.html.

64. Cited in Guy Chazan and Allstair MacDonald, "Nobel Committee's Decision Courts Controversy," *The Wall Street Journal*, October 11 2009, http://online.wsj.com/article/SB125509603349176083.html.

65. Cited in Scott Wilson, "President Obama Wins Nobel Peace Prize," *Washington Post*, October 10, 2009, http://www.washingtonpost.com/wp-dyn/content/article/2009/10/09/AR2009100900914.html.

66. Martin S. Indyk, Kenneth G. Lieberthal, and Michael E. O'Hanlon, "Scoring Obama's Foreign Policy," *Foreign Affairs* 91:3 (May/June 2012): 30.

67. "Obama's Speech to the United Nations General Assembly," *New York Times*, September 23, 2009, http://www.nytimes.com/2009/09/24/us/politics/24prexy.text.html.

68. "Obama's Second Inaugural Speech," *New York Times*, January 21, 2013, http://www.nytimes.com/2013/01/21/us/politics/obamas-second-inaugural-speech.html.

69. Daniel W. Drezner, "Does Obama Have a Grand Strategy?" *Foreign Affairs*, July/August 2011, http://www.foreignaffairs.com/articles/67919/daniel-w-drezner/does-obama-have-a-grand-strategy.

70. Cited in John Mueller, "The Iraq Syndrome Revisited," *Foreign Affairs*, March 28, 2011, http://www.foreignaffairs.com/articles/67681/john-mueller/the-iraq-syndrome-revisited.

71. "The Price of Detachment," *The Economist*, March 23, 2013, http://www.economist.com/news/united-states/21573970-shunning-foreign-entanglements-does-barack-obama-risk-losing-his-global-bully.

72. Jeffrey M. Jones and Nathan Wendt, "Americans Say UN Is Needed, but Doubt Its Effectiveness," *Gallup Politics*, March 28, 2013, http://www.gallup.com/poll/161549/americans-say-needed-doubt-effectiveness.aspx.

73. Gordon N. Bardos, "The High Cost of U.S. Foreign Policy," *The National Interest*, July 9, 2013, http://nationalinterest.org/commentary/the-high-cost-us-foreign-policy-8704.

74. Stephen G. Brooks, G. John Ikenberry, and William C. Wohlforth, "Lean Forward," *Foreign Affairs*, January/February 2013, http://www.foreignaffairs.com/articles/138468/stephen-g-brooks-g-john-ikenberry-and-william-c-wohlforth/lean-forward.

75. On shapers and restrainers/retrenchers, see James M. Parent and Paul K. MacDonald, "The Wisdom of Retrenchment," *Foreign Affairs* 90:6 (November/December 2011): 32–34; and Charles Kupchan, "Grand Strategy: The Four Pillars of the Future," *Democracy Journal* 27 (Winter 2012): 9–18.

76. Peter J. Spiro, "The New Sovereigntists: American Exceptionalism and Its False Prophets," *Foreign Affairs* 79:6 (November/December 2000), http://www.foreignaffairs.com/articles/56621/peter-j-spiro/the-new-sovereigntists-american-exceptionalism-and-its-false-pro.

77. Barry Posen, "Pull Back," *Foreign Affairs* 92:1 (January/February 2013), http://www.foreignaffairs.com/articles/138466/barry-r-posen/pull-back.

CHAPTER 3

1. Richard N. Haass, "The Age of Nonpolarity: What Will Follow U.S. Dominance," *Foreign Affairs*, May/June 2008, http://www.foreignaffairs.com/articles/63397/richard-n-haass/the-age-of-nonpolarity.

2. Laicie Heeley, "U.S. Defense Spending vs. Global Defense Spending," The Center for Arms Control and Non-Proliferation, April 24, 2013, http://armscontrolcenter.org/issues/securityspending/articles/2012_topline_global_defense_spending.

3. Cited in "U.S. Prepares First-Strike Cyber-Forces," *BBC*, October 12, 2012, http://www.bbc.com/news/technology-19922421.

4. "S.1939—War Powers Consultation Act of 2014," 113th Congress (2013–2014), https://www.congress.gov/bill/113th-congress/senate-bill/1939/text.

5. Cited in Jonathan Masters, "Debt, Deficits, and the Defense Budget," February 22, 2013, Council on Foreign Relations, http://www.cfr.org/defense-budget/debt-deficits-defense-budget/p27318.

6. Cited in Elise Labott, "Kerry's Mission: Mideast Buy-In for Anti-ISIS Effort," *CNN.com*, September 9, 2010, http://www.cnn.com/2014/09/09/politics/kerry-middle-east-trip-isis.

7. Cited in Ibid.

8. "Public Sees U.S. Power Declining as Support for Global Engagement Slips: America's Place in the World 2013," Pew Research Center for People and the Press, December 2, 2013, http://www.people-press.org/2013/12/03/public-sees-u-s-power-declining-as-support-for-global-engagement-slips.

9. Hal Brands, *The Promise and Pitfalls of Grand Strategy* (Carlisle, PA: Strategic Studies Institute, August 2012), 15, http://www.strategicstudiesinstitute.army.mil/pdffiles/PUB1121.pdf

10. George F. Kennan, *Memoirs 1925–1950* (Boston, MA: Little Brown, 1967), 557.

11. Cited in Melvyn P. Leffler, *A Preponderance of Power: National Security, the Truman Administration, and the Cold War* (Stanford, CA: Stanford University Press, 1992), 366.

12. "Vietnam Statistics—War Costs: Complete Picture Impossible," *CQ Almanac 1975*, 31st ed. (Washington, DC: Congressional Quarterly, 1976): 301–305, http://library.cqpress.com/cqalmanac/cqal75-1213988.

13. Cited in David M. Aatry, *Diplomacy at the Brink: Eisenhower, Churchill, and Eden in the Cold War* (Baton Rouge, LA: LSU Press, 2014), 103.

14. Michael Krepon, *Better Safe Than Sorry: The Ironies of Living with the Bomb* (Stanford, CA: Stanford University Press, 2009), 33.

15. Thomas C. Schelling and Morton H. Halperin, *Strategy and Arms Control* (New York, NY: Twentieth Century Fund, 1961).

16. U.S. State Department Bureau of Arms Control, Verification, and Compliance, "Treaty Between the United States of America and the Union of Soviet Socialist Republics on the Limitation of Offensive Arms (SALT II)," http://www.state.gov/t/isn/5195.htm.

17. Nuclear Threat Initiative, "Strategic Arms Limitation Talks (SALT II)," http://www.nti.org/treaties-and-regimes/strategic-arms-limitation-talks-salt-ii/.

18. Krepon, *Better Safe Than Sorry,* 69–70.

19. Arms Control Association, "START I at a Glance," http://www.armscontrol.org/factsheets/start1.

20. James R. Locher III, "Has It Worked? The Goldwater-Nichols Reorganization Act," *Naval War College Review* 54:4 (2001): 95–115.

21. The White House, *The National Security Strategy of the United States,* January 1988, 3, http://nssarchive.us/NSSR/1988.pdf.

22. UN Security Council Resolution 677, 28 November 1990, http://www.un.org/en/ga/search/view_doc.asp?symbol=S/RES/678 (1990).

23. George H. W. Bush and Brent Scowcroft, *A World Transformed* (New York: Knopf, 1998), 487.

24. U.S. Department of Defense, "Defense Casualty Analysis System," as of February 3, 2014, https://www.dmdc.osd.mil/dcas/pages/report_gulf_storm.xhtml.

25. Leslie Gelb, "Quelling the Teacup Wars: The New World's Constant Challenge," *Foreign Affairs,* November/December 1994, http://www.foreignaffairs.com/articles/50541/leslie-h-gelb/quelling-the-teacup-wars-the-new-worlds-constant-challenge.

26. "Authorization for Use of Military Force," (PL 107-40, September 18, 2001), https://www.congress.gov/bill/107th-congress/senate-joint-resolution/23/text.

27. "The National Security Strategy of the United States," September 2002, National Security Strategy Archive, http://nssarchive.us.

28. Donald Rumsfeld, "Transforming the Military," *Foreign Affairs*, May/June 2002, http://www.foreignaffairs.com/articles/58020/donald-h-rumsfeld/transforming-the-military.

29. *U.S. Government Counterinsurgency Guide,* January 2009, http://www.state.gov/documents/organization/119629.pdf.

30. Cited in Robert M. Cassidy, *War, Will and Warlords* (Quantico, VA: Marine Corps University Press, 2012), 40.

31. Jonathan Medalia, "Comprehensive Nuclear-Test-Ban Treaty: Background and Current Developments," June 10, 2013, RL33548, CRS Reports, 5, http://www.fas.org/sgp/crs/nuke/RL33548.pdf.

32. Cited in Thom Shanker, "Former Commander of U.S. Nuclear Forces Calls for Large Cuts in Warheads," *New York Times,* May 15, 2012, http://www.nytimes.com/2012/05/16/world/cartwright-key-retired-general-backs-large-us-nuclear-reduction.html.

33. Quadrennial Defense Review 2014, http://www.defense.gov/pubs/2014_Quadrennial_Defense_Review.pdf.

34. Congressional Budget Office, "Projected Costs of U.S. Nuclear Forces, 2015–2024," January 22, 2015, http://www.cbo.gov/publication/49870.

35. Arms Control Association, "U.S. Nuclear Modernization Programs," January 2014, http://www.armscontrol.org/factsheets/USNuclearModernization.

36. Christopher Harress, "U.S. Joins Russia in Latest Race to Modernize Nuclear Arsenal," *International Business Times,* November 14, 2014, http://www.ibtimes.com/us-joins-russia-latest-race-modernize-nuclear-arsenal-1724102.

37. Cited in William J. Broad and David E. Sanger, "U.S. Ramping Up Major Renewal of Nuclear Arms," *New York Times,* September 21, 2014, http://www.nytimes.com/2014/09/22/us/us-ramping-up-major-renewal-in-nuclear-arms.html.

38. Cited in Jim Garamone, "Obama Delineates Counterterrorism Policy," U.S. Department of Defense News, May 23, 2013, http://www.defense.gov/news/newsarticle.aspx?id=120129.

39. Linda Robinson, "The Future of Special Operations," *Foreign Affairs*, November/December 2012, http://www.foreignaffairs.com/articles/138232/linda-robinson/the-future-of-special-operations.

40. Cited in ibid.

41. Ibid.

42. Ibid.

43. Cited in "McCain Rips White House over Sony Hack," *The Hill,* December 18, 2014, http://thehill.com/policy/defense/227542-mccain-rips-administration-over-sony-hack.

44. Cited in Timothy Farnsworth, "Is There a Place for Nuclear Deterrence in Cyberspace?" *Arms Control Now,* May 30, 2013, http://armscontrolnow.org/?p=3487.

45. Cited in Ibid.

46. Cited in Maggie Ybarra, "Cyber Command Investment Ensures Hackers Targeting U.S. Face Retribution," *Washington Times,* December 22, 2014, http://www.washingtontimes.com/news/2014/dec/22/us-cyber-command-investment-ensures-hackers-target.

47. William J. Lynn III, "Defending a New Domain," *Foreign Affairs,* September/October 2010, http://www.foreignaffairs.com/articles/66552/william-j-lynn-iii/defending-a-new-domain.

48. Department of Defense Science Board, "Resilient Military Systems and the Advanced Cyber Threat," January 2013, 30–31, http://www.acq.osd.mil/dsb/reports/ResilientMilitarySystems.CyberThreat.pdf.

49. Ibid., 33.

50. Cited in David E. Sanger, "U.S. Blames China's Military Directly for Cyberattacks," *New York Times,* May 6, 2013, http://www.nytimes.com/2013/05/07/world/asia/us-accuses-chinas-military-in-cyberattacks.html?pagewanted=all.

51. Richard Bejtlich, "Don't Underestimate Cyber Spies," *Foreign Affairs,* May 2, 2013, http://www.foreignaffairs.com/articles/136559/richard-bejtlich/dont-underestimate-cyber-spies.

52. David E. Sanger, "As Chinese Leader's Visit Nears, U.S. Is Urged to Allow Counterattacks on Hackers," *New York Times,* May 21, 2013, http://www.nytimes.com/2013/05/22/world/asia/as-chinese-leaders-visit-nears-us-urged-to-allow-retaliation-for-cyberattacks.html?pagewanted=all.

53. William C. Hannas, James Mulvenon, and Anna B. Puglisi, *Chinese Industrial Espionage* (New York, NY: Routledge, 2013), 2.

54. Cited in Didi Kirsten Tatlow, "U.S. Is a 'Hacker Empire,' Says Chinese Military Analyst," *IHT Rendezvous,* June 26, 2013, http://rendezvous.blogs.nytimes.com/2013/06/26/u-s-is-a-hacker-empire-says-chinese-military-analyst/.

55. Cited in David E. Sanger, "Differences on Cybertheft Complicate China Talks," *New York Times,* July 10, 2013, http://www.nytimes.com/2013/07/11/world/asia/differences-on-cybertheft-complicate-china-talks.html.

56. Cited Thomas Catan and Josh Chin, "Leaks Muddy U.S. Position in Chinese Talks," *The Wall Street Journal,* July 9, 2013, A14.

57. Sarah Kreps, "Ground the Drones?" *Foreign Affairs*, December 4, 2013, http://www.foreignaffairs.com/articles/140318/sarah-kreps/ground-the-drones.

58. Kate Brannen, "Air Force's Lack of Drone Pilots Reaching 'Crisis' Levels," *Foreign Policy*, January 15, 2015, http://foreignpolicy.com/2015/01/15/air-forces-lack-of-drone-pilots-reaching-crisis-levels.

59. Micah Zenko cited in John Kaag and Sarah Kreps, *Drone Warfare* (New York, NY: Wiley, 2014), 32.

60. "Drone Wars Yemen: Analysis," International Security Data Site, http://securitydata.newamerica.net/drones/yemen/analysis.

61. "Afghanistan Drone Strike Data No Longer Reported by U.S. Air Force," *The World Post,* March 10, 2013, http://www.huffingtonpost.com/2013/03/10/afghanistan-drone-strike-data-no-longer-reported-us-air-force_n_2847296.html.

62. Cited in Thom Shanker, "Simple, Low-Cost Surveillance Drones Provide Advantage for U.S. Military," *New York Times*, January 24, 2013, http://www.nytimes.com/2013/01/25/us/simple-scaneagle-drones-a-boost-for-us-military.html.

63. Joshua Foust, "A Liberal Case for Drones," *Foreign Policy*, May 14, 2013, http://foreignpolicy.com/2013/05/15/a-liberal-case-for-drones.

64. Kaag and Kreps, *Drone Warfare*, 2.

65. Bill Briggs, "Study: U.S. Drone Strikes More Likely to Kill Civilians Than U.S. Jet Fire," *NBC News*, July 2, 2013, http://www.nbcnews.com/news/investigations/study-us-drone-strikes-more-likely-kill-civilians-us-jet-v19254842.

66. "Obama's Speech on Drone Policy," *New York Times*, May 23, 2013, http://www.nytimes.com/2013/05/24/us/politics/transcript-of-obamas-speech-on-drone-policy.html.

67. Aaron Stein, "Drone Decrees," *Foreign Affairs,* December 19, 2013, http://www.foreignaffairs.com/articles/140584/aaron-stein/drone-decrees.

68. Audrey Kurth Cronin, "Drones over Damascus," *Foreign Affairs*, September 2, 2013, http://www.foreignaffairs.com/articles/139889/audrey-kurth-cronin/drones-over-damascus.

69. Scott Peterson, "Iran Hijacked U.S. Drone, Says Iranian Engineer," *Christian Science Monitor,* December 15, 2011, http://www.csmonitor.com/World/Middle-East/2011/1215/Exclusive-Iran-hijacked-US-drone-says-Iranian-engineer-Video.

70. Cited in Sam Jones, "Drone Strikes on ISIS Loom Large in Allies' Strategy," *Financial Times,* October 12, 2014, http://www.ft.com/cms/s/0/e5f4397a-48cf-11e4-9d04-00144feab7de.html#axzz3RkxHdTXB.

71. Steven Metz, "The Strategy behind U.S. Drone Strikes," *World Politics Review*, February 27, 2013, http://www.worldpoliticsreview.com/articles/12747/strategic-horizons-the-strategy-behind-u-s-drone-strikes.

72. Cited in Joe Cirincione, "How Big a Nuclear Arsenal Do We Really Need?" *Los Angeles Times,* October 21, 2014, http://www.latimes.com/opinion/op-ed/la-oe-cirincione-nuclear-weapons-20141022-story.html.

73. Hans M. Kristensen, "Nuclear Weapons Modernization: A Threat to NPT?" *Arms Control Today,* May 1, 2014, http://www.armscontrol.org/act/2014_05/Nuclear-Weapons-Modernization-A-Threat-to-the-NPT.

74. Cited in Helene Cooper, "Obama Cites Limits of U.S. Role in Libya," *New York Times,* Marcy 28, 2011, http://www.nytimes.com/2011/03/29/world/africa/29prexy.html.

75. Sarah Dutton, Jennifer De Pinto, Anthony Salvanto, and Fred Backus, "Do Americans Want to Send Ground Troops to Fight ISIS?" *CBS News*, February 19, 2015, http://www.cbsnews.com/news/do-americans-want-to-send-ground-troops-to-fight-isis.

76. Minxin Pei and Sara Kasper, "Lessons from the Past: The American Record on Nation Building," *Policy Brief* 24, Carnegie Endowment for International Peace, May 2003, http://carnegieendowment.org/files/Policybrief24.pdf.

77. Henry Farrell, "The Political Science of Cybersecurity III—How International Relations Theory Shapes U.S. Cybersecurity Doctrine," *Washington Post,* February 20, 2014, http://www.washingtonpost.com/blogs/monkey-cage/wp/2014/02/20/the-political-science-of-cybersecurity-iii-how-international-relations-theory-shapes-u-s-cybersecurity-doctrine.

78. Thomas Rid, "Cyberwar and Peace," *Foreign Affairs*, November/December 2013, http://www.foreignaffairs.com/articles/140160/thomas-rid/cyberwar-and-peace.

79. Jason Healey, "Commentary: Cyber Deterrence Is Working," *DefenseNews*, July 30, 2014, http://archive.defensenews.com/article/20140730/DEFFEAT05/307300017/Commentary-Cyber-Deterrence-Working.

80. Peter W. Singer and Allan Friedman, "What About Deterrence in an Era of Cyberwar?" *Armed Forces Journal,* January 9, 2014, http://www.armedforcesjournal.com/what-about-deterrence-in-an-era-of-cyberwar.

81. Lynn, "Defending a New Domain."

82. Cited in Cory Bennett, "Senators Hopeful on Cyber Info Sharing Bill," *The Hill*, January 28, 2015, http://thehill.com/policy/cybersecurity/231048-senators-hopeful-on-cyber-info-sharing-bill.

83. Cited in Cory Bennett, "President Makes Unprecedented Cybersecurity Speech," *The Hill,* January 20, 2015, http://thehill.com/policy/cybersecurity/230157-obama-makes-unprecedented-cyber-pitch.

84. "Obama's Speech on Drone Policy," *New York Times,* May 23, 2013, http://www.nytimes.com/2013/05/24/us/politics/transcript-of-obamas-speech-on-drone-policy.html.

85. Daniel Markey, "A New Drone Deal for Pakistan," *Foreign Affairs,* August 8, 2013, http://www.foreignaffairs.com/articles/139584/daniel-markey/a-new-drone-deal-for-pakistan.

86. Daniel Byman, "Why Drones Work," *Foreign Affairs,* July/August 2013, http://www.foreignaffairs.com/articles/139453/daniel-byman/why-drones-work.

87. Dwight R. Lee and Richard K. Vedder, "The Political Economy of the Peace Dividend," *Public Choice* 88 (1996): 36–37.

88. Joe Gould, "Odierno: With Commitments Up, U.S. Must Rethink Cuts to Army End Strength," *Army Times,* November 21, 2014, http://www.armytimes.com/story/military/pentagon/2014/11/19/odierno-army-end-strength/19275911.

CHAPTER 4

1. George Perkovich, "Bush's Nuclear Revolution: A Regime Change in Nonproliferation," *Foreign Affairs* 81:2 (March/April 2003), http://www.foreignaffairs.com/articles/58804/george-perkovich/bushs-nuclear-revolution-a-regime-change-in-nonproliferation.

2. Dean Rusk, "Address to the Virginia State Bar Association," *Survival* 5:6 (July 15, 1963): 251.

3. Hal Brands, "Rethinking Nonproliferation: LBJ, the Gilpatric Committee, and U.S. National Security Policy," *Journal of Cold War Studies* 8:2 (Spring 2006): 88–89.

4. John F. Kennedy Presidential Library and Museum, "JFK Address at U.N. General Assembly, 25 September 1961," http://www.jfklibrary.org/Asset-Viewer/DOPIN64xJUGRKgdHJ9NfgQ.aspx.

5. John F. Kennedy Presidential Library and Museum, "John F. Kennedy Speeches, 'Face-to-Face, Nixon-Kennedy' Vice President Richard M. Nixon and Senator John F. Kennedy Third Joint Television-Radio Broadcast, October 13, 1960," http://www.jfklibrary.org/Research/Research-Aids/JFK-Speeches/3rd-Nixon-Kennedy-Debate_19601013.aspx.

6. Eric A. Croddy and James J. Wirtz, eds, *Weapons of Mass Destruction: An Encyclopedia of Worldwide Policy, Technology, and History* (Santa Barbara, CA: ABC-CLIO, 2015) vol 1, 181–182.

7. Paul Bracken, "The Structure of the Second Nuclear Age," *Orbis* 47:3 (Summer 2003): 402.

8. Ibid., 405.

9. "Text of President Bush's 2003 State of the Union Address," *Washington Post,* January 28, 2003, http://www.washingtonpost.com/wp-srv/onpolitics/transcripts/bushtext_012803.html.

10. The White House, Office of the Press Secretary, "Remarks by President Obama," Prague, Czech Republic, April 5, 2009, http://www.whitehouse.gov/the_press_office/Remarks-By-President-Barack-Obama-In-Prague-As-Delivered.

11. Council of Foreign Relations, "The Global Nuclear Nonproliferation Regime," Updated June 25, 2013, http://www.cfr.org/arms-control-disarmament-and-nonproliferation/global-nuclear-nonproliferation-regime/p18984.

12. United Nations Security Council Resolution 1540, 28 April 2004, S/RES/1540 (2004), http://www.un.org/en/sc/documents/resolutions/2004.shtml.

13. Gerald Felix Warburg, "Nonproliferation Policy Crossroads," *The Nonproliferation Review* 19:3 (2012): 453.

14. Ibid., 452.

15. Daniel Painter, "The Nuclear Suppliers Group at the Crossroads," *The Diplomat*, June 10, 2013, http://thediplomat.com/2013/06/10/the-nuclear-suppliers-group-at-the-crossroads.

16. Ibid.

17. "Proliferation Security Initiative: Ten Years On," *Arms Control Now*, http://armscontrolnow.org/?p=3480.

18. Council on Foreign Relations, "The Global Nuclear Nonproliferation Regime," July 25, 2013, http://www.cfr.org/arms-control-disarmament-and-nonproliferation/global-nuclear-nonproliferation-regime/p18984.

19. Cited in Aaron Dunne, "The Proliferation Security Initiative: Legal Considerations and Operational Realities," SIPRI Policy Paper 36, May 2013, 5, http://books.sipri.org/product_info?c_product_id=459.

20. Wade Boese, "Bush Shifts Fissile Material Ban Policy," *Arms Control Today,* September 2004, http://www.armscontrol.org/act/2004_09/FMCT.

21. UN Special Commission (UNSCOM), "Chronology of Main Events," December 1999, http://www.un.org/Depts/unscom/Chronology/chronologyframe.htm.

22. UN Security Council, Resolution 1441, November 8, 2002, http://www.un.org/depts/unmovic/documents/1441.pdf.

23. Cited in "Iraq War Illegal, Says Annan," *BBC News*, September 16, 2004, http://news.bbc.co.uk/2/hi/middle_east/3661134.stm.

24. "National Security Strategy," March 2006, The National Security Strategy Archive, http://nssarchive.U.S.

25. "National Security Strategy," May 2010, The National Security Strategy Archive, http://nssarchive.U.S.

26. "Text of President Bush's 2002 State of the Union Address," *Washington Post*, January 20, 2002, http://www.washingtonpost.com/wp-srv/onpolitics/transcripts/sou012902.html.

27. "Interview: North Korea's Nuclear Needs," Council on Foreign Relations, February 2, 2013, http://www.cfr.org/north-korea/north-koreas-nuclear-needs/p29907.

28. William Burr, "A Brief History of U.S.-Iranian Nuclear Negotiations," *Bulletin of the Atomic Scientists* 65:21 (January 2009): 24–25.

29. Greg Bruno, "Iran's Nuclear Program," *Council on Foreign Relations Backgrounder,* March 10, 2010, http://www.cfr.org/iran/irans-nuclear-program/p16811.

30. "UN Nuclear Agency IAEA: Iran 'Studying Nuclear Weapons,'" *BBC News*, November 8, 2011, http://www.bbc.co.uk/news/world-middle-east-15643460.

31. Cited in Rick Gladstone, "Iran's New President Preaches Tolerance in First UN Appearance," *New York Times*, September 24, 2013, http://www.nytimes.com/2013/09/25/world/middleeast/irans-new-president-in-first-un-appearance-preaches-tolerance-says-his-country-is-no-threat.html.

32. Cited in ibid.

33. Cited in Rick Gladstone and Thomas Erdbrink, "Temporary Deal with Iran Takes Effect," *New York Times,* January 20, 2014, http://nyti.ms/1cLkyPE.

34. Cited in Tom Cohen, "5 Reasons Diverse Critics Oppose Iran Nuclear Deal," *CNN,* November 25, 2013, http://www.cnn.com/2013/11/25/politics/iran-deal-opponents-5-things.

35. Cited in Holly Yan and Josh Levs, "Iran Nuclear Deal: One Agreement, Wildly Different Reactions," *CNN*, November 24, 2013, http://www.cnn.com/2013/11/24/world/iran-deal-reaction.

36. Ibid.

37. Cited in Michael R. Gordon and David E. Sanger, "Iran Agrees to Detailed Nuclear Outline, First Step toward a Wider Deal," *New York Times,* April 2, 2015, http://www.nytimes.com/2015/04/03/world/middleeast/iran-nuclear-talks.html.

38. Cited in Peter Baker, "A Foreign Policy Gamble by Obama at a Moment of Truth," *New York Times,* April 2, 2015, http://www.nytimes.com/2015/04/03/world/middleeast/a-foreign-policy-gamble-by-obama-at-a-moment-of-truth.html.

39. Cited in ibid.

40. "P5+1 Nations and Iran Reach Historic Nuclear Deal," Arms Control Association, July 14, 2015, http://us10.campaign-archive2.com/?u=94d82a9d1fc1a60f0138613f1&id=ba4273f1a0&e=6fc14e143a.

41. Cited in Carlo Muñoz, "Sens. Levin, McCain Push Obama to Take Military Action in Syria," *The Hill*, March 21, 2013, http://thehill.com/blogs/defcon-hill/policy-and-strategy/289659-senators-push-obama-to-establish-safe-zone-in-syria-with-airstrikes.

42. "Government Assessment of the Syrian Government's Use of Chemical Weapons on August 21, 2013," The White House Office of the Press Secretary, August 30, 2013, http://www.whitehouse.gov/the-press-office/2013/08/30/government-assessment-syrian-government-s-use-chemical-weapons-august-21.

43. John Mueller, "Erase the Red Line," *Foreign Policy*, April 20, 2013, http://www.foreignaffairs.com/articles/139351/john-mueller/erase-the-red-line.

44. Ibid.

45. Betcy Jose, "Civilians vs. Chemicals," *Foreign Affairs,* September 26, 2013, http://www.foreignaffairs.com/articles/139959/betcy-jose/civilians-vs-chemicals.

46. "Text of President Obama's Remarks on Syria," *New York Times,* August 31, 2013, http://www.nytimes.com/2013/09/01/world/middleeast/text-of-president-obamas-remarks-on-syria.html.

47. Vladimir V. Putin, "A Plea for Caution from Russia," *New York Times,* September 11, 2013, http://www

.nytimes.com/2013/09/12/opinion/putin-plea-for-caution-from-russia-on-syria.html.

48. Andrew Dugan, "U.S. Support for Action in Syria Is Low vs. Past Conflicts," *Gallup Politics*, September 6, 2013, http://www.gallup.com/poll/164282/support-syria-action-lower-past-conflicts.aspx.

49. "About the OPCW," Organization for the Prohibition of Chemical Weapons," http://www.opcw.org/about-opcw.

50. U.S. Department of State, "Framework for Elimination of Chemical Weapons," September 14, 2013, http://www.state.gov/r/pa/prs/ps/2013/09/214247.htm.

51. Cited in Alan Rappeport, "Syria's Chemical Arsenal Fully Destroyed, U.S. Says," *New York Times,* August 18, 2014.

52. Kenneth Waltz, "Why Iran Should Get the Bomb," *Foreign Affairs* 91:4 (July/August 2012), http://www.foreignaffairs.com/articles/137731/kenneth-n-waltz/why-iran-should-get-the-bomb.

53. Matthew Kroenig, "Still Time to Attack Iran," *Foreign Affairs*, January 7, 2014, http://www.foreignaffairs.com/articles/140632/matthew-kroenig/still-time-to-attack-iran.

54. Colin H. Kahl, "Not Time to Attack Iran," *Foreign Affairs,* March/April, 2012, http://www.foreignaffairs.com/articles/137031/colin-h-kahl/not-time-to-attack-iran.

55. Cited in Rebecca Shabad, "Top Dems Divided on More Iran Sanctions," *The Hill*, December 19, 2013, http://thehill.com/blogs/global-affairs/middle-east-north-africa/193669-dems-divided-on-tougher-iran-sanctions-as-bill.

56. Edward Levine, "Analysis of Faults in the Menendez-Kirk Iran Sanctions Bill (S. 1881)," The Center for Arms Control and Non-Proliferation, http://armscontrolcenter.org/issues/iran/articles/analysis_of_faults_in_the_menendez-kirk_iran_sanctions_bill_s_1881.

57. Cited in Shabad, "Top Dems Divided on More Iran Sanctions."

58. "Full Transcript: Obama's 2014 State of the Union Address," *Washington Post*, January 28, 2014, http://www.washingtonpost.com/politics/full-text-of-obamas-2014-state-of-the-union-address/2014/01/28/e0c93358-887f-11e3-a5bd-844629433ba3_story.html.

59. Kate Brannen, "Syria's Most Lethal Chemical Weapons Destroyed with Little Fanfare," *Foreign Policy*, August 18, 2014, http://complex.foreignpolicy.com/posts/2014/08/18/syria_s_most_lethal_chemical_weapons_destroyed_with_little_fanfare.

CHAPTER 5

1. "Bernanke Warns about Economic Isolationism," *NBCNews.com*, May 1, 2007, http://www.nbcnews.com/id/18417161/ns/business-stocks_and_economy/t/bernanke-warns-about-economic-isolationism/#.VBx3f0tlI5M.

2. Lydia Saad, "Americans Remain Positive about Foreign Trade," *Gallup,* February 21, 2014, http://www.gallup.com/poll/167516/americans-remain-positive-foreign-trade.aspx.

3. Charles P. Kindleberger, "Two Hundred Years of American Foreign Policy: US Foreign Economic Policy, 1776–1976," *Foreign Affairs,* January 1977, http://www.foreignaffairs.com/articles/27041/charles-p-kindleberger/two-hundred-years-of-american-foreign-policy-us-foreign-economic.

4. David A. Lake, *Power, Protection, and Free Trade* (Ithaca, NY: Cornell University Press, 1988), 4.

5. "The First Bank of the United States," The Federal Reserve Bank of Philadelphia, June 2009, http://www.philadelphiafed.org.

6. Bureau of the Public Debt, "Our History," http://www.publicdebt.treas.gov/history/1800.htm.

7. "The Slumps That Shaped Modern Finance," *The Economist*, April 12, 2014, 50; Hugh Rockoff, "Banking and Finance, 1789–1912," in Stanley L. Engermand and Robert E. Gallman, eds., *The Cambridge Economic History of the United States* (Cambridge, MA: Cambridge University Press, 2000), 647.

8. Kindleberger, "Two Hundred Years of American Foreign Policy: US Foreign Economic Policy, 1776–1976."

9. Philip Scranton, "The World War I Debts That Wouldn't Go Away," *BloombergView*, February 4, 2013, http://www.bloombergview.com/articles/2013-02-04/the-world-war-i-debts-that-wouldn-t-go-away-.

10. Cited in Michael Lind, *Land of Promise* (New York, NY: HarperCollins, 2012), 265.

11. "The Battle of Smoot-Hawley," *The Economist,* December 18, 2008, http://www.economist.com/node/12798595.

12. Cited in ibid.

13. Ibid.

14. Cited in Carolyn Rhodes, *Reciprocity, U.S. Trade Policy, and the GATT Regime* (Ithaca, NY: Cornell University Press, 1993), 55.

15. Robert L. Tontz, "U.S. Trade Policy: Background and Historical Trends," in *U.S. Trade Policy and Agricultural Exports* (Ames: Iowa State University Press, 1973): 20, 22.

16. Paul Kennedy, *The Rise and Fall of the Great Powers* (New York, NY: Random House, 1987), 358.

17. Michael Mandelbaum, *The Case for Goliath* (New York, NY: Public Affairs Press, 2005), 118.

18. Joanne Gowa, *Closing the Gold Window: Domestic Politics and the End of Bretton Woods* (Ithaca, NY: Cornell University Press, 1983), 22–23.

19. Robert Gilpin, *Global Political Economy: Understanding the International Economic Order* (Princeton, NJ: Princeton University Press, 2001), 179.

20. Dylan Matthews, "QE3 Is On! Fed to Buy $85b through December, and Then Keep Going," *Washington Post,* September 12, 2012, http://www.washingtonpost.com/blogs/wonkblog/wp/2012/09/13/qe3-is-on.

21. Cited in Andrew Huszar, "Andrew Huszar: Confessions of a Quantitative Easer," *The Wall Street Journal*, November 11, 2013, http://online.wsj.com/articles/SB10001424052702303763804579183680751473884.

22. Jon Hilsenrath, "Hilsenrath Analysis: Fed Likely to Continue Taper, Consider Changing Forward Guidance," *The Wall Street Journal*, March 7, 2014, http://blogs.wsj.com/economics/2014/03/07/hilsenrath-analysis-fed-likely-to-continue-taper-consider-changing-to-forward-guidance.

23. Thomas Wright, "How G20 Keeps World Away from Economic Brink," *CNN*, September 6, 2013, http://www.cnn.com/2013/09/05/opinion/wright-g20-summit.

24. Communique, Finance Ministers and Central Bank Governors Meeting, Berlin, Germany, December 15–16, 1999, accessed September 7, 2015, http://www.g20.utoronto.ca/1999/1999communique.htm.

25. G20, "G20 Members," https://g20.org/about-g20/g20-members.

26. "Realtime Economics: Geithner Statement on Delay of Report on China Currency Policies," *The Wall Street Journal,* April 3, 2010, http://blogs.wsj.com/economics/2010/04/03/geithner-statement-on-delay-of-report-on-china-currency-policies.

27. WTO, International Trade Statistics 2013, "World Trade Developments," http://www.wto.org/english/res_e/statis_e/its2013_e/its13_highlights1_e.pdf.

28. WTO, International Trade Statistics, 2014, "World Trade Developments," http://www.wto.org/english/res_e/statis_e/its2014_e/its14_highlights1_e.pdf.

29. Christopher Alessi and Robert McMahon, "U.S. Trade Policy," Council on Foreign Relations, March 14, 2012, http://www.cfr.org/trade/us-trade-policy/p17859.

30. "Trade Policy: Taking Aim at Imports," *The Economist*, February 22, 2014, http://www.economist.com/news/united-states/21596939-protectionists-congress-could-scupper-crucial-free-trade-deals-taking-aim-imports.

31. Aaditya Mattoo and Arvind Subramanian, "From Doha to the Next Bretton Woods," *Foreign Affairs* 88:1 (January/February 2009): 16.

32. Rhodes, *Reciprocity, U.S. Trade Policy, and the GATT Regime*, 75.

33. Robert Gilpin, *Global Political Economy* (Princeton, NJ: Princeton University Press, 2001), 219.

34. John Gerard Ruggie, "International Regimes, Transactions, and Change: Embedded Liberalism in the Postwar Economic Order," *International Organization* 36:2 (Spring 1982): 379-415.

35. WTO, "Disputes by Country/Territory," accessed September 7, 2015, http://www.wto.org/english/tratop_e/dispu_e/dispu_by_country_e.htm.

36. "Doha Delivers," *The Economist*, December 9, 2013, http://www.economist.com/blogs/freeexchange/2013/12/world-trade-organisation; "Global Trade Suffers Another Setback," *New York Times,* August 3, 2014, http://www.nytimes.com/2014/08/04/opinion/global-trade-talks-suffer-another-setback.html.

37. J.P. Singh, "India's Multi-Faceted WTO Refusal," *Washington Post*, August 5, 2014, http://www

.washingtonpost.com/blogs/monkey-cage/
wp/2014/08/05/indias-multi-faceted-wto-refusal.

38. Cited in "U.S. Nuclear Firms Urge Ex-Im Bank
    Renewal," *World Nuclear News*, July 30, 2014, http://
    www.world-nuclear-news.org/NP-US-nuclear-firms-
    urge-ex-im-bank-renewal-30071401.html.

39. Nicola Clark, "Boeing Optimistic That Export-Import
    Bank Will Get Funding," *New York Times*, July 13,
    2014, http://www.nytimes.com/2014/07/14/business/
    international/boeing-optimistic-that-export-import-
    bank-will-get-funding.html.

40. Gary Clyde Haufbauer and Jeffrey J. Schott,
    NAFTA Revisited: Achievements and Challenges
    (Washington, DC: Institute for International
    Economics, 2005), 3.

41. Carla A. Hills, "NAFTA's Economic Upsides: The View
    from the United States," *Foreign Affairs*, January/
    February 2014, http://www.foreignaffairs
    .com/articles/140348/carla-a-hills/naftas-economic-
    upsides.

42. Gary Hufbauer, "Ross Perot Was Wrong about
    NAFTA," *New York Times*, November 25, 2013, http://
    www.nytimes.com/roomfordebate/2013/11/24/what-
    weve-learned-from-nafta/ross-perot-was-wrong-
    about-nafta.

43. "Free Trade Area of the Americas-FTAA," Official
    Website of the Free Trade Area of the Americas,
    accessed September 7, 2015, http://www.ftaa-alca
    .org/view_e.asp.

44. Cited in Larry Rohter and Elisabeth Bumiller,
    "Hemisphere Meeting Ends without Trade
    Consensus," *New York Times*, November 6, 2005,
    http://www.nytimes.com/2005/11/06/international/
    americas/06prexy.html.

45. Cited in ibid.

46. Ian F. Fergusson, William H. Cooper, Remy Jurenas,
    and Brock R. Williams, "The Trans-Pacific Partnership
    (TPP) Negotiations and Issues for Congress," *CRS
    Report R42694,* December 13, 2013, https://www
    .fas.org/sgp/crs/row/R42694.pdf, 3.

47. Lydia DePillis, "Everything You Need to Know about
    the Trans Pacific Partnership," *Washington Post,*
    December 11, 2013, http://www.washingtonpost
    .com/blogs/wonkblog/wp/2013/12/11/everything-
    you-need-to-know-about-the-trans-pacific-
    partnership/; "Trans-Pacific Partnership: Summary
    of US Objectives," Office of the United States Trade

Representative, http://www.ustr.gov/tpp/Summary-
of-US-objectives.

48. Cited in ibid.

49. Cited in Mitsuru Obe, "Will the TPP Go the Way
    of the WTO's Doha Round?" *The Wall Street
    Journal,* May 23, 2014, http://blogs.wsj.com/
    economics/2014/05/23/will-the-tpp-go-the-way-of-
    the-wtos-doha-round.

50. Ian Bremmer and David Gordon, "Two Key Foreign
    Policy Openings for Obama," *New York Times*,
    February 25, 2013, http://www.nytimes
    .com/2013/02/26/opinion/global/two-key-foreign-
    policy-openings-for-obama.html.

51. "European Union." Office of the United States Trade
    Representative, accessed September 5, 2015, http://
    www.ustr.gov/countries-regions/europe-middle-east/
    europe/european-union.

52. United States-European Union High Level Working
    Group on Jobs and Growth (HLWG), "Final Report
    High Level Working Group on Jobs and Growth,"
    February 1, 2013, http://trade.ec.europa.eu/doclib/
    docs/2013/february/tradoc_150519.pdf.

53. Cited in James Kanter, "E.U. Tries to Assuage Fears
    over U.S. Trade Deal," *New York Times,* March 27,
    2014, http://www.nytimes.com/2014/03/28/business/
    international/eu-tries-to-assuage-fears-over-us-
    trade-deal.html.

54. Charlemagne, "Transatlantic Trading," *The
    Economist,* February 2, 2013: 44.

55. Cited in David Jolly, "More Hope Than Headway So
    Far in U.S.-Europe Trade Talks," *New York Times,*
    March 14, 2014, http://www.nytimes
    .com/2014/03/15/business/international/more-hope-
    than-headway-so-far-in-us-europe-trade-talks.html.

56. "U.S. Trade in Goods by Country," U.S. Census
    Bureau, accessed September 7, 2015, http://www
    .census.gov/foreign-trade/balance.

57. "Top Ten Countries with Which the U.S. Has a Trade
    Deficit for the Month of April 2013," U.S. Census
    Bureau, http://www.census.gov/foreign-trade/top/
    dst/current/deficit.html.

58. Ian Talley, "U.S. Trade Gap with China, 80% of
    Trade Deficit, Hits Historic High," *The Wall Street
    Journal,* November 4, 2014, http://blogs.wsj.com/
    economics/2014/11/04/u-s-trade-gap-with-china-80-
    of-trade-deficit-hits-historic-high; "Slicing an Apple:
    How Much of an iPhone Is Made by Samsung," *The*

Economist, August 10, 2011, http://www.economist.com/blogs/dailychart/2011/08/apple-and-samsungs-symbiotic-relationship.

59. Bruce Stokes, "U.S.-China Economic Relations in the Wake of the U.S. Election," *Pew Research Global Attitudes Project,* December 10, 2012, http://www.pewglobal.org/2012/12/10/u-s-china-economic-relations-in-the-wake-of-the-u-s-election.

60. Ibid.

61. Cited in David E. Sanger, "A New Cold War, in Cyberspace, Tests U.S. Ties to China," *New York Times,* February 24, 2013, http://www.nytimes.com/2013/02/21/business/global/china-says-army-not-behind-attacks-in-report.html.

62. Cited in Zachary A. Goldfarb, "China Less of a U.S. Creditor as It Becomes More of an Election Issue," *Washington Post,* October 16, 2012, http://articles.washingtonpost.com/2012-10-16/business/35501537_1_china-and-japan-government-debt-eswar-prasad.

63. James W. Paulsen, "Will the U.S. Run a Trade Surplus Again?" *Barron's,* August 6, 2014, http://online.barrons.com/articles/SB50001424053111904329504580075513173336640.

64. Goldman Sachs economist Jim O'Neill first coined the name BRICs in 2001, to which South Africa was added in 2010.

65. "GDP Growth (Annual %)," The World Bank, http://data.worldbank.org/indicator/NY.GDP.MKTP.KD.ZG; "When Giants Slow Down," *The Economist,* July 27, 2013, http://www.economist.com/news/briefing/21582257-most-dramatic-and-disruptive-period-emerging-market-growth-world-has-ever-seen.

66. The Bretton Woods Committee, March 5, 2013, http://www.brettonwoods.org/sites/default/files/publications/Bretton%20Woods%20Comm_Bipartisan%20Officials%20Letter%20to%20Support%20IMF%20Quota%20Changes%202013.pdf.

67. Nick Timiraos, "5 Questions on Trade Adjustment Assistance," *The Wall Street Journal,* June 15, 2015, http://blogs.wsj.com/briefly/2015/06/15/5-questions-on-trade-adjustment-assistance.

68. "Grand Central: Currency Mismatch Seems Likely to Deepen as Central Banks Diverge," *The Wall Street Journal,* December 8, 2014, http://blogs.wsj.com/economics/2014/12/08/grand-central-currency-mismatch-seems-likely-to-deepen-as-central-banks-diverge.

CHAPTER 6

1. Michael Ignatieff, "No Exceptions?" *Legal Affairs* 59 (2002), http://www.legalaffairs.org/issues/May-June-2002/review_ignatieff_mayjun2002.msp.

2. William Korey, "Human Rights Treaties: Why Is the U.S. Stalling?" *Foreign Affairs*, April 1967, http://www.foreignaffairs.com/articles/23875/william-korey/human-rights-treaties-why-is-the-us-stalling.

3. Felice D. Gaer, "Protecting Human Rights," in Charles Mayes and Richard Williamson, eds., *U.S. Foreign Policy and the United Nations System* (New York, NY: W.W. Norton & Company, 1996), 148.

4. Cited in Sydney Blumenthal, *The Rise of the Counter-Establishment* (New York, NY: Union Square Press, 2008), 142.

5. Andrew Moravcsik, "The Paradox of U.S. Human Rights Policy," in Michael Ignatieff, ed., *American Exceptionalism and Human Rights* (Princeton, NJ: Princeton University Press, 2005), 154.

6. Cited in Louis Henkin, "U.S. Ratification of Human Rights Conventions: The Ghost of Senator Bricker," *American Journal of International Law* 89:2 (1995): 347.

7. Cited in ibid., 349.

8. David P. Forsythe, "Human Rights and U.S. Foreign Policy," *Political Science Quarterly* 105:3 (1990): 437.

9. Cited in Roberta Cohen, "Integrating Human Rights in U.S. Foreign Policy: The History, Challenges, and the Criteria for an Effective Policy," Foreign Service Institute, April 2008, 2, http://www.brookings.edu/research/speeches/2008/04/human-rights-cohen.

10. Douglas Brinkley, "Democratic Enlargement: The Clinton Doctrine," *Foreign Policy* 106 (Spring 1997): 116.

11. Gordon S. Wood, cited in David P. Forsythe, "U.S. Foreign Policy and Human Rights: Situating Obama," *Human Rights Quarterly* 33:3 (2011): 769–770.

12. Arthur M. Schlesinger, Jr., "Human Rights and the American Tradition," *Foreign Affairs*, 57:3 (1978), http://www.foreignaffairs.com/articles/31960/arthur-m-schlesinger-jr/human-rights-and-the-american-tradition.

13. Laurence J. Haas, *Sound the Trumpet: The United States and Human Rights Promotion* (Lanham, MD: Rowman and Littlefield, 2012), 69.

14. Henkin, "U.S. Ratification of Human Rights Conventions," 341.

15. Ibid., 346.

16. Cited in Haas, *Sound the Trumpet,* 90.

17. Ibid.

18. Cited in "'Legitimate Concerns' over Outcome of Michael Brown and Eric Garner Cases—UN Rights Experts," UN High Commissioner for Human Rights, December 5, 2014, http://www.ohchr.org/EN/NewsEvents/Pages/DisplayNews.aspx?NewsID=15384&LangID=E.

19. Cited in Robert Mackey, "Russia, Iran, and Egypt Heckle U.S. about Tactics in Ferguson," *New York Times*, August 19, 2014, http://www.nytimes.com/2014/08/20/world/europe/russia-iran-and-egypt-heckle-us-about-tactics-in-ferguson.html.

20. Cited in Robin Wright, "Dictators: Upbraid U.S. for Racial Unrest in Ferguson," *The Wall Street Journal*, August 19, 2014, http://blogs.wsj.com/washwire/2014/08/19/dictators-upbraid-u-s-for-racial-unrest-in-ferguson.

21. Mackey, "Russia, Iran, and Egypt Heckle U.S. about Tactics in Ferguson."

22. Wright, "Dictators."

23. Cited in "Rodong Sinmun Brands U.S. as Worst Human Rights Abuser," *KFA United Kingdom,* April 29, 2015, https://www.facebook.com/permalink.php?story_fbid=811146578977439&id=223522167739886.

24. Cited in Mary E. Stuckey, *Jimmy Carter, Human Rights, and the National Agenda* (College Station, TX: Texas A&M University Press, 2009), 56, 57.

25. Cited in Forsythe, "U.S. Foreign Policy and Human Rights," 770.

26. Cited in Tamar Jacoby, "The Reagan Turnaround on Human Rights," *Foreign Affairs,* Summer 1986, http://www.foreignaffairs.com/articles/41064/tamar-jacoby/the-reagan-turnaround-on-human-rights.

27. Kathryn Sikkink, *Mixed Signals: U.S. Human Rights Policy and Latin America* (Ithaca, NY: Cornell University Press, 2004), 182–185.

28. Remarks of Anthony Lake, "From Containment to Enlargement," Johns Hopkins University School of Advanced International Studies, Washington, DC, September 21, 1993, http://www.fas.org/news/usa/1993/usa-930921.htm.

29. "Chinese Politics and the WTO: No Change," *The Economist*, December 20, 2011, http://www.economist.com/node/21541461.

30. Cited in John W. Dietrich, "U.S. Human Rights Policy in the Post-Cold War Era," *Political Science Quarterly* 121:2 (2006): 274.

31. John Kerry, Press Statement, "Special Envoy for the Human Rights of LGBT Persons," Department of State, February 23, 2015, http://www.state.gov/secretary/remarks/2015/02/237772.htm.

32. Luisa Blanchfield, "The United Nations Human Rights Council: Issues for Congress," *CRS Report for Congress*, April 20, 2013, 12, https://www.fas.org/sgp/crs/row/RL33608.pdf.

33. Cited in Colum Lynch, "U.S. to Seek Seat on UN Human Rights Council," *Washington Post,* April 1, 2009, http://www.washingtonpost.com/wp-dyn/content/article/2009/03/31/AR2009033104115.html.

34. Ibid.

35. Brett D. Schaeffer, "UN Human Rights Council: A Flawed Body That Should Be Replaced," The Heritage Foundation Issue Brief #4088, November 19, 2013, http://www.heritage.org/research/reports/2013/11/un-human-rights-council-a-flawed-body-that-should-be-replaced.

36. Jackson Nyamuya Maogoto, *War Crimes and Realpolitik* (Boulder, CO: Lynne Rienner 2004), 219–220.

37. The White House, "National Security Strategy" (May 2010), https://www.whitehouse.gov/sites/default/files/rss_viewer/national_security_strategy.pdf, 48.

38. The UN Refugee Agency (UNFR),"Child Soldiers Global Report 2001—Sudan," UN High Commissioner for Refugees, http://www.refworld.org/docid/498805cb32.html.

39. Asteris Huliaras, "Evangelists, Oil Companies, and Terrorists: The Bush Administration's Policy towards Sudan," *Orbis* 50:4 (Autumn 2006), 714.

40. Cited in Ty McCormick, "Unmade in the USA," *Foreign Policy,* February 25, 2015, http://foreignpolicy.com/2015/02/25/unmade-in-the-usa-south-sudan-bush-obama.

41. "Conflicts in South Sudan," Enough Project, October 1, 2014, http://www.enoughproject.org/conflicts/sudans/conflicts-south-sudan.

42. "South Sudan: United States Provides Support for Justice and Accountability," U.S. Department of State Press Release, May 5, 2015, http://www.state.gov/r/pa/prs/ps/2015/05/241927.htm.

43. Rochard Cockett, *Sudan: Darfur and the Failure of an African State* (New Haven, CT: Yale University Press, 2010), 188.

44. "Genocide in Darfur," United Nations Human Rights Council, accessed September 7, 2015, http://www.unitedhumanrights.org/genocide/genocide-in-sudan.htm.

45. Convention on the Prevention and Punishment of the Crime of Genocide, Adopted by the General Assembly of the UN on 9 December 1948, https://treaties.un.org/doc/Publication/UNTS/Volume%2078/volume-78-I-1021-English.pdf.

46. Ibid.

47. "Report of the International Commission of Inquiry on Darfur to the United Nations Secretary-General," January 25, 2005, 4, http://www.un.org/news/dh/sudan/com_inq_darfur.pdf.

48. "Security Council Refers Situation in Darfur, Sudan, to Prosecutor of International Criminal Court," United Nations Security Council Press Release, March 31, 2005, http://www.un.org/press/en/2005/sc8351.doc.htm.

49. Nicholas Kristof, "Angelina Jolie and Darfur," *New York Times,* October 20, 2008, http://kristof.blogs.nytimes.com/2008/10/20/angelina-jolie-and-darfur.

50. Dugald McConnell and Brian Todd, "Cuban Prisoners Said to Make Videos Exposing Prison Conditions," *CNN,* March 17, 2012, http://www.cnn.com/2012/03/16/world/americas/cuban-prison-videos.

51. Cited in "Obama's Cuba Opening Hits Early Obstacles, Faces Struggle with Congress," *New York Times,* January 3, 2015, http://www.nytimes.com/reuters/2015/01/03/world/americas/03reuters-cuba-usa.html.

52. Cited in "Bush Mixes Diplomacy, Sports in Beijing," *CNN,* August 11, 2008, http://www.cnn.com/2008/POLITICS/08/11/bush.olympics/index.html.

53. Human Rights Watch, "World Report 2014," accessed September 7, 2015, http://www.hrw.org/world-report/2014/country-chapters/china.

54. Cited in Perry Bacon, Jr., "Obama Meets Privately with Dalai Lama," *Washington Post,* July 16, 2011, http://articles.washingtonpost.com/2011-07-16/politics/35236863_1_dalai-lama-tibet-concerns-support-tibetan-independence.

55. Cited in "Xi Jinping: China Will 'Smash' Tibet Separatism," *BBC News,* July 19, 2011, http://www.bbc.co.uk/news/world-asia-pacific-14205998.

56. René Värk, "The Status and Protection of Unlawful Combatants," *Juridica International Law Review,* University of Tartu, 2005, http://www.juridicainternational.eu/?id=12632.

57. "Convention (III) Relative to the Treatment of Prisoners of War," Article 3, Geneva, August 12, 1949, https://www.icrc.org/applic/ihl/ihl.nsf.

58. For a complete list, see Open Society Justice Initiative, *Globalizing Torture: CIA Secret Detention and Extraordinary Rendition* (New York, NY: Open Society Foundation, 2013), 6.

59. Ibid., 16.

60. Cited in Dana Priest, "CIA Holds Terror Suspects in Secret Prisons," *Washington Post*, November 2, 2005, http://www.washingtonpost.com/wp-dyn/content/article/2005/11/01/AR2005110101644_2.html.

61. Paul Elias, "Court Sides With CIA on 'Extraordinary Rendition,' Grants President Broad 'State Secrets' Privilege,'" *Huffington Post*, September 9, 2010, http://www.huffingtonpost.com/2010/09/08/extraordinary-rendition-court-sides-with-cia_n_709911.html.

62. Jonathan Hafetz, "The Importance of European Court's Ruling against Extraordinary Rendition," *AlJazeera,* January 7, 2013, http://www.aljazeera.com/indepth/opinion/2013/01/20131595119662381.html.

63. Statement of Tom Malinowski, Washington Advocacy Director, Human Rights Watch, Washington, D.C., Hearing before the Committee on Foreign Relations United States Senate, July 26, 2007, http://www.gpo.gov/fdsys/pkg/CHRG-110shrg40379/html/CHRG-110shrg40379.htm.

64. Barack Obama, "Renewing American Leadership," *Foreign Affairs* 86:4 (July/August 2007), 14.

65. Cited in Jo Becker and Scott Shane, "Secret 'Kill List' Proves a Test of Obama's Principles and Will," *New York Times,* May 29, 2012, http://www.nytimes.com/2012/05/29/world/obamas-leadership-in-war-on-al-qaeda.html?pagewanted=all.

66. Cited in Mark Mazzetti, Eric Schmitt, and Robert F. Worth, "Two-Year Manhunt Led to Killing of Awlaki in Yemen," *New York Times,* September 30, 2011, http://www.nytimes.com/2011/10/01/world/middleeast/anwar-al-awlaki-is-killed-in-yemen.html?pagewanted=all.

67. "Remarks of President Barack Obama," The White House, May 23, 2013, http://www.whitehouse.gov/the-press-office/2013/05/23/remarks-president-barack-obama.

68. "Memorandum for Alberto R. Gonzales Counsel to the President," August 1, 2002, http://www.washingtonpost.com/wp-srv/nation/documents/dojinterrogationmemo20020801.pdf.

69. George W. Bush, *Decision Points* (New York, NY: Crown Publishers, 2010), 169–171.

70. Cited in "Senate Ignores Veto Threat in Limiting Detainee Treatment," *CNN*, October 6, 2005, http://www.cnn.com/2005/POLITICS/10/06/senate.detainees.

71. White House, "Executive Order 13491—Ensuring Lawful Interrogations," January 22, 2009, http://www.whitehouse.gov/the_press_office/EnsuringLawfulInterrogations.

72. Mark Mazzetti, "Panel Faults CIA over Brutality and Deceit in Terrorism Interrogations," *New York Times,* December 9, 2014, http://www.nytimes.com/2014/12/10/world/senate-intelligence-committee-cia-torture-report.html.

73. "Un-American by Any Name," *New York Times,* June 5, 2005, http://www.nytimes.com/2005/06/05/opinion/05sun1.html.

74. Jimmy Carter, "A Cruel and Unusual Record," *New York Times,* June 24, 2012, http://www.nytimes.com/2012/06/25/opinion/americas-shameful-human-rights-record.html.

75. "Text: Obama's Speech in Cairo," *New York Times,* June 4, 2009, http://www.nytimes.com/2009/06/04/us/politics/04obama.text.html?pagewanted=all.

76. Justin McCarthy, "Americans Continue to Oppose Closing Guantanamo Bay," Gallup, June 13, 2014, http://www.gallup.com/poll/171653/americans-continue-oppose-closing-guantanamo-bay.aspx.

77. Barack Obama, "Statement on Signing the Ike Skelton National Defense Authorization Act for Fiscal Year 2011," January 7, 2011, The American Presidency Project, http://www.presidency.ucsb.edu/ws/?pid=88886.

78. Cited in "Perpetuating Guantanamo's Travesty," *New York Times,* January 17, 2015, http://www.nytimes.com/2015/01/18/opinion/sunday/perpetuating-guantanamos-travesty.html.

79. Helene Cooper, "U.S. Moves Five Yemenis from Guantánamo," *New York Times*, January 14, 2015, http://www.nytimes.com/2015/01/15/world/middleeast/us-moves-five-yemenis-from-guantnamo.html.

80. "Guantánamo: By the Numbers," *Miami Herald,* September 19, 2014, http://www.miamiherald.com/news/nation-world/world/americas/guantanamo/article2163210.html.

81. "Global Opposition to U.S. Surveillance and Drones, but Limited Harm to America's Image," Pew Research Center, July 14, 2014, http://www.pewglobal.org/2014/07/14/global-opposition-to-u-s-surveillance-and-drones-but-limited-harm-to-americas-image.

82. ACLU, "Surveillance under the USA Patriot Act," accessed September 7, 2015, https://www.aclu.org/surveillance-under-usa-patriot-act.

83. James Risen and Nick Wingfield, "Web's Reach Binds N.S.A. and Silicon Valley Leaders," *New York Times,* June 19, 2013, http://www.nytimes.com/2013/06/20/technology/silicon-valley-and-spy-agency-bound-by-strengthening-web.html?pagewanted=all.

84. "Edward Snowden: Leaks that Exposed U.S. Spy Program," *BBC News*, January 17, 2014, http://www.bbc.com/news/world-us-canada-23123964.

85. "Statement by H. E. Dilma Rousseff, President of the Federative Republic of Brazil, at the Opening of the General Debate of the 68th Session of the United Nations General Assembly," New York, September 24, 2013, http://gadebate.un.org/sites/default/files/gastatements/68/BR_en.pdf.

86. Cited in Michael D. Shear, "In Pushing for Revised Surveillance Program, Obama Strikes His Own Balance," *New York Times,* June 3, 2015, http://www.nytimes.com/2015/06/04/us/winning-surveillance-limits-obama-makes-program-own.html.

87. David Scheffer, "America's Embrace of the International Criminal Court," *Jurist*, July 2, 2012, http://jurist.org/forum/2012/07/dan-scheffer-us-icc.php.

88. Cited in Josh Rogin, "Obama's Sudan Envoy: Bashir Indictment Makes My Job Harder," *Foreign Policy*, July 16, 2010, http://foreignpolicy.com/2010/07/16/obamas-sudan-envoy-bashir-indictment-makes-my-job-harder.

89. Mark Kersten, "The Complementarity Turn in International Criminal Justice," Justice in Conflict Blog, September 30, 2014, http://justiceinconflict.org/2014/09/30/the-complementarity-turn-in-international-criminal-justice.

90. Mark Anderson, "South Sudan's Warring Leaders Should Be Barred from Caretaker Government, Says African Union," *The Guardian,* March 6, 2015, http://www.theguardian.com/global-development/2015/mar/06/kiir-machar-caretaker-government-african-union-civil-war.

91. Joshua Partlow and Peyton M. Craighill, "Poll Shows Vast Majority of Cubans Welcome Closer Ties with U.S.," *Washington Post,* April 8, 2015, http://www.washingtonpost.com/world/the_americas/poll-shows-vast-majority-of-cubans-welcome-closer-ties-with-us/2015/04/08/6285bfe4-d8c3-11e4-bf0b-f648b95a6488_story.html.

92. Cited in "Enough to Make You Gag," *The Economist*, May 4, 2013, http://www.economist.com/news/leaders/21577065-prison-deeply-un-american-disgrace-it-needs-be-closed-rapidly-enough-make-you-gag?, 12.

93. Robert Jervis, "The Torture Blame Game," *Foreign Affairs*, May/June 2015, https://www.foreignaffairs.com/reviews/review-essay/2015-04-20/torture-blame-game.

94. Ibid.

95. Bruce Drake, "Americans' Views on Use of Torture in Fighting Terrorism Have Been Mixed," Pew Research Center, December 9, 2014, http://www.pewresearch.org/fact-tank/2014/12/09/americans-views-on-use-of-torture-in-fighting-terrorism-have-been-mixed.

96. Ibid.

97. Daniel Byman and Benjami Wittes, "Reforming the NSA: How to Spy after Snowden," *Foreign Affairs,* May/June 2014, https://www.foreignaffairs.com/articles/united-states/2014-04-17/reforming-nsa.

98. Jane Harman, "Disrupting the Intelligence Community: America's Spy Agencies Need an Upgrade," *Foreign Affairs*, March/April 2015, https://www.foreignaffairs.com/articles/united-states/2015-03-01/disrupting-intelligence-community.

CHAPTER 7

1. Cited in Michael Barnett, *Empire of Humanity: A History of Humanitarianism* (Ithaca, NY: Cornell University Press, 2011), 104.

2. Cited in Harold Jackson, "Obituary: Jesse Helms," July 4, 2008, *The Guardian,* http://www.theguardian.com/world/2008/jul/04/usa.

3. Curt Tarnoff and Marian Leonardo Lawson, "Foreign Aid: An Introduction to U.S. Programs and Policy," CRS Report for Congress, R40213, February 10, 2011, https://www.fas.org/sgp/crs/row/R40213.pdf.

4. Peace Corps, "About Us," October 8, 2014, http://www.peacecorps.gov/about.

5. Stephen R. Rock, *Faith and Foreign Policy: The Views and Influences of U.S. Christians and Christian Organizations* (London, UK: Continuum, 2011), ch. 4.

6. George Herring, *From Colony to Superpower: U.S. Foreign Relations since 1776* (New York, NY: Oxford University Press), 786.

7. Steven A. Holmes, "Jesse Helms Dies at 86; Conservative Force in the Senate," *New York Times,* July 5, 2008, http://www.nytimes.com/2008/07/05/us/politics/00helms.html.

8. Madeleine Bunting and Oliver Burkeman, "Pro Bono," *The Guardian,* March 18, 2002, http://www.theguardian.com/world/2002/mar/18/usa.debtrelief.

9. United Nations Development Program, UN Human Development Report (Oxford, UK: Oxford University Press, 1994), 22.

10. "Understanding the Iran-Contra Affairs," accessed June 16, 2015, http://www.brown.edu/Research/Understanding_the_Iran_Contra_Affair/index.php.

11. Russell Crandall, *Gunboat Diplomacy: U.S. Interventions in the Dominican Republic, Grenada, and Panama* (Lanham, MD: Rowman and Littlefield, 2006), 139.

12. Ibid., 154–155.

13. Seymour M. Hersh, "Panama Strongman Said to Trade in Drugs, Arms, and Illicit Money," *New York Times,* June 12, 1986, http://www.nytimes.com/1986/06/12/world/panama-strongman-said-to-trade-in-drugs-arms-and-illicit-money.html.

14. Michael Shifter, "Plan Colombia: A Retrospective," *Americas Quarterly,* Summer 2012, http://www.americasquarterly.org/node/3787.

15. June S. Beittel, "Colombia: Background, U.S. Relations, and Congressional Interest," *CRS Report to Congress,* RL32250, November 28, 2012, https://www.fas.org/sgp/crs/row/RL32250.pdf.

16. "Text of President Clinton's Address on Haiti," *Washington Post,* September 16, 1994, http://www .washingtonpost.com/archive/politics/1994/09/16/ text-of-president-clintons-address-on-haiti/1bd152b0-10e9-48aa-a995-c688c19f4583.

17. Ruth Ellen Wasem, "U.S. Immigration Policy on Haitian Migrants," *CRS Report for Congress,* May 17, 2011, 2, https://www.fas.org/sgp/crs/row/RS21349.pdf.

18. Victor C. Ferkiss, "Foreign Aid: Moral and Political Aspects," in Kenneth W. Thompson, ed., *Moral Dimensions of American Foreign Policy* (New Brunswick, NJ: Transaction, 1984), 209.

19. Joseph S. Nye, Jr. "The Decline of America's Soft Power," *Foreign Affairs*, May/June 2004, https:// www.foreignaffairs.com/articles/2004-05-01/decline-americas-soft-power.

20. W. Haven North and Jeanne Foote North, "Transformation in U.S. Foreign Economic Policy Assistance," in Louis A. Picard, Robert Groelsema, and Terry F. Buss, eds., *Foreign Aid and Foreign Policy: Lessons for the Next Half Century* (New York, NY: Taylor and Francis, 2015), 281.

21. Steven Radelet, "A Primer on Foreign Aid," Center for Global Development Working Paper No. 92, July 2006, http://www.cgdev.org/publication/primer-foreign-aid-working-paper-92, 12.

22. Louis A. Picard and Zachary A. Karazsia, "The Truman Administration's Foreign Aid Legacy," in Raymond H. Heselbracht, ed., *Foreign Aid and the Legacy of Harry S. Truman* (Kirksville, MO: Truman State University Press, 2015), 19.

23. North and North, "Transformation in U.S. Foreign Economic Policy Assistance," 271–273.

24. Ibid., 273.

25. Margaret Daly Hayes, "The U.S. and Latin America: A Lost Decade?" *Foreign Affairs*, February 1989, https://www.foreignaffairs.com/articles/central-america-caribbean/1989-02-01/us-and-latin-america-lost-decade.

26. Michael J. Mazarr, "The Rise and Fall of the Failed-State Paradigm," *Foreign Affairs*, January/ February 2014, https://www.foreignaffairs.com/ articles/2013-12-06/rise-and-fall-failed-state-paradigm.

27. "Fragile States Index," *Foreign Policy*, 2014, http:// foreignpolicy.com/fragile-states-2014.

28. James A. Schear, "Washington's Weak-State Agenda," *Foreign Affairs,* May/June 2014, https://www.foreignaffairs.com/articles/united-states/2014-04-17/washingtons-weak-state-agenda.

29. "A National Security Strategy for a New Century," May 1997, http://nssarchive.us/NSSR/1997.pdf.

30. The White House, National Security Strategy, February 2015, 1, http://nssarchive.us/national-security-strategy-2015.

31. Michael O'Hanlon, "Obama's Weak and Failing States Agenda," *Washington Quarterly,* Fall 2012, http:// www.brookings.edu/research/articles/2012/10/ obama-weak-failing-states-agenda-ohanlon.

32. "2015 UNHCR Country Operations Profile— Democratic Republic of the Congo," http://www .unhcr.org/pages/49e45c366.html.

33. UNDP, Congo (Democratic Republic of the), Human Development Reports, 2013, http://hdr.undp.org/en/ countries/profiles/COD.

34. Alexis Arieff, "Democratic Republic of Congo: Background and U.S. Policy," Congressional Research Service Report R43166, February 24, 2015, Summary, https://www.fas.org/sgp/crs/row/R43166 .pdf.

35. Lydia Polgreen, "West Africa Wins Again, with Twist," *New York Times*, February 27, 2005, http://www .nytimes.com/2005/02/27/international/africa/27togo .html; Samantha Power, "How to Kill a Country," *Atlantic Monthly*, December 2003, http://www .theatlantic.com/magazine/archive/2003/12/how-to-kill-a-country/302845.

36. Craig J. Richardson, "How the Loss of Property Rights Caused Zimbabwe's Collapse," *Economic Development Bulletin,* No. 4*,* CATO Institute, November 14, 2005, http://www.cato.org/ publications/economic-development-bulletin/how-loss-property-rights-caused-zimbabwes-collapse.

37. "Cholera in Haiti," Centers for Disease Control and Prevention, n.d., http://www.cdc.gov/cholera/haiti/ index.html.

38. Nick Davis, "Corruption Fears Stalk Haiti after the Quake," *BBC News*, February 7, 2010, http://news .bbc.co.uk/2/hi/8502616.stm.

39. José de Córdoba, "Rise of Drug Cartel Brings Wave of Mexican Violence," *The Wall Street Journal,* May 3, 2015, http://www.wsj.com/articles/

wave-of-mexican-violence-reflects-drug-cartels-rise-1430690576; "Mexico's Disastrous Drug War 'Success,'" *The Daily Beast*, March 31, 2015, http://www.thedailybeast.com/articles/2015/03/31/mexico-s-disastrous-drug-war-success.html.

40. Patricio Asfura-Heim and Ralph H. Espach, "The Rise of Mexico's Self-Defense Forces," *Foreign Affairs*, July/August 2013, https://www.foreignaffairs.com/articles/mexico/2013-06-11/rise-mexico-s-self-defense-forces.

41. Clare Ribando Seelke and Kristin Finklea, "U.S.-Mexican Security Cooperation: The Mérida Initiative and Beyond," *CRS Report for Congress,* R41349, May 7, 2015, https://fas.org/sgp/crs/row/R41349.pdf.

42. The White House, Office of the Press Secretary, "Remarks by the President at the Millennium Development Goals Summit in New York, New York," September 22, 2010, https://www.whitehouse.gov/the-press-office/2010/09/22/remarks-president-millennium-development-goals-summit-new-york-new-york.

43. Official Development Data, 2014, Organisation for Economic Co-operation and Development, http://www.compareyourcountry.org/oda?page=0&cr=oecd&lg=en.

44. Poncie Rutsch, "Guess How Much of Uncle Sam's Money Goes to Foreign Aid. Guess Again!" *NPR*, February 10, 2015, http://www.npr.org/sections/goatsandsoda/2015/02/10/383875581/guess-how-much-of-uncle-sams-money-goes-to-foreign-aid-guess-again.

45. Cited in John W. McArthur, "Own the Goals," *Foreign Affairs,* March/April 2013, https://www.foreignaffairs.com/articles/2013-03-01/own-goals.

46. Luisa Blanchfield and Marian Leonardo Lawson, "The Millennium Development Goals: The September 2010 U.N. High-level Meeting," December 9, 2010, https://www.fas.org/sgp/crs/row/R41410.pdf.

47. Steven Radelet, "Bush and Foreign Aid," *Foreign Affairs,* September/October 2003, https://www.foreignaffairs.com/articles/2003-09-01/bush-and-foreign-aid.

48. "Heavily Indebted Poor Country (HIPC) Initiative," *World Bank Brief*, October 10, 2014, http://www.worldbank.org/en/topic/debt/brief/hipc.

49. World Health Organization, "Ebola Virus Disease," August 2015, http://www.who.int/mediacentre/factsheets/fs103/en.

50. "2014 Ebola Outbreak in West Africa," Centers for Disease Control and Prevention, June 9, 2015, http://www.cdc.gov/vhf/ebola/outbreaks/2014-west-africa.

51. Maggie Fox, "Report Slams U.S. Ebola Response and Readiness," *NBC News*, February 26, 2015, http://www.nbcnews.com/storyline/ebola-virus-outbreak/report-slams-u-s-ebola-response-readiness-n313251.

52. Princeton N. Lyman and Stephen B. Wittels, "No Good Deed Goes Unpunished," *Foreign Affairs*, July/August 2010, https://www.foreignaffairs.com/articles/africa/2010-07-01/no-good-deed-goes-unpunished.

53. "HIV and AIDS in Sub-Saharan Africa," Avert, http://www.avert.org/hiv-aids-sub-saharan-africa.htm; "UNAIDS Report Shows That 19 Million of the 35 Million People Living with HIV Today Do Not Know That They Have the Virus," UNAIDS, July, 16. 2014, http://www.unaids.org/en/resources/presscentre/pressreleaseandstatementarchive/2014/july/20140716prgapreport.

54. Katherine E. Bliss, Judith Twigg, and J. Stephen Morrison, "U.S. Priorities for Global Health Diplomacy," in J. Stephen Morrison, ed., *Global Health Policy in the Second Obama Term*, Center for Strategic and International Studies, February 2013, 13, http://csis.org/publication/global-health-policy-second-obama-term.

55. Rutsch, "Guess How Much of Uncle Sam's Money Goes to Foreign Aid. Guess Again!"

56. "Americans Remain Wary of 'Foreign Aid' but Are More Supportive of Spending to Improve Health Abroad," The Henry J. Kaiser Family Foundation, September 23, 2010, http://kff.org/global-health-policy/press-release/americans-remain-wary-of-foreign-aid-but-are-more-supportive-of-spending-to-improve-health-abroad.

57. UNAIDS, "The Gap Report," 2014, 9, http://www.unaids.org/sites/default/files/media_asset/UNAIDS_Gap_report_en.pdf.

58. The White House Office of the Press Secretary, "Fact Sheet: U.S. Response to the Ebola Epidemic in West Africa," September 16, 2014, https://www.whitehouse.gov/the-press-office/2014/09/16/fact-sheet-us-response-ebola-epidemic-west-africa.

59. Kevin Sieff, "U.S.-Built Ebola Treatment Centers in Liberia Are Nearly Empty as Outbreak Fades," *Washington Post,* January 18, 2015, http://www.washingtonpost.com/world/africa/us-built-ebola-

treatment-centers-in-liberia-are-nearly-empty-as-disease-fades/2015/01/18/9acc3e2c-9b52-11e4-86a3-1b56f64925f6_story.html.

60. Fran Quigley, "The Poor and the Sick," *Foreign Affairs*, October 19, 2014, https://www.foreignaffairs.com/articles/africa/2014-10-19/poor-and-sick.

61. Todd Summers, "The Global Fund," in Morrison, ed., *Global Health Policy in the Second Obama Term* (Washington, DC: Center for Strategic and International Studies, 2013), 64.

62. Kareem Shaheen, "World Leaders Accused of Shameful Failure over Refugee Crisis," *The Guardian,* June 15, 2015, http://www.theguardian.com/world/2015/jun/15/worst-refugee-crisis-since-second-world-war-report-middle-east-africa-syria.

63. Somini Sengupta, "60 Million People Fleeing Chaotic Lands, U.N. Says." *New York Times,* June 18, 2015, http://www.nytimes.com/2015/06/18/world/60-million-people-fleeing-chaotic-lands-un-says.html?_r=0.

64. Cited in Somini Sengupta, "UN Calls on Western Nations to Shelter Syrian Refugees," *New York Times,* April 17, 2014, http://www.nytimes.com/2015/04/18/world/middleeast/un-calls-on-western-nations-to-shelter-syrian-refugees.html.

65. Alicia A. Caldwell, "Deportations of Illegal Immigrants Drop to Lowest Level since 2006," *Christian Science Monitor*, April 29, 2015, http://www.csmonitor.com/USA/Society/2015/0429/Deportations-of-illegal-immigrants-drop-to-lowest-level-since-2006-video.

66. "You Don't Have Rights Here," Human Rights Watch, October 16, 2014, http://www.hrw.org/reports/2014/10/16/you-don-t-have-rights-here-0.

67. "Cartagena Declaration on Refugees," International Refugee Rights Initiative, accessed May 9, 2015, http://www.refugeelegalaidinformation.org/cartagena-declaration-refugees.

68. Lourdes Medrano, "Border Crisis from the Other Side: One Guatemalan Mother's Journey," *Christian Science Monitor*, October 5, 2014, http://www.csmonitor.com/USA/2014/1005/Border-crisis-from-the-other-side-One-Guatemalan-mother-s-journey.

69. Marian L. Tupy, "U.S. Should Scrap Trade Barriers with Africa," CATO Institute, August 4, 2014, http://www.cato.org/publications/commentary/us-should-scrap-trade-barriers-africa.

70. Cited in Evelyn Iritani, "Tsunami Aid Creates Trade Bind," *Los Angeles Times,* January 24, 2005, http://articles.latimes.com/2005/jan/24/business/fi-tsunami24.

71. Robert Calderisi, "Why Foreign Aid and Africa Don't Mix," *CNN.com*, August 18, 2010, http://www.cnn.com/2010/OPINION/08/12/africa.aid.calderisi.

72. James Bovard, "How 'Food for Peace' Hurts Foreign Farmers," *The Wall Street Journal,* April 29, 2013, http://www.wsj.com/articles/SB10001424127887324482504578452751341751038.

73. "The 169 Commandments," *The Economist,* March 28, 2015, http://www.economist.com/news/leaders/21647286-proposed-sustainable-development-goals-would-be-worse-useless-169-commandments.

74. Amar Bhattacharya, "Worthy of Support," *The Economist,* April 8, 2015, http://www.economist.com/blogs/freeexchange/2015/04/our-piece-sustainable-development-goals; My World Survey, updated June 15, 2015, http://data.myworld2015.org.

CHAPTER 8

1. David Peterson del Mar, *Environmentalism* (New York, NY: Pearson, 2006), 36, 25.

2. Peter Lin, "Thomas Jefferson and the Environment," *History Today* 54:1 (2004), http://www.historytoday.com/peter-ling/thomas-jefferson-and-environment.

3. National Park Service, "Theodore Roosevelt and Conservation," accessed September 8, 2015, http://www.nps.gov/thro/historyculture/theodore-roosevelt-and-conservation.htm.

4. Theodore Roosevelt, "At the Opening of the Conference on the Conservation of Natural Resources," May 13, 1908, http://www.theodoreroosevelt.com/images/trenvpics/conservationconferencespeech1908.txt.

5. Kristina Alexander, "The Lacey Act: Protecting the Environment by Restricting Trade," *Congressional Research Service,* Report R42067, January 14, 2014, https://www.fas.org/sgp/crs/misc/R42067.pdf.

6. Elizabeth DeSombre, "The United States and Global Environmental Politics: Domestic Sources of U.S. Unilateralism," in Regina S. Axelrod, Stacy D. Vandeveer, and David Leonard Downie, eds.,

The Global Environment: Institutions, Law, and Policy (Washington, DC: CQ Press, 2010) 194–195.

7. Paul G. Harris, "Ozone Diplomacy Revisited: Did Morality Influence United States Policy?" *International Journal on World Peace* 12:2 (June 1995), 27.

8. Stephen O. Andersen and Madhava Sarma, *Protecting the Ozone Layer* (London, UK: Earthscan, 2002), 44.

9. Karen Litfin, *Ozone Discourses* (New York, NY: Columbia University Press, 1994), 62–63.

10. "The Donora Smog Disaster October 30–31, 1948," *Pennsylvania Historical & Museum Commission,* http://www.portal.state.pa.us/portal/server.pt/community/documents_from_1946_-_present/20426/donora_smog_disaster/999079.

11. Cited in Ann Murray, "Smog Deaths in 1948 Led to Clean Air Laws," *NPR,* April 22, 2009, http://www.npr.org/templates/story/story.php?storyId=103359330.

12. Cited in Paul G. Harris, "Ozone Diplomacy Revisited: Did Morality Influence United States Policy?" *International Journal on World Peace* 12:2 (June 1995): 24.

13. Cited in Reiner Grundmann, *Transnational Environmental Policy* (London, UK: Routledge, 2001), 147.

14. Amy Below, "U.S. Presidential Decisions on Ozone Depletion and Climate Change: A Foreign Policy Analysis," *Foreign Policy Analysis* 4:1 (January 2008): 6.

15. Litfin, *Ozone Discourses,* 106.

16. "EPA Extends Deadline for Methyl Bromide to Nov. 30, 2014," *Golf Course Superintendents Association of America,* 2013, http://www.gcsaa.org/newsroom/news/government-relations/2013/epa-extends-regulatory-deadline-on-methyl-bromide.

17. EPA, "The Phaseout of Methyl Bromide," February 18, 2014, http://www.epa.gov/ozone/mbr.

18. Juliet Eilperin, "U.S., China Agree to Work on Phasing out Hydroflourocarbons," *Washington Post,* September 6, 2013, http://www.washingtonpost.com/politics/us-china-agree-to-work-on-phasing-out-hydrofluorocarbons/2013/09/06/9037e072-170c-11e3-a2ec-b47e45e6f8ef_story.html.

19. Below, "U.S. Presidential Decisions on Ozone Depletion and Climate Change," 2.

20. Cited in Colleen McCain Nelson, "Obama Climate Push Faces Lukewarm Public," *The Wall Street Journal,* May 8, 2014, A4.

21. Cited in Ibid.

22. IPCC, "Organization," accessed September 8, 2015, http://www.ipcc.ch/organization/organization.shtml.

23. Ian H. Rowlands, *The Politics of Global Atmospheric Change* (Manchester, UK: Manchester University Press, 1995), 134.

24. Al Gore, "Earth's Fate Is the No. 1 National Security Issue," *Washington Post,* May 14, 1989, http://www.washingtonpost.com/wp-dyn/content/article/2007/10/12/AR2007101200827_pf.html.

25. Amy Royden, "U.S. Climate Change Policy under President Clinton: A Look Back," *Golden Gate University Law Review,* 32:4 (2002): 420–421.

26. William J. Clinton, "Remarks on Earth Day," April 21, 1993, http://www.presidency.ucsb.edu/ws/?pid=46460.

27. Cited in David Kaye, "Stealth Multilateralism," *Foreign Affairs,* September/October 2013, http://www.foreignaffairs.com/articles/139649/david-kaye/stealth-multilateralism.

28. Cited in David Biello, "Bush Administration Pushes Climate Change Action into the Future," *Scientific American*, September 28, 2007, http://www.scientificamerican.com/article/bush-administration-pushes-climate-change-action-into-future.

29. "Obama Addresses the Clinton Global Initiative," *Washington Post,* September 25, 2008, http://www.washingtonpost.com/wp-dyn/content/article/2008/09/25/AR2008092501675.html.

30. Hillary Rodham Clinton, *Hard Choices* (New York, NY: Simon & Schuster, 2014), 500.

31. "Who's On Board with the Copenhagen Accord?" *U.S. Climate Action Network,* January 31, 2010, http://www.usclimatenetwork.org/policy/copenhagen-accord-commitments.

32. Cited in David A. Fahrenthold and Juliet Eilperin, "White House Takes a More Modest Plan B to Cancun Climate Talks," *Washington Post,* November 20, 2010, http://www.washingtonpost.com/wp-dyn/content/article/2010/11/20/AR2010112003296_pf.html.

33. Cited in Suzanne Goldberg, "Barack Obama Urged to Change U.S. Stance at UN Climate Summit," *The Guardian*, November 20, 2011, http://www.theguardian.com/environment/2011/nov/30/barack-obama-us-stance-climate-summit.

34. T.N., "Climate Policy: Obama's Green Gamble," *The Economist*, June 3, 2014, http://www.economist.com/blogs/democracyinamerica/2014/06/climate-policy.

35. "Inaugural Address by President Barack Obama," The White House, January 21, 2013, http://www.whitehouse.gov/the-press-office/2013/01/21/inaugural-address-president-barack-obama.

36. "Remarks by the President on Climate Change," The White House Office, June 25, 2013, http://www.whitehouse.gov/the-press-office/2013/06/25/remarks-president-climate-change.

37. "Transportation and Climate," U.S. Environmental Protection Agency, http://www.epa.gov/otaq/climate/basicinfo.htm; "Clean Vehicles," Union of Concerned Scientists, revised January 31, 2014, http://www.ucsusa.org/clean_vehicles/why-clean-cars/global-warming.

38. Cited in David J. Unger, "EPA Carbon Limits: An 'Obamacare' for Climate Change," *Christian Science Monitor*, June 2, 2014, http://www.csmonitor.com/Environment/Energy-Voices/2014/0602/EPA-carbon-limits-an-Obamacare-for-climate-change-video.

39. Sonia Van Gilder Cooke, "Q&A: Biodiversity," *The Guardian*, April 6, 2010, http://www.theguardian.com/science/2010/apr/06/q-and-a-biodiversity.

40. David Biello, "How Biodiversity Keeps Earth Alive," *Scientific American*, May 3, 2012, http://www.scientificamerican.com/article/how-biodiversity-keeps-earth-alive.

41. William J. Snape, III, "Joining the Convention on Biological Diversity: A Legal and Scientific Overview of Why the United States Must Wake Up," *Sustainable Development Law and Policy*, Spring 2010, 6.

42. Stephen J. Kobrin, "Diffusion as an Explanation of Oil Nationalization: Or the Domino Effect Rides Again," *Journal of Conflict Resolution* 29:1 (March 1985): 26.

43. Statista, "Average Prices for OPEC Crude Oil from 1960 to 2013 (in U.S. dollars per barrel)," 2013, http://www.statista.com/statistics/262858/change-in-opec-crude-oil-prices-since-1960.

44. Robert S. Walters and David H. Blake, *The Politics of Global Economic Relations* (Englewood Cliffs, NJ: Prentice Hall, 1987), 184.

45. Daniel Yergin, *The Prize: The Epic Quest for Oil, Money & Power* (New York, NY: Free Press, 2008), 392.

46. Cited in "Analysis: Awash in Oil, U.S. Reshapes Mideast Role 40 Years after OPEC Embargo," *Reuters*, October 17, 2013, http://www.reuters.com/article/2013/10/17/us-usa-energy-geopolitics-analysis-idU.S.BRE99G14P20131017.

47. Mark Thompson, "U.S. to Become Biggest Oil Producer—IEA," *CNNMoney*, November 12, 2012, http://money.cnn.com/2012/11/12/news/economy/us-oil-production-energy/index.html.

48. Cited in Matthew L. Wald, "Shale's Effect on Oil Supply Is Not Expected to Last," *New York Times*, November 12, 2013, http://www.nytimes.com/2013/11/13/business/energy-environment/shales-effect-on-oil-supply-is-not-expected-to-last.htm.

49. Cited in Clifford Krauss, "Texas Refinery Is Saudi Foothold in U.S. Market," *New York Times*, April 4, 2013, http://www.nytimes.com/2013/04/05/business/texas-refinery-is-saudi-foothold-in-us-market.html.

50. Jonathan L. Ramsur, Richard K. Lattanzio, Linda Luther, Paul W. Parfomak, and Nicole T. Carter, "Oil Sands and the Keystone XL Pipeline: Background and Selected Environmental Issues," *CRS Report R42611*, April 14, 2014, 16, https://www.fas.org/sgp/crs/misc/R42611.pdf.

51. Lawrence Kumins and Robert Bamberger, "Oil and Gas Disruption from Hurricanes Katrina and Rita," *CRS Report for Congress*, October 21, 2005, http://fpc.state.gov/documents/organization/55824.pdf.

52. David Biello, "How Much Will Tar Sands Oil Add to Global Warming?" *Scientific American*, January 23, 2013, http://www.scientificamerican.com/article/tar-sands-and-keystone-xl-pipeline-impact-on-global-warming; Ramsur et al., "Oil Sands and the Keystone XL Pipeline: Background and Selected Environmental Issues."

53. Environmental Protection Agency, "The Social Cost of Carbon," updated July 21, 2015, http://www.epa.gov/climatechange/EPAactivities/economics/scc.html.

54. Jacques Leslie, "Shipping Crude Oil by Rail: New Front in Tar Sands Wars," *Yale Environment 360*,

December 5, 2013, http://e360.yale.edu/feature/shipping_crude_oil_by_rail_new_front_in_tar_sands_wars/2717.

55. White House, "Remarks by the President on Climate Change," Georgetown University, Washington, DC, June 25, 2013, http://www.whitehouse.gov/the-press-office/2013/06/25/remarks-president-climate-change.

56. Erica Meltzer, "Boulder Issue 2A: Voters Approve Carbon Tax Extension by Wide Margin," *Daily Camera,* November 6, 2012, http://www.dailycamera.com/ci_21941854/boulder-issue-2a-carbon-tax-appears-likely-be.

57. Jane A. Leggett, "Climate Change: Conceptual Approaches and Policy Tools," *CRS Report for Congress,* August 29, 2011, http://www.fas.org/sgp/crs/misc/R41973.pdf., 22; Richard Coniff, "The Political History of Cap and Trade," *Smithsonian.com*, August 2009, http://www.smithsonianmag.com/air/the-political-history-of-cap-and-trade-34711212.

58. Michael Specter, "The Climate Fixers," *The New Yorker,* May 14, 2012, http://www.newyorker.com/reporting/2012/05/14/120514fa_fact_specter.

59. Ruth Greenspan Bell, Barry Blechman, and Micha Ziegler, "Beyond the Durban Climate Talks," *Foreign Affairs*, October 30, 2011, http://www.foreignaffairs.com/articles/136627/ruth-greenspan-bell-barry-blechman-and-micah-ziegler/beyond-the-durban-climate-talks.

60. "U.S. Imports of Crude Oil and Petroleum Products," U.S. Energy Information Administration, http://www.eia.gov/dnav/pet/hist/LeafHandler.ashx?n=PET&s=MTTIMU.S.1&f=M.

61. Cited in Brad Plummer, "China Is Using Up Oil Faster Than We Can Produce It," *Washington Post,* April 29, 2013, http://www.washingtonpost.com/blogs/wonkblog/wp/2013/04/29/china-is-using-oil-faster-than-we-can-produce-it.

62. "U.S. Imports by Country of Origin," U.S. Energy Information Administration, accessed September 8, 2015, http://www.eia.gov/dnav/pet/pet_move_impcus_a1_NMX_ep00_im0_mbbl_m.htm.

63. Cited in Juliet Eilperin, "Obama Proposes Vast Expansion of Pacific Ocean Sanctuaries for Marine Life," *Washington Post,* June 17, 2014, http://www.washingtonpost.com/politics/obama-will-propose-vast-expansion-of-pacific-ocean-marine-sanctuary/2014/06/16/f8689972-f0c6-11e3-bf76-447a5df6411f_story.html.

64. Cited in Justin Gillis, "Bipartisan Report Tallies High Toll on Economy from Global Warming," *New York Times,* June 24, 2014, http://www.nytimes.com/2014/06/24/science/report-tallies-toll-on-economy-from-global-warming.html.

65. Cited in Andrew Mayeda, "Incentives for Carbon to Help Keystone Bid, Canada's Liberal Party Leader Says," *Bloomberg*, June 26, 2014, http://www.bloomberg.com/news/2014-06-26/trudeau-says-incentinves-for-carbon-to-help-keystone-bid.html.

CHAPTER 9

1. Max Rodenbeck, "Midnight at the Oasis," *New York Times,* January 28, 2007, http://www.nytimes.com/2007/01/28/books/review/Rodenbeck.t.html.

2. "Our Mission," *AIPAC,* accessed September 8, 2015, http://www.aipac.org/about/mission.

3. "How We Work," *AIPAC*, accessed September 8, 2015, http://www.aipac.org/about/how-we-work.

4. Walter Russell Mead, "Jerusalem Syndrome: Decoding the Israel Lobby," *Foreign Affairs* 86:6 (November/December 2007): 163.

5. Cited in David D. Kirkpatrick, "For Evangelicals, Supporting Israel Is 'God's Foreign Policy,'" *New York Times,* November 14, 2006, http://www.nytimes.com/2006/11/14/washington/14israel.html?pagewanted=all.

6. Pew Research Center, "Evangelical Support for Israel," April 6, 2011, http://www.pewresearch.org/daily-number/evangelical-support-for-israel.

7. William B. Quandt, *Peace Process: American Diplomacy and the Arab-Israeli Conflict Since 1967* (Washington, DC and Berkeley, CA: The Brookings Institute and the University of California Press, 2005), 1. Emphasis in original.

8. Cited in "1977: Egyptian Leader's Israel Trip Makes History," *BBC News*, n.d., http://news.bbc.co.uk/onthisday/hi/dates/stories/november/19/newsid_2520000/2520467.stm.

9. Michael Oren, *Power, Faith, and Fantasy: America in the Middle East: 1776 to the Present* (New York, NY: W. W. Norton, 2007), 570.

10. Cited in ibid.

11. Cited in William Safire, *Lend Me Your Ears* (New York, NY: W. W. Norton, 2004), 171, 172.

12. Israel Ministry of Foreign Affairs, "The Israel-Palestinian Interim Agreement," September 28, 2005, http://www.mfa.gov.il/MFA/Peace+Process/Guide+to+the+Peace+Process/THE+ISRAELI-PALESTINIAN+INTERIM+AGREEMENT.htm.

13. Ibid.

14. The Jewish Peace Lobby, "The Clinton Parameters," n.d., http://www.peacelobby.org/clinton_parameters.htm.

15. "The Covenant of the Islamic Resistance Movement," August 18, 1988, Avalon Project, Yale Law School, http://avalon.law.yale.edu/20th_century/hamas.asp.

16. Cited in Kareem Fahim, "Palestinians Find Show of Support Lacking from Arab Leaders amid Offensive," *New York Times,* July 19, 2014, http://www.nytimes.com/2014/07/20/world/middleeast/palestinians-find-show-of-support-lacking-from-arab-nations-amid-offensive.html?_r=0.

17. Cited in Mark Landler, "Gaza War Strains Relations between U.S. and Israel," *New York Times,* August 4, 2014, http://www.nytimes.com/2014/08/05/world/middleeast/gaza-is-straining-us-ties-to-israel.html.

18. Cited in Jay Solomon, "U.S. Moves against Hezbollah 'Cartel,'" *The Wall Street Journal,* April 23, 2013, http://online.wsj.com/article/SB10001424127887323735604578441251544900808.html.

19. Cited in Jo Becker, "Beirut Bank Seen as a Hub of Hezbollah's Financing," *New York Times,* December 13, 2011, http://www.nytimes.com/2011/12/14/world/middleeast/beirut-bank-seen-as-a-hub-of-hezbollahs-financing.html?pagewanted=all.

20. Human Rights Watch, "Why They Died" 19:5(E), September 2007, http://www.hrw.org/sites/default/files/reports/lebanon0907.pdf, 4.

21. Cited in Mark Landler, "Israel's U.S. Envoy Shares Thoughts as He Prepares for a New Chapter," *New York Times,* July 18, 2013, http://www.nytimes.com/2013/07/19/world/middleeast/israeli-envoy-shares-thoughts-as-he-prepares-for-a-new-chapter.html?pagewanted=all.

22. Cited in "Israel's Netanyahu Says Iran Closer to Nuclear 'Red Line,'" *Reuters,* July 14, 2013, http://www.reuters.com/article/2013/07/14/us-nuclear-israel-iran-idUSBRE96D08H20130714.

23. Cited in Jodi Rudoren, "Netanyahu Dismisses Iranian President's Remarks," *New York Times,* September 20, 2013, http://www.nytimes.com/2013/09/21/world/middleeast/prime-minister-netanyahu-on-iranian-president-rouhani.html?ref=iran.

24. Cited in David E. Sanger and Jodi Rudoren, "Split on Accord on Iran Strains U.S.-Israel Ties," *New York Times,* November 18, 2013, http://www.nytimes.com/2013/11/19/world/middleeast/split-on-accord-on-iran-strains-us-israel-ties.html.

25. "Text of Obama's Speech in Israel," *The Wall Street Journal,* March 21, 2013, http://blogs.wsj.com/washwire/2013/03/21/text-of-obamas-speech-in-israel.

26. Cited in Mark Landler, "Discussing Iran, Obama and Netanyahu Display Unity," *New York Times,* September 30, 2013, http://www.nytimes.com/2013/10/01/us/politics/tensions-over-iran-seem-to-ebb-between-netanyahu-and-obama.html.

27. Cited in "Obama Says Iran Nuclear Row 'Larger' Than Syrian Crisis," *BBC News,* September 15, 2013, http://www.bbc.co.uk/news/world-middle-east-24102723.

28. Cited in David E. Sanger, "Quick Turn of Fortunes as Diplomatic Options Open Up with Syria and Iran," *New York Times,* September 19, 2013, http://www.nytimes.com/2013/09/20/us/politics/on-mideast-heads-spin-over-shift-in-diplomacy.html.

29. Pew Research Global Attitudes Project, "Despite Their Wide Differences, Many Israelis and Palestinians Want Bigger Role for Obama in Resolving Conflict," May 9, 2013, http://www.pewglobal.org/2013/05/09/despite-their-wide-differences-many-israelis-and-palestinians-want-bigger-role-for-obama-in-resolving-conflict.

30. Cited in Michael R. Gordon and Jodi Rudoren, "Kerry Achieves Deal to Revive Mideast Talks," *New York Times,* July 19, 2013, http://www.nytimes.com/2013/07/20/world/middleeast/kerry-extends-stay-in-mideast-to-push-for-talks.html?pagewanted=all.

31. Cited in Michael R. Gordon and Isabel Kershner, "Israel and Palestinians Set to Resume Peace Talks, U.S. Announces," *New York Times,* July 28, 2013, http://www.nytimes.com/2013/07/29/world/middleeast/israel-agrees-to-prisoner-release-clearing-way-for-talks.html.

32. Cited in Yolande Knell, "Reconsidering the Two-State Solution," *BBC News,* March 21, 2013, http://www.bbc.co.uk/news/world-middle-east-21850739.

33. Cited in "Netanyahu Says Abbas Must Abandon Unity Deal with Hamas," *BBC News*, April 24, 2014, http://www.bbc.com/news/world-middle-east-27142594.

34. Cited in Jodi Rudoren and Isabel Kershner, "Arc of a Failed Deal: How Nine Months of Mideast Talks Ended in Disarray," *New York Times,* April 28, 2014, http://www.nytimes.com/2014/04/29/world/middleeast/arc-of-a-failed-deal-how-nine-months-of-mideast-talks-ended-in-dissarray.html.

35. Cited in Isabel Kershner, "Israel Says It Is 'Deeply Disappointed' by Kerry's Remarks on Peace Talks," *New York Times*, April 9, 2014, http://www.nytimes.com/2014/04/10/world/middleeast/middle-east-peace-effort.html.

36. Cited in Michael R. Gordon, "Kerry Expresses Regret after Apartheid Remark," *New York Times,* April 28, 2014, http://www.nytimes.com/2014/04/29/world/middleeast/kerry-apologizes-for-remark-that-israel-risks-apartheid.html.

37. Cited in Jodi Rudoren, "Israel 'Troubled' by U.S. Plan to Work with Palestinian Unity Government," *New York Times,* June 3, 2014, http://www.nytimes.com/2014/06/04/world/middleeast/israel-troubled-by-us-plan-to-work-with-palestinian-unity-government.html.

38. Cited in Mark Landler, "Hamas Looms over Latest Israel-U.S. Dispute," *New York Times,* June 4, 2014, http://www.nytimes.com/2014/06/05/world/middleeast/hamas-looms-over-latest-israel-us-dispute.html?_r=0.

39. Cited in Mark Landler, "A 'Battered' Mideast Envoy Steps Downs, but Keeps a Bag Packed," *New York Times*, July 3, 2014, http://www.nytimes.com/2014/07/04/world/middleeast/martin-indyk-mideast-peace-talks.html.

40. Cited in "The Masochism Tango," *The Economist,* December 15, 2012, 49.

41. "Text: Obama's Speech in Israel."

42. Thomas L. Friedman, "A Wonderful Country," *New York Times,* February 1, 2014, http://www.nytimes.com/2014/02/02/opinion/sunday/friedman-a-wonderful-country.html.

43. Cited in Jodi Rudoren, "Netanyahu's History on Palestinian Statehood," *New York Times,* March 20, 2015, http://www.nytimes.com/interactive/2015/03/20/world/middleeast/netanyahu-two-state-solution.html.

44. Cited in Julie Hirschfeld Davis, "Obama Says He Told Netanyahu That Talk before Election Hurt the Peace Process," *New York Times,* March 21, 2015, http://www.nytimes.com/2015/03/22/world/middleeast/obama-says-he-told-netanyahu-that-campaign-talk-hurt-the-peace-process.html.

45. Cited in Rudoren, "Netanyahu's History on Palestinian Statehood."

46. Cited in "Haniyeh Calls for Formation of Palestinian State on 1967 Lines," *Haaretz,* December 19, 2006, http://www.haaretz.com/news/haniyeh-calls-for-formation-of-palestinian-state-on-1967-lines-1.207641.

47. Cited in Arnold Wesker, "My Brother the Quarryman," *The Guardian,* May 28, 2004, http://www.theguardian.com/books/2004/may/29/highereducation.israeland thepalestinians.

48. "Text of Obama's Speech in Israel."

49. Cited in Jodi Rudoren, "Israeli Move over Housing Poses a Threat to Peace Talks," *New York Times,* November 12, 2013, http://www.nytimes.com/2013/11/13/world/middleeast/netanyahu-halts-some-settlement-plans-but-others-to-proceed.html.

50. "Text: Obama's Speech in Cairo," *New York Times*, June 4, 2009, http://www.nytimes.com/2009/06/04/us/politics/04obama.text.html?pagewanted=all.

51. "Text of Obama's Speech in Israel."

52. The White House, "Letter from President Bush to Prime Minister Sharon," April 14, 2004, http://georgewbush-whitehouse.archives.gov/news/releases/2004/04/20040414-3.html.

53. Cited in Adiv Sterman, "'Abbas Was Ready to Compromise on Right of Return,'" *Times of Israel,* March 11, 2013, http://www.timesofisrael.com/abbas-was-willing-to-compromise-on-right-of-return.

54. Cited in Harriet Sherwood, "Mahmoud Abbas Outrages Palestinian Refugees by Waiving His Right to Return," *The Guardian*, November 4, 2012, http://www.theguardian.com/world/2012/nov/04/mahmoud-abbas-palestinian-territories.

55. Cited in Jay Solomon and Carol E. Lee, "Strains with Israel over Iran Snarl U.S. Goals in Mideast," *The Wall Street Journal,* November 18, 2013, A11.

56. Cited in Adam Entous and Julian E. Barnes, "Pentagon Bulks Up 'Bunker Buster' Bomb to Combat Iran," *The Wall Street Journal,* May 2, 2013, http://online.wsj.com/article/SB10001424127887324 582004578459170138890756.html.

57. Trita Parsi, "Pushing Peace," *Foreign Affairs,* October 1, 2013, http://www.foreignaffairs.com/ articles/139981/trita-parsi/pushing-peace.

58. Ibid.

59. Jim Zanotti, "U.S. Foreign Aid to the Palestinians," *Congressional Research Service,* January 18, 2013, http://www.fas.org/sgp/crs/mideast/RS22967.pdf.

60. See Jihan Abdalla, "Israel Denies Palestinians Equal Water Access," *Al-Monitor*, April 8, 2013, http://www .al-monitor.com/pulse/originals/2013/04/westbank-water-restrictions-israel.html; and Amira Hass, "Two Pipes for Two Peoples: The Politics of Water in the West Bank," *Haaretz*, September 23, 2012, http:// www.haaretz.com/news/features/two-pipes-for-two-peoples-the-politics-of-water-in-the-west-bank-1.466250.

61. Cited in Somini Sengupta, "Palestinian Leader Urges U.N. to Back a Deadline to End Israeli Occupation," *New York Times,* September 26, 2014, http://www .nytimes.com/2014/09/27/world/middleeast/un-general-assembly-abbas-israel.html?_r=0.

62. Cited in Jodi Rudoren, "Region Boiling, Israel Takes Up Castle Strategy," *New York Times,* January 18, 2014, http://www.nytimes.com/2014/01/19/world/ middleeast/region-boiling-israel-takes-up-castle-strategy.html.

63. "Text: Obama's Speech in Cairo."

64. Cited in "A Peace Process that Is Going Nowhere," *The Economist*, April 12, 2014, 39.

65. Dennis R. Ross, "To Achieve Mideast Peace, Suspend Disbelief," *New York Times,* March 2, 2013, http:// www.nytimes.com/interactive/2013/03/03/opinion/ sunday/opinion-israel-palestine-mideast-peace.html.

66. "Text of Obama's Speech in Israel."

67. Cited in Michael R. Gordon and Jodi Rudoren, "Kerry, Invoking Mandela, Says Peace in Mideast Is Possible," *New York Times,* December 6, 2013, http://www.nytimes.com/2013/12/07/world/ middleeast/kerry-invoking-mandela-says-peace-in-mideast-is-possible.html.

CHAPTER 10

1. Edward D. Mansfield and Jack Snyder, "Democratization and the Arab Spring," *International Interactions* 38:5 (2012): 723.

2. Cited in Ryan Lizza, "The Consequentialist," *The New Yorker,* May 2, 2011, http://www.newyorker .com/reporting/2011/05/02/110502fa_fact_ lizza?printable=true&currentPage=all.

3. "Modern History Sourcebook: Sir Henry McMahon: Letter to Ali ibn Husain, 1915," July 1998, http:// www.fordham.edu/halsall/mod/1915mcmahon.html.

4. David Fromkin, *A Peace to End All Peace: The Fall of the Ottoman Empire and the Creation of the Modern Middle East* (New York, NY: Henry Holt, 1989), 9.

5. John C. Campbell, "The Soviet Union and the United States in the Middle East," *Annals of the American Academy of Political and Social Science* 401 (May 1972): 127.

6. John Lewis Gaddis, *We Now Know: Rethinking Cold War History* (Oxford, UK: Oxford University Press, 1997), 171.

7. John Lewis Gaddis, *The Cold War: A New History* (New York, NY: Penguin Press, 2005), 128.

8. Philip Anderson, "'Summer Madness': The Crisis in Syria, August–October 1957," *British Journal of Middle East Studies* 22:1/2 (1995): 34.

9. Richard M. Nixon, "Address to the Nation on the War in Vietnam," November 3, 1969, http:// www.nixonlibrary.gov/forkids/speechesforkids/ silentmajority/silentmajority_transcript.pdf.

10. Jimmy Carter, "The State of the Union Address Delivered before a Joint Session of the Congress," January 23, 1980, *The American Presidency Project,* http://www.presidency.ucsb.edu/ws/?pid=33079.

11. Cited in Craig A. Daigle, "The Russians Are Going: Sadat, Nixon and the Soviet Presence in Egypt, 1970–1971," *Middle East Review of International Affairs* 8:1 (March 2004): 1.

12. Anwar al-Sadat, *In Search of Identity* (New York, NY: Harper & Row, 1978), 187; cited in NSA, "Moscow's Realignment with Cairo: A Look at Gorbachev's New Political Thinking," *Cryptologic Quarterly*, n.d., unclassified, 3, http://www.nsa.gov/public_info/_ files/cryptologic_quarterly/Moscows_Realignment_ with_Cairo.pdf.

13. Charles E. Butterworth, "Political Islam: The Origins," *Annals of the American Academy off Political and Social Science* 524 (November 1992): 29.

14. Carrie Rosefsky Wickham, "The Path to Moderation: Strategy and Learning in the Formation of Egypt's

Wasat Party," *Comparative Politics* 36:2 (January 2004): 205.

15. Abul A'la Maududi, *Jihad in Islam* (Beirut: The Holy Koran Publishing House, n.d.), 5, http://www.muhammadanism.org/Terrorism/jihah_in_islam/jihad_in_islam.pdf.

16. Seyyed Vali Reza Nasr, *Mawdudi and the Making of Islamic Revivalism* (Oxford, UK: Oxford University Press, 1996), 68.

17. Beverley Milton-Edwards, *Islamic Fundamentalism since 1945* (New York, NY: Routledge, 2005), 27.

18. Rupe Simms, "'Islam Is Our Politics': A Gramscian Analysis of the Muslim Brotherhood (1928–1953)," *Social Compass* 49:4 (December 2002): 573.

19. Leon Carl Brown, *Religion and State: The Muslim Approach to Politics* (New York, NY: Columbia University Press, 2000), 146.

20. Ibid.

21. Robert S. Leiken and Steven Brooke, "The Moderate Muslim Brotherhood," *Foreign Affairs* 82:2 (March/April 2007): 110.

22. Sana Abed-Kotob, "The Accommodationists Speak: The Goals and Strategies of the Muslim Brotherhood of Egypt," *International Journal of Middle East Studies* 27:3 (August 1995): 331.

23. Simms, "'Islam Is Our Politics,'" 574.

24. Bernard Lewis, *The Crisis of Islam: Holy War and Unholy Terror* (New York, NY: Random House, 2003), 111–112.

25. Stephen M. Saideman, "When Conflict Spreads: Arab Spring and the Limits of Diffusion: Empirical and Theoretical Research in International Relations," *International Interactions* 38:5 (2012): 717.

26. Economist Intelligence Unit, "Democracy Index 2010: Democracy in Retreat," Table 3, p. 5, http://www.eiu.com/Handlers/WhitepaperHandler.ashx?fi=Democracy_Index_2010_Web.pdf&mode=wp&campaignid=demo2010. The remaining three were ranked as "hybrid regimes," a category just above "authoritarian" but below "flawed democracies."

27. Muzammil M. Hussain and Philip Howard. "What Best Explains Successful Protest Cascades? ICTs and the Fuzzy Causes of the Arab Spring," *International Studies Review* 15:1 (March 2013): 49, 51.

28. Anthony Billingsley, "Writing Constitutions in the Wake of the Arab Spring," *Foreign Affairs,* November 30, 2011, http://www.foreignaffairs.com/articles/136699/anthony-billingsley/writing-constitutions-in-the-wake-of-the-arab-spring.

29. Cited in Kavitha A. Davidson, "Democracy Index 2013: Global Democracy at a Standstill, The Economist Intelligence Unit's Annual Report Shows," *Huffington Post*, March 21, 2013, http://www.huffingtonpost.com/2013/03/21/democracy-index-2013-economist-intelligence-unit_n_2909619.html.

30. Cited in "Tunisia Counts Votes in Historic Free Election," *BBC News,* October 24, 2011, http://www.bbc.co.uk/news/world-africa-15425407.

31. Cited in Lyse Doucet, "Tunisians' Frustrations, Two Years On," *BBC News,* December 10, 2012, http://www.bbc.co.uk/news/world-20663981.

32. Cited in Maria Golovnina, "World Raises Pressure on Libya, Battles for Key Towns," *Reuters,* February 28, 2011, http://www.reuters.com/article/2011/02/28/us-libya-protests-idUSTRE71G0A620110228.

33. Cited in Devin Dwyer and Luis Martinez, "U.S. Tomahawk Cruise Missiles Hit Targets in Libya," *ABC News,* March 19, 2011, http://abcnews.go.com/International/libya-international-military-coalition-launch-assault-gadhafi-forces/story?id=13174246#.T35yGdl0SZR.

34. Cited in Amy Chozick, "Clinton Calls Benghazi Her 'Biggest Regret' as Secretary," *New York Times,* January 27, 2014, http://www.nytimes.com/2014/01/28/us/politics/clinton-calls-benghazi-attack-her-biggest-regret-as-secretary.html.

35. "Obama's Speech to the United Nations General Assembly—Text," *New York Times,* September 25, 2013, http://www.nytimes.com/2012/09/26/world/obamas-speech-to-the-united-nations-general-assembly-text.html.

36. Jason Pack, "Libya on the Brink," *Foreign Affairs*, July 28, 2014, http://www.foreignaffairs.com/articles/141666/jason-pack/libya-on-the-brink.

37. George Joffé, "Navigating the Nile," *Foreign Affairs*, September 21, 2012, http://www.foreignaffairs.com/articles/138128/george-joffe/navigating-the-nile.

38. Cited in "Obama: I Told Mubarak He Must Deliver on His Promises," *CNN World,* January 28 2011, http://www.cnn.com/2011/WORLD/africa/01/28/egypt.protests.u.s..response/index.html.

39. "Remarks by the President on the Situation in Egypt," The White House, February 1, 2011, http://www.whitehouse.gov/the-press-office/2011/02/01/remarks-president-situation-egypt.

40. Cited in Andrew Quinn, "Clinton Warns of 'Perfect Storm' in Middle East," *The Independent,* February 5, 2011, http://www.independent.co.uk/news/world/politics/clinton-warns-of-quotperfect-stormquot-in-middle-east-2205407.html.

41. Thomas L. Friedman, "Can Egypt Pull Together?" *New York Times,* July 6, 2013, http://www.nytimes.com/2013/07/07/opinion/sunday/friedman-can-egypt-pull-together.html.

42. Cited in Hamza Hendawi, "Morsi's Constitutional Declarations Grant Egypt's President Far-reaching Powers," *Huffington Post,* November 22, 2012, http://www.huffingtonpost.com/2012/11/22/morsi-constitutional-declaration_n_2175651.html.

43. Cited in Human Rights Watch, "Egypt: New Constitution Mixed on Support of Rights," November 30, 2012, http://www.hrw.org/news/2012/11/29/egypt-new-constitution-mixed-support-rights.

44. Nathan J. Brown, "Redoing the Egyptian Revolution," *Foreign Affairs,* July 3, 2013, http://www.foreignaffairs.com/articles/139555/nathan-j-brown/redoing-the-egyptian-revolution.

45. Cited in Mark Landler, "Political Turmoil in Egypt Is Replay for White House," *New York Times,* July 2, 2013, http://www.nytimes.com/2013/07/03/world/middleeast/political-turmoil-in-egypt-is-replay-for-white-house.html.

46. Cited in Jeff Martini "The Egyptian Military's Playbook," *Foreign Affairs,* July 2, 2013, http://www.foreignaffairs.com/articles/139547/jeff-martini/the-egyptian-militarys-playbook.

47. Cited in Mark Landler and Peter Baker, "His Options Few, Obama Rebukes Egypt's Leaders," *New York Times,* August 15, 2013, http://www.nytimes.com/2013/08/16/world/middleeast/obama-statement-on-egypt.html.

48. Cited in Michael R. Gordon and Kareem Fahim, "Kerry Says Egypt's Military Was Restoring Democracy in Ousting Morsi," *New York Times,* August 1, 2013, http://www.nytimes.com/2013/08/02/world/middleeast/egypt-warns-morsi-supporters-to-end-protests.html.

49. Cited in Peter Baker, "A Coup? Or Something Else? $1.5 Billion in U.S. Aid Is on the Line," *New York Times,* July 4, 2013, http://www.nytimes.com/2013/07/05/world/middleeast/egypts-arrests-of-islamists-pose-test-to-us-over-military-aid.html.

50. Cited in Adam Entous, "White House's Egypt Debate Heralds Shift," *The Wall Street Journal,* July 30, 2013, A6.

51. Cited in Jonathan Weisman, "Military Aid to Egyptians Loses Support in the Senate," *New York Times,* April 29, 2014, http://www.nytimes.com/2014/04/30/us/politics/egypt.html.

52. Cited in Kim Ghattas, "U.S. Credibility 'in Tatters' over Egypt Crisis," *BBC News,* August 16, 2013, http://www.bbc.co.uk/news/world-middle-east-23721918.

53. UNHCR, "UNHCR Chief Warns That Syrian Crisis at Dangerous Tipping Point, as Humanitarian Needs Outpace Funding," March 31, 2015, http://www.unhcr.org/551aa6736.html.

54. Cited In Scott Wilson and Joby Warrick, "Syria's Assad Must Go, Obama says," *Washington Post*, August 18, 2011, http://articles.washingtonpost.com/2011-08-18/politics/35271355_1_syrian-government-assets-syrian-president-bashar-al-assad-syrian-people.

55. Cited in Michael R. Gordon, "Kerry Criticizes Iran and Russia for Shipping Arms to Syria," *New York Times,* March 4, 2013, http://www.nytimes.com/2013/03/05/world/middleeast/syria-russia-iran-arms.html.

56. Cited in Michael R. Gordon, Eric Schmitt, and Tim Arango, "Flow of Arms to Syria Through Iraq Persists, to U.S. Dismay," *New York Times,* December 1, 2012, http://www.nytimes.com/2012/12/02/world/middleeast/us-is-stumbling-in-effort-to-cut-syria-arms-flow.html.

57. Cited in Adam Entous, "Inside Obama's Syria Debate," *The Wall Street Journal*, March 30–31, 2013, A10.

58. Hillary Rodham Clinton, *Hard Choices* (New York, NY: Simon & Schuster, 2014), 463, 464.

59. Cited in Entous, "Inside Obama's Syria Debate."

60. Cited in Mark Mazzetti, Robert F. Worth, and Michael R. Gordon, "Obama's Uncertain Path amid Syria Bloodshed," *New York Times,* October 22, 2013, http://www.nytimes.com/2013/10/23/world/middleeast/obamas-uncertain-path-amid-syria-bloodshed.html?hp.

61. Cited in Glenn Kessler, "President Obama and the 'Red Line' on Syria's Chemical Weapons,"

Washington Post, September 6, 2013, http://www.washingtonpost.com/blogs/fact-checker/wp/2013/09/06/president-obama-and-the-red-line-on-syrias-chemical-weapons.

62. Cited in Peter Baker, Mark Landler, David E. Sanger, and Anne Barnard, "Off-the-Cuff Obama Line Put U.S. in Bind on Syria," *New York Times,* May 4, 2013, http://www.nytimes.com/2013/05/05/world/middleeast/obamas-vow-on-chemical-weapons-puts-him-in-tough-spot.html.

63. John Mueller "Erase the Red Line," *Foreign Affairs,* April 30, 2013, http://www.foreignaffairs.com/articles/139351/john-mueller/erase-the-red-line.

64. Cited in Susan Jones, "Obama's Blurry Red Line," *The Wire*, September 6, 2013, http://www.factcheck.org/2013/09/obamas-blurry-red-line.

65. Cited in Mazzetti, Worth, and Gordon, "Obama's Uncertain Path amid Syria Bloodshed."

66. Cited in Helene Cooper, "Obama Seeks Money to Train 'Appropriately Vetted' Syrian Rebels," *New York Times,* June 26, 2014, http://www.nytimes.com/2014/06/27/world/middleeast/obama-seeks-500-million-to-train-and-equip-syrian-opposition.html?_r=0.

67. Mark Mazzetti, "C.I.A. Study of Covert Aid Fueled Skepticism about Helping Syrian Rebels," *New York Times,* October 14, 2014, http://www.nytimes.com/2014/10/15/us/politics/cia-study-says-arming-rebels-seldom-works.html.

68. Cited in Michael R. Gordon, Mark Landler, and Anne Barnard, "U.S. Suspends Nonlethal Aid to Syria Rebels," *New York Times,* December 11, 2013, http://www.nytimes.com/2013/12/12/world/middleeast/us-suspends-nonlethal-aid-to-syrian-rebels-in-north.html.

69. Cited in Thom Shanker, "General Says Syrian Rebels Aren't Ready to Take Power," *New York Times,* August 21, 2013, http://www.nytimes.com/2013/08/22/world/middleeast/general-says-syrian-rebels-arent-ready-to-take-power.html.

70. Cited in Anne Barnard, "Syrians on Both Sides of the War Increasingly See Assad as Likely to Stay," *New York Times,* November 8, 2013, http://www.nytimes.com/2013/11/09/world/middleeast/syrians-and-observers-increasingly-see-assad-as-likely-to-stay.html.

71. Cited in Mazzetti, Worth, and Gordon, "Obama's Uncertain Path amid Syria Bloodshed."

72. Cited in David D. Kirkpatrick, "Overwhelming Vote for Egypt's Constitution Raises Concern," *New York Times,* January 18, 2014, http://www.nytimes.com/2014/01/19/world/middleeast/vote-validates-egypts-constitution-and-military-takeover.html.

73. Mara Revkin, "Worse Than Mubarak," *Foreign Affairs*, February 11, 2014, http://www.foreignaffairs.com/articles/140729/mara-revkin/worse-than-mubarak.

74. Cited in Steven Lee Myers, "To Back Democracy, U.S. Prepares to Cut $1 Billion from Egypt's Debt," *New York Times,* September 3, 2012, http://www.nytimes.com/2012/09/04/world/middleeast/us-prepares-economic-aid-to-bolster-democracy-in-egypt.html?pagewanted=all.

75. Cited in Peter Baker, "Egypt Crisis Finds Washington Largely Ambivalent and Aloof," *New York Times,* July 5, 2013, http://www.nytimes.com/2013/07/06/world/middleeast/egypt-crisis-finds-washington-ambivalent-and-aloof.html.

76. Cited in Mark Landler and Peter Baker, "His Options Few, Obama Rebukes Egypt's Leaders," *New York Times,* August 15, 2013, http://www.nytimes.com/2013/08/16/world/middleeast/obama-statement-on-egypt.html?ref=middleeast.

77. Cited in David D. Kirkpatrick and Kareem Fahim, "U.S. Warns Egypt's Generals against Jeopardizing 'Second Chance' at Democracy," *New York Times,* July 15, 2013, http://www.nytimes.com/2013/07/16/world/middleeast/us-steps-up-public-diplomacy-in-egypt-crisis.html.

78. "Egyptians Increasingly Glum," *Pew Research Global Attitudes Project,* May 16, 2013, http://www.pewglobal.org/2013/05/16/egyptians-increasingly-glum.

79. Cited in Thom Shanker and Eric Schmitt, "Ties with Egypt Army Constrain Washington," *New York Times,* August 16, 2013, http://www.nytimes.com/2013/08/17/world/middleeast/us-officials-fear-losing-an-eager-ally-in-the-egyptian-military.html.

80. Robert Springborg, "The Nasser Playbook," *Foreign Affairs,* November 5, 2013, http://www.foreignaffairs.com/articles/140242/robert-springborg/the-nasser-playbook.

81. UNHCR, "Syria Regional Refugee Response," April 14, 2015, http://data.unhcr.org/syrianrefugees/regional.php.

82. UNHCR, "Syria Regional Refugee Response," April 10, 2015, http://data.unhcr.org/syrianrefugees/country.php?id=122.

83. Cited in "Million Syria Refugees Registered in Lebanon—UN," *BBC News*, April 3, 2014, http://www.bbc.com/news/world-middle-east-26864485.

84. UNHCR, "Syria Regional Refugee Response," April 14, 2015.

85. USAID, "Syria," March 31, 2015, http://www.usaid.gov/crisis/syria.

86. Cited in Michael R. Gordon, "U.S. Seeks to Bypass Assad So More Aid Can Reach Syrian Civilians," *New York Times*, May 15, 2014, http://www.nytimes.com/2014/05/16/world/middleeast/us-seeks-ways-to-make-aid-reach-syrian-civilians.html.

87. Cited in Michael R. Gordon, "Criticism of United States' Mideast Policy Increasingly Comes from Allies," *New York Times,* October 23, 2013, http://www.nytimes.com/2013/10/24/world/middleeast/kerry-reassures-israel-on-iran-but-divisions-remain.html.

88. Cited in Ben Hubbard, "Islamist Rebels Create Dilemma on Syria Policy," *New York Times,* April 27, 2013, http://www.nytimes.com/2013/04/28/world/middleeast/islamist-rebels-gains-in-syria-create-dilemma-for-us.html.

89. Clinton, *Hard Choices*, 461.

90. Cited in David Rothkopf, "National Insecurity," *Foreign Policy* 208 (September/October 2014): 47.

91. Ibid.

92. Cited in Mark Landler and Thom Shanker, "Pentagon Lays Out Options for U.S. Military Effort in Syria," *New York Times,* July 22, 2013, http://www.nytimes.com/2013/07/23/world/middleeast/pentagon-outlining-options-to-congress-suggests-syria-campaign-would-be-costly.html.

93. "Syria's Neighbors Want Assad to Step Down, but No Appetite for Aid to Rebels," *Pew Global Attitudes Project,* June 10, 2014, http://www.pewglobal.org/2014/06/16/syrias-neighbors-want-assad-to-step-down-but-no-appetite-for-aid-to-rebels.

94. Michael Ignatieff, "With Syria, Diplomacy Needs Force," *New York Times,* February 25, 2014, http://www.nytimes.com/2014/02/26/opinion/with-syria-diplomacy-needs-force.html.

95. Cited in David D. Kirkpatrick, "As Moderate Islamists Retreat, Extremists Surge Unchecked," *New York Times,* June 18, 2014, http://www.nytimes.com/2014/06/19/world/middleeast/as-moderate-islamists-retreat-extremists-surge-unchecked.html.

96. "The Rule of the Gunmen," *The Economist*, October 11, 2014, 57.

97. Gerald F. Seib, "Few Good Choices for U.S. in Mideast," *The Wall Street Journal,* July 30, 2013, A4.

98. Seth Jones, "The Mirage of the Arab Spring," *Foreign Affairs* 92:1 (January/February 2013): 56.

99. Cited in David D. Kirkpatrick, "Benghazi and Arab Spring Rear Up in U.S. Campaign," *New York Times,* October 21, 2012, http://www.nytimes.com/2012/10/22/us/politics/benghazi-and-arab-spring-rear-up-in-us-campaign.html.

100. Cited in Mark Landler, "Rice Offers a More Modest Strategy for Mideast," *New York Times*, October 26, 2013, http://www.nytimes.com/2013/10/27/world/middleeast/rice-offers-a-more-modest-strategy-for-mideast.html.

CHAPTER 11

1. Francis Fukuyama, "The End of History," *The National Interest* 16 (Summer 1989): 3. Emphasis in original.

2. Cited in Peter Baker, "How Obama Came to Plan for 'Surge' in Afghanistan," *New York Times,* December 5, 2009, http://www.nytimes.com/2009/12/06/world/asia/06reconstruct.html?pagewanted=all.

3. Paul L. Yingling, "An Absence of Strategic Thinking," *Foreign Affairs,* December 16, 2011, http://www.foreignaffairs.com/articles/134033/paul-l-yingling/an-absence-of-strategic-thinking.

4. Hillary Rodham Clinton, *Hard Choices* (New York, NY: Simon & Schuster, 2014), 190.

5. Robert M. Gates, *Duty: Memoirs of a Secretary at War* (New York, NY: Knopf, 2014), 585.

6. Leon Panetta, "The CIA Is Proud to Be on the Frontlines against al-Qaeda," *Washington Post*, January 10, 2010, http://www.washingtonpost.com/wp-dyn/content/article/2010/01/08/AR2010010803588.html.

7. Cited in Clinton, *Hard Choices*, 469.

8. Andrew Dugan, "Fewer in U.S. Support Iraq Withdrawal Decision Now vs. 2011," *Gallup Politics,* June 25, 2014, http://www.gallup.com/poll/171923/fewer-support-iraq-withdrawal-decision-2011.aspx.

9. "Wide Support for Striking ISIS, but Weak Approval for Obama," Washington Post-ABC News Poll, *Washington Post,* September 9, 2014, http://www.washingtonpost.com/page/2010-2019/WashingtonPost/2014/09/09/National-Politics/Polling/release_361.xml.

10. Ole Holsti, *American Public Opinion on the Iraq War* (Ann Arbor: University of Michigan Press, 2011), 132. Emphasis in original.

11. Ibid., 137.

12. Gallup, "Iraq," accessed January 6, 2015, http://www.gallup.com/poll/1633/iraq.aspx.

13. Cited in Eric Lipton, "As Wars End, a Rush to Grab Dollars Spent on the Border," *New York Times,* June 6, 2013, http://www.nytimes.com/2013/06/07/us/us-military-firms-eye-border-security-contracts.html?pagewanted=all.

14. George W. Bush, Second Inaugural Address, January 20, 2005, in "Inaugural Addresses of the Presidents of the United States," *Bartleby.com,* http://www.bartleby.com/124/pres67.html.

15. William Safire, "Bush's 'Freedom Speech,'" *New York Times,* January 21, 2005, http://www.nytimes.com/2005/01/21/opinion/21safire.html.

16. Nick Danforth, "The Myth of the Caliphate," *Foreign Affairs,* November 19, 2014, http://www.foreignaffairs.com/articles/142379/nick-danforth/the-myth-of-the-caliphate.

17. "Muslims," *Pew Research Religion & Public Life Project,* December 18, 2012, http://www.pewforum.org/2012/12/18/global-religious-landscape-muslim.

18. John L. Esposito, *What Everyone Needs to Know about Islam* (Oxford, UK: Oxford University Press, 2011), 55–56.

19. Ibid., 133.

20. Ibid.

21. Gilles Kepel, *Jihad: The Trail of Political Islam* (Cambridge, MA: Harvard University Press, 2003), 276.

22. Bruce Livesey, "The Salafist Movement," *Frontline,* n.d., http://www.pbs.org/wgbh/pages/frontline/shows/front/special/sala.html.

23. Robert S. Leiken and Steven Brooke, "The Moderate Muslim Brotherhood," *Foreign Affairs* 82:2 (March/April 2007): 110–111.

24. "The CIA's Intervention in Afghanistan: Interview with Zbigniew Brzezinski," *Le Nouvel Observateur,* Paris, 15–21 January 1998, http://www.globalresearch.ca/articles/BRZ110A.html.

25. William Malley, *The Afghanistan Wars,* 2nd ed. (New York, NY: Palgrave Macmillan, 2002), 223. Emphasis in original.

26. Bill Roggio, "The Seven Phases of the Base," *The Long War Journal,* August 15, 2005, http://www.longwarjournal.org/archives/2005/08/the_seven_phase.php.

27. "Al Qaeda's Second Fatwa," *PBS NEWSHOUR,* February 23, 1998, http://www.pbs.org/newshour/updates/military/jan-june98/fatwa_1998.html.

28. Cited in Philip Shenon, "U.S. Fury on 2 Continents; Clinton's Words: 'There Will Be No Sanctuary for Terrorists,'" *New York Times,* August 21, 1998, http://www.nytimes.com/1998/08/21/world/us-fury-2-continents-clinton-s-words-there-will-be-no-sanctuary-for-terrorists.html?n=Top%2fReference%2fTimes%20Topics%2fPeople%2fC%2fClinton%2c%20Bill.

29. Ned Zeman, David Wise, David Rose, and Bryan Burrough, "The Path to 9/11: Lost Warnings and Fatal Errors," *Vanity Fair*, November 2004, http://www.vanityfair.com/politics/features/2004/11/path-to-9-11-200411.

30. "Interview Michael Scheuer," *Frontline*, July 21, 2005, http://www.pbs.org/wgbh/pages/frontline/torture/interviews/scheuer.html.

31. "Text for Authorization of Military Force," September 18, 2001, https://www.govtrack.us/congress/bills/107/sjres23/text.

32. "Text of Bush's Speech at West Point," *New York Times,* June 1, 2002, http://www.nytimes.com/2002/06/01/international/02PTEX-WEB.html.

33. Cited in Michael R. Gordon and Eric Schmitt, "A Nation Challenged: The Hunt; Marines and Army May Scour Caves, U.S. General Says," *New York Times,* December 20, 2001, http://www.nytimes.com/2001/12/20/world/a-nation-challenged-the-hunt-marines-and-army-may-scour-caves-us-general-says.html.

34. "The Big Retrograde," *The Economist*, April 27, 2013, 38.

35. Cited in Azam Ahmed, "Misgivings by U.S. General as Afghan Mission Ends," *New York Times,* December 8, 2014, http://www.nytimes.com/2014/12/09/world/asia/us-general-joseph-anderson-mission-in-afghanistan.html.

36. Cited in Aamer Madhani and Tom Vanden Brook, "U.S., Afghans, Taliban to Begin Peace Talks in Qatar," *USA Today,* June 18, 2013, http://www.usatoday.com/story/news/politics/2013/06/18/us-taliban-afghan-peace-talks/2433879.

37. Cited in Matthew Rosenberg, "U.S. Softens Deadline for Deal to Keep Troops in Afghanistan," *New York Times,* December 23, 2013, http://www.nytimes.com/2013/12/24/world/asia/us-softens-deadline-for-deal-to-keep-troops-in-afghanistan.html?hpw&rref=us.

38. Cited in Helene Cooper, "Hard Talk Aside, Little Desire by the West to Leave Afghanistan," *New York Times,* February 26, 2014, http://www.nytimes.com/2014/02/27/world/asia/hard-talk-aside-little-desire-by-west-to-leave-afghanistan.html.

39. *IntelCenter: Words of Osama bin Laden*, vol. 1 (Alexandria, VA: Tempest, 2008), 75.

40. "President Bush Announces Major Combat Operation in Iraq Have Ended," White House, May 1, 2003, http://georgewbush-whitehouse.archives.gov/news/releases/2003/05/20030501-15.html.

41. "Declassified Key Judgments of the National Intelligence Estimate 'Trends in Global Terrorism: Implications for the United States' dated April 2006," http://www.dni.gov/files/documents/Special%20Report_Global%20Terrorism%20NIE%20Key%20Judgments.pdf.

42. Cited in Daniel Schorn, "Bush Talks about His Biggest Fear," *CBS News,* February 11, 2009, http://www.cbsnews.com/2100-500923_162-1980081.html.

43. "Transcript of Interview with Vice-President Dick Cheney on *Meet the Press,* 8 September 2002," http://www.leadingtowar.com/PDFsources_claims_aluminum/2002_09_08_NBC.pdf.

44. "President Bush, Colombia President Uribe Discuss Terrorism," White House, September 25, 2002, http://www.hsdl.org/?view&did=476019.

45. Paul R. Pillar, "Intelligence, Policy, and the War in Iraq," *Foreign Affairs* 85:2 (March/April 2006): 18.

46. Cited in R. Jeffrey Smith, "Hussein's Prewar Ties to Al-Qaeda Discounted," *Washington Post,* April 6, 2007, http://www.washingtonpost.com/wp-dyn/content/article/2007/04/05/AR2007040502263.html.

47. "The 9/11 Commission Report," 334, http://www.leadingtowar.com/claims_sources/911%20fullreport.pdf.

48. Cited in Kim Sengupta, "Occupation Made World Less Safe, Pro-War Institute Says," *The Independent*, May 26, 2004, http://www.independent.co.uk/news/world/middle-east/occupation-made-world-less-safe-prowar-institute-says-6169169.html.

49. Cited in Dana Priest, "Iraq New Terror Breeding Ground," *Washington Post,* January 14, 2005, http://www.washingtonpost.com/wp-dyn/articles/A7460-2005Jan13.html.

50. Leon Panetta, "Leon Panetta: How the White House Misplayed Iraqi Troop Talks," *Time,* October 1, 2014, http://time.com/3453840/leon-panetta-iraqi-troop.

51. Cited in "Bin Laden Raid: Barack Obama Describes 'Huge Risks,'" *BBC News*, May 9, 2011, http://www.bbc.co.uk/news/world-us-canada-13331762.

52. Cited in Adrian Brown, "Osama Bin Laden's Death: How It Happened," *BBC News,* September 10, 2012, http://www.bbc.co.uk/news/world-south-asia-13257330.

53. Clinton, *Hard Choices*, 197.

54. Bill Roggio, "Charting the Data for US Airstrikes in Pakistan, 2004–2015," *The Long War Journal*, April 13, 2015, http://www.longwarjournal.org/pakistan-strikes.

55. Cited in "London Transit Attacks Bombings Were Bin Laden's Last Successful Operation: U.S. Officials," *The World Post*, August 7, 2014, http://www.huffingtonpost.com/2011/07/13/bin-laden-london-attacks-failed-airline-plots-_n_896790.html.

56. Cited in "The Unquenchable Fire," *The Economist,* September 28, 2013, 21.

57. Cited in Robert F. Worth, "Al Qaeda-Inspired Groups, Minus Goal of Striking U.S.," *New York Times,* October 27, 2012, http://www.nytimes.com/2012/10/28/world/middleeast/al-qaeda-inspired-groups-minus-goal-of-striking-us.html?pagewanted=all&_r=0.

58. Cited in Ben Hubbard, "The Franchising of Al Qaeda," *New York Times,* January 25, 2014, http://www.nytimes.com/2014/01/26/sunday-review/the-franchising-of-al-qaeda.html.

59. William McCants, "How Zawahiri Lost al Qaeda," *Foreign Affairs,* November 19, 2013, http://www.foreignaffairs.com/articles/140273/william-mccants/how-zawahiri-lost-al-qaeda.

60. Jacob N. Shapiro, *The Terrorist's Dilemma: Managing Violent Covert Organizations* (Princeton, NJ: Princeton University Press, 2013), 4.

61. Cited in Adam Entous, "Regrouped Al Qaeda Poses Global Threat," *The Wall Street Journal*, August 5, 2013, A8.

62. Cited in Eric Schmitt, "Qaeda Affiliates Gain Regional Influence as Central Leadership Fades," *New York Times,* April 30, 2014, http://www.nytimes.com/2014/05/01/world/middleeast/qaeda-affiliates-gain-regional-influence-as-central-leadership-fades.html.

63. Cited in Mark Landler, "Obama Warns U.S. Faces Diffuse Terrorism Threats," *New York Times,* May 28, 2014, http://www.nytimes.com/2014/05/29/us/politics/obama-foreign-policy-west-point-speech.html.

64. "Shoe Bomber" Richard Reid tried unsuccessfully to ignite PETN hidden in the hollowed-out bottoms of his shoes to destroy an American Airlines flight from Paris to Miami in 2001.

65. Cited in Brian Knowlton, "Holder Voices 'Extreme Concern about Terrorist Bomb Makers," *New York Times,* July 13, 2014, http://www.nytimes.com/2014/07/14/world/middleeast/holder-expresses-concern-about-terrorist-bomb-makers.html.

66. Stig Jarle Hansen, *Al-Shabaab in Somalia* (New York, NY: Columbia University Press, 2013), 72.

67. Cited in Jay Solomon and Julian E. Barnes, "Terror Threat Prompts U.S. Rethink on Africa," *The Wall Street Journal,* January 19–20, 2013, http://online.wsj.com/article/SB10001424127887324468104578250211314357762.html.

68. Paul Hidalgo, "Al Shabab's Last Stand?" *Foreign Affairs*, September 11, 2014, http://www.foreignaffairs.com/articles/141975/paul-hidalgo/al-shababs-last-stand.

69. Cited in Benjamin Weiser, "U.S. Charges Algerian in Deadly Gas Plant Attack," *New York Times,* July 19, 2013, http://www.nytimes.com/2013/07/20/nyregion/us-charges-algerian-in-deadly-gas-plant-attack.html.

70. Cited in Steven Lee Myers, "Clinton Suggests Link to Qaeda Offshoot in Deadly Libya Attack," *New York Times,* September 26, 2012, http://www.nytimes.com/2012/09/27/world/africa/clinton-cites-clear-link-between-al-qaeda-and-attack-in-libya.html?pagewanted=all.

71. Cited in Chris McGreal, "Clinton Demands US Takes Lead to Combat 'Jihadist Threat' in North Africa," *The Guardian,* January 23, 2013, http://www.guardian.co.uk/world/2013/jan/23/hillary-clinton-north-africa-jihadist-threat.

72. U.S. House of Representatives Committee on Homeland Security Subcommittee on Counterterrorism and Intelligence, "Boko Haram Emerging Threat to the U.S. Homeland," November 30, 2011, 2, http://homeland.house.gov/sites/homeland.house.gov/files/Boko%20Haram-%20Emerging%20Threat%20to%20the%20US%20Homeland.pdf.

73. M. J. Kirdar, "Al-Qaeda in Iraq," Center for Strategic & International Studies, June 2011, http://csis.org/files/publication/110614_Kirdar_AlQaedaIraq_Web.pdf, p. 4.

74. Cited in Tim Arango and Eric Schmitt, "U.S. Actions in Iraq Fueled Rise of a Rebel," *New York Times,* August 10, 2014, http://www.nytimes.com/2014/08/11/world/middleeast/us-actions-in-iraq-fueled-rise-of-a-rebel.html.

75. Cited in Ben Hubbard, "ISIS Threatens Al Qaeda as Flagship Movement of Extremists," *New York Times,* June 30, 2014, http://www.nytimes.com/2014/07/01/world/middleeast/isis-threatens-al-qaeda-as-flagship-movement-of-extremists.html.

76. Cited in Tim Arango, Kareem Fahim, and Ben Hubbard, "Rebels' Fast Strike in Iraq Was Years in the Making," *New York Times,* June 14, 2014, http://www.nytimes.com/2014/06/15/world/middleeast/rebels-fast-strike-in-iraq-was-years-in-the-making.html.

77. Charles Lister, "ISIS a Fanatical Force—with a Weakness," *CNN,* June 17, 2014, http://www.cnn.com/2014/06/16/opinion/lister-isis-iraq.

78. Cited in David S. Joachim, "Obama to Meet Congressional Leaders over Iraq," *New York Times,*

June 18, 2014, http://www.nytimes.com/2014/06/19/world/middleeast/obama-iraq.html.

79. Cited in Ben Hubbard, "ISIS Threatens Al Qaeda as Flagship Movement of Extremists," *New York Times,* June 30, 2014, http://www.nytimes.com/2014/07/01/world/middleeast/isis-threatens-al-qaeda-as-flagship-movement-of-extremists.html.

80. Cited in Peter Baker, "Obama, with Reluctance, Returns to Action in Iraq," *New York Times,* August 7, 2014, http://www.nytimes.com/2014/08/08/world/middleeast/a-return-to-action.html.

81. "Transcript of Obama's Remarks on the Fight against ISIS," *New York Times,* September 10, 2014, http://www.nytimes.com/2014/09/11/world/middleeast/obamas-remarks-on-the-fight-against-isis.html.

82. Cited in Peter Baker, "Obama Defends Progress against Extremists," *New York Times,* December 15, 2014, http://www.nytimes.com/2014/12/16/us/politics/obama-says-coalition-forces-have-halted-islamic-state-momentum.html.

83. Cited in Jeffrey Goldberg, "Hillary Clinton: 'Failure' to Help Syrian Rebels Led to the Rise of ISIS," *The Atlantic,* August 10, 2014, http://www.theatlantic.com/international/archive/2014/08/hillary-clinton-failure-to-help-syrian-rebels-led-to-the-rise-of-isis/375832.

84. Cited in Robert F. Worth and Eric Schmitt, "Jihadist Groups Gain in Turmoil across Middle East," *New York Times,* December 3, 2013, http://www.nytimes.com/2013/12/04/world/middleeast/jihadist-groups-gain-in-turmoil-across-middle-east.html.

85. Cited in Helene Cooper, "U.S. and Allies Form Coalition with Intent to Destroy ISIS," *New York Times,* September 5, 2014, http://www.newsdiffs.org/diff/668927/668939/www.nytimes.com/2014/09/06/world/europe/nato-summit.html.

86. Cited in Scott Shane, "A Homemade Style of Terror: Jihadists Push New Tactics," *New York Times,* May 5, 2013, http://www.nytimes.com/2013/05/06/us/terrorists-find-online-education-for-attacks.html.

87. Cited in ibid.

88. Cited in Eric Schmitt, "Worries Mount as Syria Lures West's Muslims," *New York Times,* July 27, 2013, http://www.nytimes.com/2013/07/28/world/middleeast/worries-mount-as-syria-lures-wests-muslims.html?pagewanted=all.

89. Charlie Savage, "Secret Papers Describe Size of Terror Lists Kept by U.S.," *New York Times,* August 5, 2014, http://www.nytimes.com/2014/08/06/us/secret-papers-describe-size-of-terror-lists-kept-by-us.html.

90. Cited in Andrew McAfee, "Enterprise 2.0 Is a Crock: Discuss," *Andrew McAfee's Blog,* September 2, 2009, http://andrewmcafee.org/2009/09/e20-is-a-crock-discuss.

91. The White House, "Remarks of President Barack Obama," May 23, 2013, https://www.whitehouse.gov/the-press-office/2013/05/23/remarks-president-barack-obama.

92. Cited in ibid.

93. Cited in Mark Landler, "U.S. Troops to Leave Afghanistan by End of 2016," *New York Times,* May 27, 2014, http://www.nytimes.com/2014/05/28/world/asia/us-to-complete-afghan-pullout-by-end-of-2016-obama-to-say.html.

94. Cited in Thom Shanker, "Pentagon Sees Support for Afghans after 2014," *New York Times,* July 30, 2013, http://www.nytimes.com/2013/07/31/world/asia/pentagon-report-foresees-continued-support-for-afghanistan.html.

95. Cited in ibid.

96. Dalia Sussman, "How Americans View the Afghan War," *New York Times,* May 27, 2014, http://www.nytimes.com/2014/05/28/upshot/how-americans-view-the-afghan-war.html?action=click&contentCollection=Asia%20Pacific&module=RelatedCoverage&region=Marginalia&pgtype=article.

97. Husain Haqqani, "Breaking Up Is Not Hard to Do," *Foreign Affairs* 92:2 (March/April 2013): 64, 65.

98. Cited in Alissa J. Rubin and Rod Nordland, "Sunnis and Kurds on Sidelines of Iraqi Leader's Military Plans," *New York Times,* June 16, 2014, http://www.nytimes.com/2014/06/17/world/middleeast/sunnis-and-kurds-on-sidelines-of-iraq-leaders-military-plans.html.

99. Cited in Peter Baker, "Obama Finds He Can't Put Iraq War behind Him," *New York Times*, June 13, 2014, http://www.nytimes.com/2014/06/14/world/middleeast/obama-finds-he-cant-put-iraq-behind-him.html.

100. Daniel Byman and Jeremy Shapiro, "Homeward Bound?" *Foreign Affairs,* September 30, 2014,

http://www.foreignaffairs.com/articles/142025/daniel-byman-and-jeremy-shapiro/homeward-bound.

101. Jytte Klausen, "They're Coming," *Foreign Affairs*, October 1, 2014, http://www.foreignaffairs.com/articles/142129/jytte-klausen/theyre-coming.

102. Cited in Gregory S. McNeal, "Americans Fighting for ISIS Could Face Array of Criminal Charges," *Forbes,* June 13, 2014, http://www.forbes.com/sites/gregorymcneal/2014/06/13/americans-fighting-for-isis-could-face-array-of-criminal-charges/print.

103. Peter Bergen, *Holy War, Inc.: Inside the Secret World of Osama bin Laden* (London, UK: Phoenix, 2002), 38.

104. Cited in Eric Schmitt, "A U.S. Reply, in English, to Terrorists' Online Lure," *New York Times,* December 4, 2013, http://www.nytimes.com/2013/12/05/world/middleeast/us-aims-to-blunt-terrorist-recruiting-of-english-speakers.html.

105. Cited in Brian Knowlton, "Digital War Takes Shape on Websites over ISIS," *New York Times,* September 26, 2014, http://www.nytimes.com/2014/09/27/world/middleeast/us-vividly-rebuts-isis-propaganda-on-arab-social-media.html.

106. "Transcript of Obama's Remarks on the Fight against ISIS," *New York Times,* September 10, 2014, http://www.nytimes.com/2014/09/11/world/middleeast/obamas-remarks-on-the-fight-against-isis.html.

107. "Obama's Speech on Drone Policy," *New York Times,* May 23, 2013, http://www.nytimes.com/2013/05/24/us/politics/transcript-of-obamas-speech-on-drone-policy.html?pagewanted=all&_r=0.

108. Cited in Mark Mazzetti and Mark Landler, "Despite Administration Promises, Few Signs of Change in Drone Wars," *New York Times,* August 2, 2013, http://www.nytimes.com/2013/08/03/us/politics/drone-war-rages-on-even-as-administration-talks-about-ending-it.html?pagewanted=all.

109. Institute for Economics & Peace, *Global Terrorism Index 2014* (2014), http://www.visionofhumanity.org/sites/default/files/Global%20Terrorism%20Index%20Report%202014_0.pdf, 12.

110. "Jihadism: Tracking a Month of Deadly Attacks," *BBC News,* December 10, 2014, http://www.bbc.com/news/world-30080914.

CHAPTER 12

1. Cited in Mark Landler, "An Inconvenient Protest for Both China and the U.S.," *New York Times,* October 3, 2014, http://www.nytimes.com/2014/10/04/world/asia/an-inconvenient-protest-for-china-and-us-relations-obama-jinping.html?hp&action=click&pgtype=Homepage&module=first-column-region&region=top-news&WT.nav=top-news&_r=0.

2. Cited in "China and U.S. Hail 'Shared Interests,'" *BBC News,* March 19, 2013, http://www.bbc.co.uk/news/world-asia-china-21840071.

3. Zalmay Khalilzad, "Congage China," *Rand Issue Paper* (1999), http://www.rand.org/content/dam/rand/pubs/issue_papers/2006/IP187.pdf, 1, 6. See also Joseph S. Nye, Jr., "Our Pacific Predicament," *The American Interest* (March/April 2013), http://www.the-american-interest.com/article.cfm?piece=1388; and Aaron Friedberg, *A Contest for Supremacy* (New York, NY: W.W. Norton, 2011), 89–90.

4. Thom Shanker, "U.S. Forecast as No. 2 Economy, but Energy Independent," *New York Times,* December 10, 2012, http://www.nytimes.com/2012/12/11/world/china-to-be-no-1-economy-before-2030-study-says.html?_r=0.

5. Juan Pablo Cardenal and Heriberto Araújo, *China's Silent Army: The Pioneers, Traders, Fixers and Workers Who Are Remaking the World in Beijing's Image*, trans. Catherine Mansfield (New York, NY: Crown, 2013), xi.

6. David Shambaugh, *China Goes Global: The Partial Power* (Oxford, UK: Oxford University Press, 2013), 6, 7. Emphasis in original.

7. Cited in Wang Chien-Hui, "Bombardment of Quemoy," *Taiwan Review*, August 1, 1988, 4, http://taiwantoday.tw/ct.asp?xItem=107119&CtNode=124.

8. "McCarthy Publicly Attacks Owen Lattimore," 2009, http://www.history.com/this-day-in-history/mccarthy-publicly-attacks-owen-lattimore.

9. Cited in Mohammed M. Zaki, *America's Global Challenges: The Obama Era* (New York, NY: Palgrave Macmillan, 2011), 36.

10. Cited in "Bush Opposes Taiwan Independence," *Fox News,* December 9, 2003, http://www.foxnews.com/story/0,2933,105239,00.html.

11. Andrew J. Nathan and Andrew Scobell, "How China Sees America," *Foreign Affairs* 91:5 (September/October 2012): 43.

12. Kenneth Lieberthal, "The American Pivot to Asia," *Foreign Policy,* December 21, 2011, http://www.foreignpolicy.com/articles/2011/12/21/the_american_pivot_to_asia.

13. Hillary Rodham Clinton, *Hard Choices* (New York, NY: Simon & Schuster, 2014), 45,

14. Cited in "US Pledges Wider Military Presence across Pacific Rim," *BBC News,* June 4, 2011, http://www.bbc.co.uk/news/world-us-canada-13652176.

15. The White House, "Remarks by President Obama to the Australian Parliament," November 17, 2011, http://www.whitehouse.gov/the-press-office/2011/11/17/remarks-president-obama-australian-parliament.

16. The White House, "Remarks by Tom Donilon, National Security Advisor to the President, 'The United States and the Asia-Pacific in 2013,'" March 11, 2013, http://www.whitehouse.gov/the-press-office/2013/03/11/remarks-tom-donilon-national-security-advisory-president-united-states-a.

17. Lieberthal, "The American Pivot to Asia."

18. Nathan and Scobell, "How China Sees America," 33, 34.

19. Cited in Jane Perlez, "China Looks West as It Bolsters Regional Ties," *New York Times,* September 7, 2013, http://www.nytimes.com/2013/09/08/world/asia/china-looks-west-as-it-strengthens-regional-ties.html.

20. Nathan and Scobell, "How China Sees America," 36.

21. Usha C. V. Haley and George T. Haley, *Subsidies to Chinese Industry: State Capitalism, Business Strategy and Trade Policy* (Oxford, UK: Oxford University Press, 2013), 4.

22. Chris Giles, "China Poised to Pass US as World's Leading Economic Power This Year," *Financial Times,* April 30, 2014, http://www.ft.com/intl/cms/s/0/d79ffff8-cfb7-11e3-9b2b-00144feabdc0.html?siteedition=intl#axzz33A0ZMQ00.

23. Martin Wolf and David Pilling, "China: On Top of the World," *Financial Times*, May 2, 2014, www.ft.com/intl/cms/s/0/c355e0e6-d1d1-11e3-8ff4-00144feabdc0.html?siteedition=intl#axzz33A0ZMQ00.

24. Lant Pritchett and Lawrence Summers, "Asiaphoria Meet Regression to the Mean," November 6, 2013, http://www.frbsf.org/economic-research/events/2013/november/asia-economic-policy-conference/program/files/Asiaphoria-Meet-Regression-to-the-Mean.pdf.

25. CIA, "Country Comparison: GDP per Capita," *The World Factbook,* 2012, https://www.cia.gov/library/publications/the-world-factbook/rankorder/2004rank.html.

26. Wayne M. Morrison, "China-U.S. Trade Issues," *Congressional Research Service,* March 17, 2015, http://www.fas.org/sgp/crs/row/RL33536.pdf, 2.

27. Cited in Dana Mattioli, Dana Cimilluca, and David Kesmodel, "China Makes Biggest U.S. Play," *The Wall Street Journal,* May 30, 2013, A6.

28. "Top Outsourcing Countries," *SourcingLine,* 2012, http://www.sourcingline.com/top-outsourcing-countries.

29. Richard D. Fisher, Jr., *China's Military Modernization: Building for Regional and Global Research* (Westport, CT, Greenwood, 2008), viii.

30. Cited in Jane Perlez and Chris Buckley, "China's Leader, Seeking to Build Its Muscle, Pushes Overhaul of the Military," *New York Times,* May 24, 2014, http://www.nytimes.com/2014/05/25/world/asia/chinas-leader-seeking-to-build-its-muscle-pushes-overhaul-of-the-military.html?ref=world.

31. Fisher, *China's Military Modernization*, viii–ix.

32. Cited in Christian Le Mière, "China's Unarmed Arms Race," *Foreign Affairs,* July 29, 2013, http://www.foreignaffairs.com/articles/139609/christian-le-miere/chinas-unarmed-arms-race.

33. Fisher, *China's Military Modernization*, ix.

34. Cited in Siobhan Gorman and Siobhan Hughes, "U.S. Steps Up Alarm over Cyberattacks," *The Wall Street Journal,* March 13, 2013, A1.

35. Cited in David E. Sanger, "In Cyberspace, New Cold War," *New York Times*, February 24, 2013, http://www.nytimes.com/2013/02/25/world/asia/us-confronts-cyber-cold-war-with-china.html.

36. Cited in Julian E. Barnes, Siobhan Gorman, and Jeremy Page, "U.S., China Ties Tested in Cyberspace," *The Wall Street Journal,* February 19, 2013, http://online.wsj.com/article/SB10001424127887323376480457831459185728900 4.html.

37. Cited in David E. Sanger, David Barboza, and Nicole Perlroth, "Chinese Army Unit Is Seen as Tied to

Hacking Against U.S.," *New York Times,* February 18, 2013, http://www.nytimes.com/2013/02/19/technology/chinas-army-is-seen-as-tied-to-hacking-against-us.html?pagewanted=all&_r=0.

38. Cited in Siobhan Gorman, "U.S. Eyes Pushback on China Hacking," *The Wall Street Journal*, April 22, 2013, A12.

39. Edward Wong and Chris Buckley, "China's Military Budget Increasing 10% for 2015, Official Says," *New York Times,* March 4, 2015, http://www.nytimes.com/2015/03/05/world/asia/chinas-military-budget-increasing-10-for-2015-official-says.html.

40. "US Department of Defense, Military and Security Developments Involving the People's Republic of China, 2012, May 18, 2012," USC US-China Institute, http://china.usc.edu/us-department-defense-military-and-security-developments-involving-people%E2%80%99s-republic-china-2012-may.

41. Cited in Martin Fackler, "China Is Seen Nearing U.S.'s Military Power in Region," *New York Times,* May 1, 2013, http://www.nytimes.com/2013/05/02/world/asia/china-likely-to-challenge-us-supremacy-in-east-asia-report-says.html?ref=world.

42. Nathan and Scobell, "How China Sees America," 37–38.

43. Kevin Rudd, "Beyond the Pivot," *Foreign Affairs,* March/April 2013, http://www.foreignaffairs.com/articles/138843/kevin-rudd/beyond-the-pivot, 4.

44. Cited in David E. Sanger, "In the East China Sea, a Far Bigger Test of Power Looms," *New York Times,* December 1, 2013, http://www.nytlmes.com/2013/12/02/world/asia/in-the-east-china-sea-a-far-bigger-test-of-power-looms.html.

45. Christopher C. Joyner, "The Spratly Islands Dispute in the South China Sea: Problems, Policies, and Prospects for Diplomatic Accommodation," in Ranjeet Singh, ed., *Investigating Confidence Building Measures on the Asia Pacific Region* (Washington, DC: The Henry Stimson Center, 1999), 78.

46. Ibid., 57.

47. Cited in Jane Perlez, "Kerry, in Asia, Urges Focus on Law in China Disputes," *New York Times,* October 9, 2013, http://www.nytimes.com/2013/10/10/world/asia/kerry-asean-china.html.

48. Cited in Bonnie Glaser, "Trouble in the South China Sea," *Foreign Policy,* September 17, 2012, http://www.foreignpolicy.com/articles/2012/09/17/trouble_in_the_south_china_sea?page=full.

49. Ibid.

50. Ibid.

51. Cited in Thom Shanker, "Hagel Criticizes Chinese Navy, Citing Near Miss," *New York Times,* December 19, 2013, http://www.nytimes.com/2013/12/20/world/asia/hagel-criticizes-chinese-navy-citing-near-miss.html.

52. Hillary Clinton, "America's Pacific Century," *Foreign Affairs*, October 11, 2011, http://www.foreignpolicy.com/articles/2011/10/11/americas_pacific_century.

53. Cited in Jennifer Steinhauer and Martin Fackler, "Japan and U.S. Agree to Broaden Military Alliance," *New York Times,* October 3, 2013, http://www.nytimes.com/2013/10/04/world/asia/japan-and-us-agree-to-broaden-military-alliance.html.

54. Cited in Helene Cooper, "Hagel Spars with China over Islands and Security," *New York Times,* April 8, 2014, http://www.nytimes.com/2014/04/09/world/asia/united-states-and-china-clash-over-contested-islands.html.

55. Cited in Andrew Ross Sorkin, "Anxiety Rising over Relations between Japan and China," *New York Times,* January 27, 2014, http://dealbook.nytimes.com/2014/01/27/anxiety-rising-over-relations-between-japan-and-china.

56. Cited in Thom Shanker, "U.S. Sends Two B-52 Bombers into Air Zone Claimed by China," *New York Times,* November 26, 2013, http://www.nytimes.com/2013/11/27/world/asia/us-flies-b-52s-into-chinas-expanded-air-defense-zone.html.

57. Cited in Jane Perlez, "China Scrambles Jets for First Time in New Air Zone," *New York Times,* November 29, 2013, http://www.thetruthseeker.co.uk/?p=85378.

58. Cited in Austin Ramzy and Chris Buckley, "Pacific Rim Deal Could Reduce Chances of Conflict in Contested Seas," *New York Times,* April 23, 2014, http://www.nytimes.com/2014/04/24/world/asia/deal-could-reduce-chance-of-conflict-in-contested-pacific-seas.html.

59. Cited in Mark Landler, "Biden Backs Ally Japan but Avoids Roiling China," *New York Times,* December 3, 2013, http://www.nytimes.com/2013/12/04/world/asia/biden-in-japan-calibrates-message-over-tensions-with-china.html.

60. Cited in Mark Landler, "Biden Finds Political Instincts Handy in Asia," *New York Times,* December 6, 2013, http://www.nytimes.com/2013/12/07/world/asia/biden-in-asia.html.

61. Clinton, "America's Pacific Century."

62. Cited in Annie Lowrey, "U.S. and China to Discuss Investment Treaty, but Cybersecurity Is a Concern," *New York Times,* July 11, 2013, http://www.nytimes.com/2013/07/12/world/asia/us-and-china-to-discuss-investment-treaty-but-cybersecurity-is-a-concern.html.

63. Noah Feldman, *Cool War: The Future of Global Competition* (New York, NY: Random House, 2013), xii.

64. Cited in David E. Sanger and Mark Landler, "Obama's Strategic Shift to Asia Is Hobbled by Pressure at Home and Crises Abroad," *New York Times,* April 21, 2014, http://www.nytimes.com/2014/04/22/world/asia/obamas-strategic-shift-to-asia-is-hobbled-by-pressure-at-home-and-crises-abroad.html.

65. Article 8, Anti-Secession Law adopted by NPC, Taiwan Affairs Office of the State Council PRC, http://www.gwytb.gov.cn/en/Special/OneChinaPrinciple/201103/t20110317_1790121.htm.

66. Cited in "Taiwan Strait 21 July 1995 to 23 March 1996," *GlobalSecurity.org,* accessed September 9, 2015, http://www.globalsecurity.org/military/ops/taiwan_strait.htm.

67. Cited in Mark Landler, "An Array of Relations for Obama to Strengthen and Redefine," *New York Times,* November 7, 2012, http://www.nytimes.com/2012/11/08/world/obamas-other-cliff-is-in-foreign-policy.html.

68. "China Seen Overtaking U.S. as Global Superpower," *Pew Research Global Attitudes Project,* July 13, 2011, http://www.pewglobal.org/2011/07/13/china-soon-overtaking-us-as-global-superpower.

69. "America's Global Image Remains More Positive Than China's," Pew Research Center, July 18, 2013, http://www.pewglobal.org/files/2013/07/Pew-Research-Global-Attitudes-Project-Balance-of-Power-Report-FINAL-July-18-2013.pdf.

70. Cited in David E. Sanger, "Obama and Xi Try to Avoid a Cold War Mentality," *New York Times,* June 9, 2013, http://www.nytimes.com/2013/06/10/world/asia/obama-and-xi-try-to-avoid-a-cold-war-mentality.html?pagewanted=all.

71. Cited in ibid.

72. Cited in Mark Landler, "Chinese Claim Forces Obama to Flesh Out His Asia Strategy," *New York Times,* November 27, 2013, http://www.nytimes.com/2013/11/28/world/asia/airspace-claim-forces-us-to-flesh-out-china-strategy.html.

73. Cited in "Obama and Xi End 'Constructive' Summit," *BBC News,* June 9, 2013, http://www.bbc.co.uk/news/world-us-canada-22828678.

74. Banyan, "One Model, Two Interpretations," *The Economist,* September 28, 2013, 42.

75. Cited in Jennifer Steinhauer, "Back in Asia, Hagel Pursues Shift to Counter China's Goals in Pacific," *New York Times,* October 2, 2013, http://www.nytimes.com/2013/10/03/world/asia/chuck-hagel-in-asia.html.

76. Cited in Sanger and Landler, "Obama's Strategic Shift to Asia Is Hobbled by Pressures at Home and Crises Abroad."

77. Clinton, "America's Pacific Century."

78. James B. Steinberg and Michael O'Hanlon, "Keep Hope Alive," *Foreign Affairs* 93:4 (July/August 2014): 109.

CHAPTER 13

1. James K. Jackson, "U.S. Direct Investment Abroad: Trends and Current Issues," Congressional Research Service, December 11, 2013, 3, http://fas.org/sgp/crs/misc/RS21118.pdf.

2. Freedom House, *Freedom in the World 2013,* http://www.freedomhouse.org/sites/default/files/FIW%202013%20Booklet.pdf, 10.

3. Bruce M. Russett and John R. ONeal, *Triangulating Peace: Democracy, Interdependence, and International Organizations* (New York, NY: W.W. Norton, 2001).

4. Winston S. Churchill, "The Russian Enigma," *The Churchill Society* (London), October 1, 1939, http://www.churchill-society-london.org.uk/RusnEnig.html.

5. Cited in "On This Day 22 June," *BBC,* accessed June 5, 2015, http://news.bbc.co.uk/onthisday/hi/dates/stories/june/22/newsid_3526000/3526691.stm.

6. "X," "The Sources of Soviet Conduct," *Foreign Affairs* 25:4 (July 1947): 576, 582.

7. OECD, "The 'Marshall Plan' Speech at Harvard University, 5 June 1947," http://www.oecd.org/general/themarshallplanspeechatharvarduniversity5june1947.htm.

8. Lucius Clay, *Decision in Germany* (London, UK: Heinemann, 1950), 354.

9. Ibid., 361.

10. Cited in David Reynolds, *The Origins of the Cold War in Europe* (New Haven, CT: Yale University Press, 1994), 13.

11. NATO, "The North Atlantic Treaty," April 4, 1949, http://www.nato.int/cps/en/natolive/official_texts_17120.htm.

12. John Lewis Gaddis, *The Cold War: A New History* (New York, NY: Penguin Press, 2005), 127.

13. Ibid., 128.

14. Ibid.

15. Robert S. McNamara, "The Damage-Limiting Strategy," in Arthur L. Waskow, ed., *The Debate over Thermonuclear Strategy* (Boston, MA: Heath, 1965), 45.

16. Cited in Elie Abel, *The Missile Crisis* (New York, NY: Bantam Books, 1966), 96.

17. North Atlantic Treaty Organization, "Partnership for Peace: Framework Document," January 10–11, 1994, http://www.nato.int/cps/en/natolive/official_texts_24469.htm.

18. Alvin Z. Rubinstein, Albina Sheyevich, and Boris Zlotnikov, eds. *The Clinton Foreign Policy Reader: Presidential Speeches with Commentary* (Armonk, NY: M.E. Sharpe, 1999), 65.

19. North Atlantic Treaty Organization, "Founding Act on Mutual Relations, Cooperation and Security between NATO and the Russian Federation Signed in Paris, France," May 27, 1997, http://www.nato.int/cps/en/natolive/official_texts_25468.htm.

20. "Russia and NATO after the Rome Summit," *North Atlantic Treaty Organization,* February 7, 2003, http://www.nato.int/cps/en/SID-38AD4C0F-1EA8664D/natolive/news_19927.htm?selectedLocale=en.

21. Lenard J. Cohen, *Broken Bonds: Yugoslavia's Disintegration and Balkan Politics in Transition* (Boulder, CO: Westview Press, 1995), 46.

22. "BALKAN ACCORD; Clinton's Words on Mission to Bosnia: 'The Right Things to Do,'" *New York Times,* November 28, 1995, http://www.nytimes.com/1995/11/28/world/balkan-accord-clinton-s-words-on-mission-to-bosnia-the-right-thing-to-do.html.

23. UN Security Council Resolution 1244, June 10, 1999, http://www.securitycouncilreport.org/atf/cf/%7B65BFCF9B-6D27-4E9C-8CD3-CF6E4FF96FF9%7D/kos%20SRES%201244.pdf.

24. Montenegro became independent in 2006.

25. Cited in David Jackson, "Obama: Libyan Bloodshed Is 'Outrageous' and 'Unacceptable,'" *USA Today*, February 23, 2011, http://content.usatoday.com/communities/theoval/post/2011/02/obama-libyan-attacks-on-civiliamns-are-outrageous-and-unacceptable/1#.Uv72rfldWUI.

26. Derek E. Mix, "The United States and Europe: Current Issues," Congressional Research Service, May 4, 2011, http://fpc.state.gov/documents/organization/168024.pdf.

27. UNAMA, http://unama.unmissions.org/Default.aspx?tabid=12255&language=en-US, accessed April 10, 2014.

28. Zachary Laub, "The Taliban in Afghanistan," Council on Foreign Relations, February 25, 2014, http://www.cfr.org/afghanistan/taliban-afghanistan/p10551#p6.

29. Cited in Alison Smale and David E. Sanger, "Spying Scandal Alters U.S. Ties with Allies and Raises Talk of Policy Shift," *New York Times,* November 11, 2013, http://www.nytimes.com/2013/11/12/world/spying-scandal-alters-us-ties-with-allies-and-raises-talk-of-policy-shift.html

30. Cited in ibid.

31. Cited in Rachel Donadio, "Italy Convicts 23 Americans for C.I.A. Renditions," *New York Times,* November 4, 2009, http://www.nytimes.com/2009/11/05/world/europe/05italy.html.

32. Bill Bradley, "A Diplomatic Mystery," *Foreign Policy*, August 24, 2009, http://www.foreignpolicy.com/articles/2009/08/13/a_diplomatic_mystery.

33. Cited in Adrian Blomfield and Mike Smith, "Gorbachev: U.S. Could Start New Cold War," *The Telegraph,* May 6, 2008, http://www.telegraph.co.uk/news/worldnews/europe/russia/1933223/Gorbachev-US-could-start-new-Cold-War.html.

34. Mary Elise Sarotte, "A Broken Promise?" *Foreign Affairs* 93:5 (September/October 2014): 91.

35. North Atlantic Treaty Organization, "Membership Action Plan (MAP)," April 24, 1999, http://www.nato.int/cps/en/natolive/official_texts_27444.htm?selectedLocale=en.

36. Cited in Steven Erlanger and Steven Lee Myers, "NATO Allies Oppose Bush on Georgia and Ukraine,"

New York Times, April 3, 2008, http://www
.nytimes.com/2008/04/03/world/europe/03nato
.html?pagewanted=all. Russian

37. Cited in "Trading Insults," *The Economist,* August 24, 2013, 49.

38. Cited in "EU Warns Russia over Trade 'Threats' to Ex-Soviet Bloc," *BBC News,* September 12, 2013, http://www.bbc.co.uk/news/world-europe-24061556.

39. Jonas Grätz, "Freedom of Association," *Foreign Affairs,* November 20, 2013, http://www.foreign
affairs.com/articles/140280/jonas-graetz/freedom-of-
association.

40. Cited in David M. Herszenhorn, "Facing Russian Threat, Ukraine Halts Plans for Deals with E.U.," *New York Times,* November 21, 2013, http://www.nytimes
.com/2013/11/22/world/europe/ukraine-refuses-to-
free-ex-leader-raising-concerns-over-eu-talks.html.

41. Grätz, "Freedom of Association."

42. Cited in Andrew Higgins, "Ukraine Upheaval Highlights E.U.'s Past Miscalculations and Future Dangers," *New York Times,* March 20, 2014, http://
www.nytimes.com/2014/03/21/world/europe/
ukrainian-tumult-highlights-european-unions-errors
.html?hpw&rref=world.

43. Cited in "Ukraine Unrest: EU and US Clash with Russia in Munich," *BBC News,* February 1, 2014, http://www.bbc.co.uk/news/world-europe-25996453.

44. Cited in Mark Felsenthal, "Obama Warns Ukraine Military Not to 'Step over the Line,'" *Reuters,* February 19, 2014, http://www.reuters
.com/article/2014/02/19/us-ukraine-obama-
idUSBREA1I1AJ20140219.

45. Cited in Steven Erlanger, "Eastern Europe Frets about NATO's Ability to Curb Russia," *New York Times,* April 23, 2014, http://www.nytimes.com/2014/04/24/
world/europe/eastern-europe-frets-about-natos-
ability-to-curb-russia.html.

46. See "Responding to Mr. Putin," *The Economist,* March 22, 201423.

47. Cited in Andrew Higgins and David M. Herszenhorn, "Ukraine Signs Trade Agreement with European Union," *Boston Globe,* June 28, 2014, http://www
.bostonglobe.com/news/world/2014/06/27/ukraine-
signs-trade-agreement-with-european-union/
RIBcuXrrPxsLydsLD4QV2H/story.html.

48. Raphael Cohen and Gabriel Scheinmann, "The Hollow Coalition," *Foreign Affairs*, November 5, 2014, http://www.foreignaffairs.com/articles/142336/
raphael-cohen-and-gabriel-scheinmann/the-hollow-
coalition.

49. Cited in NATO, "NATO Secretary General Urges EU Nations to Invest in Capabilities," December 19, 2013, http://www.nato.int/cps/en/natolive/
news_105954.htm?selectedLocale=en.

50. Michael R. Gordon, "Survey Points to Challenges NATO Faces over Russia," *New York Times,* June 10, 2015, http://www.nytimes.com/2015/06/10/world/
europe/survey-points-to-challenges-nato-faces-over-
russia.html.

51. "Obama's Statement on New Sanctions against Russia," *New York Times,* March 17, 2014, http://
www.nytimes.com/2014/03/18/world/europe/obamas-
statement-on-new-sanctions-against-russia.html.

52. Cited in Michael D. Shear and Peter Baker, "Obama Renewing U.S. Commitment to NATO Alliance," *New York Times,* March 26, 2014, http://www.nytimes
.com/2014/03/27/world/europe/obama-europe.html.

53. Cited in Steven Erlanger, "Russia's Aggression in Crimea Brings NATO into Renewed Focus," *New York Times,* March 18, 2014, http://www.nytimes
.com/2014/03/19/world/europe/russias-aggression-
in-crimea-brings-nato-into-renewed-focus.html.

54. Cited in ibid.

55. Cited in James Kanter, "Citing Russian Moves, NATO Plans New Deployments," *New York Times,* April 16, 2014, http://www.nytimes.com/2014/04/17/world/
europe/nato-ukraine.html.

56. Cited in "A New Ostpolitik," *The Economist,* November 29, 2014, 48.

57. Cited in Tony Paterson, "Merkel Fury after Gerhard Schroeder Backs Putin on Ukraine," *The Telegraph,* March 14, 2014, http://www.telegraph.co.uk/news/
worldnews/europe/ukraine/10697986/Merkel-fury-
after-Gerhard-Schroeder-backs-Putin-on-Ukraine
.html.

58. Cited in ibid.

59. Cited in Alison Smale, "Germany Urges Russia to Help Solve Ukraine Crisis," *New York Times,* March 13, 2014, http://www.nytimes.com/2014/03/14/
world/europe/germany-urges-russia-to-help-solve-
ukraine-crisis.html.

60. Cited in Peter Baker, "Top Russians Face Sanctions by U.S. for Crimea Crisis," *New York Times,* March 3, 2012, http://www.nytimes.com/2014/03/04/world/

europe/top-russians-face-sanctions-by-us-for-crimea-crisis.html.

61. Cited in Peter Baker, "Doubting Putin, Obama Prepares to Add Pressure," *New York Times,* June 24, 2014, http://www.nytimes.com/2014/06/25/world/europe/doubting-putin-obama-prepares-to-add-pressure.html.

62. Cited in Alison Smale and Danny Hakim, "European Firms Seek to Minimize Russia Sanctions," *New York Times,* April 25, 2014, http://www.nytimes.com/2014/04/26/world/europe/european-firms-seek-to-minimize-russia-sanctions.html.

63. Cited in Stanley Reed, "A Conduit for Russian Gas, Tangled in Europe's Conflicts," *New York Times,* June 30, 2014, http://www.nytimes.com/2014/07/01/business/international/south-stream-pipeline-project-in-bulgaria-is-delayed.html.

64. Alison Smale, "Germany Puts Curbing Russia ahead of Commerce," *New York Times,* August 13, 2014, http://www.nytimes.com/2014/08/14/world/europe/ukraine-crisis-hardens-germany-against-russia-an-old-partner.html.

65. Cited in Michael R. Gordon, "NATO Weighs Assistance for Ukraine to Dissuade Further Moves by Moscow," *New York Times,* March 19, 2014, http://www.nytimes.com/2014/03/20/world/europe/nato-chief-russia-europe.html.

66. Mitchell A. Orenstein, "Get Ready for a Russo-German Europe," *Foreign Affairs,* March 9, 2014, http://www.foreignaffairs.com/articles/141018/mitchell-a-orenstein/get-ready-for-a-russo-german-europe.

67. Cited in Peter Baker, "If Not a Cold War, a Return to a Chilly Rivalry," *New York Times,* March 18, 2014, http://www.nytimes.com/2014/03/19/world/europe/if-not-a-new-cold-war-a-distinct-chill-in-the-air.html.

CHAPTER 14

1. Tom W. Smith, "The Polls: American Attitudes toward the Soviet Union and Communism," *Public Opinion Quarterly* 47:2 (Summer 1983): 280.

2. Ibid., 277.

3. Cited in Geoffrey Best, *Churchill: A Study in Greatness* (New York, NY: Oxford University Press, 2001), 93.

4. Harry S. Truman, *Memoirs: 1946–52 Years of Trial and Hope* (New York, NY: Doubleday & Co., 1956), 332–333.

5. *History Matters,* accessed June 2, 2015, http://historymatters.gmu.edu.

6. Bogdan Szajkowski, *Next to God, Poland: Politics and Religion in Contemporary Poland* (New York, NY: Palgrave Macmillan, 1983), 72

7. Timothy Garton Ash, *History of the Present: Essays, Sketches, and Dispatches from Europe in the 1990s* (New York, NY: Random House, 1999), 315.

8. Cited in Douglas C. Waller, *Congress and the Nuclear Freeze* (Amherst, MA: University of Massachusetts Press, 1987), 30.

9. Dimitri K. Simes, "Losing Russia," *Foreign Affairs* 86:6 (November/December 2007): 38.

10. Ibid.

11. Cited in Timothy J. Colton, *Yeltsin: A Life* (New York, NY: Basic Books), note 78, 553.

12. Simes, "Losing Russia," 39, 40.

13. Joshua Yaffa, "Reading Putin: The Mind and the State of Russia's President," *Foreign Affairs* 91:4 (July/August 2012): 127.

14. Ibid.

15. Cited in Caroline Wyatt, "Bush and Putin: Best of Friends," *BBC News,* June 16, 2001, http://news.bbc.co.uk/2/hi/1392791.stm.

16. Cited in "Clinton Goofs on Russian Translation, Tells Diplomat She Wants to 'Overcharge' Ties," *Fox News,* March 6, 2009, http://www.foxnews.com/politics/2009/03/06/clinton-goofs-russian-translation-tells-diplomat-wants-overcharge-ties.

17. Cited in "Vladimir Putin Steps Out," *The Economist*, June 16, 2012, 61.

18. "Northern Distribution Network (NDN)," *Center for Strategic and International Studies,* 2012, http://csis.org/program/northern-distribution-network-ndn.

19. U.S. Department of State, Office of Cooperative Threat Reduction (ISN/CTR), accessed September 11, 2015, http://www.state.gov/t/isn/offices/c55411.htm.

20. Justin Bresolin, "Fact Sheet: The Nunn-Lugar Cooperative Threat Reduction Program," July 2013, updated by Sam Kane and Kingston Reif, http://armscontrolcenter.org/publications/factsheets/fact_sheet_the_cooperative_threat_reduction_program.

21. Stephen Blank and Carol R. Saivetz, "Playing to Lose? Russia and the 'Arab Spring,'" *Problems of Post-Communism* 59:1 (January/February 2012): 1, 2.

22. Cited in Ellen Barry, "Russians Say Anti-U.S. Attack in Libya Vindicates Their Position," *New York Times*, September 12, 2012, http://www.nytimes.com/2012/09/13/world/europe/russians-say-anti-american-attack-in-libya-vindicates-their-position.html.

23. Blank and Saivetz, "Playing to Lose? Russia and the 'Arab Spring,'" 4.

24. Cited in Steven Lee Myers and Michael R. Gordon, "Kerry Castigates Russia over Syria-Bound Missiles," *New York Times,* May 31, 2013, http://www.nytimes.com/2013/06/01/world/middleeast/kerry-castigates-russia-over-syria-bound-missiles.html?pagewanted=all.

25. Cited in ibid.

26. Cited in David M. Herszenhorn, "Putin Says Proof of Chemical Arms Attack Not Enough to Justify U.S. Action," *New York Times,* September 4, 2013, http://www.nytimes.com/2013/09/05/world/europe/putin-says-proof-of-chemical-arms-attack-not-enough-to-justify-us-attack.html.

27. Cited in David E. Sanger, "Kerry's Comments on Syria Are a Shift over Strike," *New York Times,* September 9, 2013, http://www.nytimes.com/2013/09/10/world/middleeast/kerrys-comments-on-syria-mark-a-shift-over-strike.html.

28. Fiona Hill, "Putin Scores on Syria," *Foreign Affairs,* September 11, 2013, http://www.foreignaffairs.com/articles/139905/fiona-hill/putin-scores-on-syria.

29. Cited in David E. Sanger, "Quick Turn of Fortunes as Diplomatic Options Open Up with Syria and Iran," *New York Times,* September 19, 2013, http://www.nytimes.com/2013/09/20/us/politics/on-mideast-heads-spin-over-shift-in-diplomacy.html.

30. Cited in Peter Baker, "Debate over Who in U.S. Is to Blame for Ukraine," *New York Times,* March 5, 2014, http://www.nytimes.com/2014/03/06/world/europe/debate-over-who-in-us-is-to-blame-for-ukraine.html.

31. Cited in Somini Sengupta, "With Tumult around Him, Russian Diplomat Keeps Calm," *New York Times,* February 21, 2014, http://www.nytimes.com/2014/02/22/world/europe/with-tumult-around-him-russian-diplomat-keeps-calm.html.

32. Cited in Alexei Anishchuk and Gabriela Baczynska, "Russia's Putin Warns of Endless Conflict in Syria," *Reuters,* December 20, 2012, http://mobile.reuters.com/article/worldNews/idUSBRE8BJ0GF20121220.

33. Cited in David M. Herszenhorn, "Iran Mentions New Plan at Nuclear Talks as Stalemate Continues," *New York Times*, April 5, 2013, http://www.nytimes.com/2013/04/06/world/middleeast/talks-resume-on-curbing-irans-nuclear-program.html?pagewanted=all.

34. Stephen J. Blank, *Threats to Russian Security: The View from Moscow* (Carlisle, PA: Strategic Studies Institute, U.S. Army War College Commandant, 2000), 4.

35. Simes, "Losing Russia," 42.

36. "Russia," *World Public Opinion.org,* http://www.americans-world.org/digest/regional_issues/russia/russia3.cfm.

37. Charles A. Kupchan, "NATO's Final Frontier: Why Russia Should Join the Atlantic Alliance," *Foreign Affairs* 89:3 (May/June 2010), 100.

38. "Statement on the Situation in South Ossetia," August 8, 2008, http://archive.kremlin.ru/eng/speeches/2008/08/08/1553_type82912type82913_205032.shtml.

39. Jeffrey Mankoff, "The Politics of U.S. Missile Defense Cooperation with Europe and Russia," *International Affairs* 88:2 (March 2012): 338.

40. Ibid., 339, 340.

41. "Budapest Memorandums on Security Assurances, 1994," Council on Foreign Relations, December 5, 1994, http://www.cfr.org/arms-control-disarmament-and-nonproliferation/budapest-memorandums-security-assurances-1994/p32484.

42. Cited in Somini Sengupta, "Ukraine Premier Makes Plea at the U.N.," *New York Times,* March 13, 2014, http://www.nytimes.com/2014/03/14/world/europe/ukraine-premier-makes-plea-at-the-un.html.

43. Cited in Steven Lee Myers, Ellen Barry, and Alan Cowell, "Defying West, Putin Signs Treaty to Annex Crimea," *New York Times,* March 18, 2014, http://www.nytimes.com/2014/03/19/world/europe/ukraine.html?hpw&rref=world.

44. Cited in Michael R. Gordon, "Kerry Takes Offer of Aid to Ukraine and Pushes Back at Russian Claims," *New York Times,* March 4, 2014, http://www.nytimes

.com/2014/03/05/world/europe/secretary-of-state-john-kerry-arriving-in-kiev-offers-1-billion-in-loan-guarantees-to-ukraine.html.

45. Cited in Steven Lee Myers, "Putin Engages in Test of Will over Ukraine," *New York Times,* March 2, 2014, http://www.nytimes.com/2014/03/03/world/europe/putin-engages-in-test-of-will-over-ukraine.html.

46. Cited in Michael D. Shear and Peter Baker, "Obama Answers Critics, Dismissing Russia as a 'Regional Power,'" *New York Times,* March 25, 2014, http://www.nytimes.com/2014/03/26/world/europe/hague-summit-focuses-on-preventing-trafficking-of-nuclear-materials.html.

47. "Obama's Statement on New Sanctions against Russia," *New York Times*, March 17, 2014, http://www.nytimes.com/2014/03/18/world/europe/obamas-statement-on-new-sanctions-against-russia.html.

48. Cited in Andrew E. Kramer, "In Ukraine's East, Russians Are Blending Right In," *New York Times,* April 14, 2014, http://www.nytimes.com/2014/04/15/world/europe/russians-blending-in-among-ukraine-separatists.html.

49. Cited in "Wearily Back to the Battlefield," *The Economist,* April 12, 2014, 43.

50. Cited in Andrew Higgins, Michael R. Gordon, and Andrew E. Kramer, "Photos Link Masked Men in East Ukraine to Russia," *New York Times,* April 20, 2014, http://www.nytimes.com/2014/04/21/world/europe/photos-link-masked-men-in-east-ukraine-to-russia.html.

51. Cited in ibid.

52. Cited in Andrew Higgins, "In Ukraine, Russia Plays a Weighted Word Game," *New York Times,* April 16, 2014, http://www.nytimes.com/2014/04/17/world/europe/in-ukraine-russia-plays-a-weighted-word-game.html.

53. Cited in David M. Herszenhorn, "Putin Asserts Right to Use Force in Eastern Ukraine," *New York Times,* April 17, 2014, http://www.nytimes.com/2014/04/18/world/europe/russia-ukraine.html.

54. Cited in Michael R. Gordon, "U.S. and Russia Agree on Pact to Defuse Ukraine Crisis," *New York Times*, April 17, 2014, http://www.nytimes.com/2014/04/18/world/europe/ukraine-diplomacy.html?hpw&rref=world.

55. Marjorie Connelly, "Ukrainians Favor Unity, Not Russia, Polls Find," *New York Times,* May 8, 2014, http://www.nytimes.com/2014/05/08/world/europe/ukrainians-favor-unity-not-russia-polls-find.html.

56. "Into Battle," *The Economist,* May 17, 2014, 50.

57. Cited in Peter Baker, "U.S. Expands Sanctions, Adding Holdings of Russians in Putin's Financial Circle," *New York Times,* April 28, 2014, http://www.nytimes.com/2014/04/29/world/asia/obama-sanctions-russia.html.

58. Cited in Andrew E. Kramer and Stanley Reed, "For Western Oil Companies, Expanding in Russia Is a Dance around Sanctions," *New York Times,* June 9, 2014, http://www.nytimes.com/2014/06/10/business/international/for-western-oil-companies-expanding-in-russia-is-a-dance-around-sanctions.html.

59. Andrew E. Kramer, "Putin Indicates He'll Respect Result of Ukrainian Election," *New York Times,* May 23, 2014, http://www.nytimes.com/2014/05/24/world/europe/putin-indicates-hell-respect-result-of-ukrainian-election.html?ref=world.

60. Cited in Peter Baker and Rick Lyman, "With Ukraine Still Unsettled, Obama Sets Off to Soothe European Friends," *New York Times,* June 1, 2014, http://www.nytimes.com/2014/06/02/world/europe/with-ukraine-crisis-cooling-obama-sets-off-to-soothe-european-friends.html?_r=0.

61. Cited in Peter Baker, "Doubting Putin, Obama Prepares to Add Pressure," *New York Times,* June 24, 2014, http://www.nytimes.com/2014/06/25/world/europe/doubting-putin-obama-prepares-to-add-pressure.html.

62. Cited in Mark Landler and Michael R. Gordon, "NATO Chief Warns of Duplicity by Putin on Ukraine," *New York Times,* July 8, 2014, http://www.nytimes.com/2014/07/09/world/europe/nato-chief-warns-of-duplicity-by-putin-on-ukraine.html.

63. Cited in Sabrina Tavernise, "In Ukraine War, Kremlin Leaves No Fingerprints," *New York Times,* May 31, 2014, http://www.nytimes.com/2014/06/01/world/europe/in-ukraine-war-kremlin-leaves-no-fingerprints.html.

64. Stephen Holmes and Ivan Krastev, "Putin's Losing Streak," *Foreign Affairs,* July 30, 2014, http://www.foreignaffairs.com/articles/141663/stephen-holmes-and-ivan-krastev/putins-losing-streak.

65. Cited in "Alleged Phone Call: 'We Have Shot Down a Plane,'" *CNN,* July 18, 2014, http://www.cnn.com/2014/07/18/world/europe/ukraine-mh17-intercepted-audio/.

66. Cited in "Putin's War of Words: A Roundup," *New York Times,* September 2, 2014, http://www.nytimes.com/2014/09/03/world/europe/putins-war-of-words-a-roundup.html.

67. Cited in Andrew E. Kramer, "U.S. Companies Worry about Effect of Russia Joining W.T.O.," *New York Times*, August 21, 2012, http://www.nytimes.com/2012/08/22/business/with-russia-joining-wto-us-companies-worry-about-losing-business.html?pagewanted=all.

68. Cited in David M. Herszenhorn, "Gays in Russia Find No Haven, Despite Support from the West," *New York Times,* August 11, 2013, http://www.nytimes.com/2013/08/12/world/europe/gays-in-russia-find-no-haven-despite-support-from-the-west.html?pagewanted=all.

69. Cited in Peter Baker, "Obama May Cancel Moscow Trip as Tensions Build over Leaker," *New York Times,* July 18, 2013, http://www.nytimes.com/2013/07/19/world/europe/moscow-trip-for-obama-may-be-off-as-snowden-tensions-build.html?pagewanted=all.

70. Cited in David M. Herszenhorn and Michael R. Gordon, "U.S. Cancels Part of Missile Defense That Russia Opposed," *New York Times*, March 16, 2013, http://www.nytimes.com/2013/03/17/world/europe/with-eye-on-north-korea-us-cancels-missile-defense-russia-opposed.html.

71. John J. Mearsheimer, "Why the Ukraine Crisis Is the West's Fault," *Foreign Affairs* 93:5 (September/October 2014): 77.

72. Jeffrey Mankoff, "Russia's Latest Land Grab," *Foreign Affairs* 93:3 (May/June 2014): 60.

73. Alexander J. Motyl, "The Sources of Russian Conduct," *Foreign Affairs,* November 16, 2014, http://www.foreignaffairs.com/articles/142366/alexander-j-motyl/the-sources-of-russian-conduct.

74. "Russian Defense Budget to Hit Record $81 Billion in 2015," *Moscow Times,* October 16, 2014, http://www.themoscowtimes.com/business/article/russian-defense-budget-to-hit-record-81bln-in-2015/509536.html.

75. Cited in Fred Weir, "Circling the Wagons? Putin Urges 'Drastic Upgrade' to Russia's Military," *Christian Science Monitor*, February 28, 2013, http://www.csmonitor.com/World/Europe/2013/0228/Circling-the-wagons-Putin-urges-drastic-upgrade-to-Russia-s-military.

76. Cited in Helene Cooper and Steven Erlanger, "Military Cuts Render NATO Less Formidable as Deterrent to Russia," *New York Times,* March 26, 2014, http://www.nytimes.com/2014/03/27/world/europe/military-cuts-render-nato-less-formidable-as-deterrent-to-russia.html.

77. Cited in David M. Herszenhorn, Andrew E. Kramer, and Alan Cowell, "Russian Forces Release Ukraine Naval Commander," *New York Times,* March 20, 2014, http://www.nytimes.com/2014/03/21/world/europe/crimea.html.

78. Cited in "Obama's Statement on New Sanctions against Russia," *New York Times,* March 17, 2014, http://www.nytimes.com/2014/03/18/world/europe/obamas-statement-on-new-sanctions-against-russia.html.

79. Joshua Yaffa, "Peace on Putin's Terms," *Foreign Affairs,* September 7, 2014, http://www.foreignaffairs.com/articles/141966/joshua-yaffa/peace-on-putins-terms.

80. Cited in Peter Baker, "Obama's Test: Can Penalties Change Russia's Course?" *New York Times,* March 18, 2014, http://www.nytimes.com/2014/03/19/world/europe/obamas-test-can-penalties-change-russias-course.html.

81. Cited in Coral Davenport and Steven Erlanger, "U.S. Hopes Boom in Natural Gas Can Curb Putin," *New York Times,* March 5, 2014, http://www.nytimes.com/2014/03/06/world/europe/us-seeks-to-reduce-ukraines-reliance-on-russia-for-natural-gas.html.

82. Cited in Peter Baker, "3 Presidents and a Riddle Named Putin," *New York Times,* March 23, 2014, http://www.nytimes.com/2014/03/24/world/europe/3-presidents-and-a-riddle-named-putin.html.

83. Cited in ibid.

84. Anton Barbashin and Hannah Thoburn, "Putin's Brain," *Foreign Affairs*, March 31, 2014, http://www.foreignaffairs.com/articles/141080/anton-barbashin-and-hannah-thoburn/putins-brain.

85. Cited in "Clinton Criticizes Russia on Europe Policy, Human Rights," *Voice of America*, December 6, 2012, http://www.voanews.com/content/clinton-criticizes-russia-on-europe-policy-human-rights/1559739.html.

86. Cited in Peter Baker, "U.S.-Russian Ties Still Fall Short of 'Reset' Goal," *New York Times,* September 2, 2013, http://www.nytimes.com/2013/09/03/world/europe/us-russian-ties-still-fall-short-of-reset-goal.html?pagewanted=all.

87. Ariel Cohen, "Why Russia Roots for Obama," *The National Interest,* November 5, 2012, http://nationalinterest.org/commentary/why-russia-roots-obama-7696.

88. Andrei Shliefer and Daniel Treisman, "Why Moscow Says No: A Question of Russian Interests, Not Psychology," *Foreign Affairs* 90:1 (January/February 2012): 125.

89. Luke March, "Nationalism for Export? The Domestic and Foreign-Policy Implications of the New 'Russian Idea,'" *Europe-Asia Studies,* 64:3 (May 2012): 421, 422.

90. Robert Coalson, "Obama and the Russians: Moving On to the 'Post-Reset,'" *Radio Free Europe/Radio Liberty,* November 7, 2012, http://www.rferl.org/content/obama-russia-moving-on-post-reset-relations/24763754.html.

91. Brian D. Taylor, "Putin's Own Goal," *Foreign Affairs,* March 6, 2014, http://www.foreignaffairs.com/articles/141010/brian-d-taylor/putins-own-goal.

92. Cited in "CNN Poll: Most See Russia as a Threat to U.S.," *CNN Politics,* March 14, 2014, http://politicalticker.blogs.cnn.com/2014/03/14/cnn-poll-most-see-russia-as-a-threat-to-u-s/?hpt=hp_t2.

93. Pew Global Attitudes Project, "Russia's Global Image Negative amid Crisis in Ukraine," July 9, 2014, http://www.pewglobal.org/2014/07/09/russias-global-image-negative-amid-crisis-in-ukraine/.

94. Cited in Peter Baker, "If Not a Cold War, a Return to a Chilly Rivalry," *New York Times,* March 18, 2014, http://www.nytimes.com/2014/03/19/world/europe/if-not-a-new-cold-war-a-distinct-chill-in-the-air.html.

95. Shliefer and Treisman, "Why Moscow Says No," 138.

96. Cited in David Herszenhorn and Andrew E. Kramer, "Another Reset with Russia in Obama's Second Term," *New York Times,* February 1, 2013, http://www.nytimes.com/2013/02/02/world/europe/another-reset-of-relations-with-russia-in-obamas-second-term.html?pagewanted=all.

CHAPTER 15

1. Warren G. Harding, "Return to Normalcy," May 14, 1920, TeachingAmericanHistory.org, http://teachingamericanhistory.org/library/document/return-to-normalcy.

2. "X" (George F. Kennan), "The Sources of Soviet Conduct," *Foreign Affairs* 25:4 (July 1947): 566–582, http://www.foreignaffairs.com/articles/23331/x/the-sources-of-soviet-conduct.

3. Robert Kagan, "Superpowers Don't Get to Retire," *New Republic,* May 26, 2014, http://www.newrepublic.com/article/117859/allure-normalcy-what-america-still-owes-world, 11.

4. G. John Ikenberry, "The Illusion of Geopolitics," *Foreign Affairs* 93:3 (May/June 2014): 84, 89.

5. Robert Kagan, *The World America Made* (New York, NY: Vintage Books, 2012).

6. William C. Martel, "America's Grand Strategy Disaster," *The National Interest,* June 9, 2014, http://commentators.com/americas-grand-strategy-disaster-the-national-interest.

7. Randall L. Schweller, "The Age of Entropy," *Foreign Affairs,* June 16, 2014, http://www.foreignaffairs.com/articles/141568/randall-l-schweller/the-age-of-entropy.

8. Kagan, "Superpowers Don't Get to Retire," 21.

9. John Mueller, "Iraq Syndrome Redux," *Foreign Affairs,* June 18, 2014, http://www.foreignaffairs.com/articles/141578/john-mueller/iraq-syndrome-redux.

10. Kagan, "Superpowers Don't Get to Retire," 26.

11. Cited in Robert Kagan, "The September 12 Paradigm," *Foreign Affairs* 87:5 (September/October 2008): 29.

12. Ibid., 30, 36.

13. Cited in "The War on Terror, Part Two," *The Economist,* May 31, 2014, 23.

14. Cited in ibid.

15. Cited in Peter Baker, "Rebutting Critics, Obama Seeks Higher Bar for Military Action," *New York Times,* May 28, 2014, http://www.nytimes.com/2014/05/29/us/politics/rebutting-critics-obama-seeks-higher-bar-for-military-action.html.

16. Cited in ibid.

17. Cited in Peter Baker, "Crises Cascade and Converge, Testing Obama," *New York Times,* July 22, 2014, http://www.nytimes.com/2014/07/23/world/crises-cascade-and-converge-testing-obama.html.

18. Cited in "The Decline of Deterrence," *The Economist,* May 3, 2014, 23.

19. Cited in ibid., 24.

20. Cited in ibid., 25.

21. Cited in Thomas L. Friedman, "Obama on the World," *New York Times,* August 8, 2014, http://www.nytimes.com/2014/08/09/opinion/president-obama-thomas-l-friedman-iraq-and-world-affairs.html.

22. Cited in Mark Landler, "A Rift in Worldviews Is Exposed as Clinton Faults Obama on Policy," *New York Times,* August 11, 2014, http://www.nytimes.com/2014/08/12/world/middleeast/attacking-obama-policy-hillary-clinton-exposes-different-worldviews.html.

23. Richard N. Haass, "The Unraveling," *Foreign Affairs* 93:6 (November/December 2014): 70.

24. "Remarks by the President at the Acceptance of the Nobel Peace Prize," The White House, December 10, 2009, http://www.whitehouse.gov/the-press-office/remarks-president-acceptance-nobel-peace-prize.

25. Cited in Mark Landler, "Ending Asia Trip, Obama Defends His Foreign Policy," *New York Times,* April 28, 2014, http://www.nytimes.com/2014/04/29/world/obama-defends-foreign-policy-against-critics.html.

26. Cited in David E. Sanger, "Global Crises Put Obama's Strategy of Caution to the Test," *New York Times,* March 16, 2014, http://www.nytimes.com/2014/03/17/world/obamas-policy-is-put-to-the-test-as-crises-challenge-caution.html.

27. Kagan, *The World America Made,* 94.

28. Cited in Peter Baker, "As World Boils, Fingers Point Obama's Way," *New York Times,* August 15, 2014, http://www.nytimes.com/2014/08/16/world/middleeast/as-world-boils-fingers-point-obamas-way.html.

29. Haass, "The Unraveling," 73–74.

Index

About the Authors

Richard Mansbach (BA Swarthmore College, DPhil Oxford University) is a former Marshall Scholar and three-time Fulbright Scholar. He has authored, coauthored, or edited seventeen books and numerous articles and book chapters largely concerning theory in global politics and foreign policy. His scholarship has extended our understanding of global politics beyond the traditional notion of territorial states interacting in an anarchic system to encompass a wide variety of actors complexly related across a variety of issues. Increasingly, his work has moved from the dominant role of "states" in international relations theory to encompass a changing cast of actors in a globalizing world and toward the concept of "identity" and the role of psychological, as opposed to geographic, distance in determining loyalties and behavior. His scholarship focuses on the critical role of history and norms in understanding change and continuity in global politics and in the movement from preinternational to international and, ultimately, postinternational politics in a globalizing world. Among his books, several are routinely used in major graduate programs, notably, *The Web of World Politics*; *In Search of Theory: Toward a New Paradigm for Global Politics*; *The Elusive Quest: Theory and International Politics*; *Polities: Authority, Identities, and Change*; *The Elusive Quest Continues: Theory and Global Politics*; *Remapping Global Politics*; and *Globalization: The Return of Borders to a Borderless World?* In addition, Professor Mansbach was the coeditor of the field's flagship journal, *International Studies*. He has also served as department chair at Rutgers University (New Brunswick) and at Iowa State University.

Kirsten L. Taylor (BA University of Pittsburgh, PhD McGill University) is associate professor and department chair of Government and International Studies at Berry College, a private liberal arts college in Northwest Georgia. Her scholarship focuses on the development and transformation of international institutions and norms, with particular emphases on security and environmental institutions, teaching with simulations. Her articles have appeared in *International Studies Perspectives, Canadian Journal of Political Science,* and *Comparative Strategy.* Dr. Taylor also is coauthor of a textbook, *Introduction to Global Politics*, with Richard Mansbach.